EDITED BY DAVID REID

West of the West: Imagining California
(with Leonard Michaels and Raquel Scherr)

Sex, Death and God in L.A.

THE BRAZEN AGE

THE BRAZEN AGE

New York City and the American Empire:

Politics, Art, and Bohemia

DAVID REID

PANTHEON BOOKS, NEW YORK

Pantheon Books and colophon are registered trademarks
of Penguin Random House LLC.

Grateful acknowledgment is made to Random House for permission
to reprint excerpts from "The Age of Anxiety," copyright © 1947
by W. H. Auden and renewed 1975 by the Estate of W. H. Auden,
and "Refugee Blues," copyright © 1940 and renewed 1968 by W. H. Auden,
from *W. H. Auden Collected Poems* by W. H. Auden.
Reprinted by permission of Random House, an imprint and division
of Penguin Random House LLC. All rights reserved.

Library of Congress Cataloging-in-Publication Data
Reid, David [date], author.
The brazen age : New York City and the American empire :
politics, art, and bohemia / David Reid.
pages ; cm
Includes bibliographical references and index.
ISBN 978-0-394-57237-6 (hbk. : alk. paper). ISBN 978-1-101-87066-2 (eBook).
1. New York (N.Y.)—History—1898–1951.   2. New York (N.Y.)—Civilization.
3. New York (N.Y.)—Intellectual life—20th century.   4. Greenwich Village (New York,
N.Y.)—Intellectual life—20th century.   5. Bohemianism—New York (State)—
New York—History—20th century.   I. Title.
F128.5.R45   2015 974.7'043—dc23   2015024900

www.pantheonbooks.com

Jacket image: Courtesy of the Library of Congress, Washington, D.C.
Jacket design by Janet Hansen

Printed in the United States of America

First Edition

2 4 6 8 9 7 5 3 1

To my wife, Jayne L. Walker,
and to the memory of our dear son,
Stephen David Reid
1977–1995

Farewell the plumed troops and the big wars
That make ambition virtue—O, farewell!

—SHAKESPEARE, Othello, III.3

We are divided of course between liking to feel the
past strange and liking it to feel familiar; the difficulty
is, for intensity, to catch it at the moment when the
scales of the balance hang with the right evenness.

—HENRY JAMES

Contents

In the patio-garden of Café Nicholson, the celebrated gathering place for café society, artists, and writers, *from left to right:* Tanaquil Le Clercq, Donald Windham, Buffie Johnson, Tennessee Williams, and Gore Vidal, with Virginia Reed in the background, 1949

Introduction

THIS BOOK'S REMOTEST ORIGIN IS AN ESSAY, "The Art and Arts of E. Howard Hunt," by Gore Vidal, first published in the *New York Review of Books*, in the dark days of Richard Nixon's presidency. Howard Hunt was a hack novelist considered promising in the 1940s who became a career CIA agent and achieved ill fame as a Watergate "plumber."

"From December 7, 1941, to August 15, 1973," Vidal wrote, presumably on that date, "the United States has been continuously at war except for a brief, too little celebrated interregnum. Between 1945 and 1950 the empire turned its attention to peaceful pursuits and enjoyed something of a golden or at least for us not too brazen an age. The arts in particular flourished. Each week new genius was revealed by the press; and old genius decently buried." The principal setting of the golden—or at least not-too-brazen age—was, of course, New York City.

It was a queer, liminal half-decade between wars. Despite bravado in the Truman White House, the political temper of the times was jittery and suspicious: fearful of a return to the Great Depression, unrelieved almost until mid-century; fearful of international communism (the attorney general's infamous list of "subversive organizations" was drawn up in 1947). Bordered on one side by the bottomless abyss we have sentimentalized into "the Good War," and on the other by the Kodachrome mythology of "the fifties," America was harassed by a host of phantoms.

In popular iconography—television documentaries, coffee-table history books, and the annals of pop sociology—the postwar era typically lurches from V-J Day (always Alfred Eisenstaedt's photograph in

Life magazine of a jubilant sailor in Times Square kissing a girl flung over backward in his arms) to Harry S. Truman triumphantly waving the *Chicago Tribune* ("Dewey Defeats Truman") in November 1948, past the mud and murk of the "police action" in Korea (the obscurest of our wars since 1812) and on to the hydrogen bombs and hula hoops of the age of Ike, leaving a curious blank in popular memory, except for the vague but well-founded sense that a stampede to the suburbs was already foreboding the abandonment of the city. The moody genre films of the time that we now call film noir projected a sense of grim and baffled fatalism.

Yet, what span of American experience since the Jazz Age has been so brilliantly represented in novels as the forties—a decade that was also the last time fiction was at the center of popular culture? Saul Bellow's *Victim*, Norman Mailer's *Barbary Shore*, J. D. Salinger's *Catcher in the Rye*, and Jack Kerouac's *On the Road* unfold in whole or in part in New York, during what Mailer calls in his novel "the orgiastic hollow of the century." Truman Capote's novella *Breakfast at Tiffany's* (1958) is dated exactly to the summer and autumn of 1943: during some of the worst fighting of the war, the snooping narrator notices that his call-girl neighbor, Holly Golightly, "received V-letters by the bale. They were all torn into strips like bookmarks." In Vladimir Nabokov's *Lolita* (1958), doomed Humbert Humbert and Dolores Haze, his "nymphet," are fictionally on the road in 1947–49, at the same time as the Beats in *On the Road*. Because of their publication dates or movie adaptations, these novels are almost always connected with what Robert Lowell called "the tranquilized *Fifties*." When John Cheever came to collect his stories, he observed that the earliest of them, dating from when he was honorably discharged from the army in 1945, "seem to be stories of a long-lost world when the city of New York was still filled with a river light, when you heard the Benny Goodman quartets from a radio in the corner stationery store, and when almost everybody wore a hat."

For the young Vidal, who published his first novel at nineteen, the moment was full of cultural excitements, from W. H. Auden's *Age of Anxiety*—that great, unread masterpiece—to his friend Tennessee Williams's plays, to Antony Tudor's ballets, to "Bernstein's enthusiasms," that seemed to open up the prospect of a second American renaissance. When he wrote about the postwar forties in 1974, there was still a great cloud of witnesses alive, most of them in vigorous middle age; now, forty years separate us from that time, and the men and women for whom the 1940s represent a "visitable past" have become a vanishing crowd.

The postwar years would also be a golden age for real-estate speculators, developers of tract housing, Wall Street lawyers, professional anticommunists, offshore oil drillers, uranium prospectors, and "whiz kids." After his surprise election to the presidency in 1948, Harry Truman relied, in foreign affairs, as much on northeastern patricians like W. Averell Harriman, on Wall Street bankers, and on Washington, DC, white-shoe lawyers as Franklin D. Roosevelt had ever done, if not more so, thus frustrating, bitterly, those who hoped and expected to see the direction of the country restored to Middle America, socially and geographically. If America had attained the summit of the world during the war, as Winston Churchill said, then New York's power elite stood at the summit of the summit.

In urban history, the 1840s and the 1940s are at either end of a great arc, representing a period when cities in Europe and North America were growing at the fastest rate in history until the present urban explosion in what used to be called the Third World. In both decades, there was a brisk traffic in intellectuals and literary fashions, mostly from Europe, such as zoologist and geologist Louis Agassiz, and Fourierism (a type of Utopian socialism), lurid, urban novels of the 1840s, and in the 1940s the Frankfurt School, surrealism, and existentialism. In *The Decline of the West*, Oswald Spengler, the gloomy German historian whose long perspectives were much consulted in the forties by intellectuals and policy makers alike, wrote that "the rise of New York to the position of world-city during the Civil War of 1861–1865 may perhaps prove to have been the most pregnant event of the nineteenth century." Many of these writers, intellectuals, and policy makers, past and present, would have appreciated the irony that a "world-city" built on a grid like New York was "the Stone Colossus" at the end of a culture's life span, a sign of old age and decay, not vigor and promise. During the war, William S. Burroughs, an elderly twenty-nine to their early twenties, insisted his young friends Jack Kerouac and Allen Ginsberg read Spengler, and they were forever after haunted by a sense that they were living in the last days of the big cities. Sooner rather than later, joining the eternal Fellahin of the earth after the bomb was dropped, they would creep, like beatified mice, among the ruins in a world that had outlasted history. As E. B. White wrote in *Here Is New York*, a flight of planes "no larger than a wedge of geese" could destroy the most stupendous monument ever created by mankind for itself.

The photographer and diarist Cecil Beaton vaingloriously claimed that his 1938 book *Cecil Beaton's New York* was "more incomplete than any other book about New York." Really, what book on the subject could *not* be incomplete? *The Brazen Age* is at heart an interpretive historical essay, mostly along old-fashioned literary and political lines; and tracing them, I have often found myself being drawn far into the past to explain what was happening during its brief span.

If asked how I came to write the book as I have done, I might plead simply that in the New York panorama certain persons, places, and evolving themes (such as its mastery of the media as the reason for its "supremacy") came to exercise a fascination that I hope will communicate itself to the reader. I admit there is a great deal about the Roosevelts, that ancient clan of Manhattan. The maguslike figure of FDR, who made New York City his citadel while always identifying himself as an upstate squire, dominated the politics of the age while he lived and haunted them after he was gone. Having reordered American society with the New Deal, he contrived during the few years of the war to create an American empire unlike any the world had ever seen. The Korean War's proximate origins began with an imperialist escapade by his older distant cousin Theodore Roosevelt.

By adjusting the historical parallax by lining up the figures in the landscape along certain sightlines and not others, we can make New York resemble Alexandria or Rome, a "glittering metropolis" or an aging one. Looking back seventy years after the end of the Second World War, New York in the forties presents quite another aspect than it did in 1961, when Jane Jacobs celebrated Greenwich Village in *The Death and Life of Great American Cities* as a watchful, mini-cooperative community; or than it did ten years later, when W. H. Auden, a long-term tenant on St. Mark's Place, portrayed the Village as a postapocalyptic wasteland. More recently, there is Russell Shorto's charming conceit that Dutch Manhattan in the seventeenth and eighteenth centuries was "the Island at the Center of the World," because we now understand that multiculturalism is the essential fact of the city's rise.

One of the greatest historical ironies of the postwar era is that a time that began in the West—most especially in America, so comparatively opulent—with fears of a renewed depression after the great machinery of war was shut down, is now seen as the portal for what historians call a golden age (or, in France, "the thirty glorious years," *les trente glorieuses*), of 1945 to c. 1974: a period of rising income, more diffused prosperity, and declining inequality. Now that we can appreciate (or despair at!) the massive historical statistical analysis of Thomas Piketty in *Capital in the Twenty-first Century*, we know what a singular time that was: a bright, shining moment in what looms as an endless series of ages gilded for the few and dark for the many. Meanwhile, wars and rumors of war continue to define our American condition; if our wars since 1945 have been undeclared, it is because Harry Truman set the precedent with the "police action" in Korea that brought an end to what I call the Brazen Age. The intervals have been, in the title of David Halberstam's book about the George H. W. Bush and Bill Clinton interventions, *War in a Time of Peace.*

These are not the notes of a native son, or a sojourner. All histories are a form of time travel, or perhaps the better figure would be diving into the wreck. I had no foreboding the first time I followed Vidal into lost time in New York that I would ever come to write about it, let alone spend so many years attempting its circumnavigation.

Brief portions of this book have previously appeared in essays, reviews, or lectures, almost all of them published under academic auspices and addressed to "fit audience though few." Any readers who experience a shock of recognition are likely to be old friends.

David Reid
May 2015
Berkeley, California

President Roosevelt, with his Scottie dog, Fala, in Brooklyn in the midst of his New York campaign tour, October 21, 1944

THE LAST HURRAH
OF FRANKLIN D. ROOSEVELT

No memento mori is so clinching as a photograph of a vanished crowd.

—JOHN UPDIKE

SATURDAY MORNING, OCTOBER 21, 1944, a dark, cold, rainy day in New York City: the train carrying the president's armor-plated private Pullman car, the *Ferdinand Magellan*, pulled into the Bush Terminal in Brooklyn at dawn. A hurricane passing by at sea had been drenching the northeastern seaboard. The day before, at a White House press conference, his 974th since March 1933, the commander-in-chief had hailed the landing of American troops led by General Douglas MacArthur at Leyte in the Philippines. "We promised to return; we *have* returned," he read from his official statement to boisterous reporters crowding the Oval Office, before entertaining questions. With such news, the Democrat in the White House could afford to blandly sidestep the latest Republican attacks on his administration of "tired, quarrelsome, old men."

"I say I'm tough this morning," he replied when asked about the weather awaiting him in New York. "I hope you don't get wet, those who are going."

Franklin Delano Roosevelt, whose candidacy for an unprecedented third term in 1940 had caused the *Saturday Evening Post* to warn grimly, "He is the one whom the Founders feared," was now seeking a hitherto unimaginable fourth. With sixteen days remaining until the first wartime presidential election since 1864, the Gallup, Crossley, and Roper polls showed the president narrowly leading his Republican opponent, Thomas E. Dewey, the taut, contained, inquisitorial governor of New York, aged forty-two—twenty years Roosevelt's junior and a head shorter—whom FDR privately called "the little bastard."

So far, the election was turning out to be a bitter and morose affair on the Republican side. Dewey, who had achieved his fame as a prosecutor, caravanned through deserted streets to halls packed with GOP faithful, where, to the satisfaction of his core constituency of Roosevelt haters, he would arraign the president as a power-mad bungler. "You ought to hear him," Roosevelt wondered to Robert E. Sherwood, the Broadway playwright who moonlighted as a presidential speechwriter and had just returned from an Office of War Information (OWI) assignment in Europe. "He plays the part of a heroic racket-buster in one of those gangster movies. He talks to the people as if they were the jury and I the villain on trial for his life."

With the exception of his address to the Teamsters union banquet in Washington, DC, a month before, Roosevelt had disdained to campaign in the routine way, citing his responsibilities as commander-in-chief. Until then, and to the alarm of his wife, Eleanor, and his closest aides, he seemed frankly bored with electoral politics, odd behavior for the creator of the modern Democratic Party. The vibrant, omnipresent FDR of the 1930s, grinning and chain-smoking on the dais at Washington banquets; dedicating the great public works: dams and bridges and monuments, constructed by the New Deal "alphabet agencies," the WPA and the PWA; democratically eating picnic lunches with the young men of the Civilian Conservation Corps; demagogically scourging "organized money" at monster rallies ("They are unanimous in their hate for me—*and I welcome their hatred!*" he roared at Madison Square Garden as a candidate for reelection in 1936)—this American Caesar had all but disappeared into the aloof and cloistered routines of a warrior-king.

"I ought not to say it, even to you," old Marvin McIntyre, his confidential assistant of a quarter-century, whispered to a younger White House aide, "but he's getting to be one of those Olympian gods." But if ever Franklin Roosevelt was indifferent to his reelection, Tom Dewey's insufferable prosecutorial style, the insinuations about the state of Roosevelt's health, the strident immigrant- and Red-baiting of the opposition had rekindled his incomparable political instincts.

"Who was president during the depression that lasted from 1933 until 1940 when war orders from all over the world began to bring us full employment again?" demanded the governor, who was running as the candidate of youth and snappy efficiency. (It was as if he were counting on younger voters to forget that the Depression had begun under Herbert Hoover.) *"It's time for a change!"* Reporters on his chartered train, who mostly disliked him, called Dewey "Mr. Warmth." His campaign, which drew heavily on alumni of the *New York Times* for its top staff, was a very New York affair. In contrast to FDR, the upstate patrician in politics, the metallic, jumped-up Dewey was a New York archetype: one of those hyper-ambitious young men of small-town, middle-class, usually midwestern origins (Dewey grew up in Owosso, Wisconsin) who laid siege to the city, establishing themselves in law firms, industries, banks, foundations—or more rarely, as in Dewey's case, in public service—and after a decent interval were rewarded by admission to the old-money society of the "Perfumed Stockade" on the Upper East Side.*

After finishing Columbia Law School, where he excelled (unlike FDR), Thomas Edmund Dewey's dream was to join a big downtown law firm "and make a hell of a lot of money." Instead, in 1931, when the Prohibition-era rackets were threatening to turn New York into a kleptocracy, he was recruited as chief assistant to the United States attorney for New York's Southern District, the legendary George Z. Medalie; and within a few years he rose to national fame as the headline-grabbing special prosecutor in charge of pursuing such notorious male-factors as "Lucky" Luciano, "Legs" Diamond, "Waxey" Gordon, and "Dutch" Schultz (born Arthur Flegenheimer). John Gunther's *Inside U.S.A.* (1947) recalled that what amazed everybody about Dewey—not least the gangsters he put in the dock—was not the hugger-mugger and the Star Chamber methods he brought to the game, all the wiretap-ping and the boy-detective shenanigans, but the glaring fact that he was *honest.* This amounted to "a considerable reflection on the state of civilization in New York City at the time."

In 1940, aged thirty-eight, with no more experience in politics other than a single term as the district attorney of Manhattan and a narrow loss in a race for governor against Herbert H. Lehman (who had appointed him special prosecutor), the gangbuster was considered a plausible contender for the presidency. "I will be president," Dewey

---

* Along with Eastern arrivistes and the livelier heirs of Eastern fortunes, these men comprised the inner circle of the financial and political "Establishment," much writ-ten and railed about in the 1960s, which among other things effectively dominated Republican Party politics from 1940 to 1964. For a reliable but highly colored portrait of the group in its heyday, see Theodore H. White, *The Making of the President 1964* (1965; rpt. Signet Books, 1966), 80ff.

told friends with fond assurance. "It is written in the stars." When a reporter unfamiliar with this horoscope asked what effect Franklin Roosevelt's renomination might have, he exploded: "You make me sick. You're like all the rest of them. Don't you realize that Franklin Roosevelt is the easiest man in the world for me to beat?" But the stars betrayed him. A grassroots movement "sweeping through every country club in America," as Alice Roosevelt Longworth humorously observed, mightily assisted by Henry Luce's Time-Life magazine empire, handed the Republican nomination to the charismatic and frantically loquacious Wendell Willkie, a utilities executive originally from Indiana, whose party affiliation was still listed as Democratic in *Who's Who*. Roosevelt, who rather liked Willkie, easily beat him down. Ohio senator Robert A. Taft, who also contested the nomination in 1940 and would again in 1948 and 1952, did not run in 1944. His core constituency of isolationists—die-hard anti–New Dealers, the proprietors of small family businesses, and the more bunkered corporate industrialists, mostly situated in the Midwest—assembled under the banner of John W. Bricker, the handsome, vacuous governor of the Buckeye state. His nomination for vice president was their consolation prize after he lost to the liberal and internationalist Dewey. Personally, Bricker was harmless, but if the New Deal had failed and fascism had come to America, it is more likely its protagonists would have enlisted someone like this intellectual nonentity as a figurehead president, rather than march to the Capitol under the leadership of a florid demagogue like Huey Long or such a charismatic hero as Charles Lindbergh, whose dictatorship Philip Roth imagines in his counterfactual *The Plot Against America*. But in 1944 the GOP was not going to succumb to a robber bridegroom again.

Elected governor of New York in 1942, Dewey claimed the Republican nomination. If elected, he would be the youngest man to occupy the White House since Theodore Roosevelt, and the first to be born in the twentieth century. Then, he promised, there would be an end to the New Deal's "bungling" and "confusion." The Republican platform duly deplored the New Deal's bureaucratic excesses and drift toward regimentation and one-man rule: "Four more years of the New Deal would centralize all power in the President, and would daily subject every act of every citizen to regulation by his henchmen; and this country would remain a Republic only in name." At the same time, the platform promised to keep in place most of the regime's principal regulatory props, including the Securities and Exchange Commission; and it conceded Social Security, which Dewey wanted to enlarge, the Wagner Act, and the minimum wage. The Republicans also endorsed what his biographer Richard Norton Smith describes as "the strongest civil rights plank yet to appear in a major party platform, including support for the Fair Employment Practices Commission."

For all the rant, it was a liberal platform, in some respects a more liberal one than the Democrats'. But then, liberalism carried no taint in 1944; quite the contrary, left and right disputed who were the *real* liberals. For his part, FDR had declared in the class-conscious election of 1936: "'Liberalism becomes the protection for the far-sighted conservative . . . Reform if you will preserve.' I am that kind of liberal because I am that kind of conservative."

Until the *Ferdinand Magellan* arrived in New York City, the voters had only heard from Roosevelt as a candidate when he spoke to the Teamsters in Washington, DC, in a nationally broadcast address.

But that occasion found him in legendary form. "Well, here we are together again—after four years—and what years they have been!" he led off. Admitting to being four years older than in 1940, "which is a fact that seems to annoy some people," he ridiculed the Republican mythologists who, he said, had borrowed the Hitlerian technique of the "big lie" to advance the bizarre notion that the Depression was the work of the Democrats. "Now, there is an old and somewhat lugubrious adage which says: 'Never speak of rope in the house of a man who has been hanged.' In the same way, if I were a Republican leader speaking to a mixed audience, the last word in the whole dictionary that I think I would use is that word 'Depression.'" And then he moved on to a passage of elaborate drollery that he had personally composed in reply to a heaven-sent piece of absurdity that a Republican congressman from Minnesota had handed him.

"These Republican leaders have not been content with attacks on me, or my wife, or my sons," he said mournfully. "No, not content with that, they now include my little dog, Fala. Well, of course, I don't resent attacks, and my family doesn't resent attacks, but Fala *does* resent attacks. You know, Fala is Scottish, and being a Scottie, as soon as he learned that the Republican fiction writers in Congress and out had concocted a story that I had left him behind on the Aleutian Islands and had sent a destroyer back to find him—at a cost to the taxpayers of two or three or eight or twenty million dollars—his Scotch soul was furious. He has not been the same dog since. I am accustomed to hearing malicious falsehoods about myself—such as that old, worm-eaten chestnut that I have represented myself as indispensable. But I think I have a right to resent, to object to libelous statements about my dog."

These sallies convulsed the banquet hall and tickled most of the country, and afterward it was said that the race was between "Roosevelt's dog and Dewey's goat." Carried over the radio, the "Fala" speech, which is about all that popular memory preserves of the 1944 campaign, is now reckoned FDR's single most virtuosic performance in the medium—the quintessential modern medium—that he made peculiarly his own; and all the more remarkably so because the famous "Fireside Chats" were usually delivered in the privacy of the White House, when he could address, alone at the microphones, a vast but unseen audience. At the time, however, for every letter that came into the White House congratulating FDR on a "humdinger" of a speech, a letter to the editor complained that the president was comparing Dewey to Hitler, cracking adolescent jokes, and commiserating with his dog while American boys were fighting and dying in stinking jungles or frozen wastes. Predictably, wartime had inflamed the wide streak of priggishness that has been noticed by so many foreign observers of American life. But the speech clearly had the effect of bringing both campaigns to life, which was Roosevelt's aim. Much of the electorate was jaded, bored, distracted, impatient, or simply apathetic—a state of affairs more threatening to FDR's prospects than to Dewey's, since Republicans (who enjoyed a slight edge in registration nationally) were far more reliable voters than Democrats: so many of them young and in arms.

Nine a.m., Eastern War Time. Anxious to rebut rumors that he was in failing health, even dying—rumors he blamed on concerted Republican whispers and deeply resented—Roosevelt had scheduled a fifty-mile automobile procession through the boroughs of Brooklyn, Queens, the Bronx, and Manhattan; this was to demonstrate in the most vivid possible way that, as Sherwood put it, he was alive and laughing. It was a huge gamble, and left only the briefest respite before a well-advertised address to the Foreign Policy Association of New York at the Waldorf Astoria Hotel. Despite protests by his wife and his personal physician, Dr. Ross McIntire, he would not hear of disappointing the voters because of stormy weather.

"I'm going," he said, and ordered Mike Reilly, the head of the Secret Service, to remove the canvas top of the huge green Packard touring car brought up from Washington as he set off for the Brooklyn Army Base, adjacent to the Bush Terminal. But Roosevelt was not alone. Joining him was New York's ebullient mayor, Fiorello La Guardia, known as the "Little Flower" (he was five feet two and rotund, a bowling ball of man with tousled hair). Though nominally a Republican, he had enjoyed a zestful partnership with Roosevelt that began when he was still in Congress—a "New Dealer before there was a New Deal"—and lasted the length of his mayoralty, beginning January 1, 1934.

Throughout the day, as the *New York Times* reported on Sunday, October 22, the president would be the "sole object of solicitude and protection" for 10,400 uniformed policemen, as his twenty-seven-car motorcade wound through the four boroughs. The motorcycle cops had donned heavy rubber jackets, and the Secret Service agents on the Packard's running boards were in raincoats, but Roosevelt wore no more visible protection from the elements than his Navy cape and good-luck gray fedora. (A heater at his feet and a fur lap robe were out of sight.) Only he seemed to realize that the clouds' obstinate failure to part was the greatest possible political good fortune. Braving the storm would be an infinitely more effective rebuttal to the whispers of fading health than a comfortable ride in the sunshine. Throughout the day Roosevelt gloated over his good luck in having such bad weather to contend with.

At the Brooklyn Army Base, anyone wondering how the commander-in-chief looked saw him peering at jeeps and howitzers. At the Navy Yard, a few miles away, the sights were more grandiose: the immense "hammerhead crane," which could lift four hundred tons, and the storied battleship *Texas*, former flagship of the fleet, being readied for transfer to the Pacific theater and the bloody invasion of Iwo Jima.

After acknowledging the cheers of forty thousand war workers and servicemen at the Army Base, he was greeted by another seventy thousand at the Brooklyn Navy Yard, where, reported the *Times*, "women riveters, in working hoods and slacks, stood alongside Navy personnel and men workers in their overalls." Eleanor Roosevelt and Fala now joined him and Mayor Fiorello La Guardia for the rest of the journey. The big car turned into blue-collar Flatbush: down Park Avenue, Tillary Street, Fulton Street, and Bedford Avenue, all lined with cheering men, and women blowing kisses. Drenched and beaming, he arrived at Ebbets Field, home of the Brooklyn Dodgers. An enthusiastic crowd of fifteen thousand was waiting in the stands, huddled under umbrellas, as he was driven onto the playing field, where a ramp and speaker's stand had been constructed on second base. Crouching on hands and knees, Mike Reilly locked the president's knee braces. Doffing his fedora and cape, FDR stood and gripped the makeshift podium; "and while the rain beat down," his correspondence secretary, William Hassett, recorded in his diary, "he waved his greeting to the crowd—with his best smile, too, dynamic, radiant—his very presence in the storm giving the lie to his detractors who have carried on unremittingly a whispering campaign, a vendetta, against his health."

"I have never been to Ebbets Field before," Franklin Roosevelt confessed, "but I have rooted for the Dodgers. And I hope to come back here someday and see them play." His voice had lately begun to lose some of its old timbre and force, so his traveling party was amazed when it seemed to boom across the ballpark. "But the chief reason I am here today is to pay a little tribute to my old friend [Senator] Bob Wagner. We were together in the Legislature—I would hate to say how long ago—thirty-some years ago—in the Senate of the State of New York. We have been close friends ever since, I think largely because we have the same ideas of being of service to our fellow men." (Roosevelt liked to reminisce for the benefit of impressionable young reporters that he and Wagner had been denounced as "Communists" for supporting unemployment insurance and other radical measures.) Organized labor's staunchest friend in the Senate was in a tough race for reelection and needed Brooklyn's votes to prevail. FDR urged Brooklyn to give theirs to him.

From Brooklyn the motorcade passed into Queens and paused at

Flushing Meadows. Where the "master builder" Robert Moses had staged the World's Fair of 1939–40, there remained a skating rink, a handful of pavilions, the famous Unisphere (but not the eighteen-story Trylon, which had been torn down). It was said by insiders that Moses was one of the two men in public life that FDR truly hated. (The other was his isolationist congressman from Hyde Park, Hamilton Fish, long ago his classmate at Harvard, where Fish, a famous athlete, had been the bigger man on campus.) The World's Fair, signaling as it did America's emergence from the Depression, was one Moses triumph FDR approved.

Before the cheering stopped, Roosevelt was back in his car and speeding to a nearby Coast Guard station. Carried into the infirmary, he was rubbed down with heavy towels, braced with a short whiskey, dressed in a fresh suit, and, wrapped in his cape, carried back to his car. The rain, which had not let up, seemed to exhilarate him: he said he felt "fine, fine," and somehow he looked it. Crossing the Triborough Bridge, they headed to the Bronx, where, as in Brooklyn, Democrats regularly outpolled Republicans by three to one. Irish, Italians, and, predominantly, Jews lived in the apartment blocks along the Grand Concourse, whose aspiring "modern" architecture and modest comfort seemed in 1944 to be part of the gleaming future promised by the New Deal order. And here coming down the Grand Concourse in the rain was the paradoxical avatar of modernity—an elderly aristocrat in a cape, raising his battered fedora, raindrops gleaming on his old-fashioned pince-nez.

The citizens of the Bronx cheered and cheered.

As the presidential procession moved into its teeming streets, Franklin Roosevelt might have pondered the remarkable history of Upper Manhattan, once old family territory. (Early in the nineteenth century, FDR's great-grandfather James Roosevelt owned four hundred acres situated between the river and what became Fifth Avenue and 110th and 125th Streets, comprising almost all of what was later known as Spanish Harlem in the 1940s; when the land proved too rocky and barren for farming he sold it to John Jacob Astor for $25,000.) Nieuw Haarlem was settled in the 1650s by Dutch farmers and enterprising French Huguenots, mainly, and they were followed by a great mix, including Danes and Swedes. Between its three rivers, Harlem remained remote and pastoral until the mid-nineteenth century, when Germans arrived in numbers. It was briefly a fashionable address and later one of the densest Jewish quarters in the city (and in the world); then, as real-estate prices fell, it drew black migrants from the South after the First World War, followed by immigrants from Russia, Mexico, Puerto Rico, and what became the largest Finnish colony in the country. By 1944, "Negro Harlem," which FDR's procession had now entered, had an African American population of 310,000, the largest in the country, outnumbering the entire population of Atlanta or Dallas.

In 1932 most black voters outside New York remained loyal to the party of Lincoln; there, Roosevelt was known as a charismatic and effective governor in hard times. After his election as president, he won over a majority with the New Deal relief and recovery programs, which at their height gave jobs to a third of the black workforce, the fireside chats, "which gave many a feeling of belonging that they had never experienced before," and the inspiration they derived from his example of overcoming a handicap. As the historian John Hope Franklin sums up: "He had overcome his; perhaps someday they could overcome theirs." By 1936, Roosevelt's following among black voters across the country was overwhelming, and those who could not vote sometimes sent poignant "notes" to the White House to declare their support. It was the same from the streets to the lights of the Apollo Theater and the heights of Sugar Hill. W. E. B. Du Bois—sooner than A. Philip Randolph, though he was parlaying with the White House by 1942—gave his imprimatur to the New Deal; and "Fats" Waller declared: "The three greatest men who ever lived are Johann Sebastian Bach, Abraham Lincoln, and Franklin D. Roosevelt."

Now, in 1944, Harlem's handsome, hyperkinetic Reverend Adam Clayton Powell Jr., who had followed his father into the ministry of the huge Abyssinian Baptist Church, was running a strong race for Congress as a Democrat, vying to become the third black congressman to be elected since the end of Reconstruction. (Chicago had elected two black Republicans to Congress since the 1920s, one of whom converted to a New Deal Democrat.) In the 1944 presidential election Governor Dewey had much to recommend him to African Americans, notably, pushing a bill to create a strong state Fair Employment Practices Committee through the New York legislature. Needing the votes of Southerners in Congress to pass other legislation, FDR had failed to endorse even the anti-lynching bills strongly favored by liberals in his party, including Eleanor Roosevelt and his vice president, Henry Wallace. But nothing seemed to shake his hold on the affections of America's eligible black voters. By autumn the only question that remained was the size of FDR's margin. On this October day, the number of voters waving from the windows of Lenox Avenue as the president's car passed augured a big one.

Briefly, the procession came out of the rain when the Packard was driven into the Park Avenue Armory near Hunter College, where Roosevelt raised his hat in salute to rows of uniformed WAVES. Returning to the drenched streets, the motorcade turned south, down Seventh Avenue, onto Broadway, down to Times Square, and into the jammed streets of the Garment District, where an immense crowd, several hundred thousand strong, huddled beneath newspapers and umbrellas, thundered its deafening welcome, which enveloped the procession as Roosevelt lifted his good-luck fedora again and again. In front of Roosevelt's car rode a truck with newsreel cameras. Around it roamed the photographers with Speed Graphic cameras assigned by newspapers friendly and hostile; around them surged the crowd.

The garment industry, the biggest employer in the city, and until the wartime boom in armaments the fourth largest industry in the country, had migrated from the Lower East Side to the West Side earlier in the century; and in 1944 FDR had no more loyal constituency than the workers in the garment and fur trades—predominantly Jewish and Italian, and thoroughly, competitively unionized by the Amalgamated Clothing Workers of America, Sidney Hillman's organization, and the International Ladies Garment Workers' Union, headed by David Dubinsky. In the teens and twenties, these unions had developed complex interpenetrating relations with New York's flourishing Jewish gangland. Impartially supporting strikes—or cracking skulls and providing escorts for scabs to break them—the gangs paradoxically added a principle of stability to the volatile scene. In the battle between the Communists and the Socialists for control of the needle trades in the twenties, both sides had hired dubious allies and enforcers: the Com-

munists relied on goons provided by the legendary gambler Arnold
Rothstein—most famously Louis "Lepke" Buchalter, later of Murder,
Inc. ill fame. Freelancing after Rothstein's abrupt end, Lepke went to
work on the side of the Socialists, who eventually prevailed in the garment trade. The furriers, however, preserved their Communist affilia-
tions, terrifying opposing unionists and hired guns with their cutting
hooks.

This ancient struggle had found Hillman, Roosevelt's most enduring labor partner, allied with his temperamental opposite, the expansive, explosive Dubinsky. But neither then nor later did Hillman share
Dubinsky's fervent anticommunism. In his youth, Hillman had met
with Lenin and Trotsky—both "practical idealists" in his view—and
had worked with American Communists until 1924, when the Kremlin
banned such compromising alliances during the International's most
sectarian phase. The question of what exactly Hillman had known
about Lepke's activities back in the twenties had pursued him, like his
revolutionary past, into the 1944 campaign, when "Check it with Sidney" became a Republican catchphrase. The words, sometimes quoted
as "Clear everything with Sidney," were supposedly FDR's instructions
to his aides at the Democratic convention, specifically in regard to Truman's vice-presidential nomination. In certain political and gangland
circles it was believed that Lepke, now facing the electric chair, was
being kept alive by Dewey in the hope he would implicate Hillman in
the contract murder of the gangster's former associate "Little Augie"
Orgen, long ago the hired protector of the Communist Party.

A practiced hand with organized labor since the First World War,
FDR had allied himself with unionism since the New Deal turned to
the left in 1934. In 1936, against the advice of Democratic machinists
like Jim Farley and Ed Flynn, the "Boss of the Bronx," he approved
Hillman's plan to form the American Labor Party (ALP), which then
endorsed Roosevelt from the left, polling almost three hundred thousand votes for him, and as many for the Democratic governor, Herbert Lehman, and the nominally Republican mayor, La Guardia. The
ALP was a vehicle for the mostly Jewish Socialists and their families
who supported FDR but were spared the culture shock of voting for
a Democratic ticket and being associated with the Irish-dominated
Tammany Hall. These were union votes and old-time Socialist votes,

as the *New York Times*'s veteran political reporter Warren Moscow wrote, "but they also came from the mothers and grandmothers of union members, old people who had never voted before. They came out of their tenements to vote for the man they had heard on their installment-payment radio sets, for the man who to many of them was the new Messiah."

After so many years FDR remained the Messiah on the radio, but by 1944 Hillman and Dubinsky were fiercely at odds over the issue of Communists in the labor movement. Now, with the proviso that they not run as candidates or stand as officers, Hillman favored accepting Communists into the ALP, which, after all, had been formed as a vehicle for the longtime Socialists and their families who supported FDR but could not abide the culture shock of joining the Democratic Party. But Hillman's compromise was one that Dubinsky and his associate Alex Rose of the American Hatters' Union vehemently opposed. The result was a bitter split from the ALP and the birth of the Liberal Party, whose support of Roosevelt was untainted with Communist associations.

At Twenty-third Street, the procession paused, and Dave Dubinsky handed the president a bouquet on behalf of the ILGWU.

The great organizational novelty in the 1944 campaign was the CIO Political Action Committee, the prototype of the "PACs" that have been part of the political landscape ever since. The idea came from Philip Murray, the head of the CIO since 1940, when its cofounder, the United Mine Workers' turbulent president, John L. Lewis, followed through on his threat to resign if FDR was elected to a third term. A lifelong Republican, Lewis had worked closely with Roosevelt in his first term, as an ally, advisor, and high-level appointee, but felt betrayed when the president abandoned labor to pronounce "a plague on both your houses" during the Little Steel strike in 1937. "It ill behooves one who has supped at labor's table . . . to curse with equal fervor and fine impartiality both labor and its adversaries when they become locked in deadly embrace," he declaimed. Relations came embittered, at least on Lewis's part, and in 1940 he assailed the third term, while privately hinting that his nomination for vice president might assuage his

concerns. When this was not forthcoming, he denounced FDR more
fervently in the election than his actual opponent, Wendell Willkie,
ever did.*

As it happened, Earl Browder, the Communist Party leader, came
of old-settler stock and so could not be counted among the immigrant
riffraff like Hillman. Apart from that, he made a serviceable bogey
for the Republicans. Browder's famous slogan was "Communism is
twentieth-century Americanism." In May 1944, dutiful to the line
dictated by Moscow but undoubtedly in accordance with his own convictions, he had dissolved the old Communist Party, the CP, in favor
of a Communist Political Association, or CPA. At a tumultuous rally
in Madison Square Garden, the CPA had then endorsed Roosevelt's
reelection in the "spirit of Teheran."

Whatever hopes he might be reposing in a postwar settlement with
Stalin, FDR was anticommunist, as the Communist Party knew full
well. Willing to bend in the interests of wartime unity, he had par-
doned Browder, who had been convicted on dubious grounds of violating passport laws, and allowed the Communist leader to write him at
the White House, through a friend of Eleanor's. Nor was he about to
call off Sidney Hillman's troops in the American Labor Party. But the
burden of a CP endorsement, whatever the party called itself, was not
one that he was prepared to shoulder, and he promptly repudiated its
support. Roosevelt's disavowal of a Communist endorsement was then
seized upon as an excuse to belabor him with it.

"I shall be compelled to discuss it quite openly," Dewey said. Unlike
his running mate, Governor Bricker of Ohio, Dewey stopped short
of declaring the national Democratic ticket a front for the "Hillman-
Browder axis." Rather, as *Time* approvingly stated, Dewey attributed
Browder's support of "Term IV" to the New Deal's corporate-statism—
look at all those thousands of factories Franklin Roosevelt had created,
he said, "that and the fact that the Communists 'love to fish in troubled
waters,' and know that 'their aims can best be served by unemployment
and discontent.'"

---

* Lewis's once-enormous fame has faded, and is now quite exceeded by that of his
acolyte, Saul Alinsky, the pioneer community organizer, a hero to the New Left, and
a bugbear to the right, who published a deeply admiring biography of Lewis in 1949.

. . .

As the huge touring car passed through the Garment and Fur districts (and the Flower Market, too), one thousand policemen, standing shoulder-to-shoulder, separated the crowd from the president. Labor's was the only organized demonstration during the entire tour, according to the *Times*, except for a dance by some black teenagers in Harlem. Historically, it was a poignant one, as Michael Barone, a leading historian of elections, writes: "In New York—the city, which in October 1944 was economically, demographically, and intellectually the greatest city in the world—Franklin Roosevelt was happy to parade as a vulgar politician seeking the votes and acknowledging the cheers of the polyglot masses whom he was content to count as his equals. Together, they were celebrating his forthcoming political victory, but even more they were with a sense of wonderment and exultation beginning to understand that their country—the country which had seemed ruined and stagnant just eleven years before—was now the most powerful and prosperous and beneficent country in the world."

Earlier, the route down Fifth Avenue had brought the procession alongside the Empire State Building. It was still raining. Did FDR pause to remember Al Smith, who had inadvertently hurried him on his way to the presidency in 1928, pressing him to run for governor against his, Roosevelt's, private schedule (which called for him to reenter electoral politics no sooner than 1932)?

A political back number after 1936, when he supported the reactionary Liberty League, which had formed to oppose the New Deal, and moved to Park Avenue, Al Smith had spent his later years working as the president of this skyscraper, the tallest and emptiest in the world. And now he was dead. He had died on October 4, and although he had supported for president the Republicans Alfred Landon in 1936 and Willkie in 1940, Eleanor Roosevelt had dutifully attended his funeral at St. Patrick's Cathedral. It had been a long time since Smith had mattered in the councils of the Democratic Party, and even longer since his and FDR's friendship of convenience had broken up. But Roosevelt had bigger things on his mind than the Empire State Building.

. . .

As the afternoon waned, the motorcade was heading south on Fifth Avenue, in a misty rain out of an old Alfred Stieglitz photograph. At 29 Washington Square, where Eleanor Roosevelt had purchased an apartment in a modern building two years before, the Packard stopped. With police cordoning off either end of the block from a curious crowd of fifteen thousand, and a knot of protective Secret Service agents blocking him from view, the president was carried from his car into the building. It had taken his caravan four hours to travel fifty-one miles, and the police commissioner, a Democrat, estimated that FDR had been seen by three million people.

Washington Square presented Greenwich Village's most sedate and dignified face. Long after newer money had surged north, it remained a bastion of old New York aristocracy, digging down in the Greek Revival houses of the northern row. Greenwich Village, too, inevitably had Roosevelt associations. "Isaac the Patriot," the ancestor of whom FDR was proudest, had spent his old age in a fine house on Bleecker Street, not far from where Tom Paine lived more humbly, and close to where his great-great-grandson now came out of the rain.

Refreshed by another rubdown, FDR beamed as he sat propped up by pillows in bed and drank a medicinal glass of whiskey prescribed by Dr. McIntire. Plainly exhilarated, he called for a second bourbon, then a third, after he was dressed and wheeled into the library to join the little company that had been invited to share his triumph: Bill Hassett, Dr. McIntire, and FDR's cousin Daisy Suckley. Eleanor proudly noted that the apartment could be reached without climbing steps and had a self-contained suite of two rooms and a bath for his use. After an austere lunch of eggs and rice, he retired to rest and bathe. An hour or so later, he reappeared, dressed in black tie for his address to the Foreign Policy Association. FDR mixed drinks for his guests before departing with Eleanor for his speech.

Preceded by a motorcycle escort on Park Avenue, they were at the Waldorf Astoria in no time. The cold, rainy day had yielded to a cold, blustery night. Fifteen hundred uniformed policemen and a thousand detectives had been detailed to protect the president. In the grand ballroom two thousand members and guests of the Foreign Policy Association awaited his appearance. An organist played "Hail to the Chief." Roosevelt's usual practice at banquets and other big affairs was to arrive early so that he would already be seated when the guests began filing in. But whenever this was not possible, it was the custom of his entourage, going back to the twenties, to form an enthusiastic claque around him to prevent the rest of the crowd from witnessing the awkward moment when he was being transferred from his wheelchair to his place at the table; so it was this night.

The ovation lasted seven minutes, suggesting how the Perfumed Stockade would receive his speech. In his procession through the city, Roosevelt had shown himself to the millions, saluting them as they cheered for him. Now, in the grand ballroom of the Waldorf Astoria Hotel, he was speaking to a considerable part of New York's power elite. It was "a Republican audience, at least two-thirds of it," FDR's correspondence secretary, Bill Hassett, estimated. "Every place was taken at the closely placed tables on the main floor and in the double rows of upper galleries—most of the diners fifty years old, many of them more than sixty. At a table adjacent to mine sat John Dewey, who has just passed his eighty-fifth birthday." Seated on either side of the president on the dais were the secretary of war, the venerable Henry L. Stimson, and the vigorous secretary of the navy, James V. Forrestal, along with ex-Governor Herbert Lehman and, in from California, the industrialist Henry J. Kaiser, builder of Liberty Ships.

"Colonel" Stimson, as he was known for his service as an artillery officer in the First World War, personified the foreign-policy establishment and the class from which it was drawn: old family, Yale (Phi Beta Kappa, Skull and Bones), Harvard Law School, partner at Root and Clark on Wall Street. He was a friend and supporter of Theodore Roosevelt, secretary of war under William Howard Taft, governor-general of the Philippines, and secretary of state under Herbert Hoover. Stimson was seventy-three years old in 1940 when he accepted FDR's invitation to return to an office he had held thirty years before. It outraged Republican stalwarts that one of their most venerated elder statesmen had consented to be so blatantly co-opted, but the Colonel was happy to join what was shaping up to be a war cabinet. In 1942 Stimson, who could boast of a few skirmishes in the Indian "wars" of the last century, was put in charge of "S-1," the project to build an atomic bomb, whose authorization by FDR was the darkest and most expensive secret of the war effort. His counterpart, James Forrestal, the civilian builder of history's greatest navy, had climbed from lace-curtain origins about which he tended to be mysterious to the heights of Wall Street as president of the great private bank Dillon, Read—heights to which Herbert Lehman, as a scion of the German-Jewish banking clan, was born. One of Roosevelt's oldest and closest allies in New York politics, Lehman had succeeded him as governor and was now serving as head of the United Nations Relief and Rehabilitation Administration.

Henry J. Kaiser was a phenomenon, the most daunting industrialist of the day, chief contractor of the Hoover Dam, the San Francisco–Oakland Bay Bridge, the Bonneville Dam, and a myriad of other projects *and* the greatest shipbuilder in history, with facilities in Northern California and elsewhere that accounted for a third of the merchant navy built during the war, as well as fifty small aircraft carriers for combat. Kaiser, ready to tackle any challenge, boasted that "problems were just opportunities with their work clothes on." Republicans found Kaiser a distinctly ominous figure: by registration he was one of them, but he was a supremely successful capitalist who declared, "To break a union is to break yourself." He was a paternalistic employer who offered health insurance to his hundred thousand employees, and all his magnificent projects as well as his corporate statesmanship were financed with government money. (The most recent was the Fontana, California, steel mill that the Reconstruction Finance Corporation (RFC) had lent him $110 million to build.) In short, the great Henry Kaiser was a *state* capitalist, a "coddled New Deal pet," as the Hearst chain called him, as feared and shunned by conservatives as he was lionized by progressives. Hulking and mostly bald, Kaiser in his early sixties looked like the shopkeeper he once was. In New York he worked out of a suite of offices in Rockefeller Center, "luxuriously crisp and modern," with an unlisted telephone number and no name on the door; but his many enterprises were headquartered in Oakland, California. When John Gunther visited his sprawling shipyards on San Francisco Bay, the first thing that struck him was the line of streetcars from the old Sixth Avenue El that Kaiser had bought to ferry his workers to and from their dormitories.

Such were the men with whom "Dr. Win the War" had variously gathered to oversee one of the most formidable military machines in history—in Kaiser's case to supply its need, and in Lehman's to relieve suffering. Two came from old money, two were self-made millionaires, three came from Wall Street and one from the Far West, as it was known in those days, which the New Deal was transforming, partly through his agency. The only Democrat was Forrestal, but that affiliation was merely ancestral; the former head of Dillon, Read was no New Dealer.

It cannot be imagined that very many of those in attendance had stood in the rain to cheer Roosevelt earlier in the day. Yet, to their surprise, a good many were bracing themselves to vote for him. Unlike the elites of Detroit, Cleveland, St. Louis, Chicago, or even Boston, the power elite of New York City was overwhelmingly internationalist, or rather Atlanticist. When New York replaced London as the world's financial capital in 1914, the United States having become a creditor nation, Britain a debtor, their collective power, prestige, and self-esteem rose commensurately. The coming victory would bring the United States, and thus themselves, as the masters of its greatest and richest city, New York, to what Churchill called "the summit of the world." He was commander-in-chief.

For a moment Roosevelt smiled and waved, exaggerating his pleasure at seeing familiar faces in the crowd, until the waiters began serving, and he bent over his speech. Dinner was crabmeat, turtle soup, and breast of chicken. Then the spotlight was turned on the president, and immediately his features were animated, his manner and gestures expansive and elaborate, the old actor once more reviving in the limelight. It was a long speech, beginning with the First World War, when

> we helped to save our freedom, but we failed to organize the kind of world in which future generations could live—with freedom.
>
> Now, the question of the men who will formulate and carry out the foreign policy of this country is in issue in this country—*very much* in issue. It is in issue not in terms of partisan application, but in terms of sober, solemn facts—the facts that are on the record.
>
> If the Republicans were to win control of the Congress in this election—and it is only two weeks from next Tuesday, and I occupy the curious position of being president of the United States, and at the same time a candidate for the presidency—if the Republicans were to win control of the Congress, inveterate isolationists would occupy positions of commanding influence and power.

"Let's be fair," said Roosevelt. "There have been Democrats in the isolationist camp, but they have been relatively few and far between, and so far they have not attained great positions of leadership. And I am proud of the fact that this administration does not have the support of the isolationist press. You know, for about a half-century, I have been accustomed to naming names. I mean specifically, to take the glaring examples, the McCormick-Patterson-Gannett-and-Hearst press." (The *Daily News*, owned by the *Chicago Tribune*'s Colonel Robert R. McCormick, and William Randolph Hearst's *Journal-American* had both sent photographers fanning across the city with the mission of catching the president in a weary, distracted moment. A wan, fatigued-looking Roosevelt duly appeared in their late editions; the next morning in the *Times*, which was reluctantly supporting him, he appeared wide-eyed and animated.)

Turning to the future of the proposed United Nations Organization, he addressed a question that had been put by Senator Joseph Ball of Minnesota about whether it would have to seek authority from member states before authorizing peacekeeping operations.

"The council of the United Nations must have the power to act quickly and decisively to keep the peace, if necessary," Roosevelt said. "A policeman would not be a very effective policeman if, when he saw a felon break into a house, he had to go to the town hall and call a town meeting to issue a warrant before the felon could be arrested.

"So to my simple mind it is clear that if the world organization is to have any reality at all, our American representative must be endowed in advance by the people themselves, by constitutional means through their representatives in Congress, with authority to act."

"Vast Throng Sees Roosevelt" was the headline in the *New York Times* the next morning. The story reported the cheering "less frenzied" than it had been for him four years before, but improved the commissioner's estimate of the crowd to three and a half million. It was sparsest in Queens, liveliest in Upper Manhattan, noisiest in the Garment District.

FDR's tour of the four boroughs set the pattern for the remainder of the campaign—a triumphal progress. There were motorcades and rallies in Chicago; a motorcade through Philadelphia on another rainy day; and a rally in Boston, where Fenway Park was the most intimate venue of the whole campaign, and the teen idol Frank Sinatra substituted as guest celebrity for an ailing Orson Welles (the prodigy who directed *Citizen Kane* and, with his collaborator John Houseman, had been responsible for some of the most notorious triumphs of the Federal Theatre Project, including the so-called voodoo *Macbeth* with an all-black cast and Marc Blitzstein's *The Cradle Will Rock*. Welles adulated Roosevelt, who reciprocated his esteem, and was devoting himself almost exclusively to politicking at this time.) Again and again, Roosevelt arraigned the Republicans for a history of isolationism and ridiculed Dewey's campaign against "quarrelsome, tired old men" when it was precisely these supposedly "incompetent blunderers and bunglers" who were winning the war. He stood strong for the social democracy implicit in his Economic Bill of Rights and promised sixty million jobs—"a good round figure," he said privately—which even the radical Henry Wallace, who provisionally proposed it, thought utopian. It had been a high-wire act by a president afflicted by hypertension and congestive heart disease and who was dying by inches but who, in his last year, laid the architecture for the future: the United Nations, the Bretton Woods international monetary system, the atomic bomb, the GI Bill, and the Economic Bill of Rights, which projected a social democratic America yet to be realized. He replied with "unvarnished contempt" to Dewey's charge that he had sold out the Democratic Party to the CIO PAC and the Communist Party to perpetuate himself in office as a monarch. "Now, really—which is it—communism or monarchy?" he drawled sarcastically.

November 6, the last day before the election, Roosevelt made his customary "sentimental journey" through the Hudson Valley, where he had first campaigned for the state senate in 1912. Eleanor had declined to join him because they were always the *same* places, but his old friend the secretary of the treasury, Henry Morgenthau Jr., sat beside him in his small, hand-controlled Ford convertible, its canvas top pulled down in defiance of a drizzle. In the misty autumn chill the little procession was like a sentimental pendant to the big motorcades as it passed through the old river towns, Kingston, Poughkeepsie, Newburgh, where Roosevelt delivered rambling, inconsequential remarks. The

prospect of handing Tom Dewey his round, pomaded head had invigorated Roosevelt for a while, but the strain of the campaign was beginning to tell. Somewhere along their route, a UPI photographer caught
Roosevelt in a private moment with Morgenthau. A king-size cigarette
dangles from his lips, no holder. Seen in profile, his expression is one of
tired command, quite unlike either the exaggerated delight he usually
affected in public or the grave statesman's mask assumed on solemn
occasions. It is, in the Irish expression, the face of a hard man.

Once the candidates had made their last appeals on radio, the hour
had come for their surrogates in show business. Though the wartime
workweek was more arduous than anything most Americans endure
today, and a majority of the country was only a generation away from
the early-to-bed rigors of agricultural life, political broadcasts typically occurred late in the evening (the customary time for one of FDR's
Fireside Chats was 10:30 p.m., Eastern Time), and on election night in
1940 and again in 1944 the politicking was prolonged into the wee
hours by cavalcades of partisan movie stars, comedians, singers, and
the occasional well-spoken writer.

Dewey did not lack show-business supporters, but as *Time* conceded, "Excitement among the Hollywood Republicans was as tightly
rationed as gasoline." (On Broadway, more so.) Even with Cecil B.
DeMille directing and star turns by Ginger Rogers and Cary Grant,
nothing made up for the dismal speech that Dewey gave at the Hollywood Bowl in September. By contrast, the Hollywood Democratic
Committee could draw on deep reserves of admiration and affection
for Roosevelt, who for his part was quite clear that showmanship
had become a department of statesmanship. "You know, Orson," he
is supposed to have told Welles, "there are only two great actors in
this country right now, and you're one of them." Support for Roosevelt
among Communists and their fellow travelers, mostly screenwriters
and lesser directors, had no doubt waxed and waned according to the
Party line, but many were glad when the "spirit of Teheran" licensed an
enthusiasm they were happy to share with millions of less ideological
Americans. Perhaps communism really was twentieth-century Americanism. Of course, most Hollywood New Dealers were simply that,

although some, like Melvyn Douglas and his wife, Helen Gahagan Douglas, elected to Congress in 1944, and Ronald Reagan belonged to the left wing of the Roosevelt-Democratic coalition. When Norman Corwin, the master of the portentous radio drama, was drafted to write a script for the Democratic National Committee's four-network election-eve broadcast, he found an eager cast in Judy Garland, James Cagney, Groucho Marx, Humphrey Bogart, John Garfield, Lana Turner, George Raft, Jane Wyman, Gene Kelly, and Joan Bennett, broadcasting live from the CBS studio in Los Angeles.

Corwin's script varied sketches and endorsements by the stars with appearances by a railroad brakeman, a housewife, and other exemplars of the ordinary. They were all, as Bennett said, voting "for the Champ." Jane Wyman, then married to Reagan, signed off, and the broadcast was turned over to a studio in New York, where Franchot Tone, Frank Sinatra, Dorothy Parker, and Charles Boyer added their endorsements. Back in Hollywood, Corwin went to Chasen's to celebrate, and Tallulah Bankhead, though she had made the extraordinary sacrifice of giving up alcohol for the duration of the war, kissed his hand as he entered. Election night 1944 was the giddiest hour of the last Popular Front campaign.

The next day, November 7, 1944, Franklin Delano Roosevelt was elected to a fourth term as president of the United States. On Election Day, Roosevelt cast his own ballot with some difficulty. Seated in his wheelchair, he fumbled trying to close the curtains of the voting booth and pull the lever of an unfamiliar new voting machine. After *Time* magazine broke the story, a raft of censorious clergymen were deeply shocked that the exasperated president had exclaimed in his booming voice, "Tom, the goddamned thing won't work." The newsreel photographers, he later claimed, had laced their cables over the booth, "fouling the curtains and making everything inoperable." Faced with clerical disapproval, he would stoutly insist that irritation had not tempted him beyond a mild "damn," though six reporters were ready to testify otherwise.

"Tom," the neighbor whom Roosevelt asked for help, was seventy-five-year-old Tom Leonard, a house painter by profession, who had helped launch Roosevelt's political career thirty-four years earlier. Leonard, one of the three Democratic committeemen for Hyde Park, was one of the first men whose support the twenty-eight-year-old Roosevelt solicited in a run for the state senate after being approached as a prospective candidate by the local Democratic leaders in Poughkeepsie, who reasoned that at least he could pay for his own campaign. Leonard happened to be working as a helper at the summer house of FDR's half-brother, Rosy, when FDR appeared at the door. In his biography Ted Morgan proposes what happened next as "perhaps the most important in Franklin's political development."

"Hello, Tom."

"How do you do, Mr. Roosevelt?"

"No, call me Franklin. I'm going to call you Tom."

"With that phrase," Morgan writes, "he was doing something his father had been incapable of, placing himself on an equal footing with one of the villagers. He was paying obeisance to his new master, the voter . . ."

Despite being so green that he had to be instructed it would not make a good impression to call upon some local politicians wearing jodhpurs and riding boots, Roosevelt displayed an instinct for connecting with crowds and a flair for bravura gestures. He toured Dutchess County district in a red Maxwell, inaugurating the custom of the election-eve automobile tour he would still be following decades later in the midst of a world war. He declared that the fedora was his lucky hat, after one of them saved his head from a nasty scrape in a streetcar crash, and adopted the habit of addressing audiences as "my friends" from the example of a local perennial candidate for Congress. The great process of self-fashioning, which polio would accelerate and refine, began early. On the road to the White House and inside it, he would leave behind the successful politician's usual trail of discarded mentors, disappointed friends, and betrayed allies, though rather fewer than one might expect considering the dazzling heights he climbed, the length of his career, and the controversy aroused by his policies; but both the practical and the sentimental in him appreciated an old companion-in-arms, especially one in Hyde Park, where there were so few left.

Somehow, Tom Leonard freed the lever and FDR cast his vote.

FDR, who always slept late in Hyde Park, had been at the town hall to cast his vote by noon in time to be photographed for the afternoon newspapers. When asked, as custom required, his occupation, he replied, "Tree grower." At the Big House, there were cocktails and dinner for a small party of Delano cousins, old friends, courtiers, and politicians and their wives—the Morgenthaus, the Samuel Rosenmans, the Robert Sherwoods. By nine o'clock Teletype machines in the smoking room were clattering early results, and radios blared in the library, the dining room, and the "snuggery." The appearance of a television set was token. Seated beside him, the president's personal secretary, Grace Tully, kept an open telephone line to Democratic headquarters at the Biltmore in New York. Roosevelt placed or took a few calls, inspected the memoranda prepared by Bill Hassett, and chatted with Morgenthau, Sherwood, Rosenman, and other operatives who wandered in from the library.

In those days it was understood that until mid-evening the U.S.A. would appear to be a Republican country: the small-town gentry who voted early were obdurately GOP, as were many of the small businessmen with whom the New Deal carried out an increasingly unrequited affair. But by ten p.m., when reporters arrived from the Nelson House in Poughkeepsie, a groundswell of Roosevelt support in the Northeast presaged the inevitable victory: New York, Pennsylvania, Massachusetts were solidly in his column. Ohio, Michigan, California would follow. "Bill, see those figures?" FDR said to Hassett. "Everything is all right now. We can forget about New York State." Around eleven, with the trend clear, a torchlight parade wound its way from the village; seated on the portico, wearing the Navy cape, which Eleanor was photographed wrapping protectively around his shoulders, he reminisced about seeing his first torchlight parade "right here in 1892"—for Grover Cleveland's second election. "And I got up and appeared here in an old-fashioned nightgown of some kind, on this porch, and I wrapped up in an old buffalo robe that came out of a wagon. And I had a perfect grand night." Cautiously, he declined to claim reelection, while noting that things were going well in the big states. "It's good to see you, and I will have to go back and do some more telephoning," he concluded weakly, waved, and was gone. Back in the Big House, he remarked to

Bill Hassett that the parade was larger than previously. As he surely noticed, two busloads of students from Vassar College had received permission to join the celebration.

In London, Winston Churchill was kept informed by a series of cables from Harry Hopkins, FDR's closest advisor and only confidant, who had overseen the New Deal's relief agencies, and was the first head of the Lend-Lease program that came to England's rescue in the darkest days of the war in Europe. "I have no reason for changing my opinion that it will be a Roosevelt landslide," read the first. "The voting is very heavy in industrial centers. We are not likely to know definitely before 10:00 our time which will make it pretty late even for you." The hours passed. The prime minister stayed up until Hopkins's final assurance: "It's in the bag."

Sitting at the dining table, Roosevelt occasionally remarked on the returns, until about midnight he tossed away his pencil and tally sheets. "It's all over, so what's the use of putting down the figures," he said to no one in particular. Not until past three a.m. did Tom Dewey appear in front of a shrunken, dispirited crowd in the ballroom of the Roosevelt Hotel in New York City to concede the election and express the pious hope that "divine Providence" would guide TR's fifth cousin in the difficult days ahead. In Hyde Park, FDR, who had stayed up irritably waiting for the concession, dictated a crisp telegram addressed to "His Excellency Governor Dewey": "I thank you for your statement, which I heard over the air a few minutes ago." It was past four in the morning. As Hassett chatted with Eleanor Roosevelt about the term to come, simultaneously fielding telephone calls, he suddenly realized that the president had wheeled his chair away from the table and started upstairs by himself. Catching him in the corridor, Hassett asked if there was anything he needed. Roosevelt said no. He was backing himself into an old dumbwaiter he used for an elevator.

"Good night, Mr. President."

The president considered the evening. "I still think he is a son of a bitch," he said, and closed the door.

Since September, when unexpectedly high registration figures in the big industrial cities—the good work of the CIO PAC—presaged a large turnout in November, Roosevelt had felt little suspense about the outcome. The old Democracy, as the Democratic Party was still sometimes called in those days, was expansive enough to embrace office holders as disparate as Theodore Bilbo of Mississippi and Vito Marcantonio of East Harlem, who might fairly be said to represent the ideological extremes of American electoral politics, right and left. But the party-line Democrats were simply the biggest component in what the columnist William S. White later called "that astonishing one-man opus, the *Roosevelt*-Democratic Party," whose elements were even more mixed.

In a cover story on Hillman in July, *Time* had referred to the "P.A.C.'s attempt to turn at least part of C.I.O.'s 5,000,000 members into politicians." It aimed to turn them into canvassers, bell ringers, occasional public speakers, certainly, and at the least to see that its members were registered and got to the polls. "Every Worker a Voter" was the motto. The committee's stated purposes were educational and nonpartisan, to enlarge participation in the political process by getting out the vote and to promote a progressive agenda, including full employment and racial justice—the "People's Program of 1944." The PAC endorsed Roosevelt and Truman, leaving local affiliates to decide on endorsements in state and local races, but everyone knew that a large turnout of CIO voters favored the Democrats. The national committee was headquartered in an unpretentious suite of offices high in the Bartholomew Building on Forty-second Street, overlooking the East River. From here went out the orders for 138,000 lapel buttons and millions of copies of pamphlets: "What Every Canvasser Should Know," "The Negro in 1944," "This Is Your America," "Jobs for All After the War." Pamphleteering was still an important and lively political art in 1944, and Dr. J. Raymond Walsh, the former Harvard economist who directed the PAC's publications and research staffs, made sure that the committee's many tracts were written in the sort of Popular Front basic English he preferred: "Can you tell an American by the color of his skin? No, you cannot tell him by his race. He might be white or black or red or any combination of these—and be as good an American as any." The graphic equivalent of this style and these sentiments appeared in the posters whose design was overseen by Ben Shahn, who drew some that became famous: a pair of welders, one black, one white ("for full employment after the war: Register—Vote"); a pair of black hands holding wheat ("from workers to farmers ... Thanks!"); and a pensive profile of FDR, "Our Friend," looming over outstretched hands, black and white, lifted hats, and a child held high. Shahn's posters were emblems of the renewed Popular Front, the definitive graphic expression of its hopes and expectations for the postwar era.

At 8:30 on a raw, blustery Thursday morning, the election just two days past, faithful Democrats had been shivering in the plaza outside Washington's Union Square for an hour when FDR's train pulled in, his arrival, for once, emphatically on the record. The police band played ruffles and flourishes and "Hail to the Chief." The crowd roared. The civilian and war bureaucracies had given their clerks the morning off to welcome back the commander-in-chief, and the district's schoolchildren were given a holiday. Stretched along the broad avenues—Constitution, Delaware, Pennsylvania—a crowd of 300,000, entertained by eight bands along the route, cheered the procession as it roared by, the president holding tight the collar of his soaked overcoat, smiling gamely, but ashen-faced.

Emphasizing party unity, Roosevelt had invited his incoming and outgoing vice presidents to share his limousine. Truman, behind rain-spattered spectacles, only two years younger than FDR, looked every day of his sixty years, but youthful by comparison. Nobody had expected Truman to be a particularly effective campaigner, and he had not exceeded expectations. Wallace, in contrast, had crisscrossed the country energetically, sometimes standing up all night in packed trains, to much greater effect, rallying the liberal faithful, lionized by the CIO PAC. Eager to repay him, Roosevelt had determined that the former vice president would have a high place in the new administration. Truman, with his excellent relations with all factions in the Senate, could perhaps make himself useful when the time came to shepherd the postwar settlement—the United Nations organization— through the upper house. But never in Truman's brief vice presidency would FDR ever show any inclination to share his burdens with the Missourian or take into his confidence.

The crowd along the way broke up as Roosevelt passed, dispersing in the direction of trolley stops, returning to the now-familiar office routines of Washington at war. At 9:30 the motor procession passed through the White House gates, and by 11:00, freshly dressed in baggy tweeds and in a teasing good humor, the president-elect was conducting his 979th press conference. When the reporters insisted on knowing his bet on the Electoral College in the office pool, FDR made an elaborate show of rummaging through his desk drawers for the yellow slip containing the figure. "Well, mine was 335—for *me*," he said, "to 196 for my opponent . . . so I wasn't very accurate, was I?"

The final tally was 432 electoral votes for Roosevelt, 99 for Dewey: there would be no interval of suspense waiting for the soldiers' votes to be counted. No, as one reporter was quick to say, Roosevelt had erred on the conservative side. "Mr. President in 1948?" he inquired. FDR's laughter rang out above the others'.

Roosevelt's Electoral College sweep belied a much tighter popular margin: 25,602,505 to Dewey's 22,006,278, the narrowest win since Woodrow Wilson's reelection in 1916. The result was decisive nonetheless, and Roosevelt's triumph was at once endowed with the air of inevitability it has worn ever since. On the morning after, wistful Republican mathematicians calculated that a shift of only 343,414 votes would have added fifteen states to Dewey's column, and given him a narrow victory. Democrats retorted that 282,000 more votes for Roosevelt, properly distributed, would have given him all forty-eight states. Registration and voting in numbers far higher than expected in early October had preserved FDR's strength in New York, Detroit, St. Louis, and other big industrial cities, despite all the obstacles thrown in the way of new voters, the distractions of wartime routine, and often the physical difficulty of getting to a polling place; and for this the CIO PAC was conceded a big part of the credit.

Though he easily carried the small-town and rural vote, the support Dewey received from the fields of the Midwest to California's Central Valley simply did not materialize in numbers sufficient to redress FDR's strength in the factories and the union halls, the streets and tenements of the urban nation. His 59 percent in the sixteen big-city counties, compared with Dewey's 40 percent, decided the "absolutely crucial margin," since outside the South, Dewey carried the rest of the country by 52 percent to 48 percent.

What most certainly would have delivered Roosevelt a popular majority many millions bigger was a federal ballot for soldiers on the battlefield such as Roosevelt had argued for in his State of the Union address in 1944. But that bill was emasculated in Congress by a combination of Republicans who assumed that most of the men in arms would vote for their commander-in-chief; Southerners who did not wish to enfranchise blacks and poor whites serving in the military; and courthouse politicians who did not want a federal ballot to compromise their local control of the voting process. Without a federal ballot, only eighty-five thousand soldiers out of eleven million on active duty managed to cast a vote. In Bill Mauldin's cartoon for *Stars and Stripes*, Willie consoled Joe: "Well, at least we can bet."

"The 1944 election, more than any other election in the Roosevelt era, was the prototype of American politics to come," Michael Barone writes in *Our Country*. "For the next twenty years, the Democrats would be represented by presidential candidates who wholeheartedly favored the New Deal, received strong support from big labor and big-city machines, and retained some traditional support in the South"; the Republicans would be led by candidates who, while drawing support from big business and nonurban Middle America, were at least resigned to the New Deal at home and committed, like the Democrats, to internationalism abroad. "To get political support, [FDR] looked to young voters, especially soldiers, and to labor union members—Americans arrayed in constituencies assembled, even created, during his administration"; on the whole they were to remain loyal for a generation.

Roosevelt's immense standing abroad was something without precedent for an American president. In Enlightenment Europe, Washington was acknowledged a great man. Lincoln's career and his death were noted respectfully. Ex-President Theodore Roosevelt was greeted like a great celebrity, more than as a statesman, when he toured Europe in 1910; "as cowboy, Rough Rider, and hunter he seemed, to the people of Europe, to typify the slightly mad national characteristics of the republic across the sea." In 1919, arriving for the Versailles Conference, Woodrow Wilson was received as a messiah by ecstatic crowds in ancient cities, but they were soon disillusioned. The belief in Roosevelt as the champion of democracy and a better life for the greatest number only grew with the years.

Isaiah Berlin wrote in 1955: "As the skies of Europe grew darker, in particular after war broke out, he seemed to the poor and the unhappy in Europe a kind of benevolent demigod, who alone could and would save them in the end. His moral authority—the degree of confidence which he inspired outside his own country—and far more beyond America's frontiers than within them at all times—has no parallel."

There was, of course, a parallel in his relation to those who cheered him on the rainy streets of New York in that late October 1944. The aristocrat who has "betrayed" his class and retains its manners while deprecating its values in favor of those of a "revolted class" makes for a "fascinating and attractive type," Berlin suggests. "This is what makes the figures of such men as Condorcet or Charles James Fox, or some of the Russian, Italian and Polish revolutionaries in the nineteenth century, so attractive; for all we know this may have been the secret also of Moses or Pericles or Julius Caesar."

After 1932, when he ran as the non-Hoover, Roosevelt drew his following from the margins of American society, from African Americans, Jews, and "ethnics," poor southern whites (and not a few southern aristocrats), intellectuals and academics—groups who shared his distance from and disaffection for the dominant business culture that had been discredited by the Depression. "The more businessmen hated Roosevelt because, as they correctly thought, he despised business as a way of life, the more intellectuals and academicians clung to him," Alfred Kazin wrote, in the fifties. "They had all been thrown together by their common exclusion from 'normal,' commercial, American experience." Reminiscing one day in the thirties with Frances Perkins, the secretary of labor, Roosevelt recalled Big Tim Sullivan, the Tammany boss with whom he had tangled in his priggish youth. Big Tim, he said, did not understand modern politics, but he sensed that "the America of the future would be made out of the people who had come over in steerage and who knew in their own hearts and lives the difference between being despised and being accepted and liked." The prince had thrown in with the paupers.

· · ·

In the afternoon of April 12, 1945, Franklin Delano Roosevelt died of a massive cerebral hemorrhage at the "Little White House" in Warm Springs, Georgia.

In every newsroom in the world tickers rang five bells—a "flash"—and pressmen, as stunned as their readers were about to be, hauled out the big wooden "End of the World" block type that had been reserved for the end of the war: FDR DEAD. In New York City, all the firehouses rang the bells that saluted a fallen comrade. Many shops and businesses were closed for "a death in the family." Buttons were stamped: "We Mourn Our Loss." The *New York Times* editorialized that men in a hundred years would go down on their knees in gratitude that Franklin Roosevelt had been president during the war. (Posterity is never so grateful.) *PM*, Ralph Ingersoll's liberal daily newspaper published in New York from 1940 to 1948, financed by Marshall Field III, printed the news of his death in white against black, which gave an eerie effect. The radio networks, wanting solemn music, played over and over an unfamiliar work—Samuel Barber's Adagio for Strings—which became famous as the saddest music known to Americans. Most citizens mourned, but others, not too privately, rejoiced. He had been a figure of looming proportions for such a long time, like the "semi-divine stranger with superhuman powers, some Gilgamesh or Napoleon, some Solon or Sherlock Holmes," come to the city's rescue, whose death interrupts Auden's *Age of Anxiety*.

> *Mourn for us now,*
> *Our lost dad,*
> *Our colossal father.*

PART I

EMPIRE AND COMMUNICATIONS

––––––––––––

The rumor of a great city goes out beyond its borders, to all the latitudes of the known earth. The city becomes an emblem in remote minds; apart from the tangible export of goods and men, it exerts its cultural instrumentality in a thousand phases: as an image of glittering light, as the forcing ground which creates a new prose style or a new agro-biological theory, or as the germinal point for a fresh technique in metal sculpture, biometrics or the fixation of nitrogen.

—*New York Panorama* (1938)

O dark, dark, dark, amid the blaze of noon . . .

—MILTON, *Samson Agonistes*

The newsroom of *The New York Times* in 1942, showing, *center,*
the city copy desk; *right,* the foreign desk; and *left,* the telegraph desk

I

City Lights

IN MARCH 1946 the young French novelist and journalist Albert
Camus traveled by freighter from Le Havre to New York, arriving
in the first week of spring. Le Havre, the old port city at the mouth
of the Seine, had almost been destroyed in a battle between its German occupiers and a British warship during the Normandy invasion;
huge ruins ringed the harbor. In his travel journal Camus writes:
"My last image of France is of destroyed buildings at the very edge of
a wounded earth."

At the age of thirty-two this Algerian Frenchman, who had been
supporting himself with odd jobs when the war began, was about to
become very famous. By 1948, he would become an international
culture hero: author of *The Stranger* and *The Plague*, two of the most
famous novels to come out of France in the forties, and of the lofty and
astringent essays collected in *The Myth of Sisyphus*.

Camus's visit to the United States, sponsored by the French Ministry of Foreign Affairs but involving no official duties, was timed to
coincide with Alfred A. Knopf's publication of *The Stranger* in a translation by Stuart Gilbert, the annotator of James Joyce's *Ulysses*. In the
spring of 1946 France was exporting little to the United States except
literature. Even most American readers with a particular interest in
France knew of Camus, if at all, as a distant legend, editor of the Resistance newspaper *Combat* and an "existentialist."

Reviewing *The Stranger* in the *New Yorker*, Edmund Wilson, usually omniscient, confessed that he knew absolutely nothing about existentialism except that it was enjoying a "furious vogue." If there were rumored to be philosophical depths in this novel about the motiveless murder of an Arab on a North African beach, they frankly eluded him. For Wilson the book was nothing more than "a fairly clever feat"—the sort of thing that a skillful Hemingway imitator like James M. Cain had done as well or better in *The Postman Always Rings Twice*. America's most admired literary critic also had his doubts about Franz Kafka, the writer of the moment, suspecting that the claims being made for the late Prague fabulist were exaggerated. But still, like almost everyone else, especially the young, in New York's intellectual circles Wilson was intensely curious about what had been written and thought in occupied Europe, especially in France.

"Our generation had been brought up on the remembrance of the 1920s as the great golden age of the avant-garde, whose focal point had been Paris," William Barrett writes in *The Truants*, his memoir of the New York intellectuals. "We expected history to repeat itself: as it had been after the First, so it would be after the Second World War." The glamorous rumor of existentialism seemed to vindicate their expectations. Camus's arrival was eagerly awaited not only by *Partisan Review* but also by the *New Yorker*, which put him in "The Talk of the Town," and *Vogue*, which decided that his saturnine good looks resembled Humphrey Bogart's.

Although a brilliant travel writer, Camus was not a lucky traveler. When he was young and unknown, he blamed poverty for cramping his journeys, and when he was older and could afford more, he was a martyr to celebrity, always dreading its exposures and demands right up to the day he went to Stockholm to accept the Nobel Prize. Travel made him anxious, which he concluded was the proper state for a traveler, and often physically sick. As he records in his diary, after a sociable crossing, he came down with the flu just in time to arrive in New York.

On March 27, around noon on a gray, windy day, as his ship entered the Narrows, his first glimpse of New York was of Coney Island, a dismal sight under a flat painted sky. In the distance, the skyscrapers of Manhattan rose out of the mist. "Deep down, I feel calm and indifferent, as I generally do in front of spectacles that don't move me." Anticlimactically, his ship rode at anchor for the night.

"Go to bed very late. Get up very early. We enter New York harbor. A terrific sight despite or because of the mist. The order, the strength, the economic power are there. The heart trembles in front of so much admirable inhumanity."

"Order" manifested itself at once. At the dock, Camus found himself singled out for sustained scrutiny. "The immigration officer ends by excusing himself for having detained me for so long: 'I was obliged to, but I can't tell you why.'" The mystery was dispelled many years later. Alert to the left-wing politics of *Combat*, the FBI had opened a file on him, and passed on its suspicions to the Immigration Services.

Feeling weak from his flu, Camus was welcomed by two journalists from France and a man from the French consulate. The crowded streets alarmed him. His first impression of New York was of "a hideous, inhuman city. But I know that one changes one's mind." He did note the orderliness of things confirmed by how smoothly the traffic moved without policemen at intersections, and by the prim gloves worn by garbagemen. That night, crossing Broadway in a cab, his flu made worse by a bad hangover (he had stayed up drinking until four the night before), feeling "tired and feverish," Camus was "stupefied by the circus of lights."

Bright lights, big city had been the New York formula for a century. On his first visit, in 1842, Charles Dickens found the gaslights of lower Broadway as brilliant as those of London's Piccadilly, but he also discovered New York could be a strangely dark and vacant place—catacombesque—and secretive, like the oysters that its citizens devoured in such prodigious quantities. The streets were often empty except for pigs that foraged at all hours. The slums, like the infamous Five Points, to whose low haunts the great man was escorted by two policemen, were as noisome as any in London.

In the 1870s and '80s, gaslight began yielding to electricity. The Bowery, with its popular theaters, was the first district to be lit by Edison's eerie new light, followed by the stretch of Broadway from Twenty-fourth Street to Twenty-sixth. A commercial visionary from Brooklyn named O. J. Gude seized on electricity for display advertising. In 1891 Madison Square was astonished by a giant sign advertising a Coney Island resort ("Manhattan Beach Swept by Ocean Breezes"). Verbally inventive too, Gude coined the phrase "Great White Way." The most wondrous electric advertisement in New York was a fifty-foot pickle in green lightbulbs advertising Heinz's "57 Varieties." This "pioneer spectacle," as Frederick Lewis Allen hails it in *The Big Change*, stood at the intersection of Fifth Avenue, Broadway, and Twenty-third Street, since 1902 the site of the Flatiron Building. In 1913, Rupert Brooke came to marvel at the gaudiness of Times Square. At street level, the effect was disconcerting. "The merciless lights throw a mask of unradiant glare on the human beings in the streets, making each face hard, set, wolfish, terribly blue." Above, the street was filled with wonders. Brooke could not help noticing an advertisement starring two bodies electric, "a youth and a man-boy, flaming and immortal, clad in celestial underwear," who boxed a round, vanished, reappeared, and fought again. "Night after night they wage this combat. What gods they are who fight endlessly and indecisively for New York is not for our knowledge."

City lights were mostly white in the 1920s. "For anyone interested in period detail, there were almost no colored lights then," Gore Vidal recalls in his essay "On Flying." "So, on a hot, airless night in St. Louis, the city had a weird white arctic glow." In the 1930s, the planners at the New Deal farm agencies expected an influx of urbanites to flee the stricken cities for a new life in the countryside: the prospective exurbanites were called "white-light refugees." In time, of course, the refugees came, only the process was called suburbanization. Neon light, first imported from France before the First World War by a West Coast automobile dealer, Earle C. Anthony, remained unusual for a long time even in New York. Edwin Denby, the dance critic and poet, remembered "walking at night in Chelsea with Bill [de Kooning] during the depression, and his pointing out to me on the pavement the dispersed compositions—spots and cracks and bits of wrappers and reflections of neon-light—neon-signs were few then—and I remember the scale in the compositions was too big for me to see it."

Throughout the Jazz Age and the Depression the white and many-colored lights of Broadway blazed, now concentrated in Times Square, where they advertised Four Roses whiskey, Camel cigarettes, Planters Peanuts ("A Bag a Day for More Pep"), Coca-Cola, the Astor Hotel. It took the blackouts during the war to dull the blaze, but by 1946 even the more prolonged dimout was becoming a distant memory. New York had resumed its old habits of brilliance.

"I am just coming out of five years of night," says Camus in his journal, "and this orgy of violent lights gives me for the first time the impression of a new continent. An enormous, 50-foot-high Camel billboard: a G.I. with his mouth wide-open blows enormous puffs of *real* smoke. Everything is yellow and red."

2

Cultural Capital

I N AN AGE OF PRINT, New York was a city of words, ruling an empire of signs, and of all its powers and dominions its command of the arts and the mass media was apparently the most secure. "The most important single thing to say about Manhattan in relation to the rest of the United States is that it dominates what, for want of a better phrase, may be called American culture," John Gunther wrote in 1947. "New York is the publishing center of the nation; it is the art, theater, musical, ballet, operatic center; it is the opinion center; it is the radio center; it is the style center." There was no definitive success in American life, material or intellectual, unless it was ratified by New York opinion. "I do not assert that this is necessarily a good thing. I merely say that it is true."

New York opinion was an industry to which *Reader's Digest* and the *Daily Worker*, mandarin intellectuals and gossip columnists, the born-again conservative Raymond Moley at *Newsweek*, and the about-to-become-Marxist W. E. B. Du Bois all contributed. In style and temper, the range was spanned by the "two Walters"—the gravitas of Lippmann's column in the *Herald Tribune* and the demotic rush of Winchell's in Hearst's *Daily Mirror*. Winchell's Sunday-night radio broadcast on ABC was, in his idiom, the "New Yorkiest" thing on the airwaves, noisy as a klaxon in the night, and between print and radio it was estimated that his words reached fifty million Americans every week. (What did it matter that Lippmann composed his grave sentences in a mansion on Woodley Road in Washington, DC, or that Winchell's show usually originated from a studio in Miami Beach? Their mere origins were incidental to their true provenance; and besides, Miami was in those days a remote dependency of Manhattan, just as the Hawaiian Islands were of San Francisco, and Las Vegas of the Mob.)*

New York was *Time* and *Life*, Harper & Brothers, the *New Yorker*, the *New Republic*, Random House, *Partisan Review*. It was the collection of the Metropolitan Museum of Art; the robber baron's spoils in the Frick; Jackson Pollock at Peggy Guggenheim's gallery, the Art of This Century; a Ben Shahn show at the Museum of Modern Art. New York was Arturo Toscanini conducting the NBC Symphony Orchestra, Sinatra at the Paramount, Billie Holiday at the Onyx; *Oklahoma!* and *On the Town* on Broadway and Ned Rorem's song "The Lordly Hudson." For several hundreds of thousands of culturally aspiring radio listeners across the country, New York was the Saturday-afternoon broadcasts of the Metropolitan Opera, sponsored by Texaco and introduced by Milton Cross.

For serious theatergoers, it was a golden age: Tennessee Williams's *Glass Menagerie* in 1945 was followed by Eugene O'Neill's late masterpiece, *The Iceman Cometh*, which opened in 1946; Williams's *A Streetcar Named Desire* and Arthur Miller's *All My Sons* in 1947; Williams's *Summer and Smoke* in 1948; Arthur Miller's *Death of a Salesman* in 1949; and his adaptation of Ibsen's *Enemy of the People* in 1950. But the golden age was shadowed by the ironic fact that fewer than ever New Yorkers were seeing plays of any kind. In John Cheever's story "The Enormous Radio," Jim and Irene Westcott, a college-educated, decently prosperous couple living near Sutton Place (like the John Cheevers in the forties), attend the theater "an average of 10.3 times a year"—an average that for such a couple would have fallen sharply

---

* It was a golden age for publicists of all kinds and qualities. Gunther tells of how an "estimable Bourbon" of his acquaintance once maintained that the most powerful single influence on American life was the city of Minsk, in Soviet Byelorussia. "His train of thought went like this. Minsk is the birthplace of Max Lerner, the well-known editorial writer and political scientist. Lerner runs *PM*. *PM* runs the American Labor Party. The American Labor Party runs New York City. New York City runs New York state and New York state of course runs the country."

by 1950, when there were 81 shows on Broadway as compared to 144 in the last season of the war. It was by no means apparent to Mary McCarthy, the brilliant and acidulous theater critic of *Partisan Review*, that she was chronicling anything like a golden age. In 1945, when *The Glass Menagerie* and *Carousel* were on offer, she wrote that "the stage presents such a spectacle of confusion, disintegration and despair that no generalization can cover the case." In 1947, the year the French critic Nino Frank coined the term "film noir," also the year when Marlon Brando and Jessica Tandy were Stanley and Blanche at the Barrymore Theatre, McCarthy declared firmly that "there were no good Hollywood movies, no good Broadway plays—only curios," and she ridiculed a "visiting Existentialist" (Simone de Beauvoir) for suspecting otherwise. (No wonder Beauvoir was "merely confirmed in her impression that American intellectuals were 'negative.'") McCarthy was nothing if not critical—she particularly disparaged what she called "A Streetcar Named Success"—but her joyously destructive prose is a reminder that the forties were also a glorious season for critics and criticism. Vision was armored.

Gunther's inclusion of ballet among the arts of the city seems obvious, yet this performing art had been overlooked entirely in the WPA's *New York Panorama* in 1938. (Although the WPA sponsored a Federal Dance Project, Martha Graham and modern dance were similarly neglected.) Lincoln Kirstein invited George Balanchine to New York in 1933, and in 1934, along with Edward Warburg, founded for him the School of American Ballet in a studio on Fifty-ninth Street and Madison Avenue; it was in fact a space that at the turn of the century Paris Singer had taken for Isadora Duncan. Their American Ballet Company grew out of that; it had its first two-week season in New York at the Adelphi Theatre, then became the resident ballet company of the Metropolitan Opera until 1938. Confusingly, there were two Ballet Russe companies, Colonel de Basil's Original Ballet Russe, and Serge Denham's Ballet Russe de Monte Carlo, "sometimes the same company and sometimes bitter rivals," Agnes de Mille recalls, both claiming descent from the great Diaghilev and his troupe. In 1939 American Ballet Theatre (originally Ballet Theatre) was formed, with Lucia Chase as its main benefactor, and its venue became the old Metropolitan Opera House, whose famous curving horseshoe of boxes had enabled old money to contemplate itself. Among the first choreographers was Jerome Robbins, who rewarded Chase with his ballet *Fancy Free* (1944), which he adapted for Broadway later that year as the musical *On the Town*, again with a score by Leonard Bernstein. From London, Ballet Theatre brought over Antony Tudor, on the recommendation of de Mille, soon to be famous as the choreographer of *Rodeo* and *Oklahoma!* Tudor's *Pillar of Fire* (1942), set to music by Schoenberg (*Transfigured Night*) and with Chase, Nora Kaye, Hugh Laing, and Tudor in the principal roles, captured the Freudian, myth-haunted cultural atmosphere and, according to Gore Vidal, "managed to define an entire generation that was finding a transient religion in psychoanalysis."

As a realized cultural presence, American ballet had a wartime birth—like bebop and film noir. "In the late forties," Vidal writes, "balletomania hit New York City . . . Between Tudor ballets and Tennessee Williams's new plays, something visceral was happening to those of us lucky enough to be in New York at the time, and able to go from play to ballet . . . That passionate, hungry, postwar audience no longer exists." Until *Theme and Variations* in 1941, Ballet Theatre had no use for Balanchine. But in 1948 he and Kirstein were invited to establish a resident company, the New York City Ballet, at City Center by its director, Morton Baum. Originally built as the Shriners' Mecca Temple, the huge auditorium adorned with Masonic scimitar and crescent was saved from the wrecker's ball by La Guardia in 1943 and converted into the first publicly supported performing-arts space in the country. Oliver Smith, the codirector of Ballet Theatre, once described it as "one of the most hideous rooms in America," but Baum's offer gave City Ballet a unique civic status.

New York was the radio and the television capital, virtually monopolizing the new medium at a time when it remained a futuristic rumor for most of the country. Although the manufacture of television sets was interrupted by the war, in 1939, NBC had begun regular broadcasting from Studio 3H in Radio City and "remote locations," including the World's Fair. CBS's prototype station occupied a warren of makeshift studios in the mezzanine of Grand Central Terminal. "In

January 1948 about two thirds of the television sets in the United States were owned by viewers in the metropolitan area," according to *The Encyclopedia of New York City*, "whose affection for Milton Berle and other Jewish comedians dictated the content of network programs; eventually these performers were eclipsed by others considered less identifiably ethnic by viewers from the rest of the country." Berle's raucous stay at the top was cruelly prolonged—so far as the rest of the country was concerned—by technical difficulties. Though a million television sets were sold in 1948, the Federal Communications Commission closed the year with a ukase ordering a stop to the licensing of new television stations, pending a study of "interference." This standstill was extended to three and a half years by the Korean War, marking what the media historian Erik Barnouw calls a "strange twilight period," in which television remained a metropolitan rather than a truly national medium, with its biggest audiences in New York and Los Angeles. (In *Mary Kay and Johnny*, an early series set in New York which aired from 1947 to 1950, the eponymous married couple actually shared a double bed—a daring stroke of urban realism not to be repeated on television for many years.) In 1945 a mere six thousand television sets diverted an audience almost entirely concentrated in the city, most of them watching in public places, sometimes department stores, most often in taverns, which, as Barnouw notes, earlier had pioneered movies and radio. Television's colonization of the world began in the bars along Lexington Avenue.

Once New York had also been at the center of moviemaking. During the early silent era, small studios were scattered throughout the greater city, from the Lower East Side, where D. W. Griffith shot one- or two-reelers for Biograph on the teeming streets, to Yonkers and Fort Lee, New Jersey. Sometimes brutish, always short, movies were exhibited in storefront nickelodeons, of which by 1910 there were over five hundred in New York; they were concentrated in the Lower East Side, along Fourteenth Street, and on Broadway between Herald and Union Squares, the old theatrical Rialto; their typical audience was working-class, mostly men and children, largely immigrant. "Hollywood," Eric Hobsbawm observes in *The Age of Empire*, "was based on the junction between nickelodeon populism and the culturally and morally rewarding drama and sentiment expected by the equally large mass of middle Americans." This union was achieved on Broadway in venues like the old Astor Theater, where the eight-reel Italian epic *Quo Vadis?* ran for twenty weeks in 1913, when the geographical Hollywood was still a stuffy little hamlet inclined to be distrustful of "movie people." As movies became longer and more decorous, the moviegoing audience, which had stood at twenty-six million around 1908, doubled to fifty million by 1914, now enlarged to include respectable women.

Movie exhibition graduated from peep shows to palaces in the era of the First World War (the Mark Brothers' prototype Strand Theatre opened on Broadway and Forty-seventh Street in 1914), at the same time that feature filmmaking was shifting to the West Coast, the industry's aspiring moguls being attracted by the climate and by the distance from Edison's movie trust and its enforcers. After Cecil B. De Mille directed *The Squaw Man* there in 1913, Hollywood became "Hollywood," a mythic place on the map as well as a formula. Metropolitan critics like Edmund Wilson would always regret how much livelier and more intelligent the movies might have been if only they had remained in the East instead of transmigrating to "the Coast" and becoming infected with its "torpid unreality"; yet there was historical logic and a compelling symmetry in the westward shift. Eadweard Muybridge's pioneering studies in stop-motion photography, which laid the technical basis for the industry, had been performed in San Francisco three decades earlier. As Norman Mailer observed, it was a cunning fate that arranged for the dream factories of Hollywood to rise at the end of the American road at the same time that the frontier was officially closed.

New York remained a lively secondary center of movie production for another decade, with Paramount and Fox, along with such independents as William Randolph Hearst and the silent-movie star Norma Talmadge and her husband, Joseph Schenck, building or expanding their facilities in or close to Manhattan, even after Southern California had become synonymous with the movies.* But Hollywood still answered to New York, even in such a grand personage as Louis B.

---

* In "The Work of Art in the Age of Mechanical Reproduction," Walter Benjamin quotes the French writer Georges Duhamel's condemnation of motion pictures as a worthless diversion for the masses, "which kindles no light in the heart and awakens no hope other than the ridiculous one of someday becoming a 'star' in Los Angeles."

Mayer, who ran the storied MGM studio in Culver City, but whose boss, Nicholas B. Schenck (Joseph's brother), exercised long-distance control from an office at 1540 Broadway. The bold outline of the Paramount Building, towering thirty-five stories over Broadway and housing the famous theater, and the blazing sign in Times Square that announced the "Home of Columbia Pictures" were monumental testimonies to the fact that the real power in the movies—the money power—had never left New York in the first place.

In 1919, abandoning the cyclopean sets of *Intolerance*, his "Sun Play of the Ages," to crumble along Sunset Boulevard, D. W. Griffith returned to New York, which, in pointed contrast to Hollywood, he described as the home of "money and brains." For the huge sum of $375,000, he bought the Henry Flagler estate near Mamaroneck, and there on the Long Island Sound built a studio that his biographer Richard Schickel describes simply as "beautiful, perhaps the most imposing combination of grounds and structures anyone has ever employed for the manufacture of motion pictures (only Pinewood, in England, compares)." Among his last important films, *Way Down East* and *Orphans of the Storm* were shot on Long Island; but Griffith's career was in terminal decline, and his private studio so far from Hollywood was a ruinous indulgence.

Compared to Griffith's "seigneurial" facility, the studio opened in September 1920 by Famous Players–Lasky (renamed Paramount in 1927), in the Astoria section of northwest Queens, was industrial (its vaulted top-floor main studio was 120 by 128 feet) and at capacity could accommodate eight productions at a time. A twenty-six-year-old Walter Wanger was made general manager of FPL productions, which he supervised from Paramount's headquarters in Manhattan, in competition for the studio's resources with Ben P. Schulberg in Hollywood. Gloria Swanson, who moved her entourage to Astoria in 1923, recalled it as being "full of free spirits, defectors, refugees, who were all trying to get away from Hollywood and its restrictions. There was a wonderful sense of revolution and innovation in the studio in Queens." Rudolph Valentino, the Gish sisters, Clara Bow, Adolphe Menjou, Claudette Colbert, Enrico Caruso, Jimmy Durante, and Gary Cooper worked there, in its heyday. Astoria seemed to bring out the aspiring intellectual in movie actors. During World War II, when it was turned over to the army for making training films, Arthur Laurents, the play-wright, went up to the roof one day to sunbathe and found William Holden reading T. S. Eliot's poem "Gerontion."

Hearst's Cosmopolitan Productions studio on the Harlem River, on the site of a former casino between 126th and 127th Streets on Second Avenue, was only large enough for two productions at a time. But then, Hearst had faint interest in Cosmopolitan movies unless they starred his mistress, Marion Davies, even when they featured such stars as Swanson, Ramon Novarro, Lionel Barrymore, or the sadly heroin-addicted Alma Rubens, who played the lead in *Humoresque*, the studio's only success in 1920. In the early twenties, Hearst was engaged in two great campaigns: to make Davies a top star, like Mary Pickford, and to wrest control of the state Democratic Party from Al Smith; fail-ing at both, but still besotted with Davies and the movies, in 1924 he moved Cosmopolitan and his court to Los Angeles, where soon he was bestriding the MGM lot like the print colossus he was.

The arrival of talking pictures briefly erased Hollywood's advan-tages of climate since—to accommodate the early sound cameras, which were practically immobile—moviemaking was forced indoors. Rather than enlarging production in the East, the industry's moguls elected to build vast new facilities with sound stages in Southern Cali-fornia, where real estate was cheap, and put the stage actors, direc-tors, playwrights, and voice coaches they hired in New York on the *20th Century Limited* express train to Burbank and Culver City. Movie-making in New York slowed, then virtually ceased, until a year passed, 1937, in which not a single studio picture was produced in the city where American film began.

Rather than making movies, New York became the place where they were most lavishly presented, to the largest audiences, to the greatest publicity—the world capital of motion-picture exhibition. The Strand, the Rivoli, the Roxy, the Paramount, and the Capitol around Broad-way, along with the huge neighborhood houses scattered elsewhere on the island and in the outer boroughs—most imposingly, Loew's Para-dise in the Bronx and Kings Theatre in Brooklyn—were monuments to the brief, gorgeous age (c. 1913–33) of the "moving-picture palaces." Architects like Thomas Lamb and showmen like his frequent collabo-rator Samuel L. Rothafel, known as "Roxy," translated moviegoing into daily pageants, in which silent pictures were accompanied by music and light shows, interspersed with elaborate vaudeville turns (including ballet and recitations), and troops of ushers performed military drills before wielding their flashlights. (The *New Yorker* declared that the Roxy's ushers were "young men of far greater beauty and politeness than any other clique in town.") The movie palaces were the grandest spaces devoted to popular recreation since the baths of Caracalla and Domitian and, after a sober neoclassical start, tended to architectural delirium; ornamentation ranged from Aztec to Louis XIV. The moviegoers, Hart Crane's "multitudes bent upon the flashing scene," were themselves, of course, part of the spectacle, conscripted into a fantastic total work of art, grander than any opera, enacted nightly.

In the twenties, every downtown in America came to boast its own movie palace, sometimes several; and the grandest, in places like Chicago, Philadelphia, Detroit, and Cleveland, were as fantastic and as commodious as any in New York. Even more extravagant were the facades of the Moorish-Egyptian-Mayan-Chinese pagodas in Southern California. But New York had a vastly larger movie audience, the biggest and perhaps most devoted in the world, and it boasted the studios' flagship theaters, the hubs of their national chains, which, although typically they ran at a loss, were valued for prestige and treasured for advertising. Ironically, the last and most enduringly successful of Manhattan's movie palaces, Radio City Music Hall, had been designed to be the ultimate vaudeville house (Roxy, its first manager, whose heart was in operettas and live acts, swore that never would movies be shown in its sleek "modern rococo" auditorium), and converted to picture exhibition only after a famously disastrous debut as a theatrical venue. Believing firmly that nothing succeeds like excess (in his phrasing, "Don't give the people what they want—give 'em something better"), Roxy at last exceeded himself with an opening-night extravaganza that began at 8:45 on the evening of December 27, 1932, with a full house of 6,200 (Amelia Earhart, Mrs. William Randolph Hearst, Leopold Stokowski, Walter Lippmann, Gene Tunney, Walter P. Chrysler, Rose Kennedy, and Al Smith were all in attendance), and lasted well into the next morning. The festivities wound disastrously to conclusion with an ill-received *Choric Dance for an Antique Greek Tragedy* by Martha Graham and her company, followed by the moldering vaudevillians Weber and Fields; after five or six hours, much of the audience had already fled. The Rockefellers waited a decent interval before firing Roxy—the dancing "Roxyettes" became the Rockettes—but moving-picture exhibition at the Music Hall began almost at once, on January 10, 1933, with *The Bitter Tea of General Yen*.

To the surprise of exhibitors, talking movies seemed not to require the familiar extravagant accoutrements and even to discourage them. In small art cinemas, modest neighborhood houses, and newsreel theaters like the Trans-Lux, movie exhibition in the thirties retreated into the storefronts where it had begun not so many decades before. Cinephiles had their own small, sleek venues: the Film Guild Cinema, the Little Carnegie Playhouse, the Thalia, and the Sutton, formerly the Bandbox. ("Unable to offer mother-of-pearl washroom fittings, the little cinemas held out ping-pong tables, demi-tasses, and cigarettes in the lounge," noted *New York Panorama*.) Although the film scholar Peter Wollen has maintained that the mid-twentieth-century cult of cinephilia originated in the clandestine ciné-clubs of occupied Paris, the "little cinema" movement in New York decades before the war testifies otherwise. Experimental and documentary filmmaking had never left the city, and for "cinemaddicts," as *Time* called them, there were "new releases, old pictures, foreign pictures." As early as the twenties, New York's little cinemas were attracting such film cultists as the young Dwight Macdonald and the even younger James Agee.

The war would pack movie houses—the newsreel theaters, the art houses, and the aging palaces, which featured few of the old amenities like smoking rooms; the postwar era was about to empty them. It was evident that the mass public was losing the habit of regular moviegoing. Contrary to settled mythology, the audiences began to drift away from the movie palaces in advance of television; attendance fell from a peak of eighty million per week in 1946 to sixty-seven million in 1948, when there were not many more than a million television sets operating. In Nicholas Ray's *In a Lonely Place* (1950), set in the jittery Hollywood of 1949, Humphrey Bogart, playing a near-psychotic screenwriter, says to restaurateur–tsarist pretender Mike Romanoff, playing himself: "How's business?" Romanoff: "Like show business. There's no business." The huge and proudly ornate Alhambras, Paramounts, Orpheums, Foxes, Loew'ses, Rialtos, in cities small and large, were becoming tarnished and fading. As well as palaces, they had advertised themselves as cathedrals and temples; now they were being deserted. As Théophile Gautier says, "Nothing is sadder than an abandoned temple."

Leaving the provision of celluloid images to the Hollywood movie colony, New York in its own cultural production was supremely the city of words: the printed word in books, in the city's seventeen daily newspapers and dozens of smaller ones, in pulp and slick magazines; the words spoken or sung on stage; the lyrics crafted in Tin Pan Alley; most pervasively and ubiquitously, the words broadcast on radio.

Even more than the movies, radio was the quintessential modern medium. Movies may have been ethereal in conception, but movie reels were fragile, bulky, cumbersome to transport; radio shows were comparatively cheap to produce, and radio waves went everywhere. No other medium ever imposed itself on the world so quickly. After Gutenberg's invention of movable type between 1430 and 1450, four centuries passed before print completed its conquest of the world: it took radio less than twenty years.* As William Randolph Hearst observed, reading a newspaper, even one of his tabloids, required an effort; listening to the radio involved none at all. A "tribal drum," according to Marshall McLuhan, radio was impalpable, portable, requiring no particular setting, not even a room of one's own, and peculiarly urgent and pervasive.

The technical challenges involved in radio transmission had largely been solved around the turn of the twentieth century through the overlapping efforts of the Italian Guglielmo Marconi, the American Lee de Forest, and the Englishman John Ambrose Fleming; it became possible to send first dots and dashes in Morse code and then sounds.

---

* It is well known that various forms of movable type existed at least a century before in China and even earlier in Korea; East Asia was also several hundred years ahead of Western Europe in other forms of printing, such as multiple copies made from wooden blocks. As Henri-Jean Martin details in *The History and Power of Writing*, "If I adopt the point of view of the West here, it is not out of intellectual short-sightedness but because it was from that part of the globe that typography conquered and imposed its logic on the entire world."

The spoken word and music that came with radio *broadcasting* was much slower to develop and was pioneered by amateurs who were kept off the airwaves during the First World War. "A great postwar future was foreseen for radio—a future of rescues at sea, espionage and counterespionage, detection of smugglers, direction of planes to lost explorers, exchange of messages with island outposts," Erik Barnouw recalls. "In short, a future of point-to-point communication." The Radio Corporation of America was organized as a cartel in 1919, under the direction of the Navy Department, whose top officials, the southern populist secretary of the navy, Josephus Daniels, and his deputy, Franklin D. Roosevelt, were unwilling to have such a valuable technology remain in the hands of the British-controlled firm American Marconi, whose takeover by RCA followed. (Its original partners were General Electric, Westinghouse, AT&T, and the United Fruit Company, a major shipper with huge interests in Latin America.) Yet for a medium carrying news and messages (as early as 1904, the *New York Times* signed with Marconi for exclusive American rights to his news agency's coverage of the Russo-Japanese War), radio's lack of privacy was reckoned a nuisance and possibly a fatal flaw.

It was David Sarnoff who, in the forties as the president of RCA, had foreseen that radio's destiny was to be in every home. Sarnoff had made his name as the boy telegrapher in Wanamaker's department store and helped to keep New York in wireless contact with the *Titanic* as it sank in 1912. Four years later, he proposed to his superiors at the American Marconi Company a "plan of development that would make radio a household utility": a box receiving music, lectures, and news like baseball scores, all transmitted through the air. Soon radio stations, beginning with Westinghouse's experimental station 8XK in Pittsburgh, were operated by appliance manufacturers, department stores, hotels, automobile dealers, colleges, and the clergy, with the commercially minded selling time to confectioners, cigar makers like the Paleys of Philadelphia, and a host of other advertisers. To the great satisfaction and relief of advertising agencies, this uncontrolled, expansive moment was terminated by the founding of the Federal Radio Commission in 1924 and the subsequent rationalization of the industry by the two great radio networks, the National Broadcasting Company and the Columbia Broadcasting System—an arrangement

unparalleled elsewhere in the West, where radio typically remained a
state monopoly. So drastically condensed was the history of broadcast
radio, it seemed unremarkable that Sarnoff, who had been present at
its creation, was preparing with his usual self-confidence to bring the
nation into the television era in 1945, drawing up his latest "plan of
development" from his magnificent office on the fifty-third floor of
the RCA Building in Rockefeller Center. A young immigrant from
Minsk, or so legend said, Sarnoff had learned to read English from
newspapers he plucked out of trash bins on the Lower East Side.

As before with the movies, the radio industry had recruited some of
the brightest talents on Broadway and then repatriated them to Hollywood. Among them, Bob Hope, Jack Benny, and George Burns and
Gracie Allen, all of whom had been vaudevillians, starred in the most
popular entertainment shows on radio. But the big four radio networks, NBC's "Red" and "Blue" chains, Columbia, and Mutual, were
headquartered in New York; so were most of their biggest advertisers. NBC at Rockefeller Center and CBS with its corporate offices at
415 Madison Avenue were close to the advertising agencies, which also
produced the soap operas, comedies, and variety shows that their corporate clients sponsored on the air. (This golden triangle was satirized
by Frederic Wakeman, a former copywriter at Foote, Cone & Belding,
in his novel *The Hucksters*, a great sensation in 1947. Setting out for his
first postwar job interview, the protagonist famously selects a "sincere"
necktie.)

The advertising industry had emerged from the war confident of the
country's need for its services, buoyed up by the increasing academic
respectability of market research, which combined opinion sampling
with Freudian psychology, but also by a related sense that the arts of
persuasion had been greatly advanced by propagandists during the
war. It was well known on Madison Avenue that the advertising faction
had routed New Deal intellectuals for control of the Office of War
Information. Although there were many schools of advertising, they
shared a general bravado: the intuitionists, like Bill Bernbach of Doyle
Dane Bernbach (founded in 1949), were surer of their hunches; the
market researchers everywhere of their polls and their depth psychology; the hard salesmen, like Rosser Reeves at the Ted Bates agency,
of their USPs ("unique selling points"); the prescriptivists, like David

Ogilvy, who cofounded Hewitt, Ogilvy, Benson & Mather in 1948, of their rules (he had thirty-nine for making layouts). "I feel that if the agency makes an ad and the client doesn't like it, the client ought to run it anyway," a candid Bernbach said a few years later.

During the war the trade had produced advertisements that hectored citizens into doing their patriotic duty: "That's good, brother. Just sleep through this war. Let some other guy do your share! What's it to you that a kid just got bumped off in the Solomons . . . because you couldn't be bothered with scrap collection?" After the war, no longer committed merely to selling particular products, Madison Avenue discovered that its higher calling was to sell products in general, for as the industry now maintained, it was only by the incessant creation of new wants such as they specialized in arousing that prosperity could be assured. As Raymond Rubicam, who cofounded Young & Rubicam in 1923, wrote in 1946, "Mass desire does not exist unaided. Higher standards of living call for imagination and enterprise in the consumer no less than in the producer."

Television, whose advent as a universal medium had been delayed by the Depression and war, would soon become a major household appliance; the role of print as a time killer had been compromised not only by the phonograph, the radio, and the movies, but also by the automobile, which offered in addition to transportation the opportunities for diversion and casual sex. But like the rest of the civilized planet, America in the forties remained part of the "Gutenberg Galaxy" and continued to be a mass society organized according to perceptions and habits of mind founded on literacy. For most adult Americans, reading afforded entertainment, distraction, instruction, consolation; it was a daily habit, a principal means of organizing experience, and an addiction. More Americans got their news from newspapers than from any other source; radio was essentially a headline service, and television news was prenatal. In general, newspapers and magazines were more densely printed than they are today. The *New York Times*, for example, had eight columns on its front page, as opposed to the current six. Printed advertisements were wordier. ("Advertisements are *words*," reminded Ogilvy, who believed in giving the consumer a lot of copy to read, and favored the *New Yorker* as a venue.) An issue of *Life*, the dominant picture magazine, would be highly illustrated and still con-

tain as much type as *Time* does now. A review of a forgettable novel
in the back pages of *Time* might run for five or six pages and be written anonymously by a young Irving Howe. Blithely presuming on the
patience of its readers, the *New Yorker* often ran "Profiles" in several
parts, at lengths now unheard of: in 1940, St. Clair McKelway's profile
of Walter Winchell, a work of elaborate loathing, required six install-
ments and was later published as a book.[*]

Sales of print in all its forms—hardcover books, paperbacks, magazines, and newspapers—soared during the war, and people seemed
avid for distraction and edification in almost equal measure. Sales
might have been even greater except for the rationing of paper, which
limited print runs and compelled the Book-of-the-Month Club to its
membership to 600,000. *Time*, the *New Yorker*, and a hundred lesser
magazines turned away advertisers. Newspapers sold so furiously that
even the moribund Hearst empire was revived. A clerk at Brentano's
on Fifth Avenue between Forty-seventh and Forty-eighth Streets told
a reporter from *Time*, during the Christmas rush in 1944, that his job
was to open the doors at nine o'clock in the morning and get out of the
way of the customers rushing in.

People with even a casual interest in books read *about* them with
avidity that now seems impossible. The country's two most influential
book reviews were published by the *New York Times* and the *Herald Tribune*; and as the late André Schiffrin pointed out, a typical issue of the
former would often run to sixty-four or more pages, twice its present
size. (The *Herald Tribune*'s, as edited for thirty-seven years by Irita Van
Doren, was generally agreed by writers to be the livelier.) The leading
monthlies, *Harper's* and the *Atlantic*, regarded book reviewing as one
of their most serious responsibilities, as did the newsmagazines and the
leading journals of opinion, the *Nation* and the *New Republic*. The *Saturday Review*, founded by Henry Seidel Canby in 1925, was originally
entirely devoted to reviews. Promising young novelists were lionized
in the pages of *Life*, and the consumption of what Gore Vidal—one of
the lionized—calls "bookchat" was as frenzied as Grub Street could
desire.

---

[*] According to Ben Yagoda in *About Town: The New Yorker and the World It Made*
(2000), the longest ever to run was S. N. Behrman's "unprecedented" seven-part
profile of Sir Max Beerbohm in 1960, which was about three times as long as John
Hersey's *Hiroshima*.

New York City was the capital of the Gutenberg Galaxy—print's great factory town and emporium. Just as New Yorkers had indulged an addiction for print in the nineteenth century while maintaining a passion for the theater (more than thirty people died in the Astor Place Riot of May 1849, which grew out of a politically charged dispute over the respective merits of an American and an English tragedian), so in the twentieth they had succumbed to new distractions—the movies, the phonograph, radio—without losing their hunger for words, words, words on the page. Indeed, the cultural historian William R. Taylor has called Broadway "the Place That Words Built," noting that in the thirties, when the theater district around Times Square was becoming the symbolic heart of the city, the press (Sime Silverman's *Variety*, Winchell's column, Damon Runyon's stories) was replacing the theater as its voice, "a transfer of energy, one might say, from stage to page." New Yorkers bought newspapers around the clock, enjoyed the world's most luxuriant selection of magazines, shopped for used books on Fourth Avenue (musty "Book Row" between Union Square and Astor Place), bought the latest best sellers at Scribner's or Brentano's or Macy's department store, which in the forties was the biggest bookseller in the country. In Greenwich Village, the young and intellectually aspiring browsed translations of Sartre and Artaud at the Wilentz brothers' Eighth Street Bookshop, where the obscurest little magazines were displayed on spindly revolving stands. "Kafka and Brecht, Artaud and Ionesco glower from book jackets; the clerks look through you; Eli Wilentz, the owner, sighs when you mispronounce a writer's name," Pete Hamill recalled fondly in "My Lost City."

The city's packed newsstands, with their cunning juxtapositions like cubist collages, delighted photographers from Weegee to Cecil Beaton. Hamill describes Weegee's picture taken on V-E Day, of what was probably a stand in Yorkville with its array of now-dead newspapers like the *Journal-American*, the *World-Telegram*, and *PM* and such magazines as *Liberty*, *Air News*, *Argosy*, *Song Parade*, *American*, *White's Radio Log*, *Cartoon Digest*, *Die Hausfrau*, and *Die Welt*, as "one of the saddest photographs I've ever seen."

3

The Greater City

A S IN THE 1920S, so in the 1940s it seemed to European visitors like Sartre and Camus that all the wealth and dynamism of a continent were concentrated on the island of Manhattan, slightly less than thirteen miles from north to south and no more than two and a half miles from east to west, about half the size of the city and county of San Francisco, a statistic that always surprises. Brooklyn (Kings County) and the Bronx had bigger populations, but Manhattan remained the citadel of Greater New York, and Greater New York, with a population of 7.9 million, was the second-largest city in the world after London. As early as the teens and twenties, certain foreign observers and resident boosters had spoken of New York City as the world's leading metropolis. Now—sometime during the war, it would seem—it had become the capital of the twentieth century, just as Paris, according to Walter Benjamin, had been the capital of the nineteenth century.

Stamped in gold on the cover of the "Green Book," the official directory of its municipal departments and officeholders, was the motto "The World's Greatest City," which the war had made good. At the end of 1945, Fiorello H. La Guardia's long, turbulent reign as mayor of New York came to an end; his Democratic successor was William O'Dwyer, a lawyer and onetime policeman, whom he had once compared to a cabbage. After twelve years, New York and La Guardia had each tired of the other's intensities. Even tired, La Guardia would have liked another term, but having over the course of his career run on Socialist, Democratic, Republican, American Labor, and Fusion tickets, he had at last run out of parties to nominate him. The amiable O'Dwyer promised a progressive but less exigent administration, without the storm and stress. He was born in Bohola, County Mayo, Ireland, in 1890, the son of schoolteachers, and his success story seemed to vindicate the myth of the melting pot as vividly as that of his first-generation Italian-Jewish predecessor.* More so, really, since no one could have invented La Guardia except himself, while O'Dwyer was the cop on the corner who rose to power with the help of his friends at Tammany Hall.

Arriving in New York in 1910, at the age of twenty, with a worldly fortune of $23.35 (about average for an Irish immigrant at that time), O'Dwyer had to scramble to support himself with odd jobs, including grocery man, deckhand, plasterer's helper, stoker, hod carrier, and, rising in the world, bartender at the Plaza Hotel, until joining the police force. Acquiring a night-school law degree at Fordham University and the favor of various Democratic bosses, he rose to become district attorney of Kings County, in which office he became famous for prosecuting the entrepreneurs of "Murder, Inc.," the enforcement agency of organized crime. Despite his successful pursuit of the noted extortionist and executioner Louis "Lepke" Buchalter, many suspected then, and many more later, that His Honor's relation to the underworld was not always as distant or adversarial as it might have been.†

---

* O'Dwyer was one of eleven children. When he was still a young man, one of his brothers was killed in a robbery, causing the future mayor to swear eternal enmity to the criminal class. His youngest brother, Paul O'Dwyer, followed him into the law, embraced labor and civil rights activism, ran unsuccessfully against Jacob K. Javits for the United States Senate in 1968, served as president of the City Council of New York from 1974 to 1977, and until his death in 1998 personified some of the best instincts of postwar urban liberalism.

† Lepke was eventually electrocuted. In 1943 he was lodged in the West Side Jail in Manhattan, where Robert Lowell, passing through on his way to the Federal Correction Institution in Danbury, Connecticut, to serve his time as a conscientious objector, remembered having pointed out to him "the T-shirted back/of *Murder Incorporated*'s Czar Lepke." Although O'Dwyer's supporters credited him with eighty-seven murder convictions during his term as DA in 1940–41, it was widely noticed that after his prosecution of Lepke he showed no inclination to indict other figures as notable in the criminal field, such as Albert Anastasia and Joe Adonis. O'Dwyer was in the army

The mayor was a considerable raconteur, with many admirers in the press. One of his closest friends was the founder and editor of the *New Yorker*, Harold Ross. As the *New Yorker* writer Philip Hamburger wrote, "These two colorful, exotic men loved to sit on the porch of Gracie Mansion, gossip, joke, and swap tall stories of their youth—one man from Ireland, the other from the Far West."

As New York's one hundredth mayor, counting from Dutch colonial days, it fell to O'Dwyer to preside over the "golden anniversary" of Greater New York in 1948. Fifty years before, led by the visionary reformer Andrew Haswell Green, the politicians of old New York had agreed to combine the municipalities of the city (Manhattan and the Bronx) with Brooklyn, along with Queens and Richmond (Staten Island), into the modern City of New York. In the first moments of January 1, 1898, as flares and fireworks had burst over a jubilant crowd, the ensign of the Greater City was raised up the flagstaff of City Hall. From an island metropolis of 23 square miles, and 1.5 million people, New York was transformed into a city of 299 square miles and 3.4 million.

Greater New York was an imperfect union—more of a confederacy than a true merger, the *New York Times*'s Warren Moscow observed many years later, as shown to this day by the respect dutifully paid to the borough boundaries by gangs and racketeers, not to mention mere politicians, if they are wise. But consolidation served the purposes of efficiency, especially in transportation, and apart from a few recalcitrant politicians and clergymen in predominantly Protestant Brooklyn, it had long been recognized as inevitable. In fact, the real symbolic moment of union had occurred years before, on May 15, 1883, when New York's mayor, Franklin Edson, accompanied by the president of the United States, Chester A. Arthur, and the governor of New York, Grover Cleveland, had met the mayor of Brooklyn, young Seth Low, midway on the span of the Brooklyn Bridge on the day of its dedication.

Most important, consolidation disposed of the threat that New

---

during the war and an emissary of FDR in Italy. In the course of the 1945 contest for mayor, it emerged that he had paid a friendly social call on Frank Costello, one of the city's leading mobsters, who was supporting his election. None of this history prevented O'Dwyer, who had run unsuccessfully against La Guardia in 1941, from being elected by a margin of 700,000, the biggest in the city's history to that date.

York would be overtaken in population by upstart, faster-growing Chicago—1,150,000 in 1890, having doubled in a decade—with all the loss of prestige, trade, corporate headquarters, and political sway that such a terrible event would have threatened. With its primacy on the American scene secured, New York was ready to advance globally. In *The Greater City*, an official history commissioned for the 1948 jubilee, Allan Nevins, a former newspaperman turned Columbia University professor, rejoiced that in the last half-century Greater New York had so far surpassed all other cities in its combined distinctions,

> it might almost call itself the world metropolis . . . Down to the first World War, it had yielded precedence in financial fields to London, in artistic fields to Paris, and in musical fields to Berlin. In the period between wars these European capitals had struggled bravely to regain their old position. But at the end of the Second World War New York stood alone. Even in population, London, which had kept abreast of it only by annexing outlying suburbs, was ready to yield first place to its eight millions. In wealth, resources, and volume of hopeful energy no city of battered, impoverished Europe, of adolescent Latin America, or of the interior United States, could challenge its primacy.

As ever, the Empire City exaggerated the overall American condition. New York had gone from being Depression-bound to being the "supreme metropolis of the present" according to the British literary critic Cyril Connolly, while actually changing less than in any comparable span since 1800. The brute fact was, New York had succeeded in the race of cities not by advancing but almost by standing still—even as so many huge cities outside of North America were fading, or falling, or sinking downward to darkness.

In London, its only rival for size, whole districts were in ruins.* There were still fancy-dress balls: at one of the fanciest of these, the tart-tongued Lady Cunard was told by someone, pointing to the glit-

---

* After the war the most populous cities in the world were London, New York, Shanghai, Berlin, Moscow, Chicago, and Paris.

tering crowd, "This is what we were fighting for," to which she tersely replied, "What, are they all Poles?" But in postwar Britain unemployment soon exceeded Depression levels; most Londoners were miserably cold during the first winter of peace, and even colder in the terrible second; and rationing continued to be stringent—it would not be entirely lifted until 1954. In Paris most people found their living conditions were worse just after the war than they had been at the end of the German occupation. In the USSR, Leningrad and Moscow were drawn into the morbid isolation dictated by Stalin's dread of foreign influences. Almost a whole generation of men had been lost in the war and the Terror, the gulag archipelago was swollen with new prisoners, and in the wreckage of their cities people lived on thin gruels of cabbage and potato scraps.

In Berlin the dead were too many to bury, yet the city was filling up with refugees from the south and the east—"displaced persons." As the historian Hugh Thomas writes, "An accurate picture of life in Central and Eastern Europe in the winter of 1945–46 should thus include the sight of hundreds of trains, themselves in bad condition, carrying thousands of victims of international conflict to places where neither they nor their immediate ancestors had ever been, each refugee clutching a sack or two of possessions, cold, hungry, ill, bewildered." Bombing, fighting, disease, and, most of all, flight had reduced the population of Berlin, which stood at a peak of 4.3 million in 1943, by a third. Nearly 95 percent of its built-up area was in ruins; almost half of its residential units had been entirely destroyed. Most of what remained of its industrial plant had been removed by the Soviets; even railways had been stripped and carted away. Surveying the wreckage, the poet Stephen Spender imagined that for centuries to come visitors would gape and wonder at the grandiose broken hulks of the Reichstag and the Chancellery, "the scenes of a collapse so complete that it already has the remoteness of all final disasters." (Unimaginable then that by century's end the Reichstag would be "wrapped" by the Bulgarian artist Christo and restored as the capitol of a reunified Germany by an English architect, Sir Norman Foster.)

Vienna, formerly the second city of the Third Reich, was divided, like Berlin, into occupation zones—doubly divided, since the inner city had also been quartered by the Allies. The fighting and bombing in April 1945 had ripped up much of its infrastructure, including sewer lines, with the resulting threats of typhoid and dysentery. (American moviegoers would soon be acquainted with Vienna's sewers through Carol Reed's movie *The Third Man*, adapted by Graham Greene from his novel, in which Orson Welles played the black-marketer Harry Lime.) Cold, hunger, and physical desolation were facts of daily life in the famous European cities that once had vied with New York for political, economic, or cultural preeminence, regardless of the side on which the war had found them.

In the East, the damage to Japan's urban fabric was apocalyptic, literally so in the atomic-bombed cities of Hiroshima and Nagasaki. Kyoto had been spared at the insistence of Secretary of War Henry Stimson; so much of the built-up area of Tokyo had been destroyed in the fire raids that American military planners felt that the bomb would have been wasted on it. Briefly Tokyo had ruled a vast empire extending from the mid-Pacific to the gates of India, from the Aleutians to Java, and deep into China; now it had been stripped of all overseas possessions. (Japan's warlords hoped almost to the end to retain Korea, having occupied and brutalized this ancient kingdom the longest.) Most Japanese, including the political elite, were extremely surprised when the American occupation forces, as they began to arrive in September 1945, did not demand to be fed, which would have led to mass starvation. Food remained scarce. Just after the war, on any given day, a third of Tokyo's population could be found foraging in the countryside.

Yokohama, the seaport on Tokyo Bay from which the imperial warships had sailed, was "a sad place that had been flattened by bombs and the inhabitants were living in shacks made of rubble, propped up in fields of rubble," wrote Anatole Broyard, who was in command of a stevedore battalion with the dismal assignment of "scrap[ing] a solid crust of shit off a dock a quarter of a mile long. I didn't realize at first that it was human shit. As I figured it out later, Japanese stevedores and embarking soldiers had had no time for niceties toward the end and had simply squatted down wherever they stood. The entire dock was covered with a layer that was as hard as clay. The rain and traffic had packed it down." The real work was done by a huge crew of Japanese equipped with "axes, shovels, sledgehammers, picks, crowbars—whatever we could find."

Shanghai, Singapore, Hong Kong, and Manila, Asia's other great modern cities before the war, were shaken shadows of their former selves. As the novelist James Salter reveals in *Burning the Days*, in the Pacific, though the war was over, "its vast, shabby landscape remained. In Manila Bay the water was the color of rust from sunken ships. Unidentified masts and funnels were sticking above the surface. Manila was half destroyed; the tops were blown off the palm trees, the roads were ruined, the air filled with dust." At the end, the Japanese commander had mounted a prolonged and desperate defense, which became a brutal slaughter. By the time the last Japanese were routed from the old walled inner city, the Intramuros, a hundred thousand Filipino civilians had been killed, and most of the city was bloodied and ruined.

From one end of Eurasia to the other, one might behold, as Spender wrote of Germany, "ruins, not belonging to a past civilization, but the ruins of our own epoch, which make us suddenly feel that we are entering upon the nomadic stage when people walk across deserts of centuries, and when the environment which past generations have created for us disintegrates in our own lifetimes."

Just as the lights in its office buildings seemed positively incandescent after the dimout, it was against this dismal wasteland background in Europe and Asia that New York dazzled—"the incomparable, the brilliant star city of cities, the forty-ninth state, a law unto itself, the Cyclopean paradox, the inferno with no out-of-bounds, the supreme expression of both the miseries and the splendors of contemporary civilization, the Macedonia of the United States," as John Gunther rhapsodizes in *Inside U.S.A.*

Nor did any other American city come close to rivaling it in power or panache, as theater of ambition or simply as spectacle. Philadelphia (as New York viewed its ancient rivals) was staid and stultified, and Boston, Oliver Wendell Holmes's "Hub of the Universe," was too self-absorbed to notice how provincial it had become. The cities of the West Coast were peripheral in a world system still centered on the Atlantic, if no longer on Europe; something had gone out of San Francisco after the earthquake and fire of 1906, while Los Angeles, "the great anti-cultural amusement-producing center," as Edmund Wilson described it, had a well-deserved *Day of the Locust* reputation for apocalyptic natural disasters. St. Louis and New Orleans were in visible decline. Houston, which was somewhere in Texas, was a bit crude and grasping; Detroit was a company town; and Chicago, which once aspired to become the First City of the world, was now resigned to being merely Second City in the country. (Notwithstanding, Colonel Robert McCormick, the publisher of the *Tribune*, stoutly maintained that Greater "Chicagoland" was as powerful and populous as Greater New York, and had a much higher moral tone.)

Since Roosevelt's Hundred Days, in 1933, Washington, DC, had finally begun to exercise power commensurate to the grandeur of its avenues. No potentate of Wall Street could presume to deal with the president of the United States as his equal, as within living memory the senior J. P. Morgan had attempted to deal with Theodore Roosevelt, saying to him, "If we have done anything [wrong], send your man to my man and they can fix it up." But lacking any distinctions besides the political, Washington was nobody's idea of a metropolis, in the forties or the fifties, for that matter, when the senator from Massachusetts John F. Kennedy famously quipped that it was "a city of Southern efficiency and Northern charm."

But New York was the richest city in the world, the greatest seaport, and the biggest manufacturing center, employing more workers— mostly Jewish and Italian—in the needle trades alone than labored on Detroit's assembly lines or sweated in Pittsburgh's steel mills. New York, said D. W. Brogan, a Cambridge University don specializing in America, was the only American city big enough to boast of being little. ("Little Old New York," a fond phrase, he thought, like "Dear, Dirty Dublin." Brogan was Irish.)

New York did not officially celebrate its marriage to the sea, like Venice, but after three hundred years it was still reasonably faithful: the Port of New York remained a "floating traffic-jam" of red- and green-painted ferries, lighters, lumbering car floats, barges, riverboats, and smoking tugboats escorting majestic ocean liners. From the windows of the newly constructed apartment blocks around Washington

Square, Brogan wrote, those restored floating palaces the *Queen Eliza-beth*, the *Île de France*, and the *Nieuw Amsterdam*, seemed almost close enough to touch as they glided on their way to the piers on the lordly Hudson, their arrivals and departures as gigantically emblematic of the city as the skyscrapers. From her youth on Central Park West, Marya Mannes remembered in 1961 two sounds: horses' hooves clat-tering on the pavement at four o'clock in the morning, "not before and not after," as a Plaza Hotel brougham headed homeward, and the "bull roar of ocean liners," outward bound.

From 1820 to 1960 the Port of New York was the busiest in the world. It possessed superb advantages. It was never icebound, rarely dangerously foggy, and several channels led into the harbor, the broad, deep-dredged Ambrose being the most important. Counting all the navigable waterways within a twenty-mile radius of the Statue of Lib-erty, the entire port included seven bays, four rivers, four estuaries, several creeks—altogether, some 772 miles of shoreline, of which 285 miles of water frontage were developed, crowded with piers, bulkheads, groins, wharves, and "those warehouses," as recalled by Mannes, "dark red or old yellow, with blind-bricked windows, that on any waterfront spell the movement of goods and produce, ship chandlers, and the smell of hemp and iron."

The Chelsea Piers were full of maritime drama and labor strife; South Street still fragrant with memories of the old whorehouses and grogshops on Cherry Street, of the sailors' boardinghouses with names like Blind Dan's and Mother Bastard's; redolent, too, of yesterday's catch. And how like the prow of some immense ship was the tip of the island, the melancholy Battery. "There is some sense to this conceit," wrote the maritime officer and author of maritime histories and fiction Felix Riesenberg, "for I have felt it when pinned there by my imagina-tion, as if the oncoming city were pushing me back into the sea."

The great seaport was also a great entrepôt, a great emporium, and—which even many natives did not suspect—a great industrial city, whose output measured in dollars exceeded Detroit's. It supported as many odd occupations, and tempted with as many luxuries and exoti-cisms, as all the bazaars of the rest of the world combined. John Gun-ther, surveying a Midtown block in 1946:

I have just walked around the block to see concretely what illimitable variety this neighborhood affords. Within a hundred yards I can go to church, have my hair cut, admire flowers, visit two banks (both low Georgian buildings in red brick), and dine in one of the supreme restaurants of the world or at Hamburger Heaven. Within a slightly greater radius I can buy a Cézanne ($55,000), a chukar partridge ($7.50), a pound of Persian caviar ($38), or a copy of the Civil Service *Leader* (10 cents). Within two hundred yards are three competing pharmacies comfortably busy, a shop for religious goods and missals, a delicatessen squeezed into a four-foot frontage, windows full of the most ornately superior English saddlery, a podiatrist, a good French bookstore, a Speed Hosiery repair shop, and, of course, the inevitable small stationery shop with its broad red band across the window advertising a variety of cigars.

Thumbing through the sixteen hundred closely printed pages of the classified telephone directory, he discovered that the occupations supported by New York included "cinders, chenille dotting, bullet-proof equipment, breast bumps, bungs, boiler baffles, glue room equipment, abattoirs, flow meters, eschatology, mildew-proofing, pompons, potato chip machinery, rennet, spangles, solenoids, and spats."

This otherwise chaotic enumeration suggests why New York was a great manufacturing city that, however, did not feel like one, or look the part. Led by garment making, printing, machinery, food products, and chemicals (including perfumes and cosmetics), its industries were light. Its small loft factories operated behind office facades. In the text accompanying Andreas Feininger's superb photographs in *New York in the Forties*, John von Hartz writes that many of the shoppers patronizing Macy's, Gimbels, or Saks at Thirty-fourth Street could easily have been unaware that the suits, dresses, and underwear they were buying were manufactured a few blocks away in the Garment District, where the only signs of industry were the bursts of steam that spilled from windows, released from pressing machines.

4

Babylon Revisited

B EFORE THE CIVIL WAR," Lewis Mumford writes, "New York shared its intellectual distinction with Boston, its industrial place with Philadelphia, and its commercial supremacy with Baltimore and New Orleans. Though it had become the mouth of the continent, thanks to the Erie Canal, it was not yet the maw. After the Civil War, despite the energetic rise of Chicago, New York became an imperial metropolis, sucking into its own whirlpool the wealth and the wreckage of the rest of the country and of the lands beyond the sea."

The seventeenth-century Dutch and English world empires coveted "Manhattoes" for its superb geographical situation; urban amenities came later. As late as 1800, Henry Adams wrote in his *History of the United States*, "if Boston resembled an old-fashioned English market-town, New York was like a foreign seaport, badly paved, undrained, and as foul as a town surrounded by the tides could be." In an age of capital New York perhaps had the advantage of its historic single-minded devotion to commerce, uncompromised by the higher aspirations of Puritan Boston and Quaker Philadelphia, notwithstanding the bankers of Boston were famously keen and the lawyers of Philadelphia proverbially sharp. But the urban theorist Raymond Vernon suggests there was something about the "fluid social structure" of the city life that drew a perhaps new kind of driven businessman who would be able to rise socially with his new fortune. New York entrepreneurs were responsible for such innovations as regularly scheduled packet ships to Liverpool after 1818; they made themselves middlemen in the cotton trade and took full advantage of the Erie Canal, which opened in 1825.

Dismissing these "advantages" as secondary or overblown, the historian Eric Lampard traces the beginnings of New York's commercial supremacy to the era of the Seven Years' War, 1756–63, when its merchants succeeded in establishing a special relationship with the military-industrial establishment in London. In 1755 New York was made "the general Magazine of Arms and Military Stores," involving the very profitable provision of food, alcohol, uniforms, shoes, and other goods, and the terminus of a monthly postal ship two years later. From the 1750s, the city was involved with the growing interconnections between Britain and Europe. New York would be two days closer to, say, London or Amsterdam than other East Coast cities, more than fifty years before there was "a monthly scheduled commercial packet from New York to Liverpool in 1818 or its 1822 equivalent to Le Havre." In 1815, as the Napoleonic era with all its disruptions ended, the merchants of New York could draw on the "experience and institutional assets" that had been accumulating on the island ever since.

When cotton was king, New York was the port through which most of the crop was shipped to Europe's mills. After the South was defeated in the Civil War, New York only became richer; the pigs that once rooted in the streets were transformed, according to Mumford, into financiers and entrepreneurs who worked on Wall Street. In addition to its initial advantages as a port, the city grew wealthier as its bankers underwrote the railroads across the country. The import-export trade attracted the bank reserves that underwrote the corporate securities whose issuance made and kept New York the nation's preferred location for corporate headquarters. The skyscrapers (originally a nautical term) that rose to house these corporations were wired for light, connected by telegraph and telephone lines.

With the redeeming exception of Central Park, which opened to the public in 1859, and a few charming Greek Revival houses on Washington Square, New York in the Gilded Age, when it became a world city, was without charm or distinction, or so declared the most sensitive witnesses. The built-up part was prevailingly flat and brown—brownstone buildings of Triassic sandstone having become fashionable

in the 1840s and ubiquitous by the fifties—and as the island was electrified in the eighties it became forested with telegraph, telephone, and
electric-light wires. Until the blizzard of '88, which tumbled many of
them and led to undergrounding, the utility poles stood as much as
ninety feet tall beside the Hudson and in other places. The streets
were filthy with horse droppings, the air was permeated by crystal-
lized manure, and the tread of horses on the new asphalt streets made
a constant din, to which the new elevated railways were soon adding
their metallic screeching and clanging.

Toward the end of her life, Edith Wharton remembered how "intolerably ugly" New York had appeared to her as a privileged ten-year-old
just returned from Europe in 1872—"this cramped horizontal grid-
iron of a town without towers, porticoes, fountains or perspectives."
New York was built no higher than Liverpool, or Berlin on its plain.
As in Old World cities, the heights were still mostly ecclesiastical. For
decades its tallest building was the downtown Gothic Revival Trinity Church, whose spire rose 280 feet above the church steps. Mark
Twain, passing through town in 1867 as a correspondent for a California newspaper, described its "domed and steepled solitude."

The description hardly applied thirty-three years later when the
now-famous Twain came to live in Greenwich Village, at 14 West
Tenth Street. As the century waned, New York became loftier, denser,
richer, noisier, more various and extreme. Arguably, New York's first
true skyscraper was the Tower Building at 50 Broadway, designed by a
bold young architect, Bradford Lee Gilbert, for an enterprising young
merchant, John N. Stearns; like the revolutionary high-rises already
going up in Chicago, it was supported, up to a height of seven stories, by a steel skeleton; another six stories stood above them. Skep-
tics predicted that the "Idiotic Building" would topple over in a strong
wind, but were confounded when the almost-completed structure
easily withstood a hurricane in the winter of 1889.* The safety eleva-

* In his *Power and Style: A Critique of Twentieth-Century Architecture in the United States*
(New York, 1995), Robert Twombly sensibly observes that while there are various tax-
onomies of the skyscraper and claims for historical priority, "all the layperson—and
the expert, for that matter—needs to know is that they rise noticeably higher than the
norm of their built surroundings, which meant they were approaching twenty stories
in 1900 when the great majority were devoted to office space."

tor was displayed by the Yonkers inventor Elisha Graves Otis at the Crystal Palace Exhibition in 1854; subsequent improvements made the new towers plausible as investments and places to work. By 1900, the thirty-story, 392-foot Park Row Business Building was the tallest of a dozen or so skyscrapers rising on the lower part of the island. "The outline of the city became frantic in its effort to explain something that defied meaning," Henry Adams wrote in his *Education.* "Prosperity never before imagined, power not yet wielded by man, speed never reached by anything but a meteor, had made the world irritable, nervous, querulous, unreasonable and afraid." The hyper-ambitious scale of architecture in New York was like nothing else on earth. By 1906, H. G. Wells, arriving for an inspection, would be struck by how *small* against the skyline his steamship seemed, which had loomed so large in Liverpool's harbor.

If Chicago built skyscrapers earlier, New York built more, and taller, and more fanciful. Where utilitarian Chicago's typically featured flat roofs and plain facades, New York's were crowned with fantastic cupolas, obelisks, pyramids, and temple fronts, elaborated with details Greek or Gothic, soaring impossibly high, occupying whole blocks, casting their vicinity into shadow. The principle of the "zoning envelope," requiring setbacks at particular heights in given zones, was anticipated by Ernest Flagg's phallic, bulbous-crowned Singer Building, which occupied only a quarter of its site; such setbacks were codified into law in 1916, and the skyline began to fill with Babylonian ziggurats. At forty-seven stories the Singer Building was briefly the tallest office building in New York and the world, until overtaken by the Metropolitan Life Tower, a huge campanile, in turn exceeded by Cass Gilbert's fifty-five-story American Gothic Woolworth Building, which retained the title until the construction of the Chrysler Building in 1930. (The story went that the Metropolitan Life Company aroused Frank Woolworth's ire as well as his competitive instincts when it refused him a loan; travelling to Calcutta, he happened to see a postcard displaying its tower; sweet revenge and a brilliant advertising triumph were accomplished by ordering Gilbert to design a taller structure.) Unlike Chicago's, most of New York's most distinctive skyscrapers were as much promotional as they were functional office buildings; during the 1940s, when it seemed that no more of them would be built, Jean-Paul Sartre described the tall buildings as "votive offerings to success."

The misfortunes of the Old World—"potato famine, political oppression, and pogroms"—impelled the mass migrations of the nineteenth century. During the "old migration" spanning the Civil War, the larger number of arrivals were Irish, especially during and after the famine of 1845–50, and German, many of the latter seeking political or religious asylum. The Irish tended to scatter around the city, wherever work was to be found, while the Germans were concentrated on the later Lower East Side in *Kleindeutschland* (Little Germany), between Canal and Rivington. The tide of immigration from England, Scotland, Ireland, and Germany continued strong even as a more exotic and eventually more numerous "new migration" from Southern and Eastern Europe was beginning. In John Dos Passos's novel *Manhattan Transfer* (1925) the old fisherman tells his son: "When I was a boy it was wild Irish came in the spring with the first run of shad . . . Now there aint no more shad, an them folks, Lord knows where they come from."

Between 1892, when it replaced Castle Garden off the Battery as a reception center, and 1924, 16 million immigrants passed through Ellis Island. Along with Balkan Slavs, Slovaks, Turks, and Poles, that number included the great majority of the 1.9 million Italians and 2,562,000 Jews from the Russian empire who came to the U.S. during that time. Edwin G. Burrows and Mike Wallace note in their *Gotham*, "The Eastern Europeans were predominantly families, Jewish, and urban; and the Italians mainly bachelors, Catholic, and rural." Unlike the Jewish families, many, perhaps most, of the Italians regarded their residence in the New World as temporary; and in the end as many as forty-three out of one hundred returned to the homeland.

The new arrivals were as bafflingly alien to one another as they were to the old Anglo-Dutch ascendancy and other "native Americans," as whites of established families were then known. With few exceptions the immigrants crowded into tightly packed pockets of ethnicity scattered around the island: the Italians into the "Mulberry Bend" and other "Little Italies," including one in Harlem; the Jews from Russia, Poland, and elsewhere into the Lower East Side, around Ludlow,

Hester, and Essex Streets; and so on. In New York their settlements seemed to respect the boundaries of the ancient empires and old countries from which they had come, or so a clever writer claimed in 1924, when it seemed that the great tide of immigration had splashed over the city for the last time. "A map of Europe superimposed upon the map of New York could prove that the different sections of the city live in the same proximity to one another as in Europe," the Romanian American journalist and author Konrad Bercovici wrote, "the Germans near the Austrians, the Russians and the Rumanians near the Hungarians, and the Greeks behind the Italians. People of Eastern Europe live in the eastern part of the city. Northerners live in the northern part of the city and southerners in the southern part. Those who have lived on the other side near the sea or a river have a tendency to live here as near the sea or the river as possible."

Non-European immigrants were comparatively few—there was a miniature Chinatown around Mott Street, mostly laborers from California who had worked on the railroad or come to escape the rabid anti-Asian prejudice of the West Coast. There were much smaller numbers of Japanese, Koreans, Filipinos, and Indians, most of whom had also come overland from the West. In a curious way Little Italy resembled the demographic of Chinatown; both were composed mostly of single men because of restrictive immigration, which allowed the importation of male laborers when convenient for the capitalists of the West Coast, but not of families.

In the 1890s, the Tenth Ward in the Lower East Side, the heart of the Jewish ghetto, was the most crowded place on earth, with a density of 747 persons per acre, or 478,080 per square mile, more than four times that of Calcutta in recent times. By the time the population of Manhattan peaked at 2.3 million in 1910, 350,000 persons were living to the square mile in the area bordered by the old Madison Square, Houston Street, the Bowery, and the East River, a density almost four times greater than that of Shanghai. The comparable figure for the densest parts of Boston or Chicago was 18,000 per square mile.

On his American tour of 1905–06, Henry James marveled at the "ubiquity of the alien" in the city of his birth, wondering how the latest "installed tribes" could possibly be assimilated and with what effect on them and America. (His paternal grandfather, known in the family as William of Albany, was an Irish Protestant who immigrated after the Revolutionary War and died in 1832, leaving a fortune of three million dollars.) James brooded over the Italians, worrying that submersion in the melting pot might cost them their charm and vivacity—they seemed cold and remote compared with the *contadini* who had remained in Italy. Not so Jews, who now accounted for a quarter of the city's four million and did not seem to be diminished by America in the least: "The denizens of the New York Ghetto, heaped as thick as the splinters on the table of a glass-blower, had each, like the fine glass particle, his or her individual share of the whole hard glitter of Israel."

James toured the slums whose squalor had been exposed to the world by Theodore Roosevelt's friend Jacob Riis in *How the Other Half Lives*, concluding: "There is such a thing, in the United States, it is hence to be inferred, as freedom to grow up to be blighted, and it may be the only freedom in store for the smaller fry of succeeding generations."

In contrast to the privations of the many was the astonishing opulence of the few, expressing itself in a parvenu passion for show, which, considering this was New York, amounted to "gilding the temporary." Dutifully, James visited the latest temples to Mammon: the original Waldorf Astoria Hotel on Fifth Avenue, on the site later occupied by the Empire State Building; the new Tiffany Building; the new Metropolitan Museum. At the Waldorf he was amused by the "immense promiscuity" of the place. Of the museum, equally a monument to conspicuous consumption: "There was money in the air, ever so much money—that was, grossly expressed, the sense of the whole intimation. And the money was to be for *all* the most exquisite things—for all the most exquisite except for creation, which was to be off the scene altogether; for art, selection, criticism, for knowledge, piety, taste."

The First World War slammed shut the golden door on Europe's wave of immigration, and when peace came, Congress passed legislation intended to ensure that it was kept shut, with the result that immigration did not resume with anything like its former force until the 1970s, and then with an almost entirely different ethnic cast. The United States succeeded Great Britain as the world's leading creditor nation, New York City replacing London as the international capital of finance. Led by the House of Morgan, Wall Street bankers had organized the loans to pay for the Allied war effort. (Morgan partner Edward J. Stettinius Sr., father of the future secretary of state, orchestrated arrangements from a yacht on the Long Island Sound, where he could avoid distractions and presumably unwanted callers as well.)

The war, which enforced sobriety through state and federal prohibition of alcohol, and a spirit of sober sacrifice in the hinterlands, had something of the opposite effect in New York, which prospered as the ratio of exports over imports to Europe rose tenfold in a single year. "Café society celebrated with an orgy of conspicuous consumption, spending as much as two dollars to enter one of the newly-fashionable cabarets." During the preceding neutrality period, one observer wrote, "only New York was really excited" by the unfolding events in Europe. The doughboys sailing to Europe sent New Yorkers into transports of patriotism, and likewise their triumphant return. After the Armistice, wrote a distinguished literary visitor, Sir Philip Gibbs, New York "seemed to be excited by its own historical significance. There was a vibration about it as sunlight splashed its gold upon the topmost stories of the skyscrapers."

From the soberer perspectives of the thirties and forties, New York in the Jazz Age was pandemonium. George Gershwin's melodies and those of the young Eubie Blake, Hart Crane's *The Bridge* and William Van Alen's fantastic Chrysler Building, Texas Guinan's speakeasies, and Mayor Jimmy Walker's insouciant corruption, all the glories and excesses that F. Scott Fitzgerald epitomized as "the greatest spree in history," seemed as remote and unreal as Oz.

The French writer Paul Morand was one of the most acute and excitable of the European writers who came to see the great spectacle of New York when, as *New York Panorama* puts it, the city had been "not only the symbol of America but the demonic symbol of the modern." "Skyscrapers!" Morand exclaims in his *New York* (1930): "Some are women, others are men; some are like sun-temples, others recall the Aztec pyramid of the moon . . . From these great follies New York derives her grandeur, her strength, her aspect of To-morrow. Roofless, crowned with terraces, they seem to be awaiting the rigid balloons, the helicopters, the winged men of the future." And New York by night:

The lines vanish; no more walls, no more solids, no more relief; all the skyscrapers are merged and simplified, looking like a vast, square, checkered conflagration fanned by the wind from the open sea. The moon never has a chance. Those cathedral towers, fired surely by the devil, are a mirage from some fantastic world, looking not eternal but astride of time.

Visiting in 1925, the Soviets' top bard, Vladimir Mayakovsky, professed to be unmoved: the headline of an interview with the radical Michael Gold in the *New York World* read, "Russia's Dynamic Poet Finds New York Tame: We're Old-Fashioned, Unorganized to Mayakovsky; 'Manhattan Is an Accident Stumbled On by Children,' He Declares."

The assertive futurist, world-famous at thirty, moved into a room near Washington Square, to smoke and declaim. "Eh, it's boring here . . ."

But even Mayakovsky was struck by Broadway: "It really is white . . . Brightness, brightness, brightness."

Never before or since has the metropolitan element in America been as assertive, as clamorous, as concentrated, or as insular. Though otherwise different in their focus and artistry, *The Bridge*, *Manhattan Transfer*, and *The Great Gatsby* share a background sense of multitudes in furious motion, delighting in their own swarming, drawn mothlike to the bright lights, transfixed by spectacles.

"Mongrel Manhattan," as Ann Douglas writes, was "recklessly provincial." Thus, *Time*, *Reader's Digest*, and the *New Yorker*, the three most important magazine success stories of the twenties, were all launched in New York, but it was Harold Ross's *New Yorker* that flaunted its proud insularity, boasting that it was not "for the old lady from Dubuque." (Ross was from Aspen, Colorado.) According to the census, the list of city dwellers grew by 14,365,512 between 1920 and 1930; though its pace was slowing, the New York region's growth still exceeded the national average and, even more offensively to the hinterlands, its income was a third higher.

Furiously, Middle America defended itself against metropolitan

America. Having acted to shut down their saloons and beer gardens with the enactment of Prohibition, nativist legislators, mostly
from the heartland, moved to intercept immigrants themselves. The
Johnson-Reed Act of 1924 allotted small national quotas on the basis
of a formula based on the composition of the United States in 1890,
thus cutting off almost all immigration from Southern and Eastern
Europe, and barring Asians entirely, exceptions being made for the
rich and the very accomplished. Touring Ellis Island in 1929, Morand
was surprised to find it practically deserted: "Nowadays," he concludes
sardonically, "America is purifying herself. She has closed her doors to
Orientals, like a large club."

Paradoxically, the quotas actually had the effect of increasing ethnic
diversity and "tribalism," as Alan Dawley notes in *Struggles for Justice*. "No amount of Anglo-Saxon ancestor worship or eugenics fantasy
could erase the fact that America was a multiethnic society in which
the descendants of British Protestants were in a minority. That is why
the logic of immigration restriction was self-contradictory; intending
to preserve a fictional homogeneity, it froze the actual heterogeneity."

But Cosmopolis was also a small town. Governor Al Smith, the
dominant figure in New York State politics during the twenties and
the Democratic Party candidate for president in 1928, was the classic
urban provincial. A mixed German and Irish child of the Lower East
Side—fond of saying that he had received his higher education working in the Fulton Fish Market—Al Smith had rarely ventured outside
the city limits before 1928 except to govern in Albany. Profoundly distrusted by the South and by small-town America for his Catholicism
and brash city airs, Smith scarcely bothered to disguise his boredom
with, and incomprehension of, the strange folkways to be found west
of the Hudson. Once, somewhere out west, watching from his campaign train as the dark fields of the republic rolled on under the night,
he was heard by reporters to exclaim, "My God, how do they stand it?
How do they stand it?"

His opponent, Herbert Hoover, was both reassuringly Middle
American—born in Iowa, a Quaker, a self-made man—and impres-
sively worldly; the dynamic secretary of commerce was a multimillionaire mining engineer with a degree from Stanford University, who had
spent most of his adult life abroad (at one time maintaining offices in

San Francisco, New York, Melbourne, Shanghai, and London) and had become a world figure organizing relief during the First World War. Narrowly elected governor of New York in 1928, FDR was appalled by the inept presidential campaign Al Smith ran, which included such follies as moving the headquarters of the Democratic Party into the General Motors Building, as if to symbolize its Babylonian captivity to the big-business interests represented by his great friend John J. Raskob, who was an executive for DuPont and General Motors and built the Empire State Building. Although prejudice played its part, almost certainly any Democrat would have been beaten by the Republican in the prosperous year of 1928, let alone a Republican as superbly capable as Herbert Hoover was then credited with being.

But the real energies of "Mongrel Manhattan" were cultural, aesthetic, sexual, commercial, not political. "It was characteristic of the Jazz Age that it had no interest in politics at all," says Fitzgerald, who certainly had none that were noticeable before the thirties. In his classic *The Crisis of the Old Order* (1957), Arthur M. Schlesinger Jr. attributes this disaffection to a rebellion on the part of the intellectuals against an overbearing business culture: "It was an age of art, of excess, of satire, of miracle; but who was to care about economics, when business policy seemed so infallible? Or about politics, when business power seemed so invincible?" And there was an interest in the less traditional, more vulgar side of culture, as Gilbert Seldes, in his 1924 book *The Seven Lively Arts*, reveals, coming out in favor of vaudeville, movies, newspaper humorists, comic strips, ragtime, and jazz; his admiration, even idolatry, went out to Florenz Ziegfeld, Charlie Chaplin, Al Jolson, Irving Berlin, and George Herriman, the creator of *Krazy Kat.**

By any account, New York in the Jazz Age concentrated all the furies of a theatrically disillusioned time, all the license and bravura, all the movements of artistic, sexual, and political liberation. Ann Douglas

---

* In the spirit of the times, Edmund Wilson had written what he described to a friend as "a great super-ballet of New York," in which he hoped to interest Charlie Chaplin; it was "written for Chaplin, a Negro comedian, and seventeen other characters, full orchestra, movie machine, typewriters, radio, phonograph, riveter, electromagnet, alarm clocks, telephone bells and jazz band." Remarkably, *The Shores of Light*, Wilson's literary chronicle of the twenties and thirties, never mentions the Harlem Renaissance or any of its leading figures: Charles Evans Hughes, the chief justice of the U.S. Supreme Court, is in the index, but not Langston Hughes.

suggests that all these were present in the many-splendored Harlem Renaissance, whose organizers and leading figures included Charles S. Johnson, Alain Locke, James Weldon Johnson, Countee Cullen, Zora Neale Hurston, Langston Hughes, Walter White, Arna Bontemps, Aaron Douglas, and Palmer Hayden. With their white supporters and promoters such as Carl Van Vechten, these critics, sociologists, poets, polemicists, aesthetes, and novelists had complicated psychological, social, and professional relations, which have been variously characterized as cocreation, co-optation, and subordination, and included elements of all three. Langston Hughes's rueful "When the Negro Was in Vogue" is the essential account. At the time, Alain Locke wrote, Harlem was bringing together "the Negro of the North and the Negro of the South; the man from the city and the man from the town and village . . . In Harlem, Negro life is seizing upon its first chances for group expression and self-determination. It is—or promises at least to be—a race capital." Harlem above 125th Street was also the nighttime haunt of affluent whites mad for jazz or merely avid for the exotic. As Peter Conrad observes in *The Art of the City*, black Harlem became "a synecdoche for the whole of New York, a symbolic center, as Fifth Avenue had been for Henry James and Edith Wharton, and as Broadway would be for novelists, columnists, and moviemakers in the thirties and forties."

After October 1929 brightness fell from the air. It began to seem that the whole gaudy spectacle had been illusory all the while, a "splendid mirage," as Fitzgerald wrote. The Wall Street crash seemed an appropriate conclusion for a spree that had gone on for too long.

The speculative frenzies that Wall Street had sponsored in the twenties were widely blamed for the miseries of the Depression, not least by Franklin Roosevelt in his inaugural address in 1933. A "Hooverville" sprang up in Central Park, swarming with hoboes and the formerly respectable; there were more than a hundred thousand homeless camped out along Riverside Drive, and several documented cases of starvation. Worse to be down and out in New York, well-traveled observers maintained, than in London, Paris, Berlin.

"Mongrel Manhattan" sobered up, its building craze now regretted or ridiculed, its miscegenetic energies apparently spent. Abroad when the stock market crashed, the Fitzgeralds returned to New York in 1931 to find that the deepening Depression had reduced the scene of their former revels to an "echoing tomb." Having bid farewell to the city from the roof of the Plaza in the old days, Fitzgerald rode to the top of the Empire State Building, "the last and most magnificent of towers," to mark his return.

> Then I understood—everything was explained: I had discovered the crowning error of the city, its Pandora's box. Full of vaunting pride the New Yorker had climbed here and seen with dismay what he had never suspected, that the city was not the endless succession of canyons he had supposed but that *it had limits*—from the tallest structure he saw for the first time that it faded out into the country on all sides, into an expanse of green and blue that alone was limitless. And with the awful realization that New York was a city after all and not a universe, the whole shining edifice that he had reared in his imagination came crashing to the ground.

Murray Kempton has noted how those touting the thirties were determined to destroy the myth of the twenties. They condemned their predecessors for frivolity and selfishness, a fundamental unseriousness. Nowhere perhaps was the reaction swifter or more severe than in New York City. Among the city's artists and intellectuals, including some who had glittered in the twenties, "reckless provincialism" was an objectionable and unaffordable luxury. Yesterday's disdain for politics was discarded as ruthlessly as the vogue of the flapper. Fitzgerald took to reading Marx. And as for the once overweening pretensions of business, Edmund Wilson wrote, "One couldn't help being exhilarated at the sudden, unexpected collapse of the stupid gigantic fraud. It gave us a new sense of freedom; and it gave us a new sense of power."

By the winter of 1930, it was plain that the Hoover administration was hopeless in the face of the great slump, and for an interval between that general realization and the renewal of hope by the coming of the New Deal, a mood of defeatism and foreboding seized the city. In novels it is pictured most vividly in two very different books: John

O'Hara's *BUtterfield 8*, a roman à clef inspired by the career of a call girl on the Upper East Side, Starr Faithfull, and Tess Slesinger's *The Unpossessed*. For O'Hara it was the extremely uneasy end of the speakeasy era; his characters pursue their old extravagances in the gathering gloom. The drinking is just as hard in *The Unpossessed*, but here the principal characters are frustrated intellectuals in their early thirties, drawn to communism while dismissing themselves as "members of the lost tribe, the missing generation, the forgotten regiment, outcasts, miscast, professional expatriates." At a drunken fund-raising party, one of them exclaims to a salvageable young Communist, "Go west, young man, go south, go north—go anywhere out of our god-damned city."

But to radicals of the younger generation it seemed that living in the new dark ages concentrated the mind wonderfully. "I have never recovered from the thirties or wanted to," one of the most brilliant, the literary critic Alfred Kazin, would write many decades later. "Bliss it was in that dawn to be a literary radical (mostly *literary)*." The cafeteria at City College resounded with the disputes of his radical contemporaries: "Socialists who were Norman Thomas Socialists, old-line Social Democrats, Austro-Marxists; Communists who were Stalinist centrists, Trotskyite leftists, Lovestoneite right-wingers, Musteites and Fieldites; Zionists who were Progressive Labor Zionists, left Socialist Zionists and Religious Zionists." No doubt he could have extended the inventory; the distant echoes of this ideological Babel are still audible today. The left had been just as fissiparous in the twenties, but hardly anybody had cared beyond its circle; now anathema rang like thunder in the cafeterias where the young gathered. In places like the Greenwich Village apartment of V. F. Calverton, the young Alfred Kazin might encounter old-school scholars who had never joined the Party and rebellious types who had been thrown out by the Communists alongside survivors, "the characteristically lean, straight, bony Yankee individualists with ruddy faces and booming laughs, the old Harvard dissenters, leftover Abolitionists, Tolstoyans, single-taxers, Methodist ministers, Village rebels of 1912, everlasting Socialists and early psychoanalysts."

But for the ideologically engaged, New York was not the center of the world that it had been for Fitzgerald. Most often, the causes that engaged the passions of the young radicals were focused on events unfolding far away. The action was in San Francisco during the general strike of 1934, or in Harlan County, Kentucky, or later in the occupied plants in the industrial Midwest. Above all, Popular Front New York was transfixed by Hitler's assumption of power and the Nazi depredations, the Spanish Civil War, the five-year plans and the show trials in Stalin's Soviet Union, and the shock of the Hitler-Stalin Pact. "Besides, New York was then a very Russian city, so we had Russia all over the place," Saul Bellow writes in *Humboldt's Gift*, in the voice of Charlie Citrine. "It was a case, as Lionel Abel said, of a metropolis that yearned to belong to another country. New York dreamed of leaving North America and merging with Soviet Russia."

5

Wandering Rocks

IN A BRILLIANT STYLISTIC MOVE, John O'Hara modeled the opening sections of *BUtterfield 8* after the "Wandering Rocks" chapter of Joyce's *Ulysses*, which it follows in mapping the synchronous, mutually indifferent, and ironically interacting lives of its several characters. If the energies of Jazz Age Manhattan had been powerfully convergent, in the Depression-bound city, divergences and distances were increasing. Putting down, in 1938, his impressions of New York, the fashionable English photographer Cecil Beaton was struck by the divisions even within the "pleasure class" that entertained him.

"People divide themselves into various groups: those who like or dislike the President, those who worship Miss Dorothy Thompson, listen to the pianist Serkin, read the novels of John O'Hara or the poetry of Wallace Stevens," he observed. Café society had its haunts— the Stork Club, El Morocco, and "21." The Herbert Bayard Swopes, the Howard Dietzes, the George S. Kaufmans, and the Harpo Marxes composed what Cecil Beaton called the "West Point set." In another sphere, the former Russian nobility, "scattered as hotel managers, clerks, mannequins, water-colorists and sales-ladies," exhibited some of their old éclat on holidays, cooking elaborate banquets in kitchenettes and enjoying the hospitality of the still-prosperous Prince Serge Obolensky on New Year's. The publishing heir Cass Canfield and his wife were among the "social intellectuals"; couples like the Carter Burdens shared "the country pursuits and family interests of country people." The Stettheimer sisters had a salon on Seventh Avenue and Fifty-eighth Street at the Alwyn Court frequented by artists, writers, and the literary critic A. R. Orage, a follower of the mystic Gurdjieff. Carrie had spent her life working on a dollhouse with art by their friend Marcel Duchamp, Ettie wrote novels for their friend Alfred Knopf, and Florine edged briefly into the spotlight when she designed the sets for Virgil Thomson's opera *Four Saints in Three Acts*, and then tiptoed away.

This division into sets and sects was particularly apparent among artists and intellectuals. In *New York Intellect*, Thomas Bender contrasts the New York intellectuals, as they were later known, headquartered at Columbia University, City College, and *Partisan Review*, whose salons were clamorous cafeterias, with the more affluent "civic intellectuals," who had the resources to pursue more of the performing arts less available to the former, who were people of the book and generally from modest circumstances at best. The civic intellectuals—the "uptown bohemians"—included the budding cultural impresario Lincoln Kirstein; the composer Virgil Thomson; the architectural historian (he was not yet an architect) Philip Johnson and his friend and collaborator Henry-Russell Hitchcock; and Alfred Barr, who would be the long-time director of the Museum of Modern Art. The Museum of Modern Art was uptown Bohemia's public venue. At MoMA their patron Abby Aldrich Rockefeller's son Nelson headed an influential advisory committee that included Kirstein, Johnson, and the difficult banking heir "Eddie" Warburg. Independently wealthy but not, as subsequent decades would show, lacking energy, Johnson endowed and headed the architecture department.

There is a vivid group portrait of "the avant-garde art distributors," as he calls them (alternatively "the eye-and-ear people") in the memoirs of Virgil Thomson, who arrived back from Paris in 1932. Their meeting places included various galleries on the East Side, including Pierre Matisse's, but the liveliest was the lofty East Sixty-second Street brownstone of the art dealer Kirk Askew—born in Kansas City, like Thomson—and his wife, Constance.

"The drink, till Prohibition went, was homemade gin," Thomson remembered in 1967. "Evenings it was diluted with ginger ale or soda. For cocktails it was shaken with a nonalcoholic vermouth that produced a flocculation in the glass not unlike that which snows around Eiffel's Tower or New York's *Liberty* when rotated in their filled-with-liquid globes. The furniture was splendidly Victorian, with carpets, seats, and curtains richly colored. In the early thirties all pictures there were modern, but by decade's end some Italian Old Masters had been inherited."

Many of the civil intellectuals had gone to Harvard College: Johnson, Kirstein, Barr, Thomson himself, and their great friend and ally A. Everett (Chick) Austin. Austin, who seemed to the composer to be "the most spectacular of all," was a professor at Trinity College and director of the Wadsworth Atheneum in Hartford, Connecticut. But Thomson's group was much wider than just the modern-art-distributing group. The Askews' afternoon teas, nightly cocktails, and Sunday-night at-homes brought together theater people (including the yet unknown John Houseman and the very young Joseph Losey); poets (E. E. Cummings to Kirstein); the black performer Taylor Gordon, a singer and vaudevillian; the actress Edna Thomas; various curators; and painters such as Florine Stettheimer, Pavel Tchelitchew, and Eugene Berman. Sometimes Elizabeth Bowen would come over from London and stay for a month.

In the early thirties, the Askews' guests, but rarely Kirk or Constance, would often set out for Harlem after midnight, as if pursuing the last enchantments of the twenties. Thomson had completed his opera *Four Saints in Three Acts*, with a libretto by Gertrude Stein. One night in Harlem, listening to the jazz singer Jimmy Daniels (then Johnson's lover) in some small club, he had the idea of having *Four Saints* performed by black singers: "Next morning I was sure, remembering how proudly the Negroes enunciate and how the whites just hate to move their lips." In due course *Four Saints* was staged in Hartford, at the Atheneum, with Houseman directing an all-black cast and designs by Stettheimer that featured dangerously flammable cellophane curtains. Subsequently, Houseman collaborated with Orson Welles in producing the famous "voodoo" *Macbeth*, set in Haiti, with another all-black cast, for the Federal Theatre Project.

While the *Partisan Review* group tended to be strenuously heterosexual, many of the leading civic intellectuals (male) were homosexual or bisexual. There was an element of camp about such projects as the celebrated Paper Ball in February 1936, which was organized by Chick Austin at the Hartford Atheneum in the depths of the Depression and attended by such New York notables as Abby Aldrich Rockefeller, Fernand Léger, George Gershwin, and Buckminster Fuller, who arrived in a curvy "Dymaxion" car with Clare Boothe Luce in tow. Pavel Tchelitchew designed the decor and costumes, which made heavy use of newspaper cuttings, black-and-white text, and vivid comic-strip colors. Tchelitchew's partner was Charles Henri Ford, the editor of the exotic magazine *View*. Ford and the film critic Parker Tyler coauthored the 1933 novel *The Young and Evil* and were among the six men who shocked old Hartford with their appearance—"almost as nature made them, and nature made them well"—supporting a carriage bearing Ford's sister, the actress Ruth Ford, posing as the Muse of Poetry, enveloped in cellophane. Of course, as in the person of Nelson Rockefeller, who escorted his mother to the ball, the civic intellectuals boasted some vigorous heterosexuals as fellow travelers.

By the late thirties, the last flashes of "Mongrel Manhattan" had come and gone. The light faded even from the Askews' salon, though instead of bathtub gin, they drank good Scotch whiskey. "I only know we never laughed again there," Thomson writes sadly. Fashionable Manhattan stopped going uptown to Harlem, noted Beaton. "The large colored night-clubs, to which the negroes were never welcomed, have moved downtown to Broadway, the financial depression ruined the smaller *boites*. Paris has claimed the torch singers, the Blackbirds have scattered and the waiters spin trays no more."

The photographer had an eye as multifaceted as a fly's, and it took in many curious glimpses of what he called the pleasure class. In a typical scene from *Cecil Beaton's New York* (1938), Tchelitchew is in his apartment on East Seventy-third Street, still at work after two years "on his vast picture, his interpretation of the universe in terms of freaks." He gossips on the telephone with George Balanchine about Lincoln Kirstein and the crowd of "grotesques" that comprised the audience for a recent performance of *Norma*, while in the kitchen Charles Henri Ford and Parker Tyler are cooking duck with olives and raisins and arguing about Wystan Auden and Stephen Spender. Have they perverted

Marxism or has Marxism perverted them? Tyler is writing for *Partisan Review* one of those baroque essays on film that will appear in *Magic and Myth of the Movies* (and be rediscovered a generation later via Gore Vidal's *Myra Breckinridge*).

A precocious nineteen-year-old who spoke with the heavy accent of Brownsville, Alfred Kazin presented himself one summer day in 1934 at the office of the *New Republic* in Chelsea—altogether elsewhere so far as the pleasure world was concerned. He carried an introduction ("Here's an intelligent radical") from John Chamberlain, the daily book reviewer at the *New York Times*, then an influential man of the left. After an interview Malcolm Cowley, who had succeeded Edmund Wilson as literary editor, invited him to join the other starvelings on the "hunger bench" reserved for would-be reviewers. "Handsome and as coolly macho as Clark Gable in his vivid seersucker suit," Cowley would dole out assignments and, for desperate cases, unwanted review copies that might be worth a few pennies. Quick and fluent, full of passionate judgments, Kazin was soon writing reviews not only in the *New Republic* but also for the *Times*, the *Herald Tribune*, and venerable magazines like *Scribner's*. He was born for the writer's trade, and Cowley marveled that from the start his copy never needed fixing.

Since its founding in 1914 the *New Republic* had been published from the same address on West Twenty-first Street, settling like the neighborhood into shabby gentility but remaining, as Arthur Schlesinger writes, "the voice of Eastern, metropolitan progressivism." The editors lunched together three or four times a week, attended by a cook and a butler, a married couple who lived in the basement. Through the *New Republic*, Kazin was introduced to ancient eminences like the philosopher John Dewey, who once made a great impression at a cocktail party with a sweeping gesture that knocked fifty brimming glasses of gin off a table, as well as to prodigies of his own generation like John Cheever, whose first published short story appeared in the *New Republic* when he was eighteen—a handsome, graceful youth recently expelled from his prep school.

Kazin graduated from City College in 1935, but like many of his generation of New York intellectuals, he educated himself at the New

York Public Library, where he did the reading for his path-breaking *On Native Grounds* (1942). Whole sets of the old *Masses*, crumbling catalogues, shelves of forgotten novels, along with the writings of Henry James, Stephen Crane, Theodore Dreiser, H. L. Mencken, James G. Huneker, Irving Babbitt, Edmund Wilson, and Allen Tate, were retrieved by the librarians to be digested by the young critic. Often he was joined at one of the polished tables in the reading room by his friend Richard Hofstadter, whose *The American Political Tradition* (1948) was also destined to be famous. A great walker, Kazin would think as he passed these landmarks of "Mark Twain in his old house on Tenth Street, Dreiser and Millay in Washington Square, Willa Cather on Bank Street." He wrote *On Native Grounds* on his parents' kitchen table in Brownsville.

Kazin was befriended by Otis Ferguson, who, eight years older, was the *New Republic*'s movie and radio reviewer. Ferguson was an intense young man given to delivering pungent opinions from the corner of his mouth. While working his way through Clark University, he won a top prize in a *New Republic* college writing contest; soon after, or so the story went, he turned up at the magazine's doorstep and refused to budge until he was hired. Ferguson worshipped jazz and jazzmen. A decade before Jack Kerouac began his efforts in this vein ("bebop prosody"), he was attempting jazz rhythms in the "Nertz to Hertz" essay that he wrote sitting up all night in the rat trap he rented above a movie theater on Union Square; reeking of the Four Roses whiskey he drank for inspiration, he would deliver his copy at the last possible minute directly to the printer. Otis Ferguson feared and hated the gods of high culture like T. S. Eliot, whom Kazin admired; he despised the "cozy, Algonquin-lunching people" who wrote for the newspapers and the *New Yorker*. "Otis hated them with all the righteous fury of the sans-culotte who feels that his hour has come. Otis allied himself to the toughness of the times, to the militant new wind, to the anger which was always in the air." Yet, such was Kazin's sense of himself as the embattled son of Brownsville that he thought of his friend Ferguson as a "have," and thus ignorant of the real intensities of the struggle going on all around them. It was a shock to him when his friend, whom he invited to Brownsville for dinner ("I surreptitiously thought of him as a visitor from the great literary world"), seemed to find his family commonplace. Though embarrassed by his father's table manners and eagerness to please, Kazin thought of his parents' poverty and crudity, as it might strike an outsider, as being "sacramental." Out of such poor, unworldly Jews had come Christianity; out of such *would* come the great socialist revolution.

Otis Ferguson died in 1943 when his ship was bombed in the Bay of Salerno. Kazin would never imitate his excesses. He was disciplined and purposeful and though he was awkward and stammering at parties, envying John Cheever's precocious ease, he was avid and ambitious. The world of "New York intellect" was sufficiently village-like that only one or two degrees separated him, in his obscure literary beginnings, from the avant-garde art distributors or from middlebrow penthouse dwellers like the popular critic Alexander Woollcott. They would have glanced at his book reviews, or shared nodding acquaintances, people like Malcolm Cowley or the biographer Matthew Josephson, who seemed to know everybody. But his world was not yet the great world.

Later in the thirties, married to a young scientist, Natasha Dohn, and living in a two-room apartment in Brooklyn Heights, Kazin thought of their austere work-filled days, their modest pleasures of walking and listening to recordings of Schubert and Bach and César Franck, the occasional concert, as the very pattern of a postrevolutionary world, when "life would be purified and beautiful and everyone would live as Natasha and I lived in the radiance of cultural truth." Needless to say, Cecil Beaton's pleasure world would have regarded this prospect with horror and dismay. Really, what had an Alfred Kazin to do with the likes of the revelers at the Paper Ball, or the revelers with him?

Poet W. H. Auden in his beach shack in the Pines on Fire Island, 1945

PART II

CITY OF REFUGE

How bitter is the taste of another man's bread, and how hard to tread another man's stair.

—DANTE, *Paradiso*, Canto XVII

I

———

Exiles and Émigrés

THE BITTER AIR OF EXILE settled on New York in the war years, 1939–45, and made the city immeasurably more brilliant. As Virgil Thomson, in those years the music critic of the *New York Herald Tribune*, recalls: "If America in the 1920s exiled its artists, the 1940s, especially their first half, saw a meeting of talent here, both foreign and domestic, that made us for the first time an international center for intellectuals."

In October 1940, the *Saturday Review of Literature* published an issue devoted to "the Exiled Writers," timed to coincide with a dinner for their benefit at the Hotel Commodore organized by Cass Canfield, Nelson Doubleday, Bennett Cerf, and other sympathetic publishers. Based on a somber oil painting by the Belgian-born Georges Schreiber, the magazine's cover showed a bedraggled couple trudging against the wind in a cornfield, storm clouds overhead. Inside, a mix of exiled eminences and American best sellers—Jules Romains, Albert Einstein, André Maurois, Hermann Broch, and Wolfgang Köhler; Pearl S. Buck and Fannie Hurst contributed statements. Benjamin Appel, a young writer of leftist views known for tough-guy novels of the street with titles like *Brain Guy* and *Runaround*, went out on assignment to find the writers who had "got through" to New York.*

———

* Born and raised in Hell's Kitchen, Appel (1907–77) boasted the usual résumé of odd jobs, including farmer, bank clerk, factory hand, and lumberjack, found on dust

"And the writers fled. Behind them, their books lit the sky from Germany to the Atlantic." Appel's prose is Popular Front purple; but then, the fall of 1940 was not the time for their American friends to understate the value of the cultural capital the exiles brought with them.* America was not at war, New York was a neutral city, and while the Nazis had few professed adherents, the great majority of Americans devoutly hoped that the European conflict would remain none of their affair. In the year before Pearl Harbor, most Americans, according to the polls, felt little sympathy with the European refugees. The whole lot, most especially the Jews, were thought to be burdensome people—actual or potential competitors for jobs if they were not candidates for relief in an economy still recovering from the Depression; needy people who in some obscure way were responsible for the plight in which they found themselves. The few so-called "refugees de Luxe," who had escaped with means, were censured by a letter writer to *Life* magazine for crowding resort hotels and being rude and toplofty.

Appel found the novelist Jules Romains, author of the huge multi-volume novel translated into English as *The Men of Good Will*, undaunted at fifty-five, by his present dislocation: "Hugo stayed eighteen years in exile and his most important work was *Les Miserables*, which is mostly full of French things." Franz Werfel and his wife, the redoubtable Alma Mahler Werfel, had made a daring escape across the Pyrenees, during part of which they were hidden in Lourdes. Like Thomas Mann, Werfel had the knack of falling upstairs, if he had to fall. His latest novel, *Embezzled Heaven*, had already been selected by the Book-of-the-Month Club, enabling him to make his Atlantic crossing in style. Sigrid Undset, the Norwegian novelist awarded the

---

jackets in the days before the advent of the creative writers' workshop. Like the better-known proletarian writer Arthur Hayes, he began by writing poetry. His novel *Fortress in the Rice* (1951), based on his wartime service in the Philippines as a civilian advisor, was adapted for the movies in 1963 as *Cry of Battle*, starring Rita Moreno, Van Heflin, and James MacArthur.

* History and dictionary usage distinguishes between "émigrés," who depart voluntarily from their homelands for whatever political or personal (aesthetic, social) motives; "exiles" cast out by the state, from Ovid to Heine and Marx and Joseph Brodsky; and "refugees," who flee out of compulsion and terror. In twentieth-century circumstances, the categories bleed into one another. Thomas Mann, for example, was an émigré who became an exile, like many others less distinguished.

Nobel Prize in 1928 for *Kristin Lavransdatter* and other historical fictions, was one of Alfred A. Knopf's most popular European imports, along with Thomas Mann. She had fled occupied Norway with only a handbag, flying from Sweden to Moscow, traveling across Russia, voyaging to San Francisco via Japan, and then to New York. Soon after she left Norway her oldest son, Anders, was killed in an encounter with the Nazi occupiers. "All the events I think of—is Europe," she told Appel. "Impossible—I can't write a book—I don't know."

There was an honored place in New York for Wystan Hugh Auden, the most brilliant and influential poet of his generation in England and America, who strictly speaking was neither exile nor émigré nor refugee; rather, many in England bitterly said then and later, a defector, like his friend Christopher Isherwood and the novelist-sage Aldous Huxley. In "Refugee Blues" he made common cause with a situation far more dire than his own. He did not lack a passport, or a roof, or powerful friends like Bennett Cerf, his and Isherwood's American publisher. Even though he had chosen his exile, he felt the loss that comes with dislocation: "In Europe, facts were concealed by tradition," he told Appel. "The attractiveness of America to a writer is its openness and lack of tradition. In a way it's frightening. You are forced to live here as everyone will be forced to live. There is no past. No tradition. No roots—that is in the European sense."

The intellectual migration from the Europe of the dictators to America—catching up artists, intellectuals, scientists; architects, philosophers, art historians, composers; painters, physicists, publishers, and poets; playwrights, actors, opera singers, and impresarios—was an event in the history of culture and science whose influence, far from being exhausted almost eighty years after it began, continues to spread and circulate. The émigrés changed how Americans lit their movie sets, understood their motives, explained their elections; how they built and decorated their houses and skyscrapers and apartments; how they studied and collected art; how they painted, how they practiced science, and how they waged war. Did not a Hungarian émigré, Leo Szilard, persuade a German exile, Albert Einstein, to put his signature to the letter that first led Franklin Roosevelt to consider building an

atomic bomb? And when that led to the construction of a secret city in
New Mexico for the design of such a weapon, Los Alamos became perhaps the most fateful grouping of European minds to ever have come
together in America, under the direction of a German-Jewish prodigy
raised on Riverside Drive, J. Robert Oppenheimer.

As fascism spread and war was imminent, the arrival in New York of
Einstein or Mann, Chagall or Dalí, Toscanini or Stravinsky, was front-
page news. By 1939, the *New York Times* was comparing these distinguished refugees to the Greek scholars who sparked the Renaissance
with their flight from Constantinople to Italy; in 1942 the *American
Mercury* reviewed a show of "Artists in Exile" at Pierre Matisse's gallery as "Hitler's Gift to America." But it seemed to require the distance
of a generation to appreciate fully the significance of the "Great Migration." It was only toward the end of the 1960s, as H. Stuart Hughes
writes in *The Sea Change* (1975), when the older generation of émigrés
had mostly died and the younger was in mid-career—when one part
of the emigration had recrossed the ocean to be "Europeanized" and
the other had stayed on to be "Americanized"—that the flight of the
European intellectuals from fascism came to loom as "the most important cultural event—or series of events—of the second quarter of the
twentieth century."

The German-speaking group has been the most closely studied. In
his classic *Weimar Culture* (1968), Peter Gay names Albert Einstein,
Thomas Mann, Erwin Panofsky, Bertolt Brecht, Walter Gropius,
George Grosz, Wassily Kandinsky, Max Reinhardt, Bruno Walter,
Werner Jaeger, Wolfgang Köhler, Paul Tillich, and Ernst Cassirer
as the outsiders who had become insiders during Weimar's glorious,
precarious day and then, sooner or later, became fugitives under the
Nazis. Comparing their exile, again, to the flight of Greek scholars to
Italy during the fall of the Byzantine Empire in the early fifteenth century, and also to the dispersal of the Huguenots from France and the
foundation of New England by Puritan "refugees" in the seventeenth,
Gay felt these intellectual migrations were overmatched by what he
called "the greatest collection of transplanted intellect, talent, and
scholarship the world has ever seen."

By count, 104,098 German and Austrian refugees entered the
United States between January 1933 and December 1941, represent-

ing about two-thirds of the entire emigration from Europe. No other country came close to offering refuge to so many, but such were the obstacles they faced both in escaping from Europe and in entering the U.S. that the immigration quotas for their countries were actually unfulfilled during these years. As opposed to what Martin Jay has called "the silent majority" of exiles with whom historians are less likely to identify, and thus to write about, the Austro-German part of the "intellectual migration" consisted of 7,622 academics and about 1,500 artists and intellectuals of various description. About three-quarters were of "Jewish origin." Out of Hungary came the "Budapest galaxy," a wizardly band as brilliant and as various as the Austro-German: among them, the physicists Edward Teller, Leo Szilard, and Eugene Wigner; the mathematician John von Neumann, the photojournalists André Kertész and Robert Capa; the novelist and controversialist Arthur Koestler; the movie producer Alexander Korda and director Michael Curtiz—the nine subjects of a book by Kati Marton—as well as the psychoanalyst Franz Alexander, the architect Marcel Breuer, and the historian John Lukacs, who came after the war. Prophetically, their great gathering place during Budapest's "Golden Age" had been the opulent Café New York in the inner city.

It must not be forgotten that until after December 7, 1941, the refugees were arriving in a neutral city, where German officers in Nazi dress circulated freely, and Hitler's victories and atrocities were cheered in particular moviehouses—witnessing such a spectacle at a theater in Yorkville turned W. H. Auden back into a Christian. Irwin Shaw's story "Sailor Off the Bremen," published in *The New Yorker* in 1939, captures this strange interval, which is recalled from a long distance by George Steiner, then a frighteningly precocious schoolboy at the French *lycée*, in his memoir, *Errata*. In *A Life in the Twentieth Century*, Arthur M. Schlesinger, Jr., commends the accuracy of the atmosphere in John P. Marquand's novel *So Little Time* (1943), in which the story is stolen by the protagonist's friend, a bullying, rich boy, who is based on George Merck, the pharmaceutical heir, and who is forever saying, "Come the revolution!" from the back of his town car.

The "illustrious immigrants" comprised only a minute fraction of a continental flux of exiles, émigrés, and relatively anonymous refugees during the length of what has been called Europe's second Thirty

Years' War, from 1914 to 1945. Millions fled as dictatorships were imposed from Portugal to Poland, as civil wars raged from Russia to Spain. For many of the intellectual emigrants who found their way there, New York was only the latest city of refuge, or "vast waiting room," succeeding Vienna, Berlin, Paris, London. White Russian émigrés, for example, who had congregated in Berlin after the Bolshevik Revolution and then made their way to Paris in 1933–34, if they were lucky, crossed the Atlantic in a second, continental expatriation during and after the fall of France. Vladimir Nabokov, destined to be the most famous writer in the group, thought of his crossing more as a "homecoming." The French emigration which Nabokov joined on the last ship from Cherbourg was smaller, more abruptly assembled, and destined to be briefer than the Central European.* The equally eminent but even smaller Italian emigration, including Salvador Luria, Arturo Toscanini, Enrico Fermi, and Renato Poggioli, assimilated brilliantly into the American scene; the Spanish, with centuries of practice at exile, kept their eyes on Iberia. Migration to the New World, which had been interrupted when the United States entered the war, was resumed for a few years after 1945 in the time of the Displaced Person.

America was big and various enough to be hospitable to both White and Red emigrations, almost always starting from a beachhead in New York City. Thus, at about the same time Franz Neumann and Herbert Marcuse began their American careers at the Institute for Social Research at Columbia, around 1940, Leo Strauss was a lecturer on starveling terms at the New School (1938–48); Ludwig von Mises became a professor at NYU in 1946; in 1949, Strauss moved to the University of Chicago, where he became the éminence grise of neoconservatism; Marcuse's fame as the intellectual godfather of the New

---

* Yet what a long shadow it would cast across the intellectual landscape of the century. As Jeffrey Mehlman writes: "Wartime New York was the city where French Symbolism, in the person of Maurice Maeterlinck, came to live out its last productive years; where French surrealism, in the person of André Breton, came to survive; and where French structuralism, in the person of Claude Lévi-Strauss, came to be born. As such, in those brief years the city was curiously traversed by three of the four cultural vanguards bequeathed to the world over the last century." The fourth, French existentialism, then made its appearance in the waning days of the war "in the person of Jean-Paul Sartre." *Émigré New York: French Intellectuals in Wartime Manhattan, 1940–1944* (Baltimore: Johns Hopkins, 2000), 1.

Left found him at retirement age at the University of California at San Diego. There were, as it turned out, many places—honored, lofty places, very often—for the émigrés. As an older Auden sang:

> *God bless the U.S.A., so large,*
> *So friendly, and so rich.*

American intellectuals of the 1930s and '40s were Eurocentric; it seemed to be part of their calling. Had not the American writers most admired at *Partisan Review*—Henry James, T. S. Eliot—chosen to live abroad? On the other hand, the idea that Europe was the "biggest thing in North America," as the poet-critic Delmore Schwartz liked to say—or that Manhattan was an island that yearned to merge with Russia, as Saul Bellow quotes Lionel Abel in *Humboldt's Gift*—was a version of a conceit that only a native could indulge. To actual Europeans, New York on first impression presented itself as unreal, frighteningly grandiose, and overpowering. Surprisingly few of the Germans, for example, even those who were or had been rich or famous, had ever visited as tourists before they arrived as refugees. And since almost all came by sea across the Atlantic, it was what the German expressionist writer Leonhard Frank called "the grand silhouette of unreal, giant buildings" that prefigured the conditions of their existence—along with the Statue of Liberty, which most found anything but welcoming (although Maria Weiss, an imaginative poet, was reminded of Eleanor Roosevelt). The theme of the modern as the primordial occurs again and again. Thus, the novelist Hans Natonek marveled at how "the piled-up, monolithic hulks of the buildings resemble jagged meteorites cast down by awful forces of original creation"; the designer Eric Godal saw the skyline rising like "castles of the Cyclopes, unreal and terrifying."

Christopher Isherwood, though he arrived with a reputation and the benefit of a previous visit, felt the same alarm when he and Auden returned as immigrants, faced with the prospect of earning a living in America. "God, what a terrifying place this suddenly seemed! You could feel it vibrating with the tension of the nervous New World, aggressively flaunting its rude steel nudity. We're Americans here—

and we keep at it, twenty-four hours a day, *being* Americans. We scream, we grab, we jostle. We've no time for what's slow, what's gracious, nice, quiet, modest."

The sheer forbidding bulk of New York was both challenging and oddly reassuring—"for how could the country that manifested such great strength ever be endangered by the lunatic dictator from Branau?" True, H. G. Wells had imagined New York air-raided and laid waste by Germany as long ago as 1908, the Mexican moralist Orozco had painted its ruin, and in 1929 the Spanish poet Federico García Lorca, visiting New York, had seen, or imagined he had seen, ruined millionaires leaping to their deaths. These imaginary examples of its destruction were noted by Mike Davis, the author of *City of Quartz*, after September 11, 2001. H. L. Mencken had also written an essay in this vein. "What will finish New York in the end, I suppose, will be an onslaught from without, not from within. The city is the least defensible of great capitals." But such visions seemed almost as fantastic as Stephen Vincent Benét's poem about a city doomed by termites that could feed on steel. The 1930s and early '40s were the last time that New York City really seemed to be invulnerable.

The busyness of the harbor and the streets invigorated some, stunned others, and for almost everybody the first encounter with uniformed American authority at customs was apt to be fearful. Hans Natonek recalled unconsciously bending so far over for the inspection of his papers that he was suspected of having a "forbidden hunchback." Anyone whose papers or person was doubtful was dispatched to Ellis Island for further inspection, where typically their treatment was "well organized, factual, with a reserved friendliness, devoid of emotion." Vladimir Nabokov always remembered his first encounter with American officialdom as slapstick fun. He, his wife, Vera, and their six-year-old son, Dmitri, arrived "in the lilac mist of a May morning, May 1940," on the *Champlain*, the ocean liner that had delivered Auden and Isherwood almost a year earlier, and was sunk off the coast of France a few weeks later when it struck a mine. At customs a nervous Vera forgot that the key to a padlocked trunk was in her jacket pocket. Nabokov "stood bantering," as he later recalled, "with a diminutive Negro porter and two large Customs men until a locksmith arrived and opened the padlock with one blow of his iron hammer."

The operation had to be repeated when the "merry little porter," fascinated by the operation, fiddled with the padlock until it snapped shut again. At last reopened for inspection, the trunk revealed its topmost contents: two pairs of boxing gloves used for little Dmitri's practice sessions. They were promptly snatched up by the customs men, who put them on and began to spar, circling about Nabokov. Attracted by the commotion, a third officer was fascinated by an album of butterfly specimens, even venturing a name for a species. "As Nabokov retold the story decades later," Brian Boyd writes, "still enchanted by America's easygoing, good-natured atmosphere, he repeated with delight: 'Where would that happen? Where would that happen?'"

When Nabokov wondered aloud to Vera where he might buy a newspaper, one of the helpful customs men volunteered, "Oh, I'll get one for you," and returned with the *New York Times*. When their contacts in America, a Russian relation and an English friend, failed to appear, the Nabokovs, released by the authorities into the rush and glare of Manhattan, hailed a bright-yellow Checker taxicab, resembling a scarab, and were driven to 32 East Sixty-first, the apartment of the missing relative—Nathalie Nabokov, the ex-wife of Nabokov's cousin Nicolas. Misreading the meter's 9.0 for "o, oh God, ninety, ninety dollars," Vera forlornly handed over the one hundred dollars that was all of their capital. The driver: "'Lady, I haven't got a hundred dollars. If I had that kind of money, I wouldn't be sitting here driving this cab.' . . . Of course the simplest way for him would have been to give us the ten dollars' change and call it a day," Nabokov would finish the story. His day of arrival struck a note of good humor and informality that colored his view of America ever after.

Tall, insouciant, with a certain kind of aristocrat's instinctive democratic ways, and fluent in English since the nursery, Nabokov enjoyed advantages that the hundreds of other émigrés milling in the great customs shed that day did not; and the views he formed of his "second home" were reflections of them. Countess Alexandra Tolstaya, the novelist's youngest daughter, who ran a relief agency for displaced persons in New York, told him categorically: "All Americans are completely uncultured, credulous fools." (Presumably, this harsh judgment extended to the Tolstoy Foundation's honorary chairman, ex-President Herbert Hoover.) To the contrary, Nabokov assured a friend who was about to follow him a year or two later: "This is a cultured and exceedingly diverse country. The only thing you must do is deal with genuine Americans and don't get involved with the local Russian emigration."

The first job that the Tolstoy Foundation found for Nabokov was another fine comedy. In Vermont, where he was staying with other Russian émigrés, he received a cable with the good news that a job in publishing was being held for him, but returning to New York he was told to report not to the editorial offices of the publisher, Scribner's, but to its bookstore a floor below in the same Fifth Avenue building, and be sure to stand up straight when he did. "At Scribner's he was received by a man named Wreden, whom he had known in Europe, and who was somewhat nonplussed to see who had been sent over, since the job opening was for a delivery boy on a bicycle."* Moreover, he was supposed to wrap the books to be delivered to the post office, working from 9 a.m. to 6 p.m. for a weekly emolument of sixty-eight dollars. Nabokov politely declined the job, which would not have sufficed to support his family; also, he did not know how to wrap packages. If he had been handier and more desperate, he might have found himself tying parcels to be delivered to Scribner's authors, such as Ernest Hemingway, whom he did not admire, and F. Scott Fitzgerald, whom he did. But Nabokov, unlike his hapless creation Timofey Pnin, had well-placed Russian-born admirers in the academy, and soon had acquired influential American admirers in publishing, such as Allen Tate and Edmund Wilson, who recommended him to the *New Yorker*. He published his first novel in English, *The Real Life of Sebastian Knight*,

---

* His fellow émigré Nicholas R. Wreden (1901–54), the son of the former private physician to the tsar and his family, had fought as a royal cadet during the First World War, and against the Bolsheviks during the revolution and civil war, experiences he described in a memoir, *The Unmaking of a Russian* (1935); he arrived in New York in 1920. After pursuing various other occupations, he drifted into publishing, first as a traveling salesman, and was manager of Scribner's bookstore when Nabokov was presented to him as a prospective delivery boy in 1940. Moving to E. P. Dutton as editorial director later in the forties, he published Gore Vidal's early novels, most notably *The City and the Pillar;* it seems not to have occurred to him to publish Nabokov, although his Park Avenue apartment was a popular gathering place for anti-Soviet émigrés.

in 1941, and was awarded a research fellowship at Harvard University to study entomology and a lectureship at Wellesley College in the next term (both were continued until 1948). A Guggenheim fellowship and citizenship followed, and before the decade was out he was appointed professor of Russian and European literature at Cornell University, where world fame found the author of *Lolita* in 1958.

For those to whom glittering prizes began to arrive more slowly, or not at all, a brush with menial labor was nothing to laugh about. In *Illustrious Immigrants* Laura Fermi tells the story of the political scientist Hans Morgenthau, later a great eminence at the University of Chicago and "realist" critic of the Vietnam War, who applied to an agency in New York that placed refugee scholars and was told by the young woman interviewing him that his two published books and previous teaching appointments in Frankfurt, Geneva, and Madrid hardly made him stand out, and he would be better advised to look for a job as an elevator boy. Morgenthau's wife, Irma, was told by a Jewish relief agency that at thirty-one she was too old to be a saleswoman. The couple persevered, and their efforts were rewarded with a night-school job at Brooklyn College that paid by the hour for him, and a sales job at Macy's for her. Nevertheless their joint earnings were scant. One time, the bedbugs in their furnished room bit Irma so badly that her supervisor told her to stay away until her sores had healed. A shy man, Hans Morgenthau was grateful when his students decided to teach him English; but despairing of making a life in New York, they traveled to Kansas City, where an employment agency placed him at the University of Kansas. His *Politics Among Nations*, published in 1948 after he had moved to Chicago, made his reputation, and remained a standard text for a generation. Morgenthau returned to New York after retiring from the University of Chicago, spending valedictory years at the Graduate Center at City University of New York and then at the New School. It is doubtful he ever remembered his first attempts to make his way in New York with any amusement.

Although the immigrants or their sponsors were compelled to show that they would not be wards of the state, their material circumstances varied from rich and famous to obscure and threadbare. Maurice

Maeterlinck, the Belgian symbolist poet and playwright, best known in America for his play *The Blue Bird* and his 1911 Nobel Prize, was reported to be both when he appeared in July 1940. The *New York Times* headlined "Maeterlinck, Impoverished Exile, Arrives with Wife from France"; but when the *New Yorker* caught up with him at his suite at the Plaza Hotel, it noted that the "impoverished couple" had come with "a tiny French motor car," thirty-two pieces of luggage, two Pekingese dogs, and a pair of parakeets, which were confiscated at customs in Hoboken. "Perhaps it is for the best," Maeterlinck sighed; "bluebirds are the symbol of happy times." (The elderly poet spent most of his exile in Palm Beach, Florida.)

For all but a super-cosmopolitan few, there was a period of adjustment in which at the same time they attempted to remake their lives and acquire a new language, the newcomers learned to cope with such American peculiarities as doors that had knobs rather than proper handles and opened the "wrong" way (when you left a building rather than entered it), and windows that had to be pushed up or down rather than casements. According to Helmut Pfanner, "The loud noises from their neighbors' apartments, the result of insufficient insulation in cheap New York housing projects, made the émigrés think that Americans liked to hear these sounds to compensate for their loneliness." Some were disconcerted by the homely proximity of "laxatives, syringes, and toilet paper" to the lunch counter in the ubiquitous drugstores. There were the usual complaints about the lack or inconspicuousness of post offices and public toilets, the absence of "public clocks" such as adorned Europe's piazzas, and of piazzas themselves, in the proper sense.

Americans' well-advertised obsession with "regularity" was another surprise, as was the compulsory good humor. ("Not to grin is a sin" is the way Sartre epitomized the ethos of millions of cheery Americans in his novel *Iron in the Soul*, set in 1940 and published in 1949, after he had spent considerable time in the U.S.) There was not even a suitable public place to air such grievances and discoveries. The émigrés complained that the cafeterias, which were the cheapest places to eat, served neither wine nor beer. There were bars, but no bistros or brasseries and, worst deprivation of all, no coffeehouses in the European style, in which to read, talk, or play chess hours at a time, for the price of a coffee or glass of wine. In all of New York there was no Café New York.

· · ·

Few of the exiles escaped a lapse in professional status and income, which many had to endure permanently. The tendency to compensate for present indignities by dwelling on past glories was almost irresistible, epitomized by the prolific writer and scholar Helmut Hirsch's poetic fable about the two émigré dachshunds who happened to meet on Broadway. "Once when I was a St. Bernard . . ." one of them begins. The story became proverbial. In fact, a few St. Bernards stayed St. Bernards—in literature, Thomas Mann, Franz Werfel, Lion Feuchtwanger, notably; in music, Stravinsky and Schoenberg, most famously; in scholarship, Erwin Panofsky, Paul Kristeller, Ernst Kantorowicz, among many others; in the sciences, Einstein, above all.

Scientists, established scholars, and musicians typically negotiated the transition most easily. Experimental and theoretical physicists, Gestalt psychologists, Bauhaus architects, art historians, and professors of comparative literature attained honored places in the ivory tower, and some adaptable social scientists eventually found their way to Madison Avenue. In the thirties, foreign conductors were on the podiums of symphony orchestras from San Francisco (Pierre Monteux) to Minneapolis (Dimitri Mitropoulos) to New York (Artur Rodzinski, Bruno Walter). Arturo Toscanini, the conductor of his own NBC Symphony Orchestra, which broadcast from Studio 8-H in Rockefeller Center, was an international culture hero.

Middle-aged or elderly doctors and lawyers, legally obliged to reestablish their credentials in a foreign language, were often stalled and frustrated. (New York State had automatically accepted foreign medical credentials until 1936, but this generous practice did not survive the Depression.) "What would American doctors do if they had to master Viennese grammar at the age of seventy?" Richard Berczeller asked in the poignantly titled *Displaced Doctor* (1943). Younger scholars forced to drop their studies to flee had to resort to menial work until they acquired a Ph.D. (the "union card"). American colleges and universities were far less overtly hierarchical than Europe's but even more demanding about degrees. "Without the Union Card of a Ph.D., some of them became secretaries, furniture painters, physical education instructors, even helping to sell the huge Hearst art collection at Gimbels, taking any one of the few available jobs for funds to complete their degree or help establish a reputation through publication." In the first years of the emigration it was not uncommon to find ex-professors hauling furniture, surgeons waiting tables in restaurants, litterateurs coaching tennis, and philosophers washing dishes. (At least, Ernst Bloch told Theodor Adorno he had been reduced to this extremity.)

Reflexively, we picture the exile as solitary, even while knowing that Dante fathered seven children by his wife, Gemma Donati; that Heine was nursed faithfully by Crescence Eugénie Mirat, the shopgirl he married in Paris; that Marx had his "Jenny" beside him in Soho; and Mme de Staël enjoyed the virile companionship of Benjamin Constant. Even so, the intellectual migration was "more than any other period in exile, a family matter," with for the first time the female contingent outnumbering the male. With fewer restrictions on their foreign travel, wives often went ahead of their husbands—who might be liable for arrest or even put in a concentration camp—to New York or some other destination to do the paperwork for a visa and to raise the money for their husbands' boat passage. Often as not, the wife was obliged to remain the family mainstay for some time after the former professor, banker, or accredited doctor arrived, some to be un- or underemployed for months or years. Usually with little fuss, women who had run households in Germany but rarely had professional careers of their own became housemaids, factory workers, babysitters, worked in the needle trade, sold encyclopedias or baked goods.

Finding a job and learning English were the joint perplexities that bedeviled the émigrés, whether it was a writer determined to find a new audience in a new language, a singer or actor, or, perhaps most poignantly, a lawyer or doctor required to reestablish his credentials by examination. French or Italian, not English, was the second language in which an educated German of the émigré generation was likely to have any fluency; the struggle to master English in middle age was bound to be an arduous and incomplete project, although the émigré wives almost uniformly learned faster, and spoke more idiomatically, than their husbands. Grammars and night schools, magazines and newspapers instructed the newcomers in English, and the movies, the radio, and the streets imparted it by immersion. The novelist Claudia Martell "prayerfully" practiced such difficult English sounds as "the," which she called "the enemy of all immigrants"; Jimmy Stern, a professor of theater history at Columbia later, confessed: "I could live here two hundred years (God forbid), and I'd still not learn its language."

When it was a matter of what someone called "a race between the language and the bank account," however, it was natural to pretend to rapid progress. As Hannah Arendt sardonically wrote in the *Menorah Journal* (1943), "With the language, however, we find no difficulties: after a single year optimists are convinced they speak English as well as their mother tongue; and after two hours they swear solemnly that they speak English better than any other language—their German is a language they hardly remember." There were those like Oskar Maria Graf, the Bavarian novelist, who refused on principle to learn English; and almost all of the most notable German émigrés, including Thomas Mann, Albert Einstein, Hannah Arendt, and Stefan Zweig contributed to the *Aufbau* ("construction" in German), subtitled "America's Only German-Jewish Publication," founded by the German-Jewish Club in New York in 1934 and published until 2004, which reached a circulation of a hundred thousand during the war. But the one language could prosper only as the other one waned—Arendt's "optimists" were right about that—and in time even the writers who remained loyal to German found it more and more difficult to keep up their mastery in an English-speaking environment; not even a Broch or a Mann was immune to this coarsening effect.

The academy, within limits, was the big American institution most hospitable to the émigrés, and the New School of Social Research in Greenwich Village led the way by establishing the University in Exile for refugee scholars in 1933. From its founding in 1919 by John Dewey and the historians Charles Beard and James Harvey Robinson—they had all quit Columbia University in protest of Nicholas Murray Butler's imposition of a loyalty oath during the First World War and accompanying limits on faculty free speech—the New School was intended to be an arena for freethinking. Thorstein Veblen joined the faculty early on. Alvin Johnson, an economist originally from the Great Plains, took over as director in 1921; reoriented the fledgling college as a night school with open enrollment; enlarged the curriculum to include arts, letters, and psychology; and in place of permanent faculty recruited visiting lecturers such as Lewis Mumford, the composer Henry Cowell, and the painter Thomas Hart Benton. Into this lively and experimental downtown milieu were welcomed a select group of refugee scholars in the first year of Hitler's rule, with funding provided by the Rockefeller Foundation and Hiram Halle, a wealthy business- man and inventor specializing in improvements to the typewriter. A shy tycoon who was a partner in Gulf Oil, Halle ran a sort of private Jewish-emigrant relief agency in the thirties and forties, employing refugees to restore the dozens of historic houses he owned in Pound Ridge in New York's Westchester County.

The Rockefeller Foundation was the financial mainstay of the Emer- gency Committee in Aid of Displaced Foreign (originally "German") Scholars, which had been formed to find temporary or permanent jobs in American colleges and universities for the refugees. In practice those placed were limited to "mature scholars of distinction who had already made their reputations," since younger ones would be compet- ing with their American contemporaries in the Depression, and older ones would be expensive to pension (fifty-eight was adopted as the shadow line). On behalf of the committee, the Rockefeller Foundation proposed that it transfer as many as one hundred refugee scholars to America, to teach at the University in Exile within the New School. A solid job offer satisfied the stringent immigration standards of the isolationist thirties, and, once authorized to grant advanced degrees by the state of New York, the exile academy was solemnized as the gradu- ate faculty of the New School in 1935.

"The New School practically determined the receptivity of the intellectual world of America to the scholars from abroad," its then- dean Clara W. Meyer said later, although for most of the refugees it was a way station to better-paying and more secure employment else- where, usually outside New York City. Between 1933 and 1940, the diverse talents recruited to the New School included the theologian Paul Tillich, a cadre of experimental psychologists led by Max Wert- heimer, and two scholars associated with the Frankfurt Institute, the sinologist Karl Wittfogel and the sociologist Leo Lowenthal.

The philanthropy of New York's German-Jewish financial and mercantile elite—familiarly, "Our Crowd"—helped make New York University's Institute of Fine Arts (IFA) an unparalleled haven for refugee art historians. Thanks to such benefactors as Colonel Michael Friedsam, the heir to the B. Altman department store fortune, art history at NYU was already being taught by "an unusually cosmopolitan, European-oriented faculty" by 1931, when it was still a division of the College of Fine Arts. Friedsam gave his backing to the design of two NYU administrators, General Charles H. Sherrill and Walter W. S. Cook, to create an independent graduate program in art history, with research professors spending half the year abroad and teaching courses at the Ecole du Louvre and in Berlin and Munich. The Nuremberg Decrees mooted this transatlantic dream, but the IFA was launched on its ambitious way.

Erwin Panofsky was invited to join the budding Institute of Fine Arts as a visiting professor in 1931, when it numbered just a dozen or so students and three or four professors. "Both lecture and seminar courses were held in the basement rooms of the Metropolitan Museum, commonly referred to as 'the funeral parlors,' where smoking was forbidden under penalty of death and stern-faced attendants would turn us out at 8:55 p.m., regardless of how far the report or discussion had proceeded," Panofsky wrote in a 1953 memoir, "Three Decades of Art History in the United States: Impressions of a Transplanted European." "The only thing to do was to adjourn to a nice speakeasy on Fifty-second Street."

It was the waning days of Prohibition, and Panofsky, writing in the third person, "tells how he found himself surrounded by an atmosphere of cozy dissipation which is hard to describe and harder to remember without a certain nostalgia—the European art historian was at once bewildered, electrified, and elated. He feasted on the treasures assembled in museums, libraries, private collections, and dealers' galleries . . . He was amazed that he could order a book at the New York Public Library without being introduced by an embassy or vouched for by two responsible citizens; that libraries were open in the evening, some as late as midnight; and that they actually seemed eager to make material accessible to him." Even the Museum of Modern Art, in its old quarters, "permitted visitors to leave unsnubbed in those days." Americans seemed genuinely to like going to lectures—something he supposed an anthropologist could explain—and lectures on art history were "delivered not just in the seats of learning but also in the homes of the wealthy," with the audience arriving "in twelve-cylinder Cadillacs, seasoned Rolls-Royces, Pierce-Arrows, and Locomobiles."

Panofsky had the advantage of being established in America before being cast out of his profession at home, when Jews were fired from German universities in 1933. "I fondly remember the receipt of a long cable in German, informing me of my dismissal but sealed with a strip of green paper which bore the inscription 'Cordial Easter Greetings, Western Union.'" The IFA's genial director was Walter William Spenser Cook, a WASP gentleman scholar (Harvard, 1913; Ph.D. 1924), to whom Panofsky pays fond tribute in his memoir. Cook had had a genius for strategic self-deprecation: "'Hitler is my best friend,' he used to say, 'he shakes the trees and I collect the apples.'" No doubt, as Colin Eiser suggests, it was just because this generous and well-connected establishmentarian "was personally nothing like his protégés, that he could persuade so many deans to find a place for them in their faculties, and raise the money necessary to hire those he wanted for the Institute. 'I just passed the hat around,'" he would say, explaining how he hired other distinguished visiting professors. The IFA graduated from the Metropolitan's stygian depths to an apartment in an old brownstone, where the "magic lantern" slides were projected in a darkened living room and the syllabuses were stacked in the bathtub, next moving to the six floors of Paul Warburg's old mansion.

The Institute of Fine Arts could only have flourished in New York City, where the adjacency of great museums and collections obviated the need for one of its own. "You may spend your money on a museum," Cook told the administrator of another fine arts department, "but we are going to move right next to a museum and let it buy our works of art, while we spend it on the professors and get the best there are." Under his entrepreneurial wing the "native Americans" on the faculty, himself and Richard Offner, were joined by the refugee eminences such as the classical archaeologist Karl Lehmann, from Münster, and the baroque specialist Walter Friedlaender, from Freiburg.

Panofsky was offered an appointment to the Institute for Advanced Study in Princeton in 1934, where he moved full-time in 1935; there he produced his celebrated *Studies in Iconology* (1939), *The Life and Art of Albrecht Dürer* (1943), and the essay collection *Meaning in the Visual Arts* (1955). At the IAS, he wrote, "its members do their research openly and their teaching surreptitiously, whereas the opposite is true of so many other institutions of learning."

Though written under the shadow of McCarthyism, Panofsky's memoir-survey is cheerful, often very funny; in a few pages it condenses the rise of art history in America from the hobby of rich, cultivated men like Henry Adams and Charles Eliot Norton in the late nineteenth century into a full-fledged academic specialization capable of challenging Germany's preeminence after the First World War. It was not only the material resources available to universities such as Princeton and Harvard that made the decade from 1923 to 1933 a golden age for building and enlarging museums and collections, for opening up and enriching a new field of scholarship, and for excavations; it was the unprecedented vantage point that America's empire city offered to postwar Europe's present and past. Panofsky wrote:

> Where the communications between the European countries, too close for speedy reconciliation and too poor for a speedy resumption of cultural exchange, remained disrupted for many years, the communications between Europe and the United States had been kept intact or were quickly restored. *New York was a gigantic radio set capable of receiving and transmitting to a great number of stations which were unable to reach each other* [emphasis added]. But what made the greatest impression on the stranger when first becoming aware of what was happening was this: where the European art historians were conditioned to think in terms of national and regional boundaries, no such limitations existed for the Americans ... Historical distance (we normally require from sixty to eighty years) proved to be replaceable by cultural and geographical distance.

And what was true for art history applied, mutatis mutandis, to art, architecture, political science, psychology. New York was not only the transmitter of its own "cultural instrumentalities in a thousand phases," as the WPA writers said, but also where all the signals were picked up, amplified, and redirected.

2

———

The City at War

O N DECEMBER 29, 1940, in a radio address from the White
House, Franklin D. Roosevelt proclaimed America "the great
arsenal of democracy," and promised to furnish Britain with the ships,
airplanes, and arms it needed to fight Nazi Germany, doing so under
the no-cash-terms arrangement that a few days later was unveiled as
"Lend-Lease." It was the most historic Fireside Chat since the first in
March 1933, and its announced subject, "national security," immediately and permanently entered the national vocabulary. What FDR
called "our gigantic efforts to increase the production of munitions"
had already put the country on the path to full employment: what
his biographer Conrad Black calls the Fourth New Deal. But not in
New York City, the citadel of the New Deal, and not even after Pearl
Harbor.

"Wartime spending had brought recovery to many cities," Thomas
Kessner writes in his essential biography of La Guardia. "But New
York drew only bitter consequences from the war: Its population was
fragmented, its mayor was preoccupied, and its light industry could not
exploit the open-fitted programs for defense spending. Moreover, as
federal budget dollars were allocated to defense, they were withdrawn
from relief and public works of the type that had sustained the city
during the thirties. As a result, there were 50,000 more persons unemployed in New York in 1942 than in the Depression year of 1929."
Federal authorities urged New Yorkers looking for work to move out

of the city, and apartments went vacant as job seekers heeded their advice. La Guardia appealed to Roosevelt; the president instructed his warlords in charge of manpower and procurement, along with the Office of Price Administration and the Treasury, to confer with the mayor; and in a short time Washington obliged with "a great affirmative action program for the metropolis," a sheaf of contracts launched on the rising tide of the wartime economy, which brought New York to full employment in the next year. But other industrial cities and regions, old and new, had prospered at the expense of New York, which got less war work but still paid a disproportionate share of taxes. The redistribution of population and industry during the war had the effect of accelerating what the political reporter Richard Rovere, writing in the *American Mercury* in December 1944, described as New York's "relative (if not absolute) decline."

It is doubtful that most New Yorkers noticed any such decline, while for many observers, foreign and domestic, Gotham seemed to be aloof and unconstrained by the world struggle. In his twenties, Eric Sevareid was one of the "boys" recruited for CBS Radio by Edward R. Murrow to report the war in Europe. A student radical at the University of Minnesota in his undergraduate days, not long past, and full of a messianic sense of generation, in *Not So Wild a Dream*, his best-selling memoir of 1946, Sevareid tells how disengaged New York seemed to him in the fall of 1940, when he was fresh from reporting the fall of France and the Blitz. "I marveled at this city which seemed so integrated, intact, oblivious, and I could find no purpose in the ceaseless rushing to and fro upon the streets, in and out of the great fortress buildings, up and down the clicking elevators. When I noticed a husky, grown man on a bus deeply absorbed in the page of comic strips, I felt astonished. In time I began to apply moral judgments to all this, as did others who came back from Europe; but at first there was no feeling save the purest wonder."

Lesser cities and innumerable towns saw their worlds turned upside-down by the routines of a new defense plant or swarms of uniformed men on leave from a nearby military camp. In *WWII*, James Jones remembers how in Memphis, Tennessee, for example, his convalescent army buddies took over the one fashionable hotel and crowded out the gentry with their clamorous round-the-clock drinking parties. Frederic Wakeman's *Shore Leave* (1944), nicely described by James Salter in *Burning the Days* as "a then-irresistible novel," pictures a similar carousal by a gang of edgy aviators at the St. Francis Hotel in San Francisco. New York was simply too rich, too self-absorbed, too populous to be overrun by soldiers and sailors on leave, or to have its sociology rearranged overnight, even by the fallout from a global war. (In *Shore Leave*, the flyboys, having moved on to Manhattan, observe the less glamorous servicemen milling forlornly in Times Square, "most of them looking so sad and bewildered.") The musical *On the Town* opened on Broadway in the last week of 1944, on December 28, with choreography and music by the precocious talents of Jerome Robbins and Leonard Bernstein. Developed from *Fancy Free*, their ballet of earlier that year (although Bernstein always denied the musical connection), this wartime offering about three sailors doing the town ("The Bronx is up, but the Battery's down") was an immediate and lasting hit, flattering the New Yorker's secret sense of being kind and generous to new arrivals and those passing through.

The writer and scholar John Tytell arrived in New York in 1940 when he was a year old; his family were diamond traders. In *Reading New York*, he writes, "The city was saturated with an awareness of the war, with soldiers constantly in transit, incessant appeals for war bonds, omnipresent propaganda posters, and grim newsreel accounts of bloody battles." We must remember that this is reconstruction, not memory, but any photograph of the waiting rooms at Grand Central Terminal or Pennsylvania Station taken during the war will support his description of the military on the move, and the monumental and inescapable propagandizing.

As we have seen, it appeared otherwise at the time to more grown-up observers, from more embattled democracies, from homelands closer to battle zones or having come under fire themselves. Many of them privately accused New York of being heartlessly detached about the great struggle. New York seemed to be the "city without a country" that an earlier French writer, Ernest Duvergier de Hauranne, had found it to be in 1864, "the cosmopolitan market, the vast hostelry which America opens to all people," where "sacrifice occurs without devotion."

In 1942, having just escaped from Bataan, the Filipino statesman

Carlos P. Romulo was scandalized by what seemed to be New York's perpetual state of "fiesta": "There is no war here." The city seemed frantic for pleasure and distraction; the multitudes were looking for cheap thrills on Broadway, while café society danced to the music of Xavier Cugat and his orchestra in the Starlight Room of the Waldorf Astoria. (How Romulo found his way to the Starlight Room on his first night in town, he does not say.) Two and a half years later his surface impression remained much the same, despite the soldiers scattered in the crowds and the war-bond drives glamorized by the appearances of movie stars. There did not seem to be many privations that money could not evade; and without the censorious neighbors of small-town America looking over their shoulders, New Yorkers could shop on a black market abundantly stocked with steaks and nylons. "One read of rationing and shortages, but one also seemed able to buy pretty much anything one desired, if the price were in his pocket. And most New Yorkers seemed to have the price." Many soldiers suspected the civilians who insisted on paying for their drinks of paying a pittance for a guilty prosperity.

It took several more visits to bring Romulo around to "a great and awed respect": when he considered that New York too was sending its sons off to the armed services (in fact, 900,000 of them, along with women in the WAVES and the WACs), that its young women gave at the blood bank, and that its old men volunteered to be air wardens. "New York, I found, had a fighting spirit of its own, developed in its own peculiar and insulated fashion while America was deep in war."

During the Battle of the Atlantic, blackouts and dimouts were imposed, so that merchant ships would not be silhouetted against the city lights. Edward Robb Ellis notes that other precautions included painting over the gold leaf on the dome of the Federal Building in Foley Square because it shone in moonlight, turning off the torch on the Statue of Liberty, and shutting down the electronic loop of news on the Times Tower. "Air raid wardens patrolled the streets and bellowed up at apartment buildings lacking black window shades." On hot summer nights during the blackouts, Brooklynites enjoyed the amazing spectacle of the darkened city across the East River.

Manhattan never ceased to make a splendid show, as Cecil Beaton noted when he passed through on official business in 1944.

After the shabbiness of four war-time years on a besieged island, I was greatly amazed by the smartness and comfort to be seen everywhere in New York, the new paint, the alluring window displays, the diamond lights, the crocodile file of taxis, the long hot baths, the short cold drinks, the succulent dishes . . . Certain people expressed compassion for a few of the rarefied cliques in New York, saying that they had been left out of the great change that had taken place everywhere, and might now find it difficult to face the post-war world. Needless to say, we all "faced" the post-war world with them, returning to our former frivolities and selfishness. And why not? Only elephants remember. But seeing these cliques, I didn't have the impression that they were living in the past.

Yet there was, as hopeful liberal observers agreed, a rough consensus among natives and visitors alike that the Depression, the war, and the progressive administration of La Guardia that spanned them, had generally sobered and humanized the city. Together, they had curbed a little its commercial avidity, revivified a sense of neighborhood, and strengthened the civic culture.

PART III

WORDS, WORDS, WORDS

———————

New York has its own insubstantiality that is due to the impermanence of its people, of its buildings, of its business, of its thoughts; but all the wires of our western civilization are buzzing and crossing here.

—EDMUND WILSON,
The Boys in the Back Room (1940–41)

Avid for books, GIs crowd the 31st Division's Mobile Library, August 18, 1943.

I

———

Books Are Bullets

THE PUBLISHING INDUSTRY prospered mightily during the war. Owing to their war coverage, *Time* and *Life* came to exercise an almost imperial sway, and for the same reason the *New Yorker* gained a moral authority that would have been inconceivable to its frivolous Jazz Age self or its readers.* So-called "pony," or reduced-size, versions of *Time* and the *New Yorker* (but not, for obvious reasons, the pictorial *Life*) were dispatched to the troops—shorn of advertisements, which undoubtedly the soldiers missed.

The war sold mysteries, bibles, atlases, dictionaries, prayer books, historical romances, westerns, comic books (see Michael Chabon's *Kavalier and Klay*), and classics. Jane Austen and Anthony Trollope both enjoyed huge revivals in England and had respectable ones in the United States. The millions of restive soldiers and fully employed civilians alike seemed possessed by a hunger for print profounder than and without precedent in peacetime; in England and America, writers

---

* That discerning literary visitor, Cyril Connolly, found in these three publications an index to the state of civilization in New York. "It is easy to make fun of these three papers, but in fact they are not funny. Although they have very large circulations indeed, they only just miss being completely honorable and serious journals, in fact 'highbrow.' Hence the particular nemesis, ordeal by shiny paper, of those who manage them; they work very hard, and deliver *almost* the best work of which they are capable . . . Thurber's drawings, Hersey's Hiroshima, the essays of Edmund Wilson or Mary McCarthy, *Time*'s anonymous reviews, show that occasionally the gap *is* closed." ("Introduction," *Horizon*, October 1947, 7)

and publishers wondered that the less time people had for recreation, the more they read. Books were a distraction and an escape that could be indulged in foxholes, dugouts, and boring training camps. Some soldiers in the field tore out signatures of paperback books as they finished reading them, in order to pass them on to their comrades.

The new paperbacks from Pocket Books, Avon, Bantam, and Dell were sold in the tens of millions in drugstores, newsstands, railway stations, and dime stores, most of them priced at twenty-five cents. This publishing "revolution" had been launched in Great Britain by Allen Lane's Penguin Books, and followed almost immediately in America by Robert de Graff's Pocket Books. Their shared formula—a cheap price, about the cost of a package of cigarettes, and unadvertised but widespread, demotic distribution—achieved a lasting success that had eluded the earlier paperback revolutionists of the dime novel. Pocket Books sold thirty-eight million books in 1943, prompting Bennett Cerf, the founder of Random House, to exclaim: "It's unbelievable. It's frightening." Inevitably, they were promoted as reading for the millions in uniform. Avon advertised: "Because the new Avon Books are easy to open, light to hold, thrilling to read and compact to carry or store in clothing or bags, they are ideal gifts to the boys in the Armed Forces." Paul Fussell, who quotes the advertisement in his survey of wartime reading, recalls how his father ordered him four Modern Library books, at ninety-five cents each, every month; and for servicemen of aspiring taste whose parents were not so thoughtful, a hundred different Modern Library titles could be ordered through the *Infantry Journal*. They, too, were compact, and, durably bound, also cheap at the price.

Considering a few years later the implications for hardcover publishers, which at first seemed to be dire—no more gatekeepers!—Malcolm Cowley conceded the logic of the paperback. "Isn't this in the spirit of a new civilization bent on distributing the greatest number of commodities to the widest possible circle of consumers at the lowest possible prices? Books are the chief cultural commodity."

Between July 1943 and V-J Day, 122,951,031 paperback books in pocket-sized Armed Services Editions (ASEs) were printed and distributed for six cents to soldiers and sailors by a consortium of major publishers operating as the Council on Books in Wartime. ASEs were launched with the slogan "Books Are Weapons in the War of Ideas," but in practice, even *The Great Gatsby*, a surprise best seller helping to boost Fitzgerald's revival, and *The Fireside Book of Verse: Poems of Romance and Adventure* were weaponized. ASE's first list included Dickens's *Oliver Twist*, Joseph Conrad's *Lord Jim*, John Steinbeck's *Tortilla Flat*, James Thurber's *My World and Welcome to It*, Ambassador Joseph Grew's *Report from Tokyo*, and *The Fireside Book of Dog Stories*. In the months that followed, along with more forgettable fare, soldiers were offered *The Education of Henry Adams*, Emerson's essays, Melville, and Browning, and contemporary fiction by Faulkner, Isherwood, Huxley, and Mann. Whether by policy or silent agreement, the selection committee excluded the classics of disillusionment written after the First World War, from *All Quiet on the Western Front* to *A Farewell to Arms*, Fussell notes. As the publishers no doubt expected, the preferred reading of soldiers and sailors, apart from those who stuck with comic books, were westerns, mysteries, self-improvement, sex, and humor. The authors most reprinted were Ernest Haycox and Max Brand (the pseudonym of Frederick Faust), two prolific purveyors of westerns, followed by the late Thorne Smith, author of the two Topper novels and *The Night Life of the Gods*. Humorists, including Thurber, Dorothy Parker, Robert Benchley, Ring Lardner, and Ludwig Bemelmans, were tonic for bored or frightened GIs. Some of the most battle-scarred felt restored by Betty Smith's *A Tree Grows in Brooklyn*, one of the few publishing success stories of the war that can be considered poignant.

In all, 1,322 titles were selected by committees of critics, librarians, and booksellers, each with a service representative armed with a veto. Every month, forty new titles were selected, and the books were bundled in boxes and shipped to thousands of destinations around the world, with each box intended for 150 GIs, although many copies were waylaid by the officers in charge of their distribution. Every soldier at the Normandy landing was given a book for his kit; and 155,000 boxes were dispatched in spring 1945. Soldiers reportedly "ripped open" the crates of precious books, and while some might have been dismayed to have been allotted poetry or history by the officers in charge, others who were given more popular fare might be ordered to read it aloud. The army and navy paid publishers an extremely modest royalty of half a cent per copy, but the ASEs were reckoned bread upon the waters, a patriotic thing to support, and a way of enlarging the audience for books after the war.

Most GIs wanted simple distraction in their reading, and they were fairly easily satisfied. Fussell notes: "In April, 1945 a *Stars and Stripes* survey found that among soldiers in Europe the most popular titles were *The Pocket Book Dictionary* (help in writing letters); *The Pocket Book of Cartoons, The Pocket Book of Boners*, and (the best selling paperback of the war) *See Here, Private Hargrove* (levity); Erle Stanley Gardner's *The Case of the Curious Bride* (mystery with a whiff of sex); Zola's *Nana* (French: promise of considerable sex); and *The Pocket Book of Verse*," edited by Professor Morris E. Speare, whose popularity must have surprised even the anthologist. Ezra Pound found a copy on the seat of an outhouse in the Disciplinary Training Center near Pisa, where he was caged as a military prisoner in 1945, accused of treason.

Promising a great deal of diversion for the dollar, anthologies became enormously popular and great money spinners for the trade. Their editors, like Clifton Fadiman (*Reading I've Liked*) and Allen Tate and John Peale Bishop (*American Harvest*), enjoyed large audiences and critical authority. "Wartime was notably the age of anthologies," says Fussell, who, discounting price and brevity, discerns a propagandistic motive in the variety encompassed by such collections, "a way of honoring the pluralism and exuberance of the 'democratic' Allied cause . . . A reader of them over forty years afterward will be astonished to find what admirable people Americans are, how generous, tolerant, imaginative, and charming, how resolute in pursuing Victory, how selfless in sacrifice and noble in courage. As well as how literate and tasteful in their reading. It is as if the whole country were the invention of E. B. White."

In 1943 the Viking Portable Library was launched with a 655-page miscellany, *As You Were*, addressed to the armed forces and merchant marine, edited by the *New Yorker* columnist and beloved epicene radio personality Alexander Woollcott, supposedly the inspiration for the title character in *The Man Who Came to Dinner*, the 1939 comedy by George S. Kaufman and Moss Hart. Published in stout, squarish hardcovers costing a dollar, the Portable Library contained one-volume selections from single authors, including over the years Shakespeare,

Cervantes, Twain, Coleridge, Blake, Dorothy Parker, Oscar Wilde, Edward Gibbon, Melville, Hawthorne, Hemingway, Fitzgerald, Steinbeck, and Matthew Arnold. *The Portable Faulkner*, in 1946, edited and with an introduction by Malcolm Cowley, is credited with reviving his reputation at a time when most of his books were out of print, "little read and often disparaged." In James Jones's semi-autobiographical novel *Some Came Running* (1957)—which, if nothing else, is the longest novel devoted to the period between the war and Korea, exhausting the reader at a biblical 1,226 pages—his fictional alter ego, Dave Hirsh, a failed novelist washed up in his Indiana hometown after the war, fishes the precious volumes from his duffel bag and arranges them reverently in his hotel room. "There were five, all Viking Portables. FITZGERALD, HEMINGWAY, FAULKNER, STEINBECK, WOLFE—the five major influences his sister Francine had called them. She had sent them to him in Europe from Hollywood one by one as they came out." (The scene is faithfully re-created in the 1959 movie directed by Vincente Minnelli and starring Frank Sinatra.)

During the war the balance in book sales shifted from fiction to nonfiction: not necessarily good news for publishers, because foreign-policy tracts and battlefield accounts rarely age well, and so are less likely than novels to become reliable backlist sellers. (The books with the largest individual sales were still mostly novels, though novels now mostly forgotten: Kathleen Winsor's *Forever Amber*, Elizabeth Goudge's *Green Dolphin Street*, Lillian Smith's *Strange Fruit*, and Elliot Paul's *The Last Time I Saw Paris*, whose title was also borrowed from a song.) As war began in Europe, the CBS radio correspondent William L. Shirer's *Berlin Diary* sold almost as well (nearly 500,000 copies) as A. J. Cronin's *The Keys of the Kingdom*. Beginning in 1941, war reportage on the best-seller lists included *They Were Expendable*, *Thirty Seconds Over Tokyo*, *God Is My Co-Pilot*, *Guadalcanal Diary*, and Ernie Pyle's *This Is Your Army*. Wendell Willkie's *One World* was a phenomenal million-seller in 1944. Walter Lippmann had a large success with a small tract on *U.S. Foreign Policy*, as did Sumner Welles, who led the nonfiction list with *The Time for Decision*, until toppled by Bob Hope's *I Never Left Home*.

Not unexpectedly, few war novels of any distinction were written while the war was actually being fought: the only two that appeared on best-seller lists were John Steinbeck's *The Moon Is Down*, which aroused controversy by portraying some of the Nazis occupying Norway as human beings, and John Hersey's *A Bell for Adano*, about an American military governor in Sicily. No military man sold more books than Marion Hargrove, a North Carolina GI whose humorous letters home from boot camp, *See Here, Private Hargrove*, were a phenomenon. Bill Mauldin's grimy, unshaven dogfaces Willie and Joe, wearily engaged like their creator in the Italian campaign, reached the best-seller list when Mauldin's cartoons for *Stars and Stripes*, the army newspaper, were collected in *Up Front* in 1945.

"Literature as a business is prospering as never before," Malcolm Cowley wrote in 1943, "with book after book selling more than a quarter of a million copies in hardcovers, but literature as an art is in a dead season." At forty-five Cowley was a close and canny observer of the literary marketplace, following events from his farm in Sherman, Connecticut. He had expected a more active war, but his appointment as chief information analyst for the Office of Facts and Figures, the predecessor agency to the Office of War Information headed by his friend Archibald MacLeish, was waylaid by opposition in Congress and the press. Westbrook Pegler of the Hearst press and Martin Dies Jr., the vehement (and, as it turned out, venal) Texas Democrat who led the House Un-American Activities Committee, had pointed with alarm to his past fellow-traveling.

Cowley complained that the best-selling volumes of war reporting "might as well have been mailed by slow boat and sunk in mid-ocean." "Written for heroes who found God in a foxhole and a contract waiting in Hollywood," the GI memoirs occupied the bookstalls next to historical romances or the memoirs that read as if they had been written "in collaboration by Miss Ginger Rogers and Parson Weems." Where—as opposed to these mass-manufactured goods—were the novels that told about occupied Europe, or the aircraft plants in Southern California, or the wartime bureaucracy in Washington, DC? Where was the war reportage to compare with that of the Spanish Civil War, and the war poets, as opposed to the propagandists? If the younger writers were living in a GI world, which afforded neither time nor privacy for writing novels, that did not explain the low level of books that were written by the "women, 4Fs, and over-thirty-eights" who remained in civilian life. His own generation, born in the 1890s, seemed to be falling silent, baffled and disillusioned by ideological cross-currents; meanwhile, the younger writers he had taught before the war—the first literary generation to enroll in creative-writing classes—had seemed oddly cloistered. They were admirers of the hermetic masters Rilke and Kafka, and besotted with "symbolism." "The one thing for which they were not prepared, intellectually or emotionally, was to be seized and transported into a world without solitude, where their time would be measured by the top sergeant's whistle."

In the midst of the greatest events in history, the reading public was mostly content with worthy Ernie Pyle, Ellery Queen, and Bob Hope; with historical romances like *The Black Rose* (about a Saxon knight's adventures in Asia) by Thomas B. Costain, *Captain from Castile* (a conquistador riding with Cortés into Mexico) by Samuel Shellabarger, *The Foxes of Harrow* (a fortune hunter has dynastic ambitions in antebellum New Orleans) by Frank Yerby, and Winsor's *Forever Amber* (a saucy wench in Restoration England), each of which sold over a million copies in various formats; and with uplifting religiose novels, including A. J. Cronin's *The Keys of the Kingdom*, about the life and good works of a missionary; Lloyd C. Douglas's *The Robe*, about Christianity in the first century, and Franz Werfel's *The Song of Bernadette*, about the visionary French peasant girl.

The fact that almost nobody reads any of these novels anymore and that they are unwanted by even the least discriminating used-book stores that remain does not diminish the significance of their former popularity and what it says about the wartime mood. As James D. Hart, then a young professor at Berkeley, wrote in *The Popular Book* (1950), the transient best seller is usually the indicative book. "If a student of taste wants to know the thoughts and feelings of the majority who lived during Franklin Pierce's administration, he will find more positive value in Maria Cummins's *The Lamplighter* or T. S. Arthur's *Ten Nights in a Bar-Room* than he will in Thoreau's *Walden*—all books published in 1854." And similarly, *Forever Amber* and *The Robe* might tell us more about popular feeling toward the end of the war than *Dangling*

Man, Saul Bellow's first novel, which was published to modest sales in 1944 (1,056 copies in the first edition); although *Dangling Man*, whose last sentence is "Hail regimentation!," tells us something too.

Leaving aside mere literature, the top best-selling novelists of the war—mostly historical romancers—arrived on the commercial heights by very different routes. Costain, a Canadian, had been an editor at *Maclean's* and the *Saturday Evening Post*, a story editor at Twentieth Century–Fox, and an executive at Doubleday before publishing *The Black Rose*, his first novel, in 1943, at the age of fifty-five. Shellabarger, the headmaster of a girls' school in Columbus, Ohio, a Ph.D. from Harvard who knew six languages and had published scholarly monographs, was fifty-seven when he published *Captain from Castile*, his first novel. Their fellow best seller W. Somerset Maugham once wrote that with "advancing years the novelist grows less and less inclined to describe more than what his experience has given him." Mr. Costain and Dr. Shellabarger waited until a ripe age to write very profitably about matters of which they could not possibly have known anything at all from personal experience.

Very few of his readers suspected that Frank Yerby, a comparative youngster at thirty, who had worked in the Chicago office of the Federal Writers' Project, was African American. Kathleen Winsor was an undergraduate at the University of California, Berkeley, when she began the research for her first novel, which was published when she was twenty-five. Her interest in Restoration England was aroused by a class project of her husband's, a football star. When the book clubs declined *Forever Amber* as too racy for adoption, its success was ensured. Macmillan put the attractive young author in a seductive pose on the front cover of *Publishers Weekly*. (Not to be outdone, Bennett Cerf advertised Gertrude Stein's *Wars I Have Seen* with a photograph of the author and her companion, Alice B. Toklas, headlined "Shucks, we've got glamour girls too!")

Franz Werfel, a friend of Kafka's in his youth, and his wife, Alma Mahler Werfel (more precisely, Alma Schindler Mahler Gropius Werfel), belonged to the circle of expatriates and émigrés in Los Angeles that included Thomas Mann, Lion Feuchtwanger, Igor Stravinsky, and Aldous Huxley. *The Song of Bernadette* fulfilled a vow that the author had made when he and his wife were fleeing across the Pyrenees in 1940 and passed by the shrine at Lourdes, where St. Bernadette

had her visions. No cosmopolite, Lloyd C. Douglas was a Congregationalist minister who was past fifty when his first novel, *Magnificent
Obsession*, was published in 1929 and became a best seller. Four of his
books were made into major motion pictures, and this one is about
Robert Merrick, who is rescued after a boating accident, but because
they are saving him, the rescue crew cannot get across the lake to
save the famous Dr. Hudson, beloved for helping people, and he has a
fatal heart attack. Merrick decides to make up for the doctor's loss by
becoming a doctor himself. The film, however, had a very different but
equally absurd plot.

Another of his books, *The Robe* has as its protagonist the Roman cen-
turion who supervised the crucifixion. By August 1944, when it came
to Edmund Wilson's belated notice in the *New Yorker*, it had stood at or
near the top of the best-seller list for almost two years, during which it
had sold 1,450,000 copies, for each of which his publisher, Houghton
Mifflin, claimed an average of five readers. Wilson confessed to being
"astounded and terrified at the thought that seven million Americans
have found something to hold their attention" in an old-fashioned historical novel on the order of *The Last Days of Pompeii* or *Ben-Hur*, only
worse. Douglas himself, as he noted, ventured modestly that books
about Jesus usually sold if the author avoided theological brambles,
and that it might be a relief to hear about somebody who was interested in healing the blind and the crippled rather than in blinding and
crippling them. In *The Table Talk of W. H. Auden*, Alan Ansen notes
the poet venturing that *Partisan Review* went wrong in spending too
much time with "people who don't matter," but "of course, if one had
a chance to do something like *The Robe*, where one could do a very
elaborate and detailed analysis of an important, bad work, that would
be different."

Spiritual disquiet sold during the war—on the lower and higher
frequencies—as Gore Vidal, a youthful and later guarded admirer,
recalls in an essay on Maugham. *The Razor's Edge* might be said to have
bridged the audiences of Mann's *Doctor Faustus* and Lloyd C. Douglas.
In fact, this novel, about a young man's spiritual quest after the First
World War—set in Chicago, Germany, a monastery in the Himalayas,
and the South of France—was a genuinely prophetic book. Maugham's
glamorous dropout Larry Darrell, an aviator in the war who might
or might not have achieved Vedanta enlightenment and is last heard

of living anonymously as a cabdriver in New York, prefigured the eastward-journeying spiritual nomads and dropouts of the sixties— French and English as well as American—not only earlier but more exactly than the "Zen lunatics" (inspired by the poets Gary Snyder and Philip Whalen) in Kerouac's *The Dharma Bums* (1957), who were too radically individual to prefigure anything other than their later selves, although Snyder prophesied a "rucksack revolution." *Time* reported a rumor that Maugham had modeled his hero on Christopher Isherwood, and indeed he had consulted the younger novelist, a disciple of the Vedanta guru Swami Prabhavananda in Hollywood, on some fine points of translating from Sanskrit. But Isherwood had not lost, and indeed never did, his worldly attachments to sex and alcohol, and rather than dropping out was profitably writing screenplays for MGM.

Maugham, whose fascination with the Mysterious East went back decades, was sixty-nine when *The Razor's Edge* was published in 1944, almost half a century after his first novel, *Liza of Lambeth*, appeared in 1897, and the year *Quo Vadis?* was the most popular book in America. In her historical study of best sellers, based on the files of *Publishers Weekly*, Alice Payne Hackett writes that *The Razor's Edge* had "almost reached the ultimate in all types of sales," having been serialized in *Redbook*, a best seller in the Doubleday trade edition, a Literary Guild and Dollar Book Club selection, and in paperback everywhere for twenty-five cents. Maugham had millions of readers abroad, and for many years, as Vidal notes, was the most revered foreign-language author in Japan. And of course the book was sold to the movies. Maugham "dominated the movies at a time when movies were the lingua franca of the world. Although the French have told us that the movie is the creation of the director, no one in the Twenties, Thirties, Forties paid the slightest attention to who had directed *Of Human Bondage, Rain, The Moon and Sixpence, The Razor's Edge, The Painted Veil, The Letter.* Their true creator was W. Somerset Maugham, and a generation was in thrall to his sensuous, exotic imaginings of a duplicitous world."

Between 1946 and 1953, after which interest languished, the most plausible best sellers were bought by Hollywood and expensively translated into movies. Tyrone Power, Fox's leading man, starred as the Anglo-Saxon adventurer in *The Black Rose* (1950), as the hidalgo fleeing the Inquisition in *Captain from Castile* (1947), and as the mystic Larry Darrell in *The Razor's Edge* (1946), as well as a carnival hustler in *Nightmare Alley* (1947), based on William Lindsay Graham's best seller of 1946. Linda Darnell, who played the saucy wench in *Forever Amber* (1947), appeared unbilled as the Virgin Mary, Our Lady of Lourdes, in *The Song of Bernadette* (1943). Although fading, the studio contract system was obviously still in flower.

The best-seller lists, along with the translation of novels into movies—and the writing of novels whose real purpose was to *become* movies—are cited by Daniel J. Boorstin in *The Image* (1961) as examples of the "dissolving forms" in which experience in America has been increasingly submerged as a result of the Graphic Revolution that began with high-speed printing in the nineteenth century, now giving rise to what he calls "pseudo-events." Movies were a more accessible and popular narrative form than the prose fictions on which so many of them were based, and in turn changed the way people read books, and authors wrote them. With the prospect of being abridged, condensed, paperbacked, and adapted for the movies, a published novel became the instance for various metamorphoses. Or as Joan Didion explains in her essay "In Hollywood": "A book or a story is a 'property' only until the deal; after that it is 'the basic material,' as in 'I haven't read the basic material on *Gatsby*.'"

John Steinbeck's novel *The Wayward Bus*, regarded by critics as a lesser effort, was a leading fiction best seller in 1947, along with Laura Z. Hobson's *Gentleman's Agreement* and Sinclair Lewis's *Kingsblood Royal* (and *The Foxes of Harrow* and Shellabarger's new book, *Prince of Foxes*). Steinbeck, who in the early thirties lived in a little cottage owned by his father in Pacific Grove, California, surviving along with his friends on what they could grow in truck gardens, beg or steal from farmers, or fish from the sea, was a great grizzled celebrity when he moved permanently to New York in 1943. *The Grapes of Wrath* had made him famous; the movie directed by John Ford and starring Henry Fonda had put him on the way to being rich. The controversy over his Broadway play *The Moon Is Down*, adapted from his novel, enlarged his celebrity: his journalism was sought after; and he was welcomed to Roosevelt's White House, even producing a draft (rejected) for FDR's fourth inaugural address. Now, dining in the front room of "21," which prided itself on turning away more hopeful diners than any other restaurant in the world, he could afford to indulge, as freely as David Sarnoff, Moss Hart, Cole Porter, Lawrence Tibbett, or Leland Hayward, what the arch snob Lucius Beebe called a whim of iron. In 1953, Steinbeck wrote an often-quoted essay for the *New York Times Magazine* in which he declared: "But there is one thing about it—once you have lived in New York and it has become your home, no place else is good enough." But his was a cautionary tale. After the years rolled away, and he died, his reputation in steep decline, his friend Elia Kazan wrote: "I don't think John Steinbeck should have been living in New York. I don't think he should have been writing plays. I don't think he should have hung out with show people. He was a prose writer, at home in the West, with land, with horses, or on a boat; in the big city, he was a dupe."

Old forms seemed to be dissolving all the more swiftly after the war as Hollywood began to lose its mass audience and searched frantically for ways to recapture it, tempting "the public, that moody tyrant," as Ben Hecht called it, with expensive costume dramas, film noir, "problem pictures," and problematic male leads imported from Broadway: Clift, Brando, Dean. Characters were in constant transmigration from one medium to another: Blondie and Dagwood went from the comics to the movies; Hammett's detective Sam Spade became a comic strip; and Orson Welles's greatest role was to be himself in all the available media as theatrical impresario, movie director and actor, radio voice, and left-wing newspaper columnist.

As Daniel Boorstin wrote, "Thus the multiplying kinds of images—from the printed page to the photograph to the movie to radio and television, to the comic book and back again—make our literary-dramatic experience a limbo. In that limbo there are no forms but only the ghosts of other forms." In *Understanding Media*, Marshall McLuhan dismisses all this as so much elitist literary nostalgia. What Boorstin calls pseudo-events have been enriching life since antiquity, while the "content" of any medium, McLuhan famously maintains, was always another medium. Novels and plays furnished the content of movies. "The electric light is pure information." In the forties, neither of these theories had yet been mounted; but the confusion of realms which we have since agreed to call "postmodern" was everywhere becoming apparent.

New York Discovers America

"NEW YORK IS NOT AMERICA," Ford Madox Ford declared in 1927. A sentiment endorsed by many others before and since, but New York City *was* the fountainhead of Americana, and not only because that was where most of it was published. Wartime cast a rosy glow on the American past, which shone in every medium, but the vogue for Americana had begun in the very different atmosphere of the Jazz Age, when Stephen Vincent Benét published *John Brown's Body*. This long narrative poem, with its incantatory rhythms (much later to be rehearsed in the rhetoric of Ronald Reagan), became a main selection of the Book-of-the-Month Club, was awarded the Pulitzer Prize in 1929, and over the next twenty years sold more than one hundred thousand copies, a popular success that no other American poet had enjoyed since Henry Wadsworth Longfellow.

Along with Robert Frost and Carl Sandburg, Benét was one of the few American moderns who became a household poet like Longfellow and Whittier in the nineteenth century; and as a friend of young talent and a man of letters, he has been compared to William Dean Howells. His short stories "The Devil and Daniel Webster" (which became a movie and an opera) and "By the Waters of Babylon" (1937; the original post-apocalyptic fiction, set in the burnt ruins of New York City) are still anthologized; but he has fallen out of fashion and almost out of literary history. How many of the millions who have thrilled to the words "Bury my heart at Wounded Knee" know that they were written by a paleface New York poet with a good Upper East Side address? Benét was an ardent New Dealer and dedicated wartime propagandist—a title he did not disdain—whose poetry was read on state occasions by Roosevelt, who publicly mourned Benét's premature death of a heart attack brought on by overwork in 1943. The growth of Americana, which Benét helped to launch from Paris and New York, was not a movement or a school, but rather an all-enveloping nostalgic mood which persisted through the Depression and the war, sweeping over the whole republic of letters.

Novels as various as Edna Ferber's *Cimarron* and George Santayana's *The Last Puritan*, Thomas Wolfe's *Of Time and the River*, John P. Marquand's *The Late George Apley*, and Marjorie Kinnan Rawlings's *The Yearling* are its expressions in the novel. It engendered historical romances like Kenneth Roberts's *Northwest Passage* and Walter D. Edmonds's *Drums Along the Mohawk* and huge biographies like Sandburg's *Life of Lincoln* (which cruel wits said was the worst thing to happen to the sixteenth president since Ford's Theatre) and Douglas Southall Freeman's *R. E. Lee*, a favorite of Harry Truman, whose Confederate ancestors he revered.

In 1950, James Hart suggested that Americana "smacked of psychological regression among a people frustrated by the present and hoping to find comfort in the happier, younger days of their land." Sentimental and undiscriminating, it included the Federal Writers' Project's *Highway One*; the memoir *Lanterns on the Levee*, by the Louisiana aristocrat William Alexander Percy, uncle of the novelist Walker Percy, a book that was on FDR's desk when he died; as well as A. B. Guthrie Jr.'s *The Big Sky*. In 1942, Alfred Kazin conceded, after a careful survey, "So the new literature of American folkways, of the river legends and regional cultures, while often shallow enough, was anything but museum-like."

Earlier, Malcolm Cowley ventured that novels like *Gone with the Wind* and historical plays like Robert Sherwood's *Abe Lincoln in Illinois* had their place among the pastimes and consolations of a middle class that had lowered its expectations and was learning to make the best of what it had. The Americans who had turned to small pleasures like home cooking, bridge, gardening, croquet, gossip, and "community affairs" were collecting a "glorious past" in the same spirit that they might collect antique furniture. As a prophecy of what was to come for the American middle classes, this could not have been more mistaken—but it should be remembered that the so-called First New Deal was launched in the same expectation that America's great days of expansion were over, and now it was about, "the soberer, less dramatic business of administering resources already in hand," as Roosevelt said in his address at the Commonwealth Club in San Francisco, the most thoughtful address of his 1932 presidential campaign. Cowley also shrewdly noted that what was then perceived as the need to preserve natural resources—what we now call the environmental movement—grew out of the same resigned mood of "Shall I at least put my lands in order?"

The New Deal had a complex and contradictory relationship to Americana. Hart notes that "by upsetting established relations between citizen and government, [it] paradoxically helped to focus attention on tradition." At the same time, the WPA relief programs for writers and artists, collectively known as Federal One, fostered the growth of regional history; subsidized the burgeoning art of oral history, including slave narratives; enlivened the theater; and adorned post offices and courthouses with social-realist depictions of the American past and present, sometimes varied with the work of future abstract expressionists.

The great monument of the Federal Writers' Project was the American Guide Series to the forty-eight states, supplemented with volumes on Washington, DC, Puerto Rico (a sort of New Deal laboratory), and Alaska, and thirty volumes on individual cities, including the two on New York City. Federal One was an immense collective enterprise in a collectivist time, which employed several hundred writers, including over the years Saul Bellow, Richard Wright, Kenneth Rexroth, Lionel Abel, Ralph Ellison, Willard Motley, Maxwell Bodenheim, John Cheever, Jack Conroy, and Margaret Walker. According to policy, chapters and essays were unsigned (the contributors were listed at the top of the volumes), although it is well known by students of the series that, for example, Wright wrote the section on Harlem in *New York Panorama* and Conrad Aiken the "Literature" survey in the New England volume. (To placate the Marxists on the staff who objected to

Aiken's emphasis on individualism, a chapter on "Literary Groups and Movements" was added.)

Though subsequently neglected by professional historians, the vast treasury of writing about the lore, landscape, and literature of America found in the guides would be mined by later generations of fiction writers, poets, and essayists. While Aiken was already an authority on the literature of New England, Philip Rahv, the cofounder of *Partisan Review*, had to be persuaded that the literature of New York City was worth writing about. Informed by his editorial supervisor, Vincent McHugh, that such writers as Henry James, Stephen Crane, Walt Whitman, Herman Melville, and Edgar Allan Poe had vital connections to the city, he agreed to his assignment with a "doleful sigh." In her 1947 essay "America the Beautiful," when Mary McCarthy ironically concedes that America—it was, increasingly, "America" or "our country," for intellectuals after the war, rather than a distanced "U.S.A.," as in Dos Passos's trilogy—was "deficient in objects of virtue" that might strike a "visiting Existentialist" like Simone de Beauvoir, one senses the not-so-distant influence of the Federal Writers' Project in her inventory of supposedly deficient "objects": "The Grand Canyon, Yellowstone Park, Jim Hill's mansion in St. Paul, Jefferson's Monticello, the blast furnaces of Pittsburgh, Mount Rainier, the yellow observatory at Amherst, the little-theatre movement in Cleveland, Ohio, a Greek revival house glimpsed from a car window in a lost river-town in New Jersey—these things were too small for the size of the country."

Writers of the Popular Front embraced Americana with a passion. As the Communist Party, led by Earl Browder, emerged from catacombs, its intellectual cadres discovered grace and vitality in the forms of popular culture the Party had formerly scorned, and inspiration in the American past. Just as communism was redefined as "twentieth-century Americanism," so illustrious forebears Tom Paine, Thomas Jefferson, Andrew Jackson, and Abraham Lincoln were conscripted into the pantheon of Marxist heroes. According to Eric Foner, in 1937 the Young Communist League made a point of celebrating the anniversary of Paul Revere's midnight ride "and chided the Daughters of

the American Revolution for failing to mark the occasion." The pioneering scholarship that Communist historians produced in the fields
of African American and labor history was largely unknown to the
reading, or listening, public, which only knew, and sometimes rather
liked, the sentimentality of "Ballad for Americans." Historical fiction
turned out to be a much better way of reaching readers than horny-
handed proletarian novels, and for a time it seemed that Howard Fast
would be to Americana what Clifford Odets was to the theater. *Citizen
Tom Paine* was adopted by the Modern Library and issued as a "Giant,"
alongside George Eliot, Dostoevsky, Plutarch, and *Capital*, volume 1.

Fast, who grew up desperately poor on Tenth Avenue, published
his first novel, a romance set in the Revolutionary War era, in 1934,
at the age of nineteen. Along with Jack London, he was one of the few
professional writers to come out of the working class. A Communist
friend, Sarah Kunitz, criticized him for betraying his background and
suffering by writing historical fairy tales, but Fast's contemporary fictions are merely dutiful; his gift was for popular history, and he soon
found a way of infusing novels like *Freedom Road*, about Reconstruction in South Carolina, with his radical politics. (*Freedom Road* became
one of the most widely read and translated novels of the last century:
Sartre personally intervened with Fast to acquire the French rights for
his publisher, Gallimard.)

Perversely, having shunned the Communist Party in the thirties
because of the Moscow Trials and the Hitler-Stalin Pact, Fast joined
the Party in 1944, when events were about to march it back to the
catacombs. In retrospect Fast would wonder why he had not seized his
opportunity to escape when he was threatened with expulsion for the
thought crime of failing to understand that it was "white chauvinism"
to refer to black teenagers as boys and girls rather than as "youths."

"But retrospect has no validity," Fast wrote, "and this was 1946, not
1990, and as crazy as this moment might have been, this was the party
of Bill Foster and Big Bill Haywood and Elizabeth Gurley Flynn, the
party that had organized the French Resistance and fought the Nazis
to the death and taught the world a new lesson in courage and honor,
the party that created the Abraham Lincoln Brigade and never stinted
at the price paid for freedom." Rather than allow himself to be expelled
from such a vanguard, he would submit to their "loony" prescriptions.

On May Day 1946, a host of 150,000, including many thousands of uniformed veterans, men and women, cheered Communist speakers and left-wing sympathizers at the last and greatest such rally at Union Square; and that seemed to augur well. His fealty to the Party would be costly, but in 1944 he did not believe that America jailed authors.

By the forties, strands of Americana were spread out over the whole literary and subliterary landscape, from the editorials in *Life* magazine to the Book-of-the-Month Club to local historical societies to radio dramas to Broadway, with the moody *Carousel* and the ebullient *Oklahoma!* from Rodgers and Hammerstein. The combination of official and commercial propaganda on behalf of a largely imaginary past reinforced "the mood of evangelical patriotism" that led Henry Luce, in a famous moment of hubris, to proclaim the American Century.*

"The peculiar power of American nostalgia," V. S. Pritchett writes, "is that it is not only harking back to something lost in the past, but suggests also the tragedy of a lost future." In the forties, Americans were being borne, like Fitzgerald voyagers, ceaselessly into the past, as they faced a more-than-usually clouded future.

---

* When Van Wyck Brooks set to work on *The World of Washington Irving* (1944), he wrote his friend Lewis Mumford that he would try to show "that America has *a monopoly of Revolution*, that we really started the whole thing and have our chance *for the last word also.*" Alas, no neoconservative in the twenty-first century could put it better.

3

Limousines on Grub Street

FOR A YEAR OR TWO after the war was over the boom roared on. Publishers dared to hope that along with civilians who subscribed to the Book-of-the-Month Club, soldiers who had kept fear or tedium at bay with Armed Services Editions and Pocket Books would maintain the reading habits they had acquired in wartime. Hopes were vindicated when book sales continued strong even after movie admissions and, in New York, theater attendance, began to plummet: in both cases soon after V-J Day. The lonely crowd was deserting public places, but private pursuits like reproducing (innocent demographers and sociologists had not yet noticed the baby boom) and reading flourished.

The competition for promising manuscripts and the wartime tax on "excess" profits had put publishers in a mood of unaccustomed generosity. A large advance on a book could be deducted from their taxable income; by the time a manuscript was delivered (*if* it was delivered), the tax would almost certainly be repealed. A similar calculation led big-circulation magazines like the *Saturday Evening Post* that published fiction and freelance journalism to increase their top rates for the first time since the days when Jack London commanded ten cents a word. Although "synergy" was still a learned word, the lucrative idea was hardly unknown to magazine editors, publishers, or movie moguls. In many ways the popular tastes and publishing arrangements of the time were more apt to foster multimedia coups then than later. Stories are a likelier source of movie scenarios than articles, and in the forties magazines as various as the *Post, Collier's, Cosmopolitan, Harper's Bazaar,* the *Atlantic Monthly,* and *Esquire,* as well as the *New Yorker,* still published a great many short stories.

The search for a usable past was profitably extended into the day before yesterday by a steady flow of histories and memoirs by statesmen and soldiers, such as General Eisenhower's *Crusade in Europe* and Henry Stimson's *On Active Service in Peace and War* (written for the grand old man by his friend Harvey Bundy's son McGeorge, who received coauthor's credit); by Upton Sinclair's hugely popular Lanny Budd novels, which even Thomas Mann praised, about a well-traveled rich boy who was a secret agent for FDR and turned up everywhere and met everybody, like a glamorous anticipation of Woody Allen's Zelig; and not least by books about FDR, written not only by the public figures in his court, like his speechwriters Robert E. Sherwood and Samuel Rosenman, but also by the secretaries, housekeepers, and bodyguards in his entourage. Considering some other fads of the day— the simple life and psychoanalysis—James D. Hart suggested that as a guaranteed best seller the old reliable formula of *Lincoln's Doctor's Dog* (traditionally attributed to Bennett Cerf) could be replaced with *Roosevelt's Psychiatrist's Egg Ranch.*

Writing in the *New Republic,* Malcolm Cowley spotted the amazing sight of "Limousines on Grub Street." A book club adoption combined with a movie sale could make the author of a successful novel practically a millionaire overnight.* Liquor was poured more freely at

---

* "In those days a romantic novel that was chosen by one of the major book clubs and sold to the movies might yield its author as much as half a million dollars [$5–6 million in current dollars]. There weren't many of these bonanzas, but most books were selling well, many publishers were making excess profits, and even the authors of unsuccessful novels could find well-paid writing jobs in Hollywood or on the staffs of big-circulation magazines. A large share of their literary earnings went to the Bureau of Internal Revenue, for the income-tax laws have never been kind to writers, actors, glamour girls, professional athletes, national heroes, and others with brief periods of prosperity." This is true, but in the forties the IRS was incomparably kinder to such mayflies than later on. Tax law then permitted income to be averaged over a period of seven years (a period that seemed unconscionably short to the best-selling nonfiction author and radio correspondent William L. Shirer, later to be even more famous as the author of *The Rise and Fall of the Third Reich*). In the 1980s, income averaging would be eliminated entirely—curiously enough, as part of a tax reform engineered in large part by a former professional actor, Ronald Reagan, and a retired athlete, then-Senator Bill Bradley.

publishers' parties than it had been since the revels of the Jazz Age were ended. Only a few years later, in the soberer fifties, Cowley would recall almost with disbelief "a brief period at the end of World War II when writing books was a profession that supported hundreds in comfort or luxury."

During the boom, as at almost any other time in publishing, the big money was divided among an assortment of sturdy professionals who had learned how to please a large public (*The Mixture as Before* was the candid title Somerset Maugham gave to one of his story collections) and newcomers who by force of style or personality—or publicity, or beguiling theme, or rumors of sex—aroused its curiosity. Kathleen Winsor's *Forever Amber* continued its amazing stay on the best-seller lists, where it was joined by Samuel Shellabarger's *Captain from Castile*, Richard Wright's *Black Boy*, and Sinclair Lewis's *Cass Timberlane*, which earned the fading legend a half-million dollars, including a large movie sale. Winsor's good fortune was prolonged in 1946 when the Massachusetts Superior Court upheld a lower court's clearance of *Forever Amber* of obscenity charges. Alluding to Judge John M. Woolsey's famous decision declaring *Ulysses* more "emetic" than arousing, Judge Frank J. Donahue characterized *Forever Amber* as more of a "soporific . . . than an aphrodisiac." Buyers, however, were not discouraged.

Not so lucky in the courts was Edmund Wilson, whose brief limousine ride was brutally interrupted by the morals police. The country's leading literary critic also wrote stories, poems, parodies, and plays, although he really only excelled as a parodist (one wonders how the reputation of Archibald MacLeish survived "The Omelet of A. MacLeish" to the extent it did). His collection of linked short stories, *Memoirs of Hecate County*, was banned in New York State after it caught the unfavorable attention of the Society for the Suppression of Vice and the Roman Catholic Legion of Decency, and was successfully prosecuted for obscenity by the New York district attorney's office.

Sex and rumors of sex reliably sell, and it is customary to observe that after the Second World War younger readers especially wanted a franker treatment of sex than commercial fiction had previously given them. John Updike recalls reading a copy of *Hecate County* he had dis-

covered sitting "placidly" on the open shelves of the Reading, Pennsylvania, public library even as it was being banned in New York. In
1946 Updike was fourteen years old, a very young reader. He imagines
his younger self must have skipped or skimmed a lot of the contents
of "that slightly sinister volume, a milky-green in the original Doubleday edition," but he recalls having been "blinded" by the journal
entry in "The Princess with the Golden Hair" that begins "——ing in
the afternoon, with the shades down and all her clothes on—different
from anything else—rank satisfactory smell like the salt marine tides
we come out of." He confesses that when Wilson's journals of *The
Thirties* were published in the seventies, he was a little disappointed to
find that "——ing" was just fucking.

An operative definition of obscenity in the forties was a description
of the human genitalia in a literary context. Wilson told friends that
Scribner's and Houghton, Mifflin were "scared to death of the story,"
and he even considered publishing *Hecate County* himself with some
of his *New Yorker* money before Doubleday, in an adventurous mood,
accepted it. It was published in March 1946 (the month that Winston
Churchill declared in Missouri that "an iron curtain has descended
across Europe"), and fifty thousand copies were in print by the second week of July; one, it was reported, had been bought by the White
House. (In a letter to Louise Bogan, Wilson said, "I'm charmed by the
idea of the Trumans with my book.")

By July, *Hecate County* was seized by the police; it was prosecuted
in October and effectively outlawed by November, when the verdict
of the Court of Special Sessions was upheld by the Appellate Division
of the State Supreme Court. (An appeal to the U.S. Supreme Court
failed in 1948.) During the interval, the author of *Axel's Castle* and *To
the Finland Station* enjoyed unaccustomed notoriety, having surprised
his mother by publishing a popular book.

Wilson was never named as a defendant in any of the trials of *Hecate County*, thus sparing New York the spectacle of its leading man of
letters in the dock. By custom rather than statute, obscenity cases were
prosecuted against publishing companies (not individual publishers)
and booksellers rather than authors. The New York legislature and the
Hearst press wished to correct this oversight, but the *New York Times*
and other respectable newspapers were opposed, and the enabling legislation was vetoed by Governor Thomas Dewey.

But in another way, *Memoirs of Hecate County* did set Edmund Wilson upon a life of crime. As he relates in *The Cold War and the Income Tax: A Protest* (1963), for many years he had been "living on a shoestring" as a freelance. Then, for a brief spell between 1943 and 1946, he enjoyed a season of comparative affluence, earning as much as $10,000 a year as a book reviewer and foreign correspondent for the *New Yorker* (more than $100,000 in current dollars), while *Memoirs of Hecate County* brought in $50,000, a small fortune, before sales were halted by the obscenity trials and, having quit his regular job at the *New Yorker*, he returned to his customary penury. Between 1947 and 1951 America's leading man of letters estimated his income averaged about $2,000 a year.

With two divorce settlements to pay for, his own and his future wife's, Elena Mumm Thornton's, a house to keep up in Wellfleet, Massachusetts, and one thing or another, he neglected to file any income returns between 1945 and 1954. "It may seem naive, and even stupid, on the part of one who had worked for years on a journal which specialized on public affairs, that he should have paid so little attention to recent changes in the income tax laws," he conceded. When he belatedly decided to put his affairs in order (his book on the Dead Sea Scrolls was selling well, and Jason Epstein was putting his previous work in paperback at Anchor Doubleday), it came as a distinct shock to learn from his horrified lawyer that he had exposed himself to jail time and fines that exceeded his original windfall. His battle with the Internal Revenue Service dragged on for several years (at one point his lawyer advised him to take up citizenship in another country to escape the IRS's punitive measures), and was only resolved on terms Wilson could afford when President John F. Kennedy, who had heard of his troubles from his special assistant, Arthur M. Schlesinger Jr., personally intervened. The IRS was indignant when the president announced his intention of awarding a tax delinquent the Medal of Freedom, the preeminent civilian award which he had restored. Kennedy, who did not live to present Wilson with his medal, replied that it was awarded for accomplishment, not virtue.

4

Scenes of Writing

New york's claim to being the nation's literary capital was weaker than it had been before the First World War, when Greenwich Village was in bloom, or in the thirties, when Union Square and Astor Place comprised a hotbed of ideology, or farther back in the late 1890s, when Stephen Crane and Frank Norris had briefly blazed and, toward the decade's end, Mark Twain—not only the most famous American writer but also the most recognizable American on the planet—could regularly be seen in his white serge walking up Fifth Avenue, perhaps to dine with his close friend William Dean Howells.[*]

In 1938 *New York Panorama* had ventured that as the "ideological seat" of proletarian literature, New York was perhaps nearer than ever to being the country's literary capital, because of all the great critical fights that had taken place over "literary-social-economic questions." After a lull, it was imagined that, along with left-wing drama, proletarian prose would be due for a revival. Such expectations were not entirely misplaced: beginning with *All My Sons* in 1946, Arthur Miller's problem plays and other less distinguished works in that vein

---

[*] Such was Howells's prestige as author, editor, and publicist, it was said that when he gave up the editing of the *Atlantic Monthly* in Boston to move to New York, the literary capital of the country went with him. *A Hazard of New Fortunes* (1890), which reflects his radicalization by the Haymarket massacre in Chicago, is the first great panoramic novel of New York; significantly, it is set in the publishing milieu.

did forward the political (and familial) preoccupations of the thirties. But for most American writers the particular kind of "literary-social-economic questions," such as the status of proletarian literature, that had been a heated subject of discussion in the cafeterias of City College and Union Square during the Red Decade were as extinct as the quarrel of the Raven and the Whale a century before.

The two most generally admired and influential American writers—the poet and critic T. S. Eliot, the novelist and adventurer Ernest Hemingway—lived abroad (as indeed for many years Twain had done, explaining reasonably, "The United States is fit for many things, but not for living"); both were on more or less remote terms with New York and the American scene in general. Although Eliot, born in St. Louis, Missouri, in 1888, was almost eleven years older than Hemingway (born in Oak Park, Illinois, in 1899), their fame was contemporary: *The Waste Land* came out in 1922, the year before *Three Stories and Ten Poems* was published in Paris by Contact Publishing, introducing Hemingway to the cognoscenti. Eliot had lived in England ever since 1914, when the outbreak of the First World War had caught him there. In the later forties he shared a tenebrous bachelor flat at 19 Carlyle Gardens in London with his friend John Hayward, a crippled bibliophile. It was rumored that he celebrated being awarded the Nobel Prize in 1948 by buying a more powerful lightbulb for his bedroom-study. (It somewhat spoils the story that Eliot happened to be in residence as a fellow at the Institute for Advanced Study at Princeton when the news came, but perhaps he bought the lightbulb when he returned home.)

Hemingway and his fourth wife, the former Mary Welsh, lived on thirteen acres in the country town of San Francisco de Paula, fifteen miles outside Havana, Cuba. The comforts of Finca Vigía (Lookout Farm) included flower and vegetable gardens, an orchard, a swimming pool, a tennis court, a wood-frame guesthouse, a writing tower, and a rambling hilltop villa as well as a staff of ten: "three gardeners, a houseboy, a chauffeur, a Chinese cook, a carpenter, two maids, and a man who tended the fighting cocks." By strict definition Hemingway was not an expatriate like Eliot, who had renounced his American citizenship to become a British subject, and only visited the United States at long intervals. After returning from Paris in 1928, Hemingway had moved to Key West, Florida; he made occasional trips to New York, where he stayed at the Sherry-Netherland and drank at the Stork Club and Toots Shor's, always surrounded by his claque. His friend Leonard Lyons, the gentle gossip columnist of the *New York Post*, faithfully chronicled his movements.

Between them Hemingway and Eliot exercised an ascendancy over the literary life in America that it is now difficult to imagine. If, as maintained by Philip Rahv, who had learned much from his time at the Federal Writers' Project, American literature was divided between the palefaces and the redskins, "and despite occasional efforts at reconciliation no love is lost between them," Hemingway and Eliot were the reigning archetypes. They had succeeded Henry James and Walt Whitman, Melville and Mark Twain: Eliot as the most refined possible paleface, Hemingway as the most vital and instinctive redskin. It hardly mattered that Eliot had boxed at Harvard, that he drank martinis five at a time, adored music halls, comic strips, and the Marx Brothers; or that Hemingway was a morbidly sensitive man and intensely bookish—the author, as Dwight Macdonald wickedly observed later, of the most exquisitely mannered prose since Walter Pater's *Marius the Epicurean*. "One seems to become a myth, a fabulous creature that doesn't exist," Eliot said to a reporter from the *New York Times* after he won the Nobel Prize. "One doesn't feel any different. It isn't that you get any bigger to fit the world, the world gets smaller to fit you. You remain exactly the same."

Younger poets wanted to write like Eliot; younger novelists wanted to *be* Hemingway. People had been striking attitudes after him since the twenties, as Edmund Wilson recalls. "It was the moment of gallantry in heartbreak, grim and nonchalant banter, and heroic dissipation. The great watchword was 'Have a drink'; and in the bars of New York and Paris the young people were getting to talk like Hemingway." Sartre, who considered New York to be "the most conformist city in the world," wrote that in America you must become a success in order to acquire the right to be yourself, to be an individual. "There are individuals in America, just as there are skyscrapers," he explained. "There are Ford and Rockefeller and Hemingway and Roosevelt. They are models and examples." Perhaps it was not essential to their mystique that Hemingway and Eliot never lived in the city which contained the world's greatest concentration of their admirers and emulators, but it does not seem to have hurt.

Papa Hemingway (as he preferred to be addressed by the time he reached his thirties) and Old Possum (as Eliot signed himself in letters to intimate friends) would seem to be striking exceptions to Alfred Kazin's contention that sooner or later almost all major American writers are obliged to come to terms imaginatively with the fact of New York City—as a challenge, a locale and place in the mind and not only as a place to publish books. The settings of Eliot's poetry are Cambridge drawing rooms, the New England coast, the banks of the Mississippi, old English churchyards: a sort of vast historical Interzone where the most prominent landmarks are in London. Hemingway's soldiers, pugilists, deserters, footloose young men, and burnt-out cases are to be found in upstate Michigan, in Paris bars and the South of France, in Spain, Italy, Africa, Key West, and other exotic locales. In the opening pages of *Green Hills of Africa* Hemingway notoriously compared "writers in New York" to "angleworms in a bottle, trying to derive knowledge and nourishment from their own contact and from the bottle."

In *Terrible Honesty* Ann Douglas argues that Hemingway and Eliot *were* engaged with New York; indeed, she refers to the former's "complicated and obsessive relationship" with the city, which, following his biographer James Mellow, she sees as representing to him his "darker side": his affinities with homosexuality, dissolution, and failure, aspects of himself he wanted to write about, not live." Perhaps, but homosexuality is associated with all sorts of milieus in his fiction—most importantly Paris—and in his most ambitious story Harry, the dying novelist, contemplates his failure as a writer and as a man in the shadow of Mount Kilimanjaro. Douglas is on firmer ground when she suggests that "pathologically competitive" Hemingway, sensing the terrain was occupied, conceded New York to F. Scott Fitzgerald in the twenties, subsequently finding "he could and did rule the American metropolis more effectively at a distance." Eliot was no more indifferent to the applause of the metropolis, and more cunning about soliciting it; he too liked what Walter Winchell called "New Yorky" things, like the Marx Brothers, just as Hemingway was a great admirer of Winchell himself, whom he considered to be the greatest newspaperman who ever lived. The fact remains that in the forties neither had ever lived in the city, or written much, if anything, explicitly about it, and in general visited only on business, to deliver a book or celebrate a triumph.

William Faulkner, the third American writer to be awarded the Nobel Prize in the decade after the war, although living at home in Oxford, Mississippi, was more often in the city, and sometimes spent the night on a couch at Random House (then still in the Villard Mansion on Madison Avenue). Once, he says, Bennett Cerf talked to him sternly about becoming so drunk in his hotel room that he fell on a radiator and had to be hospitalized for burns, spoiling his vacation. "But this *is* my vacation," Faulkner replied. In his *Collected Stories*, only one is set in New York City, the unpleasant "Pennsylvania Station," about a thankless young man—the same number he devoted to Los Angeles, which he detested ("Golden Land").

What is striking is how little of their time or literary attention, aside from making business arrangements with their publishers, most of the canonical American writers of the first half of the twentieth century after James and Wharton ever gave to New York City. Willa Cather (though not in her major works), Scott Fitzgerald, during his Plaza Hotel and Great Neck, Long Island, days, which produced *The Great Gatsby*, and Marianne Moore in Brooklyn were conspicuous exceptions rather than the rule. Though within commuting distance of the city, Wallace Stevens and William Carlos Williams kept a distance in New Haven and Rutherford, though Williams was vividly engaged with Greenwich Village bohemia when he was young. "Have you ever noticed that no American writer of any consequence lives in Manhattan?" Mencken once asked. "Dreiser tried it . . . but he finally fled to California."

For at least the previous decade, however, events (politics, sociology) had conspired to disperse rather than to concentrate art and intellect. Between 1935 and 1943, the Federal Writers' Project had given work in their home states to hundreds, and over time thousands, of unemployed published and would-be writers who might otherwise have tried their luck in New York (and possibly starved). Instead they helped to prepare, write, and edit the always useful and sometimes glorious

WPA state and city guides, as well as performing lesser jobs that Bernard DeVoto disparaged as "antiquarian leaf-raking." The Roosevelt administration gave serious consideration in 1940–41 to establishing a Bureau of Fine Arts that would have extended and enlarged the writing and other arts projects of the WPA, and in time might have evolved into a cultural ministry on the European model. (This would have been part of what some historians regard as the abortive Third New Deal, involving a great increase in regional planning and the reorganization of the executive branch, which was incompletely realized.) But the war came, and federal patronage of the arts, including literature, was delayed for another generation and never again resumed with the panache and inventiveness of the New Deal "projects."

On matters of literary opinion, New York still had a decisive say. It spoke in many different voices that did not quite add up to a chorus: besides newspapers, the middlebrow monthlies like *Harper's*, the news-magazines *Time* and *Newsweek*, the weekly journals of opinion like the *New Republic* and the *Nation*, and the quarterlies, most powerfully and conspicuously *Partisan Review*, although the *Hudson Review*, founded in 1946 by a Morgan heir, had an even higher tone.

Partisan Review was founded in 1934 as an official publication of the Communist-sponsored John Reed Club; or as its editors, Philip Rahv and William Phillips, said later, it "emerged from the womb of the depression crying for a proletarian literature and a socialist America." But they were resistant to the Party's attempt to dictate a cultural line (a fidelity that the *New Masses* confused with aesthetic merit on principle), and over the next two years Rahv and Phillips became convinced that such "intellectual vulgarities" were ultimately traceable to the boundless corruption and "totalitarian essence" of Stalinism.

After a confused hiatus and a search for money, *Partisan Review* was relaunched as a highbrow journal devoted to modernism and radicalism in the arts—still avowedly Marxist but anti-Stalinist. By 1946, when the Dial Press brought out *The Partisan Reader*, edited by Phillips and Rahv, it had published stories by Franz Kafka, James T. Farrell, Mary McCarthy, Saul Bellow, Isaac Rosenfeld, James Agee, Lionel Trilling, Paul Goodman, and Delmore Schwartz; poems by Kenneth Fearing,

Kenneth Patchen, Wallace Stevens, E. E. Cummings, Louise Bogan, John Berryman, Horace Gregory, W. H. Auden, Robert Lowell, Karl Shapiro, Allen Tate, William Carlos Williams, Randall Jarrell, and Stephen Spender; "interpretations" by Edmund Wilson, André Gide, Clement Greenberg, T. S. Eliot, John Dewey, and Dwight Macdonald: the richest gathering by any American literary magazine in that period—perhaps by any since the original transcendentalist *Dial*.

Partisan Review, Irving Howe once observed, had a gift for making enemies and the even rarer one of keeping them. To which may be added the quite infectious self-regard on the part of its inner circle. Its six thousand readers on an average year—never more than ten thousand—included a fair proportion of what counted as America's intelligentsia; anyone who considered himself an intellectual would have been very much aware of *Partisan Review* even if he did not read it.

In the forties *PR* was still published in Astor Place, from an office in the old Bible House, which for a long time put the staff of *PR* at comically close quarters to their ex-comrades at the *New Masses* in the same building. It was scant distance, too, from the packed tenements of the Lower East Side, of which, it seemed to William Barrett, writing in *The Truants*, to be an offshoot, "as if the editors in choosing this place were returning to the locale of their forebears." Actually, none of the "new" *PR*'s founding editors in 1937 had direct "forebears" on the Lower East Side. Philip Rahv had emigrated as a boy from the Ukraine, William Phillips grew up in the Bronx, Dwight Macdonald was a child of privilege from the Upper East Side, and Mary McCarthy (Rahv's "girl," as she much later described her qualifications as its theater critic) was from Seattle and recently graduated from Vassar. The forties, however, found most of the principals in Greenwich Village: Rahv in a town house on West Tenth Street, Phillips in an apartment on West Eleventh. *PR*'s literary dictatorship was in setting, style, ambition, atmosphere, and sensibility very much a downtown affair—as yet unacademicized—a kind of long conversation and, especially if Dwight Macdonald was in the room, a loud argument, constantly being renewed at the editors' parties, at editorial conferences, in the Eighth Street and other bookstores, in furnished rooms, cafeterias, bars, and in street-corner exchanges (McCarthy called the art historian Meyer Schapiro "a mouth in search of an ear") by figures like

Schapiro, Greenberg, Barrett, Schwartz, Harold Rosenberg, Lionel Abel, and the Trillings, Lionel and his wife, Diana.

As its fame and transatlantic connections grew, *PR* entertained visiting existentialists (Simone de Beauvoir wondered at their hatred of John Steinbeck) and British mandarins like Cyril Connolly, the editor of *Horizon*, whose bad manners made a vivid impression when he deliberately stubbed out his cigar in a chocolate soufflé prepared by Diana Trilling. The living god T. S. Eliot actually proposed himself for a visit to Dwight Macdonald's house on East Tenth Street to discuss the essays on mass culture Macdonald was publishing in *politics*, the anarchopacifist journal he had established in opposition to *PR*, but then, complaining of backache, he lay down on the couch and fell asleep. (Macdonald was struck by the great man's winning simplicity.) But for all these sightings and increasing access to the great world, *PR*'s circle remained at this time urban provincial. "However intense in its personalities, and however cosmopolitan in its ideas, it was the social life of a sealed-off circle," Barrett recalls, "and it seemed to transpire largely beneath Fourteenth Street. 'Midtown' was for us the name of an alien territory, the haunt of the middlebrows and philistines of the cultural. And carrying this ghettolike mentality with us, we were not likely to widen our circle of acquaintance within that uptown world."

By the forties *PR*'s influence on literary opinion was increasingly exercised in informal alliance (a "School of Letters," Leslie Fiedler says) with the New Critics, a group whose origins were in the South and whose politics were in earlier days (and in some cases much later) professedly reactionary. Having begun at such places as Vanderbilt University in Nashville, Louisiana State University (where the *Southern Review* had been published under Huey Long's patronage), and Kenyon College in Gambier, Ohio, poet-critics like John Crowe Ransom and Allen Tate were busy colonizing university English departments in the north. The New Critics' doctrine of the "verbal icon," their recoil from history, their intense focus on metaphor and professed unconcern with "intention" or "affect" had little enough to do with the "Marxian" criticism practiced, for example, by Rahv.

Both groups, the future New Critics in the 1920s and the Parti-

sans in the thirties, had started out on the margins of American society, but on opposite margins, and with opposed aesthetic agendas and
political commitments. While *PR* professed radicalism in politics and
the arts, Ransom and Tate, Robert Penn Warren and Cleanth Brooks
(who coedited the ubiquitous college textbook *Understanding Poetry* in
1938) were "Fugitives" and "Agrarians," espousing hierarchy, formal-
ism, regionalism, and the Lost Cause. They had wished to escape the
industrial society that the Partisans had once wished to revolutionize:
in their collective manifesto, *I'll Take My Stand* (1930), Warren argued
that Negroes would be terribly damaged if they ever attained social
equality with whites.

Up close the association must have looked more like a mésalliance
to those involved. Even with the changes that time brought (Warren
recanted his racial bigotry, for example), the Southerners remained
"Tory Formalists," while New York continued to think of itself as an
avant-garde. William Barrett in a 1946 essay in *PR* denounced a supposed middlebrow conspiracy against modernism: the enemy camp
included "tweedy professors of English," "Book-of-the-Month Club
businessmen," and "the nostalgic fantasists of Americana." Tenure-
bound, the New Critics considered pedagogy an important part of
their mission and sponsored the fashion of "close reading" of approved
texts. The New York Intellectuals (as a then very young Irving Howe
would later call them) deplored intellect's institutionalization and
viewed the university with keen reserve even when they found a place
within it. In his essay "The Teaching of Literature," Lionel Trilling,
the group's leading academician, admitted as late as the sixties: "I know
pedagogy is a depressing subject to all persons of sensibility."

But the times and their own ambitions threw them together. They
published one another in their quarterlies and swarmed to the same
symposiums. Rahv, Trilling, Delmore Schwartz, Isaac Rosenfeld, Paul
Goodman, and William Barrett were published in *Kenyon Review*. John
Crowe Ransom and Allen Tate appeared in *PR*. By the fifties—Allen
Ginsberg's *Howl* would shake the milieu—it seemed to outliers like the
Beats and the Black Mountain poets that the ex-Trotskyist Partisans
and the recusant Fugitives had conspired to impose a stifling critical
orthodoxy. In San Francisco Kenneth Rexroth maintained that poetry
flourished in proportion to its distance from Astor Place or Kenyon
College.

What would have amazed the *PR* group about 1945 was how quickly and decisively most of them would be conscripted into the university, where the former Fugitives were already dug in. In sentimental ways their assumed environment would always be a kind of higher Grub Street, in which (once they had ceased to think of themselves as Marxist revolutionists) the independent radical journalist like Edmund Wilson, rather than a tenured scholar, was the ideal type. "Without a Ph.D. I had no hope of finding the skimpiest instructorship in a university," Irving Howe writes, adding poignantly, "and who, in those years, wanted that sort of job anyway, who so much as even thought of it? Imagine being locked away in some drab university town, swallowing martinis with waspish English professors and 'teaching' Emerson's essays to bored lunkheads?" But when the great enemy of talent, *Time* magazine, offered him a job as a reviewer, Philip Rahv, the "Commander of Partisans," advised him that it was better to do dirty work for one boss who paid well than a dozen who paid ill. He was soon tenured at Brandeis and a distinguished visiting professor at Stanford.

For reasons of economy or fashion (or both) many writers had been rusticating themselves, moving to Connecticut, or Bucks County, Pennsylvania, or remoter places—a trend that Whittaker Chambers ridiculed in *Time* magazine, referring to the "lonely remodeled farmhouses" in which ex–fellow travelers had taken refuge, although he had done the same, buying a working farm in Maryland that he called Cold Friday. But then, "Our metropolitan civilization is not a success," Mumford had declared in 1922, and never saw any reason to alter this judgment, only to repeat it in ever more alarmed tones, from the distance of Amenia, a hundred miles from New York City.

"The United States was born in the country and has moved to the city," Richard Hofstadter writes at the start of *The Age of Reform* (1956), but by the time this book was published most Americans who could afford it were moving to the suburbs; and in this exodus writers and intellectuals—the inheritors of an ancient quarrel with the city—had taken the lead.

But for the time being, in the forties New York intellect was still city-pent, and usually in no great comfort. "When you visited Saul Bellow in his tiny room on Riverside Drive," Alfred Kazin recalls, "you had to stand on the toilet to get a glimpse of the Hudson." In the desperate housing shortage, Kazin was lucky to latch on to an apartment with a studio from Bellow's friend Arthur Lidov, "who had prospered in commercial art" (he drew covers for *Time*), on Pineapple Street in Brooklyn Heights. Brooklyn Heights was a great staging ground for talent just after the war: Norman Mailer began writing *The Naked and the Dead* in his parents' apartment in a converted house at 102 Pierrepont Street, where, as it happened, Arthur Miller had a duplex and was writing *All My Sons* (not, as Mailer recalls, *Death of a Salesman*). "Seeing him get his mail downstairs day after day, the two of us exchanging small talk, I can remember thinking, 'This guy's never going anywhere.' I'm sure he thought the same of me."

PART IV

THAT WINTER—AND THE NEXT

———————

There was a time when New York was everything to me: my mother, my mistress, my Mecca . . .

—HARVEY SWADOS,
Nights in the Gardens of Brooklyn

Mulberry Street in Little Italy, New York, celebrating V-J Day, 1945

I

A Fractious Peace

V-J DAY, AUGUST 14, 1945, in New York City quickly turned into parties all over town and a crowd of two million milling in the vortex of Times Square, strangers embracing, couples just met exchanging fervent kisses, conga lines, bottles being passed, the bright lights restored, flags on Park Avenue, and Mayor La Guardia pleading after a while for some decorum. In New York, as elsewhere as Eric F. Goldman points up in *The Crucial Decade*, "Americans had quite a celebration and, yet, in a way, the celebration never really rang true. People were so gay, so determinedly gay." After a few hours in some places, but two days and two nights in Manhattan, the crowd dispersed, to mixed auguries and with great expectations.

Popular memory of the "good war" long ago erased the thousands of work stoppages, including hate strikes; racial strife in Detroit, Los Angeles, New York, and Philadelphia; labor leader John L. Lewis's brutal duel with Roosevelt, which Truman inherited; the congressional attack on the New Deal; Dewey's Red baiting in the 1944 presidential election. There was no great opposition to the war, but rather a grim determination to see it won, which is why the handful of dissenters were mostly treated indulgently—at least as compared to the long prison sentences, mass repression, and mass deportations of the First World War.

Japan formally surrendered on September 2, 1945. Within the month, notional home-front "solidarity" dissolved into the largest

strike wave in American history, albeit less bitter and revolutionary in temper than that of 1919. A half-million unionized workers,
no longer restrained by no-strike clauses, had walked out of automobile factories, oil refineries, meatpacking factories, and other industries. A futile labor-management conference called in November by
President Truman, including representatives of the AFL, the CIO,
the National Association of Manufacturers, and the national Chamber of Commerce, adjourned in early December without agreeing on
a single recommendation. By January 1946, the number of workers
on strike numbered almost 2.2 million autoworkers, a comparable
number of electrical workers, and 750,000 steelworkers. Altogether,
almost 5 million workers, a tenth of the labor force, would walk off the
job in the course of the year. What the nineteenth-century historian
George Bancroft had called the feud between capitalist and laborer,
"the house of Have and the house of Want," which could not be completely quieted—not even in wartime—had resumed with a vengeance.

The great industrial unions, led by Walter Reuther's United Automobile Workers, were demanding a pay increase on the order of 30
percent in hourly wages; this would compensate for the loss of overtime
pay, as the workweek reverted from the forty-eight hours of wartime to
the previous forty. Union leaders, "the new men of power," as the brilliant young Columbia University sociologist C. Wright Mills called
them, maintained that having prospered so mightily during the war,
big business could easily absorb the cost and still make a decent profit.
Higher wages would mean increased spending, which would translate
into a prosperous nation and a richly deserved increase in the standard of living for American workers. To the contrary, retorted those
represented by the National Association of Manufacturers (NAM),
the Chamber of Commerce, and other business organizations, corporations would be ruined if they agreed to these exorbitant demands,
but they could agree to more reasonable ones only if wartime price
controls were lifted. As the picket lines lengthened, Truman pursued
a wayward course. Publicly supportive of the Office of Price Administration (OPA), he blurted out at a press conference that price controls
in time of peace smacked of "police state methods." Facing an unprecedented housing shortage, he threw out controls on building materials
in October and then reinstated them in December; with the public

impatiently demanding beefsteaks, meat rationing was dropped, reimposed, dropped again. By the end of his first turbulent year, Truman would intervene in a half-dozen major labor disputes, threaten to seize whole industries—the mines, the railroads—and draft their workers. "To err is Truman," said the wits.

The strike wave reached New York City on September 24, 1945, when fifteen thousand elevator operators and building maintenance workers walked off the job, shutting down thousands of businesses, including all those financial enterprises housed in skyscrapers. A sympathy strike by garment workers shut down that industry: a million and a half workers were off the job, either unable or unwilling to work. At issue was whether landlords would abide by contract recommendations drafted by the War Labor Board in Washington, DC. After five days, Governor Dewey intervened, persuading both sides to accept arbitration, which eventually went in the strikers' favor. On October 1, stevedores on the Chelsea docks began a wildcat strike, joined by longshoremen, who for two weeks disregarded orders from their International Longshoremen's Association's president-for-life, Joseph P. Ryan, to return to work.

In February 1946 the city faced a strike by the tugboat men who steered the ocean liners and other big ships into port, but whose more essential work was to keep moving the barges that supplied New Yorkers with coal, fuel oil, and food. (The owners refused to arbitrate.) Declaring it was "the worst threat ever made to the city," Mayor William O'Dwyer waited a week, then began shutting the city down: first lowering thermostats and dimming outdoor advertising lights, then closing schools, stores, museums, amusements, and bars. Policemen stood at the entrances to subway stations, telling would-be passengers to go home. On February 12, the Disaster Control Board was put in charge: an eighteen-hour ban on most uses of electrical power was decreed, gradually bringing the city to a standstill. "Until the strike was settled," said *Time*, "the city was dead."

It was, at least, becalmed, something that neither nature nor war had ever achieved. Reflecting the vagaries of historical witness, the day that *Time* reported as a slow-motion apocalypse—"industrial paralysis"— was a larky urban idyll according to the *New Yorker*. Admitting to "a great deal of nervousness everywhere," "The Talk of the Town" joined up with a smiling, idle crowd which, "armed with infants, cameras, and portable radios, seemed to fill every nook and dingle of Central Park." The weather was fine: "More like May. More like a feast day," a peanut vendor told the *New Yorker*'s omniscient correspondent, who agreed. "We are all equally children excused from our chores. It was indeed, as the vendor had said, a feast day, the feast day of Blessed William the Impatient, and we spent it as if we were under the equivalent not of Martial Law but of Mardi Gras."

On February 14, the tugboat operators agreed to arbitration, but within a week New York was confronted by the prospect of another major strike. Michael J. Quill, disapprovingly described in *Time* as "belligerent, Communist-line boss of the disaffected 110,000 Transport Workers Union, C.I.O.," was threatening a walkout that would shut down subways, elevated railways, streetcars, and bus lines if the city sold back to a private utility the three power plants that employed union workers. "Red Mike," who also served the public as a councilman from the Bronx, had given the city his demand for a two-dollar-a-day raise and exclusive bargaining rights for the city's thirty-two thousand transit workers, with a deadline of midnight the next Tuesday to comply. Once again, "industrial paralysis" seemed to impend. "In desperation, the Disaster Control Board alerted police, combed other city departments for amateurs who could run the trains if ruthless Mike Quill should say strike."

This crisis, too, passed; but the dramatic succession of threatened strikes and real walkouts, of emergency measures and disrupted routines—the darkened marquees in Times Square, the deserted docks, the silent shop floors and inaccessible skyscrapers, the policemen warning people to stay away from the city—all contributed to the "enveloping anxiety felt by millionaires and straphangers, poets and tabloid journalists alike," said *Time*. Like a gigantic seismograph New York registered the shock when miners climbed out of the pits in West Virginia, when a national railroad strike loomed, when telephone operators nationwide walked off the job and pilots on transatlantic flights left their controls. There was no general strike in New York, as there was in Oakland, California, no blackout like Pittsburgh's when the strikers shut down the power stations. But New York was peculiarly vulnerable to labor disruptions, as Joshua B. Freeman points out in *Working-Class New York.* After a century of organizing, there was scarcely a niche in the life of the city that was not unionized. The roll call was "Whitmanesque" in its sweep: every occupational group from transport workers and machinists to barbers and beauty culturists, funeral chauffeurs, screen publicists, sightseeing guides, and seltzer-water workers being represented. "In New York, the breadth and complexity of the labor movement gave it access to multiple pressure points capable of crippling the city."

During the war, blue-collar workers had been lionized in movies, murals, music, and poster art (Ben Shahn's most notably) for providing the muscle essential to victory. Most of the lionizing, however, had been done by government propagandists, left-wing artists, sympathetic Hollywoodians, or the trade-union movement itself. Salaried white-collar workers suspected that the proletarians were indecently prospering at their expense, and as the polls attested, the middle classes remained deeply suspicious of the trade unions, which now numbered 14.5 million workers, and indignant when they began demanding what seemed huge wage increases, upwards of 25 percent; not only their leaders but the rank-and-file of particular unions were suspected, not always wrongly, of consorting with gangsters and sympathizing with Communists.

The wave rolled on, until one day in September there were forty strikes going on in New York, and it was impossible to cross Midtown without being interdicted by a picket line. Twelve thousand mutinous AFL truck drivers, joined in sympathy for another fifteen thousand drivers in New Jersey, threatened to deprive New Yorkers of cigarettes, candy, soap, razor blades, and anything else they ordinarily purchased over the counter; deliveries of food and drugs were promised by the union leaders, but the rank-and-file, which shouted down orders from their chief, Dan Tobin, to get back to work, would not supply chain stores, forcing A&P and Safeway to shut down. Newspapers shrank as the strike cut off supplies of newsprint: Hearst's *Daily Mirror* dropped to eight pages, including two of essential comics. Even the *Daily News,* which had laid in a huge hoard of paper, was forced to drop department-store display advertising, along with the other eight dailies. But then, there was less on offer at Macy's and Gimbels and Saks: a walkout by the United Parcel Service had interrupted deliveries. As *Time* summarized for the benefit of the hinterland: "New Yorkers had suffered since V-J Day from elevator tieups, two tugboat strikes that periled fuel and power supplies . . . a war of nerves over a subway standstill, and now this. They had learned two things: 1) how easily one union can put the brakes on the Big Town; 2) there was nothing they could do about it."

The receding roar of the strike wave continued until 1949, but labor was deprived of some of its most potent weapons, including sympathy strikes and secondary boycotts, by the Taft-Hartley Act, which President Truman publicly denounced as the "slave labor act" but privately approved of. The feud between the houses of Want and Have was less embittered than in the nineteenth century and up to the thirties. The great strike wave of 1946 produced no Haymarket Affair, no Homestead, no Ludlow Massacre; no lynching, no plant occupations, no significant pitched battles with police. But in New York there was still power in a union.

All the more noticeable, then, was how conspicuous consumption and frank privilege were also making *their* comeback. Town cars (discreetly garaged during the war) and fancy dress reappeared. A season of "almost hysterical voracity," vividly evoked in Frederic Prokosch's novel *The Idols of the Cave* (1946), followed the peace: restaurants were thronged, theaters sold out weeks in advance, decent hotel rooms were objects of desire; the would-bes strained against the velvet ropes of El Morocco, the Stork Club, and "21." "In other ways, too, the city's atmosphere was changing. There was a growing stream of returning soldiers and sailors, with the flush of adventures still on them, and a rather ominous glint in their eyes." In counterpart was the "wistful migration" of the wartime exiles and the officers and diplomats of Allied or occupied nations, whose presence had made wartime New York as cosmopolitan as it was ever to be. "An air of nostalgia, of coming disintegration pervaded the European cliques."

As the months lengthened and people looked around, they wondered what had become of the new society, rebuilt on social-democratic lines, that so many had expected after the war, and that did seem to be materializing in England, where Labour ruled. "The Englishman who crosses the Atlantic today is no longer crossing from the Old World to the New," the seasoned America watcher Beverley Nichols said a few years later in *Uncle Samson*, "he is crossing from the New World to the Old . . . Just as Park Avenue is now, in spirit, a million miles from Park Lane, so is Wall Street a million miles from Lombard Street." In New York the people riding in the back of town cars were no longer saying, "Come the revolution . . ."

2

———

New York Observed

WAS NEW YORK ever more of a cynosure for brilliant foreign observers—continental, English, and even Asian—than during and after the war? Not since Tocqueville, Dickens, and Mrs. Trollope had visited in the 1830s and '40s had so much alien intelligence been directed at New York's buildings and manners and the physiognomy of its citizens. Here were the existentialists Sartre, Camus, Beauvoir; the English critics and novelists Cyril Connolly, V. S. Pritchett, Stephen Spender, and J. B. Priestley, who came to see and judge the postwar American scene and sometimes were taken around by such expatriate friends as Christopher Isherwood and W. H. Auden, ex-Englishmen who were going native in, respectively, Los Angeles and New York. (Connolly compared the welcome he got from Auden to that of the town mouse condescending to the country mouse in the Disney cartoon.)

From Middle Europe, the future historian John Lukacs arrived as an unknown "displaced person" of twenty-two in 1946, having fled Budapest under the Soviets. A dockers' strike on the East Coast diverted the Liberty Ship on which he had sailed from Bordeaux to Portland, Maine. Traveling down to the city, he experienced "the surprising and disconcerting impression that so many things in New York *looked* old." The "shattering iron clangor" and catacomb depths of the subway were out of Kafka, not Piranesi; the "steely rows of windows" in office and industrial buildings recalled the "windrows" of Theodore Roosevelt's teeth; the "Wurlitzer sounds and atmosphere" of the streets seemed from 1910 or 1920.

Places familiar from the movies or magazines—the Waldorf Astoria, Rockefeller Center, Fifth Avenue, Wall Street—looked exactly as he had expected, but he felt the people often looked older than their years. Americans clung to outmoded fashions like high-buttoned shoes and steel-rimmed spectacles (restored to fashion by John Lennon in the sixties, now superseded again by horn-rims) or were old-fashioned physical types, like the millionaires with "round Herbert Hoover faces" encountered in the expensive vicinity of the Waldorf. (Their archetype, the ex-president, who looked like Mr. Heinz Tomato of the advertisements, lived in the tower.) Bernard Baruch, the financial and political oracle (self-appointed), somehow resembled the Flatiron Building. Even in summertime American men kept on their hats and undershirts. American women typically wore longer skirts and primmer bathing suits than European women. "There were entire classes of American women who inclined to age more rapidly than their European contemporaries," Lukacs recalls ungallantly. "This had nothing to do with cosmetics or even with their physical circumstances; it had probably much to do with their interior lives"—the failure, perhaps, of youthful dreams that turned fresh-faced girls into middle-aged women before they reached thirty.

Jean-Paul Sartre proposed that the salient fact about New York's social geography was its tremendous linearity, "those endless 'north–south' highways," the avenues, that demarcated the separate worlds of Park, Fifth, Sixth, and Seventh Avenues, and "the No Man's Land of Tenth Avenue." "The space, the great, empty space of the steppes and pampas, flows through New York's arteries like a draught of cold air, separating one side from the other." Beyond the Waldorf Astoria and the handsome facades of "smart" apartment buildings canopied in blue and white, he catches a glimpse of the Third Avenue Elevated, carrying from the Bowery a whiff of old-fashioned poverty. Unchanged in its tawdry essentials since Stephen Crane wrote *An Experiment in Misery* in 1898, the Bowery was a great magnet for philosophical Frenchmen like Sartre, Claude Lévi-Strauss, and Albert Camus, who delighted in the "authenticity" of its flophouses and sleazy entertainments. "Nuit de Bowery," Camus wrote in his travel journal. "Night on

the Bowery, Poverty—and a European wants to say 'Finally, reality.'"
The elevated railroads and a place like the Bowery were "survivals,"
"islands of resistance," which the armies of progress had encircled and
would overwhelm at leisure; though doomed to extinction, they were
America's true monuments. Let it be remembered that there were still
horses drawing ice carts and milk wagons, tenements that Jacob Riis
would have recognized with a shudder, and countless furnished rooms
that might have housed Sister Carrie or Lily Bart on her way down.
One of La Guardia's last campaigns was banning pushcarts and putting grocery vendors into sanitary markets.

Cyril Connolly declared New York "the supreme metropolis of the
present"—one of the most-quoted remarks ever about the city, but
almost never in context. New York, as he said, would be the most beautiful city in the world if one never needed to descend below the fortieth
floor; the light is southern, the vegetation and architecture northern,
the sky the royal-blue velvet of Lisbon or Palermo. "A southern city,
with a southern pullulation of life, yet with a northern winter imposing
a control; the whole Nordic energy and sanity of living crisply enforc-
ing its authority for three of the four seasons on the violet-airy babel
of tongues and races; *this tension gives New York its unique concentration
and makes it the supreme metropolis of the present*" (my italics). This ultra-
modern metropolis to which Connolly pays tribute is not as gone as
the gaslight New York of O. Henry, but it is more than half-vanished:

> [The] glitter of "21," the old-world lethargy of the Lafayette, the
> hazy views of the East River or Central Park over tea in some
> apartment at the magic hour when the concrete icebergs suddenly
> flare up; the impressionist pictures in one house, the exotic trees
> or bamboo furniture in another, the chink of 'old fashioneds' with
> their little glass pestles, the divine glories—Egyptian, Etruscan,
> French—of the Metropolitan Museum, the felicitous contemporary
> assertion of the Museum of Modern Art, the snow, the sea-breezes,
> the late suppers, with the Partisans, the reelings-home down the
> black steam-spitting canyons, the Christmas trees lit up beside the
> liquorice ribbons of cars on Park Avenue, the Gotham Book Mart,
> the shabby coziness of the Village, all go to form an unforgettable
> picture of what a city ought to be: that is, continuously insolent and

alive, a place where one can buy a book or meet a friend at any hour of the day or night . . .

Those secondhand-book stores that stayed open all night, like the one off Washington Square where Connolly bought a first edition of E. E. Cummings at two a.m., are as extinct as the particular fashionable Manhattan into which he was made welcome: a "concrete Capri" and "a noisily masculine society," where wit and wisecracks flowered rather than art.

Another alert British observer, Cecil Beaton, found fashionable New York women to be "hard and awe-inspiring." They had an "Indian elegance" that might be attributable to the rocky ground on which they flourished, displaying "legs, arms and hands of such attenuated grace; wrists and ankles so fine, that they are the most beautiful in the world." In his view, it was the men who fell apart too young in America. "Few men over twenty-five are good-looking; often those most charming college boys with faces fit for a collar 'ad,' concave figures, heavy hands, fox-terrier behinds and disarming smiles, run to seed at a tragically early age, and become grey-haired, bloated and spoilt." The generic American businessman, who was of course the generic American type, had a "foetus face." The photographer suspected that the American's bland features betrayed an empty soul: the man of letters more generously suggested that they masked a tragic sense of life. "Why, after midnight, do so many Americans fight or weep?" he asked. "Almost everyone hates his job. Psychiatrists of all schools are as common as monks in the Theibeid."

Affluent New Yorkers seemed to lack a capacity for relaxation, from which followed the rigors of "leisure time" activities: golf, backgammon, bridge, plays, movies, sports, "culture," not to mention the conspicuous consumption of whiskey and cocktails, which made the hangover one of the perils of the American scene. Cigarette smoke was another, but hardly anyone protested—certainly not Europeans, who smoked as much. From Voisin, the Colony, and Chambord (said to be the costliest restaurant on earth just after the war, with a typical dinner costing as much as twenty-five dollars) to Schrafft's, to Woolworth's and the humblest corner drugstore fountain, everybody smoked—big bankers, laborers, society women, *Partisan Review* intellectuals, movie

stars, ribbon clerks—before, after, and often during meals, adding to
the great pall hanging over New York in the forties; and every meal
was drowned in ice water, which European visitors found extremely
unhealthy.

Like its great singer Walt Whitman ("I am large, I contain multitudes"), New York contradicted itself: its multitude of observers contradicted one another. Was Manhattan remarkably clean, neat, and
decorous, as Cecil Beaton maintained? Sartre was struck by the filth
on the streets, the muddy, discarded newspapers blown by the wind
and the "blackish snow" in winter: "this most modern of cities is also
the dirtiest." At least wherever the grid extended it was impossible to
get lost ("One glance is enough for you to get your bearings; you are
on the East Side, at the corner of 52nd Street and Lexington Avenue").
Beaton retorted it was all too easy to lose one's way: street signs were
few, entrances to the subway obscure, post offices unmarked, public
lavatories invisible or nonexistent. Appurtenances like awnings, which
in England actually signified something (a party, a wedding), in New
York sheltered the entrances to grand hotels and flophouses alike.

Or consider the Automat: "a high point of civilization," according
to Connolly, who was known as a gourmand, extolled for offering an
endless selection of food for nickels and dimes: "strawberries in January, leberwurst on rye bread, a cut off the roast, huge oysters, a shrimp
cocktail, or marshmallow cup-cake." Switching for a moment to an
American observer, the same cuisine was remembered at a distance
of a quarter-century by Elizabeth Hardwick (in the forties, recently
arrived from Lexington, Kentucky) for "its woeful, watery macaroni,
its bready meat loaf, the cubicles of drying sandwiches; mud, glue and
leather, from these textures you made your choice. The miseries of the
deformed diners and their revolting habits; they were necessary, like a
sewer, like the Bowery, Klein's, 14th Street." Thus, we are reminded
that the past is not only another country, where things are done differently, as the novelist L. P. Hartley instructs us—it is also a matter
of taste.

Literally and figuratively, the atmosphere was supercharged: the traffic lights, which even dogs were said to heed, went straight from red
to green. Simone de Beauvoir wrote of "something in New York that

makes sleep useless." And Sartre: "There is the wailing of the wind, the electric shocks I get each time I touch a doorbell or shake a friend's hand, the cockroaches that scoot across my kitchen, the elevators that make me nauseous and the inexhaustible thirst that rages in me from morning till night. New York is a colonial city, an outpost. All the hostility and cruelty of Nature are present in this city, the most prodigious monument man has ever erected to himself."

And yet postwar New York was a quieter and less changeable place than before or since. New Yorkers experienced nothing in these years like the usual incessant building up and tearing down, "the new landmarks crushing the old quite as violent children stamp on snails and caterpillars," as Henry James put it in *The American Scene* (1907). It was quieter after the demolition of the elevated subways, the Els, beginning in 1930 and completed in the fifties.

The United Nations complex (1947–52) and, appropriately for a collectivist age, two giant housing blocks—Metropolitan Insurance's Stuyvesant Town, which Lewis Mumford denounced as "the architecture of the Police State," and the publicly funded Peter Cooper Village—comprised the most important additions to the cityscape in these years. The pace of commercial construction did not become energetic until around 1952, when Gordon Bunshaft's Lever House began the march of glass-walled postwar skyscrapers up Park Avenue in the same year that the United Nations complex was completed. Neither Lever House nor the Seagram Building (1958) contained more than a small fraction of the floor space of the Empire State or the Chrysler Building. It was not until Walter Gropius's Pan Am Building in 1963 that a corporate monument imposed itself on the city like the Jazz Age behemoths or Rockefeller Center (1930–39) as an ensemble. Indeed, it is significant that rather than the Empire State or the Chrysler Building, it was the timeless-seeming, end-of-history architecture of Rockefeller Center—"Egyptian," some said, although Cyril Connolly was reminded of Stonehenge—that seemed the high-rise most emblematic of the city. In the forties, New York was actually scaled down, as many old money-losing buildings of ten or twelve stories were pulled down and replaced with thrifty "taxpayers" of two or three, a sign of diminished expectations applauded by the *New York Times* and by Lewis Mumford in the *New Yorker.*

It was in the forties that New York began defining itself ever more as a constellation of self-contained urban enclaves, "an island of islands." The housing shortage during and after the war, along with rent regulation (imposed by the state in 1947 after the OPA controls lapsed), eventually turning much of the housing market into a lottery, discouraged the old nomadism. Increasingly New Yorkers were apt to hive into particular neighborhoods and stay there. One thinks of Mrs. H. T. Miller in Truman Capote's career-making story "Miriam": "For several years, Mrs. H. T. Miller had lived alone in a pleasant apartment (two rooms with a kitchenette) in a remodeled brownstone. She was a widow: Mr. H. T. Miller had left a reasonable amount of insurance. Her interests were narrow, she had no friends to speak of, and she rarely journeyed farther than the corner grocery store."

New York was showing its age. What old-fashioned relics the skyscrapers of the twenties appeared to a French visitor like Sartre, who had so admired American movies and American jazz, which now seemed to him to have outlived their future! "Far away I see the Empire State or the Chrysler Building reaching vainly toward the sky, and suddenly I think that New York is about to acquire a History and that it already possessed its ruins."

Beneath the aging skyscrapers, most of the built city was still Walt Whitman's "Babylonish brick-kiln," not high but deep, not futuristic but fraying, and grimy beneath the glitter.

In Europe the winter of 1946–47 was the coldest in three hundred years, freezing and threatening to starve victors and vanquished alike; coal and foodstuffs were in shorter supply in London and Paris than during the worst of the war. There was snowfall in Saint-Tropez, and wolves were sighted on the road from Rome to Naples. The era of the Cold War began in a cold season.

New Yorkers were generally sheltered against the cold, but in summer, with home air-conditioning almost as rare as television before 1947, they sweltered in the most intense heat waves that anyone could remember. The eight million made their way to the Roxy, the Capitol, Radio City Music Hall, and the other giant movie palaces that had air-conditioning; or went to Coney Island, Brighton Beach, or Jones Beach, passing amid scenes unchanged since the turn of the century, but that would barely last out the decade: whole families spending the night on tenement roofs, small children wedged together on fire escapes, old people sitting up late on kitchen chairs by the stoop—the lost world that lives on vividly in Alfred Kazin's memoirs and Helen Levitt's photographs.

Truman Capote writes of a particular August day in 1946 when "the heat closed in like a hand over a murder victim's mouth, the city thrashed and twisted." Central Park was like a battlefield, whose "exhausted fatalities lay crumpled in the dead-still shade," as documented by newspaper photographers. "At night, hot weather opens the skull of a city, exposing its brain and its central nerves, which sizzle like the inside of an electric-light bulb."

"On some nights, New York is as hot as Bangkok." The famous opening line of Saul Bellow's *The Victim* (1947) might have been inspired by the heat wave of the preceding year; it is definite that Bellow had never spent a sultry night in Bangkok, but from the next sentence it is obvious that he had read Spengler. "The whole continent seems to have moved from its place and slid nearer the equator, the bitter gray Atlantic to have become green and tropical, and the people, thronging the streets, barbaric fellahin among the stupendous monuments of their mystery, the lights of which, a dazing profusion, climb upward endlessly into the heat of the sky."

3

Soldier's Home

Probably I was in the war.

—NORMAN MAILER,
Barbary Shore (1951)

No ONE SPOKE, as Scott Fitzgerald had done after the First World War, of a generation waking up "to find all Gods dead, all wars fought, all faiths in man shaken." As a group, the veterans of the Second World War had fought, or been prepared to fight, to preserve a way of life which Fascists and Nazis had put in jeopardy and the empire of Japan under direct assault. On V-J Day, the armed forces of the United States, which had numbered fewer than Belgium's five years before, had grown to 11,913,639. How to reassimilate so many millions of soldiers into American society and the economy was a question being pondered by the thoughtful long before the war was over in Europe; it became abruptly more urgent when the war in Asia and the Pacific ended so much sooner than most people expected.

The soldier's homecoming was an event eagerly awaited; repeated twelve million times, it threatened to throw society into a profound crisis. How could their vast numbers be absorbed into the workforce in an economy that was no longer racing to fill military orders—even if all the women in heavy industry quit or were laid off, as mostly they were? The addition of twelve million veterans to the labor force might entirely disrupt the economy, plunging it into uncertainty, perhaps the renewed depression that almost everyone apprehended, and certainly labor strife. Many leftists and liberal New Dealers hoped that veterans might be organized as a powerful progressive force; many conservative politicians were fearful that they would succeed. If times were hard, would the soldier's mood turn resentful, even mutinous? Women's magazines like *McCall's* warned veterans' wives to be prepared for moodiness, which might last for weeks.

Journalists like the *New York Times* political correspondent Anne O'Hare McCormick warned of the need for "psychic reconversion." Writing from Rome in December 1944, McCormick had been struck by how shocked a group of visiting congressmen had been at the hardships of the Italian campaign, to which the GIs had become inured. "There is no getting away from the fact that millions of men in battle zones are leading abnormal lives in an abnormal world that comes in time to seem more normal than the one they have left," she wrote. "War is a long exile in a strange world, and the future of America depends on the mood and spirit in which the exiles return."

Thronged troopships steaming into New York Harbor punctuated that autumn. The *Queen Mary*, which along with Britain's other great ocean liners, the *Queen Elizabeth* and the *Aquitania*, had been converted to American service during the war, delivered 14,526 uniformed Americans into New York Harbor, where they were met by a jubilant crowd of a quarter of a million. "Flags cracked and whipped in the jubilant wind everywhere, and ships' whistles and horns brayed in the huge demented medley of war's end—something furiously sad, angry, mute, and piteous was in the air, something pathetically happy too": so Jack Kerouac recalls such occasions in *The Town and the City*. Later in the fall, as Truman was compelled to scale down the projected rate of discharges in line with available shipping, soldiers' wives, along with their mothers and fathers, organized "Bring Back Daddy" clubs, which besieged the White House with baby booties and buried Congress in letters and telegrams of complaint. The soldiers gave vent to their impatience in massive demonstrations, from Berlin and Tokyo to London, Paris, and the Philippines—an ominous breakdown in discipline which Truman ordered Eisenhower to make his first order of business after his appointment as Army Chief of Staff. "The President worried aloud to his Cabinet that the 'frenzied' rate at which men were being discharged—he estimated about 650 an hour—was turning into a rout: it was 'the disintegration of our armed forces.'" General Lewis B. Hershey, the head of Selective Service, indiscreetly ventured that if too many servicemen threatened to flood the job market, their enlistment could always be extended indefinitely, thus causing another furor.

The dead were coming home too. On October 25, 1946, Meyer Berger reported in *The New York Times* that the bodies of 6,248 Americans had arrived on USS *Joseph V. Connolly*. A single coffin was selected to represent them all in a service in the Sheep Meadow in Central Park after it was carried there in a procession escorted by six thousand past and present servicemen and attended by a crowd of four hundred thousand. In the Sheep Meadow, Protestant, Catholic, and Jewish clergy prayed over the coffin. A band from Fort Jay played "Taps." "In a front row seat, a woman started up. She stretched out her arms and screamed the name 'Johnny.'" Within a few days another death ship with its freight of several thousand coffins arrived at the Port of New York, but this time there was no procession, no service in the park.

Wherever you went, recalls the narrator of Merle Miller's novel *That Winter* (1948), you saw "some of the fourteen million comrades—the word is not yet illegal, is it?—buddies, pals, former brothers-in-arms, easily identifiable, most of them, and not many were any longer wearing discharge buttons." Regardless of how grateful they were to be home, many of them did cling to some totemic vestiges of their former service: a navy sweater or peacoat, a pair of khakis, a webbed belt, making identification easy. "After all, we had—all of us—won the great imperial war, and thanks to us, the whole world was briefly American": Gore Vidal picked up the story fifty years later in *Palimpsest*.

Because fiction was still bringing the news in the forties, novels and short stories about the returning war veteran received much attention. Decently, these could only be written by one of the brotherhood. In the twenties, Edith Wharton—not only old but a woman—scandalized Hemingway and the rest of the "Lost Generation" by presuming to write a novel, *A Son at the Front* (1923), about *their* war. After the Second World War, civilians ceded the territory to such variously promising veteran-writers as Vidal, Vance Bourjaily, Merle Miller, and J. D. Salinger. And Norman Mailer, as he revealed in *Advertisements for Myself*, questioned the idea of writing about a war he had not been part of: "Was I to do the book of the returning veteran when I had lived like a mole writing and rewriting seven hundred pages in those fifteen months?" In *Barbary Shore*, he sidestepped the issue by depriving Mike Lovett of his past: he was "probably in the war." Admirers of *The Naked and the Dead* were deeply disappointed by what looked suspiciously like a Marxist allegory, or rather an allegory about Marxism, set in a Brooklyn boardinghouse.

Merle Miller's *That Winter*, on the other hand, was the returning-veteran novel that most exactly satisfied standard expectations: it was published in 1948, and immediately, as the novelist Alice Adams remembered many years later, it was the book "we were all reading."

"We all drank too much that winter," says the narrator, "some to forget the neuroses acquired in the war just ended, others in anticipation of those expected from the next, but most of us simply because we liked to drink too much." For a generation, bookish youths had attempted to drink and talk like the characters in Hemingway's novels: Miller's novel flattered them that they had succeeded. The great sodality of ex-soldiers was drifting back into civilian life on a tide of alcohol, all the while exchanging arch, tight-lipped dialogue lifted from Jake Barnes's fishing trip with Bill Gorton in *The Sun Also Rises*. " 'I find I no longer give a damn what's happening in or to the world,' he said. 'Any special reason?' 'Not much. I decided when I got out I'd spend the rest of my life leading the inner life. Hear that inner life is a fine thing.' "

The narrator, Peter Anthony, is a young man from the provinces (Iowa was Miller's home state). He has published a novel, and works at "the news magazine"—i.e., *Time*, the great devourer of talent. To comfort himself, he drinks a lot and is regularly joined in his alcoholic haze by his friends, casual acquaintances, and especially his two housemates in an apartment in Murray Hill, both former enlisted men like himself: Ted Hamilton, a futile rich boy, was a hero in the war (Omaha Beach), but is now bitter, sodden, and missing an arm; and Lew Cole, a young Jewish radio writer who is unhappily aware that anti-Semitism has not merely lingered but flourished as a result of the war.

Life at *Time*: "On the sixth day of the week, most men play, and on the seventh they rest and recover from hangover. But those of us who worked in that Park Avenue model of cold glass, colder steel, and indirect lighting and soundproof offices and two-inch carpets did not play on the sixth day, and we did not rest on the seventh." In other words, *Time* magazine closed on Mondays, so the real work of writing was done on Saturdays and Sundays, tight against deadline: "Each sentence in each of the stories must be polished, terse, brittle, and smart, and perfect for publication in the news magazine but for no other purpose whatsoever."

Referring to such deeply unimaginative and deeply revealing fiction, Paul Fussell asks in *Wartime*: "What did people want to believe in the forties? What struck them as important?" Right off, he notes the huge moral significance attached to the choice of career; this was so to an extent that now appears either laughably naive or priggish—the idea of a calling or "true" vocation now seeming an ancient luxury, like traveling through life with a steamer trunk. *That Winter* was one of a number of popular novels—Fussell names Frederic Wakeman's *The Hucksters*, Helen Haberman's *How About Tomorrow Morning?*, and Herman Wouk's *Aurora Dawn*—that "explore[d] the degree of dishonor attaching to 'the parasitical professions'": advertising, the vending of cosmetics, radio, low journalism, making a living by working for Henry Luce, even selling. (*Death of a Salesman* was the Broadway hit of 1949.)

Nowhere in *That Winter* appear the stoic, purposeful veterans, bursting with the optimism of "the greatest generation" mythologizing, whom memory welcomed home with parades and brass bands. His veterans are at loose ends even when they are fully employed; as a generation they have been maimed by the successive blows of the Depression and the war; many have made marriages they regret and fathered children they did not want. The wife of a sold-out novelist, Martha Westing, the lone sympathetic member of the older generation, remarks to Peter that the enraged, suicidal Ted was "like the rest of you, only more so." What *was* it about his generation? "I tried to explain, but I'm not sure I succeeded," Peter replies. "I talked about all the thousands, the tens of thousands, the millions of us who had been away for a while and had returned. *Without any bands, without any committees of welcome, without banners* [my emphasis]. We hadn't wanted these, we tried to think we hadn't wanted anything; yet we had, and the difficulty was that we didn't know what we wanted, and neither did anybody else. That was the difficulty."

. . .

In his first novel, *The Town and the City*, Jack Kerouac divides himself into four brothers and multiplies his sister, Nin, into three girls to create the saga of the Martin family, whose hometown, "Galloway," is Kerouac's native Lowell, Massachusetts. In later years, Kerouac would disparage his first novel as "conventional," although many of its themes would be with him for the rest of his career, and a number of his trademark phrases are on display, including his fondness for the word "huge" to describe anything from a landmark event to a letter, and the phrase "afternoon of the world." It was written under the spell of his first literary idol, Thomas Wolfe, and mines Wolfe's rhapsodic vein of Americana, alloyed somewhat by the influence of William Saroyan's whimsy, until in the latter sections, set in New York, Kerouac begins to write himself out of Wolfe's shadow. The youngest Martin brother is still a boy when the war, which has "uprooted" the family, ends; the other four play their parts. One is killed in combat; another is in the air force. The brothers of whom we see the most—and between whom Kerouac distributed his wartime experiences—are Francis, a flighty, implicitly homosexual aesthete who is ashamed of his regrettably common family, and Kerouac's more obvious stand-in, Peter, who cannot abide military discipline, stages the nervous breakdown that Kerouac actually suffered, and is medically discharged from the army, as was Kerouac from the navy. Peter, like Kerouac, joins the merchant marine and makes treacherous crossings during the Battle of the Atlantic; he drifts into the hipster circles that are materializing in New York during and after the war.

Kerouac was a great walker in the city, like his lecturer at the New School Alfred Kazin, taking in not only his university and bohemian haunts but also the "dark, somber, ancient part of the city" above Chinatown and the Bowery, where the patriarch, George Martin, who has lost his business gambling, goes to work in a printing press; or at the water's edge, where "the sudden loom" of huge ships' hulls along the East River are "high as though docked at the very curbstones." The obligatory tour of Times Square:

> He looked about him at the people passing by—the same people he
> had seen so many times in other American cities on similar streets:

soldiers, sailors, the panhandlers and drifters, the zoot-suiters, the hoodlums, the young men who washed dishes in cafeterias from coast to coast, the hitch-hikers, the hustlers, the drunks, the battered lonely young Negroes, the twinkling little Chinese, the dark Puerto Ricans, and the varieties of dungareed young Americans in leather jackets who were seamen and mechanics and garagemen everywhere.

It was the same as Scollay Square in Boston, or the Loop in Chicago, or Canal Street in New Orleans, or Curtis Street in Denver, or West Twelfth in Kansas City, or Market Street in San Francisco, or South Main Street in Los Angeles.

The same girls who walked in rhythmic pairs, the occasional whore in purple pumps and red raincoat whose passage down these sidewalks was always so sensational, the sudden garish sight of some incredible homosexual flouncing by with an effeminate greeting to everyone, anyone: "I'm just *so* knocked out, and you *all*, know it, you *mad* things"—and vanishing in a flaunt of hips.

In Harvey Swados's novella *Nights in the Gardens of Brooklyn* (1963), the postwar scene is recalled from the rueful distance of middle age in suburbia—a fate once unimaginable. The unnamed narrator graduated from college in 1943, "a bad year for nostalgia or avowals of future reunions." His brother dies in the fighting in North Africa; he is relieved of his "undergraduate radical platitudes" in Mississippi, England, Normandy; returns home with shrapnel wounds. Released from service, he joyously wanders the "bright and unblasted streets" of New York, wondering that all of the other cities in America had not been "depopulated" now that the young were free to do and to live as they pleased. Miraculously, he finds an apartment on Remsen Street in Brooklyn, when he happens upon the landlady putting out a To Let sign at dawn, and gets a makeshift job as an "enumerator" at the Census Bureau in the Federal Building on Christopher Street. The period detail is deftly handled. Riding the Seventh Avenue subway, he is dazzled by his future bride, Pauline Friede, who happens to be reading *Partisan Review*. "That was what first caught my eye, that and her legs." This was before Dior's New Look, he specifies, noting that her skirt was short and revealing in the approved wartime manner, when short skirts and bright red lipstick were considered patriotic. "That a girl with legs like that would be reading *Partisan*!" He introduces himself by asking what she thinks of the story by Isaac Rosenfeld, thus establishing the intellectual milieu, and almost at once they are a couple, heading out at twilight to dinner in Red Hook, Ridgewood, or East Harlem, ending up in a bar where he sleepily watches the brand-new television and Pauline, who works at a refugee agency, worries over her charges' job losses and diseases.

Visits with her family in the Bronx are a trial because of her small-minded father. He runs a men's furnishings store on Fordham Avenue, fretting when he cannot supply his customers with white shirts, and regaling the young couple with secondhand political opinions that he got from the radio, subjecting them nightly to "Gabriel Heatter, Lowell Thomas, Elmer Davis, Raymond Gram Swing, H. V. Kaltenborn, and Drew Pearson" and readings of his letters to *Reader's Digest* and the *New York Post*. Thank God for his own flat, the narrator thinks, since otherwise he and Pauline would have been reduced, like other unmarried couples, to coupling in the backseats of taxis, balcony seats, a friend's borrowed apartment, or else having to deal with censorious hotel keepers obliged in those days to enforce public morals. Lovemaking in Brooklyn would be followed by a dreary, freezing ride on the Woodlawn Express at three o'clock in the morning, since the pretense had to be maintained that they were *not* making love. Soon enough, they are married and living together on Remsen Street.

One night at City Center, where they have gone to see Bernstein conduct the New York City Symphony (they sit in the second balcony, where the teenage girls are screaming " 'Lenny! Lenny!' as though they were at the Paramount"), he is reunited with his best friend from college, Barney Meltzer, who is standing "a head taller than any of the chattering young fairies or serious young couples around him" as they smoke during intermission. A mathematics major with hopes of a Ph.D., Barney cheerfully confesses to being a draft dodger, keeping up his technical deferment with classified work in a research laboratory. "As if he were drawing her from his raglan-sleeved topcoat," Barney produces his "expensive-looking and enormously self-possessed" girlfriend, Cordelia Spencer, whose family in Greenwich, degree from

Bennington, and "patina of avant-garde" are a considerable contrast to
the "flat-heeled girl radicals and harpsichord players" he had dated in
college. They all adjourn to the Russian Tea Room, for tea and baklava
("We were rewarded for our extravagance: Marian Anderson sat regally
with S. Hurok only two tables away"), and the four are soon inseparable: rowing in Central Park, bicycling in Prospect Park, clowning
on the Brooklyn Bridge, going to baseball games at Ebbets Field, and
attending Meyer Schapiro's lectures at the New School, relaxing over
PM, dining on a card table on the anchovies, oysters, and Argentine
ham that Barney has shoplifted from Gristedes or Esposito's, pickled
herring in a mason jar from his mother in Flatbush, and canned mul-
ligatawny soup cooked on a hot plate. Can such good times last? "Have
we really earned it, the whole country?" asks Barney.

The narrator's work requires him monthly to check the household,
job status, work hours, and income of a small gallery of New Yorkers: the old Italian woman in Bay Ridge who supports herself sticking
bobby pins into cardboard for a notions store; the wholesale diamond
merchant in River House, "rising every month to greet me punctili-
ously across half an acre of Baluchistan carpeting"; the "Jewish FBI
agent, self-satisfied, but wary," who explained that even the number
of hours he worked was a state secret; the cranky househusband, who
greets him with: "So it's Henry Wallace's stooge again." He develops
a fascination with a lonely old Jewish woman who has outlived her son
and daughter, living alone on welfare in a dreary tenement on a block
slated for demolition on Avenue C: "Cousin Marya," as he thinks of
her, imagining she is possibly a relation of Barney's. One day he arrives
for a visit to find her door padlocked; Marya has been relocated by the
"welfare people." In the abrupt way of New York, they had been sun-
dered "as effectively as though she had indeed died."

The gang dines beneath the hanging sausages at Katz's delicatessen, negotiates the Festival of San Gennaro in Little Italy on the day
when all the radios are tuned to the Lower East Side favorite Rocky
Graziano fighting a title bout with Tony Zale (September 27, 1946, the
first of their three encounters). "We followed the mounting roar from
radio to radio, stand to stand, block to block." Ambition, infidelity, the
prospect of children, a chill in the political climate—these soon put an
end to the idyll. Pauline becomes pregnant, and in that light the flat

on Remsen Street looks impossibly small and shabby, lacking even a kitchen, with just a bathroom tap to rinse out diapers or bottles. Barney is fired from his classified work, possibly because of guilt by association with his friend's youthful radicalism. Dante Brunini, a would-be actor studying with Stella Adler, has joined their circle, and although Dante is no highbrow, he is handsome and purposeful, and "the only one of our crowd who knew enough to wear a knit tie with a plaid shirt." At a mobbed cocktail party where people are talking of "Sartre, Henry Wallace, Chaplin, Le Corbusier, Stravinsky," Dante arrives with Cordelia on his arm, neither bothering to hide their affair. Barney bolts from the room, and a few pages later everyone is marooned in what Swados elsewhere called "the fat and frightened fifties."

Our narrator has prospered with a music and record store, founded on a GI loan: "LP's came out, and I rode the wave of the culture boom. Who could go wrong?" Although they keep in touch, Barney is no longer good company: "not just balding, he is embittered," yet he has a "pleasant enough" wife and children in a big house on Avenue J, "and he has done well—even better than I—as an executive in a toilet supply service owned by a wealthy brother-in-law. Always the brothers-in-law!" Dante Brunini is "Dan Bruno," a television actor, and faithless Cordelia, having gone through him and two husbands, is promoting a sculptor who works in pistons and crankcases. No longer his mother, his mistress, or his Mecca, New York has shed its magic and mystery: as part of his remembered youth, it remains "an internal capital, aflame with romance and infected with disillusion."

As one might suspect, Swados's novella is broadly autobiographical: like the narrator, he was in the war, as a seaman and radio operator in the merchant marine; he lived in Brooklyn Heights with his wife, Bette Beller Swados, began publishing stories and articles, moved—censoriously, it would appear—among "the throng of ambitious decorators and editors and academics on the make" that occupied New York after the war. His sister, Felice, who inducted him into radical politics when he was a teenager, was married to Richard Hofstadter and died of cancer at the age of twenty-nine. C. Wright Mills was his close friend and dedicated his *Sociological Imagination* to "Harvey and Bette." Unusually for one of the New York intellectuals, Swados, who never renounced his radicalism, supported himself for a decade with odd jobs (including one for the Census Bureau), manual labor, and unemployment benefits (far more liberal then than now). His article "Why Resign from the Human Race?," published in *Esquire* in 1959, is said to have helped inspire the Peace Corps, although it must be said that the connection was indirect at best. The sixties found him on the creative-writing circuit, including Sarah Lawrence, the Iowa Writers' Workshop, and San Francisco State, and finally a professorship at the University of Massachusetts Amherst—all a long way from Mecca— before his premature death in 1972, when he was only fifty-two.

It would be an incomplete picture of the soldiers coming home—and, thanks to the GI Bill, going to college—that did not include the perspective of the younger generation soon to be named "silent" (although in literature it was anything but), for whom the returning veterans were neither conquering heroes nor worrisome "social problems" but unwelcome interlopers into *their* college life.

"The truth is, I despised these anxious grown-ups, in their seasoned khaki, with their sticky domestic worries and ugly practical needs," Cynthia Ozick writes in a memoir, "Alfred Chester's Wig," which mostly remembers her tragic friend, but is uncommonly frank about what their likes—teenage aesthetes at Washington Square College, the ex-factory building where the downtown liberal-arts branch of New York University was then housed—thought about the returning heroes. "I felt them to be intruders, or obstacles, or something worse: contaminants. Their massive presence was an affront to literature, to the classical vision, to the purity of awe and reverence, to *mind*. There were so many of them that the unventilated lecture halls, thronged, smelled of old shoes, stale flatulence, boredom. The younger students sprawled or squatted in the aisles while the veterans took mechanical notes in childishly slanted handwriting." They were trespassers, these coarse, pragmatic beneficiaries of the GI Bill, "grave, patient, humorless old men. Some of them actually were old: twenty-seven, thirty-two, even thirty-five."

Her friend Alfred Chester—sixteen to her grown-up seventeen— wore an unpersuasive yellow wig to disguise his baldness; as a result of a childhood disease, he was "a completely hairless boy." They met in the crowded composition course taught by a Mr. Emerson, whose subsequent suicide made him glamorous. Alfred announced himself a writer and had a tropism for bohemia ("a term then still in its flower") and worshipped Truman Capote. Ozick, who lived with her parents in Pelham Bay, was "infatuated with German and Latin"; she had learned about lust from reading about Dido and Aeneas. The inseparable pair spent rainy afternoons—it always seemed to be raining in the spring of 1946—exploring the catacomb depths of the secondhand-book stores that lined Fourth Avenue: "Everywhere those thousands of books had the sewery smell of cellar—repellent, earthen, heart-catching."

Back in class, the doomed Mr. Emerson gave them special assignments, coolly snubbing the veterans, whom he found as lumpish as his prodigies did. If Alfred Chester and Cynthia Ozick, brother and sister in their love of literature, had ventured into Anatole Broyard's little bookstore on Cornelia Street, with its cheerful shelves and cozy stamped-tin ceiling, would they have identified the conspicuously handsome proprietor as belonging to the same cohort, even the same species, as their classmates—"diffident Midwesterners with names like Vernon and Wendell, wretchedly quartered in Long Island Quonset huts" at government expense with their "old-fashioned wives and quantities of babies"? It is doubtful. But Broyard, too, was educating himself with the assistance of the GI Bill, albeit in the rather different atmosphere of the New School, of which he writes, "People went to the New School the way you go to a party. Education was chic and sexy in those days. It was not yet open to the public."

Like everything else in the American scene, the nature of the university was changing in the light of the war. There were anomalous moments: men who had fought at Anzio or in the Ardennes, or who at least were in service during the war, were still obliged to endure the ritual humiliations at the hands of the younger men who guarded access to fraternities, secret societies, school newspapers, and other places to launch a career, particularly in the Ivy League. There was outrage in some quarters when even the wounded were not spared. The veterans in Ozick's memoir are not the young romantics feasting on New York's plenty, as Harvey Swados remembers himself and his friends; not at all the disillusioned drunks of *That Winter;* they have nothing in common—except the war—with the hipsters that Kerouac was consorting with, or with the upper bohemia adorned by a young Gore Vidal. To the eye of a teenager the differences were too subtle to be registered:

"They were too old, too enervated, too indifferent. In the commons I would hear them comparing used cars. They were despoiling my youth."

PART V

THE CITY IN BLACK AND WHITE

As usual in New York, everything is torn down
Before you have had time to care for it.

—JAMES MERRILL,
"An Urban Convalescence"

Like the collector, the photographer is driven by a
passion that, even if it appears to be for the present, is
animated by a sense of the past.

—SUSAN SONTAG, *On Photography*

Montgomery Clift, Kevin McCarthy, and Jack Kerouac (*far right*), with
unidentified companions at the San Remo Café, 93 Macdougal Street at the
corner of Bleecker, a popular hangout in the 1940s and '50s for such poets,
musicians, and theater folk as Allen Ginsberg, Miles Davis, Frank O'Hara,
James Baldwin, Gore Vidal, Julian Beck, and Judith Malina

I N THE LATTER PART of the nineteenth century, the Ninth Ward, making up most of what would become Greenwich Village, was celebrated for its lack of diversity. The Ninth Ward was the "American Ward," in which the descendants of English, Dutch, Scotch-Irish, and other so-called native Americans were predominant. Fewer than a third of its dwellers were foreign-born, as opposed to far higher percentages in other parts of Manhattan, and two-thirds overall by 1900.

"A sprinkling of French and Italians is found within these limits," a writer in *Harper's Magazine* conceded in 1893, "together with the few Irish required for political purposes; and in the vicinity of Carmine Street are scattered some of the tents of the children of Ham. But with these exceptions the population is composed of substantial well-to-do Americans . . . As compared with the corresponding region on the east side—where a score of families may be found packed into a single building, and where even the bad smells have foreign names—this American quarter of New York is a liberal lesson in cleanliness, good citizenship, and self-respect."

The Fifteenth Ward, detached from the Ninth in 1832, and centered on Washington Square Park, was the "Empire Ward." In its mid-century prime it was home to merchant princes, bankers, brokers, doctors, old money, and respectable strivers—the fashionable suburb where Henry James was born in 1843 and set *Washington Square*, his novel of old New York. It offered, as James says in the book, "a kind of established repose which is not of frequent occurrence in other quarters of the long, shrill city." It was, as he says elsewhere, "as if the wine of life had been poured for you, in advance, into some pleasant old punch bowl."[*]

---

* Set a century before, *Washington Square* was adapted on-screen as *The Heiress* (1949), based on the Broadway play, directed by William Wyler, and memorable for Mont-

Stupendous new money made a splash in the punch bowl when Cornelius Vanderbilt, the rough-hewn shipping magnate from Staten Island, moved into the imposing four-story redbrick town house that he had built on Washington Place in 1846. The Commodore, as he was known, who had been a brawler in his youth and barely literate, remained at this address for three fabulously acquisitive decades, during which he launched a fleet of steamships, monopolized overseas transport to San Francisco during the California Gold Rush, averted a panic, built a railroad empire (headquartered at the original Grand Central Depot), bribed legislators if necessary, cheated friends when the opportunity presented itself, and otherwise enlarged a fortune that was estimated at an unheard-of $105 million at the time of his death in 1877.[*] Most of it was piled up when the Commodore had reached old age; or as Gustavus Myers writes in his muckraking *History of the Great American Fortunes* (1915): "Nearly a century of fraud was behind the Astor fortune. The greater part of Cornelius Vanderbilt's wealth was massed together in his last fifteen years." Plutocracy was thus entrenched in the Village in advance of bohemia; but dissidence and brooding eccentricity, in the persons, respectively, of old Tom Paine and doomed Edgar Allan Poe, had already made their mark.

Even after progress had breached what James calls "the grassy waysides of Canal Street," the ancient maze of streets, deriving from Indian trails, cow paths, and country lanes, in the future Village resisted New York's grid. Its handsome brick dwellings further distinguished it as enclave after enclave of brownstone was poured over much of the rest

gomery Clift's ravishing performance as a fortune hunter, complete with "beautifully achieved" "upper class tough boy accent" (Gore Vidal), and the Academy Award–winning musical score by Aaron Copland. Olivia de Havilland costarred and received an Oscar for Best Actress.

[*] His latest and most authoritative biographer, T. J. Stiles, calculates that if, *per impossibile*, it had been possible to liquidate the Commodore's estate at full market value, it would have taken one-ninth of all the dollars in circulation to buy it up; one in twenty if demand deposits in banks are included. By contrast, as of 2008, Bill Gates's $57 billion of net worth accounted for a mere one dollar of every $138 in circulation. See Stiles, *The First Tycoon: The Epic Life of Cornelius Vanderbilt* (New York: Alfred A. Knopf, 2009), 569–70.

of the island. The little bastion of privilege did not include the "green wave" of Irish Catholic immigrants who arrived in the 1840s. Washington Square and the streets to the west and north were subsiding into a genteel backwater when the lower orders renewed their assault in the 1890s. Tenements spread along the Hudson River on the west and on the shabby blocks to the southeast, teeming with Irish and Italians, who by the first decade of the twentieth century had displaced most of the "native" Americans and all but a few of the African-Americans who had been living on Carmine and Gay Streets. It seemed for a moment that the writers and painters of the Mauve Decade who were already infiltrating Washington Square might serve as a bulwark against the immigrant masses. But the newcomers simply swarmed past their rampart, leaving a few tenacious aristocrats entrenched on the north side and a colony of bohemians occupying the south ("Genius Row")," while they were in possession of Sheridan Square.

"By 1910 the transformation of Greenwich Village had been completed," the *WPA Guide to New York City* noted in 1939. "The American Ward had become Ward 9, a foreign ward, leading its life of pushcart, café, fiesta, and bar, its land values as cheap as in nearly any settled section of the city, its people faithful followers of the Roman Catholic Church and of Tammany."

Into the mews and alleyways of Ward 9 the "moderns" of the teens launched *their* colonization, pioneered around the turn of the century, as we have seen, by teachers, lawyers, and settlement-house workers, very often women of advanced opinions, like Crystal Eastman and Inez Milholland, protagonists of the "ethical bohemia" who preceded the aesthetic and cohabited with the political in the years leading up to the First World War. Gertrude Vanderbilt Whitney, the Commodore Vanderbilt's great-grandchild, who had discovered her vocation as a sculptor in Paris and was married to the even more opulent Harry Payne Whitney, moved into a studio in Macdougal Alley in 1907. The Whitney Museum of American Art, which she endowed, was established in an adjoining row of town houses in 1931, after the infant Museum of Modern Art uptown politely but firmly declined the offer of her collection of American paintings and sculptures, including works by John Sloan, George Bellows, Marsden Hartley, Edward Hopper, Stuart Davis, and Maurice Prendergast. The rents below Fourteenth Street were low, and bohemia delighted in the high-ceilinged rooms and marbled fireplaces the gentry had abandoned, as fashion moved northward and the newly moneyed appeared. Though it would never be what it used to be, Greenwich Village developed the mystique that has been periodically renewed ever since, like Brigadoon, the magical Scots village in the 1940s musical, which materializes for a day once a century—more often, if a miracle is required for a curtain.

Fascinated by the politically obsessed and culture-mad Jews of the Lower East Side, the Villagers were incurious about the Irish and the Italians—the locals—with whom they shared the mazy streets: "Already the lines between groups were sharply drawn; there were as yet no big business neighbors, no white-collar workers, no respectable well-to-do drawn here by the love or glamour of the arts. There was only the Villager and Ward Niner, and the former walked from home to Polly's and from Polly's to the Brevoort through a little world of their own." Popular with artists and the politically active, like Sherwood Anderson, Theodore Dreiser, and Emma Goldman, Polly's was owned by the anarchist Polly Holladay. From 1915 to 1919 it was located at 137 Macdougal Street, and then moved to around the corner. The generations of Villagers who drank and dined at Italian restaurants like Bertolotti's and Squarcialupi's were *in* but definitely not *of* the milieu. Unfamiliarity bred contempt; or as the left-leaning sociologist Caroline F. Ware put it in mid-Depression: "To the Villagers the Italians were 'grasping'—to the Italians the Villagers were 'crazy.'" Nothing in the unhappy relation had significantly changed by the forties or even into the fifties, when the waiters at the San Remo sometimes set upon their customers with chairs, and the hipsters called young Italian males "Goths."

Coming after the dissolute twenties, the militant thirties, and a second world war, even newcomers to the Village who were very young and very merry—like the lovers in Edna St. Vincent Millay's "Recuerdo," who go back and forth all night on the ferry—wondered if they had not come too late for the party, or even if they had arrived at the right place.

"It is not too easy for a native of the Village, let alone a visitor, to know whether he is in Bohemia when he enters the neighborhood," William Barrett advised the readers of the *New York Times Magazine* in 1950. The territorial boundaries of the Village had always been disputed; now the temporal ones were looking blurry too. "In comparison with the twenties and thirties, which had definite intellectual climates, the forties seem pretty vague," said Barrett. "'What happened during the Forties?' The older Villagers, when asked, return your question. 'I don't know. Mostly the war, I guess.'"

The indiscriminate nostalgia that made an interminable Broadway hit of *Life with Father* (3,224 performances, lasting more than the length of the war) and a best seller and acclaimed movie of Betty Smith's *A Tree Grows in Brooklyn*—the one set in the 1880s, the other at the turn of the twentieth century—also cast a glow on the decades from 1910 to 1930 when Greenwich Village was "New York's Montmartre." The historian of bohemia, Albert Parry, revisited old haunts, and the ex-radical Max Eastman, who had once been described as so Red that he burned the bushes in Union Square, devoted nearly a thousand pages to telling the story of his life to the age of thirty-five in an autobiography he called *Enjoyment of Living*.

On December 26, 1940, *My Sister Eileen*, the play adapted by Jerome Chodorov and Joseph Fields from Ruth McKenney's short-story collection, directed by George S. Kaufman, and starring Shirley Booth and Jo Ann Sayers, opened at the Biltmore Theater on Broadway, and ran for 864 performances. McKenney, who published her Eileen stories in the *New Yorker*, was a Communist Party member, who wrote a column, "Strictly Personal," for the *New Masses* and considered her proletarian novels, of which *Industrial Valley* (1939) was the most successful, to be her "real" work; she was married to Richard Bransten, a leading reporter at the *Daily Worker*, who came from a prominent family in San Francisco (the Branstens were the "B" in MJB coffee). Chodorov, another Party member, and Fields had made a screwball comedy out of just two of her semi-fictional sketches set in Greenwich Village, where the brainy would-be writer Ruth and the beautiful would-be actress Eileen launch their conquest of New York from a noisome one-room basement apartment on Gay Street, complete with, of course, a zany landlord. Four days before the opening, Eileen McKenney and her husband, the screenwriter and novelist Nathanael West, were killed in an automobile accident a few miles outside of El Centro, California, when West drove their 1939 Ford station wagon through a four-way boulevard stop amid lettuce fields and crashed into another car crossing legally; the author, most recently, of *The Day of the Locust*, was a notoriously careless driver. Kaufman decided it would be pointless to postpone the premiere, and *My Sister Eileen* was a hit. Alexander Trachtenberg, the Communist Party literary functionary, delighted at Ruth McKenney's box-office success, exclaimed at the *Daily Worker*, "She's getting more publicity than Marx and Engels put together."

When George Abbott asked the team of Betty Comden and Adolph Green to write the lyrics for a musical adaptation of the play in 1953, they were glum about the assignment until Leonard Bernstein agreed to write the music. As Green recalled a few years later, "*Eileen* seemed so awfully Thirties-bound, sort of a post-Depression play, full of over-exploited plot lines and passé references. We were discussing it all when suddenly Lenny stands in the doorway. 'The Thirties!' he said. 'My God, those were the years! The excitement there was around! The political awareness! The optimism! Franklin Delano! Fiorello! Real personalities! And the wonderful fashions. Glorious! Hey, and the songs! What beat! Remember the songs?' And he rushed to the piano and began to belt out five nostalgic hits."

Wonderful Town, starring a droll Rosalind Russell as Ruth, opened in February 1953 and played to packed houses for 559 performances. Even the Red hunters of the day (led by the Broadway columnist Ed Sullivan) could not prevail against its charms, although Bernstein had been named, or rather, pictured as a Communist dupe by *Life* magazine as far back as the Waldorf Conference of 1949, and Chodorov (who, along with Fields, wrote the musical's book), was blacklisted in Hollywood after he was denounced as a Communist by Jerome Robbins (and other informers) before the House Un-American Activities Committee. (Chodorov and Fields continued to flourish on Broadway, with another musical and a play running simultaneously in 1954.) On the other side of the barricades, McKenney and Bransten, who had been enjoying a prosperous season writing comedies in Hollywood, were expelled from the Communist Party in 1946, accused of "ultra-leftism." During the McCarthy era, they moved abroad and turned to travel writing. McKenney wrote a fictionalized memoir, *Love Story*

(1950), which deals with unregretful wit about their days in the Party, although she did not spare her ex-comrades for their personal foibles; in every way it is the opposite number to Whittaker Chambers's somber, self-dramatizing *Witness*. Bransten committed suicide in 1955. Writing close to the "facts," Christina Stead, the author of *The Man Who Loved Children*, who knew the milieu firsthand, based her last novel, *I'm Dying Laughing: The Humourist*, published posthumously in 1986, on the couple, of whom she said unsparingly, "At the same time they wanted to be on the side of the angels, good Communists, good people, and also to be very rich. Well, of course . . . they came to a bad end." But in *My Sister Eileen* the Village found its most revivable version, on stage, on radio, on screen, and on stage again and again.

In the forties, Greenwich Village, or so it seemed to foreign visitors, maintained a distance from the rest of the city, resembling some misplaced quarter of Paris or London. The poet Stephen Spender, who often visited Wystan Auden at his untidy apartment on Cornelia Street, recalls in his autobiography *World Within World* (1951) that his friend was living in "Greenwich Village, that part of New York which seems an outpost of yellowing stuccoed London, where the streets have names and not numbers." Once, staying overnight, Spender incautiously parted the curtains that Auden habitually kept shut, "with the result that they fell clattering to the ground. Auden, who had been asleep, woke up, and groaned: 'You idiot! Why did you draw them? No one ever draws them. In any case there's no daylight in New York.'"

But of course there was brilliant daylight, reflected off the two rivers, and everybody walked a lot. Where history and fashion have rearranged the landscape, the camera eye has preserved the light of their days.

Berenice Abbott's Village in the City

H OW BEAUTIFULLY SOMBER and ghostly are the streets and the storefronts, the vistas, and—most of the time—the Villagers, in Berenice Abbott's *Greenwich Village, Today and Yesterday.* Photographed in the winter of 1948, published by Harper & Brothers in 1949, with a text by Henry Wysham Lanier, *Greenwich Village* is the haunting palinode to *Changing New York,* Abbott's great 1930s documentary of the city she called "the most phenomenal human gesture ever made."

A brave venture to capture time when the future was vertiginously pressing against the present and literally casting into shadow the past, as skyscrapers piled up behind frayed docks and tenements fringed by clotheslines, *Changing New York,* which occupied Abbott for ten years and was completed under the aegis of the New Deal's Federal Art Project, is one of the essential works of a time and place in which documentary photography attained a central role in American culture, unprecedented then and equaled since only in the 1960s.

Other photographers might have looked as deeply into various facets of the New York panorama in the thirties, but nobody else captured the immense physical fact of it from as many angles as Abbott: the tremendous Pisgah view of Manhattan at night seen from the Empire State Building; sublime perspectives and homely doorways; brownstones eclipsed by skyscrapers; vast ocean liners heading out to sea; innumerable densely lettered storefronts; the view from under the El and above Wall Street; the lonely crowd in Midtown; shivering hoboes on Coenties Slip.* Like her great French exemplar Eugène Atget, Abbott disdained familiar monuments, such as the Empire State Building, or City Hall, which she regarded as a "silly building"; but she had a fondness for soon-to-be-lost architectural wonders like the old City Hall Post Office—a glorious Second Empire–style monstrosity for which the city had staged an architectural competition and then taken the best features from fifteen different plans.

"I took this early in the evening; there was only one time of year to take it, shortly before Christmas": Abbott's "comment" on "Nightview" (taken from the top of the Empire State Building) captures briskly the common sense and sensibility behind her camera eye.

> I started at about 4:30 p.m. and didn't have much time . . . This was a fifteen-minute exposure and I'm surprised the negative is as sharp as it is because these big buildings do sway a bit. I knew I had no opportunity to make multiple exposures because the lights would start to go out shortly after 5 p.m. when the people began to go home, and so it had to be correct on the first try. In this case I was at a window, not at the top of the building; there would have been too much wind outside. It was, of course, hard to get permission. They always thought you wanted to commit suicide and superintendents were always tired, lazy and annoyed. They usually had to be bribed.

She arrived in Greenwich Village from Springfield, Ohio, in 1918, "in the midst of a blizzard and an epidemic of the Spanish flu"—a dropout from Ohio State University with bobbed hair and dreams of becoming a journalist, whose only connection with the city, which at first quite overwhelmed her, was a hometown friend named Sue Jenkins,

---

* "Many of these dispossessed individuals ended up trying to drown themselves in desperation; today Abbott's prophetic and visionary images are a sad reminder of the homeless populations in the big cities of our industrialized world," writes Samuel Fuller in the photo-essay *New York in the 1930s* (Paris: Editions Hazan, 1997), 20. The director of *Underworld USA* and *Shock Corridor* started out as a copy boy at Hearst's *Journal* and graduated to a teenaged police reporter at the *Evening Graphic*, "the finest paper I have ever known," he said fondly of the most lurid tabloid of all. (14)

who had paid her train fare. Her first night in town Jenkins took her to a bar at West Fourth Street and Sixth Avenue called the Golden Swan—more familiarly, the Hell Hole—where Eugene O'Neill, Edna St. Vincent Millay, and Hippolyte Havel happened to be; always susceptible to ingenuous beauty, Havel, a waiter at Polly's, "adopted" her. Soon he had presented her with two other "surrogate fathers": Sadakichi Hartmann, the "king of bohemia," and O'Neill's friend the lice-ridden philosophical anarchist Terry Carlin, destined, like Havel, to be forever a character in *The Iceman Cometh*.

According to plan, Bernice (as she spelled her name then) moved into the apartment on Macdougal Street above the Provincetown Playhouse where Jenkins was living with her fiancé, James Light, a graduate of Ohio State University with a scholarship at Columbia, who had already joined the troupe as a carpenter and occasional bit actor. (In the twenties, finding his métier, he directed the premieres of *The Emperor Jones* and other plays by O'Neill.) Abbott followed her friends to a larger apartment at 91 Greenwich Avenue, which was shared by the recently demobilized Malcolm Cowley; his friend Kenneth Burke, the future critic; and Djuna Barnes, the future sacred monster. It was the first winter after the war, Cowley recalled in *Exile's Return*, and everyone was poor. "The streets outside were those of Glenn Coleman's early paintings: low red-brick early nineteenth-century houses, crazy doorways, sidewalks covered with black snow and, in the foreground, an old woman bending under a sack of rags."

Amid such chilly scenes of winter strode Baroness Elsa von Freytag-Loringhoven, who became Abbott's idol: "The Baroness was like Jesus Christ and Shakespeare all rolled into one and perhaps she was the most influential person to me in the early part of my life." Although she did not shave her skull and paint it green or get herself arrested for indecency like the baroness, Abbott was confirmed in her own independent ways as she entered and dropped out of Columbia University in a week, abandoned dreams of journalism for theater design and sculpture, and supported herself with odd jobs: modeling, waitressing, yarn spinning. She was cast in a small role in O'Neill's *The Moon of the Caribbees*, and almost died when she and everyone else in the cast of another Provincetown production came down with the flu during rehearsals.

In 1921, joining her generation's pilgrimage, Abbott sailed to Europe, where she studied sculpture and drawing in Paris and Berlin, and later published poems in *transition* (as "Berenice" Abbott, having adopted the French spelling at Djuna Barnes's instigation), took on more odd jobs, and, by fall 1923, was on very thin ice financially. In Paris she became reacquainted with Man Ray, a friend from New York, who, among his other pursuits, had established himself as the portrait photographer of the avant-garde—"the Crowd"—with sitters that included Stein, Joyce, Léger; when he complained to Abbott about his assistant, a young man he considered a tiresome know-it-all, she breezily proposed herself as a replacement—though she knew nothing at all about photography. Ray had to concede her logic, and Abbott went to work in the upstairs darkroom of his studio at 15 rue Campagne Première, which he shared, turbulently, with his mistress, Kiki of Montparnasse. "I slaved for Man Ray, but I was glad to do it. I was very glad to have the experience."

While she was still working as Ray's assistant, Abbott began doing portrait photography of her own, and without too much mutual discomfort came to share the patronage of "the Crowd" (she charged less). Jean Cocteau (aiming a pistol at the camera), James Joyce, André Gide, Marie Laurencin became her subjects; their portraits joined Ray's on the walls of Shakespeare and Co. Most famous are those of Joyce—dandyish in a white suit and striped shirt, wearing a piratical black eye patch in one, pensive in cloak and peaked hat and dandling a cane in another; for once, the word "iconic" is justified. She worked out of a studio on the rue du Bac, which she rented and equipped with the help of Peggy Guggenheim and other benefactors, including the novelist Robert McAlmon, whom she considered to be a much solider character than did most people. (Hemingway, referring to McAlmon's marriage of convenience to the heiress-poet Bryher, called him "Robert McAlimony.")

"I had a lot of friends who just took me at face value," Abbott told her biographer Hank O'Neal; "a crazy kid, a crazy American kid. I had little money and I didn't care." Besides photography, her main interests, or favorite recreations, were "reading—Joyce was her favorite; movies—for her Charlie Chaplin and Buster Keaton reigned supreme; and dancing—in which, as far as she was concerned, *she* reigned supreme."

. . .

Not only did she discover her vocation in Man Ray's atelier, Berenice Abbott found an aesthetic and a cause in the photography of Eugène Atget. The former occurred only after she had mastered developing, printing, and mounting; the latter, in an instant of life-changing illumination one day in 1925 when she happened upon Ray's cache of the photographs that Atget sold as "DOCUMENTS POUR ARTISTES." "Their direct and humble qualities touched a documentary nerve in her: 'There was a sudden flash of recognition,' she remembered, 'the real world, seen with wonder and surprise, was mirrored in each print.'"

Since the 1890s, Atget had set out at dawn to photograph "Old Paris" in the early hours when the streets were empty, using a hooded antique of a camera incapable of registering movement except as a blur, and with results so intensely prosaic as to verge on the miraculous and uncanny; indeed, although his aims and procedures were quite the opposite of those of a modernist trickster like Ray, Atget's work was taken up by the avant-garde.* At seventy-five he professed to be "only an amateur," not an artist. Thus, his works were "documents and nothing else," and although Man Ray persuaded him to contribute four images to André Breton's *La Révolution surréaliste*, he insisted that they be anonymous. Almost all of his "documentation" of the old, prerevolutionary city was done by 1920, when the government purchased a huge cache for the Bibliothèque nationale. In the years that remained, the old man was free to divert himself with "circuses, trees, signs, ragpickers, small tradesman"—to name a few of the meticulous files and albums he kept, like any professional. Abbott befriended Atget, whom she discovered was living only a couple of blocks away, and alone since the death of his mistress of thirty years. She did his portrait, somewhat disappointed that he dressed in a suit and overcoat for the occasion

---

* Walter Benjamin notes in his "Little History of Photography" (1931) that "Berenice Abbott from New York" had collected Atget's "oeuvre of more than 4,000 photographs," from which Camille Recht had published a selection. "Indeed," he writes, "Atget's Paris photos are the forerunners of Surrealist photography—an advance party of the only really broad column Surrealism managed to set in motion." In Benjamin, *Selected Writings*, vol. 2, 1927–1934, trans. Rodney Livingston "and others" (Cambridge, MA, and London: Belknap Press of Harvard University Press, 1999), 518.

rather than in his work clothes, but pleased with his frank and haggard expression, and was running up the stairs to his rooms with the prints from their session when the concierge told her that he had died. The sign advertising "DOCUMENTS" had already been removed from his door.

Another young American in Paris who admired Atget was Julien Levy, a recent Harvard graduate and budding collector, whose father built and owned apartment buildings on Park Avenue and Central Park West. Levy traveled to Paris with his friend Marcel Duchamp in 1927 and spent a few lively months staying at the Hôtel Istria, next door to Man Ray's studio, during which he met and married Mina Loy's daughter Joella. Mina Loy was a bohemian painter, poet, and actress who was an early part of Gertrude Stein's salon in Paris and later belonged to Mabel Dodge Luhan's salon at the Villa Curonia in Arcetri. Learning of Atget from Breton's magazine, he was delighted when Ray advised him that "the eccentric old photographer" welcomed visitors. In *Memoir of an Art Gallery* (1977), Levy recalls making "dozens of visits" to Atget's "small, bare, crowded lodgings," and buying an "innumerable number of prints, which meant dozens of rewarding visits with that extraordinary man." On one of these visits, he claims in his *Memoir*, he introduced Abbott to Atget. Six months later, back in New York, Levy says, he received an urgent telegram from her: ATGET DEAD. MUST SAVE COLLECTION FROM GARBAGE. CONCIERGE WILL SELL FOR ONE THOUSAND DOLLARS. PLEASE SEND. Levy reports that he wired the thousand dollars, which she used to buy the fourteen hundred glass-plate negatives and seventy-four hundred prints in Atget's archive, filling up twenty crates that were shipped to New York in 1929.

Levy's *Memoir*, appearing decades later, when the Lost Generation was settling its accounts, sometimes in a quarrelsome fashion, was bitterly disputed by Abbott. "I never visited Atget with Levy; this is entirely false . . . The contract between us was made on May 2, 1930, some months after the 1929 crash, a year after I had returned to New York with the entire collection. Levy's subsequent claims are either due to a loss of memory or a deliberate lie." The contract gave Levy an interest in the archive in exchange for the contentious thousand dollars.

After Atget's death, Abbott worked zealously to preserve his work

and promote his reputation. *Atget Photographe de Paris*, which she conceived, was published in Paris, Leipzig, and New York in 1930; the
New York edition bore the imprint of Erhard Weyhe's Lexington Avenue bookstore, where Levy was then working: "Unfortunately, it was a
very badly made book, and very few sold." When he opened his gallery
in 1931, one of the first shows was of Abbott's reprints of Atget for ten
dollars. Except for editions, all of Atget's work was reserved: "Berenice
and I were in total agreement: all the originals must go as a complete
collection to a museum." Unfortunately, neither the "Eastman people"
in Rochester, New York, the French Institute, or the Museum of Modern Art was interested at the price of $10,000. "But for photos? After
all!" was the response.

The acclaim for Abbott's portraits at the First Independent Salon of
Photography in Paris in 1928 stole some glory from Man Ray, Nadar,
André Kertész, and Paul Outerbridge, who were also on exhibit; one
critic dizzyingly compared her to Holbein. At length homesick, she
gave a careful reading to the illustrated study *America Comes of Age* by
the French academician André Siegfried. "Yes, I am eager to go back,"
she confessed to a reporter from the *Cleveland Plain Dealer.* "When
I came here seven years ago I ran away. But I guess those who rebel
most against it love it best." In fall 1929 she arrived in New York with
the idea of returning to live there and the plan of finding a publisher
for a book about Atget. However, between various obstacles and distractions, *The World of Atget* would not be published until 1964. On
meeting Alfred Stieglitz—Man Ray's old teacher, whom he revered—
she found him not at all appealing. At an exhibition of Paul Strand,
Stieglitz compromised praise of his confrere with what she considered
niggling criticisms, and pettishly scolded a child who had touched a
photograph; immediately, she dismissed the idea that this was the figure to introduce her idol to America. "I felt there was something negative about the man . . . America had new needs and new results. There
was poetry in our crazy gadgets, our tools, our architecture. They
were our poems, and Hart Crane, perhaps our finest poet, recognized
this. Stieglitz did not recognize it."*

* Time did not improve Abbott's opinion of Stieglitz and what she considered his
"cult"; he was overrated and a continuing bad influence on American photography,

The "immense passion" she conceived at this time for documenting "the whole crazy city" was tempered with the recognition of how fantastically difficult it would be. According to O'Neill, "She was not prepared for New York in 1929 any more than she had been in 1918 as a frightened teenager from Ohio. She looked—and was—overwhelmed; the city appeared to her like one gigantic photograph that needed to be taken."

Abbott returned to Paris only long enough to wind up her affairs, and sailed back to New York with a new hand-held camera in her baggage. (The same roll of film recorded both some parting street scenes of Paris and her first shots of Manhattan.) Working out of a studio in the Hotel des Artistes, she resumed her portrait photography, producing a brilliant mini-gallery of the Jazz Age at the end of its tether: a still-waifish Edna St. Vincent Millay; A'Lelia Walker (heir to her mother's hair-straightening fortune, whose premature death was said by Langston Hughes to mark the end of the Harlem Renaissance); the novelist Elliot Paul; the jazz drummer Buddy Gilmore; Princess Eugénie Murat, granddaughter of the king of Naples anointed by Napoleon. The fat princess frowns at the camera, cigarette in hand, but evidently was up for a good time: "She was responsible for introducing me to Harlem and the dancing at the Savoy." Although her work was featured in *Vanity Fair* and even in the *Saturday Evening Post*, Abbott's portrait photography failed to find a steady clientele; the fifty dollars she charged seemed excessive to fashionable Americans. Her friend Margaret Bourke-White, the staff photographer for Henry Luce's lavish new business magazine, *Fortune*, arranged for her to photograph some of the corporate executives that Luce hero-worshipped. But having worked so successfully with the idols of the avant-garde, Abbott discovered that the tycoons were "disagreeably vain and insecure," and gave up a lucrative assignment.

---

more often admired as an oracle (a false one, needless to say) than critically appraised as an artist, in her opinion. She went after the "superpictorialism" of Stieglitz, Paul Strand, and Edward Steichen at the national conference on photography held by the newly established Aspen Institute for Humanistic Studies in 1951. Speaking on the last day of the event, which was also attended by Minor White, Ansel Adams, Eliot Porter, Ben Shahn, and Dorothea Lange as well as Steichen, she defined "pictorialism" as "essentially the making of pleasant, pretty pictures in the spirit of certain minor painters . . . Photography can never grow up and stand on its own two feet if it imitates primarily some other medium." See O'Neal, 24–25.

. . .

For six years, Abbott was able to spend only one day a week, usually Wednesday, on the project that became *Changing New York*; the others were devoted to teaching photography at the New School and free-lance work. The New-York Historical Society, the Museum of the City of New York, and the Museum of Modern Art were all sympathetic to her plea that the Empire City deserved a more complete and durable photographic record than "poorly produced and inferior photographs of yellowing and decaying newspapers"; but none came forward with a grant. (The Guggenheim Foundation declined to even consider an application, judging *Changing New York* not to be a project of "international" scope.) Hardinge Scholle at the Museum of the City of New York and Philip Johnson at the Museum of Modern Art wrote letters of support and furnished her with lists of their most generous contributors. Abbott mailed personal appeals for private subscriptions to two hundred of the culture lovers, receiving in reply thirty-five rejections: the first, received overnight, was from Rex Cole, the appliance king, the last from one of the Dodge heirs, traveling in the Middle East; along with, she vaguely recalled, a check for fifty dollars from somebody, which was lost. The rest simply ignored her.

In 1934, Abbott moved into an apartment above a restaurant on Commerce Street in Greenwich Village, which she came to share with her companion and artistic partner, the critic Elizabeth McCausland, until the latter's death in 1965. In 1935, as happened for a generation of writers and artists, the Federal Art Project of the WPA became her patron of last resort. Abbott had highly placed supporters in Audrey McMahon, the regional director for New York City, and Holger Cahill, the national director, an old friend from the Village. She was given a salary of $145 a month—handsome by WPA standards—and a staff of five, which permitted her to work in her home studio on Commerce Street. In her application she had written: "To photograph New York City means to seek to catch in the sensitive and delicate photographic emulsion the spirit of the metropolis, while remaining true to its essential fact, its hurrying tempo, its congested streets, the past jostling the present."

By now Abbott was convinced that photography was essentially a realistic and objective medium that should not be manipulated to attempt the effects of painting or theater. Even the most brilliantly staged and lit portrait can fail as a document—"which every photograph should be," she added in a telling parenthesis. Thus, the Atget she idolized was not the unaware experimentalist that some critics have discerned in his late garden photographs but rather the tireless and meticulous documentarian of Old Paris whom she called "the Balzac of the camera." Though comparably encyclopedic, Atget's spectral and history-soaked Paris and Abbott's machine-age Gotham are very different places in their historical consciousness. The former, even as it registers resistless change, compels long perspectives; the latter recognizes only what Frank Kermode calls modernism's "Cubist historiography." Significantly, Atget did not seek out heights, or point his camera sharply upward to emphasize height, as Abbott does repeatedly—for example, by standing in traffic with her 8x10 view camera to photograph the Flatiron Building. Yet, their cities share a haunting sense of vacancy, of being for the moment unoccupied or mysteriously emptied; what Walter Benjamin says of Atget's photographs of Paris is as true of Abbott's of New York: "Remarkably, however, almost all of these pictures are empty ... They are not lonely, merely without mood; the city in these pictures looks cleaned out, like a lodging that has not yet found a new tenant. It is in these achievements that Surrealist photography sets the scene for a salutary estrangement between man and his surroundings." In *Changing New York*, too, the more monumental the subject, the more uncanny the effect, even or especially in the sober sunlight she usually favored, which makes it difficult to remember the frantic getting-and-spending that was actually going on in the skyscraper ziggurats; they might be gigantic mausoleums, seeming to brood on past catastrophes and prophesy extinctions to come. "Abbott's images are obituaries," says Peter Conrad in *The Art of the City*.

A project that was conceived in the last hectic flush of the "New Era" and came to fruition under the New Deal was completed amid the premonitory rumblings of another world war. A selection of ninety-seven of Abbott's city images was published by E. P. Dutton to coincide with the World's Fair in 1939, and a set of 305 prints was exhibited by the

Museum of the City of New York the next year. *Time* magazine, in its now-accustomed role of interpreting Metropolis for the benefit of "America," approved: "Manhattan Island is a stony spine of land occupied by millions of tons of masonry and 800,000 souls. To Europe it is a dream, to itself a business, and to the U.S. at large a cultural gold fish bowl." People coming for the World's Fair and seeing New York for the first time "might remember the work of a woman who has devoted herself for ten years to seeing it, and making her camera see it, as material for history.

"A direct girl"—Abbott was forty-one—"who still talks harsh Ohio, still wears a Left Bank haircut and beret, she confesses to being scared of heights and crowds until she gets her head under the black cloth. Her dizziest shots are nevertheless sharp, hard and sense-making, although her best are meditative portraits of comely, plain buildings, dingy shop fronts, chapfallen facades selected from a vast 19th Century underbrush under Manhattan's skyscrapers."

This is appreciation acute enough that one suspects the fine hand of James Agee, but *Time*'s most eloquent captive writer had temporarily escaped Henry Luce's orbit.

As happens with grand passions, Abbott's for photographing New York did not end happily, despite the praise in *Time*, a spread in *Life*, the museum show, and acclaim by a chorus of eminent New Yorkers, led by Mayor La Guardia. Since her photographs for the FAP were considered "work for hire," she received no royalties for *Changing New York* (whose guidebook format she deplored), and retained no rights to her photographs for the whole project. When Congress slashed funding for the Federal Art Project in 1938, she lost her staff, was demoted and otherwise treated shabbily until she resigned in 1939; all this was not entirely to the dissatisfaction of some of her colleagues in the Project, who resented her being permitted to work so independently.

The FAP turned down her bid to photograph the World's Fair, and an attempt to persuade the city to appoint her New York's official photographer went nowhere. "When *Changing New York* was finished, it was just over," she said later. "I didn't want to sacrifice any more; I didn't want any more agony. The project was not ideal, but perhaps as good as was possible given the circumstances, and if I had had some encouragement I might have gone on, but I did not so it was finished."

About this time she befriended Lewis W. Hine, whose deeply humane documentary photographs had recorded Ellis Island immigrants and weary child laborers at the turn of the century, heroically muscled workers in a mechanical age (*Men at Work*), the construction of the Empire State Building, and, for the WPA, various New Deal projects in the thirties. No bohemian, Hine had studied sociology at the University of Chicago in the 1890s and gone into photography as an adjunct to his teaching at the Ethical Culture School in New York; by 1940, he found himself lacking for work, as Abbott was about to be. Abbott photographed him in a sunny, cluttered room at his house in Hastings-on-Hudson; the man who had hovered a thousand feet above Fifth Avenue in a swinging gondola to photograph the construction of the Empire State Building looks like a superannuated clerk. Abbott and McCausland got him a show at the Riverside Museum in 1939, but that same year he lost the house to a flood, and he died in poverty the next.

"His work was probably never fashionable, but it was particularly unfashionable in the years before his death. The people who found his work most unfashionable were those who gravitated around the various cults and the editors of the magazines who could have offered him employment," Abbott said, also describing her own situation. In the fashion world whose house organs were *Harper's Bazaar* and *Vogue*, their sober civic style, neither sensational nor chic, had no place.

In the twenty years after *Changing New York*, Abbott published two successful camera guides for amateurs—the first such books authored by a photographer of her stature—but her other book proposals, including one for a book of portraits, *Faces of the Twenties*, with a text by Djuna Barnes or Janet Flanner, another for a photographic history of the first half of the twentieth century, failed to interest publishers. With the gallery owner Hudson Walker and the poet Muriel Rukeyser as partners, she opened the House of Photography, where she worked on lighting and camera designs (including a "camera obscura in reverse") that were so far ahead of their time, so radically simple, that she found no commercial takers—quite the contrary, hostility and derision—although she was awarded several patents.

RIGHT Henry Luce (left), the founder of *Time* (with Briton Hadden), *Life*, and *Fortune*, and the editor in chief of all Time Inc. magazines, 1928–1964

LEFT Choreographer George Balanchine with lyricist Lorenz Hart on the Grace Line cruise ship *Santa Paula*, 1938

LEFT Leonard Bernstein, at twenty-five, in 1943, when he was assistant to Artur Rodziński, the conductor of the New York Philharmonic Orchestra. On November 14, Bernstein stood in for the ailing guest conductor, Bruno Walter, at a matinee: his debut at the podium and on CBS Radio became legend.

RIGHT Playwright Arthur Miller, age thirty-four, in 1949; his play *Death of a Salesman* was running on Broadway at the time.

ABOVE The Jamaican-born poet and novelist Claude McKay, a major figure of the Harlem Renaissance, with Max Eastman, with whom he edited *The Liberator*, successor to *The Masses*

LEFT A drawing of 91 Greenwich Avenue in the West Village, where Max Eastman moved *The Masses* in 1913. As a Red socialist weekly journal of art and politics, it featured such Ashcan artists as George Bellows, Stuart Davis, and John Sloan, and writing by Upton Sinclair, Jack London, John Reed, and Dorothy Day.

Truman Capote at twenty-four, photographed by Carl Van Vechten in 1948, the year his novel *Other Voices, Other Rooms* was published, to controversy and acclaim

A view of art patron and saloniste Mabel Dodge's gray sitting room in her apartment at 23 Fifth Avenue, where she entertained Greenwich Village writers, radicals, and artists, including her lover John Reed, Lincoln Steffens, Carl Van Vechten, and Walter Lippmann, as well as the Lower East Side agitator Emma Goldman

Art dealer Julien Levy (left), whose gallery on Fifty-seventh and Madison (1931–49) specialized in surrealism, photography, and avant-garde films, looks on as the fashionable photographer Murray Korman (center) talks to master surrealist Salvador Dalí.

These writers were among the black voices of the 1940s: Ralph Ellison (left), celebrated for his novel *Invisible Man* (1951). Langston Hughes (center), poet, playwright, memoirist, editor, and essayist. Between 1946 and 1949, James Baldwin (right) published his first review in *The Nation*, and his first essay, "Everybody's Protest Novel," in *Partisan Review*.

Berenice Abbott's dramatic shot of the Financial District's rooftops, part of her epic WPA project, *Changing New York* (1935–39)

LEFT Celebrated for his architectural landscapes and magical lighting, Samuel Gottscho captured New York at night with this shot of the newly opened RKO Mayfair on Seventh Avenue and Forty-seventh Street in 1931.

RIGHT Weegee was famous for his black-and-white photographs of low life, street urchins, disasters, and murdered gangsters, as in this image, "Harry Maxwell Shot Dead in a Car," 1941.

ABOVE Dwight Macdonald (front center, with mustache and glasses), one of the founders of the "new" *Partisan Review* in 1937 and editor of his own journal, *Politics* (1943–49), is at the center of this literary gathering in 1947. From left: Bowden Broadwater (Mary McCarthy's husband), Lionel Abel, Elizabeth Hardwick, Miriam Chiaromonte, Nicola Chiaromonte, Mary McCarthy, John Berryman; seated in front: Macdonald and Kevin McCarthy (Mary's brother). In 1949 *Horizon* published Mary's satirical short novel *The Oasis*, in which various figures from *PR* and *Politics*, including Macdonald, put in appearances, usually unflattering.

OPPOSITE, TOP Troops of the U.S. Army's 82nd Airborne Division parade through Washington Square Park, January 12, 1946.
OPPOSITE, BOTTOM Troops of the 20th Armored Division and units of the 9th Army on the SS *John Ericsson* as it nears Pier 84 in Manhattan on the Hudson River, August 6, 1945

"Wasn't that a time!" Henry A. Wallace, as insurgent presidential candidate in 1948, among schoolchildren. In the background Woody Guthrie sings.

Posing before the opening dinner of the Cultural and Scientific Conference for World Peace, March 25, 1949, at the Waldorf-Astoria Hotel (from left to right): the Soviet author and apparatchik Alexander Fadeyev, Norman Mailer, Russian composer Dmitri Shostakovich, Arthur Miller, and Olaf Stapledon, the author of *Last and First Men* and other science-fiction classics

The first secretary of defense, James V. Forrestal (far right) with Kenneth C. Royall, secretary of the army (far left); John L. Sullivan, secretary of the navy; and his future nemesis, Stuart Symington, the first secretary of the air force, March 18, 1948

Legendary CBS broadcasters Edward R. Murrow (left) and Eric Sevareid, who reported the war in Europe, shown here in New York, 1948

Avatars of the Beat Generation, Jack Kerouac (left) and Neal Cassady. In Kerouac's *On the Road*, they appear as Sal Paradise and Dean Moriarty.

Her scientific photography, which she had been pioneering since 1939 (because "we live in a scientific age") got an enormous boost from *Sputnik* in 1957, when educators and publishers rushed to fill the high-school science-textbook gap with the Russians. For a long time, her images taken on the road were unpublished and unknown.

In the early fifties, in exchange for lessons in photography, a young friend, Damon Gadd, drove her from New York to Key West and, doubling back, from Florida to Maine, fulfilling the plan she had conceived on an earlier train trip of photographing the length of Route 1. "The new photographs captured the native character of the small towns and cities along Route 1, revealing the existence of a fundamentally American spirit not found in cosmopolitan New York." As a record of the fantastically jumbled postwar mood and landscape, Abbott's Route 1 photographs belong with those of Andreas Feininger, another great photographer of New York who also went on the road, and Robert Frank's *The Americans*. Her work is severer than theirs: not as scenic as Feininger's, not as sentimental as Frank's can be.

When Abbott proposed an updated *Changing New York* in 1953, no publisher was interested. Thus, *Greenwich Village, Today and Yesterday* turned out to be her last assay at a subject she once expected to be life-long; this time at least she made her own selection of images. Harper & Brothers interspersed thirty-two black-and-white photographs, usually one to a page, with a text by Henry Wysham Lanier, a venerable man of letters whose other books included a history of banking in New York and an "as-told-to" collaboration with a deep-sea diver. Although Abbott was not happy with the imposed partnering, Lanier turned out to be a superb guide; it is possible no one has ever written so knowledgeably about the physical and historical geography of the Village in a comparable space.[*]

---

[*] Since this was written, John Strausbaugh has published *The Village: 400 Years of Beats and Bohemians, Radicals and Rogues—A History of Greenwich Village* (New York: Ecco, 2013), a worthy successor and companion to Lanier's text and Ross Wetzsteon's *Republic of Dreams: Greenwich Village, the American Bohemia, 1910–1960* (New York: Simon & Schuster, 2002): altogether the closest thing to a definitive history of Greenwich Village to its date of publication as can be found.

None of the vast perspectives, dizzying heights, encompassing views of *Changing New York* are to be found in *Greenwich Village*, in which, by contrast, the camera she pointed at Washington Square omits the looming mass of One Fifth Avenue. The panoramic first book has the emptiness of Atget, while the latter shares his uncanny intimacy: both are filled with the same melancholy of things in their vanishing. In *Greenwich Village*, the shadows are dense, the light is hard, the mood solitary, the trees naked, the sky a hazy shade of winter, like the Simon & Garfunkel song. Snow has turned to slush in Patchin Place and on West Fourth near Bank, a "typical Village street with old houses." Washington Square is "a pleasant spot on sunny days," but almost everyone in the sparse crowd by the arch is wearing an overcoat against the cold. The young man contemplating the "tiny triangular book-shop on Seventh Avenue, south," where manuscripts are typed for sixty cents a thousand words ("Carbon Free! Special rate on novels, plays") is dressed in the grown-up's version of the belted tweed jacket worn by the small boy who is watching his bonneted little sister dangling from a drinking fountain; the boy is wearing a man's cast-off wingtip shoes.

In coat, tie, and vest, an old man dines alone on smothered octopus at Joe's Tavern, 230 West Fourth. The self-absorbed bartender and distracted patrons might be the windowless monads in *The Waste Land*; the "Nighthawks" in Hopper's great work, painted a few blocks away, are a study in conviviality by comparison. At the half-empty Grand Ticino, on Thompson Street, recommended by Lanier for its calves' brains in butter, all the customers are old men who do not seem par-ticularly to be enjoying one another's company. The tradesmen and shopkeepers, the gunsmith on Christopher Street; the "birdsmith" on Hudson; the importers of art books on Bleecker—they are all alone, and in the dark.

The darkness surrounds the artists in their solitary callings. Dressed for work in sweater vest and shirtsleeves, the sculptor Isamu Noguchi is posed with a drill in his studio; during the war, he had insisted on being interned for seven months in solidarity with the incarcerated West Coast Japanese. Faithful socialist, master of the Ashcan school, long-ago art editor and illustrator of the "old" *Masses*, proclaimer of the "Republic of Washington Square," John Sloan was in his late seventies when he sat for Abbott in his heavily furnished room at the Chelsea

Hotel; all around are the portraits and nudes for which he abandoned his genre paintings of New York like *McSorley's Bar* and tremendous city images like *Wake of the Ferry*. A handsome old man with wavy white hair, Sloan looks very much the lifelong bohemian in his dark flannel shirt, showing a still-strong profile to the camera. (Recently remarried, he will die within the year.) Edward Hopper, on the other hand, his sometime student at the Art Students League, is dressed like a businessman in a three-piece suit, and stares pensively at the camera in his studio on Washington Square North, where he has lived and worked since 1913 (and would do so until he died in 1967): the impression of sobriety is nicely subverted by a fedora dangling from a stick to his side.

The last image in *Greenwich Village, Today and Yesterday*, is the only one that might be considered surrealist: a stunning carving of an antlered buck deer, flat white, suspended in midair in a designer's show window on Bleecker Street. It is nighttime. The darkness surrounds it.

The deer on Bleecker Street appears like a ghostly afterimage from the deep history of the island, when the hilly, marshy site by the river was a fecund hunting ground and fishery, known to its inhabitants as Sapokanikan, the "Tobacco Plantation," for the fineness of the tobacco it grew. As Henry Wysham Lanier reflects: "The whole region must have been one of the choice upland grounds for those original Villagers, the band of Canarsie Indians who had their settlement by the river, at Sapokanikan, when the white man arrived. Undoubtedly there was many a deer shot, many a wild turkey 'roosted' just about where we stand, along the brook, to nourish squaws and papooses at the wigwams a mile to the west."

Among the earliest settlers in "Noortwyck," as it was called by the Dutch, was a party of African slaves who in the 1640s were freed and given land in the vicinity, including Simon Congo, whose property ran for three blocks along what is now Broadway, and as many on present-day Sixth Avenue. In the eighteenth century an obelisk dedicated to General Wolfe, the "Hero of Quebec," that stood at the junction of Greenwich and Hudson became the destination of fashionable carriages.

There is a great deal of such curious lore in Lanier's text, which takes the form of a walking tour, starting at Union Square and Fifteenth Street, on the southeast corner, where the former Tiffany Building was now occupied by the headquarters of the Amalgamated Clothing Workers of America—a symbolic change in function that Lanier connects with José Ortega y Gasset's *The Revolt of the Masses*, as represented by the rise to national power and prominence of the union's leader Sidney Hillman during the New Deal and the Second World War. On this day, a loudspeaker truck is promoting a favorite liberal cause: "The big horns are pleading, demanding: Give. Give to Israel."

In the Meatpacking District, between Ninth and Tenth Avenues, our guide gazes up at the carcasses whizzing by on trolleys above the sidewalk, and picks his way carefully through the gore left behind. The New York Central freight trains pass by on their elevated viaduct— the future High Line—which is nobody's idea of an amenity in 1948. Approaching the waterfront, he passes the gigantic National Biscuit plant, and comes to the "solid wall" formed by warehouses connected to the Cunard Line piers. The way south, "along what was river bed," leads to some very up-to-date reflections on racketeering on the waterfront, as exposed by Malcolm Johnson in the ultraconservative *New York Sun*: Johnson's twenty-four-part series will become the basis of Budd Schulberg's script for *On the Waterfront*, the 1954 Academy Award–winning movie. The way east, "through a reformed swamp," encompasses the prehistory of Canal Street when it was witness to "incredible flights of ducks and geese; vast flocks of curlews, yellow-legs, jacksnipe, sandpipers and all the host of the mud-dwelling, stilt-legged birds who dropped in and grew fat on the abounding life in this black ooze."

In the forties, Broadway in the Bowery was a dreary stretch of dull commercial buildings where the city's theater district had once been. On the night of November 25, 1864, underground Confederate agents attempted a plan to burn down New York, simultaneously setting fires in hotel rooms across the city using bottles that contained a combination of turpentine, phosphorus, and rosin ("Greek fire") designed to burst into flame when exposed to air. A man named Ashbrook set off a bomb at the LaFarge House and tossed another into the adjoining Winter Garden Theatre. Edwin Booth, who was playing Brutus in

Shakespeare's *Julius Caesar*, coolly averted a panic, and the conspirators were disappointed when the fires were easily put out: they suspected their New York chemist had purposely watered down the Greek fire. Eighty-four years later the theaters and the fashionable hostelries were gone, replaced by humble shops and showrooms of wedding dresses.

In his brisk tour Lanier circumnavigates a square mile out of Manhattan's twenty-two, boasting sixty thousand residents, seven out of ten of them native-born, about the same percentage as in the 1870s, and with more than a hundred houses that were 100 to 150 years old: "more, that is, in this single square mile than in the remaining 3,089 square miles of the greater city."

If the Villagers past and present who most interest him are the writers and the artists who made the Village "a hive of expressive art," yet along the way he pauses to look into the Village's role in the history of industry and technology, such as histories of bohemia typically omit:

Robert Fulton, the inventor of the modern steamboat, set off from the Christopher Street wharf, August 17, 1807, on a demonstration voyage to the upriver estate of his patron, Chancellor Robert Livingston, at Clermont: twenty-four hours back and forth. As professor of fine arts at New York University in 1832, Samuel F. B. Morse abandoned painting to concentrate on the single-line, long-distance electromagnetic telegraph for which over twelve years he developed both a workable apparatus and a transmission code, the once familiar dots and dashes; other scientists converged on telegraphy in Britain and France, but Morse fought for international recognition as its principal inventor. One of those iron-willed nineteenth-century dynamos like Cornelius Vanderbilt, Morse devoted himself to telegraphy only after his vaunting ambitions as a painter were frustrated; and though often hard-pressed for money, he found time to introduce Louis Daguerre's photography to America, while pursuing a controversial sideline as an anti-Catholic pamphleteer. As Marshall McLuhan places him in *Understanding Media*: "Within a year of Daguerre's discovery, Samuel F. B. Morse was taking photographs of his wife and daughter in New York City. Dots for the eye (photograph) and dots for the ear (telegraph) thus met on the top of a skyscraper."

In 1896 the American Mutoscope and Biograph Company—distinguished as the first American company devoted exclusively to the production of motion pictures—began filming in a rooftop studio on lower Broadway (subsequently relocated to a brownstone mansion off Union Square, where it was the first facility to use entirely artificial light, and then to the Bronx). Chief rival to Edison's Vitascope, Biograph produced some of the earliest American fiction movies (as opposed to "actualities," which were dominant until 1903), including the novice work of D. W. Griffith. As late as the twenties, the movie crowd gathered at the Pepper Pot on West Fourth Street. "Lillian and Dorothy Gish, Francis X. Bushman, the beautiful Talmadges, and Beverly Bayne ornamented that favored restaurant regularly; Norma Shearer was hat-check girl." In the late forties, television studios were beginning to be improvised all over town, but Greenwich Village boasted few suitable facilities. One of its most famous appearances on the big screen, in Fritz Lang's *Scarlet Street* (1945), a film noir starring Edward G. Robinson, Joan Bennett, and Dan Duryea, was shot on a sound stage in Hollywood. There were actors like those Abbott posed on the south side of Washington Square; one of them, a young Lucille Ball, said, "The Village is the greatest place in the world."[*]

At the top of Henry Wysham Lanier's pantheon are the writers: "Tom Paine, Irving, Cooper, Poe, Whitman, Melville, Masefield, Eugene O'Neill. All in one century." The James brothers, William Dean Howells, Edith Wharton, Lafcadio Hearn, Edna St. Vincent Millay, Stephen Crane, Willa Cather, O. Henry, Edward Arlington Robinson, Sherwood Anderson, Sinclair Lewis. And perhaps a little farther down Parnassus he mentions Frank Norris, John Dos Passos, Alan Seeger, Maxwell Bodenheim, Carl Van Doren, Albert Payson Terhune, E. B. White, "the blithe McKenney sisters," E. E. Cummings, Fannie Hurst. Among the artists, he lauds Winslow Homer and

---

[*] Quoted in Wetzsteon, *Republic of Dreams*, ix. Ball and her husband and business partner, Desi Arnaz, moved their phenomenally successful television comedy to Hollywood in 1951, and, branching into production of other programs, made such a success that they eventually bought the old RKO studio. RKO had been the most "New Yorky" of the majors, appealing to an urban audience and "sophisticated" tastes. The so-called golden age of live television prolonged New York's brief reign as the new medium's capital.

his friends at the West Tenth Street "studios," including the painter John La Farge and the sculptor Alexander Stirling Calder. The son of a sculptor, Stirling Calder eventually passed his studio on to *his* sculptor son, Alexander (known as Sandy). Augustus Saint-Gaudens ("our supreme manifestation in art thus far") was taking a night class at Cooper Union the year Winslow Homer moved into Washington Square. Albert Pinkham Ryder painted many of his mystical canvases in his room at the Albert Hotel, which his brother, the owner, had named after him; he died in 1917, almost unknown. Boardman Robinson, Stuart Davis, Alexander Archipenko, and the cartoonist Art Young bring the story into the present, although they represented the past. The *Tiger's Eye*, a "little magazine" offered for sale on Bleecker Street, was the house organ of a coterie later to be known as abstract expressionists, and their supporters; but in 1947, like most people, Henry Wysham Lanier knew nothing of that school. His tour concludes with a backward glance to the famous night when John Sloan and his companions (unnamed) declared the independence of Washington Square. Such memories should not be lost! It was between the acts in Greenwich Village, and the season was cold.

2

———

Gottscho's Oz

ABBOTT'S OPPOSITE as an architectural photographer of the city was Samuel H. Gottscho, a great urban romancer who was enjoying well-paying commercial success at the same time that Abbott was either struggling financially or being supported but constrained by government bureaucracy. Where Abbott was midwestern by origin, a Villager by choice, a repatriate with an eye for the city sharpened by years of consorting with the transatlantic avant-garde, Gottscho, a generation older (born in Brooklyn in 1875), was self-taught, a life-long New Yorker who supported himself and his family as a traveling salesman in lace and fine linens until, at fifty, he was able to turn a sideline in real-estate photography into a full-time occupation.

Within a few years he graduated from photographing suburban houses in Queens to commissions for the River House and the San Remo in Manhattan. Gottscho boasted that during the worst of the Depression he could support himself with an annual trip to Palm Beach to photograph the estates of the nouveaux riches; and it might be said there is something of Palm Beach in his photographs of Manhattan. (The venetian-blinded interiors, mirrored walls, and zebra-striped carpets of William S. Paley's town house in Beekman Place could as easily be in one place as the other.)

In 1925, Gottscho did a stunning set of noncommissioned nocturnal photographs of Raymond Hood's American Radiator Building, catching the attention of the architect, who bought the photos and saw that

Gottscho was hired to document his next monument, the McGraw-Hill Building.* Gottscho's work with Hood culminated in his privileged access to the construction of Rockefeller Center. No one has ever photographed Rockefeller Center more ravishingly than Gottscho, but he did so without a hint of the dangerous and exalted labor that went into its construction, such as Lewis W. Hine devoted to the Empire State Building.

In a Jazz Age success story prolonged to the end of the Depression, Gottscho made himself the custodian of Manhattan's alabaster-towered and art-deco-appointed glamour, never allowing a hint of hard times to intrude on his pearlescent skylines, immaculate apartments, gleaming showrooms, glittering theater lobbies, stylish shops, aloof corporate headquarters, majestic branch banks; the whole ensemble enthralling by day, enchanting by night. His machine-age Manhattan is an Artificial Paradise in which all the great engines are kept discreetly out of sight; while, paradoxically, the domestic appliances of the everyday, like the refrigerators in Rex Cole's sumptuous General Electric emporiums, are gleaming objects of desire. (Few other photographers have ever made signage so romantic, as in the giant GE monogram in Cole's showrooms or, less expectedly, the facades of modest Peck & Peck's or Lerner stores in Midtown: there is none of the dense, chaotic enumeration to be found in the neighborhoods of the poor that Abbott found so compelling.) From Gottscho's photographs of Times Square taken in the dead seasons of 1930–32, one would never guess at the desperation of the movie industry (still deep in debt from the conversion to sound, and terrified by competition from radio), or the empty houses of the "legitimate" theaters. Half of Broadway was "dark," but in Gottscho's

---

* Of the first project we are told, "Gottscho was inspired to develop what became his trademark technique of photographing buildings at night using two separate exposures that were combined into one composite image. The first exposure was made at dusk to register the building's ziggurat silhouette against the darkening sky; the second, from the exact same spot but with a longer exposure time, was made later to capture the building's windows blazing with artificial illumination. The resulting images painted a luminous city in a surreal moment, poised between night and day." See Donald Albrecht, Introduction, *The Mythic City: Photographs of New York by Samuel H. Gottscho, 1925–1940* (New York: Museum of the City of New York, 2005), 30. Albrecht is the source for the facts of Gottscho's life and career as stated here, and an invaluable guide to his enchantments.

Times Square district the marquees blaze as confidently as ever. RKO has just opened a "new deluxe theatre," and Constance Bennett is starring in *Sin Takes a Holiday*.

Featured in *Town & Country, House & Garden, American Architect*, and innumerable glossy brochures, Gottscho was included with Abbott, Margaret Bourke-White, and Walker Evans in the Julien Levy Gallery's Photographs of New York by New York Photographers in 1933, and given an exhibition by the Museum of the City of New York in 1937; the venues attested to an appeal that transcended the commercial without ever ceasing to be answerable to it. His *Mythic City* breathes Baudelairean "luxe, calme et volupté." His photographs of the 1939 World's Fair, where again he enjoyed great patronage and access, have the look, not of Tomorrowland, but of a vast timeless Shangri-La; those of the building of the United Nations complex in the forties (again privileged access) are only a conscientious pendant to his inspired work in the thirties. After 1950 he devoted himself, with great distinction, to photographing wildflowers. His *Mythic City* represented a perfected modernism at the antipodes from Abbott's building and decaying, constantly metamorphosing metropolis. It is Oz. As for Greenwich Village, it is off his map. The rents were too low.

3
———

Weegee's Dark Carnival

Changing New York is only a fragmentary realization of Berenice Abbott's "immense dream" of recording the myriad faces of the city. The long-overdue publication of all 305 photographs from the WPA project by the New Press in 1997 only underscored the fact. "There are lots of things I could have taken in the last five years, if I had only had better cameras," she told an interviewer in 1938. "You want to get a crowd of people really protesting something. If you try to get the expression on their faces, you are stuck . . . You want to take a bunch of colored people in a dark corner . . . You want to take a subway rush at five o'clock . . . Suppose you want to catch a seething mass of people from a bus stop."

Exactly why Abbott could not buy the equipment she wanted is unclear; but for lack of a "miniature camera" she did not attempt, as she had proposed, to show "people and the way they live now," from inside their apartments to the protests and election nights in Union Square. Along with an absence of politics there is an absence of crime and punishment and entertainments, grand and small: no cops and no robbers, no precinct houses, no crime scenes, no nightclubs, no nightlife.

Berenice Abbott's night is as sober as her day. The city's wild side was left to a photographer of very different origins and intentions: Arthur H. Fellig, who stamped on the back of his photos: "CREDIT TO WEEGEE THE FAMOUS." Weegee also photographed Greenwich Village in the late 1940s, and then throughout the fifties. Compared to Abbott's wintry ghost town, his Village is a summer festival, messy, indecorous, boozed up, sexy, mostly young, and often undressed. *The Village*, published posthumously in 1989, is an amiable anticlimax to the melodramatic spectacle he made of New York in *Naked City*, the photo book that he published in 1945, in the last days of the war.

With its bloody crime scenes and car crashes, petty criminals, oblivious socialites, lewd women, dead men, transvestites in paddy wagons, glassy-eyed drunks, freaks, tenement fires, race riots, mean streets, and more dead bodies—a landscape of big-city melodrama lit up by the flash of a Speed Graphic and captioned in seen-it-all sentimental-hardboiled three-dot prose—*Naked City* might have provoked what Oscar Wilde called the rage of Caliban at seeing his face in a glass. Instead, Gotham experienced a pleasurable shock of recognition at seeing its crimes, follies, and misfortunes so vividly rendered in inglorious black-and-white. It was, people realized, a peculiar kind of love letter, dedicated (as it was) "To You, the People of New York."

A child of the Lower East Side, proudly coarse-grained and practical ("I only take off my clothes when I have company" was a typical confidence in his autobiography, *Weegee by Weegee*), Arthur Fellig went to school as a freelance photographer selling mayhem and misery to the furiously competitive tabloids. Along with the freewheeling Acme Syndicate, his most reliable customers were Hearst's *Daily Mirror* and its even less discriminating rival the Pattersons' *Daily News*. "Anything went with them, the bloodier and sexier the better." Following the famous frontispiece of lightning striking a topless tower, making darkness visible, the first image in *Naked City* is of bundles of fat Sunday papers on a dark sidewalk outside some still-closed candy store or newsstand. "New Yorkers like their Sunday papers, especially the lonely men and women who live in furnished rooms," wrote Weegee, who lived in one himself.

Naked City ran through six printings between July and December 1945, receiving high praise from *Time* and the *Saturday Review of Literature*, which found it "wise and wonderful," and even from the *New York Times*, which Weegee said he boycotted because it would not print pictures of dead gangsters, "no matter how prominent," and the *Herald*

Tribune, where he was persona non grata for refusing to wear a tie. After a decade of billing himself as "Weegee the Famous," Arthur H. Fellig actually *was* famous.

He was born in 1899 in Austrian Galicia, and came to New York at ten with his mother and brothers to join his father, a pushcart peddler on the Lower East Side who specialized in new dishes for holy days. A pious man, the elder Fellig studied, successfully, to become a rabbi.

Arthur (born Usher) was put in the "greenhorn" class at school until he learned English; though an avid student, when he turned fourteen he demanded his working papers so he could help support his family. "This was the East of the 1920s," as he explained his milieu in *Weegee by Weegee*, "with its Grand Street Playhouse, Henry Street Settlement house, Educational Alliance, music schools, synagogues, and whore-houses. I liked them and attended them all." Inspired when a street photographer took a tintype of him, he bought a mail-order kit and in a few months had found work with a commercial photographer on Grand Street who produced pictures of heavy items for traveling sales-men: brass beds, pianos, tables, and chandeliers; caskets, shrouds, and cemetery stones (photographed "on location") were a specialty. "That place looked more like a morgue than a photo studio," said Weegee, recalling that their best customer, a casket maker, promised "Happi-ness in Every Box." On his own, he rented a pony from a stable, named him Hypo, and took him around the Lower East Side on weekends when the kids were dressed up for church or synagogue, offering a ride and taking their photographs, which he sold to their proud par-ents. The 5x7 glass plates took a week to develop, and the proofs were finished on "the contrastiest paper I could get in order to give the kids nice white, chalky faces. My customers, who were Italian, Polish or Jewish, liked their pictures dead-white." This turned out to be an excellent preparation for the tabloids, which also prized starkness.

Instructive, too, was his first sexual consummation one hot night on the Lower East Side when he was eighteen. "On the roof, it was pitch-black and romantic. Couples were huddled together. Poor people are not fussy about privacy; they have other problems." Never there-after did he have any compunction about invading the privacy of others, poor or prosperous.* He left home; slept rough, eventually finding Pennsylvania Station to be the best place to lie down for the night; worked as a busboy at the Automat; slept in flophouses in the Bowery; punched holes at the Life Savers candy factory; played the violin (his other great passion), which he had studied at the Henry Street Settlement house, at silent movies in converted storefronts. "I suppose my fiddle-playing was a subconscious kind of training for my future photography. In later years, people often told me that my pictures moved them deeply to tears or to laughter."

Working in the darkroom of a passport studio, he was earning a good living of forty dollars a week, which he exchanged for twenty dollars and adventure at Acme Newspictures (later, United Press, or UP), the Scripps-Howard newspaper chain's scrappy rival to the Associated Press's Wirephoto. (He despised the AP's editors for their midwestern dullness.) There he remained for several years, developing other photographers' pictures and starting to place his own with the *World-Telegram* and other papers. It was at Acme that Arthur Fellig was nicknamed "Weegee"; most likely after the squeegee he used in the darkroom rather than the Ouija board, which was the explanation he gave for the nickname after he developed an eerie knack for turning up at photographable crime scenes, sometimes ahead of the police, or even the crime.

Striking out as a freelance in 1935, he virtually took up residence at Manhattan Police Headquarters, "the nerve center of the city I knew." His days began punctually at midnight when the teletype would be "singing a song of crime and violence," which Weegee, riding with the cops, would pursue to its origins: a dead body in the East River; a newborn abandoned in a trash can; well-dressed, just-deceased gangsters found lying in their blood; screaming families being led down the ladder from a burning tenement, clutching babies, dogs, cats, canaries, a pair of snakes in a box. "These were the pictures that I took and sold. It was during the Depression, and people could forget their own troubles

---

* "When criminals tried to cover their faces it was a challenge to me. I literally uncovered not only their faces, but their black souls as well." In *Weegee by Weegee*, the immediate reference is to burglars and gangsters, but similar unveilings, literal or metaphorical, were the lot of gay playboys who had been misbehaving at the Astor Bar, as well as transvestites ("Gay Deceivers").

by reading about others'." Friendly cops taught him to drive, and the NYPD allowed him to equip his brand-new 1938 maroon Chevrolet with a police radio—a privilege he shared with Walter Winchell, with whom he sometimes exchanged tips at the counter of Hanson's all-night drugstore; another police radio was never turned off in his furnished room, undoubtedly accounting for his amazing prescience. His nocturnal vigils instructed Weegee in the city's secret timetable. Midnight was the hour of peeping Toms; one to two a.m., of stickups at delicatessens; two to three a.m., of automobile accidents and fires; at four the bars closed, and the calls reporting burglaries and smashed windows came in. At five in the morning, people who had obsessed all night about their fears and failures began taking "dives" out the window. (Weegee was proud that he never photographed a dive.)

His standard fee was "five bucks for a shot," and although he canvassed the liberal *New York Post*, the venerable *Sun*, and the sporting *World-Telegram*, his most regular customers were always the big tabloids, the *Daily Mirror* and the *Daily News*. "Anything went with them, the bloodier and sexier the better." After a struggle the papers began printing his byline. The gangster syndicate Murder, Inc. supposedly appointed him their "official" photographer, alerting him to upcoming atrocities, and Weegee rewarded them, and his newspaper clients, with memorably ghoulish photographs of bullet-riddled bodies stuffed into baby carriages and steamer trunks. A dead gangster sprawling on the sidewalk beside his fallen gray fedora became so much a signature that editors suspected him of planting the hat. As early as 1937, his work caught the attention of *Life* magazine. In 1940 he went on a roving assignment for Ralph Ingersoll's newly launched *PM*, which, already boasting the reporting of I. F. Stone, the editorials of Max Lerner, the cartoons of Theodor Geisel (the future Dr. Seuss), and the baby advice of Dr. Benjamin Spock, now had the benefit of his lynx's eye for disaster and distress.

In 1941 the Photo League gave him an exhibition, *Murder Is My Business*, which *PM* loyally played up. (Arthur Fellig kept up his association with the leftish Photo League after the war when the Red hunters began closing in, but somehow "Weegee the Famous"—an admirer of FDR, "the greatest man of the twentieth century," but no lefty—escaped the inquisition.) In 1944, he was invited to lecture at the Museum of Modern Art, his formal initiation into the uptown art-and-fashion world, whose rites he sometimes photographed for *PM*. His uptown admirers told him he should publish a book—an idea he seized on when an unprofitable season of quiet descended upon the city. "There was a sudden drop in Murders and Fires (my two best sellers, my bread and butter) . . . but it did give me a chance to look over the pictures I had been accumulating. As I did so I saw there was a pattern."

Publishers were puzzled by the absence of clichés in the "dummy" he circulated: " 'Where's the picture of the sailor in the rowboat in Central Park?' 'Where's the Statue of Liberty?' 'Where's the picture of the Fulton Fish Market?' " Though impatient with such stuff, Weegee had never disdained to include crowd-pleasers like kittens stuffed into firemen's socks strung on a line and rescued dogs being cuddled by policemen, clichés of a different sort which he had staged and sold to the animal-loving *Sun*. Some of the most famous images in *Naked City*, such as *The Critic (Opening Night at the Opera)*, in which a demented-looking crone heckles two bejeweled grandes dames, were stage-managed (Weegee hired the heckler, just as he paid penniless actors to impersonate lovers necking in movie theaters if he was on deadline for such a shot). When *Naked City* was published by Duell, Sloan and Pearce after a determined siege, Weegee cannily declined the usual cocktail party and proposed they celebrate at Sammy's on the Bowery. "We did. Everyone came. Sammy bought a thousand dollars' worth of books, all the food and liquor were on the house, and it was really sensational."*

New York became acquainted with the newly minted celebrity, "a rather portly, cigar-smoking, irregularly shaven man," William McCleery, his editor at *PM*, described him in the foreword. Mary

---

* Founded in 1939, Duell, Sloan and Pearce published the *U.S. Camera* annual volumes, which likely explains why Weegee finally succeeded in persuading its nonfiction editor, Frank Henry, to publish a book that cost $10,000 to produce. Its other authors included John O'Hara, Archibald MacLeish, and Conrad Aiken, among literary figures, but it was also notable for books by leftist liberals, including Joseph Gaer's *The First Round*, about the CIO's role in Roosevelt's 1944 reelection, and Elliott Roosevelt's *As He Saw It*, about intimate conversations with his father, which became a global sensation for suggesting FDR mistrusted Churchill's imperialism and would not have been drawn into a cold war with Stalin.

Margaret McBride, the Terry Gross of her day, interviewed him on her daytime NBC program; the *New Yorker* published a two-part profile by Joseph Mitchell. ("Mitchell not only had a pencil and pad of paper, he had an X-ray machine stuck in the back of his head," Weegee saluted another pro.) Sales were so brisk that his publisher sped copies by taxicab to Macy's, which sold more books than any bookstore in the country.

In his essay "Human Interest Stories," Anthony W. Lee writes persuasively of how *Naked City* allowed Weegee to imagine "an entirely different audience for his work, far removed from the kinds of readers who had once given life to *PM*. 'Weegee today is Art,' *Newsweek* exclaimed in 1945, just after the book was released." Even Alfred Stieglitz, whom he had befriended, sent a kindly note, though almost certainly his idea of Weegee was befuddled. If there was a "national bout of amnesia" in 1945, as Lee suggests, which at least can be argued (more persuasive is Mailer's perception that one followed 1945), one doubts how Weegee is placed in this amnesiac phase. "It is telling that a book like *Naked City*, although coming on the heels of World War II and the Great Depression, hardly refers to them and for the most part actively disavows them.

  "'Too much war news!' Weegee had once complained in 1944. 'My free lance photographic business has taken a nose dive.'"

  But, really, how could the most sharp-eyed photographer—observer of New York at street level *during* (not "on the heels of") the war—possibly "disavow" the two overwhelming, historical facts of its time? The shabby look of the Depression lingers; the war is *always* there. It was a part of the "pattern," a very large part of the pattern, that Weegee discovered in his pictures.

  Not just in the news of remote events told in the headlines he captures ("B-29s Hit Tokyo Docks"), or the spooky appearance of begoggled air-raid wardens, but as the overwhelming fact (universally felt, therefore needless to speak of) affecting liberty, politics, visibility, sex, and the overwhelming atmosphere of dark carnival, *Naked City* belongs to wartime. The Duke and Duchess of Windsor at the circus in Madison Square Garden, the carousers at Sammy's on the Bowery, the tremulous teenage fans of Frank Sinatra at the Paramount (shot from below with a telephoto lens, the skinny crooner looks like a broadly smiling golem with a grotesquely swollen head), the zoot-suiters at "the actual birth of a riot in Harlem," the sleeping soldiers and the sailors sharing the benches with civilians in crumpled suits in Bryant Park—all were photographed under what Allen Ginsberg recalls in *Howl* as "the blue light of wartime." But the tumultuous crowding of wartime, the robust promiscuity, the etiology of the race riot, the unprecedented (and unequaled until Elvis and the Beatles) stardom of Sinatra and the orgiastic adoration of his fans, were all wartime phenomena, even if the huge backdrop eventually faded.*

Feeling "confident and happy" after the success of *Naked City*, Weegee parked his car and cut the wires of the police radio. "I was through with the newspaper game—through with chasing ambulances to scenes of crime and horror—I was saturated with the tears of women and with children sleeping on fire escapes. Now I could really photograph the subjects I liked—I was free."

Alexander Liberman hired him to cast a tabloid eye on fashion and "society" at *Vogue*, which replaced *PM* as his regular venue.† "All I needed to make the change from patrol wagon to Rolls-Royce was a tuxedo." Perhaps, but the photographs from *Vogue* that are reproduced in *Weegee's People*, his 1946 sequel to *Naked City*, are nothing like as memorable as his work for *PM*, tending to stereotypical plutocrats in top hats and their poodles. On the other hand, his stories about working for *Vogue* are superb; he claimed, for example, to have started a fashion for bottle-green tuxedos when a moldy one was all he could find to wear to the opera (it was still wartime, and the production of

---

* Gay Talese condenses volumes of history, sociology, ethnology, and show business into half a paragraph of "Frank Sinatra Has a Cold" (1966): "Sinatra gave away $50,000 worth of gold cigarette lighters before he was thirty, was living an immigrant's wildest dream of America. He arrived suddenly on the scene when DiMaggio was silent, when *paisanos* were mournful, were quietly defensive about Hitler in their homeland."

† Weegee was philosophical about the demise of his "alma mater" a very few years later. "One of the reasons *PM* eventually folded was that it was ahead of the times. There were not quite as many eggheads around as there are now. All the lost souls used to read *PM* and swear by it. You could tell *PM* readers on sight. They looked like people from another planet waiting for someone to take them back to their leader . . . which, of course, was *PM*." (Weegee, 86)

such sumptuary wear was forbidden). The models were "magnificent girls . . . with dead-pan faces and icy eyes," and overawed him more than the plutocrats who wore their own clothes. But he found ways of compensating. On his first fashion shoot he took the model down to a favorite delicatessen on Delancey Street, where he "posed her against a background of salamis, bolonies, frankfurters, and assorted cold cuts, and made my pictures . . . As a matter of fact, in my picture the main interest was the salamis." A delighted Liberman paid him two hundred dollars for "Imagination."

Now, a fair number of the subjects, from Joe the bartender at Julius's in the Village to the late-night revelers on Saturday night in Harlem, along with the churchgoers on Sunday, are smiling directly at the camera. Washington Square was the "friendliest park in the city," and he spent the season of his great success in an apartment nearby. New York noir is sublimated to the human comedy as it happened to be unfolding on a given day, and history is just a newsboy's shout in the street. On Navy Day, that triumphant day, Weegee photographed a "Negro cop against the clouds" and a black boy asleep in a telephone booth. "President Truman was there, not to mention a couple of million New Yorkers," he recalled. "That's the kind of backdrop I like . . . while other photographers were getting seasick picturing the battleships in the harbor, I was photographing the people."

As often happens with innovators, Weegee's conception of his work differed markedly from that of his subtlest critics; praised for Grand Guignol, cast as photographic voyeur, rapist, and assassin abroad in the night, he thought of his true subject as the Family of Man. (Weegee revered Steichen, whom he photographed in *Naked City* and thanked for his "help and encouragement" in his autobiography.) Although he accused its reporters of smoking cork-filtered cigarettes and other affectations, his favorite newspaper was the *New York Post*. "At the *Post* they talked the language of the common man—the language of Abe Lincoln, F.D.R., Adlai Stevenson, with a little bit of genius thrown in for good measure."

Naked City was sold to Hollywood, providing the title and some of the look and mood of the 1948 film noir produced and narrated by

Mark Hellinger, who hired Weegee as a special consultant. *The Naked City* (note the sentimentalizing effect of the definite article) was the first feature film to be shot in Manhattan since the twenties, the days of King Vidor's *The Big Parade*; and according to Universal International's publicists, more than 200,000 New Yorkers came to watch the spectacle. Unfortunately, "in the streets of New York, Hellinger only dissipated the studio-furnished darkness of film noir," David Thomson writes, in his *New Biographical Dictionary of Film*. Yet, simply as a visual record, *The Naked City*, directed by Jules Dassin, is the most sustained look we have of New York after the war. Handsome, vital, prematurely white-haired Mark Hellinger, who had started out as a Broadway columnist, died of a heart attack during previews, not so long after he had concluded his narration: "There are eight million stories in the Naked City. This has been one of them."

Weegee moved his novelty act to Hollywood, and "Hollywood, the last refuge of geniuses and scoundrels, welcomed me with open arms." Praise from Chaplin and Disney; drinks with Bogart; parties at the Gene Kellys'; limousines to ferry him to screenings at MGM, like going to a gangster's funeral: none of this sufficed to keep Weegee from despising Hollywood as the "Land of the Zombies," where the blintzes were not worthy of the Salvation Army. But he kept up a connection with the movies for the rest of his life.

(He was also married and divorced by 1950, a detail omitted from *Weegee by Weegee*, although he is matter-of-fact about his whoring.)

In the fifties, he joined the jet set, flying from New York to Hollywood or Paris or London for special assignments, and sometimes playing a bit role in a film, usually a hoodlum. (The movie work included *Dr. Strangelove*, but a more typical project was the never-released, unpromisingly titled *Holiday in Brussels*, celebrating the 1958 World's Fair, "with music by Steve Allen and narration by George Jessel.") The Speed Graphic exposures of deceased gangsters and jaundiced urchins yielded to "photo-caricatures" of celebrities shot with a Hasselblad and manipulated in a darkroom. "I've photographed everyone of importance, from the Social Register to the police files," he boasted. "Including Picasso. (I'm glad he has not taken up photography. He would be too much competition even for me.)" The parenthesis is not really facetious, since Weegee saw himself as vying to equal the effects of modern painting. "My photo-caricatures would show not only how people looked, but what they were inside," he said. But what they actually did was to use Polaroid or darkroom tricks to exaggerate grossly, say, John Kennedy's teeth, or Ed Sullivan's chin, or Jack Paar's leer, which was hardly an examination of their soul. For the rest, he devoted himself to *Police Gazette*–type cheesecake for men's magazines with names like *Swank* and *Nugget*, and one he edited, *"Photographer's Showcase, a Playboy* type of magazine"; he also appeared in *Playboy*.

In *The New York School*, Jane Livingston declares Hollywood was his "undoing as a photojournalist." Certainly none of his work after 1947 has the fascination of what he did before, but Arthur H. Fellig was undone years before he bought his ticket. This was surely his own opinion, since it was he himself who published the damning description of his later works and days in Bruce Downes's odd tribute, which prefaces his autobiography.

"But all that ended when Weegee got his first look and his first taste of fame. Then the innocence vanished and Weegee traded his radio prowl car for a mess of mirrors in a futile attempt to make photographs look like modern art. The years of the kaleidoscope and the distortion devices have netted nothing but gimmicks."

Sounding like old James Huneker, who mourned that sanitation and settlement houses had killed the romance of the old East Side, Weegee lamented the disappearance of "my beloved slums": "The place where I had spent my happy childhood was now a housing project for the under-privileged. All television programs had to be approved by Paddy Chayefsky. All street fights and rumbles were under the supervision of the Police Athletic League."

Greenwich Village, which, though it was being overrun by New York University, was still "the most sensitive spot in town . . . the soul of the city," a refuge for a new generation of internal exiles from Cold War America whom he delighted to photograph: clean-cut, well-barbered folksingers in front of Judson Memorial Church; couples, sometimes interracial, drinking jug wine and gin, smoking and embracing at rent parties (a mildly transgressive motif is a half-dressed black man being appraised by white women in street clothes); a mimeographed notice of the latest (Cocteau's *Orpheus)* by the Living Theater; a morose James Dean sitting alone at a café, a cigarette in the hand cupping his chin.

The latest photographs appear to come from the era of joyless hedonism, c. 1958–63, encompassing the last days of Ike and JFK's thousand, and best known to younger generations for being depicted in the
television series *Mad Men*. It was a time of cultural vibrancy, but Happenings either escaped or did not interest Arthur H. Fellig. He had
written an introduction and assembled a maquette for a collection of
his photographs of the Village when he died in 1968, but for whatever
reason *The Village* was not published for another twenty years, and is of
only minor interest. *Naked City* has never been out of print since 1946.
As Ezra Pound wrote after the earlier war:

> *The age demanded an image*
> *of its accelerated grimace . . .*

PART VI

GREENWICH VILLAGE: GHOSTS, GOTHS, AND GLIMPSES OF THE MOON

———————

—Where do you want to have dinner?

—At the Viareggio?

—Esme, that place is always so full of . . . well, I don't know, all the rags and relics below Fourteenth Street. It's like Jehovah's Witnesses when you sit down at a table there, everybody comes over. Why do you go there anyhow?

—WILLIAM GADDIS, *The Recognitions*

"The Irascibles"—American abstract expressionist painters. *Back row, left to right*: Willem de Kooning, Adolph Gottlieb, Ad Reinhardt, Hedda Sterne. *Center row*: Richard Pousette-Dart, William Baziotes, Jackson Pollock, Clyfford Still, Robert Motherwell, Bradley Walker Tomlin. *Front row*: Theodoros Stamos, Jimmy Ernst, Barnett Newman, James Brooks, and Mark Rothko. The *New York Herald Tribune* so titled them after their letter to the president of the Metropolitan Museum of Art, protesting the exclusion of abstract painters in juried exhibitions. Photo by *Life* photographer Nina Leen, 1950.

I
———

Bohemia Was Yesterday

c. 1837–1932

IN SPRING 1948, Albert Parry, author of *Garrets and Pretenders: A History of Bohemianism in America*, traveled down from Colgate University, the upstate campus where he taught Russian studies, a field he had pioneered, to witness the leveling of "Genius Row" in Washington Square South.

Born in Russia in 1900 and witness to the revolution, Parry had jumped ship out of the Soviet merchant marine in New York Harbor in 1921—a pioneer refugee from the Soviet Union—and, living in a house off Washington Square, had broken the ice with his neighbors in the age-old way: by complaining about the noise and then being invited to join the party. Working at a newspaper and writing freelance on the side, a wizard at languages and a walker in the Village, he conceived the idea of chronicling Bohemia—"this dreamy, chaotic way of life so alien to hard-headed America." Encouraged by H. L. Mencken, who published his articles in the *American Mercury*, Parry spent five years researching and writing his "book about all Bohemias." Unluckily, it was published by Covici, Friede in March 1933, on the weekend of Roosevelt's inauguration, when even the most avid readers were distracted and, at FDR's order, all the banks were closed. Who would throw away precious cash on a book when no grocery would accept a check for food or drink?

.   .   .

Garrets and Pretenders unfolds like a tragicomic cavalcade, with the curtain rising on Edgar Allan Poe, "The Lone One," who lived in beggarly lodgings on Waverly Place, Carmine Street, and Sheridan Square, in the 1830s, when there were still fields all around, and the only bohemian was Poe himself. To Poe's solitary reign succeeded, with some pretenders along the way, the artists, scribblers, idlers, and drunks who crowded Pfaff's cellar bar on Broadway near Bleecker Street in the 1850s and '60s: "Immediately overhead pass the myriad feet of Broadway," wrote its resident celebrity, Walt Whitman. Pfaff's did not appeal to Ralph Waldo Emerson, who disparaged its regulars as "noisy and rowdy firemen" after Whitman unwisely dragged him downstairs. Yet, their number included the fabulist Fitz-James O'Brien, the great travel writer Bayard Taylor, and the editor Henry Clapp Jr., whose *Saturday Press* launched Mark Twain in the East.

Pfaff's was beneath the notice of Herman Melville, whose *Pierre; or, The Ambiguities* (1852) goes unmentioned by Parry. Yet, this novel, which came after *Moby-Dick* and was even more disastrous to Melville's career, is the first, the strangest, and the greatest American novel ever to be set among bohemians. The Church of the Apostles where Pierre Glendinning and his dark half-sister/lover, Isabel, find refuge, is "a fearful pile of Titanic bricks" set in a lofty warehouse district downtown, where their fellow lodgers are "mostly artists of various sorts; painters, or sculptors, or indigent students, or teachers of languages, or poets, or fugitive French politicians, or German philosophers." Thus, the cast of characters is definitively assembled.* Exactly a hundred years later, the "*Pierre*-of-Melville goof and wonder of it" is Jack Kerouac's epitome of the bohemian antics in *The Subterraneans*, his novel about the cool characters who drank at the San Remo and lived in Paradise Alley in the early 1950s. (Afraid of being sued by the black woman he calls "Mardou Fox," Kerouac shifted the scene from New York to

---

* Omniscient as always, Van Wyck Brooks notes various haunts for starving artists and writers in the mid-nineteenth century: "some of them living in Chelsea among small dressmakers and stuffers of birds in houses with cast-iron balconies and wisteria vines; others in Union Square, or in the Bowery, where the local dish was goulash rather than spaghetti and tripe. But the favorite Bohemian region was the 'Quarter,' in the neighborhood of Bleecker and Houston Streets, the 'Village' where artists and writers had been dwelling for years, even before Pfaff's, the old Broadway beer-cellar that prefigured the careless tolerance of the later city." *The Confident Years: 1885–1915* (New York: E. P. Dutton, 1952), 8–9.

San Francisco, substituting North Beach for Greenwich Village; not merely changing place names, but throwing himself into the game, as the Beats and hipsters in New York are transferred into the fogs and hills of North Beach. The effect might not be entirely persuasive, as Ellis Amburn, Kerouac's sometime editor, maintains in his biography, because "claustrophobic" Lower Manhattan is not breezy San Francisco; but the novel is richer and stranger for the transplantation.)

Bohemia in America has always been a matter of life imitating art imitating, with romantic or sordid embellishments, life—usually in Paris. The crowd at Pfaff's might have claimed Poe as their dark father, but they learned to act like "bohemians" from the poor but gay Parisians in Henry Murger's *Scènes de la vie de Bohème* (1848) and his sensational play based on it, *La Vie de Bohème*, the basis for Puccini's opera (and more recently *Rent*). Living fast and dying young was a bohemian tradition scrupulously observed in America. Ada Clare, the actress "queen" of New York bohemia in the 1860s and '70s had done firsthand research in Paris and exceeded expectations by returning disgracefully unwed and bearing the child of her lover Louis Moreau Gottschalk, the composer and piano virtuoso, and in 1874 dying of rabies from a lapdog's bite. Poor Ada had dreamed of creating a Latin Quarter in New York "better and smaller" than the original, which "might show more order and cleanliness."

Bohemia did not flourish in New York during the feverish getting-and-spending of the Gilded Age. Parry suspects that Charles de Kay's *The Bohemian: A Tragedy of Modern Times* (1878), set in Washington Square, and supposedly the first novel to depict the milieu, was a pastiche based on the "Pfaffians" of yesteryear rather than "a picture of contemporary times," as the author claimed. "We do not know of any native Murgeria of this type actually existing in New York of the late 'Seventies.'"

Charles de Kay was an unlikely chronicler of bohemia in any case. Scion of an old Knickerbocker family, de Kay was a polymath who spoke fluent German, Italian, and French; read Latin, Greek, and Sanskrit. His poems and translations were approved by expert opinion: his handsome, erudite company was welcomed by Emerson, Henry James, and Browning. Old New York might have deprecated a mere lord of language; writing, as Edith Wharton recalled, was considered in polite circles "something between a black art and a form of manual labor." But de Kay was also a tremendous athlete and clubman, a founder of the Fencers Club, the National Arts Club, and the Authors Club, the latter precursors to what is now the Academy of Arts and Letters. "In the Seventies," his friend Robert Underwood Johnson, the writer, diplomat, and conservationist, reminisced half a century later, "de Kay, then recently returned from Europe, a handsome and spirited figure in New York life, was showing himself one of the best equipped and 'all around' literary men of that day. He was the master of more branches of knowledge than any man I ever met—art, science, philology, Oriental lore, general literature."

Unusually for one of his class, de Kay became a newspaperman, working as arts and literary editor, editorial writer, and book reviewer for the *New York Times* from 1876 to 1923, with a hiatus when he was appointed consul in Berlin. De Kay's brother-in-law, Richard Watson Gilder, was editor of the *Century* magazine, the flagship of the genteel tradition and the monthly expression of turn-of-the-century Brownstone culture. (Gilder was happy to befriend Whitman, but never dreamed of publishing him, and bowdlerized *Huckleberry Finn* before serializing it in the *Century*.) Gilder commissioned Stanford White to redesign a stable near Union Square into a trendy residence that he and his wife called simply "the Studio." This was an early and influential instance of what we now deplore as "gentrification," and a precedent for converting stables to studios in Macdougal Alley and Washington Mews in the age of the automobile. Thomas Bender detects a "distinctly fin de siècle quality to their social life, not quite decadent, but with at least a suggestion of extravagant aesthetic delight." Stanford White, John La Farge, Augustus Saint-Gaudens, and Eleanora Duse were among the guests regularly welcomed to their Friday-night gatherings.

De Kay and his spirited wife, also a fencer, inherited the salon when the Gilders moved uptown, leaving them their house. But Charles de Kay considered bohemia "an unwelcome tragedy," Parry sums up; "he would not have dreamed of bringing it into the Gilders' salon."

.   .   .

In the 1890s, an English novelist gave the world more gay Parisians to emulate. Like Murger's romances, George du Maurier's *Trilby* (1894), similarly set in the Latin Quarter, was an international craze: there were riots when booksellers ran out of copies. The bohemia of Washington Square South was one of a loose network that sprang up toward the end of the nineteenth century and vibrated remotely from Berlin to Berkeley (*Martin Eden*), London to Buenos Aires. San Francisco boasted its "International Quarter," the setting of Frank Norris's *Blix;* a "Streetcar Bohemia" on the beach; and the nearby art colony of Carmel-by-the-Sea, where Jack London and George Sterling were bronze gods. George Cram Cook, then a young English instructor at Stanford University, sampled the milieu a decade before founding the Provincetown Players with his wife, Susan Glaspell. Altogether Parry has dropped hundreds of names, famous and obscure, from Mary Austin to Israel Zangwill, covered thousands of miles, devoted dense chapters to "Confused Souls in Boston," "Hushed Murgeria in Philadelphia," and "Gentle Thunder in the South"; to the dill pickle in Chicago and the boomtowns of Texas, where Will Porter (O. Henry) published a humor sheet; Parry looked abroad to the expatriates of the *Yellow Book* era and made an excursion to the Lower East Side to listen for "The Yiddish Note," before circling back to Washington Square in time for the Mauve Decade of the nineties.

About 1910—overnight, it seemed—people looked around to discover that Greenwich Village was becoming "the Village," its cast of free thinkers and free lovers, students, starving artists, eccentrics, revolutionists either in place or on their way.

John Butler Yeats, the painter father of the poet, himself reputed to be the best conversationalist in Dublin, London, *and* New York, having adventurously moved there in 1909 at the age of sixty-nine, lived in a hotel in Chelsea owned by three sisters from Brittany named Petitpas; and he often held court in its downstairs restaurant, attended by the painters Robert Henri, John Sloan, and George Bellows and their writer friends, including Alan Seeger and Van Wyck Brooks. Whenever anyone asked if he was related to "the great Yeats," he would reply: "*I* am the great Yeats."

"The fiddles are tuning as it were all over America," the old man proclaimed in 1912. Nowhere with such promise, or with such intense appreciation for youthful talent, as below Fourteenth Street. Indeed, it was considered a great scandal when the *Lyric Year* prize anthology did *not* award first place to "Renascence," a long poem by nineteen-year-old Edna St. Vincent Millay of Camden, Maine.

Tearooms, flower boxes in windows, cubist paintings and poets from Chicago, and many other novelties were added to the mise-en-scène by the time the outbreak of the Great War in 1914 enlarged the cast by bringing home expatriate Americans from Paris and London, Rome and Berlin.* The reformers, aesthetes, romantic rebels, and pioneering feminists of the Village were now joined by socialist organizers, labor agitators (anarchist, socialist, anarcho-syndicalist), college boys, and streetwise camp followers, "half-radical, half-hoboes." Even nonchalant street urchins, peering into the window of a café, might register the change, as the tramp poet Harry Kemp recalled:

> *"Hey, fellas, there's a woman in there smokin' a cigarette!"*
> *"—Pipe the big guy with a beard!"*
> *"ALL the women are smokin'!"*

It is striking that the golden day dawned "on or about December 1910," when, as Virginia Woolf is often misquoted, "human nature changed" (she wrote "human character"). "All human relationships have shifted—those between masters and servants, husbands and wives, parents and children. And when human relations change there is at the same time a change in religion, conduct, and literature." It was in fact the great discovery of the Villagers in the teens that the personal was the political—Bloomsbury's sentiment exactly, and a connection that was disparaged in the fervent thirties in favor of a militant single-mindedness. By 1936, when Mabel Dodge wrote, "Looking back upon it now, it seems as though everywhere, in that year of 1913, barriers went down and people reached each other who had never been

---

* Note, however, that the war did not bring back Gertrude Stein, Ezra Pound, or T. S. Eliot, three of the writers—Eliot most especially—who would be of the greatest fascination to New York intellects.

in touch before; and there were all sorts of new ways to communicate, as well as new communications," the idea sounded merely quaint. In retrospect, fallen-away admirers realized that it had been an ominous sign that Max Eastman insisted on publishing his love poetry in the *Masses* alongside subversive cartoons and dispatches on the class war.

As a cultural emporium, New York was still almost entirely an importer, and then a transmitter to the hinterlands. Greenwich Village was becoming the place where, in Edmund Wilson's words, all the wires crossed. Warm and cold currents of socialism, anarchism, symbolism, and psychoanalysis stirred the Village discussion; events like the Ludlow Massacre, the Paterson strike, the Mexican Civil War, and at last the world war and the Russian Revolution agitated it.

When he attempted "A Spiritual Autobiography of My Own Generation in Its Literary and Social Aspects," in *Intellectual Vagabondage: An Apology for the Intelligentsia* (1926), Floyd Dell tells the story almost entirely in terms of the books they had read. Drama was Shaw, Ibsen, Strindberg, Maeterlinck. More than its politics, poetry, or painting, the theater that came out of the Village—on stage but also on the streets, in marches and pageants—was its most intense form and liveliest legacy.

Handsome Frank Tannenbaum, supposedly risen up from the anonymous masses but in fact recruited by the Industrial Workers of the World (IWW) out of the radical Ferrer School, led a "revolt of the unemployed," barging into churches and synagogues during services to demand bread and shelter, which very few clergy obliged in what Christine Stansell, in her fine study of bohemian New York, *American Moderns*, calls "a kind of proto-street theater." When Tannenbaum was convicted of inciting to riot, sentenced to a year on Blackwell's Island and fined $500, "everybody" in radical bohemia, including young Walter Lippmann, who, though already representing "the drift to respectability," as Max Eastman recalled, walked behind the black flag in a protest march down Fifth Avenue, and joined Emma Goldman, Alexander Berkman, Lincoln Steffens, and Hutchins Hapgood on the platform in Union Square to denounce the injustice.

"Who does not know the now routine legend in which the world of 1910–1917 is Washington Square turned Arcadia," Alfred Kazin wrote in 1942, youthfully condescending but with a trace of envy, "in which the barriers are always down, the magazines are always promising, the workers are always marching, geniuses sprouting in every Village bedroom, Isadora Duncan always dancing—that world of which John Reed was the Byronic hero, Mabel Dodge the hostess, Randolph Bourne the martyr, Van Wyck Brooks the oracle? No other generation ever seemed to have so radiant a youth, or has remembered it in so many winsome autobiographies written at forty." The whole thing was, in retrospect, a pageant. One cannot appreciate why the Village seemed so beaten down in the forties, so politically dull and artistically listless, without a sense of how remote the golden day seemed.

The "rebel girl" was first spotted organizing on the Lower East Side, where Emma Goldman had been a force since the 1890s, famous for agitating in Union Square.* Elizabeth Gurley Flynn, "the Joan of Arc of the East Side," addressed the Harlem Socialist Club at the age of fifteen. "Just because I'm young and a girl is no reason you shouldn't ask me questions!" she admonished when none was forthcoming. She was twenty-five but already a veteran of strikes from Paterson, New Jersey, to Spokane, Washington, when Joe Hill saluted her in song:

> *That's the rebel girl, that's the rebel girl!*
> *Of the working class she is the pearl!*
> *She's the courage, pride and joy of the fighting rebel boy!*

Max Eastman, the newly installed editor of the *Masses*, went out to observe the new breed of labor agitators at a rally in Haledon, a small town in New Jersey with a socialist mayor, during the 1913 Paterson silk workers' strike. Flynn shared the platform with her lover, the Italian American anarchist Carlo Tresca, and towering "Big Bill" Haywood. Soon to be lionized in the parlors of the Village, each was

---

* Goldman was too large to be contained, or constrained, even by the Lower East Side, let alone Greenwich Village, as Irving Howe writes. In the 1890s, when her tours exposed her to legal persecution elsewhere, "the East Side became for her a place to which she could retreat in relative safety, and during the depression of 1893 she found employment there as a social worker, serving the jobless bread and leaflets with equal zeal. But, in truth, her notoriety in the world at large was always greater than her influence among the Jewish immigrants; she was one of the first intellectuals to 'graduate' from and then move out of their milieu." (*World of Our Fathers*)

impressive in his or her own way: Flynn for her girlish command; Tresca for a speech delivered in Italian, the only words of which Eastman understood were "Occhio per occhio, dente per dente, sangue per sangue!" ("Eye for an eye, tooth for a tooth, blood for blood!"), and Haywood for his imposing presence. The IWW, Big Bill liked to say, was "socialism with its working clothes on"; and he left no extenuating hope that the socialist revolution could be achieved without bloodshed—a sentiment that was received with a frisson when he repeated it to Mabel Dodge's salon.

Mary Heaton Vorse was a New Woman in her teens before becoming a rebel girl in middle age. Born in 1874 and growing up abroad and in a twenty-four-room house in New England, Mary Heaton studied art in Paris but was summoned back by her parents for having too many good times; she married a writer of bohemian inclinations and modest talents, Bert Vorse, and took up writing while raising a family in an eighth-floor walkup on Sheridan Square. Her gift was for anodyne popular fiction, but she was "all for Labor and the Arts," and she talked politics and publishing with Theodore Dreiser; John Sloan and his wife, Dolly; Mary Harris "Mother" Jones; and occasionally Mark Twain, at the conversation club she cofounded.* In 1912, she participated in and covered the textile workers' strike in Lawrence, Massachusetts. Over the next fifty years Vorse was no stranger to raids or jailhouses or the cop's truncheon, as a labor reporter, or to wars as a foreign correspondent. In 1906 she pioneered the Village's summer exodus to Provincetown, to be followed by Hutchins Hapgood, Max Eastman, John Reed, and George Cram Cook and his wife, Susan Glaspell. Vorse owned the rackety wharf whose fish house Cook and Glaspell (expatriates out of the bohemia of Davenport, Iowa) made over into their Wharf Theatre, the first home of the Provincetown Players.

Washington Square was a place "where youth lived and reds gathered, playwrights, actors, and Bohemians, and leaders of a radical trend,"

---

* Mary Heaton Vorse must have been one of the very few opponents of American imperialism in the Philippines at the turn of the twentieth century to be around to oppose the Vietnam War in the 1960s. Ross Wetzsteon notes that she, who lived to be ninety-two, was the oldest accredited journalist in Vietnam, and had the distinction of being the oldest American to merit an active FBI file. (*Republic of Dreams*, 172)

Lincoln Steffens recalled. At forty-four and recently widowed, in 1910 he was living in a single room in the house at 42 Washington Square where Jack Reed had moved with some college chums from Harvard. After midnight Reed would wake up the middle-aged muckraker to tell him about his nightly adventures. "O life is a joy to a broth of a boy / At Forty-two Washington Square!" sang Reed in one of the poems he devoted to his bohemian days in 1913.

The Liberal Club, advertised as "a Meeting Place for Those Interested in New Ideas," occupied the first floor of a hard-worn brownstone at 137 Macdougal Street; along with Polly's restaurant in the basement, it was the daily hub of bohemia until war made bohemia a divided country. Its guiding spirit, an avant-garde high-school English teacher named Henrietta Rodman, had led the exodus downtown from the original Liberal Club, which the more radical elements she represented—upon seceding, they were surprised to find themselves a majority—had begun to find intolerably conventional, exclusive, and located in Gramercy Park. The secessionists painted their new club-house in fauve colors, exhibited cubist and futurist art, staged poetry readings and one-act plays, and followed up lectures and discussions with dancing to a player piano. Barney Gallant, an enterprising Latvian who had shared a squalid apartment on Fourth Street with Eugene O'Neill, lowered the tone by keeping an interminable poker game going in a corner. More in keeping with the club's motto, Eastman, Reed, and Floyd Dell represented the *Masses*; William English Walling and his wife, Anna Strunsky, the Socialist Party intelligentsia; Marsden Hartley, fine arts; Art Young, the political cartoon. Ruth Pickering, "a gloriously beautiful girl just down from Vassar," was the first in a notable procession from that campus to the Village. There were poets who looked the part, like Scudder Middleton, and Egmont Arens, who was muscular for an aesthete (and later a distinguished industrial designer). Gilbert Seldes had launched himself as a journalist, not yet as America's first highbrow champion of popular culture.[*]

---

[*] See Allen Churchill, *The Improper Bohemians*, 62–64. Among the later careers of those named, that of Egmont Arens, "a brawny New Yorker just back from the West who nursed an interest in books, magazines, and Bohemian life," took the least predictable path. From publishing *Playboy*, a frivolous gazette of the Village beautifully printed, in the twenties he turned to industrial design—clocks, lamps, kitchen appli-

Awkward but a compelling storyteller, Sinclair Lewis was a dedicated hanger-on.

"Incredibly naïve, preposterously reckless, believing wistfully in beauty and goodness, a Candide in petticoat and sandals, she did always manage to involve herself in complicated difficulties; but she fought those difficulties serenely, and fought her way out of them—into some new briar patch." So Floyd Dell remembers Henrietta Rodman in *Love in Greenwich Village*, and how her addiction to causes and controversies kept things lively at the "new" Liberal Club. It was entirely in character, Dell thought, that she managed to make a scandal out of doing something as conventional as getting married. She was the cynosure of a group of mostly young, mostly female social workers, newspaper reporters, professors, and schoolteachers like herself, which the Liberal Club introduced to what Dell called "those shy and timid aborigines, the artist-folk," who had hitherto themselves been living together in the crazy streets, "but in tiny groups and cliques, mutually indifferent, or secretly suspicious of each other." The effect, he says, was pyrotechnic. "She invented Greenwich Village . . . It wasn't at all what she had meant it to be—for she was a very serious young woman, and it was incurably frivolous. But she did it!"

No less than for her causes, Rodman, described as "lanky," became known for her look: cropped hair and monklike costume of a meal-sack shift and sandals with brown wool socks, which became an enduring bohemian uniform. Her dinners were famous for being sketchy: at the last minute some obliging male, such as Floyd Dell or Harry Kemp, would be sent out for bread and butter and canned spaghetti, and when he had carried dinner up the five flights of stairs to her apartment, he would be sent out again for a pail of beer. Rodman lived on the top

---

ances, and packaging—and became one of the better-known such practitioners in the country, though never achieving popular renown like Norman Bel Geddes, Raymond Loewy, and Henry Dreyfuss (whose talents included self-promotion). His redesign of the packaging of in-house products for the Great Atlantic and Pacific Tea Company (A&P) made his work familiar to millions who did not know his name. The current Eight O'Clock coffee bag alludes to his original design. His sinuously Brancusian Hobart meat slicer is in the collection of the Museum of Modern Art.

floor of her Bank Street building, which was pleasant in the summer. "At such times the hostess, a lady not conspicuous for humor, would indulge in perhaps her only light remark. 'Coming up to my apartment is like a progress of the soul,' she would declare. 'A long tortuous climb, difficult step after step, but at the top you burst into the sky . . .'"

Polly, as Paula Holladay was known, on whose plain but cheap fare the intelligentsia dined before heading upstairs, was quiet and proper and came out of respectable Evanston, Illinois. The group in her restaurant basement were wild and noisy, and no less noisy, usually more so, was Polly's lover and partner, a veteran of the black flag of anarchism named Hippolyte Havel, who was rumored to have seen the inside of half of Europe's prisons before traveling to America in 1901 as the companion (and presumably lover) of Emma Goldman. Looking exactly like a bomb thrower in a cartoon (except for owlish spectacles), Havel, doubling as waiter and cook, alternated between berating the customers as "bourgeois pigs" and cadging them for a dollar; he addressed everyone as "darling," including the red-faced desk sergeant whom he embraced (for he was actually a gentle soul) when he was arrested for public drunkenness and taken to the station house. "Darling, lend me fifty cents."

Next door to the Liberal Club and Polly's was Albert and Charles Boni's Washington Square Bookshop, birthplace of the Modern Library and the Washington Square Players, out of which came the Theatre Guild; George Cram Cook, a fallen-away classics professor from Iowa, and his wife, the writer Susan Glaspell, founded the Provincetown Players on a wharf in the beach town that the Village was busy colonizing. They occupied another house on Macdougal, where they launched their discovery, Eugene O'Neill.

No one did more to promote the new openness, or got more publicity doing it, than Mabel Dodge, as she was then, who welcomed anarchists, roaring boys, and pale poetesses—but never the press, which was naturally mesmerized—to her white-painted, gray-furnished rooms at 23 Fifth Avenue for "evenings" that might be devoted to anarchism, "sex antagonism," birth control, or psychoanalysis. Even her neighbors at 23 Fifth added to the mystique in their emphatic contrast to the "ferment of ideas" in her chic rooms. Occupying the ground floor was the owner, General Daniel Sickles, the Civil War commander, sitting ramrod in a straight-backed chair; on the floor between him and Mabel Dodge's third-floor apartment lived the ex-governor of New York William Sulzer, "a tall, gaunt Andrew Jackson of a man with a ten-gallon black hat and a madly glittering eye," who had disowned his Tammany Hall sponsors and been impeached for his disloyalty.

The stout, handsome heiress to a tidy Buffalo fortune, married to a wealthy but unfortunately dull architect, Mabel had reluctantly quit the Medici villa near Florence where they had been living for ten years so that her young son by a previous marriage could be educated. America, alas, was "ugly, ugly, ugly," her husband a bore ("I was so sick of Edwin's being commonplace"), and after the monochromatic fit of decorating in which she painted all the walls and woodwork of their apartment white and had all the furnishings covered in gray silk, she became so despondent that she had her tonsils removed as a distraction. Her spirits rose through a budding friendship with the music and dance critic Carl Van Vechten and a visit from the sculptor Jo Davidson, raised on the East Side, whom Gertrude Stein had introduced them to in Paris. Although Dodge had entertained high-bohemians like Leo and Gertrude Stein in Italy, it apparently had not occurred to her that she could do the same in New York. Their afternoon with Jo Davidson, enjoyed over pinch-bottle Scotch whiskey, Gorgonzola sandwiches, and Turkish cigarettes, was poor Edwin's undoing, for as other "movers and shakers" followed, he became superfluous, and was dispatched to live at the Hotel Brevoort next door. It was another new friend, Lincoln Steffens, who proposed that Mabel have evening gatherings. "Why, something wonderful might come of it! You might revive General Conversation!"

"All sorts of guests came to Mabel Dodge's salons," Steffens recalled in his *Autobiography*, "poor and rich, labor skates, scabs, strikers and unemployed, painters, musicians, reporters, editors, swells; it was the only successful salon I have ever seen in America." Freud's translator and leading American disciple, Dr. A. A. Brill, expounded psychoanalysis, and within days "complexes" were endemic all over the Village. Emma Goldman came over from the Lower East Side to preach anarchism, while the principle of syndicalism was monumentally represented by "Big Bill" Haywood of the IWW. A stout six feet tall, Big Bill was known as the "Polyphemus of Labor," having lost one eye while whittling a slingshot as a boy; he did not disguise its socket, although he always turned his better profile to a camera. On a Radical Evening, Goldman, Haywood, and the young socialist Walter Lippmann advocated their respective revolutions; their emphases varied, but it was agreed the expropriators could expect to be expropriated.

Max Eastman puzzled to explain what quality enabled Mabel Dodge to become such a great collector of intellectuals: "For the most part she sits like a lump and says nothing." On reflection he decided: "Many famous salons have been established by women of wit and beauty; Mabel's was the only one ever established by sheer will power." No doubt part of its appeal for the hungrier bohemians was the lavish table Dodge set after the discussions, with whole hams and turkeys, and bottles of whiskey and wine, which the New Women drank along with the Modern Men. The association of hard drinking (and cigarette smoking) with modernity and liberation was one of the Village's less fortunate and unfortunately long-lived legacies to literary life.

With great foresight Mabel Dodge found her way to Alfred Stieglitz's gallery, "291," in time to fall in with the organizers of the Armory Show, which opened in February 1913, lending them the use of her limousine and driver, among other services, and seizing the occasion to promote the works of her friend Gertrude Stein. When New York was introduced to cubism, fauvism, postimpressionism, and the most adventuresome young artists in New York, Dodge could take some small portion of the credit for an event which, she wrote Stein, was the most important in America since 1776. "The first, and possibly the last, exhibition of paintings held in New York which everybody attended," Carl Van Vechten later wrote. By now aspiring to be "the most dangerous woman in New York," Mabel Dodge rendered a comparable service to the cause of labor by sponsoring a "pageant" at Madison Square Garden to support the silk workers' strike in Paterson, New Jersey, in which the IWW was playing a conspicuous role. (When John Reed went to Paterson to report and was arrested, he shared a cell with Carlo Tresca and met Big Bill Haywood in the exercise yard; they endorsed him to their suspicious cellmates, who suspected him of being a stool pigeon.) Like the Armory Show, the Paterson Strike Pageant was a great happening, with the strikers at the textile works and their families, a thousand strong, ferried across the Hudson to play themselves in a giant performance piece, as did Elizabeth Gurley Flynn and Tresca and Haywood, all appearing against the gigantic backdrops painted by John Sloan and the hulking mill devised by Robert Edmond Jones, Reed and Eugene O'Neill's classmate at Harvard, and later the most influential American set designer of his time. Mabel and Jack Reed and the radical novelist Ernest Poole collaborated on the scenario, whose flavor is suggested by Reed's program notes, e.g.: "Episode 2: The Mills Dead—The People Alive. The gathering of the people before the mills. The picket line. The scab passes. Coming of the police. 'Boo!' Clubbing and brutality. Arrest of forty pickets. 'Boo!' "

In highest secrecy, Jack Reed (or Ernest Poole) had arranged to wire the letters "IWW" in giant electric lights on Stanford White's Spanish baroque Garden Tower, switching them on an hour before the performance. "As city police charged frantically around the premises looking for the switch to the provocative sign, Madison Square Garden became the scene of a truly rousing spectacle. Those alive today," wrote Allen Churchill in 1959, "who were among the fifteen thousand viewing the Paterson Pageant are inclined to recall it as one of the most moving experiences of a life-time." In his chapter on Greenwich Village in *The Confident Years, 1885–1915* (1952), Van Wyck Brooks writes that "the American religion of social reform expressed itself in the Paterson pageant along with the Marxian revolutionary creed and impulse," a combination also to be found in Poole's novel *The Harbor* and Arthur Bullard's *Comrade Yetta*.

In the frantic, secretive weeks spent preparing the pageant, Mabel Dodge and Jack Reed had become lovers in all but the act; "that it was no time for lovemaking was accepted between us," recalled Dodge, who then kept him "on the Threshold" for months until the opportune time came to surrender to his ardor in Paris. But the suspense undoubtedly contributed to the electricity of her "evenings," which had become such a sensation that the newshounds resorted to dressing up in overalls to impersonate anarchist laborers, or in evening dress to pass as slumming bluebloods, in order to get in. Mabel Dodge, who assumed what she hoped was an enigmatic air for these evenings, took a stern line about embargoing the press.

The notoriety of 23 Fifth Avenue might have been even more lurid if the press had got wind of a more private séance when Mabel Dodge invited a select group to a peyote party which foreshadowed her own eventual move to mystical New Mexico and, obviously, much else. In *Enjoyment of Living* (1948), Max Eastman recalls a freezing winter night in 1915 when the lunatic apparition of Mabel's downstairs neighbor ex-Governor Sulzer was the appropriate prelude to a disastrous "experiment in consciousness." Mabel's ethnologist friend Richard Harrington supplied the peyote buttons; the psychologist Raymond Dodge improvised a Kiowa Indian ceremonial, "an electric bulb with red tissue paper to represent a campfire . . . and for the mountains of the moon—I forget what he did about that," Mabel recorded. A frightening rather than an enlightening time was had by all except Mabel, who prudently hid her button in her skirt, and Eastman, who spat his out. ("She was raving mad, as well as chilled to the bone and shaking like a harp string," he wrote of one communicant, the poet Genevieve Taggard, another of his lovers.) Yet as Jay Stevens writes in *Storming Heaven: LSD and the American Dream* (1987): "Looking back on that evening from the vantage of seventy years, it is possible to imagine a psychedelic era in miniature. In less than thirty years peyote had passed from the scientists to the intellectuals to the bohemians. Had the First World War not intervened, there is no telling how far the 'dry whiskey' might have spread." But as Leonard Michaels writes of the end of the fifties, it was a matter of "not yet, not yet."

2

Conciliating Nobody: The *Masses* and the Villagers

1913–1917

THE *MASSES* WAS A MONTHLY PROVOCATION in folio, costing fifteen cents a copy (originally, five cents). A notice above the masthead proclaimed the *Masses* to be (among many other bold things): "A MAGAZINE WHOSE FINAL POLICY IS TO DO AS IT PLEASES AND TO CONCILIATE NOBODY, NOT EVEN ITS READERS." It was notorious that readership of the *Masses* included precious few of the masses. But "every agitator who really intended to overthrow capitalism and inaugurate a working-class millennium in the United States felt he had a body of friends and colleagues in the writers and artists of the *Masses*," Max Eastman, its editor, was still proud to recall in 1948. By then, he, once a notorious Red, had subsided into employment as a "roving correspondent" for *Reader's Digest*.

Upton Sinclair, Randolph Bourne, Jack London, and John Reed, one of the editors, were among the better-known writers published in the *Masses*. Sherwood Anderson, Djuna Barnes, William Carlos Williams, Konrad Bercovici, and Babette Deutsch appeared in the *Masses* when they were just starting out. A young socialist and schoolteacher, Louis Ginsberg, later wrote poetry conventional enough to be published in the *New York Times*, something his son Allen never did. John Sloan, Stuart Davis, Boardman Robinson, George Bellows, and Robert Minor were among the artists, along with, at least once, Pablo Picasso.[*] "Our

---

[*] Among the other writers and artists who contributed to the *Masses* besides its contributing editors were Amy Lowell, Carl Sandburg, Paul H. Douglas, Emma Gold-

magazine provided, for the first time in America," Eastman claimed, "a meeting place for revolutionary labor and the radical intelligentsia. It acquired, in spite of its gay laughter, the character of a crusade." It will be an interesting study to see where the crusaders who still lived had landed by the time he wrote his memoirs.

As editor of the *Masses* and its successor, the *Liberator*, from 1913 to 1922, when he left for Europe and Russia, Max Eastman was among the best-known literary radicals in the country, and the most conspicuous in Greenwich Village: it was said (by his admirers, some reluctant) that he combined the wit of a George Bernard Shaw and the looks of "a sleepy Adonis." He was born in Canandaigua, in upstate New York, in 1883—the year that Marx died, he liked to point out—and grew up in Elmira, where both of his parents were Congregationalist ministers. Samuel Elijah Eastman preferred farming to preaching, but Annis Ford Eastman was famous for her eloquence, and Max first studied the art of public speaking by listening to her sermons. The accomplished Annis Eastman was listed in *Who's Who* when that was a rare distinction for a woman, as later was Eastman's older sister Crystal, a leading feminist and labor lawyer. Mark Twain and his wife, Olivia Clemens, spent their summers in Elmira, where he wrote *Tom Sawyer*, until 1896, when their daughter Susy died. Olivia was a parishioner of the Eastmans' Park Church, where Max met Twain in the pews; over the years his parents "shared between them the melancholy honor of officiating at the funerals of that great American and of his wife and his best-loved daughter." Eastman recalls in his memoirs what Mark Twain told a nephew of his in Elmira who asked about socialism. "I can't even hope for it. I know too much about human nature." By the time he related the story, Max Eastman had come to the same conclusion.

Eastman attended Williams College, where he neglected his studies for drinking, diving, hiking, and poetry writing until his senior year, when he made up for lost time, was elected to Phi Beta Kappa, and was chosen as class orator. (His subject was Giordano Bruno, the Renais-

---

man, Dorothy Day, Clement Wood, Meyer London, Maurice Becker, Amos Pinchot, Frank Tannenbaum, and Louis Untermeyer. They are included in a handsome reader, *Echoes of Revolt: The Masses, 1911–1917*, ed. William L. O'Neill (Chicago: Quadrangle Books, 1966), 411–12.

sance philosopher who was burned alive for heresy in the Campo dei Fiori in Rome in 1600.) As a graduate student in philosophy at Columbia, Eastman was the protégé of John Dewey, who appointed him to teach a class in "logic," meaning the scientific method. Neither then nor later did Max Eastman attempt to master any particular science except psychology—then as now a very inexact science; but the cult he developed at this time for "experimentation" became the basis of his radicalism, and later of his repudiation of radicalism.

In 1907, he rented a furnished room in a house near Crystal's apartment on Charles Street, and later moved with her to an apartment on Eleventh Street. "New York was not quite the quintessence of cityhood that it is now," he recalled in 1948. "Indeed, Greenwich Village, where my sister lived, was still almost rural, for Seventh Avenue had not yet crashed down through it, biting the very houses in two. The roaring north-and-southbound monster was still confined above Eleventh Street, and below there was quietness and quaintness, there were neighbors who knew each other, there was sauntering in the streets." Claude McKay, the Jamaica-born poet and writer, who moved in their circle after 1917, remembers Crystal Eastman in his autobiography as "the most beautiful white woman I ever knew," with a "magnificent presence." Eastman tells how his sister was at the earnest heart of the crowd of social workers, professors, schoolteachers, and lawyers devoted to uplift and reform, the protagonists of "ethical" bohemia who moved to Greenwich Village ahead of the artists and aesthetes. (Note that Eastman followed the custom of the time in distinguishing the Village, a term he found cloying, from Washington Square.) After graduating from Vassar and taking a master's in sociology at Columbia, Crystal studied law at New York University, and in 1910 she published a landmark study, *Work-Accidents and the Law*, leading to New York's model workmen's compensation legislation, which she substantially drafted. Under her influence Max adopted feminism as his cause, as he was soon to become a Marxian socialist under the influence of his first wife, Ida Rauh. Beginning with his mother at the pulpit, Max Eastman was always ready to take instruction from a woman: something which became less rather than more common for male intellectuals in succeeding decades.[*]

---

[*] Mary McCarthy was appointed theater critic of the "new" *Partisan Review*, as she later said, "because I had been married to an actor. It was often debated whether we

At Crystal's instigation Max founded the Men's League for Women's Suffrage, the cause in which he gained his first notoriety and a reputation as a great platform performer. On stage, Eastman benefited from his height and extraordinary dark good looks, and the languid air in which he drawled the most outrageous heresies, hands in his pockets, eyes half-shut. His rhetorical style was unadorned, like his prose, which except when exasperated by controversy is sinewy and unfailingly lucid. His languorous air, combined with the way he had of stretching out on couches at parties and a habit of dropping book projects, earned him a quite undeserved reputation in literary circles as "the laziest man in America." However, by way of compensation, he was conceded one of the most active libidos in the Village: Max Eastman was perhaps the only man in America who ever considered that he might simplify his sex life by taking Mabel Dodge as a lover. His frank hedonism distinguished him from the usual run of revolutionists. "I have always had a strong and shameless interest in having a good time," he confessed.

One spring day in 1913, Eastman received in the mail a scrap of paper with a painted message: "You are elected editor of the *Masses*. No pay." It was addressed to him by a posse of artists and writers led by the cartoonist Art Young, to whom he had confided his hope of finding part-time work in some socialist cause that would pay the rent; instead he was offered a more-than-full-time job that paid nothing. Eastman had already tried to decline the honor, but Young, John Sloan, the journalist Mary Heaton Vorse, the youthful litterateur Louis Untermeyer, and the rest of the staff were looking for a messiah to save their impoverished socialist monthly, which had been forsaken by its founder, a Dutch communitarian named Piet Vlag whose main occupation was running the cafeteria at the Rand School, and by its millionaire angel. Eastman had as yet published little, and nothing of political note, but

---

should have a theatre column at all. Some of the editors felt that the theatre was not worth bothering about, since it was neither a high art nor a mass art, like the movies. But that was also an argument for letting me do it. If I made mistakes, who cared?" *Sights and Spectacles: Theatre Chronicles, 1937–1956* (New York: Meridian Books, 1957), p. xi.

the *Masses* gang suspected from his founding a "league"—which he did entirely on his own—that he might have organizational skills.

"They were inviting me to raise money and run the business as well as edit the magazine, and it was easy to infer, from the nature of artists and the climate of opinion then prevailing in Greenwich Village, that anyone who took on the job could change the editorial policy from 'reformist' to 'revolutionary' with a turn of the hand."

This he proceeded to do. Moving offices from Nassau Street to 91 Greenwich Avenue—from Newspaper Row, that is, to bohemia— Eastman reinvented Piet Vlag's moderate "yellow socialist" *Masses* into the ultra-bright-Red flagship of revolution, while himself remaining presentable enough to be received at the White House. (He and Woodrow Wilson were friendly acquaintances from the lecture circuit, until Wilson decided he should go to prison for thirty years for opposing America's entrance into the world war.) With good humor Eastman presided over the *Masses*' fractious monthly meetings, held usually at either Young's or Sloan's studio, to which not only its nominal owners, the "contributing editors," but interested parties as well were invited to vote on art (held up for display) and editorial matter (read aloud until the crowd groaned).

"Bourgeois pigs! Voting! Voting on poetry! Poetry is something from the soul! You can't vote on poetry!" the irrepressible Hippolyte Havel protested at such behavior. When Eastman's associate editor Floyd Dell mildly remarked that surely he and the other editors at the anarchist *Mother Earth* had to meet and decide what to include in their issues, Havel conceded: "Yes. But we don't abide by our decisions."

In later years Eastman deprecated the myth that editorial policy was ever really made at these meetings, portraying them as occasions for coddling the illusion that the *Masses* was run as a collective; in practice he and Floyd Dell—who actually put out the magazine and in Eastman's case raised the money to keep it afloat financially—decided the contents. Dell's hiring was also legend. Ben Hecht, another Chicago bohemian who passed through Greenwich Village in the teens, before heading to Hollywood in the twenties, where he became an opulent screenwriter, refers to handsome Floyd Dell in his autobiography, *A Child of the Century*, as "a Chicago literary critic in a Windsor tie who had treacherously gone to New York City to become a novelist." A few months before, Eastman had hired the Village character Harry Kemp to assist him, but the hobo bard had quit overnight, leaving behind a pile of unread manuscripts and an excuse: "Dear Max—I don't want to be an editor any more. I must live and die a poet. Please don't get mad. I leave this note because I hate to come up and tell you. Harry." Eastman was dining out in the Village with Jack Reed and the *Masses'* business manager, Berkeley Tobey, who had gallantly donated his inheritance to the cause, when a slim bohemian figure happened to pass by. "There's your associate editor—that's Floyd Dell," said Tobey. In his early twenties Dell was an adornment of the Chicago bohemian scene, to which he had graduated from Davenport, Iowa, and the boy editor of the *Chicago Evening Post Friday Book Review* before he came to New York in 1913. The wispy but industrious aesthete from Chicago was accosted and offered the job on the spot. "Life is extraordinarily simple and happy in Greenwich Village," he reflected. "One even gets a job without asking for it." Uniquely, he received a regular salary, his unbohemian condition for being conscripted.*

"The *Masses* was a luxurious magazine, in all but opinion aristocratic rather than proletarian," Eastman recalled in 1948, referring not only to the expense of producing it and its insouciant style of radical will, but more pointedly to the irony that most of the money for the venture came from rich sympathizers—some very rich indeed, like the newspaper baron E. W. Scripps and his half-sister the art-loving Ellen Browning Scripps.

Discovering a "natural genius for pasting up a dummy," Eastman uncluttered the *Masses'* pages, running text consecutively, and giving plenty of space to the art. He took no credit for the drawings of such artists as Sloan, George Bellows, and Stuart Davis, who were later known as part of the Ashcan school after a jibe by their older colleague Art Young, and who were ridiculed by Bobby Edwards, the Village's balladeer: "They draw fat women for the *Masses*/Denuded, fat,

---

* In his autobiography Dell adds the prosaic detail that he had already visited the offices of the *Masses,* and met Eastman and Reed. "Max Eastman was a tall, handsome, poetic, lazy-looking fellow; Jack Reed a large, infantile, round-faced, energetic youth." *Homecoming: An Autobiography* (New York: Farrar and Rinehart, 1933), 248.

ungainly lasses—/How does that help the working classes?" However, in later years Eastman did permit himself to boast that the *Masses* had invented the modern cartoon with a one-line caption ("Your Honor, this woman gave birth to a naked child!"), an invention for which the *New Yorker* is often credited ("I say it's spinach, and I say to hell with it!"). Eastman's biographer William L. O'Neill says succinctly that its pictorial style "made the *Masses* bold and beautiful and the *New Yorker*, which later adopted the style, wealthy." Another example for the *New Yorker* was the *Masses*' amiable self-mocking presentation of itself, best captured in H. J. Glintenkamp's cartoon exchange between a well-dressed, rakish-looking young man and his date at a Village café. "He: 'Did you know that I am an anarchist and a free-lover?' She: 'Oh, indeed—I thought you were a Boy Scout.'"

The *Masses* stood for radicalism in a progressive era, but the omens looked promising after the three-way presidential election in 1912, in which the Socialist Party's Eugene V. Debs polled almost a million votes. "The socialist idea flourished to its highest bloom in America in that exciting year," Eastman recalled, noting that even the polo-playing Harry Payne Whitney was inspired to buy the popular *Metropolitan* magazine and install a British Fabian as editor. "When Fabian socialism invades the Sixty Families, revolutionary socialism invades the labor movement and the intelligentsia."

Electorally, socialists seemed destined to become more numerous and entrenched. There were twelve hundred Socialist Party office holders in the country, among them seventy-four mayors in twenty-four states, from Bridgeport, Connecticut, to Butte, Montana, to Berkeley, California. The party's 118,000 enrolled members represented every region, accent, and shade of left-wing opinion from down-to-earth social democrats in Wisconsin (derided by the less moderate as "sewer socialists") to soapboxing, song-struck Wobblies in the Far West, to garment-trade unionists in the big cities of the East and militant tenant farmers in the South, few of them strictly bound by Marxist orthodoxy or even necessarily familiar with it. There were 323 English and foreign-language socialist publications, five in English and eight in other languages, most enduringly the Yiddish *Jewish Daily Forward* in New York City, and over two hundred weeklies: the folksy *Appeal to Reason*, published in Girard, Kansas, claimed a circulation of 760,000. The party could accommodate such diversity, Irving Howe explains, at least until after 1912, because distance mitigated difference. "What a socialist local did in the coal-mining town of Krebs, Oklahoma, seldom touched a Yiddish branch on the Lower East Side of New York . . . The country was large; it took a few days to get from New York to Oklahoma." Oklahoma, now the most reactionary of states, was a radical hotbed in 1912, with a socialist constitution.

Where did the Reds of Greenwich Village stand? Editorially and personally, Eastman stood with the revolutionists, against the reformers. "I backed the rebels in every industrial or legal battle then in progress: the IWW in Lawrence; the anarchists in San Diego; the Structural Iron Workers in Indianapolis; the Timber Workers in Louisiana; the miners waging a 'civil war' in West Virginia; and I declared that 'every vote cast for Eugene V. Debs is a vote for revolutionary socialism and the class struggle.'" A year later, when Big Bill Haywood was expelled from the Socialist Party's national committee for advocating "direct action" and industrial sabotage, Eastman endorsed both tactics; he was happy to share platforms, picket lines, and his pages with the likes of Arturo Giovannitti, the poet of the revolution who sent the *Masses* a ballad from his prison cell in Lawrence, Massachusetts; with Mary Harris "Mother" Jones, the schoolteacher and dressmaker turned socialist reformer, who joined him at Carnegie Hall in a *Masses* benefit for the striking miners in West Virginia; and with Big Bill, who asked him to publish a bulletin in the magazine.

"It was like being admitted to the inner circle of some heroic order." But even then, Eastman was not converted. "The flower of character blooms best, to my taste, in a lowly soil," he wrote in long retrospect. "But I could not deceive myself that in the mass, and still less in idea, the industrial workers were my comrades or brothers, or the special repositories of my love."

And yet, under his editorship, the *Masses* went after the American plutocracy (more recently known as the One Percent) with a fury and a wit unsurpassed in the hungry thirties, the passionate sixties, or by the Occupy movement a century later, advocating its overthrow by any means necessary. In the June 1913 issue, whose cover carried Stuart Davis's drawing of two drabs ("Gee, Mag, think of us bein' on a magazine cover!"), Eastman notes: "We endorsed the general strike in Belgium, supported the 'War in Paterson,' backed Karl Liebknecht's fight against the Social Democratic majority in the German Reichstag, affirmed that the so-called 'bandits of Mexico' were the real patriots of the country, satirized the 'fifty-seven varieties of national religion,' ridiculed an Old Testament story, and featured a lyric by a striking Paint Creek miner longing in anything but pure poetry for the coming of the spring: ... 'I want to use this GUN from undercover—/ Oh Buddy, how I'm longing for the spring.'" For such editorial provocations the *Masses* was banned from subway newsstands (it fought a long battle against this ukase) and forbidden in the Harvard Club; but the cartoons, to the pride of the artists, invariably caused the greatest offense. Eastman suspected that the indictment of himself and Art Young for criminal libel of the Associated Press had something to do with the *Masses'* Christmas issue in which a group of Episcopal prelates are gorging at a banquet, oblivious to Christ hanging on the cross above them.

Eastman aimed "to keep the *Masses* poetically alive and yet not Greenwich Villagey," a task rendered paradoxical in retrospect by his admission that when he considered what a postrevolutionary world might look like, it looked a lot like Greenwich Village. After 1914 the war in Europe and the debate over what America's course should be infected the Village with a febrile atmosphere, a sort of vague militancy that infected even bohemians. In 1916 a group at the *Masses* led by John Sloan and his acolyte Stuart Davis called a strike to depose Eastman and Dell for the crimes of imposing a "policy," captioning their illustrations, and even drawing salaries. Eastman, who had been looking for an excuse to quit, instead found himself politicking to keep his job and protect Dell's; when Sloan's proposal was voted down in a showdown meeting, he moved to expel the dissidents from the magazine, getting unexpected backing from the venerated Art Young. But fearing to go too far, Eastman's majority withdrew the amendment and instead offered offices in "the Masses Publishing Company" to Sloan and his junta. But the next day a letter from the painter arrived, ominously beginning, "If thy right hand offend thee, cut it off," tendering his resignation. The artists Stuart Davis, Glenn Coleman, and Maurice Becker followed him out the door, along with the comic writer Robert Carlton Brown, later a Dadaist and, still later, a party liner.

"They want to run pictures of ash cans and girls hitching up their skirts in Horatio Street—regardless of ideas—and without title," Art Young told a reporter. "For my part I do not care to be connected with a publication that does not try to point the way out of a sordid materialistic world." Eastman, interviewed in pajamas and raincoat at his doorway in Washington Square, disingenuously dismissed the brawl as a semiannual dustup. But John Sloan, "wearing a vivid green flannel shirt and an even vivider scarlet necktie" at his studio on Washington Place, took a sterner line. " 'It just proves that real democracy doesn't work—yet,' he said, adding the 'yet' as he remembered the future Socialist paradise."

In 1914, disregarding the hallowed slogan "The workers have no country," the socialist parties of Europe had schismatically gone to war under their various national flags. In America the socialist mainstream—more consistent with Marxist orthodoxy, or perhaps wishful thinking—wanted no part in the Great War, as it became known. When "Preparedness" became the watchword for the war party led by Theodore Roosevelt, and was embraced by some anti-interventionists who still hoped to ward off entering the conflict, the *Masses* confirmed its opposition. "The country is rapidly being scared into a heroic mood," John Reed editorialized. "The workingman will do well to realize that his enemy is not Germany, nor Japan; his enemy is that 2% of the people of the United States who own 60% of the national wealth, and are now planning to make a soldier out of him to defend their loot. We advocate that the workingman prepare himself against that enemy. That is our Preparedness." Next to such editorials were cartoons that might show Jesus Christ facing a multinational firing squad ("THE DESERTER"), or Death on horseback, asking: "America, did you call?"

Ironically in view of future developments, the political class in Greenwich Village, which had been merely intrigued by Wilson four years before, was virtually unanimous for his reelection in 1916. At the *Masses*, Eastman, Dell, and Reed supported him as likelier than any Republican to keep the country out of Europe's conflagration at a time when Theodore Roosevelt was beating the war drums, and the Republican candidate, Charles Evans Hughes, was awkwardly ambiguous. Even the unyielding pacifist Randolph Bourne at the *Seven Arts* endorsed Wilson. Until 1916, the *New Republic* followed a wavering course, reflecting the divisions between the editors, and exasperating their clay-footed idol, Roosevelt. Barging into their offices on the fringe of the Village, Roosevelt remonstrated with them, but unsatisfactorily; afterward, he brutally dismissed the *New Republic* as "a negligible sheet run by two anaemic Gentiles and two uncircumcised Jews." But they were soon bent on war. Walter Lippmann, Herbert Croly, and John Dewey, as they came to oppose America's "pernicious neutrality," discounted the pacifism of their new favorite, Woodrow Wilson. "We never believed Wilson when he said he would keep us out of war," Lippmann said later. "We were convinced he was going to get us into the war." Lippmann argued with sinuous logic that it was simply psychologically insupportable for America as a nation to stay aloof from the gigantic events in Europe. John Dewey believed that war would bring socialism that much closer. "We stand at the threshold of a collectivism which is greater than any yet planned by a socialist party," he declared once America was in. The Socialist Party's brightest theoretician, the Englishman William English Walling, turned rabidly patriotic once war was declared, and urged that his former comrades who remained antiwar be rounded up and shot.

Unconcerned with Marxist orthodoxy, Eastman attributed the war to tribalism and the herd instinct. He was no pacifist, writing editorially in January 1917: "We are not advocates of violence, but as between two current misfortunes, we much prefer domestic to international violence. For in domestic violence it usually happens that some definite benefit is being fought for, and not infrequently the fighting holds a possibility of gaining the benefit; whereas in international wars, the fighting usually arises at the bidding of blind tribal instincts . . ." As he reflected later, "There was enough dynamite in that sentiment . . . to keep me busy for two years trying to stay out of jail."

In the first months of 1917, the world was turned upside-down. In March, where it was still February by its Julian calendar, a revolution that began with a bread riot in Petrograd ended barely a week later with the abdication of Tsar Nicholas II at his military headquarters, and the overthrow of the ancient autocracy. On April 2, 1917, a month after his second inauguration, Wilson asked Congress for a declaration of war against Germany, which had resumed unrestricted submarine war.

The First World War divided America as profoundly as any event since the Civil War; and dissent was dealt with the more harshly for the fact that there was so much opposition, though as time went on, mostly cowed and silent. Under the Espionage Act, signed by Wilson a month after the declaration of war, and amended and vastly enlarged by the Sedition Act in the next year, even a "disloyal" letter was criminal if it might come to the attention of a soldier or anyone liable to the draft. "It became a crime to advocate heavier taxation instead of bond issues, to criticize the Allies, to say that a referendum should have preceded, or hold that war was contrary to Christ's teaching." The *Masses* was banned from the mails under the Espionage Act, which specifically proscribed antiwar opinion that might compromise the success of the armed services, and Eastman and the other editors were tried twice for sedition, which might have led to decades of imprisonment.

In a landmark opinion Judge Learned Hand upheld the *Masses'* suit to lift the ban based on a novel "incitement" test, which was immediately appealed and overruled, and for which he was widely reviled at the time. Opponents of the First World War were subject to far more draconian treatment than their counterparts during the Vietnam era, when antiwar publications like *Ramparts*, the *Nation*, and the *New York Review of Books* were freely available, and their editors went unmolested. Eastman was nearly lynched after an antiwar address in Fargo, North Dakota, which a company of the Home Guard had been given a night's leave to heckle. Fortunately, some local dissidents managed to smuggle him out of the hall. An antiwar couple offered to drive him out of town, and handed him a gun in case they were stopped. "I loved that gun," said Max Eastman.

Wartime divided and disheartened radical bohemia, and emptied the streets of young men. Either they went off to fight in France or, if they conscientiously objected to fighting, they were in danger of being sent to Leavenworth prison. The cafés filled up with government spies (and a few German), and the Secret Service trailed not only the strapping Max Eastman but also the slight, deformed, caped figure of Randolph Bourne.

The revolutionary hopes of a literary generation for a socialist and aesthetically enlightened America were extinguished for a generation.

The high-minded *Seven Arts* magazine, founded by James Oppenheim and Waldo Frank, which had incarnated that program, was a casualty of the war. (Aside from the magazine, Oppenheim is best known for his poem "Bread and Roses," which became a rallying cry during the Lowell, Massachusetts, textile workers' strike.) In *New York Intellect*, Thomas Bender notes that four of the five editors and contributors to the *Seven Arts* grew up in New York or its environs: Oppenheim, Frank, Van Wyck Brooks (under whose banner it was launched), Randolph Bourne, and Paul Rosenfeld; and three of them were Jewish. "Long before the *Partisan Review*, Jews, who were, in the words of Frank, 'bitter, ironic, passionately logical' critics of the arts, had assumed a significant place in the shaping of American intellectual life." Editorially, the *Seven Arts* attempted a balanced "ensemble" effect, like a symphony or a poem, quite the opposite of Eastman's slangy, eclectic *Masses*; but the most distinctive note was struck by Randolph Bourne, its great soul and the only contributor who finds many readers today, and he identified with the 1910s' "Party of Youth" from a sad distance. Deformed at birth by a doctor's forceps, he was also hunchbacked from childhood spinal tuberculosis; his huge, misshapen head sank into a dwarfish body which (others imagined) he attempted to hide under a student's cape; his appearance repelled most people until he spoke, mellifluously and brilliantly, as kindly in person as he could be cutting on the page. "He had a powerful mind, philosophical erudition, a commanding prose style, and the courage of a giant," was Eastman's tribute. A prize student of John Dewey's, who worked his way through Columbia at a Pianola factory in Newark and at other odd occupations, he was disgusted when the philosopher and his disciples at the *New Republic* began supporting the war as an expression of "creative intelligence," and even taking credit for willing it against the masses who were hanging back. "A war made deliberately by the intellectuals!" Bourne's editorials stiffened Oppenheim's opposition to the war, which cost the *Seven Arts* its patronage. Bourne died of pneumonia in the dreadful winter of 1918, while hard at work on a study of the State. "If any man has a ghost / Bourne has a ghost," John Dos Passos writes in *1919* (1932):

> *A tiny twisted unscared ghost in a black cloak*
> *hopping along the grimy old brick and brownstone*
> *streets still left in downtown New York*
> *crying out in a shrill soundless giggle:*
> War is the health of the state.

In the freezing winter of 1917–18, with bohemia divided and besieged, and its flagships going down, Dorothy Day, an assistant to Max Eastman and Floyd Dell at the *Masses* and then the *Liberator*, often spent the evening drinking hard with her friend Eugene O'Neill at the Hell Hole, a rough place on Sixth Avenue at the corner of West Fourth Street patronized by teamsters, gangsters, gamblers, street-walkers, and sometimes by actors from the nearby Provincetown Play-house and some of the more adventurous younger writers and artists. Rumor said the owner kept a pig in the cellar, which he fed with scraps from the free lunch.

As a teenage suffragist, Day had gone to jail for picketing the White House, and proclaimed herself a socialist just as that was becoming a dangerous avowal. (She turned twenty in November 1918.) "The gangsters admired Dorothy Day because she could drink them under the table," recalled Malcolm Cowley, "but they felt more at home with Eugene O'Neill, who listened to their troubles and never criticized. They pitied him, too, because he was thin and shabbily dressed. One of them said to him, 'You go to any department store, Gene, and pick yourself an overcoat and tell me what size it is and I steal it for you.'"

Day and O'Neill shared a thwarted religiousness, which he enacted by endlessly reciting Francis Thompson's incantatory poem "The Hound of Heaven," to the bemused but respectful patrons of the Hell Hole. "I fled Him, down the nights and down the days; / I fled Him, down the arches of the years . . ." After closing time, the two would head to the waterfront, stopping for more drinks at sailors' bars along the way. Sometimes, they were accompanied by their friend Irwin

Granich, a young truck driver with literary ambitions and political passions, who had met Day after he began placing the occasional poem or piece in the *Masses*, singing:

> *Bill, pipe all these cute red dolls' houses.*
> *They're jammed full of people with cold noses and bad livers*
> *Who look out of their windows as we go roaring by under the stars*
> *Disgustingly drunk with the wine of life,*
> *And write us up for the magazines.*

As the trio huddled on a pier on South Street, waiting for six a.m. to strike so O'Neill could resume drinking at the Hell Hole, Granich would sing mournful Jewish songs. In 1917, he fled the draft to Mexico, wading across the Rio Grande at night with a friend, and returned after the Armistice, wearing a sombrero and calling himself Michael Gold; he went to work at the *Liberator* and later at the *New Masses*, which he edited for two years. In 1931 he put a decade's worth of sketches and stories into the semblance of a novel called *Jews Without Money*, a small, scabrous classic which became a surprise best seller for Boni & Liveright in 1931; along the way, he had become a leading proponent of proletarian literature and art, the deadly foe of Thornton Wilder, "the Genteel Christ," and a stalwart Stalinist Party liner, although never a Party functionary.

The Hound of Heaven never caught Eugene O'Neill, who became the first American to be awarded the Nobel Prize in literature, and who, on his infrequent visits to Greenwich Village, was observed to look as haunted as before, although now very elegantly dressed; but down the labyrinthine ways the Hound did catch Dorothy Day: after years of heavy drinking, casual affairs, a brief marriage, and an abortion she bitterly regretted, she converted to Roman Catholicism, became a Benedictine oblate, the founding editor of the radical *Catholic Worker*, and, today, three and a half decades after her death in 1980, is a serious candidate for sainthood.

In Albert Parry's telling, the postwar years in Greenwich Village were a dark carnival in which the bright hopes of the preceding decade were

snuffed out. Upper bohemia had always favored the war, and most
other Villagers found reasons to embrace the Allied cause and began
cheering the men who were coming home with Distinguished Service Medals (or dying, like Alan Seeger), and shunning the likes of Art
Young and John Reed. Tearooms were thronged with tourists, some
of them having been alerted to the Village's supposed temptations by
Sinclair Lewis's satirical "Hobohemia" in the *Saturday Evening Post*.
In his book, Parry lists the Wigwam, the Mouse Trap, the Vermilion Hound, the Garret, and Trilby's Waffle Shop among other cafés
calculated to catch the tourist's eye. At Don Dickerman's Pirate's Den
in Sheridan Square, waiters wore eye patches and earrings, and rusty
cutlasses were displayed on the walls. Already disapproving of the
"sissy" element that had invaded their neighborhood, the Irish toughs
rounded on the waiters of Dickerman's establishment, thinking the
pirates were a gang. The kitschy café décor—farmhouse, jail, pirate's
den, Gypsy camp—was matched by the kitsch in shops and stores
named the Bazaar de Junk and Three Steps Down.

In November 1917, almost to the day the Bolsheviks seized power in
Petrograd, Eastman shut down the *Masses*. Banned from the mails, the
last two issues had been sold only at brave newsstands; but it seemed
the magazine's purpose had been served. "It was as though we had
achieved the revolution and could now take a rest!" But "historical
necessity" could not be denied, and a few months later, with Crystal as his partner and coeditor, he founded the *Liberator* in order to
serve "the new society coming into being in Russia." The first issue of
the *Liberator* published the account from Russia by Jack Reed that had
been advertised on the last issue of the *Masses*, and which, refined into
book form, became the classic *Ten Days That Shook the World*.
    Reed had witnessed the Bolshevik revolution's birth pangs, and hav-
ing raised the money to send him to Russia, Eastman owned the exclusive rights to his eyewitness reporting of events like the storming of
the Winter Palace; it was a cablegram from Reed that convinced him
and Crystal to go ahead with the new magazine, despite a shared sense
that it was not psychologically the right thing for either. But this time
there was no nonsense about a collective: the Eastmans owned a major-

ity of the shares in the *Liberator.* "Of necessity it would be less ram-
bunctious" than the *Masses.* As President Wilson had reminded him in
a public letter, "A time of war must be regarded as wholly exceptional,"
and a line would be drawn on what was permissible by way of speech.

Returning to New York in the dead of winter, and after a tussle
with the authorities who briefly seized his papers, Reed wrote his book
in about as many days as it describes, while holed up in a furnished
room above the new Polly's restaurant on West Fourth Street. The
newly minted Bolshevik was back in Russia on April 15, 1918, when
on the basis of four cartoons and four editorials, the principals of the
Masses were put on trial for "conspiring to cause mutiny and refusal
of duty" in the armed services, and for obstructing recruitment and
enlistment—weighty charges that carried a potential penalty of twenty
years in prison.

"It was a little like being herded into the stockyards to be put on
trial for what amounted to treason in those ominous days," Eastman
recalled from the safe distance of forty years. "But New York was a
little less out of its head than the rest of the country, and New York was
full of our influential friends. We were not without hope."

Eastman and his supposed partners in crime were tried, both times,
at the Old Post Office Building across from City Hall. The windows
of the courtroom overlooked a flag-bedecked Liberty Loan booth
in the park, where a brass band played patriotic tunes every hour or
two. Crowding the space were the friends and enemies of the *Masses,*
onlookers, swarms of reporters, and a cast such as only New York
could furnish. The defendants were Eastman, Art Young, Reed (in
absentia), the business manager of the *Masses* Merrill Rogers, the cartoonist H. J. Glintenkamp, and the poet Josephine Bell. Glintenkamp
had absconded to Mexico to avoid trial, as a number of Village radicals,
the so-called "Soviet of slackers," had done to escape the draft. Bell
stood accused of publishing a free-verse tribute to Emma Goldman
and Alexander Berkman in prison, which their chief counsel, Morris
Hillquit handed to Judge Hand. "You call that a poem?" said the judge.
"Your Honor, it is so called in the indictment." "Indictment dismissed."

The presiding judge, Augustus N. Hand, thin and grizzle-bearded,
was less impressive than his cousin Learned Hand, but had the same
integrity, it seemed to Eastman. Judge Hand's judicial temperament

was one advantage the defenders enjoyed, he decided; another was that none of the defendants were German or Austrian (let alone Russian or Russian-Jewish); "we were all, absolutely and from way back, American, and we looked it." Their chief counsel, on the other hand, Morris Hillquit, the leader of the Socialist Party in New York, was born in Riga, Latvia, and spoke with a noticeable accent as he argued their case in an academic style that Eastman admired but feared might be over the heads of the jury; as a candidate for mayor the year before, he had scored a respectable 117,000 votes, appealing to antiwar sentiment. Seconding Hillquit was Dudley Field Malone, a silver-tongued Tammany Democrat who had resigned as collector of the Port of New York when his friend President Wilson reneged on his support for women's suffrage and his lover, a suffragist, had been locked up for picketing the White House.

The trial was in its first hours when the band outside struck up "The Star-Spangled Banner," immediately bringing Merrill Rogers to his feet in a display of "five-feet-two-inches of unalloyed patriotism"—a performance that astonished Judge Hand, who bemusedly followed his example, followed by the rest of the courtroom. Aghast, Eastman gave some thought to the different means of murdering his antic colleague.

"My flag was still the red flag, and I was not in the habit of standing up for 'The Star-Spangled Banner.' To begin my trial that way was to begin by backing down, and I was possessed to an almost morbid degree by an anxiety *not to back down*." On the other hand, he and others had been accused of conspiring against the government and interfering with military recruitment—and the idea of a conspiracy being launched at the *Masses'* chaotic editorial meetings "was about the most cockeyed fantasy the war psychosis produced. I had no wish, and no intention if I could help it, to spend twenty years in jail for a crime I did not commit; but to avoid this without betraying my convictions was, in the existing hysteria, an extremely delicate operation." For if he stood up, he contradicted his published opposition to the "Religion of Patriotism"; but if he kept his seat while everyone else stood, "I might as well withdraw my plea of 'not guilty'—and hand myself over to the sergeant-at-arms." So reluctantly he stood when the band played, three times, until Augustus Hand declared: "Well, I think we shall have to dispense with this ceremony from now on."

Eastman spent almost three days on the stand, virtually conducting a tutorial on socialism with Hillquit, while enduring an inquisition on the consistency of his opinions with the prosecutor, Earl Barnes. The government had impounded his correspondence file, and Barnes, "a bald-headed, hawk-faced clothes-pole of a man, with a perpetual tight smile under his nose," held up notes and letters, trying to catch him in a contradiction between what he had written and what he was prepared to say now. When the draft was signed into law, two young men in New Orleans had written to ask if he believed it would be resisted; he wired back: "I don't know, but I hope so." When Barnes asked if he had ever individually counseled draft resistance, "I had no memory of that telegram, but I had the good sense to answer: 'I was angry enough to say something like that when the idea was first proposed.'" Inevitably, he was asked how he could reconcile his published disdain for patriotic rituals with his standing up for the national anthem in court. The truth was subtler than he could explain to a jury: "I had refrained from *refusing to stand up* in order to avoid *expressing my feelings!*" But rather than attempt to explain that subtlety, he told Barnes that his feelings had changed, that when the anthem was played he was saddened to think of "those boys over there [on the western front] who were dying by the thousands, perhaps destined to die by the millions," who were fighting for liberty while at home upright citizens like himself and the other defendants were being prosecuted by other upright men who would be better occupied going after spies and profiteers and "friends of Prussianism" at home. Villagers in no legal jeopardy themselves accused Eastman of going all "Star-Spangled Banner"; this was gall and wormwood for an avowed revolutionist, and even after fifty years Eastman would admit sarcastically to have been insufficiently "martyr-like."

After two wearisome days the jury declared itself hopelessly deadlocked, eleven-to-one for conviction; the holdout, Eastman and the others learned, was a factory manager from the Bronx and the last to be chosen, "square-shouldered, blue-eyed, young and powerful," who had dared the jurors who accused him of being pro-German to put up their fists, taking off his coat as he did. Eerily enough, Eastman and his friends had caught a glimpse of this nighttime scene in the jury room in the "imperfect reflection" in an unlighted window of the

Woolworth Building. Later, the prosecutor, who rather admired Eastman, calling him "one of the brainiest men of our time," told him: "If
I had noticed that man's jaw I would never have let him on the jury."

"War is a confused time," Floyd Dell reflects in his autobiography,
Homecoming. Before the first trial began, Wilson had freed several hundred conscientious objectors from prison and conceded pacifists the
same rights that Dell was on trial for publicly defending: "I defended
those rights in court, although I no longer expected to be a conscientious objector."

After the October Revolution, old Art Young was the only pacifist in the dock. Now that America and Soviet Russia had a common
enemy in Germany, Dell did not object to being drafted, and dutifully
reported for basic training at Spartanburg, South Carolina, where for
ten days he rather enjoyed himself until it occurred to authorities that
a man who stood accused of sedition did not belong in the army. In the
Liberator, Eastman applauded Wilson's letter to the pope on war aims,
for which the president thanked him in a public letter, while admon-
ishing that some things were dangerous in wartime that in peacetime
would be innocent, and endorsed Wilson's Fourteen Points (of which
the French premier, Georges Clemenceau, said, "God Almighty was
content with ten").

The *Liberator* applauded the friendly greetings Wilson extended to
Russia's "republic of labor unions" and his admonition to the Allied
Powers that their treatment of the new regime would be an "acid
test" of their goodwill: Eastman now urged American Socialists to
drop their opposition to the war and join Europe's Socialists in supporting Wilson's war aims. Under the circumstances, the alleged coconspirators not unreasonably hoped to escape a retrial. It seemed "a
crazy foolishness" that the administration would continue to pursue
a vendetta against the defunct *Masses* when Eastman was now supporting the president in the *Liberator*. The solicitor general, John W.
Davis, one of the whitest of white-shoe lawyers in New York City
(he was to be the Democratic Party's presidential candidate in 1924),
and even the president's intimate counselor Colonel House seemed to
agree in private. But wartime *is* confusing. Wilson's dalliance with the

Bolsheviks, unlike his on-and-off liaison with the American left, was extremely short-lived; and at the end of 1918 he had joined the Allies in sending troops to Russia to oust the Bolsheviks. On the anniversary of the October Revolution in 1919, Eastman was to tell a mass rally at the Harlem Casino: "President Wilson is waging his own private war on Russia in direct violation of the spirit, and even the letter, of the United States Constitution." Indeed, the invasion of Russia was the precedent for the undeclared wars that presidents have waged outside the Americas ever since.

The Villagers who had regretted Eastman and company's failure to be martyred in April consoled themselves that they would certainly go to prison in October; the defendants expected the same. In Cleveland, Ohio, Eugene V. Debs was also on trial for violating the Espionage Act. "I went out there, both as a reporter and to get a little training for my ordeal," Eastman recalled. Pronounced guilty, the perennial Socialist candidate for president was sentenced to ten years in prison, "and received the news as calmly as one would receive a call to supper." (In 1920 he ran for president a fifth time from his prison cell and received 915,490 votes, improving on his poll in 1916.)

With Hillquit and Malone unavailable to retry the case and their attorney of record, Seymour Stedman, stricken with a fever, it was left to the *Masses'* editors to mount their own defense. The prospective jurors were not promising. About socialism one said, "I don't know what it is, but I'm opposed to it"; another, who might as well have been wearing a vest decorated with dollar bills like a plutocrat in a cartoon, gave his occupation as "Wall Street." Eastman noted that "the new judge, Martin Manton . . . was hard, brisk, and mean-looking, unpossessed of dignity, and always in a hurry, as though he had larger interests elsewhere."

Once again, the courtroom took on the atmosphere of a classroom, as Floyd Dell, now stating his occupation as "soldier," explained why he had previously opposed the war; Art Young, "solemn as a bloodhound and yet funny underneath, confessed his absolute pacifism and explained once more why cartoons can't be explained"; and Jack Reed, boyishly shy and staring in the other direction from the jury, gave an absorbing account of his journey to socialism and Russia. This time Eastman was prepared to concede the need for some restrictions on free speech in wartime, but maintained nonetheless that the *Masses* had been within its constitutional rights to oppose the war and the draft when it did. "On our side I, being the editor, was naturally the captain or head usher, and it fell to me to make the summing up . . . I had to be the Attorney for Defense, not just play the part."

Heart pounding, he lay awake in his bed, alone for once, for seven nights, each day after court, rehearsing and polishing his points. Like T. H. Huxley, "Darwin's bulldog," who in his debate with Bishop Wilberforce seized on his opening when the bishop sarcastically asked whether he was descended from an ape on his father's side or his mother's, Eastman seized on his when the prosecutor, again Mr. Barnes, proposed that the "Bolsheviki" were in reality German agents and by association the defendants their accessories.

Eastman grasped eagerly at the fistful of nettles the prosecution had given him. Judge Manton had ruled out of order any testimony about what was happening in Russia, but did not stop Eastman from assuming the relevance to the defendants' intent of *"our opinion about what was happening in Russia,"* and with this excuse Eastman delivered an exposition of socialist doctrine and a defense of the Socialist Party's stand against the war in 1916—the position to which he had reverted after Wilson joined the Allied expedition in Siberia. Regarding the draft, he quoted Daniel Webster, "not omitting to mention he was a member of the Eastman family." But it was his quietly eloquent defense of socialism that riveted the courtroom and was soon circulating in pamphlet form around the world.

"It is either," he told the rapt jurors, "the most beautiful and courageous mistake that hundreds of millions of mankind ever made, or else it is really the truth that will lead us out of misery, and anxiety, and poverty; and war, and strife and hatred between classes, into a free and happy world. In either case it deserves your respect."

This time, the trial—perhaps the most important test of freedom of the press in New York since Peter Zenger's in 1735 regarding *The New York Weekly Journal* and its piece criticizing the corrupt royal governor, William S. Cosby—ended in another hung jury, with eight votes for acquittal, four for conviction. Eastman was inclined to attribute the verdict as well as the later omission of the government to go after the avowedly Marxist-Leninist *Liberator* (during the time of the Palmer raids, when thousands of "suspected radicals" were dragooned, and thousands more "dangerous aliens" detained and deported) to their not being "swarthy foreigners": "We were so inconveniently and awfully American." Of course Eastman and company had been no less "native Americans" in April than they were in October. Something in the air of Manhattan had shifted—as would happen thirty years plus one later in the interval between the trials of Alger Hiss, when it grew abruptly colder to that defendant. But sometimes not even a weatherman can tell which way the wind blows.

3

———

Brightness Falls

1919–1932

IN *Exile's Return* (1934), Malcolm Cowley tells of moving to Greenwich Village in 1919—and how weary and middle-aged it seemed in the Great War's aftermath. The streets were full of "former people," as Cowley brutally called them—ex-anarchists, disillusioned suffragists, discouraged settlement workers, "millionaire strike leaders," and the burnt-out editors of radical newspapers. All those who had remained from the old dispensation were resistless—or so Cowley remembered in 1933—against the gang of demobilized soldiers and recent college graduates (not so numerous in those days, still an elite) who occupied the maze below Fourteenth Street like a conquering army.*

According to him, the writers of the new generation—soon to be called "lost"—did not live in bohemia, which Cowley disparaged as a romantic concoction of the nineteenth century, but in Grub Street, a *real* place "as old as the trade of letters—in Alexandria, in Rome, it was already a crowded quarter; bohemia is younger than the Romantic movement." Grub Street, or so said Cowley in his Marxian phase, was inhabited by "intellectual proletarians," whose poverty was involuntary; bohemia was elective, but its conventions required that even

———

* Cowley's phrase "former people" is the same term that was applied to the deposed nobility, ex-officials, priests, gentry, merchants, etc., of the tsarist regime who, along with their offspring, were officially declared to be pariahs in Soviet Russia.

millionaire bohemians ape the manners of starving artists—bohemia was "Grub Street on parade." But there was another difference he neglected, perhaps as too obvious. While writers and artists may hang together, like the "Cenacle" in Balzac's *Lost Illusions*, a poor writer requires only a room or a corner or a table in a café for work; a poor painter must have light and materials and a place to prop his easel. But a bohemian always needs a milieu, even if it is only a sordid boarding-house or a sad café.

As in any town under occupation, there were places in Greenwich Village where occupiers and occupied might fraternize. The Hell Hole was one; the back room of Luke O'Connor's saloon (later, a speakeasy) at Greenwich Avenue and Christopher Street was another—it was familiarly if obscurely known as the Working Girls' Home. John Masefield, the future English poet laureate—a teenaged sailor who had deserted his ship—had emptied spittoons and slop jars at O'Connor's in the 1890s. It was here that Cowley refined his sense of the differences between the former people, who had come to the Village before 1917, and the half-Villagers, as the former people called those like himself who came after. The former people tended to dress the part, with the women especially resembling their caricatures in the *Saturday Evening Post* in bright blouses, short skirts, and Henrietta Rodman sandals-with-socks. The men were "tweedy but unpressed"; the fashion for Russian peasant blouses was fading; only a nostalgic few still wore Windsor ties. The younger men who had been in the army were accustomed to uniforms, and adopted their equivalent in mufti; the younger women were learning to dress like flappers, not feminists, in uniform short shifts.

" 'They' had been rebels: they wanted to change the world, be leaders in the fight for justice and art, help to create a society in which individuals could express themselves. 'We' were convinced at the time that society could never be changed by an act of will." (Note that they changed their minds in the thirties.) "They" had quarreled with their parents, whose opinions they wanted to correct; his generation had said, "Yes, sir" in the South and "All right" in the North, and gone about their business. The romantic rebels cared about scenery, décor, the right clothes; his gang (male) was content to argue aesthetics with their feet on the kitchen table, in a tobacco trance: their expectations were humble. "We had lost our ideals at a very early age, and painlessly"; if any remained, they did not survive turbulent 1919. As Amory Blaine says in *This Side of Paradise*, the new generation had grown up "to find all wars fought, all Gods dead, all faiths in man shaken." (Fitzgerald, of course, cared passionately about scenery, décor, wearing the right clothes; but then, he was no Villager.)

"Greenwich Village was not only a place, a mood, a way of life: like all bohemias, it was also a doctrine." The catechism had not changed in its essentials since the days of Gautier and Murger: "The idea of salvation by the child"; "paganism"; "living for the moment," like Edna Millay burning her candle at both ends; female equality. The war had disentangled the bohemian revolt and the radical, which had previously seemed to be integral. "But the war, and especially the Draft Law, separated the two currents. People were suddenly forced to decide what kind of rebels they were: if they were merely rebels against Puritanism they could continue to exist safely in Mr. Wilson's world. The political rebels had no place in it." The radicals had proved inadequate to events, even when they acted honorably; the bohemians endured, even flourished after a manner." Or so it seemed to the tenants of Grub Street like Cowley, who had driven an ambulance in the war.* In 1919 the older Villagers on either side of their generation's divide seemed obsolescent at the same historical moment that, diluted for population consumption, their version of the "doctrine" was about to be embraced in the country at large: women with bobbed hair smoking in public, cocktails, country-club adulteries dignified by knowing, if not terribly informed, references to Freud—the twenties America of Fitzgerald's

---

* But here again the witness's generation determines the angle of vision. When Kenneth Rexroth published his mostly true literary memoirs in 1960, he recalled Greenwich Village after the war, which he had been privileged to experience as a recent high-school dropout from the Midwest, as a miracle of comity. "It was an interregnum in the history of revolutionary bohemia. People were dear friends and devoted comrades and passionate lovers who have been the bitterest enemies now for over thirty years. Around 201 West Thirteenth came and went Max and Crystal Eastman, Hayes and Zenith Jones, Manny Gomez, the Becker brothers, all the bunch that had been in Yucatan during the war when it was a socialist state . . . There were all kinds of girls, but most of them were rather fugitive and came and went on their way through the Revolution to Vedanta or marriage." *An Autobiographical Novel*, 205.

Tales of the Jazz Age and John O'Hara's *Appointment in Samarra* and, remoter from the metropole, Lewis's *Babbitt* and Faulkner's *Sartoris*.

Feminism had been the overarching cause of the prewar Village. Paradoxically, the passage of the Nineteenth Amendment had reduced a legion of feminists to rebels without a cause—or rather, rebels reduced to a single cause, the Equal Rights Amendment, which the younger generation associated with dowdiness. "Female equality was a good idea, perhaps, but the feminists we knew wore spectacles and flat-heeled shoes," said Malcolm Cowley.

As for Cowley's gang, "The truth is that 'we,' the newcomers to the Village, were not bohemians. We lived in top-floor tenements along the Sixth Avenue Elevated because we couldn't afford to live elsewhere."

Of course that is what bohemians always say: they came because the rents were cheap.

In *Love in Greenwich Village*, Floyd Dell did not spare himself when he was apportioning blame for its downfall. In the golden light of 1913 it was he who had suggested drafty old Webster Hall on Eleventh Street near Third Avenue when the *Masses* was looking for a venue for a benefit masquerade. "Is yours a drinking crowd?" inquired the owner, who also happened to operate a nearby bar. "'Hell, yes,' the poetic-looking Dell replied. 'All right, you can have it for nothing,' the owner said."

Admission was a dollar for anyone in costume, two dollars for those without. The ingenuity of poverty conjured up circus dancers, cavemen and -women, hula dancers, houris and sheiks, beggar girls, Gypsies of both sexes, Pierrots and Pierrettes. Barely draped young women were reminded: "There must be SOME costume." Other big causes and little magazines followed the *Masses'* example, until it seemed there was a costume ball every night at Webster Hall. For the Liberal Club, Dell consulted *Roget's Thesaurus* and came up with "'Pagan Rout,' so potent in its appeal to the fevered imaginations of the bourgeoisie!" Posters that pictured a near-naked girl riding bareback on a leaping faun, or a brawny artist in a beret carrying off his nude model, raised orgiastic expectations, which, though rarely satisfied, were regularly renewed until the expeditions from uptown became an invasion during the war, when the city was thriving, as it always did during wartime, and mad for distractions.

After the Armistice the Liberal Club, hoping to clear a large debt, promised a "Pagan Rout" uptown at the two-thousand-room Hotel Commodore, and announced all tickets must be paid for, only to back down when Villagers, indignant at such unaccustomed high-handedness and expecting to be admitted for free, threatened to riot. Prompt upon their cue, the new generation arrived en masse, also clamoring for free admission. Cowley describes the ensuing debacle: "The dance at the Commodore was something new in Village his-tory: there were so many youngsters, such high spirits, so many people not drinking quietly as in the old days, but with a frantic desire to get drunk and enjoy themselves. After midnight there were little com-motions everywhere in the ballroom." Among the lesser commotions was the poet Laurence Vail being firmly escorted from the premises: "it took four detectives to throw him out, and he left behind a great handful of bloodstained yellow hair." A hysterical Radcliffe woman was the center of an admiring circle until she began shrieking and bit-ing people. After a climactic lunge, she leaped backward onto a huge Chinese vase, which crashed to the floor. Its replacement cost was the end of the Liberal Club, which had been fatally divided by the war any-way. Its upstairs rooms and downstairs garden were succeeded as the Village's social center by the sordid Hell Hole and the marginally less sordid Working Girls' Home, places whose whiskey-soaked ambiences did not inspire debates on truth and beauty.

Some of the most eminent Villagers had long since been searching out refuges in the "suburbs," as places like Croton-on-Hudson were then known. Always the pioneer, Mabel Dodge rented a house on Mount Airy Road in 1915, as her affair with John Reed was tumul-tuously winding down. Eastman took a tiny cottage down the road, although suspecting "that Mabel was on the hunt again, and that I was in a dangerously convenient position." Jack Reed and Louise Bryant moved into Dodge's house after she moved on to Taos, New Mexico, in 1919, bringing along Hippolyte Havel as their man-of-all-work. (When Havel inevitably accused Reed of being a "parlor socialist," Reed retorted that *he* was a "kitchen anarchist.") The quiet village filled up with practicing bohemians and professing Bolsheviks. When Floyd Dell visited with his new love, B. Marie Gage, they were met on Mount Airy Road by Jack Reed, who welcomed them on behalf of "the Mount Airy Soviet."

Ingenious hucksters were finding ways to profit from the squares' fascination with bohemia, setting an example for the notional bohemians who filled the Village with twee tearooms and Ye Olde Shoppes after the war. The most conspicuous was an operator in a brocade waistcoat calling himself Guido Bruno, whose accent and origins were mysterious ("I, Bruno, have given birth to myself," he would say when pressed), who had established an eponymous "Garret" on the top floor of an ancient roadhouse on Washington Square and Thompson Street, across from the stop of the double-decker buses of the Fifth Avenue Coach Company.

Between 1914 and 1916, Bruno's Garret furnished "First Aid for Struggling Artists" in exchange for their living up to the expectations of tourists who paid ten cents or a quarter, depending on traffic, to climb upstairs. "Gaudy, dirty, crammed with easels bearing half-finished canvases bearing half-finished works of impressionist art, the Garret was populated with artists'-model types of girls and hot-eyed young men who declared themselves poets, writers, painters": Allen Churchill's description in *The Improper Bohemians* probably exaggerates the sexiness of the crowded suite to which Bruno himself commuted, mysteriously, from Yonkers, although he did nothing to discourage libidinous rumors by confiding, "I, Bruno, sleep with all the girls." In *Oh, Lady! Lady!*, the 1918 Broadway musical by P. G. Wodehouse, Guy Bolton, and Jerome Kern, he gets a knowing nod:

> *Quite ordinary people who come and live down here*
> *Get changed to perfect nuts within a year!*
> *They learn to eat spaghetti (That's hard enough you know!)*
> *They leave off socks and wear greek smocks,*
> *And study Guido Bruno!*

No mere exhibitor-exhibitionist, Bruno was possibly the most prolific publisher of little magazines (reviews, guidebooks, gazettes, chapbooks) ever to flourish in the Village. *Bruno's Bohemia, Bruno's Review of Two Worlds, Bruno's Scrap Book, Bruno's Weekly,* and *Bruno's Review of Life, Love and Literature*: all of them advertised the romance of below Fourteenth Street—in particular, of Bruno's Garret, which "hundreds, *thousands* of uptowners and out-of-towners" rode the bus downtown to gape at. As a teenager, Hart Crane was first published in *Bruno's Weekly,* which he had discovered in a Cleveland, Ohio, bookstore, and he became a habitué of the Garret when he made his first pilgrimage to Manhattan. Djuna Barnes was another of Bruno's "discoveries," although already a successful freelance at newspapers, writing stories and sometimes illustrating them, when Bruno brought out *The Book of Repulsive Women* as one of his "chapbooks." Its price was upped from fifteen to fifty cents after Village rumor hopefully detected lubricities that had escaped authority in such lines as: *"See you sagging down with bulging / Hairs to sip / The dappled damp from some vague / Under lip, / Your soft saliva, loosed / With orgy, drip."* In her small modernist masterpiece, *Nightwood,* the character of Felix Volkbein is partly based on her colorful publisher. In her hermetic old age, she recalled the milieu for a reporter from the *New York Times*: "Ghastly days—how I miss them."

Modestly, Bruno disclaimed being "the king of bohemia," reserving that distinction for the half-Japanese, half-German symbolist poet and playwright, critic, art historian, translator, and all-around artistic provocateur, Sadakichi Hartmann. Great things were expected of the poet in his youth by Whitman and Mallarmé; and, though disparaged by Van Wyck Brooks as one of the "little Nietzsches" circulating in New York in the teens, Hartmann was considered an American Verlaine by his admirers in the Village. A philosophical anarchist, he discussed the "propaganda of the deed"—that is, the need for terrorism—with Emma Goldman in the cafés of the Lower East Side, and won H. L. Mencken's reluctant admiration as a very American sort of bohemian; a discerning champion of modernist art, he pursued avant-garde adventures of his own—in the forties, this all-too-many-sided figure would end up a whiskey-soaked satellite of John Barrymore in Hollywood, bawling "I'm Sadakichi Hartmann, and I'm so colossal goddam marvelous," out the open window of his shabby apartment above Elysian Park. In the Village, he was notorious for sponging off his friends—even Maxwell Bodenheim, himself a sponger—and invited ridicule all his life; yet Ezra Pound, who had no mean self-regard, once said, "If one hadn't been oneself, it would have been worthwhile to have been Sadakichi," and grouped him among the "legion of the lost" in *The Pisan Cantos*:

> *and as for the vagaries of our friend*
> *Mr. Hartmann,*
> *Sadakichi a few more of him,*
> *Were that conceivable, would have enriched*
> *The life of Manhattan*
> *Or any other town or metropolis*
> *The texts of his early stuff are probably lost*
> *With the loss of fly-by-night periodicals . . .*

Bohemia's "king" was born c. 1867 in Nagasaki, the son of a German trader and his Japanese bride; she died within a year of his birth. The father, Oscar Hartmann, sent Sadakichi and his slightly older brother to Hamburg to be raised by their uncle Ernst, a cultivated man who treated them to art galleries, books, museums, theater, and more books. When Sadakichi was twelve Oscar Hartmann reappeared, accompanied by a jealous new wife, and apprenticed Sadakichi's brother to a farmer, and placed Sadakichi in a naval academy, which he hated. Sadakichi ran away, and when his father caught up with him in Paris, he gave him the alternative of being shipped off to live with poor relations in Pennsylvania, a fate the boy accepted, denouncing his father as he departed. His aunt and uncle were simple, pious people who put him to work at menial labor (including cleaning spittoons at a lithographer's, like John Masefield at Luke O'Connor's), but indulged his orgies of reading books from the Mercantile Library in Philadelphia, supposedly sometimes twenty in a day, mostly drama and philosophy.

In 1882, the fifteen-year-old boy presented himself one morning at the door of Walt Whitman's house in Camden, New Jersey, across the Schuylkill River. "I would like to see Walt Whitman." "That's my name," said the Good Gray One. "And you are a Japanese boy, are you not?" Whitman fried eggs for his young caller, a story Hartmann repeated often enough that *Bruno's Greenwich Village* published a cartoon in which a tall, spindly Japanese youth is declaiming something while the aged poet is reading a book and negligently attending to the eggs: "SADAKICHI TRYING HARD TO BE A GREAT MAN, WENT FRYING EGGS WITH THE GREAT WHITMAN." Although many of his other younger admirers found Sadakichi no more than a poseur, Whitman said: "I can't see it that way. I expect good things of him—extra good things."

Beginning in the 1880s, the aspiring poet made several trips back to Europe, meeting Liszt, Mallarmé, Swinburne, and Rossetti, among other great men. Typically, he managed to insinuate himself into the closed dress rehearsal of one of the midnight spectacles staged by mad King Ludwig II of Bavaria, a Wagnerian phantasmagoria in a phosphorescent grotto, featuring girls barely clad in flesh-colored tights and seaweed. "King Ludwig would have loved Hollywood," Sadakichi reminisced many years later.

Sadakichi was the cynosure of a small band of admirers to whom he was the oracle who knew "everything" about the French symbolists and the English decadents, about occult philosophy and the mysterious Orient, completing the mystique with decadent manners and occult affectations of his own. In his early twenties, he had the satisfaction of seeing the book of his play about Christ reviewed as "blasphemous" by *Publishers Weekly*, banned and burned in Boston, and causing his arrest on Christmas Day. Kenneth Rexroth, who met Hartmann as a boy when his bohemian mother invited him to Battle Creek, Michigan, and his behavior caused a scandal, concedes his poems are awful. "Yet he knew everybody more than anybody else and he seemed to know everybody." In New York, he captivated James Huneker's beer-drinking bohemian crowd at Lüchow's, on Fourteenth Street at Irving Place at the turn of the century, as, later on, he enthralled the Village underground. "To take an imaginary case, we could think of Sadakichi saying to Carl Sandburg, 'When you get to Belgium be sure and look up Verhaeren. He's a friend of mine and speaks English,' or reading aloud from Alfred Jarry's *Ubu Roi* or the poems of Tristan Corbière to an audience of Harvard boys that included T. S. Eliot." Along with Lafcadio Hearn and Yone Noguchi, the father of the sculptor, he introduced American writers to Japanese and Chinese poetry. His performance pieces anticipate the happenings of fifty and sixty years later, but merely puzzled contemporaries. *The Trip to Japan in Sixteen Minutes*, accomplished by means of perfumed linens and a fan operated by two "geishas," was presented in a music hall in Midtown to an audience whose impatience cut the act short at four minutes. An event advertised as an "orchestral concert," in which the only instrument was a phonograph player, was derided as a con. More successful in its way was the jape in which he dined at the Grill Room of the Brevoort Hotel with a bust of himself placed on the table and then departed, saying, "The other gentleman will pay."

Like many of the former people, Hartmann made his way in the twenties to Hollywood, where he became an exotic adornment at the more culturally aspiring cocktail parties. Douglas Fairbanks cast him as the court magician to the Mongol prince in his 1924 spectacular, *The Thief of Bagdad*, for which he was paid $250 and a crate of whiskey a week. At length the prodigy of whom Whitman and Mallarmé had great expectations, the oracle for two generations of Villagers, was inducted into the hard-drinking circle of John Barrymore, who called him, not unfondly, "a living freak."

He lived to be seventy-seven, dying in 1944—when the West Coast Japanese were interned in camps—in a remote house in the desert in Banning, California. Despite abundant distractions and the disadvantage of being ahead of his time, he authored more than twenty books, some of which—on Chinese art and photography—are still consulted, and fathered eleven children by two wives. The first was the daughter of an English colonel, and although he abandoned her, she recalled: "He was three parts genius and one part devil, and I was in love with all four parts."

Guido Bruno's unlikeliest and most opulent recruit to bohemia was Charles Edison, the twenty-five-year-old son and heir of the inventor, who, according to Parry, "moved to the Village at his behest and, starting with the Summer of 1915, gave him bank notes without count." The bank notes went to pay for Bruno's magazines, to which Edison, writing as "Tom Sleeper," contributed lugubrious verse, and subsidized the Little Thimble Theater, which Bruno managed. The plays were mounted in a brownstone across from the Brevoort Hotel: "good plays by Checkov [sic] and not so good ones by Strindberg, fairly interesting witticisms by Shaw and forgotten masterpieces by Gogol." Sadly, after this promising beginning as a bohemian impresario, Edison was recalled to New Jersey by his father, where he subsided into corporate life, running the family empire and in addition serving briefly as secretary of the navy and one term as the Democratic governor of New Jersey. In later life he moved into the Waldorf Astoria, becoming a friend of Herbert Hoover, his fellow Tower dweller, and in the sixties a patron of William F. Buckley Jr. and a cofounder of the Conservative Party.

Although Guido Bruno had other rich sponsors, his enterprises did not long survive Edison's defection, but others said that he was disheartened when his great friend Frank Harris left town. The Garret was closed in November 1916, and by 1918, when Wodehouse gave Bruno a shout-out in *O, Lady! Lady!*, its master of revels had disappeared from the streets of the Village, only to turn up prosaically running a used-book store in Buffalo, and respectably married, as he had been all along (thus, the commute to Yonkers). His real name was Curt Josef Kisch, his birthplace was a town in Bohemia, then part of the Austro-Hungarian Empire. But perhaps Guido Bruno had calculated that a bohemian from Bohemia would have strained credulity.

The two Village proprietors who lasted much longer than Bruno Guido—more profitably in the one case, more legendarily in the other—were Barney Gallant and Marie Marchand, "Romany Marie." When they were young, unknown, and dissipated, Gallant and Eugene O'Neill, recently expelled from Harvard for drinking, shared sordid digs which the playwright called "the garbage apartment"; the floor was carpeted in cigarette butts, and the remains of meals were left to molder in corners. Barney Gallant had immigrated from Riga, Latvia, to work for a pawnbroker uncle, who had promised to send him to Harvard in return. His uncle's word proved unreliable, and in the winter of 1910 Boris Gallant, not yet Americanized into Barney, was at loose ends and sharing a squalid, practically unfurnished room on West Fourth Street, west of Sixth Avenue, with a handsome and dissolute young O'Neill, who needed a roommate to help pay the three-dollar-a-week rent. O'Neill would go on to worse in the next few years. (In the spring he shipped out on a Norwegian bark bound for Buenos Aires.)

Gallant, meanwhile, found his way to the Liberal Club, where he organized an ongoing poker game, his best-known occupation until he became Polly Holladay's partner in the Greenwich Village Inn in 1919. In the early days of Prohibition, he earned the distinction of being the first person in New York to be prosecuted for serving alcohol after the passage of the Volstead Act. Uncertain whom to arrest when a waiter served a customer a prohibited glass of sherry, the police were relieved when Gallant, as the publican, stepped forward. Judge Learned Hand, who despised Prohibition ("that blotch, that blazon, that stench, that enormity, that changeling, that hybrid, that monster, that nightmare, that vile stew," etc., he called it when it was repealed in 1933), sentenced him to a conspicuously short time in jail. Gallant flourished in the speakeasy era, moving his boîtes in and around Sheridan Square, and scandalizing the Village by charging sixteen dollars for a bottle of bonded whiskey and twenty-five for Champagne at the various Barney's and Club Gallants, where the Villagers never ventured. As Stanley Walker, the great chronicler of the nightclub era, wrote: "He was the first to put the tall silk hat and coattails on raffish Bohemia."

Mercenary instincts never led "Romany Marie" Marchand to neglect a starving artist. A Romanian Jew, she attributed her affinity for Gypsies to her mother's having run an inn that catered to them in the woods of Moldavia; this story was widely disbelieved, although she cooked hearty country stews and was famous for reading Turkish coffee grounds. It *was* known that, having come to America as a small child, she grew up on the Lower East Side, worked in factories, and acquired anarchist sympathies, ushering at Emma Goldman's lectures. When her husband, Dr. Ad Marchand, a fabulous linguist who supposedly could speak three hundred languages and dialects, lost his job as a translator at Ellis Island during the war and they were forced to save money by moving to the Bronx, their friends, including Goldman and Alexander Berkman, Sadakichi Hartmann, and a young Columbia University instructor, Will Durant, scraped together $150 so that she could open the first Romany Marie's. Eventually, she counted seven of these "Gypsy"-themed caravansaries, from the original garret at 133 Washington Place, to 20 Christopher Street, Waverly Place, Minetta Street, Grove Street, 40 West Eighth, 64 Washington Square South, and the basement of the Hotel Brevoort, until she retired to nurse her ailing husband in the fifties. "All the seven places were one place," she once reminisced for the *Village Voice*. "When I moved there would be a sign saying 'My caravan has gone to . . .' And they would follow."

"They" included over the years and venues such writers as O'Neill, when he was penniless, and William Saroyan, when he was flush; Edna St. Vincent Millay ("She was nicer than her work"); E. E. Cummings; Max Eastman and Floyd Dell; the Benét brothers, William Rose and Stephen Vincent; Hemingway; Elliot Paul. "They" were also the artists John Sloan, Marcel Duchamp, Arthur Dove, Stuart Davis, Marsden Hartley, Joseph Stella, Constantin Brancusi, Charles Demuth, Isamu Noguchi; the inventor and oracle-to-be Buckminster Fuller became a close friend, although the "Dymaxion" furniture he designed for the Minetta Lane café tended to pitch the patrons onto the floor. The mystagogue Gurdjieff dropped in on trips to New York, accompanied by his acolyte Brancusi. "Two kinds of people came to my place, those who were creative and those who could pay for their food."

Floyd Dell took becoming a former person harder than Max Eastman, who was too busy making love and revolution to notice. Dell was aghast as the degradation of the Village came to be personified by Guido Bruno's stunts, and wheedling "characters" like the thin young man known as Tiny Tim, who sold "psychic candies" to tourists in restaurants. "Do I really seem like that?" Dell wondered as he watched "Willy the Wisp" at work, assuring women that his bonbons were the color of their psyche. "Yes, dear lady, I have looked into your subconsciousness, and seen its secret need, and these are especially for you!" The woman might be sitting with some profiteer, her husband or her lover, both probably imagining that they were patronizing the arts as well as Willy. If only the Wisp would bang the profiteer over the head with his tray and go proudly off to jail, redeeming his honor and that of the Village!

Beautiful losers starving and dying in untidy garrets had never appealed to Floyd Dell. The young Parisians *he* admired at a safe historical distance were the students of the Latin Quarter who had stood and fallen with the workers and the revolutionists in 1848 and 1870. As a boy, he had thrilled to the traveling minstrels in Bliss Carman and Richard Hovey's *Songs from Vagabondia*; as a young writer, his ideal bohemia was not the Village but San Francisco's North Beach as limned in Gelett Burgess's stories and Frank Norris's *Blix*. The coast of bohemia was sea-breezy, like San Francisco, or full of river light like Davenport, Iowa. As for below Fourteenth Street, "I loathed what the Village had now become. It was a show-place, where there was no longer any privacy from the vulgar stares of an up-town rabble." The final indignity was one of these uptowners intruding upon his late-night cup of coffee to ask: "Are you a merry Villager?"

Politically and artistically, the years between the declaration of war in 1917 and 1922, when so many eminent Villagers seemed to flee, en masse, to the French Line and sail away, were a confused entr'acte, during which America might have lost its innocence, but most definitely advanced in its modernity. Almost nobody spoke of "Dada" in New York until after 1920, yet New York Dada was most flourishing during the war. Baroness Elsa von Freytag-Loringhoven, called the "mother" of Dada, but perhaps more like its embodiment, had been an arresting sight on the streets of the Village for several years before the cast was ever assembled at the Cabaret Voltaire, Dada's official birthplace in Zurich, in 1916.

A former chorus girl and off-and-on artist's model, born in 1874, who had moved in avant-garde circles in Munich and Berlin and traveled to America with her second husband, a novelist who abandoned her on a Kentucky farm, the former Elsa Plotz married a penniless German aristocrat eleven years her junior in New York in 1913. After a honeymoon at the Ritz, the baron went back to work as a busboy and then, patriotically, attempted to return to Germany in 1914 (intercepted and interned, he committed suicide in 1919). The baroness moved into a hovel on West Thirteenth Street, which she shared with homeless dogs and cats and adopted rats, and began living, performing, dressing, and writing the thing that had not yet been named Dada. She powdered her face chrome yellow and painted her lips flat black; ice-cream and mustard spoons and the scrolled lids of sardine tins did for earrings; lead soldiers dangled from her skirts; she cropped her hair short and dyed it vermilion. Her reputation preceded her at the salon of Walter and Louise Arensberg, a drawing-room version of Zurich-Berlin Dada at their large West Sixty-seventh Street apartment, with the painters Joseph Stella, Charles Sheeler, Charles Demuth; Man Ray and the poet William Carlos Williams; the expatriate Frenchmen Walter Pach, Francis Picabia (who was AWOL from the French army), and Marcel Duchamp in regular attendance; the baroness and the pugnacious Arthur Cravan were the most outrageous guests, even in a company that sometimes included Isadora Duncan.

When George Biddle, the rich and aristocratic Philadelphia painter to whom she had applied as a model, asked to see her nude, the baroness flung open her overcoat to reveal herself naked except for the tomato cans on her breasts and a birdcage containing a "crestfallen canary" which hung from the green string tied behind her back that connected the cans. The baroness fashioned junk sculptures out of the same detritus with which she adorned herself (a flattened tin can might do for either purpose). On a visit to the *Little Review*, which published her poetry but never gave her as much space as she thought she deserved—such as a whole issue—she brazenly pilfered sheets of the pink two-cent stamps (first-class mail at the time) which she would paste on her cheek like beauty marks.* For a mechanomorphic effect she attached an electric battery taillight to the bustle of an ordinary black dress. "Cars and bicycles have tail lights. Why not I?" she explained. "Also, people won't bump into me in the dark." Headgear included a wastepaper basket, a chocolate cake with lit candles, an upside-down colander with vegetables, and the top of a coal scuttle, fastened under her chin like a helmet. According to Margaret Anderson, she was wearing the coal scuttle at a reception for the English diva Marguerite d'Alvarez when the guest of honor piously announced that she "sang for humanity." "I wouldn't lift a leg for humanity!" the baroness replied.

Arrested at least once for public nudity, when she paraded around

---

* On her first visit to the *Little Review*'s offices, Margaret Anderson tells, the baroness was wearing a bolero jacket, a tam o'shanter dangling ice-cream spoons, and tea balls hanging from her bust. After inspecting the bookcases, this extraordinary figure announced, "I have sent you a poem." "Yes," Jane Heap agreed, and retrieved from a pile of manuscripts a submission by "Tara Osrik." "How did you know I wrote that poem?" the baroness demanded. "I am not," replied Jane Heap, "entirely without imagination." See Margaret C. Anderson, *My Thirty Years' War.*

Washington Square wearing a Mexican blanket and nothing else, and many times for shoplifting at Macy's and Wanamaker's, Baroness Elsa developed an extensive acquaintance with Manhattan's houses of detention, including the women's cells at the frightening and noisome Tombs—at least until the police, impressed with her agility at escaping from Black Marias, ceased to bother with her. "Crime is not crime in country of criminals," she told Jane Heap.

Her sexual voracity impressed the women of the Village and terrified the men, not least the major American poets who aroused her lust. According to William Carlos Williams, Wallace Stevens for years was afraid to go below Fourteenth Street because of her, and he was himself the object of a mad pursuit. To be able to fend off her advances (after unwisely encouraging them) and the physical assaults that followed when they were rebuffed, Williams applied himself to a punching bag in his cellar, "and the next time she attacked me, about six o'clock one evening on Park Avenue, I flattened her with a stiff punch to the mouth. I thought she was going to stick a knife in me. I had her arrested, she shouting, 'What are you in this town? Napoleon?'" Rejection inspired some of her greatest performances. Yearning for more than comradeship from Marcel Duchamp, but understanding for once that her "platonic lover" was an asexual flirt who would not endure even a touch, she reacted electrically when a mutual friend brought her a newspaper clipping featuring his *Nude Descending a Staircase*. "She was all joy, took the clipping and gave herself a rubdown with it, missing no part of her anatomy. The climax was a poem she had composed for Duchamp. It went 'Marcel, Marcel, I love you like Hell, Marcel.'" A handsome teenage art student whose "molten gold" tresses she admired and whose coldness she associated with his Canadian birth was memorialized in "The Cast-Iron Lover," which her biographer proposes as "New York's equivalent to T. S. Eliot's 'The Love Song of J. Alfred Prufrock.'" Chagrined but resilient, Baroness Elsa shaved her skull and began "shellacking" it persimmon red or her favorite, vermilion green, her best-known feat of personal artifice. "Shaving one's head," she said, "is like having a new love experience." The baroness lengthened her rap sheet during the war when she was arrested as a suspected spy and jailed for three weeks in Connecticut; "a person like myself sometimes *will* run up against this sort of thing," she remarked to Djuna Barnes after she was released as "mentally deranged": oddly enough, it was the first time.

"Dada cannot live in New York. All New York is dada." Quoted fragmentarily, as it usually is, Man Ray's famous letter to Tristan Tzara in 1921 reads more like an awestruck tribute than an explanation of why New York could not be interested in buying anything Dada, imported or homemade: "All New York is dada, and will not tolerate a rival, will not notice dada." On the page, Man Ray pasted a photograph of a nude, entirely shaven Baroness Elsa in a strenuous pose, accompanied by a scatological pun.

Quite exceeding all other Dadaist provocations committed in New York, the baroness at this time almost certainly created what Robert Hughes calls "one of the few exceptional images of blasphemy in American art": the upside-down cast-iron plumbing trap titled *God*. The piece was for long attributed to Morton Schamberg, a follower of Picabia, who died in the 1918 influenza epidemic; but recent scholarship suggests that it is unlikely that the fastidious Schamberg did more than mount the assembly—which much more closely resembles the baroness's junk sculptures than his sleek ones—on a miter box and photograph it. Unlike the canonical urinal that Duchamp called *Fountain* and signed R. Mutt, *God* retains shock value. "If there was anyone in New York likely to exhibit a grease trap as God, that person was probably the Baroness," says Hughes, who nominates her as "America's first punk." But the city would not tolerate a rival, as Man Ray said. In 1923, with, in George Biddle's words, "her spirit withering in the sordid materialism of New York," she fled to Europe. To loyal but not inexhaustibly loyal Jane Heap she wrote: "I have no chance here—none at all—I *hate* this country—I am nauseated to see the monstrous faces—send me to Paris." Deeply relieved to see her go, William Carlos Williams had contributed two hundred dollars to the fund organized by Heap—and by his own account gave her more, but a go-between pilfered the money. Ironically, as Ross Wetzsteon notes, Baroness Elsa—who had been the ultimate outsider-as-insider in New York—was regarded, when anybody noticed, as a "dotty old lady" in an early Weimar Germany, where a legion of outsiders had become insiders. After doing time in two madhouses, and being reduced to hawking newspapers on street corners, she fled to Paris, where she fared better for a time. Having kept her lean and boyish figure into her mid-fifties, Baroness Elsa advertised her availability as a model, with some modest success. Her work found an unlikely champion in the twenty-five-year-old Ernest Hemingway, who was assisting Ford Madox Ford at the *transatlantic review* and published a substantial sample in his absence (her "collected works," Ford said sarcastically when he returned from fund-raising in New York and discovered what his subeditor had done). At a safe distance, she recalled her days in New York with pride. When Charles Lindbergh convulsed Paris with admiration for his transatlantic flight, she boasted in a letter to her fan Peggy Guggenheim, "I dared as fine as Lindbergh in my realm." In fall 1927 she moved into a modest flat in a dismal hotel on the rue Barrault in the thirteenth arrondisement. On the cold night of December 14, all Paris was celebrating Lindbergh's arrival in Mexico City, which had been announced on radio, in movie houses, and on a big electric sign in the place de l'Opéra. The next morning, December 15, Baroness Elsa was found asphyxiated, along with her dog, Pinkie; rather than a suicide, her friends believed she must have carelessly left on the gas lights, since they could not believe she would have harmed the dog. In his autobiography Williams repeats a nasty story that went around that she was "playfully killed by some French jokester," who turned on the gas while she was asleep, although there was no evidence that such a thing happened. Berenice Abbott, who had been her worshipful disciple in New York and faithful friend in Paris, hastened to the ill-named Grand Hotel for a farewell. Djuna Barnes, who had introduced Abbott to the baroness in New York, took responsibility for settling her affairs and taking up a collection for her burial at Père Lachaise. On the day appointed for a gravesite funeral, Barnes and her turbulent lover Thelma Wood could not find the plot and, accompanied by some friends, got drunk in a convenient bar, missing the obsequies, which, no doubt to the point, had concluded when they found the unmarked and now-lost grave. Barnes commissioned a death mask, which was photographed and reproduced in *transition*, along with her tribute, which regretted that her accidental death was apparently "a stupid joke that had not even the decency of maliciousness." In death, the baroness looks as composed as a Roman senator. Barnes carried the mask with her back to America, stowing it in a closet in Patchin Place and forgetting all about it until she opened the door one day and it came tumbling out and hit her on the head; landing on the floor, the clay visage broke into pieces.

"One world war produced the Baroness," said Kenneth Rexroth. "The second world war produced thousands of Baronesses all over the world. Long ago when I was very young I asked Marcel Duchamp, 'Would you call the Baroness a Futurist or a Dadaist?' He replied, 'She is not a Futurist. She is the future.'"

Nothing dramatized so poignantly the dissolution of the old Village than Dell's last encounter with George Cram Cook at the Brevoort Hotel in spring 1922, a great season for leave-takings. His old friend was heartbroken that after the enormous success of *The Emperor Jones*, Eugene O'Neill had decided to open his plays directly on Broadway. The Provincetown Players suspended operations, and Cook and Susan Glaspell prepared to sail to Greece, fulfilling an older dream than producing O'Neill's plays.

> I was having lunch with a friend in the basement of the Brevoort, when George came in. He was drunk; he said he had been drunk for eight days. He talked about Greece, and Greek dances with an intense earnestness; and, picking up my plate, he did some kind of solemn Pyrrhic dance with it all over the floor of the restaurant; and I felt embarrassed, and ashamed of him. Then he said to me: "Floyd, let's gather the old Davenport crowd together, and go back there, and make it a new Athens!" I was touched, and ashamed of myself for being ashamed of him. It was, at least, a beautiful dream that was driving him into exile. That was the last I ever saw him."

Cook made his way to Delphi, where he adopted Greek dress and drank with the local shepherds, posed for photographs against the ruins, and four years later died a strange death from glanders, a disease he caught from his dog. The Greeks, to whom he had endeared himself, buried him under a great stone from Delphi's temple. "I would have had him die for Russia and the future, rather than for Greece and the past," Floyd Dell wrote in 1933, not realizing that in America the future was not Bolshevik revolution, which meant Stalinism, but FDR's New Deal, in whose administration so many former people like himself were finding a place.

In *Love in Greenwich Village*, Dell recounts how one night in 1917, when the old Village was already under siege, he and three friends sat up late at a bohemian party. It was snowing; they were arguing about one thing and another as the party died down, and the lively young couple who were their hosts pulled out mattresses and laid them down in a row for the remaining guests to sleep on. Awakening to broad daylight, Dell and his friends went out for breakfast at the "Purple Purp," where they discussed the diverse paths that brought them together, with America having for so long conspired to keep them distant. "Here we are—safe in Greenwich Village!" Remembering an old occasion when they might have met years earlier, they resolved to reconvene at the same spot in seven years, in December 1924. When the date rolled around, Dell somewhat doubtfully kept the appointment, knowing that Julian had committed suicide and Ben was in prison. But Paul was among the living and waiting for him in the café, probably a speakeasy, that had replaced the Purple Purp; the commercial fiction he was writing now enabled him to live, though perhaps inwardly as an alien, among the very rich, which seemed another sort of doom to Floyd Dell. Walking in the Village afterward, he saw no one he knew. Everything had changed.

"I went out from the noise and smoke into the crisp December air, feeling old. Presently I felt older than that—I felt dead. A ghost, I walked about the midnight streets, meeting other ghosts—friends and comrades and sweethearts of those lost, happy years. Together we revisited those glimpses of the moon."

In the twenties, the Village ceased to matter as it had mattered in the Progressive Era, ceased even to exist as a destination for the creative minority. Looking around in 1929, on his return from Paris, Scott Fitzgerald observed with some wonder: "In the past decade Greenwich Village, Washington Square, Murray Hill, the chateaux of Fifth Avenue had somehow disappeared, or become inexpressible of anything."

Edna Millay had married and moved upstate, and Maxwell Bodenheim was now the Village's most famous poet, but less for his conventional verses than for his reputation as a lady-killer (at least one teenage girl died for love of him); he even succeeded in writing a bestselling novel for Horace Liveright. Banned in Boston and censored in New York City, *Replenishing Jessica* sold thirty-three thousand copies, ten thousand more than *The Great Gatsby*; it was declared harmless in New York after a lengthy reading by the district attorney put the jury to sleep. The playboy mayor, Jimmy Walker, was referring to Bodenheim's masterpiece when he quipped, "No girl was ever ruined by a book." (Bodenheim, obviously, was another thing.)

Bodenheim's friend Ben Hecht, with whom he conducted a mock feud in the golden days, had graduated from Greenwich Village to a penthouse in Beekman Place, but was two months behind in the rent on the day in 1927 when a telegram arrived "from the unknown Scythian wastes of Hollywood, Calif.," offering him three hundred dollars a week to work at Paramount Pictures, all expenses paid. "The three hundred is peanuts. There are millions to be grabbed out here and your only competition is idiots. Don't let this get around. Herman Mankiewicz." Hecht leapt at the temptation. On his first day in his office at Paramount, he recalled, he was made welcome by compatriots from the East. "Men of letters, bearing gin bottles, arrived": Robert Benchley, Donald Ogden Stewart, F. Scott Fitzgerald, Edwin Justus Mayer.

Radicalism was eclipsed, and the romance of Bolshevism, which was the last great love affair the "old" Village had indulged, died down except for a relative handful of obdurate sectaries. In *Homecoming* Floyd Dell remarks intriguingly that by 1924 it was businessmen rather than bohemians who were apt to be interested in communism as a successful example of organization.

Bobby Edwards, a troubadour who accompanied himself on one of his "futuristic" cigar-box ukuleles (available for sale) and practiced "Painless Photography," furnished the postrevolutionary Village with a motto: "Why be an industrial slave when you can be crazy?" (pronounced "cr-a-a-a-zy"). If John Reed's "A Day in Bohemia" sang of boyish pleasures, Edwards, no less the master of doggerel in 1920, was the bard of a tourist trap:

Way down South in Greenwich Village
Where the spinsters come for thrillage . . .

The most famous citizen of the Village in the mid-twenties was the "millionaire poet," Robert Clairmont, a Gatsby-esque figure who squandered his fortune on other people's riotous living. The parties at his West Fourth Street apartment might last three or four days, often continuing long after he had fled to the country. (According to a Village saying, if his lights were on, he was out.) As a "dreamy clerk" in his teens, or so the story went, Clairmont had saved a steel tycoon from drowning in the pool of the men's club in Pittsburgh where he was working; his good deed was rewarded with a bequest of $350,000, or $500,000, or some such amount, when the fated tycoon died of natural causes soon after. Bob moved to New York, enrolled at Columbia's School of Journalism, and enlarged his tidy fortune into a million dollars speculating in the stock market. (Wall Street was Golconda in those days.)

Indifferent to high society, Clairmont reserved his hospitality for poets and painters—no "rich dullards"—but was ill repaid by his "boy friends," as Parry calls them, who broke down his door when he was away, helped themselves to his suits and ties, and sold his books to the used-book stores on Second and Fourth Avenues. Hans Stengel, a talented caricaturist who had been a Prussian officer in the war and did cartoons for the *Herald Tribune*, commandeered Clairmont's apartment in his absence for a party whose dramatic climax was the discovery that he had hanged himself in the bathroom; as a final touch, he had left behind a cartoon of how he expected to look when the other guests found him, tongue lolling. In an obituary in the *New Republic*, Edmund Wilson, who knew and admired him, wrote that Stengel, a proud man, suffered from being unable to impose himself as an artist on New York—although he had the actor's gift of dominating a group and could count Mencken, Dreiser, and the American fauve Robert Chanler among his friends, he could never assimilate, remaining a foreigner in the city that had become home. "It is natural to put down a failure to survive in one's own community—where we ourselves have no difficulty in prospering—to the deficiencies of the person who fails," wrote Wilson; "but it is sometimes a good idea to inquire into the deficiencies of one's civilization from the point of view of what it destroys." This was a question that was soon to become urgent when it appeared that American civilization had destroyed millions.

The long party was winding down when Robert Clairmont lost everything in the stock market crash of October 1929. "Wall Street was flooded in red ink, and I happened not to have my water wings along," he said nonchalantly when reporters came calling at the municipal boardinghouse to which he was reduced. Of his ex-friends who neglected to repay his loans, or pilfered his books, or sold his suits, he said: "It cost me just $800,000 to learn that the only art which mattered vitally to those apostles of esthetics was the art of getting dollars for nothing. Education is rather expensive, isn't it?"

All of this was a sideshow. It was "Pound's Era," and the action was abroad. "Now even New York seemed too American, too close to home," in Malcolm Cowley's telling. "On its river side, Greenwich Village was bounded by the French Line pier." Europe had never looked more civilized to the disaffected younger than now that Prohibition had, in theory at least, deprived them of the solace of alcohol. No less important, even poor bohemians were in a position to benefit from valuta—the difference between the value of the rock-solid dollar and bankrupt Europe's inflated currencies—everywhere from Prague to Pamplona, but most especially in Paris, the most shining destination of "the great migration eastward."

By 1927, the American colony in Paris, collectively known as "Montparnassia" after its favored quarter, counted as many as forty thousand expatriates, with hangers-on, remittance men, collegiate adventurers, poseurs, spongers, and wastrels greatly exceeding the genuinely aspiring writers, painters, sculptors, and musicians. Memoirs, reminiscences, and autobiographical novels began to appear almost as soon as the exodus started, and continued as long as the Lost Generation was above ground. Among the earliest was Alfred Kreymborg's *Troubadour: An Autobiography* (1925), published a year before Hemingway's *The Sun Also Rises*. The two most famous memoirs, and among the least reliable, are the relevant parts of Stein's *Autobiography of Alice B. Toklas* and Hemingway's posthumous *A Moveable Feast*. Djuna Barnes, William Carlos Williams, Sherwood Anderson, Malcolm Cowley, John Dos

Passos, Stephen Vincent Benét, Edmund Wilson, Edna St. Vincent Millay, Matthew Josephson, Max Eastman, E. E. Cummings, Anaïs Nin, Katharine Anne Porter, Elliot Paul, Louis Bromfield, Glenway Wescott, Archibald MacLeish, Lincoln Steffens, Gorham Munson, Robert McAlmon, Kay Boyle—all wrote novels or memoirs, in brief or at length, in which the City of Light is a setting, usually the principal one. As a place name "Paris" features almost as prominently in American works of or about the twenties as "America" does in those of the thirties, forties, and fifties.

The Americans were only a part, albeit the most conspicuous, of the cosmopolitan mob which had descended on the city. Spreading out from the corner of the boulevard Montparnasse and the boulevard Raspail were the formerly working-class cafés where the exiles could be found: the Dôme, which from 1919 until the Crash was "the capitol of the English-speaking avant-garde"; the Rotonde, favored by painters and Scandinavians; the Jockey Club, where Les Copeland sang Joe Hill ("Shall we be slaves and work for wages? / It is outrageous / Has been for ages"); the Select; the Dingo. Café society was the exiles' outdoor relief.

"You're an expatriate," Jake Barnes accuses himself in *The Sun Also Rises*. "You've lost touch with the soil. You get precious. Fake European standards have ruined you. You drink yourself to death. You become obsessed with sex. You spend all your time talking, not working. You are an expatriate, see? You hang around cafés."

Resonant in literary annals was Malcolm Cowley's being collared at the heart of Montparnassia in the early morning of July 15, 1923, two weeks before his scheduled departure for New York, after a fracas earlier in the evening. Amid the excitement of Bastille Day he was seated with his usual companions at the Dôme, just as Hemingway unflatteringly pictures him in "The Snows of Kilimanjaro": *"that American poet with a pile of saucers in front of him and a stupid look on his potato face talking about the Dada movement with a Roumanian who said his name was Tristan Tzara, who always wore a monocle and had a headache . . ."* Returning after midnight, and loudly denouncing the proprietor of the Rotonde one more time, he was seized by a pair of policemen, one of them drunk and in a mood to amuse himself. " 'You're lucky,' he said, 'to be arrested in Paris. If you were arrested by the brutal policemen of New York, they would cuff you on the ear—like this,' he snarled, cuffing me on the ear, 'but in Paris we pat you gently on the shoulder.'"

Nodding over a pile of saucers at the Select, Harold Stearns was a living cautionary tale. It was he who had led the exodus from Greenwich Village. In July 1921, in his basement apartment at 31 Jones Street, he completed the preface to *Civilization in the United States: An Inquiry by Thirty Americans*, the symposium that he had conceived and edited, and having delivered the completed manuscript to his publisher, Harcourt, Brace, sailed for Europe on the Fourth of July, following the succinct advice he had given other young American intellectuals in a previous book: "Get out."

Reporters had crowded the gangplank to report any parting shots; in *Exile's Return* Cowley said it was like Byron shaking the dust of England from his boots. Stearns's thirty contributors included writers already distinguished in their fields—Van Wyck Brooks (on literature), Lewis Mumford (the city), Ring Lardner (sports), Deems Taylor (music), H. L. Mencken (politics), George Jean Nathan (theater)—or about to be: Paul de Kruif (medicine) and Hendrik van Loon (popular illustrated history). Stearns congratulated himself on having the wit to assign the chapter on sex to a married woman and the chapter on marriage to a "spinster." With few exceptions, the thirty Americans were agreed on the "emotional and aesthetic" starvation of the American scene. Its politicians were venal, its cities noisome, its critics irrelevant, its journalism unserious, its pleasures crass. *Civilization in the United States*, Malcolm Cowley wrote, was like "an inquest performed over the body of a man whom nobody liked."

In Paris, Stearns entered upon what Hemingway called his "period of unreliability." Passed out at the Select, he became a melancholy landmark: "There lies civilization in the United States." Stearns pulled himself together to join the exodus home in 1932, and in 1935 he published an autobiography, *The Street I Know*: "The wind blows cold down every street / But coldest down the street I know." Despite this melancholy avowal, the chapters on the Village are sparkling and unregretful. In 1937 he conducted another "inquiry," *America Now: A Re-Appraisal*, enlisting many of the same writers as before, most of them chastened by the experience of the twenties, heartened by the New Deal, and broadened beyond the perspectives of Greenwich Village. In the same year he was remarried to a rich woman and moved into her large house in Locust Valley, Long Island. He died in 1943.

"God damn the continent of Europe," Scott Fitzgerald wrote his college chum Edmund Wilson after an unsatisfactory trip to Europe in 1921. "Rome is only a few years behind Tyre and Babylon . . . You may have spoken in jest about New York as the capital of culture but in 25 years it will be just as London is now. Culture follows money and all the refinements of aestheticism can't stave off its change of seat. We will be the Romans in the next generation as the English are now." Fitzgerald, of course, was entirely right, as sensitive Englishmen like Harold Macmillan recognized well before the end of the war. (In his diary Macmillan refers to FDR at the Casablanca Conference as "The Emperor of the West": surely, he was not the only one.) Paris is beautifully observed in "Babylon Revisited," one of Fitzgerald's great short stories; but like most Americans in Paris he seemed oblivious to his cultural, as opposed to social and material, surroundings. The "exiles" like Cowley, Hemingway, and Matthew Josephson, who knew or bothered to learn the language, who studied the paintings in museums, acquainted themselves with the literature and the indigenous avant-garde, followed European politics, or even sports like bicycle races, were few: Fitzgerald was simply more articulate in his rationalizations for being a chauvinist abroad. "You could have sworn you were only in a transplanted Greenwich Village . . . except for the fact some people stubbornly persisted in speaking French," Stearns says in his memoir, confirming that most of the Villagers in Paris observed the same obliviousness to their neighbors that they practiced at home.

Paris paid them the same disregard. "In those days," says the Canadian short-story writer Morley Callaghan in *That Summer in Paris* (1963), "a writer coming to Paris could believe he would find contemporaries and it didn't matter to him that the French themselves paid no attention to him. In no time you learned that the oddly parochial French took it for granted you were absorbed in their culture. If not, what were you doing there in the style center?" Paris was entranced by Josephine Baker, the exotic singer-dancer and life force from St. Louis, Missouri, who, at the age of nineteen, conquered the City of Light wearing little more than a flamingo feather between her legs or a skirt of artificial bananas; and Paris gave Charles Lindbergh a welcome accorded few human beings before or since. But then, as Alistair Horne points out, a few months later the same Parisians were out in the avenues in a fury at the barbarous nation that had executed Sacco and Vanzetti.* There are nested art-historical ironies in the fascination that certain French artists and intellectuals found in the brassy surfaces of American life, in the wonder of skyscrapers (as seen in photographs), the genius of Chaplin, the art of the silent Western movies starring William S. Hart, and in how this taste was to be recirculated. As Kenneth Rexroth writes, "*Americanisme* became a craze of the international avant-garde," which was of course centered in Paris, "even of the Russian Com-futurists and Constructivists—at last even of the Americans." Gilbert Seldes wrote a book, *The Seven Lively Arts*, which proved conclusively that the forms of the mass culture were greatly superior to the fine arts of the elite. It would be more exact to say, as does Ann Douglas, that Seldes championed the "popular" arts, for by 1950, as we shall see, he despaired of their mutation into "mass" media; but his example of highbrow slumming remains infectious to this day. Another American convert to *Americanisme* was the novelist Robert M. Coates, who, as art critic for the *New Yorker*, in 1946 coined the fatal phrase "abstract expressionism," the banner under which, we are ironically told by Serge Guilbaut, "New York Stole the Idea of Modern Art."

His unruly red hair and dandyish dress proclaimed him a bohemian; only his regular work habits compromised Ezra Pound's claim to be bohemia's king in the exilic twenties. "Yes, even more than Hemingway, he was the prophet and the ruler of these times and these exiles, he, Ezra Pound—the erudite, multilingual poet," says Parry, naming

* On the New York–Paris connection (and disconnection), see chapter 14 of Callaghan's *That Summer in Paris* (New York, 1963); Rexroth, *American Poetry of the Twentieth Century*, 95–97; Horne, *Seven Ages of Paris* (New York, 2002), 329–33.

the era after him. "While Hemingway stressed drink and disillusionment, Pound stressed symbolism and aestheticism, with drink and disillusionment as things not to be argued against." Pound had aspired to the literary dictatorship of London before he moved operations to Paris; and before the decade was done he had gone on to Rapallo: his reign, too, was a moveable feast.

It does not occur to Parry that the "expatriation" of the Lost Generation into the Paris of Diaghilev and Stravinsky, Proust and Joyce, Cocteau and Gide was not only an interesting time to be alive but a transformative event in the history of modern civilization, as it seems to us. But then, at the bottom of the Depression the expatriate years were apt to appear to have been nothing more than an episode in a gaudy spree. When Fitzgerald published *Tender Is the Night*—the last great literary monument of the Jazz Age he named—an early number of *Partisan Review* informed him that it was useless to hide under a beach umbrella during a revolution. Such was the crushing verdict of Union Square on Cap d'Antibes, where the party had moved for its last commotions.

Few of the Lost Generation—as it was named by Gertrude Stein, portrayed by Ernest Hemingway, and anatomized by Malcolm Cowley— were actual expatriates like T. S. Eliot, who, following the example of Henry James, became a British subject; or Stein and Ezra Pound, who, although keeping their American citizenship, returned as strangers in a strange land in the thirties: she triumphantly, having the satisfaction of seeing her arrival announced on the "zipper" of the New York Times Building; he disastrously in terms of what followed. (Puzzled and hurt that FDR had no time to hear his theories of money, Pound came to think even more highly of Mussolini, and took to denouncing Roosevelt as a "putrescence.") When the Crash cut off their lifelines to America in 1929, most of the Americans in Paris, like other foreigners dependent on valuta, dispersed like birds from the chestnut trees at sunset.

In 1929 Eric Blair, the future George Orwell, was living in a sordid boardinghouse on the rue du Pot-de-Fer, a short distance, Alistair Horne points out, from the comfortable if unpretentious bourgeois apartment on the rue de Cardinal Lemoine that Ernest Hemingway could now afford. Paris was no moveable feast for Eric Blair, miserably employed as a *plongeur* (dishwasher) in the red-hot kitchen cellar of a huge hotel. Before that job came along, his friend Boris, formerly in the tsar's service, had proposed a life of crime. "Sooner rob than starve, *mon ami*. I have often planned it. A fat, rich American—some dark corner down Montparnasse way—a cobblestone in a stocking—bang! And then go through his pockets and bolt." Nor did George Orwell remember his fellow foreigners as more than a pretentious rabble, "such a swarm of artists, writers, students, dilettanti, sight-seers, debauchees, and plain idlers as the world has probably never seen . . . It was the age of dark horses and neglected genii; the phrase on everybody's lips was '*Quand je serai lancé.*' As it turned out, nobody was '*lancé*'; the slump descended like another Ice Age, the cosmopolitan mob of artists vanished, and the huge Montparnasse cafés which only ten years ago were filled till the small hours by hordes of shrieking poseurs have turned into darkened tombs in which there are not even any ghosts." In his great essay "Inside the Whale," their multitudinous coming and going was mere prelude to the arrival of Henry Miller, son of Brooklyn, a true impoverished scavenging expatriate, not a currency tourist, swimming against the current.

Two years of exile were enough for Malcolm Cowley, who "had learned from a distance to admire [America's] picturesque qualities," if not its moral and social values. Having made his grand gesture in Montparnasse, he was conscious of returning, in 1923, to a country where his moral convictions about literature were bound to be misunderstood, where nobody knew or cared about Dada, and where he would be living "in a city where writers had only three justifications for their acts: they did them to make money, or to get their names in the papers, or because they were drunk."

In New York, which he called "the City of Anger" ("but underneath the anger is another mood, a feeling of timeless melancholy, dry, reckless, defeated and perverse")—in this "least human of all the babylons," the repatriates were to be merged, or *submerged*, into the new class working in advertising, public relations, and publishing as auxiliaries or propagandists of big business.

"In fact, once the returning exiles had been stripped of their ambitions, once they surrendered to the city and lived the common life of its peasants, they found abundant compensation in their lot . . . They were learning that New York had another life, too—subterranean, like almost everything that was human in the city—a life of writers," who met for lunch, or at coffeehouses, to talk of work and plans; perhaps a new life on a farm in Connecticut. Considering the frantic historical reputation of New York in the twenties, it is striking that Cowley should find that its real "human" life was subterranean—something which had struck Charles Dickens, too, about New York, in 1842, when it was rising to be a world city. Cowley and his second wife moved to a converted barn in Sherman, Connecticut, in 1931, to work at the writer's trade.

The New Era roared on, oblivious to the disaffection of the intellectuals, the intellectuals as indifferent to politics. Greenwich Village is again at the end of an era in "15 Beech Street," a fictional sketch that Edmund Wilson published in the *New Republic* in 1927. It is the dog days of summer. Everyone the narrator knows below Fourteenth Street is in Provincetown or Woodstock; "now that their world has shut up for the summer, the docks had closed in our sanctuary," filling the air with a rank river smell. The enormous old apartment house where his friend Jane Gooch lives, with its lofty yellow-stucco halls redolent of airless bathrooms and trickling toilets, "closed round [him] with a void of abandonment even more formidable than that of the streets." Gooch is a spirited composite, to whom Wilson attributes affairs with John Reed and Harry Kemp (under pseudonyms); who was an editor at the *Worker* (i.e., the *Masses*); and who sporadically publishes a little magazine called *Vortex*—the next issue, once "we can raise the money," will be "a big hydraulic number," with lots of photographs of pipes and oil pumps and gas stations on the West Coast. "There's a series—of wash-basins at different angles—that looks just like the tomb of the Medicis." As they talk, she is rummaging through her desk for the address of a Village poet who has recently announced his deconversion from free love in Hearst's *Cosmopolitan*; it turns out that he is writing a newsletter for an automobile club in Detroit.

"For several years before Crystal Eastman's death [in 1928], rumors circulated that Greenwich Village was dead; that after the war it had become a 'bogus and lewd bore,' a philistine swamp filled with lesbian harems and other licentious things. That interpretation, at once misogynist and mean-minded, ignores the continued dynamism of the Village as a haven for creativity and the home of choice for independent radical women." Rightly, Blanche Wiesen Cook, the biographer of Eleanor Roosevelt, complains that popular journalists like Albert Parry (Cowley, too, and Wilson would also have to be put under indictment), very often attributed the accomplishments of formidable women like Crystal Eastman to the men in their lives, and condescended to what they were undertaking into the twenties. Eleanor Roosevelt, she points out, made Greenwich Village her base as she launched herself in politics not only as a formidable spear carrier for her husband, sidelined by polio, but also as a force of her own; her allies were activists in the League of Women Voters and the Women's Committee of the Democratic Party who lived there, and who became her closest friends. During her White House years, she rented an apartment from Esther Lape and Elizabeth Read in their house on East Eleventh Street until she bought her own apartment off Washington Square. It is true the company of radical women in the Village never really died out, but like the rest of radical bohemia it was very often dispirited and divided in the twenties. Between the fading of world-revolutionary hopes after 1919 and the coming of a new militancy after 1929, it was a strange interlude.

Kenneth Rexroth's description of an evening in bohemia spent on a rooftop picnic is actually set much earlier in the decade, but the becalmed atmosphere, soon to be broken, can stand for the interval.

"About midnight the moon was overhead and Seventh Avenue had quieted down for the night into the deep stillness that once was characteristic of nighttime in lower New York. Everybody had run out of songs."

"And what of Greenwich Village of today?" asked Parry, glancing around in 1933, at the bottom of the Depression. "What came after the *Masses*, Polly's, the Provincetown Players, Old Man Clivette, Sonia the Cigarette Girl, the exiles shuttling between here and Paris, Hubert's, Bob Clairmont, and Bodenheim?"

His eye lights upon "black and silver night clubs and cordial shops," residential hotels looming over the redbrick houses, "modernistic" drugstores and glass-fronted cafés like the one where Hopper's *night-hawks* forever convene. With streets emptied of tourists, the Villagers are catching up on their sleep; the more blatant speakeasies have been shut down, the all-night taxi stands are closed for lack of customers. The rents are lower. Gnomish Joe Gould, the scrounger with a Harvard degree, enters the scene; like everybody else, Parry gullibly imagines that Gould really is transcribing all the conversations he overhears into the notebooks that will complete his immense *Oral History of the World*. Parry calls the poets sinking into middle age—the "Eli Siegels"—"good for wisps and gasps only, but not for any sustained long-range work."*

Compared to the gay revolutionists of the teens, the radicals of the thirties, even when young, seemed ponderous and doctrinaire to Parry; devotion to the "Moscow idea" meant following the Party line. When the John Reed Club staged a debate between Mike Gold and Joshua Kunitz, a middle-aged firebrand and a young one, on the value, if any, of bourgeois literature to proletarians, it was understood that they had been assigned their sides, like members of a college debating team, and in fact were entirely agreed that the value was nil (for the moment, as it turned out). Most of the celebrities of the old Village, if they were still living, had long since gone away; although Max Eastman makes a cameo, looking "debonair and visibly relaxed" on a trip down from Croton-on-Hudson.

At last, a procession that begins with Poe's poverty and despair ends with a suicide on the Hudson River and another at sea. In early April 1932, "Gal Kolski, a Polish artist of Horatio Street" becomes the first person to leap to his death from the recently completed George Washington Bridge; unfortunately he lands on the rocks below rather than

---

* Of Bob Clairmont's circle, Eli Siegel (1902–78) is the one name not almost entirely lost to fame. In 1923 his metaphysical poem "Hot Afternoons Have Been in Montana" won the *Nation*'s poetry prize and briefly gained him acclaim in the Village scarcely second to T. S. Eliot's. In 1941 he founded a school (movement, cult) called "Aesthetic Realism," based on the premise that all right perception is based on the attraction of opposites. (Since homosexuality is obviously not based on the attraction of opposites, Aesthetic Realism was sometimes said to offer a "cure," but its remaining adherents deny this interpretation.) Kenneth Rexroth, who knew Siegel in their youth, reviewed him in the sixties as a philosophical comic.

in the river, his presumed destination. On a photograph of himself Kolski had written: "To All: If you cannot hear the cry of the starving millions, listen to your dead, brothers. Your economic system is dead."

April 27, 1932, about noon, Hart Crane jumped overboard from the stern of the *Orizaba*, the ship on which he was traveling from Veracruz, Mexico, to New York, and disappeared in shark-infested waters three hundred miles off Havana. "Goodbye, everybody." A watery grave was the finishing touch that turned a tortured life into flourishing mythology. Although he made elaborate preparations for writing a poem and fanatically revised his first draft, Crane was able to compose only when he was in a fine frenzy fueled by alcohol, music, and, ideally, rough sex. "Therefore," Malcolm Cowley writes, "he got drunk night after night, always hopefully; therefore his typewriter stood close to an Orthophonic Victrola . . . and therefore he cruised the waterfront looking for obliging sailors. All his carousals had an element of self-sacrifice, almost of self-flagellation; they were undertaken partly and primarily as a means of driving himself to write great poems."

It was Cowley who gave Crane the idea of going to Mexico on his Guggenheim fellowship rather than to Paris, where on an earlier trip the flics had given him a harder time for drunkenness, vagrancy, and soliciting sex with men than the Irish cops at home. His life in Mexico City was sober and made happy for a time by an affair with Peggy Cowley, who by coincidence was there to divorce Malcolm. It was his only deviation into heterosexuality beyond indulging, up to a point, women's pursuit of him. The season of comfort did not last. "The periodicity of his excesses grew swifter; the lucid intervening times when he could write were crowded out." The delicate phrasing of Crane's friend Waldo Frank refers to such horrific occasions as Katharine Anne Porter recorded, when Crane would crash her gate after midnight in a taxicab, screaming insults at the poor driver who simply wanted his fare and cursing the moon and the flowers in the vilest language. Peggy Cowley insisted they return home after he attempted suicide by swallowing a bottle of Mercurochrome. Aboard ship he escaped from his cabin, where he had been confined for rank drunkenness, and headed toward the crew's quarters—it would seem in hopes of another, or perhaps a final, debauch; he was bearing the bruises of his last beating at the hands of a disobliging sailor when he turned up that forenoon at Peggy Cowley's cabin, wearing pajamas under his overcoat. "I'm not going to make it, dear. I'm utterly disgraced." Accustomed to his melodramatizing, she told him to put on some clothes. Instead, he went to the stern and climbed over the rail.

Waldo Frank, the editor of Crane's *Collected Poems* (1958), blamed his friend's exposure to Mexico's "cult of death" at a vulnerable moment. "He wanted to escape. But as his boat turned toward what seemed to him the modern chaos of New York, there was the sea. He could not resist it." Edward Dahlberg, writing many years later, surmised that Crane could not bear the prospect of living "once more as a penniless urchin in New York"; his friend Kay Boyle rejoined in an exchange in the young *New York Review of Books* that he could easily have done so, *if* he had produced the great poem that would have justified his myth instead of wasting his time. Crane's suicide is often compared to the rather showy suicide that Harry Crosby staged from his apartment in the Hotel des Artistes in New York City, on December 10, 1930, in conjunction with the murder of a willing victim, a Boston socialite; but Crosby prepared meticulously for his departure, including painting his toenails. Crane's leap seems to have been unpremeditated, but predestined. It is more poignant to associate his leap with that of the obscure "Polish artist of Horatio Street," as does Parry. "In these two suicides, with certain modifications of detail, there is the daring and the pain, the bewilderment and the protest, the soaring and the fall of the artist, surrounded by an alien world, whether of 1833, 1883, or 1933."

Albert Parry was drawn back to Greenwich Village in 1948, after many years, by newspaper accounts of the protests—which he found sentimental—over the destruction of "Genius Row," which its landlord, New York University, was replacing with a prosaic law school. Professor Parry, as he was now, was barely moved as he watched the wreckers set about their work on a rainy day. The rackety houses where Theodore Dreiser, John Sloan, Alan Seeger, Harry Kemp, and all the visionary company had lived and loved had been seedy and unsanitary for a long time. The first and only edition of *Garrets and Pretenders* had been remaindered long ago, and with the author's consent the plates were melted down for their metal during the war just as the remaining copies were becoming collector's items. He was in a mood to let the past bury the past, while taking a freelance tour of the present.*

Parry felt there was a new paradigm for the artist: "You get a job, work part time or for a few months at a stretch, and store up enough cash for that masterpiece of yours on your own terms. Also, there are foundations and prizes and wealthy relatives eager to stake you. It was different in Dreiser's youth. Then the capitalist world was much colder to talent, foreseeing no profits therein."

Almost seventy years on, the days when an able-bodied aspiring writer or painter—male, needless to say—could support himself on a casual basis and save up money by painting houses, working on construction, or shipping out, are sufficiently remote that it is worth pausing to consider the extent to which such opportunities once defined bohemia; the history of the Beats, for example, would have been quite a different affair without the merchant marine (not only Jack Kerouac but that unlikely mariner Allen Ginsberg went to sea), the railroad, the fire watcher's post.

Who is coming from out of town to be creative in the postwar era? Few writers could afford the rent or, if they could afford it, could not endure the noise of children at play, or the roar of the trucks near the piers and tunnels off the Hudson, where cold-water flats were still affordable.

Painters were better adapted to the noise, but the ones Parry met seemed merely to be going through the motions of bohemianism. At a large cold-water flat on the Hudson converted to one-room studios, he interviewed a young woman seated at her easel.

"'Where are you from?' I ask.

"She apologizes: 'I am only from New Jersey. So discouraging, you know, when everyone else comes from practically every part of the Union and the world!'

* "Greenwich Village Revisited: 1948" was published in *Tomorrow* magazine, June 1948, and, along with another new chapter, "Enter Beatniks: The Bohème of 1960" by Harry T. Moore, included as "Addenda to the 1933 Edition" in the Dover reprint of *Garrets and Pretenders* in 1960. This expanded volume was then republished by Dover under the title *Garrets and Pretenders: Bohemian Life in America from Poe to Kerouac* in 2012, with a new introduction by Paul Buhle.

"I reassure her that she at least looks Midwestern."

The young painter was an "abstractionist," and she and other young artists were not given much of a chance by the old-timers to display at the Washington Square outdoor exhibits in May and September; many of them had begun moving into immigrant territory on the Lower East Side, where empty stores and cold-water flats were still abundant.

Compared to former days, the political temperature was tepid, even at the once quarrelsome Waldorf Cafeteria. "A lanky, hot-eyed Trotsky-ite calls two icy-eyed Stalinists a bunch of reactionaries, but there is no fight. A Wallaceite laments to me that most of her Village friends are deaf to her pleas, that laconically they tell her they are going to vote for Truman—'Not to break up the Democratic Party, they say! Imagine that for a reason!'" It was all rather sad, like the parties which ended at midnight, when once they would have just been getting started; like Parry's discovering that the tiny bookshop on Macdougal Street where he had debated with the "dreamy proprietor" the right translation of Krylov's fables had been replaced by a gleaming-white Laundromat, while across the street had risen a "prettified, Village-styled church of Christ the Scientist."

But although the colonization had begun, it was not for another twenty years that fashion and aspiring realtors would annex the upper Lower East Side as the "East Village," just as the old Village had long ago stretched across the fields to join Washington Square.

4

———

Another Part of the Forest

I N *The Autobiography of Lincoln Steffens* (1931), the venerable muckraker tells of being introduced to New York's underworld in the
1890s by "wise," meaning streetwise, reporters like Max Fischel, the
legman for Jacob A. Riis.

"I remember one morning hearing Riis roaring, as he could roar, at
Max, who was reporting a police raid on a resort of fairies.

"'Fairies!' Riis shouted, suspicious. 'What are fairies?' And when
Max began to define the word Riis rose up in a rage. 'Not so,' he cried.
'There are no such creatures in the world.' He threw down his pencil
and rushed out of the office."

Riis, the crusading Danish-born photographer and writer, whose
book about the squalor of the Lower East Side ghetto, *How the Other
Half Lives* (1890), shocked the conscience of the city, simply could not,
would not, admit that "fairies" existed—even though their "resorts" and
recreations were very much a part of the naked city which he explored
by night with his friend Police Commissioner Theodore Roosevelt.*
"Gay New York," as masterfully negotiated by George Chauncey in
a magisterial study—that city-within-a-city with its codes and con-
cealments, its male brothels, boy whores, and discreet "bachelor"

———

* Ninety years later, homosexuality is still missing from the Lower East Side of Irving
Howe's *World of Our Fathers* (1976), although in fairness the entire topic of sex among
the young is dispatched in a single paragraph in a very long book.

fraternities—was, if not invisible, at least deniable. But in the forties, what once had been in shadows had come into unprecedented publicity and visibility, after the universal license of wartime.

At a time when novels were still expected to bring the news, fiction reflected what Joseph Allen Boon calls "libidinal currents" more candidly than movies or the theater—albeit rarely with as much subversive wit; for one thing, they were usually written in the gray naturalistic prose, a pastiche of Hemingway and James T. Farrell, that Gore Vidal called "the national style."

The prominence of gay themes in postwar fiction was such that avowedly straight critics soon began to affect an exaggerated weariness of the whole subject. (In the lordly *Hudson Review*, Leslie Fiedler, the young critic who achieved notoriety for his 1948 essay in *Partisan Review*, "Come Back to the Raft Ag'in, Huck Honey!," praised Vidal's *The City and the Pillar* for its deft portrayal of "seedy torment," but regretted its drab prose and sermonizing.) The subject of gay fiction turns up, most unexpectedly, in Kerouac's *The Town and the City*, in which the not-yet-Beat novelist multiplies himself into four brothers—the intellectual Francis is implicitly gay but married and living closeted in Greenwich Village. In an implausible literary discussion, the Martin family patriarch—based on Kerouac's coarse homophobic father, Leo Kerouac, who called Jack's friend Allen Ginsberg "the cockroach"—becomes indignant about a perverted novel he had found at a public library.

"It was all worked out with a lot of rigmarole and symbols and he even brings politics into it," he complains to his son Peter, the most consistent stand-in for the author. "It is a big world-shaking business—two big boys playing with each other like those morons who hang around men's rooms in the subway."

"There's a lot of that in New York," Peter replies, "meditatively."

Like bohemia, whose shores it overlapped, gay New York contained lower depths as well as views from the penthouse; in *The Gay Metropolis, 1940-1996* by Charles Kaiser, who picks up where George Chauncey leaves off, the secret city remained, as it had been in the previous hundred years, stratified and compartmentalized to an extraordinary degree. Otis Bigelow, one of the leading witnesses Kaiser summons, arrived in New York in 1938, a recent graduate of Exeter with hopes of becoming an actor, and for a time shared an apartment in a building next to El Morocco with two other young men: Gordon Merrick, who became famous in the 1970s for his novel *The Lord Won't Mind*, and the future Broadway impresario Richard Barr, Edward Albee's producer. In 1942 Bigelow dropped out of Hamilton College when a Broadway producer showed interest in a play he had written.

Though he did not flourish as a playwright, Bigelow's dramatic good looks ("the best-looking man in Manhattan," his admirers said, and remembered many years later), and his ways of making himself agreeable to affluent older men, recommended him to the café-society division of the gay metropolis: one of his first patrons was Maury Paul, who wrote the "Cholly Knickerbocker" society-gossip column for the Hearst papers and was credited with coining the phrase "café society" in 1919. Fifty years on, time having added its usual enchantments, Bigelow assured Kaiser: "'Everybody was very classy in those days. There was no trade. There were no bums.' (He said so moments before he described Maury Paul's kept boy.) 'Everybody that you met had a style of elegance. It was not T-shirts and muscles and so on. It was wit and class. You had to have tails and be polite. Homosexuality was an upscale thing to be. It was defined by class. There wasn't dark cruising.'" To which Kaiser rejoins: "On this subject, Bigelow was wholly misinformed."

High and low consorted in gay Gotham—as always. In his memoir *Palimpsest*, Gore Vidal tells of having a thousand sexual partners before he was twenty-five—an impressive number but no more, he modestly reckons, than his contemporaries Jack Kennedy, Tennessee Williams, and Marlon Brando could boast. "I did enjoy my daily meetings with strangers, usually encountered on the streets. We would then go to one of the Dreiserian hotels around Times Square. Most were poor youths of my age, and often capable of an odd lovingness, odd considering the fact that I did so little to give any of them physical pleasure. But then, even at twenty, I often paid for sex on the ground that it was only fair." Vidal much preferred being the pursuer than to be pursued, and in *Palimpsest* he tells of firmly rebuffing the advances of Kimon Friar, the Greek American poet, translator, and critic, who had caught sight of him at the bar of the Astor Hotel, with a Modern Library copy of Pepys's diary under his arm.

"From behind me, someone quotes, 'And so to bed': Pepys's usual last line for a journal entry. I turn. A small, grinning, bespectacled civilian . . ." The civilian and he discuss literature, and Vidal invites Friar to his father's apartment on Fifth Avenue to continue their talk. Friar is "unduly impressed" by Gene Vidal's apartment; resigned to no sex but still full of confidences, he tells Vidal about how, when he was teaching at Amherst, he had become the mentor of an undergraduate poet named James Merrill, " 'whose father,' he announced triumphantly, 'is a lot richer than yours!' " It was true; young Merrill's father, known to Wall Street as "Good Time Charlie" Merrill, the founder of Merrill Lynch, was richer than almost everybody's father.

In *The City and the Pillar*, Vidal's naturalistic exposé, Jim Willard, the available tennis pro yearning for his boyhood love, is invited to "a fairy party—very high class of course"—by his sometime lover Ronald Shaw, a closeted movie star: "There were painters, writers, composers, athletes, members of Congress, but Shaw was *the* actor, the handsomest and most legendary of them all." Jim is new to their world, though not to same-sex relations, and wonders at his friend's indiscretion in keeping such compromising company in wartime New York, when he had been the soul of discretion in peacetime Hollywood.

"They were of every age; many were handsome athletic types, many were pale and pretty, many were aging and fat and bald, but they all had very much the same expression in their eyes: a glittering awareness both bold and guarded." (This intriguing observation is omitted in revised editions of the novel, along with the word "normal" as a synonym for heterosexuality.)

"It seemed that from all over the country the homosexuals had come to New York as to a center, a new Sodom; for here, among the millions, they could be unnoticed by the enemy and yet known to each other."

Unlike "the unorganized and submerged dreamers and practitioners in the villages and small towns of the hinterland," not confessing or even knowing their desires, "the thousands in New York were either the strong and brave or else the effeminate and marked, people who had nothing to lose by being free and reasonably open in their behavior."

With impressive bravado, Truman Capote had announced himself to be one of the latter—a gesture requiring courage even if, really, there was no alternative. No one could possibly mistake the symbolic swampland of *Other Voices, Other Rooms* for a direct transcription of experience, but as his biographer Gerald Clarke writes, the notorious photograph of Capote on the back of the dust jacket matches exactly the description of the thirteen-year-old Joel Knox, who is "too pretty, too delicate and fair-skinned" to be a real boy, and who at the end is about to answer the window-tapping of his uncle Randolph, dressed up as the bewigged "queer lady," who will initiate him into homosexuality.

The publication of *The City and the Pillar*, on the other hand, was widely understood to mark Vidal either as one of the bold—or as naively indiscreet, by those who assumed it was an artless memoir. "I have read that I was too stupid at the time to know what I was doing," Vidal wrote almost forty years later, "but in such matters I have always had a certain alertness."

If gay liberation began as a literary movement, as Christopher Bram maintains in *Eminent Outlaws*—not entirely persuasively, but with panache—then Vidal was its most articulate protagonist. When the first revised edition of *The City and the Pillar* was published in 1965, Vidal claimed in an afterword that his purpose in writing a "gay" novel had been propagandistic—polemical, in fact. "By the time I came to write *The City and the Pillar*, I was bored by playing it safe. I wanted to take risks, to try something no American had done before. I decided to examine the homosexual underworld (which I knew rather less well than I pretended) and in the process show the 'naturalness' of homosexual relations, as well as making the point that there is of course no such thing as a homosexual." Inadvertently, this echoes Riis's denial that fairies existed, but what Vidal meant is that "homosexualists" no more conform to a psychological type than heterosexuals. This distinction was largely lost on the book's early readers, who usually interpreted it as a documentary. Even a critic as familiar with the milieu as

Stephen Spender, writing in the *Saturday Review*, assumed that Vidal was confessional: "Apparently I had drawn the character of the athlete Jim Willard so convincingly, that to this day aging pederasts are firmly convinced that I was once a male prostitute, with an excellent backhand at tennis."

The straight readers of 1948 learned a good deal about the "well-organized homosexual world in New York," which Vidal offered in an anthropological spirit. "A man who could not be had, who was normal, was called 'jam.' The rough young men who offered themselves for seduction but who did not practice were known as 'trade' . . . Among the homosexuals there was a saying that 'this year's trade is next year's competition.'" In 1948 Vidal was prepared to concede the word "normal" to the straights ("the enemy"), and readier to generalize about particular homosexual types in a way that rather undercuts his claim in later years to be showing that "there is of course no such thing as a homosexual."

"He did not like men who acted like women," we are told of Jim Willard. "He was repelled by the queens and long-haired young men with sensitive girlish faces. He hoped, however, that by seeing them often he could begin to accept this society and be happy in it. But he could not find what he wanted here: there was an overripe, overcivilized aura about this society . . . He turned to the bars then, finding in them at least, young men like himself who were still natural and not overly corrupted."

Upper bohemia, where Jim is uneasy but Vidal shone, is "a half-world where normal and homosexual people met with a certain degree of frankness; this was true of many theatrical and literary groups." For a sense of its ambience downtown, we can turn to the diary of Anaïs Nin, model for Maria Verlaine, the older woman attracted to younger men in *The City and the Pillar*. Nin and her banker husband, Hugh Guiler, lived in a fifth-floor walkup on Thirteenth Street, where they played at being poor bohemians; so persuasive was the performance that Vidal insisted on paying for their dinners out until she told him that Hugo, as she called him, was a banker, not a starving artist. She writes, February 1946:

I give a Party.

Guests: Luise Rainer and her husband, Robert Knittel; Maya Deren and Sasha Hammiod; Stanley Haggart; Woody Parrish-Martin; Kim Hoffman; Sherry Martinelli and Enrique Zanarte; Charles Duits; Louise and Edgard Varèse; John Stroup; Gore Vidal; Claude Fredericks; James Agee.

Took the mattresses off the beds and made a lot of low oriental divans. Invited a flamenco guitarist. Kim played his accordion. Steve, a handsome, suave, elegant Austrian, danced extremely well.

Gore asked me what I put in my nail polish that gives the color a warm gleam.

"Gold," I said.

"As in your writing?"

Enrique Zanarte's somber Spanish beauty, Stanley's intuitive analysis of people, Woody's fantasies, Steve's grace, Kim's music, Maya's films, all bloomed that night. Even Agee, who so often looks a sad Lincoln, and rather dramatic, smiled.

(Note that time has made the "real" names on Nin's guest list as romantically evocative of a lost time and place as the imaginary ones in Fitzgerald's *Gatsby*: the deeply obscure, unknown even to Wikipedia, as well as the famous like Luise Rainer, the only actress to date to win Academy Awards as best actress in two successive years, a fatal distinction from which her career not to mention her marriage to Clifford Odets never recovered. Rainer retired to England and died, too luminous to be forgotten, in 2014 at the age of 104.)

One of the great campgrounds of high bohemians in the forties (and long after) was the town house at Ninety-fourth Street and Lexington Avenue, number 1453, where Leo Lerman, a writer and editor at Condé Nast, held open house on Sunday evenings, receiving his guests sitting up in bed, dressed in pajamas and a fez. Bearded and rotund, Lerman was a vivacious talker and omnivorous reader whose admirers inevitably compared him to Oscar Wilde and fondly supposed he knew "everything": he often mentioned, for example, that 1453 was the year that Constantinople fell to the Turks. Dates were the sort of thing that Anaïs Nin did not know, and did not want to know, but he and she became great friends. Lerman once telephoned to say that he and Truman Capote were taking turns reading aloud from *The Winter of Artifice*. His parties were already legendary by 1948 when he auditioned for a job at *Mademoiselle* by inviting the editor one Sunday, and was immediately hired.

"Everybody came," his later companion, Gray Foy, said of the parties that sprawled over four floors and then in 1967 moved to a vast apartment in the Osborne on Fifty-seventh Street. "Marcel Duchamp, Marlene Dietrich, Maria Callas, William Faulkner, Evelyn Waugh, everybody you could think of." Some guests, like the lyricist John La Touche, Tennessee Williams, and Capote (whom Lerman once carried piggyback down the street), were "chums"; others undoubtedly came to gawk; a few were disasters, most notably Evelyn Waugh, whose rudeness made a vivid impression on literary New York in the winter of 1948. "'Who does that little pig think he is?' asked someone behind us," recalled John Malcolm Brinnin, who was standing with Capote. "'He's supposed to be worried about the decline of manners.'"

Mary Louise Aswell, the fiction editor of *Harper's Bazaar*, brought Capote to a party in December 1945. Nin answered the bell: "I saw a small, slender young man, with hair over his eyes, extending the softest and most boneless hand I had ever held, like a baby's nestling in mine." Deceived by appearances, she imagined he was another of the "transparent children" needing her protection in cruel New York, a city on whose conquest he was already advancing. Immediately he spotted a published author even younger than he. "How," he addressed Gore Vidal, age twenty, "does it feel to be an enfant terrible?"

In June 1947 both prodigies were featured in *Life* magazine's spread on "New U.S. Writers." Capote, dressed like a child dandy in a fussy room, described as "esoteric," was given pride of place, although he had yet to publish a book, a coup that even his publisher, Bennett Cerf, wondered at; former warrant officer Vidal is posed in a peacoat against a ship, "like Jack London." The next year, in November 1948, Vidal had the satisfaction of being included in *Life*'s famous shoot of the party at Frances Steloff's Gotham Book Mart in honor of Dame Edith and Osbert Sitwell ("the most-reproduced photo of the forties"). With Edith seated in a thronelike chair, the sibling sacred monsters are attended by, among other poets of note, Stephen Spender, Randall Jarrell, Marianne Moore, Horace Gregory, Delmore Schwartz, José Villa, Tennessee Williams, and Elizabeth Bishop. Truman Capote was nowhere in sight. Naturally he was indignant, since in his estimation Vidal (despite attempts) was no more a poet than he was. W. H. Auden, perched on a ladder and uncharacteristically well dressed, steals the show, or rather the shot, from the other poets. Capote and Vidal's wary, unaffectionate but mutually amused friendship, marked by almost-weekly lunches at the Oak Room in the Plaza Hotel, survived Vidal's introducing the horrified Capote to the Everard Baths, but not a cocktail party at Tennessee Williams's apartment at which Vidal accused Capote of stealing his plots from Carson McCullers and Eudora Welty, and Capote retorted that Vidal found *his* in the *Daily News*.

Well-born and handsome—not to mention "luminous and manly," a tribute in Nin's diary that he was surprised to find survived the decades—Vidal seemed to navigate all the strata of bohemia. Yet, "'What in the name of God am I doing here?' I kept thinking." Despite social standing, respectable sales (and until *The City and the Pillar*, respectability), an entrée into many worlds, Vidal found himself out of tune with an art world dominated by fashion. In the summer of 1946, he left his job at E. P. Dutton and, Europe still being out of reach for most Americans, moved to Guatemala, where he bought a former convent and settled into the writer's life there for two years, before taking a Greek freighter to Naples in 1948; thence, he traveled to Rome, which became the setting of *The Judgment of Paris* (1952), his first novel written in Vidalian prose, and to Paris, much later the setting for his novel-as-memoir, *Two Sisters* (1970).

Indeed, 1948 was the year upper bohemia returned to Rome, Paris, London, this time in the van of a world-conquering army. In Paris, an ambitious young writer at the Sorbonne on the GI Bill such as Norman Mailer might for the first time encounter the great world at the vast apartment in Montparnasse of the mysterious H. J. Kaplan, host to the intelligentsia-at-large, whose post as the Paris correspondent for *Partisan Review* could hardly have paid for his grand lodging. On the island of Ischia, in the Bay of Naples, W. H. Auden, whose apartment on Cornelia Street in Greenwich Village was dark and squalid, rented a half-ruined carriage house with a spacious, sunny upstairs, two reception rooms, and adjoining vineyards for the equivalent of $230 a month. Capote and his lover, Jack Dunphy, came to the island in spring 1949. "What a strange, and strangely enchanted place this is, an encantada in the Mediterranean," he wrote to his editor, Robert Linscott, at Random House. "It is an island off the coast from Naples, very primitive, populated mostly by winegrowers, goatherders, W. H. Auden and the Mussolini family."

In his *Table Talk* with Alan Ansen, recorded in the forties but published much later, in 1990, Auden has a good deal to say about the "Homintern," the ostensibly semisecret, mutually supportive gay sodality in the arts and letters: "Did you see that Mary McCarthy has joined the anti-Homintern?" "Did you see that Dewey was bidding for the Homintern vote?" Auden exasperated Edmund Wilson by insisting that Eisenhower was gay, and that he rather fancied him.

The suppositious Homintern, named after the Soviet Comintern (Harold Norse claimed the credit for the coinage, although it seems to have originated in the Federal Theatre Projects in the thirties), intersected with upper bohemia and the fashion world in something like the way that the bohemias, high and low, intersected with ethnic Greenwich Village and Midtown.

The Beats belonged to low bohemia—this "Dostoyevskian New York," as John Clellon Holmes called it—whose characteristic settings were around Times Square and the vicinity of Columbia University; the subway, the furnished room, the illegally occupied loft downtown. In *The Town and the City*, the excitable, voluble teenaged Leon Levinsky, based on Allen Ginsberg, and the sardonic, middle-aged Will Dennison, based on William S. Burroughs, are not explicitly portrayed as homosexual; nor did either Ginsberg or Burroughs regard himself as being irrevocably such for some years. Burroughs was married to the doomed Joan Vollmer Burroughs, destined to die in a fatal game of William Tell in Mexico City in 1951. Ginsberg had affairs with women, and off and on both would declare they had renounced sleeping with men, or at least disapproved of it. Auden did as well: "The reasons Americans pretend so hard about the subject is that America is really a very queer country. I've come to the conclusion that it's wrong to be queer, but that's a long story."

"For more than a half century," Gore Vidal writes in the introduction to Karl Bissinger's *The Luminous Years: Portraits at Mid-Century* (2003), "whenever anyone asks me about the postwar 1940s and what it was like, I always say look at Karl Bissinger's photograph of us in the first issue of *Flair*: There we are all."

"There" is the patio-garden of the newly opened Café Nicholson on East Fifty-second Street; "we"—they—are the ballet dancer Tanaquil Le Clercq, later married to Balanchine; the writer Donald Windham; the painter Buffie Johnson; Tennessee Williams; Vidal in a crew cut. *Flair* was the inventively designed monthly magazine—avant-gardism for the masses—in which Gardner Cowles, the publisher of *Look* magazine, indulged his wife, Fleur, for an expensive year. "And such is the magic of his [Bissinger's] art that, though we are shown in black and white, the encompassing light appears golden. And we are young." Vidal defines the time and place they shared as "the world of the arts, as well as strange celebrities like the Windsors." Housed in a brownstone, the Café Nicholson attempted to re-create the décor of the Caffè Greco in Rome. Period note: almost everybody in Bissinger's photos is smoking a cigarette. Tennessee Williams, Truman Capote, Jean Renoir, Doe Avedon, Michèle Morgan, Christopher Isherwood—each has a pack and an ashtray at hand. (Anna Magnani smokes Philip Morris.) Other shorelines of bohemia in Bissinger's photographs are Hollywood (Isherwood and Aldous Huxley), Tangiers (Paul and Jane Bowles), the Marais in Paris, Broadway dressing rooms, Havana, various locales shared with the squares (e.g., Central Park), a Roman drawing room, Bernard Berenson's villa I Tatti outside Florence. If admitted as evidence, the weather most definitely was sunnier on the loftier shores of bohemia than on the lower.

The writers who catch Bissinger's camera eye include a world-weary Janet Flanner; Henry Miller "in his Chinese phase"; Williams looking like a successful shoe salesman; Colette *en regard*. Truman Capote was "easily the most photographed writer of our brief golden age," Vidal notes, and his appearances here show the prodigy in his postwar waif mode, gazing over his shoulder on the set of Cocteau's *Les Parents terribles* in Paris in 1948, or looking upward apprehensively from the steps going down to the East River from Beekman Place. (Montgomery Clift, though rugged by comparison, affects the same stranded expression.) Capote's first book of nonfiction, *Local Color* (1950), a book of travel writing and a sort of Baedeker of upper bohemia during the Brazen Age, was illustrated with photographs by a gallery of masters, including Bissinger, Henri Cartier-Bresson, Bill Brandt, Clifford Coffin, Cecil Beaton, George Hoyningen-Huene; landscapes in black-and-white, with no photos of the precocious author.

Sacred monsters were enjoying a golden age in the forties, even if they were not always enjoying themselves. Dame Edith Sitwell and Isak Dinesen were rather more interesting examples than the desperately bored duke and duchess: they were all crocodilian survivors in an age when survival was everything. Hemingway's motto, "Il faut (d'abord) durer," might have served for them all. "One must (above all) endure." Upper bohemia was the natural habitat of such "strange celebrities," although café society sufficed for the Windsors. Hemingway, who had taken to calling himself "a strange old man," spent more time with sycophantic columnists like Leonard Lyons and publicans like Toots Shor than he did with his fellow writers when in New York, and made a fool of himself for the benefit of Lillian Ross in the *New Yorker* when he was in town to deliver the manuscript of *Across the River and Into the Trees* to his publisher. (*The New Yorker* completed its damage by publishing E. B. White's devastating parody, "Across the Street and Into the Grill.")

T. S. Eliot fulfilled a cherished ambition of seeing his name in lights when his play *The Cocktail Party* was staged on Broadway. He accepted an invitation from John Malcolm Brinnin to read at the 92nd Street Y, writing: "My overriding concern is the problem of dress. Shall I put on evening clothes?" (Brinnin told him that most poets came as they were.) Eliot impressed John Berryman and the other young poets at Princeton by condescending to attend a modest cocktail party and drinking five martinis without visible effect. He also paid social visits in New York, but apparently not to Djuna Barnes, a writer he had published and admired. She had entombed herself in her tiny apartment in Patchin Place and would shriek at would-be callers like Carson McCullers to go away. Some days her neighbor, E. E. Cummings, would shout up to her window, "Djuna, are you still alive?" But she had an answer for that. "I used to be gorgeous," she told the young men who ran errands for her. "Don't think this is the real Djuna Barnes. The real Djuna Barnes is dead."

One bright day in 1946, Gore Vidal caught up with Harold Norse after a long chase up Fifth Avenue. Norse's version of the dialogue: "You're a fast walker." "Are you a dancer? You look like one." Each identifies himself as a writer. Vidal: "My book's on display at the Gotham Book Mart. Let's go see it."

The author of *Williwaw* is crestfallen when Frances Steloff, "a white-haired ogress with pale blue eyes," fails to recognize his name ("I'm Gore Vidal, Miss Steloff," he says plaintively) or remember his book. Finally, he locates a copy, which he holds up, "like a young father holding up his firstborn, searching my face for signs of approval. His colossal vanity and conceit made me feel my own wretched poverty keenly. He had everything: youth, beauty, money, talent, brains."

Norse's late-life *Memoirs of a Bastard Angel* (1989) brings out a self-conscious abjectness about the homosexual underworld, a sordid, scary aspect that seemed practically definitive at the time, and is palpable in the early journals and letters of Allen Ginsberg and in William S. Burroughs's *Queer* (but not in Dawn Powell's *The Happy Island* [1938] or Larry Rivers's rollicking *What Did I Do? The Unauthorized Autobiography*). The moodiness of "trade," for example, was a dangerously unpredictable element in anonymous back-alley, beachside, or waterfront encounters: "those human seraphim, the sailors," who offer "caresses of Atlantic and Caribbean love" in Ginsberg's *Howl* often reciprocated a blow job with a beating. Norse was raped by two English sailors encountered in Central Park, and almost killed by a wild boy in Provincetown whom Tennessee Williams had warned him against. Upper bohemia was a sanctuary, a liberated zone, yet it is striking how so many years later, when, as Vidal liked to say, memoir time had rolled around, even a Truman Capote, darling of the gods as he seemed at the time, recalled characters like George Davis, the fiction editor of *Harper's Bazaar* and, later, *Mademoiselle*, as monsters of sexual rapacity in his unfinished novel, *Answered Prayers*.

. . .

On the subject of homosexuality, "enlightened" opinion was extraordinarily unenlightened by the standards of the early twenty-first century. "During the forties and fifties the anti-fag battalions were everywhere on the march," Vidal writes, in a reminiscent essay about Tennessee Williams. "From the high lands of *Partisan Review* to the middle ground of *Time* magazine, envenomed attacks on real or suspected fags never let up." A *Time* cover story on Auden was killed when the managing editor was told that Auden was a "fag." Vidal, who once called himself "the national fag," knew the story all too well, since after the publication of *The City and the Pillar* in 1948 none of his other novels were reviewed in *Time* or the daily *New York Times* for years. In fact, Orville Prescott, who wrote for the daily *Times*, not only declined to review what he probably believed to be Vidal's memoir, but swore never to review a book of his again—a promise he kept.

In *Intellectual Memoirs* Mary McCarthy tells the story about how Philip Rahv, her sometime lover, who spoke with a strong Russian accent and never learned to pronounce the letter "h," which Russian lacks, reacted when a "young writer" submitted a story to *Partisan Review* based on the Samuel Barber–Gian Carlo Menotti ménage: "Philip rejected it categorically, instructing the young author, '*Partisan Review* is a 'eterosexual magazine. It does not publish 'omosexual stories.'" *PR did* publish essays and reviews by writers presumably known by the editors to be homosexual: Rahv opened its pages to the unknown James Baldwin, publishing "Everybody's Protest Novel" (1949, written in Paris), which gave him his first notoriety; and although Baldwin's early miscellaneous reviews had nothing explicitly to do with homosexuality, Auden's essay about Oscar Wilde, "A Playboy of the Western World," subtitled "St. Oscar, the Homintern Martyr" (1950) most definitely did. In William Barrett's 1949 travelogue, "New Innocents Abroad," the Homintern is taking over the only-just-liberated Continent. "For me the final and parting irony was that in Italy, of all places, I should become most aware of the internationally organized network of the inverts' world." Apparently the fraternity of the gay is a network as carefully organized as the American Express, and, like the latter, now takes in the whole of Europe as its territory."

Needless to say, it is woman (implicitly, Philip Wylie's dread "Mom") who "has been accorded an unprecedented status of equality, on the basis of which she has already moved ahead to secure dominance," who is to blame—and must pay the price.

> The American mother who fears that her son, drifting about in Europe on the G. I. Bill, may be seduced by some European hussy, is no longer up-to-date. Mother, that boy of yours loitering along the European dockside at evening, gazing out at the water and apparently lost in reflection, has his eye peeled, not for the poor drab who winks vainly at him from the quay, but for the pretty young sailor boy of his dreams who just at this moment might be descending from the boat out there in the twilit harbor.*

Then was not now. Events like the Stonewall Inn riot on Christopher Street in 1969, now long in the past, were far in the future. In *Palimpsest* Vidal recalls a party at Peggy Guggenheim's when Charles Henri Ford, "the bright-eyed poet-novelist-editor and friend of Tchelitchev, approached me and said, 'You can't be a good writer because you have such lovely legs.'" (How did he know?) Indignant at being objectified, Vidal turned to another guest, James Agee, "a tall, sadly amiable man with bloodshot eyes."

"I told Agee that I'd like to break poor Charles's legs. Agee was soothing; then he said, most thoughtfully, 'Those fairies can be surprisingly tough.'"

---

* "New Innocents Abroad" is reprinted in Chandler Brossard's aggressively hip collection, *The Scene Before You*, beside essays by Harvey Swados, Manny Farber, Milton Klonsky, Anatole Broyard, Elizabeth Hardwick, and other knowing characters.

5

Culture and Anarchy: "The Sublime Is Now"

Aᴏᴏ FTER THE WAR, bohemia seemed at once besieged and becalmed. E. B. White noted the spirit of change amid continuity in *Here Is New York*: "In Greenwich Village the light is thinning: big apartment buildings have come in, bordering the Square, and bars are mirrored and chromed. But there are still in the Village the lingering traces of poesy, Mexican glass, hammered brass, batik, lamps made of whiskey bottles, first novels made of fresh memories—the old Village with its alleys and ratty one-room rents catering to the erratic needs of those whose hearts are young and gay."

The Village was no longer the literary hotbed it had been— though in the mid-fifties, it was reanimated by the Beats. Malcolm Cowley explained in *The Literary Situation* (1954) how at midcentury, even though many Greenwich Village novels were submitted to publishers—including those he called "fairy-Freudian"—the ones that "reach the bookstores, like *Who Walk in Darkness* and *Go*, are almost always Hemingway-realistic and deadly serious." George Mandel's *Flee the Angry Strangers* (1952), sometimes called the first Beat novel—a distinction usually accorded John Clellon Holmes's *Go*—is more angry and sorrowful than beaten down, while Cowley's two examples are morose and jittery. Kerouac, regarding the Beat Generation (named in conversations with the four-years-younger Holmes) as his intellectual property and ticket to fame and modest fortune—as indeed it turned out to be—was incensed when Holmes beat him to publication, and charged to their friends that Holmes had "plagiarized" from the unpublished, and for several years unpublishable, *On the Road*.

In the late forties, it was memoir time for the "old" Village. The two great literary men of the 1910s' radical Village published theirs. Floyd Dell's was an insignificant, although sweetly done, magazine article in the *American Mercury*, "Rents Were Low in Greenwich Village." Max Eastman's 1948 *Enjoyment of Living* was a substantial autobiography up to 1917, when his days as a fiery Red were still beginning. After leaving the *Liberator* in 1922, Eastman spent time in Paris, where at the celebrated annual art students' Quat'z' Arts Ball, he was "bronzed all over" to represent an American Indian and paraded through the boulevards of Paris wearing nothing but a jockstrap; lived in Moscow and became the closest American follower of Trotsky (his translation of Trotsky's *History of the Russian Revolution* remains definitive); shared a lover with Charlie Chaplin in Hollywood; and engaged in literary feuds, most famously with Ernest Hemingway, with whom he had been on friendly terms since their meeting in 1922, when they both were covering the Genoa Conference. In *Here Is New York*, E. B. White wrote that in his Midtown hotel room, he was, among other landmarks, "five blocks from the publisher's office where Ernest Hemingway hit Max Eastman on the nose." The novelist believed that Eastman had accused him of having "false chest hair," which Hemingway disproved by ripping open his shirt: in fact, it was an accusation that Eastman had leveled at his epigones. Eastman was intellectually fearless: he debated the unconscious with Freud, literary modernism with Joyce, and attempted to debate dialectic with Trotsky; no doubt, he was more often out of his depth than he realized. (Believing the dialectic was a useless mystification, Eastman helpfully produced an edition of *Capital* from which, so far as was possible, it was omitted; the result was published by Modern Library.) In 1924 his revelation of Lenin's so-called deathbed "testament," which expressed doubts about Stalin's suitability as a successor, came out; for this and other misdeeds he earned the dangerous distinction of being personally denounced by Stalin as "the American literary gangster Max Eastman." In 1934, Eastman dismayed his American comrades by publishing *Artists in Uniform*, which contradicted many sunny myths circulating on the left about the condition of worker-artists in the Soviet Union four years after Mayakovsky's suicide.

His ex-idolater Mike Gold, who specialized in denunciations, out-did himself in the *Daily Worker*. "But Max Eastman, former friend, you have sunk beneath all tolerance! You are a filthy and deliberate liar! . . . Nay, you are worse, since you yourself were once the Bolshevik leader of a generation of young intellectuals." (Victor Serge attests in *Memoirs of a Revolutionist* that Eastman got it right.) Disillusioned with Trotsky and never taken with Stalin, the only prominent American Bolshevik who never went Stalinist, Eastman wrote of his progressive disenchantment with the scientific pretensions of Marxism in books whose influence Edmund Wilson acknowledges in *To the Finland Station*. In 1948, Eastman lost his old comrade Claude McKay, who had starred in the Harlem Renaissance but disparaged its other stars in his fiction. McKay had written a poem, "If We Must Die," about the suffering and defiance of black Americans during the 1919 "Red Summer," which was recited by Churchill during the Blitz; he had also spent 1922–34 in the Soviet Union, but never joined the Party and defied every orthodoxy, like his friend Max. In 1948, Eastman was still debonair, no longer "Red," now a "roving editor" for *Reader's Digest*.

In 1948 a more dispirited and despoiled Greenwich Village appeared in *Partisan Review* and *Commentary*, the latter launched that year under the editorship of Elliot Cohen and the auspices of the American Jewish Committee. The two "little" magazines shared many of their contributors, including Leslie Fiedler, Mary McCarthy, Isaac Rosenfeld, Alfred Kazin, and, after some hesitation, Lionel Trilling. "The main difference between *Partisan Review* and *Commentary*," Cohen explained to a young Norman Podhoretz, "is that we admit to being a Jewish magazine and they don't." *Commentary* took a livelier and more sustained interest in popular culture, as in Robert Warshow's stunning essays, and life on the street. *PR* typically noticed the latter only to deplore it.

A contributor to both *Commentary* and *Partisan Review*, Milton Klonsky was the author of "Greenwich Village Decline and Fall," a portentous exercise that begins with an epigraph from Gershom Scholem, the great scholar of Jewish mysticism, "It is the abyss which becomes visible in the gaps of existence," and ends with the horrid realization that the eyes of Klonsky's junkie friend Saggy were "pitch-black! They had no whites!—like the sooty fire-place with the orange flame burning inside it before which I am writing."

In Klonsky's psychic geography, the Village is id to uptown's ego—his slangy, allusive style, sharp tongue, and aggressive manners announced the arrival of the New York intellectual as hipster, shape-shifting around earlier incarnations as aesthete and engagé, the ghostly figures haunting the Village's cunning corridors. Rampant in the Village are the "Street Goths," the "young toughs, the 'internal prole-tariat'" of the Village, who escape at night from tenements to taunt and terrorize the gentle bohemians, jealous of their sexual freedom.

This is a Village of the damned into which tourists bumble and refugees from Middle America spill, along with the wayfarers who stay for a season or two, to inhabit a nostalgic milieu dating from the golden age before the First World War: the painted floors of yellow, red, green, brown; rickety furniture; framed prints of Rouault and Picasso on the walls. Not for *their* innocent eyes is the abyss visible to Milton Klonsky, as he catches sight of a hideously disfigured man caught like him in the traffic on Sheridan Square, who disappears down one of the seven streets that converge on the square, leaving behind only a "sulphurous after-image."

It was the war, with the international hordes of Allied soldiers thronging the streets and saloons, that exposed the innocent Village as never before in American mass culture, soap operas and radio advertis-ing, Hollywood movies, and comic strips that blinded with their light. After such knowledge, the long-awaited evangels out of Europe—the new paintings by Picasso, the poetry of Éluard, even the existentialist fables of Sartre and Camus, which borrowed from the tough guys in American detective stories and movies—were somehow a letdown; at least they were to the young Milton Klonsky and his friends. And here, prompt upon his cue, comes the hipster.

"The Hipster societies—if they are such, since nobody in them thinks they belong—may be considered the draft-dodgers of com-mercial civilization, just as Villagers, in general, are the loyal opposi-tion or 'conscientious objectors' . . . The mood which infects them all is, perhaps, a tender American version of that underground nihilism which erupted in the forms of Dada and fascism in Europe—anti-art and anti-morality. What they believe in is Benzedrine, 'tea,' and jazz."

Anatole Broyard's "A Portrait of the Hipster" in *Partisan Review* declared: "As he was the illegitimate son of the Lost Generation, the hipster was really *nowhere* . . . Jive music and tea were the most important component of the hipster's life." The ancestry of the hipster is obscure, the origin of the word "hip" unknown (on the authority of the *Oxford English Dictionary*, which, however, traces "cool" to Eton, the English public school, in the early nineteenth century). An ingenious theory, tentatively proposed by the late English linguist David Dalby, and popularized by the poet and critic Clarence Major, finds the origin of "hip" in Wolof, a West African tongue carried by slaves to the Americas: specifically the verb "hepi" (to see) or "hipi" (to open one's eyes). The origins of "cool" (notwithstanding the *OED*) and words once used in cool circles such as "dig," as in "to understand," are similarly tracked back to Senegal, although it remains unclear how these words, now so essential, were unrecorded for four hundred or five hundred years after they had been transported across the black Atlantic. Yet, in this way the hipster is endowed with a rich history, stretching back centuries to colonial and antebellum slave economy, when words such as "hip," "dig," "jive," "juke," "jazz," and "honky" formed "a new argot."

Hip's anatomists at mid-century had no such remote antecedents in mind. The Greenwich Village hipster was not a trickster-revenant but a contemporary phenomenon of disputed paternity undoubtedly related to the experience of the century's two great wars, emerging from the proletariat toward the end of the Depression, and becoming a recognizable type during the war (related on the West Coast to the pachuco, whose anatomist was the Mexican poet and critic Octavio Paz). Broyard, a Louisiana Creole who did not acknowledge his own African roots, did not think the hipster was necessarily enlightened in any way—or necessarily cool, in the Etonian sense.

Broyard felt that out of some sort of delinquency came a philosophy called jive, from "jibe," to agree, or harmonize.* By getting rid of so-called aggressions symbolically, the hipster could reconcile himself

---

* *OED:* "Jibe" is an ancient word of nautical origins and Scandinavian etymology, arriving in English via Middle French.

with society; thus, a gestural minimalism, or "frequent use of meton-
ymy and metonymous gestures," another aspect of jive later associated
with the yet-unnamed beatnik, "e.g., brushing palms for handshaking,
extending an index finger, without raising the arm, as a form of greeting." And almost a full decade before Mailer announced his discovery
of the hipster as "the American existentialist," Broyard described his
apotheosis and subsequent ruin:

> The intellectuals manques, however, the desperate barometers of
> society, took him into their bosom . . .
>
> He was received in the Village as an oracle; his language was *the
> revolution of the word, the personal idiom.* He was the great instinctual
> man, an ambassador from the Id. He was asked to read things, look
> at things, feel things, taste things, and report. Was it *in there?* Was
> it *gone?* Was it *fine?* . . .
>
> With such an audience, nothing was too much. The hipster
> became, in his own eyes, a poet, a seer, a hero.

At this distance in time, it is obvious that misogyny was a trait the
hipsters shared with their anatomists, who were, of course, in their
fashion, hipsters themselves. Klonsky's friend and extravagant admirer
Seymour Krim recounts in his memoir how they felt each other out:
"Whodya like in prose right now? Chicks: Bennington or spade? Dig
a tenor or a trumpet? You a Giants fan? What about Matisse?" Krim
admired Klonsky's tremendous intellect and fantastic erudition, but
even more his successful pursuit of women. In Norman Mailer's later,
more famous anatomy of hip, the goal is the "apocalyptic orgasm"
(male): a long way from the days when the Village's moderns practiced
free love and professed feminism.

In memoirs of Greenwich Village such as Broyard's *When Kafka
Was the Rage* (1993), Ronald Sukenick's *Down and In: Life in the Underground* (1987), and Herbert Gold's *Bohemia: Where Art, Angst, Love,
and Strong Coffee Meet* (1993), the scene is lit by nostalgia: there is nothing dark and satanic about it, nor is it the futile, belated space that it
looked like to Albert Parry and William Barrett. Even before he began
to publish stories and essays in *Partisan Review*, Broyard was someone
who was noticed—a discharged navy captain with conspicuously hand-

some, slightly dark features (was he a Negro?), who had a bookshop on Cornelia Street. "If it hadn't been for books, we'd have been completely at the mercy of sex," Broyard recalls, having applied himself diligently to both.

Born in 1924, Herbert Gold spent his first season in Greenwich Village in 1941, still young enough to be a runaway (although he had said "formal good-byes to tearful parents" before setting off from Lakewood, Ohio), but already a published poet in New York. He stayed at the decrepit Mills Hotel on Bleecker Street, where it was still possible to approximate the conditions in Stephen Crane's *An Experiment in Misery* (1894) for fifty cents a night, until he "moved into a hot-sheets rooming house, one boy among the whores—it was healthier and more congenial. An older woman of nineteen shared her frozen Mars bars with me."

Gold found work as a Mercury bicycle messenger and a busboy. "It was still the Village of caped poets, red-checked tablecloths in cheap spaghetti restaurants, and pale huge-eyed seekers"; or so he remembered fifty years on. One day the underground Minetta Stream, which ran from Fifth Avenue and Twenty-first Street down to Charlton Street before flowing into the Hudson, flooded a basement on Macdougal Street, and this youth from Ohio realized that all his surroundings had once been farm and pasture land, long before E. E. Cummings came to Patchin Place. Gold enrolled at Columbia, where in a freshman class taught by Lionel Trilling, part of the university's so-called Great Books syllabus, he met Allen Ginsberg and his friend Lucien Carr. It was 1944, and the rest of the class consisted of naval cadets and army officers-in-training, who did not share the threesome's interest in the required classical literature and the Book of Job or their admiration for Trilling, who sensibly ignored them and gave most of his attention to the civilians. Gold and Ginsberg became friends, and remained friendly until Ginsberg's death, although Gold considered the Beat Generation to be a "male cult" and a fraud, publishing a hipper-than-thou critique in 1958 that compared them and their followers to "unleashed zazous."

Gold, whose opinion of the Beats eventually improved, moved to San Francisco in the fifties, arriving after Lawrence Ferlinghetti (born 1919), perhaps the most venerable, and certainly the most famous, self-professed bohemian of our time. Poet, publisher, and bookseller, Ferlinghetti, then Larry Monsanto Ferling, spent time in Greenwich Village after the war, in which he had served in the navy as the captain of a submarine chaser, escorting landing craft on D-Day on the Normandy beaches ("I have seen the educated armies / on the beach at Dover"). Like an Oliver Twist story in reverse, Ferlinghetti had grown up an orphan as the ward of a rich older couple, Presley and Anna Lawrence Bisland, in a mansion in Bronxville, in the same neighborhood as Joe and Rose Kennedy and their children, who lived in a house at 294 Pondfield Road from 1928 to 1938, and again from 1939 to 1940. Oddly, Anna had had a son named Lawrence who had died in childbirth. (Her father, a real-estate tycoon, founded Sarah Lawrence College, named for his wife.) During the war Larry Ferling discovered from magazines like the *New Republic* and the *Nation* that there were political values other than the conservative ones he had been raised with. After the war, he returned to New York, where he did graduate study at Columbia, and later commuted from Bronxville to a job at the mailroom of Time-Life. Unhappy with his prospects, he went to Paris to study literature at the Sorbonne, completing a dissertation on the poetry of the city and successfully defending it in French. By December 1950, he was back in New York, which he described in his journal as "an uneasy metropolis, featuring the new all-plastic, nylon-reinforced television mentality . . .

"It was just too tough and avaricious. Everything seemed to be sewn up. So I went west, young man."

In the late 1940s and into the mid-'50s, everybody went to the San Remo—an old-fashioned Italian restaurant and bar, with tin ceiling, black-and-white tile floors, and windows facing Bleecker Street. In his memoirs Michael Harrington, the future discoverer of *The Other America*, describes the "uneasy intersection of Greenwich Village and Little Italy, with bad, yellowed paintings over the bar and the Entr'Acte from Wolf-Ferrari's *Jewels of the Madonna* on the jukebox." A recent graduate of the University of Chicago, Harrington was curtly directed there on his first night in town by a patron at a lesbian bar on Barrow Street who, displeased at his chatting up her date, informed him, "You don't belong here, buddy. You're a San Remo type."

As Harrington became a regular, the San Remo's bohemian clientele (distinct from the neighborhood's Italians) sorted itself into types: tragic gypsies out of the past, the poet and novelist Maxwell Bodenheim being the archetype; young, lusty heterosexuals and homosexuals on the prowl; the various sectaries of the left, Socialist, Communist, Trotskyist; and a few anarchists, like the abstract expressionist Barnett Newman. Harrington was more attentive to the dissident elements in the room than others when memoir time came around, marshalling, for example, the many sailors of radical persuasion, including veterans of the Spanish Civil War. The early Cold War purges and blacklists, he observed, gave the radical mariners "plenty of time to drink and reminisce about Spain in the Remo." Dylan Thomas went to drink there on his first lecture tour, but according to his friend and American handler, John Malcolm Brinnin, he was disappointed to find himself treated by the blasé patrons like any other celebrity on a drunk.

As a teenager in 1948, Ronald Sukenick went straight to the Remo from Ocean Parkway in Brooklyn. "Every bright kid in Midwood High School in the middle of middle-class Brooklyn is campaigning his ass off for Henry Wallace," but Sukenick was not enlisting in the crusade. In his 1987 memoir, *Down and In*, with the generous benefit of retrospect, he sees who were overlooked at the Remo by Mary McCarthy in her satirical tour of the Village published in the *New York Post* about this time: Paul Goodman, John Cage, Miles Davis, Merce Cunningham, William Steig, Jackson Pollock, Julian Beck and Judith Malina, Dorothy Day, "and writers as diverse as James Agee, Brossard, Ginsberg, Corso, Kerouac . . ."

Another face in this crowd at the Remo: James Ingram Merrill. James was taken from the hospital where he was born in 1926 to a brownstone at 18 West Eleventh Street; in 1970 this would be blown up by the Weathermen, camped inside as they assembled a bomb and made a fatal electrical connection. When James was still small, Charlie and Hellen Merrill moved on to more opulent dwellings: large apartments in Manhattan; a thirty-three-room "beach cottage" in Southampton, Long Island, known as "the Orchard," with an exterior vaguely inspired by Mount Vernon, only bigger (the setting of James Merrill's "The Broken Home"); and "Merrill's Landing" in Palm Beach, whose grounds covered the distance from Lake Worth to the Atlantic. Charlie Merrill, already once divorced when he married James's mother, divorced her, remarried, and was divorced again. After St. Bernard's, where he did well until his parents were divorced and he was held back, Jimmy went on to Lawrenceville School, where he began writing poems, and then to Amherst. He was drafted into the army in 1944 and spent an uneventful eight months as a clerk, returning to Amherst at nineteen at the start of 1945. Merrill graduated summa cum laude with a thesis on metaphor in Proust, and only later learned that Charlie Merrill had considered hiring Murder, Inc. to "rub out" Jimmy's professor Kimon Friar when his mother told him Jimmy and his professor were having an affair, calling off Murder, Inc. only after Hellen Merrill talked some sense into him.

For a year, Jimmy taught at Bard College, "two hours by car from Macdougal Street," where the great event was meeting Elizabeth Bishop, the "right woman" for him. "Like her I had no graduate degree, didn't feel called upon to teach, preferred to New York's literary circus the camouflage of another culture." Though fifteen years older, she would also set him an example of sexual candor (for those with eyes to read), but it was not heeded for several years. Luckily, he was launching his career in the golden age of irony, ambiguity, and paradox. His book of poetry was accepted by Alfred A. Knopf, the first publisher to which it was submitted.

Teaching at Bard College had alleviated the feeling of being less "serious" than his friends who were starting work or graduate school. His father had canvassed opinions of his poems from various authorities, including the president of Amherst, and been assured of their high quality. One day in Delray Beach, Florida, as they were watching a polo match, Charlie Merrill thought to confide that he would rather have a first-rate poet for a son than a third-rate polo player. (But a *first-rate* polo player? Jimmy surely wondered. In accordance with psychiatric opinion at the time, Merrill assumed that homosexuals were made, not born, and in his memoir blames his parents' divorce for turning him into a "sissy.")

In the city he followed a languorous routine not unlike Anthony Patch's in *The Beautiful and Damned* before Fitzgerald's stand-in marries teenaged Gloria and his dissipation becomes heroic: lunch with his mother at her East Side apartment and "an hour or two of 'work' in order to deserve the evening's fun." He was renting an apartment on Sutton Place, a Proustian cocoon of three rooms, whose heavy bedroom curtains were permanently closed against the sun, and even the sitting room's "dark tobacco-brown walls and black, flowered carpet" needed lamplight at noon. The piano held sheet music of Mozart's sonatas and all the pieces he had learned as a child. He questioned whether it was too much cultural capital: "Wouldn't I live a wiser, freer life without twice my weight in scratchy opera recordings, and shelves overloaded with books very few of which were enduring classics? Alas, I had never thrown anything out. In its three small rooms this first apartment held all the accumulated 'signifiers' of my twenty-four years—or am I mis-using a fashionable term?"

Like almost every other writer of his generation in New York, Merrill spent innumerable evenings at the San Remo, where he might have encountered (but does not mention) jazzmen, anarchists, paint-ers, ancient bohemians, hipsters, writers, extinct or aspiring, of all descriptions, from the sleek Broyard to a broken-down, beggarly Max Bodenheim. But Merrill associated riotous nights of "being myself" at the San Remo with a circle of friends with whom he did not share his "serious" side. Night after night, they sat gossiping and laughing, "pro-tected from encounters they perhaps desired with other customers by the glittering moat, inches deep, of their allusive chatter."

One of their obsessions Merrill did not share was a legendarily self-destructive wild man named Bill Cannastra, of whom Tennes-see Williams—who caroused with him in Provincetown, where they were sometimes joined by Jackson Pollock, and in whose Harvard Law School dormitory room he finished *The Glass Menagerie*—said, "He was beat before there were beats." Cannastra amazed his friends by managing to graduate from Harvard Law School, though he took only menial jobs in New York. He was known for such rash activities as voyeurism on fire escapes, streaking, walking on the tops of cars, and kissing longshoremen in low bars, and for the parties in his gloomy loft above a lampshade factory on West Twenty-first Street; to these came W. H. Auden, Howard Moss (poetry editor of the *New Yorker*), Kerouac, Ginsberg, the other Beats, Larry Rivers, Alan Harrington, Edwin Denby, Paul Goodman. In a bizarre mishap, Cannastra was killed in October 1950 when he started climbing out the window of a subway car at the Bleecker Street station, and his handsome face was smashed against a pillar. Jack Kerouac met Joan Haverty, Cannastra's notional fiancée, the next month, and they celebrated their marriage with an awkward party at the loft, which she was preserving as a sort of shrine. Early in 1951 they moved to an apartment on West Twenty-fourth Street, where Kerouac, inspired by the frantic prose of a 28,000-word letter from Neal Cassady, rewrote *On the Road*, taping together the twenty-foot scrolls of Japanese drawing paper that had belonged to Cannastra and feeding them into his typewriter to produce a single-spaced paragraph long enough to circle the block.

In *The Recognitions* (1955), William Gaddis's description of the educated classes who patronized the Via Viareggio, as he calls the San Remo, is acidulous: "an ill-dressed, underfed, overdrunken group of squatters with minds so highly developed that they were excused from good manners, tastes so refined in one direction that they were excused for having none in any other, emotions so cultivated that the only aberration was normality, all afloat here on sodden pools of depravity calculated only to manifest the pricelessness of what they were throwing away, the three sexes in two colors, a group of people all mentally and physically the wrong size." Tourists came to be scandalized; the timid needed only to peer through the windows.

In Gaddis's set piece the jukebox is eternally playing "Return to Sorrento," and everyone in the room is a frantic poseur, including the Big Unshaven Man rumored to be Ernest Hemingway. "A damn fine painter, Mr. Memlin, he was saying, as he took a quart flask out of his pocket. Would you mind filling this up with martinis?"

"The painters could be identified by dirty fingernails," just as the writers were "by conversation in labored monosyllables and aggressive vulgarities which disguised their minds.—Yeh, I'm doing a psychoanalysis of it, said one of them, tapping Mother Goose on the table."

The elements of the Italianate San Remo were more combustible than those of the Celtic White Horse, although in the McCarthy era the latter did sometimes come under assault from neighborhood youths denouncing "Commies and fags." At the San Remo the bartenders themselves sometimes set upon the customers, and according to Ed Fancher, the first publisher of the *Village Voice*, after one such episode the whole crowd left and moved their patronage to the nearby Louis.

. . .

Even before the shutdown of the Federal Art Project in 1942, differences in practice that had divided the painters of Greenwich Village in the thirties now seemed less important than solidarity in the face of a society apparently renewed in its indifference to the fine arts and its contempt for those who practiced them. Charles Henri Ford's surrealist-inflected magazine, *View*, published from 1940 to 1947, printed a list issued by the Selective Service of workers not eligible for deferment from the draft, including: "clerks, messengers, office boys, shipping clerks, footmen, bellboys, pages, sales clerks, filing clerks, hairdressers, dress and millinery makers, designers, interior decorators and artists." The postwar promised no better.

Arshile Gorky, Willem de Kooning, Jack Tworkov, Milton Resnick, and the sculptor Philip Pavia were among the regulars who drifted into the Waldorf Cafeteria between eleven o'clock and midnight and renewed a conversation that had begun in the politically charged thirties and continued into the myth-haunted forties.

"It's hard to describe the evenings," Pavia later said. "But there was a real hunger. We all sought each other's company and it was practically daily; six out of seven nights of the week we all sat around and talked."

They talked, and they argued, said Pavia. "We'd fight about the Surrealists and French culture. Bill de Kooning talked about *his* Picasso, and Gorky talked about *his* Picasso." If Gorky brought his dogs, as he sometimes did, the argument happened on the sidewalk, because the dogs were not allowed inside. Once the Waldorf closed, the discussions were continued under the awning of a cigar store. By 1948, the *New Yorker* and *Life* magazine were writing about such disparate figures as a "school." The term "abstract expressionism" made its first appearance in print in 1946 in a review of recent work by Pollock, Gorky, and de Kooning by the *New Yorker*'s art critic, Robert M. Coates.

Clement Greenberg, the regular critic for the *Nation* and *Partisan Review*, maintained that the crucial formation had come in 1946–47, which happened to coincide with his own realization that the new work being produced in New York was simply more interesting and more expressive of the times than anything coming out of France. One day in 1946, he astonished John Bernard Myers, the young managing editor of *View* and future director of the Tibor de Nagy Gallery, saying over drinks at the Vanderbilt Bar that the next world art center would be "the place where the money is, New York."

It was Greenberg's essay for *Partisan Review*, "Avant-Garde and Kitsch," that made his reputation in 1939. After graduating from Syracuse with honors in 1931, Greenberg had moved back in with his family on Riverside Drive and then Ocean Parkway, and for most of a decade loafed, womanized, taught himself languages (Latin, French, German, Italian), until his desperate father sent him on the road to sell neckties from his factory; later, he found a civil-service job at the customhouse on Varick Street, and was working there when Dwight Macdonald, whose Trotskyism he vaguely shared, proposed that he expand a letter he had sent him about kitsch into an essay. Many years later, Greenberg wrote, "Someday it will have to be told how anti-Stalinism which started out more or less as Trotskyism turned into art for art's sake, and thereby cleared the way, heroically, for what was to come." As far as art-world advocacy goes, he was only giving himself the proper credit.

Beginning with "Avant-Garde and Kitsch," Greenberg struck a tone that was authoritative even by *Partisan Review*'s lofty standard. To an exaggerated degree, it was declarative rather than analytical, sparing of examples, sweeping in scope, distinctive in style but impersonal in tone (a *PR* signature), and uncompromising in its conclusions, so much so that the reader loses track of exactly how he has been persuaded by them.

At its most basic, Greenberg is arguing for the fundamental distinction between the degraded mass culture he calls kitsch, which was being exploited by the totalitarian regimes in Russia, Germany, and Italy, used to "ingratiate" them with the masses—and the avant-garde (modernist, formalist) art, which carries at least the potential for resistance. In poetry, the avant-garde is represented by a poem by T. S. Eliot in contrast to the kitsch of Tin Pan Alley; in painting, a work by Braque is compared to a *Saturday Evening Post* cover; the more debased, the more popular. Kitsch was born in the great cities created by the Industrial Revolution, but its sludge was now being spread by colonialism over the earth, extinguishing native arts in its path. The avant-garde began with the original bohemia's heroic struggle to avoid slipping into the "motionless Alexandrianism" of a moribund culture, in which "nothing new is produced: Statius, mandarin verse, Roman sculpture, Beaux-Arts painting, neo-republican architecture." "It was no accident" (the readers of *PR* could confidently await this cant, dropped like the other shoe) that the bourgeoisie, on which the avant-garde ultimately depends for a living, is always liable to slip back into supporting lifeless academic art or sinking into the morass of the popular and commercial.

Admired, ridiculed, resented, and feared, his uncompromised air of authority became one of the secrets of the dictatorship he exercised over the art world for over thirty years. Greenberg retained from his Trotskyist days a sense of historical mission, which encouraged him to dispatch such things as easel painting to the dustbin and to draw up lists of who was at the front of the vanguard; but in the forties he also provided a tradition for the painters below Fourteenth Street by assimilating them in to the history of bohemia, garrets and all—social and artistic territory that *PR* had previously embargoed. (Philip Rahv was scathing on the subject of the *Luftmensch*, who, in the Yiddish idiom, lived in the air with no visible means of support, although for years he had been one himself.) In "The Present Prospects of American Painting and Sculpture," the essay he contributed to *Horizon*'s famous American issue in 1947, Greenberg wrote that "international Bohemia" had imposed its taste on the dealers on Fifty-seventh Street and the Museum of Modern Art, which followed *their* lead, but "it is still downtown, below 34th Street, that the fate of modern art is being decided by young people, few of them under forty, who live in cold-water flats and exist from hand to mouth." In "The Situation at the Moment" (1948), the essay that declared that easel painting was on its way out (because it was too small for the vision of the avant-garde in New York), he contended that since America was the most industrialized country, it followed that its artists must be experienced in alienation. "The alienation of Bohemia was only an anticipation in nineteenth-century Paris; it is in New York that it has been completely fulfilled."

The legend of the New York school has been flourishing ever since that time, beginning with the artists' diverse and distant origins: de Kooning, the graybeard in the group, was born in Rotterdam in

1904, the same year as their tragic precursor, Gorky, was born in the Armenian village of Korkhom, in the old Ottoman Empire. Pollock's birthplace was Cody, Wyoming; Rothko's was in what is now Latvia; Clyfford Still's in Grandin, North Dakota; and Clement Greenberg's in the Bronx; all were distant from Greenwich Village. And the legend continued with the stories of the fruitful time most of them spent on "the Project" during the thirties, which sealed their fellowship; their turn in the war-darkened forties from the political to the primitive, the mythic, and the totemic; how the fabulous rumor of surrealism was followed by the actual New York appearance of the surrealists themselves after the fall of Paris; how, after months of staring doubtfully at the twenty-foot canvas in his studio, Pollock painted *Mural* for the entry of Peggy Guggenheim's apartment in a single night; how Guggenheim's gallery, Art of This Century, at 30 West Fifty-seventh Street, designed by Friedrich Kiesler, opening in October 1942, both exhibited the European surrealists, whose works she had smuggled out of Nazi-occupied Europe, and gave Pollock, Adolph Gottlieb, Ad Reinhardt, and Theodoros Stamos their first one-man shows.

For the first and last time, a major American art movement announced itself with solemn mottos and manifestos in the European style. Mark Rothko declared "the subject is crucial and only that subject matter is valid which is tragic and timeless"; Barnett Newman, then still known for his activity as an art journalist rather than as a painter, insisted that the artist needed to return to the condition of primordial man and his self-aware "helplessness before the void." "The sublime is now," said Newman.

By 1949, the gatherings at the Waldorf Cafeteria had drifted to the Cedar Bar and were formalized into the Artists' Club (familiarly, "the Club"), which met in a loft at 39 East Eighth Street, collected dues, and sponsored lectures; the postindustrial setting was without doubt as portentous for future artistic developments in the city as the talk. "It is disastrous to name ourselves," de Kooning declared on the famous night that Alfred Barr presided over a debate on the subject, but it was too late: fashionable opinion was about to settle on "abstract expressionism," although it could be said that those were exactly the lines along which they were divided.

Time and *Life* had been paying fitful attention to Pollock and other dissident painters in New York for several years, blowing hot and cold on their subject. In October 1948, along with Adolph Gottlieb, William Baziotes, Theodoros Stamos, and de Kooning, he was one of the "Young American Extremists"—the merits of whose representative works were considered by a "round table" panel including Greenberg, Aldous Huxley, Meyer Schapiro, James J. Sweeney, author and lecturer, James Thrall Soby, the chairman of the department of painting and sculpture at MoMA, and the art historian H. W. Janson. Picasso, Braque, Matisse, Miró, Rouault, and the surrealists Tanguy and Dalí were appraised: heady company for a band of unknown outsiders. Several of the panelists remarked that the colorful Pollock would make a lovely silk necktie or a good pattern for wallpaper. Greenberg, billed as "avant-garde critic," ventured that *Cathedral* was one of the most remarkable paintings to appear in America in recent times.

In August 1949, *Life* published an article headlined "Jackson Pollock: Is He the Greatest Living Painter in the United States?" It was supposedly Greenberg's exalted opinion of Pollock that had inspired the piece. "Recently a formidably high-brow New York critic hailed the brooding, puzzled-looking man above as a major artist of our time and a fine candidate to become 'the greatest American painter of the 20th Century.'"

Time-Life, which had come out of the war as the supreme magazine empire in America, was suffering from a corporate fit of insecurity about its continued relevance, and responsibility for maintaining the American Way of life. The editors, including the editor-in-chief, Henry Luce, were spending as much time exchanging fretful memoranda as editing the magazines. "Life as it is lived in America," Luce wrote in a typical communiqué, "is a strange and wonderful tension between the particular problems of little people (all of us and our families) and the surge of great 'historic forces.' It's enough to drive anybody crazy—and apparently does. All the more then, *Life* is required to be good-tempered and sane."

Everyone read *Life*. It was as ubiquitous as Coca-Cola and Campbell's soup, which, like Camel and Lucky Strike cigarettes, were among its biggest advertisers. According to a house advertisement published early in 1949, *Life* sold an average of 5.2 million copies every week, 5 million paid, most of which were "passed along," accumulating a total readership of 22 million, which represented fully 36 percent of all American households. Advertisers spent more money on *Life* than on any of the national radio and television broadcasting networks; and rather than retrenching after the war, when so many correspondents were coming home, Luce expanded *Life*'s staff—which, as told by its historian Loudon Wainwright, was as brilliant an assemblage of ambitious, mostly young New Yorkers as can be imagined.*

"Art" (always capitalized in his memoranda) was a domain that Luce did not intend *Life* to neglect, and that *Life* did not hesitate to police. In December 1948, *Life* published an article about Jean Dubuffet, whose cunning faux-primitive art was among the most vital coming out of France after the war, devoting a whole page to a reproduction of *Smoky Black (Lili)*; "Dead End Art: A Frenchman's Mud-and-Rubble Paintings Reduce Modernism to a Joke" was the title. With this debacle in mind, Pollock and his wife, the painter Lee Krasner, were wary when he was approached by *Life* about a feature early in July 1949; but as art-world insiders they had become aware that after *Life*'s blast, Dubuffet's dealer, Pierre Matisse, had bought back the painting in the article, correctly anticipating that the publicity would lead to more demand for Dubuffet. Pollock and Krasner duly appeared at the Time-Life Building for him to be interviewed on July 18, 1949, the artist dressed up in a respectable tweed jacket and polished loafers. Their interviewer was a young writer-researcher, Dorothy Seiberling, an alumna of Vassar and the granddaughter of the founder of Goodyear Tire; a sympathetic Seiberling found Pollock, in contrast to the articulate and composed Krasner, "all kind of knotted up inside." What he said, as opposed to how he looked in the photographs taken by Arnold

---

* "Taken all together, the staff was a vital, talented, restless, even frolicsome group. Young geniuses from Harvard and Vassar mixed with returned infantry officers and bomber pilots; jazz piano players trained in politics and economics mingled with poetry-writing science writers; pipe-smoking experts on ancient Greek culture flirted with beautiful Egyptologists [was there more than one?], hymn-singing newsmen from the farm belt shook bone-dry martinis for chic fashion consultants on the latest clothes from Chanel. The place brimmed with energy, enthusiasm, ambition and life." Loudon Wainwright, *Life: The Great American Magazine: An Inside History of Life* (1986; rpt. New York: Ballantine Books, 1988), 194.

Newman in Springs, Long Island, scarcely mattered. As his first biographer, B. H. Friedman, writes, they showed "a new, non-arty American style painter, working in dungarees, with commercial materials, crouching over canvas spread on the floor, with a can in his left hand" and a cigarette jammed in his mouth. In a single photo shoot Pollock joined the postwar rogues' gallery of moody male writers, artists, and actors: cousin to Camus, brother to Brando.

"Is Jackson Pollock a threat to the American way of life? That was the question percolating through the offices of *Life* magazine as the deadline for the August 8 issue approached." Thus, Pollock's biographers Steven Naifeh and Gregory White Smith dramatize the scene, but it seems most unlikely that anyone on that worldly-wise staff would have put the question that way; the question was whether Pollock was a fraud, like Jean Dubuffet. But, as they reveal, Pollock had his supporters as well, including, crucially, Daniel Longwell, a former managing editor of *Life* and chairman of its board of editors. It was Longwell, a "very enthusiastic, exuberant person," according to Seiberling when she was interviewed many years later, who had proposed a piece on Pollock in the first place; he had gone to his most recent opening and come away with a painting, bemused that its impasto had a fly in it.

But was it the impulse of an idle hour that had led Longwell, who had previously shown no interest in the avant-garde, to the Betty Parsons Gallery, or, conceivably, a tip from Rosalind Constable, the only person in the Time-Life hierarchy without a title, who functioned, as the biographer of her admirer Patricia Highsmith puts it, as Henry Luce's "cool-hunter, *avant la lettre*"? From her unmarked office, Constable, an Englishwoman with striking "Nordic" blond hair and features, monitored developments in the underground and the avant-garde—which in the forties typically announced themselves in little magazines like *Tiger's Eye*, pamphlets, posters, and other ephemera. Her office was piled up with signs and portents that Constable interpreted in a fortnightly report for Luce and the other top editors.

"Look at him standing there," said Willem de Kooning when he saw the article, "he looks like some guy who works at a service station pumping gas." With a cigarette dangling from his lips, arms folded, Pollock stood in his dungarees in front of the eighteen-foot canvas later titled *Summertime*; two and a half pages of fame was set in the midst of the postwar consumerist clutter of whiskey, canned soup, frozen fish fillets, television sets, airplane flights to romantic places, and cigarettes safe for the T-zone. Pollock stares back at the camera, wearing that quizzical look, guarded and challenging at the same time, that he shared with Clift, Brando, Dean. "The picture is only 3 feet high, but it is 18 feet long and sells for $1800, or $100 a foot. Critics have wondered why Pollock happened to stop this painting where he did. The answer: his studio is only 22 feet long." The generous layout and arch but not quite dismissive tone reflect the division in editorial opinion at Time-Life about this cool commodity. *Life* conceded that Pollock, who mimed his drip technique for the photographer, Arnold Newman, had his admirers: five museums and forty private collections owned his paintings, and twelve had sold in New York at his last exhibition. His work had stirred up a "fuss" in Italy and would soon be in an upcoming show in "avant-garde Paris." In short, the man with the scowl was a contender; and if there was more than a hint that he might be a confidence man, that, too, would have been in the American grain. Pollock loved the article, and often reread it, along with other favorable reviews, for reassurance; although he blushed when anyone brought it into his house on Firehouse Drive, he bought a hundred copies. If he knew, it did not bother him that the article provoked more than five hundred letters to the editor, with all but a handful objecting to *Life*'s giving space to such an obvious fraud. There had been no such outpouring since *Life* had given a cover story to Paul Robeson's *Othello*, in which the black actor appeared with Uta Hagen as Desdemona.

On November 21, 1949, Pollock's show of new work opened at the Betty Parsons Gallery, where the crowd overflowed its two rooms on the fifth floor of 15 East Fifty-seventh Street—the address that she and Sam Kootz, who rented the other half of the floor from her, had made a staging ground for the new painting. The bare wooden floors and plain white-painted walls of her gallery—a new look at the time—were exquisitely suited to her relation with the artists she represented. "I give them walls. They do the rest."

Betty Bierne Pierson was an artist herself, who religiously devoted weekends and summers to her sculpting. Her parents, well-off New

Yorkers from "old" families who divided the year between Manhattan, Newport, and Palm Beach, indulged her in art lessons after her interest had been aroused by the Armory Show, while she completed her formal education with five years at Miss Chapin's. They expected her to marry a rich man, as she did, at age nineteen. Unfortunately—or perhaps not, as things worked out—Schuyler Livingston Parsons, whose bloodline was considered positively primordial in New York society, was a jealous alcoholic who chased men as avidly as she did women. She went to Paris to divorce him in 1923 (they remained on friendly terms, but she was disinherited by her family) and then stayed on for another ten, studying sculpture alongside Isamu Noguchi and Alberto Giacometti in classes taught by Antoine Bourdelle and Ossip Zadkine. Parsons frequented the salons, including Gertrude Stein's, and became friends with Natalie Barney, Janet Flanner, and Alexander Calder. The Depression brought her back to America in 1933, and, finding sunny California more suited to a reduced income than New York, she moved to Hollywood, "where her acquaintances numbered Greta Garbo, Marlene Dietrich, Tallulah Bankhead, Dorothy Parker and Robert Benchley," and then to Santa Barbara, where she worked at various genteel occupations, painting portraits and giving drawing lessons, as well as selling French wines at a liquor store.

Parsons returned to New York in 1935, having sold her engagement ring to pay for the trip. Robert Benchley gave her an entrée to Alan Gruskin's Midtown Galleries, which showed her work. She also curated some exhibitions, and in 1939 she was introduced to Rosalind Constable, already patrolling the avant-garde at *Time*, and the next year she was invited to manage a gallery devoted to modern art at the Wakefield Bookshop. Saul Steinberg, Theodoros Stamos, Hedda Stone, and Joseph Cornell were among the artists she exhibited there. Steinberg once painted her as a spaniel dog, explaining to Calvin Tomkins, "If you look closely at Betty, you see the Sphinx, the Garbo-like quality. And strictly entre nous, the Sphinx is doggy."

When the bookshop was closing its doors in 1944, Mortimer Brandt, a hard-boiled dealer in Old Masters, offered a similar arrangement at his fifth-floor gallery at 15 East Fifty-seventh Street; when he decided to return to England after the war, Parsons was able to raise the money to sublet the space, keeping her two rooms and renting the others to the enterprising Sam Kootz. As Peter Watson writes in *From Manet to Manhattan*, it was from their galleries, and a more exiguous one run by Charles Egan, a hole-in-the-wall with irregular hours and a bohemian proprietor, that the contemporary art market was launched.

In 1947, when Peggy Guggenheim joined the surrealists in the return exodus to Europe, Parsons assumed responsibility for Pollock, keeping up his allowance and forgoing commissions, few as they were, when she feared that he and Krasner were in desperate shape at their unheated farmhouse on Long Island. Now that *Life* had confirmed him as a celebrity, Parsons was atypically leaning on prospective buyers, offering special discounts in a low whisper, and Krasner, who did not identify herself as Mrs. Jackson Pollock, was seated at the receptionist's desk with a stack of reprints of the *Life* article.

For a time, the Pollocks were living in the unaccustomed comfort of their friend Alfonso Ossorio's converted coach house in Macdougal Alley, which he lent them while he was back in the Philippines, painting a mural for his family's private chapel. An oasis of potted plants and white-painted walls bright with Ossorio's watercolors and muddy with Dubuffets, it was tended by Ossorio's companion, the dancer Ted Dragon, who was rehearsing for his first performance of the Balanchine/Stravinsky *Orpheus* for City Ballet. Steadied by the Miltown prescribed for him by a young Dr. Heller in Long Island, Pollock was spruce and sober at the opening at Betty Parsons, dressed in his uptown uniform of tweed jacket and polished loafers. He had produced a number of smaller canvases, sometimes "no bigger than one by two feet, mounted on Masonite," with calligraphic images, rather than his trademark swirls, to oblige a skittish art market, and he had cooperated with Peter Blake, a design wunderkind at the Museum of Modern Art, in a model for "The Ideal Exhibit," a design looking like an enlarged Philip Johnson Glass House, in which miniature reproductions of Pollock's abstractions were accompanied, "for scale," with miniature Pollock "sculptures."

Milton Resnick, who had come to the show with de Kooning, wondered why all the men in suits were shaking hands, a gesture that would have been needless downtown, where everybody at an opening knew everybody else. "I said to Bill, 'What's all this shaking about?' And he said, 'Look around. These are the big shots. Jackson has finally broken the ice.'" A legend later grew up that de Kooning meant that Pollock had made the breakthrough to abstraction, but, as usual, he meant exactly what he said. Alexey Brodovitch, the art director of *Harper's Bazaar*, represented the fashion world, in which White Russians were so prominent. Among the more opulent collectors were Burton and Emily Hall Tremaine, who started buying art, beginning with Mondrian's *Broadway Boogie-Woogie*, when they were married in 1945, and white-haired Edward Wales Root, the son of Theodore Roosevelt's secretary of state, whose collecting went back to the Armory Show. As one opening-night attendee asked, reasonably, "Who wouldn't be willing to pay a few hundred dollars to have a painting by 'that artist who was profiled in *Life*'?" The financier Roy E. Neuberger, who was also there, undoubtedly regretted later that he did not join the Tremaines and Root in making a buy. In the weeks to come, Alfred Barr, who had told Peter Blake, "But I don't think Pollock's work is something we should be supporting," was seen escorting Abby Rockefeller to the Parsons Gallery to select one of the small Pollocks to donate to the Museum of Modern Art; and he was not a lonely convert. Reviewers discovered not only beauties but depths hitherto undetected. In his notice of a show at the Whitney Museum following on the heels of the Parsons show, Henry McBride, who had made his critical debut with the Armory Show, ventured that the painting on view implied "a flat, war-shattered, possibly Hiroshima, as seen from a great height in moonlight."

Pollock ridiculed the idea that he had ever "expressed the city" in any way, least of all so apocalyptically, but these interpretations are no more or less plausible than the idea that he was enacting Navajo dances, or Charlie Parker's jazz, or engaged in a performance ("action painting") of which the painted canvas was merely the residue of the deed; it is the nature of a work deemed great, of the products of an artist considered a genius, that any extravagance of interpretation is licensed.

Putting aside more recent debates about what Carter Ratcliff has called "the Fate of a Gesture"—or whether "the Triumph of American Painting" represented the looting of the idea of modern art from Paris, one has to consider Greenberg. He had rearranged the historical parallax to restore the identity of bohemia and the avant-garde, and sent them both marching under the banner of the sublime. To be contemporary was to become timeless.

In April 1950, after the famous closed session at "the Club," Adolph Gottlieb proposed that the group organize a protest at the Metropolitan Museum for a juried competition there of American art that conspicuously excluded most of the abstractionists. An editorial in the *Herald Tribune* derided the artists as "the Irascible Eighteen." The epithet stuck, and six months later, after someone contacted *Life*—meaning, quite possibly, Rosalind Constable—the magazine published a photograph titled "Irascible Group of Advanced Artists Led Fight Against Show." According to Gottlieb, *Life* was surprised when the fifteen artists who came to pose for a shoot refused to stand, like supplicants, holding up their canvases on the steps of the museum, and rescheduled the shoot at its studio on West Forty-fourth Street. Pollock came in from Long Island to join Theodoros Stamos, Jimmy Ernst, Barnett Newman, James Brooks, Mark Rothko, Richard Pousette-Dart, William Baziotes, Clyfford Still, Robert Motherwell, Bradley Walker Tomlin, Willem de Kooning, Adolph Gottlieb, Ad Reinhardt, and Hedda Sterne in a group photograph by Nina Leen that became as famous as the writers doing homage to the Sitwells at the Gotham Book Mart: a classic iconostasis of the midcentury. As the lone woman, Sterne, in dark clothes, stands on a chair or stool at the back; the men, stony-faced, are wearing suits and ties, except for Stamos, who is dressed in khakis and a dark shirt under a dark jacket, the classic dressed-up bohemian look. They were all, or had been, "downtown." No one, looking at the "Irascibles," would have dared ask: "Are you a merry Villager?"

PART VII

1948: THE END OF SOMETHING

———————

We are never as happy or as unhappy as we suppose.

—LA ROCHEFOUCAULD, *Maxims*

President Harry S. Truman giving his acceptance speech
after being nominated for the presidency at the Democratic National
Convention, Philadelphia Convention Hall, July 15, 1948

I

———

Verdict

IN KEROUAC'S *On the Road*, a cold, bright January 20, 1949, finds Sal Paradise and Dean Moriarty, Moriarty's teenaged bride, Marylou, and their friend Ed Dunkel (in the "scroll" version of the novel they are given their "real" names: Jack Kerouac, Neal Cassady, LuAnne Henderson, Al Hinkle) in Washington, DC. They have come down from New York City ("'frosty fagtown New York,' as Dean called it"), bound for San Francisco, by way of New Orleans and Algiers, Texas, where they will meet up with Old Bull Lee (William S. Burroughs) at his marijuana farm. Arriving at dawn, the Beat Generation finds the capital dressed in military gear for Harry Truman's inauguration.

> Great displays of war might were lined along Pennsylvania Avenue as we rolled by in our battered car. There were B-29s, PT boats, artillery, all kinds of war material that looked murderous in the snowy grass; the last thing was a regular small ordinary lifeboat that looked pitiful and foolish. Dean slowed down to look at it. He kept shaking his head in awe. "What are those people up to? Harry's sleeping somewhere in this town . . . Good old Harry . . . Man from Missouri, as I am . . . This must be his own boat."

For most of 1948—indeed, up until late election night and into the next morning—there was no political event less expected than FDR's "accidental" successor being inaugurated as president in his own right. "Harry Truman has never been elected president of the United States and he never will be," declared Strom Thurmond, the junior senator from South Carolina, who was soon to lead a secession of Southern Democrats out of the party; privately and even publicly, the great majority of Truman's friends, and all of his foes, agreed. As Jonathan Daniels put it in *The Man of Independence* (1950), "Not only all the commentators but most of his companions shook their heads over his chances." Along with a unanimity of American pundits, Alistair Cooke, the BBC broadcaster and American correspondent for the *Manchester Guardian*, anticipated—rashly, as it turned out—the verdict not only of the electorate but of posterity in a column entitled "Harry S. Truman: A Study in Failure," published on election eve.

Consider that Truman had accomplished most of the things of large historical significance for which he is now credited with greatness by his admirers: the "decision" (it was a foregone conclusion) to drop the atomic bomb on Hiroshima and Nagasaki, bringing an end to the Pacific War; taking part in the deliberations at Potsdam and subsequent decisions about the future of Germany, including the Berlin Airlift; the Truman Doctrine and the Marshall Plan. Yet Cooke's uncompromising title and two subheads, "Ineptitude" and "Unimpressive," tell a different story, one worth recalling because it is substantially what Truman's informed contemporaries thought right up until the last votes were counted.

The expected loser emerged as a worthy man who had all the disadvantages of his virtues: his sterling qualities of straightforwardness, candor, modesty, loyalty, and steady application, which might appear to handsome effect in a small town, like Independence, Missouri, but looked faintly ridiculous in a president, and had rendered his administration "admittedly inept." (It did not help that Truman owed his rise in Missouri politics and his first election to the United States Senate to the Pendergast machine in Kansas City, one of the most malodorous in the country.) Inheriting the White House, not only had he often been outsmarted; he had allowed himself to be *seen* being outsmarted, or overawed, especially by men in uniform. As for accomplishments, even the Truman Doctrine had been enunciated under Churchill's "immense shadow."

Such a judgment now seems wildly off the mark, like Walter Lippmann's dismissal of Roosevelt in 1932 as an amiable lightweight. In *The Cycles of American History* (1986), Arthur M. Schlesinger Jr. devotes a typically incisive and witty essay to "The Vicissitudes of Presidential Reputations," in which, oddly, Truman is practically omitted—though surely no twentieth-century president, including Hoover, Eisenhower, and Kennedy, has been subject to such an improved revaluation.[*] The same qualities that made him unfit for the presidency enhanced his appeal as an endearingly plainspoken and long-lived ex-president whose straightforwardness and lack of swank gained by way of contrast with his more grandiose successors. Once out of office, the triumph of 1948 having been followed by the quagmire of Korea, as unapproved (though not as despised) as any president since Hoover, or possibly John Quincy Adams—and almost as lightly regarded by most of the political class as Warren G. Harding—Truman is now ranked by historians and political scientists in the tier of "near-great" presidents, just below the "greats" (Washington, Lincoln, FDR), putting him in the proximity of Thomas Jefferson, Theodore Roosevelt, James K. Polk, and Woodrow Wilson: previous American caesars whom, respectively, he admired, disparaged, had nothing much to say about, and idolized.

"I don't care how the thing is explained," said Robert A. Taft, the day after Dewey did not defeat Truman, November 3, 1948. "It defies all common sense to send that roughneck ward politician back to the White House." At his lofty offices in the Criminal Courts Building, New York District Attorney Frank Hogan, Dewey's close friend, admonished a staff meeting, "The best man did not win this election, and anybody who says different I will personally throw out that window."

---

[*] Writing during the Reagan era, Schlesinger observes that the "private-interest mood" that revised the standing of the thirty-first, thirty-fourth, and thirty-fifth presidents in the 1970s and '80s did not affect the reputation of the thirty-third. "Truman remains a curious exception, evidently because he is popularly remembered not as the champion of the Fair Deal but as the fellow from Missouri who told the Russians where to get off." Schlesinger, *Cycles of American History* (Boston: Houghton Mifflin, 1986), 174.

And yet, the senator from Ohio, for one, had privately noticed weeks before that Dewey was falling behind, had even confided to a reporter whose discretion he trusted that he knew Dewey would lose when his wife, Martha Bowers Taft (whom many considered the sharper politician), did not bother anymore to listen to his speeches on radio and television. "Mr. Republican" had apparently repressed the terrible thought that, if Tom Dewey was going to lose, Harry Truman was going to win.

"Up from the country came a long loud guffaw," Eric F. Goldman pictures the morning after in *The Crucial Decade*. "Even many Dewey voters went about grinning at strangers, gathering in scoffing clusters with friends. The people of the United States had made fools of all the experts. They had knocked down the smooth and the smug and lifted up the shaggy, spunky underdog. They had brought off the most spectacular upset in American history."

So the people might have celebrated their verdict in Manhattan's Garment District, where millions of bits of colored cloth were scattered like ticker tape from factory lofts; or in the vast "ethnic" wards of South Chicago; or in the solid-Democratic precincts south of Market Street in San Francisco, a labor bastion after the tumult of the thirties. Somehow, if the pollsters were to be believed, a majority of farmers in the Midwest had gone into the voting booth intending to vote for Dewey and marked their ballot for Truman instead, and they were tickled as well.

But for the rock-solid Republicans in such characteristic habitats as the apartments of the Waldorf Astoria Tower, the town houses of Rittenhouse Square, and the salons of Washington, DC; in the big houses in prosperous railroad suburbs; in country clubs and small towns—the people's verdict was a sickening shock. Dewey had spoken for *them* when he told John Gunther how "FDR had stolen the faith of people, seduced from them their self-confidence." But even his detractors— saving the most hate-filled, admittedly numerous—had to concede the late president large historical proportions: he was "a brave, bad man," like Lord Clarendon's description of Cromwell. But the election of *Harry Truman*, a man in whom almost nobody had ever detected the lineaments of greatness, not his friends, not his foes; a candidate to whom the pundits and the pollsters and the vast majority of professional politicians had not conceded the barest chance of winning— what else could it mean but that the sorcerer of Hyde Park's spell had survived his death? In the *New York Herald Tribune*, Walter Lippmann wrote that, "with much justice and without detracting from Mr. Truman's remarkable personal performance . . . of all Roosevelt's electoral triumphs, this one in 1948 is the most impressive."

If, it seemed, the American people were ready to give the dead Roosevelt a fifth term, it also seemed that 1948 threatened the Republicans with a permanent minority status, helpless to resist as the Democrats extended their control over the entire machinery of the state, according to the formula apocryphally attributed to Harry Hopkins: "We will tax and tax, spend and spend, elect and elect." In the end the dwindling band of the GOP might well be reduced to mere window dressing in a functioning one-party state, like the PRI's regime in Mexico.*

On the left, Rexford Guy Tugwell, the most prominent New Dealer (save the candidate himself) to be associated with Henry Wallace's third-party campaign, considered the verdict with a sigh. "In spite of the great contrast that everyone felt between the majestic Roosevelt and the unimpressive Truman, given a choice between a man who meant well and the arrogant, insincere, and inhuman Dewey, the electorate had chosen the lesser of the evils. Mr. Wallace, who had seemed for a while to be an acceptable alternative, and who was obviously in intellect and in moral power much more nearly in the dead Roosevelt's class, had come out simply nowhere. His vote was something over one million in some sixty millions of votes cast."

Political buffs indulged in the usual quasi-numerological might-have-beens. A shift of a mere thirty-three thousand votes in the decisive states of Ohio, California, and Illinois, favorably apportioned to Dewey, would have given him a majority in the Electoral College; if

---

* The comparison was implied, post facto, by William F. Buckley Jr. in his credo *Up from Liberalism* (Chicago: Henry Regnery, 1959). After his graduation from Yale, Buckley worked for the CIA in Mexico City, as a minor spook supervised by E. Howard Hunt, the novelist and future Watergate burglar.

he had carried any two of them, the contest would have gone to the House of Representatives. (Late election night, the governor had sent orders to Washington for party officials to consult with constitutional lawyers if this appeared likely to happen.) The fracturing of the Democratic Party after Henry Wallace announced as an independent candidate and Strom Thurmond was nominated by the southern rump on a states' rights ticket, cost Truman far fewer electoral votes than had been expected in the spring and, in the case of Wallace, allowed him to distance himself from the left while running as a fervent populist. Now, the verdict was in.

"Labor did it," Truman told his cronies at the Muehlebach Hotel in Kansas City, as they sat sipping bourbon in the predawn; and the remark was reported in the *New York Times* the following day. Publicly, Dewey was one of a host of Republicans who blamed overconfidence in their ranks, which had led one, or two, or three million supporters not to bother to vote because the polls told them it was unnecessary. In private, he was more particular, writing crisply to Henry Luce: "The farm vote switched in the last ten days, and you can analyze the figures from now to kingdom come and all they will show is that we lost the farm vote we won in '44."

Like Evelyn Waugh's Lord Copper, both the losing governor and the triumphant president were correct "up to a point." Truman would not have been returned to office without a muscular majority of the labor vote. So it was fortunate for him that his relations with labor leaders were more amiable in 1948 than they were before or after; and crucial that the rank-and-file were deceived into believing that his outrage over Congress overriding his veto of the 1947 Taft-Hartley Act was sincere, not ersatz. But the AFL, the CIO, and other organs of big labor had not intervened expensively in the election in order to return Harry Truman to the White House—something that the "new men of power" had regarded as a lost cause, like everybody else; rather, they strived to elect sympathetic Democrats to state and congressional offices by getting out the vote, providing foot soldiers, and contributing money. Big labor gave its support to candidates like Adlai Stevenson, running for governor, and Paul Douglas, running for the United States Senate, in Illinois; and Truman rode their coattails to victory. But labor's house was divided. As David McCullough points out, such leading unionists as Alvanley Johnston and John L. Lewis, reverting to his original Republicanism, supported Dewey; "and to lose in New York, New Jersey, Pennsylvania, and Michigan was hardly a sign that labor had carried the day."

It was true, as Dewey said, that farmers had been their usual fickle selves. In 1944 they had turned ungratefully against the Democrats, who during the Depression had led them out of their worst crisis since the 1890s: in part because they had so few consumer goods on which to splurge during their wartime prosperity. In 1948, given the chance to reclaim the country from the New Deal, the midwestern farm belt turned to its increasingly fevered proponent in the White House, mostly because they saw their continued prosperity as precarious, but also because of Republican missteps and parochial concerns like grain storage and price supports that the Democrats deftly exploited. It turned out that the ex-farmer from Independence, Missouri, knew them better than the sages of Manhattan and Georgetown, the likes of Walter Lippmann, Marquis Childs, and the Alsop brothers, who had agreed to consign him to history's dustbin.* Truman understood their suspicion and resentment of northeastern wealth and expertise, because he shared them. He persuaded them that it was the fault of the "no-good, do-nothing Eightieth Congress," and not his, that the price of corn had fallen.

Dewey swept the industrial Northeast, but Truman carried every state west of the Mississippi except for Nebraska, the Dakotas, and Oregon. His majority of 303 in the Electoral College was comfortable but not resounding, far short of FDR's 432 in 1944; both tallies greatly exaggerated the close popular votes. Because of the insurgent candidates Wallace and Thurmond, Truman won slightly less than half of the vote of the 52 percent of eligible voters who went to the polls, numbering about fifty million. In 1944, the distractions of wartime,

---

* Note that neither Truman nor Dewey assigned much significance to Strom Thurmond's pro-segregationist third-party candidacy, although it cost the Democrats the Deep South states of Mississippi, South Carolina, Louisiana, and Alabama. (Wallace cost Truman New York and Michigan.) The electoral vote of the South was so much smaller then than today that FDR would have won all four of his elections if he had carried not a single state in the former Confederacy. The South's political strength lay in the congressional baronies it controlled because of the seniority system.

prejudicial residence requirements, and Republican voter suppression (disenfranchising soldiers) had lowered turnout; in 1948, disgruntlement and a lack of suspense had the same effect.

In the forties, most political insiders, including the leading pollsters Gallup, Roper, and Crossley, assumed the conventional wisdom epitomized by former Democratic operative Jim Farley's law: "No souls are saved for the Democratic Party after September." Accordingly, they either failed systematically to sample the vote in the last stretch of the campaign or, assuming a Dewey victory, failed to grasp the significance of the narrowing margin they did detect. George Gallup privately advised the Dewey campaign not to waste its money on further polling, although his last tally, on October 30, put Dewey at 49.5 percent and Truman at 44.5 percent, approaching the statistical margin of error.

A "vast swing," continuing right into the balloting booth, was occurring. Yet there was no crux, no emblematic moment, no obvious turning point that explained what had happened. In the last days of the campaign, Dewey remained as calculatedly anodyne as ever; Truman's populist bombast possibly repelled as many of those who bothered to listen as it galvanized. Henry Wallace's vote seemed to dwindle the more furiously he campaigned on the sidewalks of New York, his first and last bastion. (But in Brooklyn, he electrified a crowd by addressing them in Yiddish.) Yet Farley's law was stood on its head. In 1948 a great many souls were saved for the Democratic Party not only after September, but even after the first of November, because of voters like Charles Crenshaw of New Lebanon, Ohio. "I kept reading about that Dewey fellow," Eric Goldman quotes him, "and the more I read the more he reminded me of one of those slick ads trying to get money out of my pocket. Now Harry Truman, running around and yipping and falling all over his feet—I had the feeling he could understand the kind of fixes I get into." The journalistic fraternity berated itself for neglecting the likes of Mr. Crenshaw in favor of the supposedly omniscient but fallible polls. "The plain fact of the matter is that editors, reporters, columnists, and pundits were fundamentally bored with the candidates and the seeming lack of issues as far as last summer," confessed *Life*, whose election-week cover photo of Dewey as "the Next President of the United States" crossing San Francisco Bay, was an embarrassment comparable to the *Chicago Daily Tribune*'s "Dewey Defeats Truman." "The boredom affected the pollsters; they went through the motions of scientific sampling of public opinion . . . but they weren't sufficiently suspicious or sufficiently interested to try to penetrate the great mystery of the undecided vote."

In 1944 Paul Lazarsfeld, a Viennese-born émigré scholar at Columbia University, had ingeniously adopted the mathematical methods of the social sciences to interpret the presidential election, as he did again in 1948, updating his research. But it was a veteran political journalist, Samuel Lubell, an election-night analyst for radio and television, who produced the most ambitious and provocative reading of the 1948 contest. *The Future of American Politics* (1952) is a neglected classic, which, along with John Gunther's *Inside U.S.A.* and Denis Brogan's *The American Character*, is an essential study of the shifting American political landscape of the postwar years.

Having been an assistant to Jimmy Byrnes at the Office of Economic Stabilization and an aide to the financier-gadfly Bernard Baruch, Lubell was no stranger to the corridors of power. His empiricism (unlike Lazarsfeld's cloistered Frankfurt-school version) married statistical analysis and shoe leather: after the *Saturday Evening Post* asked him to do a "postmortem" on Truman's election, as he had done for FDR's third-term race in 1940, he spent two years analyzing the returns for the three-thousand-plus counties in the country—sometimes precinct-by-precinct—to determine "the streams of voters who tend to shift together." Consulting census data since 1892, cultural and political histories, and regional lore, he was able to his satisfaction to place these groups against a historical background going back to the Populist fury of the 1880s and '90s; and the findings he reached were tested by several months on the road, meeting the voters of what he had identified as "strategic voter areas."

Resisting the temptation to parade his research, Lubell wrote with anecdotal flair, sparing the reader all but the most telling statistics. We begin, then, with the arresting comparison of Harry Truman to the

Red Queen in Lewis Carroll's *Through the Looking-Glass*. ("Now, here, you see, it takes all the running you can do, to keep in the same place," she explains to Alice.) In Truman's case it is no exaggeration to say that for almost every action, there was an equal and opposite reaction, and usually in short order, because this was a president who abhorred indecision and delay. Thus, in an inflationary economy—which he deplored—he abandoned or declined to exercise his power to impose price controls, because he was equally afraid of deflation. As a rule he was never stronger or more forceful than when proposing a course of action that he knew Congress would reject: as in price control, civil rights legislation, and the repeal of Taft-Hartley.

In foreign affairs, the abrupt cancellation of Lend-Lease—a mistake he uncharacteristically admitted (but then characteristically blamed on bad advice)—was redressed by the Marshall Plan. Chief Justice Fred M. Vinson was appointed to go to Moscow to negotiate with men whom Truman said could not be trusted, and then recalled before he could get onto his plane. The paradox was that all of this sound and fury prolonged stalemate. The New Deal was preserved but not significantly extended. Europe remained divided, but war with the Soviet Union was averted. And the Korean War was destined to end in a bitter truce.

"One doesn't have to question Truman's sincerity," Lubell wrote, "to observe that he appeared happiest when able to make a dramatic show of activity, serene in the knowledge that nothing much was going to happen . . . Harsh as that estimate may sound it was Truman's only claim to greatness. There is much to be said, after all, for the mariner who, knowing that he cannot quiet the storm, contrives somehow to stay afloat until the storm has died of itself."

The Future of American Politics relates Truman's sure instinct for planting himself at the "furiously dead center of stalemate" to his personal psychology and, more surely, to his political geography. Until the age of thirty-eight, he allowed himself to be dominated by his capricious and demanding father, a failed land speculator who managed a farm owned by his wife's family and was never out of debt. After service as an artilleryman in the First World War, in which he rose to captain, and later failing as an oilman and merchant, Truman depended for another decade on the patronage of Boss Tom Pendergast, who, when Truman most desperately needed him during the hard-fought 1940 Senate primary in Missouri, was inconveniently locked in the penitentiary. FDR was ready to cut him off at the knees at that time, and he never showed any great enthusiasm for him as a vice-presidential candidate, having agreed to his selection after party bosses, who were insisting that he dump Wallace, pressed his case; and he treated him indifferently during their few months of executive office together. No one ever doubted Truman's personal integrity; but in "Tom's Town," politics was close to being a criminal milieu, and Truman knew that most of his neighbors in Independence regarded his profession as politician with disdain. It is hardly surprising that Truman was beset with insecurity, for which he compensated with bluster, an exaggerated decisiveness, and imaginary conversational coups, but which also inclined him to caution and accommodation, going along and getting along as a senator, fulminating and beating hasty retreats as president.

Temperament and geography combined to make Truman an ideal "border-state politician," which was less a matter of coming from a border state than that he "represented a state of mind." As the breach between Roosevelt and the Democratic conservatives in Congress widened after FDR's failed "purge" in 1938, these figures held the "balance of compromise." Except for race, where they either shared or were obliged to respect local prejudice, Southerners like Jimmy Byrnes and Richard Russell, the revered senator from Georgia, were as representative of the breed as Truman or Senator Carl Hatch of New Mexico.

In this regard, Sam Lubell tells an indicative story. In January 1938, the returning Seventy-fifth Congress unhappily contemplated a debate over the antilynching legislation that had been introduced with tepid administration support by Democratic Senate Majority Leader Alben Barkley. "You know I'm against this bill, but if it comes to a vote I'll have to be for it," Harry Truman confided to one of the leading Southerners in opposition, recalling that his own grandparents had sided with the Confederacy during the Civil War. "'All my sympathies are with you,' the Senator fervently declared, 'but the Negro vote in Kansas City and St. Louis is too important.'" Truman was thus obliged to vote for the antilynching bill and to override the southern filibuster organized against it; but the South prevailed, as he knew it would, and his credit with its representatives was unimpaired. It was not that Truman consciously played the hypocrite on civil rights: on the contrary, he believed in voting rights for African Americans, and certainly believed that they had the right not to be lynched, just as he believed the North had no business monitoring the South's business, and that the better sort of "Negroes" did not desire "social equality" with whites. Nothing needed to change too much. As Lubell wrote, "It was because stalemate fitted his nature so snugly that he became President."

The question posed by the 1948 election, and answered affirmatively, was whether the Democrats had emerged as the "normal" majority party, able to govern without the charismatic leader under whom it had risen to majority status after 1932. Rather than asking why the pollsters had got it so wrong, Lubell suggested asking more fundamental questions, such as: "Why is it that our major parties always seem on the verge of flying apart, but rarely do? Why do third parties always look so formidable in May and so hollow in November?" Rejecting both the traditional bipolar interpretation of party politics as organized by "recurring themes" such as Hamiltonians vs. Jeffersonians, the people vs. plutocracy, the farmer against the city, and so on, and the opposing Tweedledum-Tweedledee interpretation which minimizes or denies any fundamental differences in the "duopoly," Lubell proposed a new theory which recognized that at any given time one party is dominant; or that, in his famous metaphor, in the political sky one is the sun and the other is the moon.

The majority party remains dominant as long as it contains its various constituencies, which are inevitably disparate, but whose contention, if it can be contained, is a source of strength because each faction is the more attached to the party as it hopes to gain control. Third parties are a register of the "agony" of the majority party from which they typically hive off. But the sun party can survive even a major secession, as the GOP did the revolt of Theodore Roosevelt's Bull Moose Party in 1912; even a series of secessions need not be fatal, as 1948 would show for the Democrats.

The pattern has held since the modern Democratic Party assembled itself under Andrew Jackson's banner in the 1820s, owing its sway not only to its majorities but, crucially, to the "timeliness" of its elements: namely, the Western frontiersmen who allied themselves with the agrarian South against the commercial interests of the Northeast. Until it split apart in 1860 (and even then, not irrevocably), the elements of the old Democracy framed the debate on civil slavery, just as the Republicans would define the issues relating to tariffs, trusts, regulation, and expansion that agitated the nation as America became an industrial and agricultural colossus in the latter part of the nineteenth century. In fact, the times have been rare when the two major parties have been fairly evenly matched, as between 1876, when the Democrats traded the White House for an end to Reconstruction, and 1896, when McKinley's victory led to almost forty years of Republican dominance.

As early as 1940, Lubell had suspected that the Democrats were assembling a lasting majority; or as he wrote in the *Saturday Evening Post* in 1941: "The people who had elected Roosevelt would vote for him for a fourth or fifth term as readily as for a third" and that "once Roosevelt is out of the picture this vote will not slip automatically into its former slots." In 1940 FDR's most gifted political henchman, James A. Farley, and his first vice president, John Nance Garner, had both opposed his candidacy for a third term, arguing that it would be fatal for the Democratic Party to attach itself so exclusively to one man; when he was gone, the party would shatter. But it turned out to be the other way around. It was during his third term—that is, during the war—that the Democrats consolidated their gains among Jews, Negroes, and other minorities. Their votes were concentrated in the big cities, from New York to San Francisco, where Roosevelt's increasingly large majorities more than compensated for his weakening rural vote.

For all the alarums and excursions of almost four years in office, Truman's signal electoral achievement was to reassemble the FDR coalition as it had existed in the North into roughly its condition of 1944; around certain edges (the European-ethnic vote in the old Northwest, the black vote) it was even marginally improved. In 1944 Roosevelt won the big-city vote, concentrated in sixteen counties, by

49 percent to 40 percent, overcoming Dewey's lead of 52 percent to 48 percent in the rest of the country: a feat Truman roughly duplicated, compensating for running slightly behind FDR in the big cities by improving on his rural vote.* Truman's defeat was assumed at the beginning of the campaign not because Dewey was a genuinely popular figure (he was not, even among many reliable Republicans), and not because Truman's poll numbers were so low (they had fallen and risen before), but because the advantages of his incumbency were underestimated and Henry Wallace's ultimate appeal was wildly overestimated. In reckoning with what happened on November 2, 1948, one begins with Lubell's question: "Where was Gideon's army?"

From March 17, 1947, when he addressed the Progressive Citizens of America (PCA) rally at Madison Square Garden, until Election Day, November 2, 1948, Henry A. Wallace had been almost constantly on the road. He set out with an excellent augury: in February, the American Labor Party candidate, Leo Isaacson, a strong supporter of Wallace, Israel, and peace, won a special election for Congress in the Bronx, handily beating Boss Flynn's man. The ex–vice president's highly publicized travels as an undeclared candidate that spring and fall led seamlessly into his barnstorming as a declared candidate in December and finally as the nominee of the Progressive Party. The pattern of these appearances before and during the campaign showed the imprint of his admirers in the arts and show business. (Wallace's third-party candidacy divided Broadway and Hollywood, the Upper West Side and Astor Place, as no presidential election since, possibly excepting the contest between Robert F. Kennedy and Eugene McCarthy in the 1968 primary season.)

---

* See Barone, *Our Country*, 179–80. "This margin has eerie similarities with the 1948 election (in which Truman ran behind Roosevelt in the South but ahead of him in some parts of the countryside, and won) and even with the 1960 election (in which John Kennedy carried the big cities, 59%–40%, as Roosevelt had, and lost the non-southern vote by only a bit more than Roosevelt, 47%–53%; the obvious difference was Kennedy's weaker performance in the South." The persistence of the 1944 pattern in presidential politics is all the eerier considering, as Barone observes, that Kennedy and Nixon in 1960 were running, economically and socially as well as politically, in another country.

In New York, Chicago, Milwaukee, or some college town, the crowd would gather and be asked to contribute a dollar or two, as little as fifty cents, to attend, although no one was turned away; to the shock and alarm of hardened politicians, most people cheerfully paid. Paul Robeson, Pete Seeger, or Woody Guthrie would sing; there were comic sketches by Zero Mostel, dramatic monologues by Canada Lee, tap dancing to classical music by Paul Draper. Over the loudspeakers an unseen announcer played master of ceremonies, following a script as he announced the local or national notables who preceded Wallace on the platform. On May 14, 1947, at a rally that crowded Chicago Stadium and spilled into the streets, this role was played by a local radio personality of radical persuasion nicknamed "Studs" Terkel (after Studs Lonigan, the rough-hewn protagonist of James T. Farrell's novels). The lights in the stadium or auditorium would dim, the name of the speaker pronounced, a spotlight shone on the stage or platform as he or she appeared; the procession might last as long as two hours. At last Henry Wallace, accompanied by drumbeats. When the crowd burst into chants of "We want Wallace!" the candidate might greet them, as he did the crowd in 1947, with: "And I say, we want peace." It was the most stirring political theater of the postwar era, far more charged than Harry Truman's scrappy appearances at some crossroads in the back of a train during the election, although not to the taste of the cynical press.

By December, Wallace's candidacy for president was a foregone conclusion: possibly it had been ever since he failed to be renominated as vice president in Chicago in 1944. The notion that a Democratic convention would desert Truman for Wallace could hardly be entertained, although it seemed conceivable that it might be stampeded into drafting General Eisenhower. Nonetheless, two or three dramatic meetings among PCA insiders were held at Jo Davidson's studio on West Fortieth Street in December to debate whether Wallace should run as an insurgent Democrat or a third-party candidate. Christmas Eve found Wallace in his offices at the *New Republic*, where he promised a Mutual Broadcasting Company address on December 29, to announce his "views" on the election. In Chicago Anita McCormick Blaine, at eighty-seven one of the richest women in America and Henry Wallace's most opulent admirer, had rented an entire floor of the Drake

Hotel. A crowd of one thousand milled as Wallace pondered, and Paul Robeson sang. That night the candidate spoke from the MBS studio in Chicago's Tribune Tower.

"We have assembled a Gideon's army, small in number, powerful in conviction, ready for action. We have said with Gideon, 'Let those who are fearful and trembling depart.'" He was running. The trumpet sounded in Philco and Emerson radios all over the nation—except in "Chicagoland," where Anita McCormick Blaine's cousin Colonel McCormick, the lord of the Tribune Tower, had no intention of opening his airwaves to the treasonous likes of Henry Wallace. But the call to arms was heard from the Bronx to Beverly Hills, two places where Wallace actually enjoyed significant support.

There had already been significant defections from the PCA, and mounting accusations that the new party was dominated by Communists. Departing were the broadcaster Frank Kingdon, the publisher and lawyer Bartley Crum, and the *New Yorker* writer A. J. Liebling; on the attack went the columnist Dorothy Thompson (whose celebrity inspired the movie comedy *Woman of the Year*, starring Katharine Hepburn and Spencer Tracy) and, in more-sorrow-than-anger vein, Max Lerner at *PM* and Walter Reuther, who called Wallace "a lost soul." "The Wallace third party campaign has been indecently exposed for what it is: an instrument of Soviet foreign policy," wrote Stewart Alsop in his column. "Since the PCA invited him to head a third party, the whole movement has been stripped bare. The bones revealed as communist bones." For all that, the polls suggested that Wallace maintained a hold on as much as 10 to 15 percent of the electorate: five to ten million votes. But third parties rarely live up to their youthful promise.

After a strenuous national campaign waged from the East Bronx to Beverly Hills, in which he qualified for the ballots of forty-six states, having campaigned in the South in the company of blacks, and having braved such physical threats and indignities as no other national politician, before or since, has endured in modern times, the former vice president of the United States carried a grand total of thirty precincts. Eighteen of them were in New York City; five were in Los Angeles;

and seven were in Tampa, Florida, where something in his message resonated with the cigar workers (mostly Cuban) in Ybor City.

In New York eight of his precincts were in Vito Marcantonio's racially mixed East Harlem congressional district, which included a growing number of Puerto Ricans. The remaining two were "'Red' precincts" in Bronx Park East, where communal workers' housing had been built in the twenties (approximately, the "dissident gardens" of Jonathan Lethem's 2012 novel). The East Bronx, which was supposed to be Wallace's redoubt, was carried for Truman by "Boss of the Bronx" Ed Flynn's machine, which combined with the Republicans and the Liberals to defeat Leo Isaacson. In Los Angeles, Wallace enjoyed the support of Thomas Mann and Katharine Hepburn in Pacific Palisades and Brentwood, but the only precincts he won were in fading Jewish neighborhoods like Boyle Heights, where African Americans were moving in. Prophetically, Lubell identified all these as belonging to an "urban frontier" that defined coming fault lines of American politics.

Altogether, New York accounted for roughly half of the 1.2 million votes cast for Wallace nationally, and California for 190,000. About three-quarters of Wallace's votes came from Jews and blacks; along with "self-identified intellectuals" these were the urban blocs in which Truman's tally came out below FDR's in 1940 and 1944. In 1948 Jewish voters composed the most agonized and conflicted part of the electorate. Overwhelmingly since 1936, they had supported Roosevelt, to the point that by 1944 there were precincts in New York City where his vote exceeded 90 percent, and even the Republican poll watchers voted for him. His death left his Jewish supporters politically "homeless." In the Squirrel Hill neighborhood in Pittsburgh, Pennsylvania, the prosperous home to one of the densest Jewish communities in the country, the Jewish vote turned Republican in 1948. But then, outside Hollywood and the Upper West Side, where they turned out not to be so numerous as once imagined, Wallace's Jewish voters were typically Mike Gold "Jews without money," trapped in a few decaying urban enclaves, their leadership and energy provided by Communist organizers and perfervid Zionists. Lubell interviewed an extended family in Brooklyn, solidly for FDR in 1940, which eight years later "split eleven for Truman, eight for Wallace, and one for Norman Thomas, while one stayed home." Wallace's African American voters were typically middle-class "strivers," Lubell specified, who subscribed to the Book-of-the-Month Club and smoked their cigarettes in holders. "'We couldn't get the poorer Negroes to understand our arguments,' confessed one Wallace worker in Harlem."

In retrospect it is clear that the majority of African American and Jewish voters were becoming durably housed within the Democratic Party, although Truman, never a great hero for blacks, carried only two-thirds of their vote; and the GOP scored respectably among these groups up until the 1960s.* Other "ethnicities," as they were beginning to be called, especially Poles, Italians, and other Southern and Eastern European Catholics, were becoming more volatile. Many had become restive and resentful under Roosevelt's rule; their social and economic instincts were conservative, and privately many believed that because of him the United States was fighting the wrong war. Lubell calculates that Truman improved on FDR's most recent tally among Roman Catholics because he got the votes of the socially conservative and economically muddle-headed followers of the radio demagogue Father Charles Coughlin, who had deserted the Democrats for William Lemke's Union Party in 1936 and restrained their enthusiasm for Democratic presidents ever after. In Boston, for example, he notes, the top ten Democratic wards consistently from 1928 to 1944 had given the Democratic presidential candidate a two-thirds majority, but FDR fared best by far in Jewish wards, where Wallace scored a decent 10 percent, and Truman in Irish and Italian ones, where his turnout compared to Al Smith's in 1928.

Without winning any votes in the Electoral College, Wallace cost Truman seventy-five, denying him New York, which the president lost

---

* In 1960 Richard Nixon, who had previously polled well with black voters in the North (as his Democratic opponent, John F. Kennedy, had done with whites in the South), lost them when he failed to reach out to Martin Luther King Jr. and his family when he was jailed in Georgia on a dubious traffic charge. JFK phoned Coretta Scott King, who was distraught, fearing her husband might be lynched, to express his sympathy, and his brother Robert separately interceded with the judge on the case, asking for King to be given bail. "In the meanwhile," Arthur M. Schlesinger Jr. tells, "King's father told newspapermen that he never thought he could vote for a Catholic, but that the call to his daughter-in-law had changed his mind. 'Imagine Martin Luther having a bigot for a father,' Kennedy said—then added quizzically, 'Well, we all have fathers, don't we?'" *A Thousand Days*, 74.

to Dewey by a scant sixty thousand votes, along with Maryland and Michigan (reflecting labor support). Within the national picture it was to Truman's advantage to have "Wallace and his Communist followers" running on his left, and Strom Thurmond's Dixiecrats to his right; with a stroke, or rather two, he was freed to denounce "subversive" elements with which otherwise the Republicans could have associated him, and forthrightly to embrace civil rights (but not "social equality") for Negroes. His opponents had done him the favor of ceding him the middle ground to which he always aspired, even when he indulged in populist rhetoric. Ever the party loyalist, Truman claimed victory not for himself personally "but a victory of the Democratic Party for the people," which was true enough. The Democrats regained control of both houses of Congress by decisive margins, and introduced attractive, mostly younger Democrats into Congress and statehouses, many of whom had lent strength to the national ticket. The best summary of what happened is in Henry Steele Commager and Samuel Eliot Morison's magisterial history: "The 1948 elections confirmed what had long been suspected: that Americans do not take kindly to splinter parties; that labor was still loyal to the Democratic party; that the midwestern farm vote was by no means irretrievably committed to the Republican party; that the political temper of the country was still liberal; and that loyalty to Franklin Roosevelt was a factor to be reckoned with in the future."

Beginning that dismal election night at his headquarters on Park Avenue, Henry Wallace reacted to his drubbing with incredulity, defiance, private fury at Truman, and a gathering bitterness at erstwhile allies and presumed supporters, although he spoke bravely of the future. "To save the peace of the world the Progressive Party is more needed than ever before," he said in a brief radio statement. To his campaign workers, he declared: "We must fight even if we left Manhattan and they," the domestic fascists, "were coming through New Jersey."

"Under no circumstances will I congratulate that son of a bitch," he snapped to his advisors when they gave him a draft telegram to Truman, and repeated his comment early that morning when he and his wife, Ilo, had gone to Marcantonio's headquarters in the Bronx and Truman appeared on television—"that lying son of a bitch." The rejected candidate rued the ingratitude of the working people and the blacks. "The Negroes," he said bitterly, "had their chance." Neither the egg throwing in the South nor his pollster Louis Bean's statistics had prepared him for the enormity of his defeat, or the meagerness of his tally. Ilo Wallace was several times heard to cry: "I knew it! I told him so all the time!"

The desertion of Gideon's army was a hard blow, and only in the immediate dazed aftermath could Wallace maintain he had only lost a skirmish, not the battle, let alone the war. For the voters had dealt far less kindly with the New Party than they had with Theodore Roosevelt's Bull Moose insurgency, which came in second with eighty-eight electoral votes and 4.1 million popular votes in 1912, or Robert La Follette's Progressive Party, which carried only his home state of Wisconsin but won 16 percent of the popular vote in 1924. No one should have expected otherwise; the ten million votes which Wallace's supporters had fondly predicted in spring had always been a pipe dream. Yet, the New Party fulfilled the traditional role of third parties in arguing for ideas that one or the other of the major parties could appropriate. An exaggerated sense of its potential draw had moved Truman perceptibly to the left in domestic affairs, a fact that did not escape the *Wall Street Journal*, which observed: "It is said by political commentators that Mr. Wallace made a bad showing because he got few votes. What they neglect is that Mr. Wallace succeeded in having his ideas adopted, except in the field of foreign affairs. From the time that Mr. Wallace announced he would run for President, Mr. Truman began to suck the wind from the Wallace sails by coming out for more and more of the Wallace domestic program."[*]

Truman's rhetorical conversion into a furious combination of old-time populist and New Deal ultra, direly warning of "fascism" in the

---

[*] In his address to the Progressive National Committee, November 13, 1948, in Chicago, Wallace contended that the American people "voted for the Democratic candidate for President after we had forced him to compete with us on the same program, on civil liberties and on the revival of an expanded New Deal with emphasis on lower prices and housing." In a November 10 letter to the *New York Herald Tribune*, he wrote: "It was the Progressive party alone that made peace an issue in the 1948 campaign. It was our insistence on a return to the Roosevelt One World policy that forced the bipartisans to slow down their Cold War program and at least make the gesture of negotiating with the Russians." Both quotations are in MacDougal, 859–60.

case of a Republican victory, was small consolation for Wallace's Progressives. As a program of active reform the New Deal (rebranded "somewhat unnecessarily," Morison and Commager observe, as the "Fair Deal") did not flourish in the Eighty-first Congress. It was simply not possible to advance significantly the agenda of the liberal state in a climate of conspiracy-minded anti-statism to which Truman had significantly contributed, not least by his appointment of Attorney General Tom Clark, a buffoon flourishing his infamous "list" of subversive organizations.

An increasingly conservative age was no time to be projecting brave new worlds. What was achieved in Truman's second term by way of expansion of Social Security, increased unemployment benefits, and (segregated) public housing were footnotes to the New Deal—substantial ones, but not a new chapter in history.

In foreign affairs, the creation of NATO, countered by the Warsaw Pact, meant that Europe would be divided into armed camps, developments which in Wallace's view threatened to put "military Fascism" and global war on the horizon. Under the circumstances Point Four, Truman's call in his inaugural address for "technical assistance" to "underdeveloped areas," seemed at least a small good thing, vindicating as it did the course that he had long advocated, especially for Latin America. In twenty years' time, when the modern civil rights revolution the progressives had championed was translated into legislation, and a few years later when Richard M. Nixon had proclaimed "détente" with the Soviet Union, the surviving Progressives enjoyed, at least among themselves, the satisfaction of having been a little band of prophets. But in 1948, though for a time Wallace bravely insisted otherwise, their eclipse was total. FDR's reelection on a social-democratic platform in 1944 had encouraged small-*p* progressives to infer more enthusiasm for social democracy than actually existed. The inflated union membership rolls, an artifact of the war, encouraged similar illusions ("Labor will rule"). The fact was that a decisive number of voters were always going to vote for Roosevelt whatever the platform said, and there were millions enrolled in unions who thought no better of them than the Chamber of Commerce. Officially disdained and tacitly accepted, the Communists' support of FDR encouraged illusions on their part and Wallace's about their acceptability in a new Popular Front. But if social democracy were to have been introduced into the

U.S.A., such a Popular Front as the Progressives presented could never have been its vehicle.

Murray Kempton writes that by discarding Wallace and uplifting Truman in 1944, Roosevelt, "having commanded his own twelve years, set with his dead hand the course of the next eight." It might be said, for much longer than that, since the end of the New Deal era has been set as late as 1980, when an apostate New Deal ultra, Ronald Reagan, was elected president.[*] In 1948 Wallace and his followers vehemently denied that the majestic dead president could possibly have intended the erratic and dangerous course that his successor pursued. But in time Wallace came to believe that if he had been renominated for vice president in 1944, and inherited the presidency in 1945, he would have been too controversial to govern. Historians who have considered the scenario tend to agree. "It would have been a national catastrophe," John Lukacs writes in *1945: Year Zero*, if Roosevelt had run again with Wallace or gone with his personal preference, William O. Douglas, another "Sovietophile." "A Wallace or a Douglas presidency, in 1945, at the beginning of the confrontation with Russia would have torn the country apart."[†] But on this score there is room for doubt. To begin with, the confrontation with Russia might have been delayed, if not indefinitely, then for a year or two, although on terms most of the future Cold Warriors would have declined. When delving into counterfactual history on this question, it should not be forgotten that in factual history most Americans did not approve of Churchill's "Iron Curtain" call to arms in 1946, and President Truman hastened to disassociate himself from it.

----

[*] See the essays in Steve Fraser and Gary Gerstle, eds., *The Rise and Fall of the New Order, 1930–1980* (Princeton, NJ, 1989), part 2.

[†] The counterfactual history of a Wallace presidency enjoyed a lively time in 2012, when the movie director Oliver Stone and his scholar-collaborator Peter Kuznick published their *Untold History*, in which the bomb was not dropped and the Cold War did not occur. And at a symposium on Whittaker Chambers at Yale, John Lewis Gaddis, the "dean" of Cold War history, indulged lurid speculations that Wallace, who had indiscreet connections with the Soviets (at his office at the Commerce Department!), would have handed over most of Europe to Stalin.

Historically, America learns to live with the next in succession when a president dies in office. Even Mark Hanna, who had warned the Republican convention in 1900 that naming Theodore Roosevelt as William McKinley's running mate would place but a single life "between this madman and the presidency," offered his services when McKinley's assassination put the madman in the White House. Especially during wartime, the country would have rallied around whomever Roosevelt had chosen to run with, as it did around the comparatively unknown and uninspiring Truman.

Invested with the dignity of the presidency, it is entirely possible that Wallace's quirks, the faddish diets, the boomerangs, the teetotalism, even the rumors of spiritualism, would have come to be regarded as lovable eccentricities. (The wisdom of the East was enjoying a great vogue in the thirties and forties. FDR was a fan of James Hilton's novel *Lost Horizon*, which he quoted in his "quarantine the aggressors" speech, and named his presidential retreat Shangri-La, after its setting.) Among the power elite, Nelson Rockefeller was one who found Wallace "wonderful"; and as vice president he was particularly well thought of by the new mandarins of science who were amassing great power and influence during the war.

In foreign affairs Wallace was a visionary like Roosevelt, as Franz Schurmann writes, and indeed, for all the wooziness of his rhetoric, he had more clearly articulated their shared vision of a "free world"—a phrase he put into circulation—that had been remade in America's image.* Wallace differed from most of the politicians, technocrats, businessmen, and soldiers who enlisted into the postwar instauration

---

* "The visionary element in American politics has always baffled and exasperated rationalist politicians of leftist and centrist political persuasions. But it has always been taken seriously by the right, who have sensed a revolutionary in just that idealism." Franz Schurmann, *The Logic of World Power*, 4. In Wallace's case, vindicating Schurmann's observation, his deadliest enemy was Jesse Jones, the so-called "banker of the New Deal," with whom he fought and lost a monumental bureaucratic battle during the war when he was running the Bureau of Economic Warfare. Jones fought in great earnest, even though he regarded Wallace's ideas as harebrained. The *Partisan Review* intellectual Dwight Macdonald, on the other hand, although he developed an obsession with Wallace, was more irritated by him as a phenomenon than anything else. Wallace was a visionary who with his gawky bearing and prophetic utterances looked and sounded like one, a disadvantage in a democratic society that the urbane Roosevelt did not suffer.

of the American empire, first in believing that it could be achieved only by advancing reform at home, particularly civil rights for minorities, and second, fearing that alienating Russia would mean war, in his determination to maintain a working relation with Stalin. Domestically, he would have pursued a consistently liberal line on price controls, labor rights, reconversion, federal aid to education, public housing, and agriculture, without Truman's waywardness and secret reservations. There is no doubt he would have been more vehement in his support of civil rights for African Americans. Wallace deeply believed in the social-democratic aims that Roosevelt had embraced during the 1944 election. Combined with the regional planning that FDR was also projecting, a Wallace administration would have attempted a revitalized New Deal, a "super New Deal," rather than the compromised Fair Deal, whose frustrated hopes haunt the political consciousness of the forties like a specter, both for progressives and for their enemies.*

"Counterfactual" history bestows circumstantial detail on the dim and indistinct outlines of what might have been. It is at best a diversion to imagine a president who was literate, scientifically speaking— indeed, a scientist of note himself; a figure of global renown, widely traveled in Asia and Latin America as well as Europe; a student of history who read in hopes of discovering laws, not improving anecdotes; a committed civil libertarian; a planner who, like Roosevelt, saw America's geography in terms of its bioregions rather than as the sum of its states and the total of its political machines.

Though surely an "irrepressible conflict," the Cold War might have been somewhat less frigid, and ended sooner, without a near-apocalypse like the Cuban Missile Crisis in between. Stalin, who found Roosevelt uncanny, at least respected Wallace as a world figure, but despised Truman. Shorn of fuzzy rhetoric, the détente that Wallace wished for with the Soviet Union was not greatly different from that negotiated by Nixon and Kissinger in the 1970s—and unsuccessfully advocated by Churchill to Eisenhower in the fifties.

The election of 1948 marked the closing of a frontier in American

---

* In the first edition of *Inside U.S.A.* (1947), we still find Gunther wondering if Wallace Progressives like Robert Kenney and Bartley Crum in California will represent the future of American politics.

life, a winnowing of possibility, which is the underground theme of the characteristic literature of the day. The New Deal order continued, and would continue for decades to come, but it was reticulated in narrower ways and in a more crabbed spirit than other democratic vistas might have been.

Call this imaginary country "Usonia," after Frank Lloyd Wright's acronym for a more perfect union—the "United States of North America"—redesigned according to his specifications; but let it stand for a future that might have materialized in the postwar era instead of "the geography of nowhere" that did.* This imaginary America could be described negatively as one in which the "anxieties of affluence," anatomized in the 1950s by such writers as John Kenneth Galbraith in *The Affluent Society*, John Brooks in *The Insolent Chariots*, and William H. Whyte in *The Organization Man*, might at least have been subtly different. The Organization Man's "nuclear" family (indicative word) need not have lived in a house that was as close to identical to his neighbor's as their work spaces in a skyscraper or industrial "park"; Brooks's "insolent chariots," meaning automobiles, need not have been given even greater centrality in American life than they had in previous decades, which had done damage enough to the urban fabric; the contrast between "private opulence" and "public squalor," Galbraith's famous complaint, might not have been quite so extreme.

The "Atlantic crossings" which still did so much to define the American mind at mid-century might have been differently arranged. In the 1930s, America's "Europeanization" had occurred mostly at the level of public policy; in the postwar era the paths diverged. While Great Britain under Clement Attlee was instituting the National Health Service, national health care in the United States, ineptly backed by Truman, was beaten back by organized opposition, led by the American Medical Association, to "socialized medicine."

. . .

---

* James Howard Kunstler calls "Broadacre City," the suburban planned community to which workers would commute from the city, "eerily prophetic," in its capitulation to the automobile and in the way that Wright's "Usonian house would be stripped down and bastardized into the ubiquitous ranch house of the suburbs," but this is to say that it was prophetic only to the extent that it was stripped of its utopian dimension. *The Geography of Nowhere*, 165.

Shepherded by titans such as John Maynard Keynes and André Malraux, provision for the arts and historical preservation became accepted responsibilities for government in England and France; while in the United States the New Deal arts projects, along with the rest of the WPA, were shut down in 1942, not to be replaced, and then quite inadequately, for two decades. When the State Department absentmindedly sent abroad an exhibition of recent paintings by American artists, Truman denounced it. FDR was as much of a philistine as Truman (though he did know his naval prints), but dealt with the avant-garde, as he did with the rest of humanity, with his usual noblesse oblige. It is possible to imagine funding for the arts being restored by FDR if he had lived, by Wallace, and even by Dewey, who after all had aspired to be an artist himself; nothing of the sort was conceivable under Truman.

Between 1933 and 1943, the New Deal arts projects had provided work for several thousand artists. The largest number of them were in New York City, and Arshile Gorky, Jackson Pollock, Mark Rothko, and Willem de Kooning, among the visual artists, were enrolled in the WPA's Federal Art Project. "Almost every major Abstract Expressionist already active in the 1930s (except for Clyfford Still who stayed in Washington state) worked for it at some point," David Anfam writes; the WPA "provided vital support to them in Depression circumstances but whether it nurtured the formation of a New York avant-garde seems dubious." However, providing them with a living, and bringing them a proximity and a fellowship that would not otherwise have existed, the New Deal was contributing to their future as an avant-garde group. In *Life and Times of the New York School* (1972), Dore Ashton quotes Edward Bruce, the Treasury Department administrator who was responsible for commissioning the murals and sculptures that still adorn so many public buildings: "The receipt of a check from the United States government meant much more than the amount to which it was drawn. It brought to the artist for the first time in America the realization that he was not a solitary worker. It symbolized a people's interest in his achievement . . . No longer was he, so to speak, talking to himself." The shutting down of "the project" meant the artist's relation to the public would once again be entirely mediated by the marketplace, the culture industry, and the cash-nexus; but the vital connections had been made.

In architecture the conversion to the international style—or, as critics like Tom Wolfe of *From Bauhaus to Our House* (1981) prefer, the surrender to the European "white gods," Gropius, Mies, Corbusier— might have been less abject, on the part of the architectural profession and its wealthy clients. Government construction might not have taken the disastrous turn to the shoddy that it did; public housing in particular need not have been so poorly conceived and shabbily executed as to turn into "instant slums," like the tenements it was supposed to replace. The Interstate Highway System, which was projected by the Roosevelt administration, might have been built without the grotesque rationale of providing motorists an escape route from cities that could have had atom bombs dropped on them, as it was during the Eisenhower administration—and with some consideration for the fate of the towns and cities it bypassed. Unlike the solid, Roman-like projects of the New Deal, built for the centuries, Ike's interstates were built on the cheap and falling apart in a few decades.

In the introduction to a new edition of *The Lonely Crowd* published in 1970, David Riesman, the master sociologist of the forties, writes that, unlike those who considered 1948 a catastrophe for progressivism, he was amazed that 1.2 million people had actually voted for the candidate of the left. Indeed, the 1.2 million Wallace voters marked the utmost number of people who were involved, if only to the extent of signing a petition or joining the occasional march, with the left during the "Red Decade" of the 1930s. In the lowering atmosphere of the Cold War, it was indeed a brave thing to declare oneself a Wallace supporter, and a bold thing to cast a vote for him. (The ex–vice president himself was cross-examined on camera by HUAC in 1950.)

In 1948 the boundary line was crossed which marked "the retreat to a more conservative existence," of which Norman Mailer would write in 1960.* Murray Kempton, in "The Trouble with Harry (and

---

* By then, Mailer, though a Wallace supporter in 1948, had come to believe that "the last large appearance of the myth [of the underground] was the vote which tricked the polls and gave Harry Truman his victory in '48. That was the last." "Superman Comes to the Supermarket," collected in *Some Honorable Men: Political Conventions 1960–1972* (1976), 17.

Henry)," deprecates might-have-beens. "But then it is a waste of time to wonder what sort of president [Wallace] might have been. He could not have been. At the end, tired as he was, Roosevelt had too keen a vision of what our future would be."

No doubt the early days after the war, when, as Mailer recalled nostalgically in 1960, "the underground river returned to earth, and the life of the nation was intense, of the present, electric," could not have been indefinitely prolonged. Even in the "orgiastic hollow of the century," the veteran's joy of simply being alive was bound to dissipate in the light of common day; according to the Beats (then unknown to fame), the shades of the prison house would darken, Moloch's skyscrapers would rise, and the suburbs would fill up. Could it have been otherwise in an "administered" world? It is in the nature of an underground river to return to earth.

2

———

Conference at the Waldorf

HOWARD FAST ALWAYS INSISTED that what was officially the Scientific and Cultural Conference for World Peace, but is known to history as the 1949 Waldorf Conference—after its incongruously grand setting, the Waldorf Astoria Hotel—was entirely his idea. It was not conceived in the Kremlin or paid for with Moscow gold. Nor did it originate with the New York City Communist Party organization, which, apart from its habitual distrust of artists and intellectuals, was distracted and financially hard-pressed by the impending trial of its leadership for violations of the Smith Act.

The great peace conference was the brainchild of the born-to-immigrants literary prodigy from Upper Manhattan, who published his first novel at eighteen and by thirty was the author of two historical novels, *Citizen Tom Paine* and *Freedom Road*, that became global best sellers; who had worked for the Office of War Information during the war and been invited to a luncheon at the White House, but who, more recently, had been convicted of contempt of Congress for declining to name the contributors to a fund for orphans of American volunteers who had died in the Spanish Civil War, and sentenced to six years in prison. In March 1949, his case was on appeal. Howard Fast did not believe that America sent its writers to prison.

"My idea was to organize a great meeting of the arts in the cause of peace. My feeling was the struggle for peace was paramount. If the march to war could be halted, other matters could be solved more easily."

On a raw cold day, March 25, 1949, what was left of Gideon's army convened once more. In his article covering the conference for *Partisan Review*, Irving Howe counted "three thousand middle-class Wallaceites," by which he meant dupes and fellow travelers being led by the nose by Stalinists; he worried that their number, although nondescript, represented "the possible appearance of a new political tendency," which might be of considerable significance if there was no war and if the Marshall Plan failed. "The Cold War rankles—why not reach a cold agreement?" Simply divide the world into "spheres" and let the Soviets do as they wished in theirs.

The auspices were officially those of the National Council of Arts, Sciences and Professions, which had spearheaded Wallace's campaign. Its remoter origin was the international peace initiative launched by the Cominform (Communist Information Bureau), which was founded in 1946 as the successor to the Comintern, which Stalin had dissolved in 1943. Howard Fast proudly recalled the conference as "the largest and most important gathering of intellectuals in the forties," and even after his break with the Party in the fifties it did not occur to him that the spontaneous outpouring of support, including lining up six hundred sponsors, which enabled them to hire this most expensive venue—not to mention finding an eager squad of event coordinators, or the dispatch of a Russian delegation that included Dmitri Shostakovich, the Soviet Union's greatest musical genius—might have been a concerted affair.

Outside every entrance of the great hotel were pickets organized by the American Legion and the Catholic War Veterans, a thousand or so altogether, but outnumbered by police, and pairs of nuns who dropped to their knees to pray for the souls of the deluded delegates. "And on the morning of the conference I actually had to step between two gentle sisters kneeling on the sidewalk as I made for the Waldorf door," Arthur Miller recalled in *Timebends* (1987). A great many of the misguided celebrities had recently been featured, in anticipation of the conference, in a two-page rogues' gallery in *Life*, rows of postage-stamp-sized photographs headlined "Dupes and Fellow Travelers Dress Up Communist Fronts"; the article was personally overseen by Henry Luce. Some, like Clifford Odets, Lillian Hellman, Dashiell Hammett, Dorothy Parker, Jo Davidson, Aaron Copland, Albert Einstein, Charles Chaplin, Frank Lloyd Wright, and Langston Hughes, had long been associated with left-wing causes; but the suspect integers also included four of the rising postwar stars: Marlon Brando, who was launching his career in Hollywood after his legendary performance in *A Streetcar Named Desire* on Broadway; Norman Mailer, who with *The Naked and the Dead* had produced the "big" novel about the war that everybody had been waiting for; Miller, whose *Death of a Salesman* had been selling out for months; and the conductor and composer Leonard Bernstein. Bernstein was a political animal, who had electrified New York's newborn Zionists with his concerts in Jerusalem and Tel Aviv in 1947 and in the Negev during Israel's war of independence, which *Time* covered under the headline "Mozart in the Desert." Bernstein had agreed to participate when he learned that Shostakovich would be a Soviet delegate, but he was already an inveterate signer of petitions and supporter of protests.

Miller, who gives a thorough account of his participation in *Time-bends*, and suffered more damage to his reputation than Mailer or Bernstein, was struck by how opinion had swung so swiftly against America's wartime ally, despite the millions of deaths it had sustained; like almost all the delegates, he seemed to give little consideration to the recent Communist coup in Czechoslovakia, which had changed so many people's minds. "Thus," he sums up, "the sharp postwar turn against the Soviets and in favor of a Germany unpurged of Nazis seemed not only ignoble but threatened another war that might indeed destroy Russia and bring down our democracy as well."

The Waldorf Conference was the latest in a succession of large international cultural congresses organized by the Communist Party, of which the most famous was the first International Congress of Writers for the Defense of Culture, chaired by André Gide in Paris in June 1935, where the delegates of the League of American Writers, Waldo Frank and Mike Gold, encountered, among others, Aldous Huxley, E. M. Forster, André Malraux, Isaac Babel, Heinrich Mann, Lion Feuchtwanger, and Bertolt Brecht. The League issued calls for American congresses in 1935, with James T. Farrell, Edmund Wilson, Lionel Trilling, and Dwight Macdonald as signatories; and again in 1937, by which time the above had become "renegades" and the league was courting celebrity writers like Archibald MacLeish, Ernest Hemingway, and even Mike Gold's bête noire, Thornton Wilder. The conference at the Waldorf followed on the heels of the World Congress of

Intellectuals in Defense of Peace, organized by the Cominform, which was held in Wrocław, Poland, in late August 1948.

Howe observed that the attendees at the Waldorf included fewer young people than at previous such confabulations: "Apparently the Stalinists are not doing well on campus. It was also interesting that in addition to the breathless middle-brows, half-grasping and half-fearful in their culture hunger (*did you* see Shostakovich?), there were untainted innocents who really thought the conference had some genuine relation to working for peace. Somehow the Stalinists always find new innocents, each batch on a lower cultural level."

By 1949, the Communist Party was no longer an answerable authority in intellectual circles, and in the unions it was besieged from within and without. Its remaining support, hardly numerous outside New York, was in the professional middle class, and on Broadway and in Hollywood—not for long.

"There can be no adequate compensation for losses in the unions, but in some ways the C. finds Hollywood a profitable substitute for the intelligentsia." The latter, which contributed far less money, raised far more troublesome questions; however, its defection meant that the conference boasted none of the literary stars that had addressed the conferences of the thirties, such as Hemingway. The only literary highbrow to distinguish the conference was the Harvard literary historian F. O. Matthiessen, author of *American Renaissance*. On the other hand, the organizers had the considerable consolation of Harlow Shapley, the Harvard astronomer, serving as chairman. Shapley, who had determined the true dimensions of the Milky Way and the insignificant location of our solar system within it, thus "overthrowing" Copernicus, was a considerable academic politician, a popular writer, and not a Party liner, despite accusations by HUAC and later McCarthy; nor was he a supporter of the Progressive Party, though he voted for his friend Henry Wallace. But he indulged many illusions about the Soviets, and for a while was a leading figure among the new scientific mandarins who were expected to exercise a growing authority after the war, but never really did, once their wings were clipped in the person of their archetype, J. Robert Oppenheimer.*

---

* Shapley was an American original, who grew up in rural Missouri, a contemporary of Harry Truman, and was a boy journalist before he went to college. His politics,

. . .

For three weeks an ad hoc committee, the Americans for Intellectual Freedom (AIF), organized by the philosopher Sidney Hook, had been agitating against the conference, and by its opening session the group was embedded at the Waldorf Astoria in a bridal suite on the tenth floor, room 1042. There, Hook was host to a hubbub of New York intellectuals and their allies: the heralded young historian Arthur M. Schlesinger Jr.; the editors of *Partisan Review*, Philip Rahv and William Phillips; Dwight Macdonald, American gadfly; the Italian journalist Nicola Chiaromonte; the émigré Russian composer Nicolas Nabokov; the fiction writer and critic Mary McCarthy and her husband, Bowden Broadwater; the poet Robert Lowell and writer Elizabeth Hardwick, soon to be married. Labor was represented conspicuously by David Dubinsky, the head of the International Ladies Garment Workers' Union, who was paying for the suite, and two associates, Arnold Beichman, a former labor reporter and editor at *PM*, now working as a union press agent, and another labor publicist, Melvyn Pitzele. Dubinsky's resources furnished the suite with extra telephone lines, installed on Sunday morning in blatant disregard of union regulations, and a mimeograph machine set up in the bathroom.

"As waiters staggered into the suite, they were met by a strange scene. Telephone cords webbed across the room, and at the end of the tangle callers were leaning animatedly into each receiver. Every available surface was occupied by a person or teetering piles of paper. The suite was heavy with cigarette smoke." All those teetering piles of paper make room 1042 sound like the Collyer brothers' rat-packed brownstone (a New York newspaper sensation in 1947, when it was opened after their deaths), but no doubt the atmosphere really was as tense and hectic as Frances Stonor Saunders suggests in *The Cultural Cold War*. Hook was intent on discrediting the conference, not disrupting it, which he thought would simply play into the hands of its organizers; but somehow its mail was intercepted, disinformation was spread, and anticommunist renegades and provocateurs of all stripes

---

which are of no interest to present-day scientists, come in for a drubbing in John Lukacs's *1945: Year Zero*, in which the author mentions his discovery that Shapley was "a fervent admirer of the Soviets and a political imbecile" (301).

roamed the corridors. The intellectuals in the room—not necessarily the laborites—all deferred to Hook's deeply informed mastery of Marxist theory and Communist tactics. It was good they did, since it was known that the author of *From Hegel to Marx* was one of the most intellectually combative men in New York, never ready to let an argument go until he had pinned his opponent to the wall; his dialectic had been refined by graduate study with John Dewey and finished by a summer at the Marx-Engels Institute in Moscow in 1929. (An academic wunderkind, Hook was already tenured at NYU, one of the first Jews to achieve such status in New York, when he announced himself a Communist in 1932, arousing the horror of the Hearst press; fifty years later he still considered himself a radical socialist when he received greetings on his eightieth birthday from President Ronald Reagan.)

The Americans for Intellectual Freedom had been organized at a meeting led by Hook at Dwight Macdonald's apartment in Greenwich Village. Typically, Hook was brutally condescending when Macdonald and Mary McCarthy, joined by Lowell and Hardwick, proposed to apply for credentials and disrupt proceedings at the conference with embarrassing questions. Not to his surprise, Hook had been turned down when he demanded that Harlow Shapley let him deliver a paper on "Science, Culture and Peace"; he declined an invitation to join a panel and, along with the rest of his group, boycotted the public sessions. Hook informed Macdonald and McCarthy that they too would be peremptorily denied passes; when, to his surprise, their credentials were accepted, he told them to report for a training session conducted by "some goon from the Intelligence Freedom Committee," as McCarthy recalled decades later. The goon told them to prepare for being harassed and thrown out by bringing ropes and chains to attach to their chairs, an idea that sent Macdonald into a fit of giggles. Ropes and chains were too much, but McCarthy and Hardwick were persuaded to equip themselves with umbrellas to bang on the floor for recognition and also for protection; and all of them wrote down the questions that they were assured they would not be allowed to ask, which were then mimeographed to be distributed afterward.

Thus prepared, the bold saboteurs arrived early at the Starlight Roof Ballroom for the session on literature and publishing: McCarthy

soignée for a recovering Trotskyist; Macdonald a tall and storklike ste-
reotype of the intellectual in horn-rimmed glasses; Hardwick, weigh-
ing "about ten pounds," "skinny, smoking"; Lowell, looking like a
patrician tough, the handsomest major poet since Byron—they seated
themselves in the second row. On the dais: Fast; W. E. B. Du Bois; the
novelist (and triple agent) Agnes Smedley; F. O. Matthiessen; the Stalin Prize novelist P. A. Pavlenko; the secretary of the Union of Soviet
Writers, A. A. Fadeyev; Shostakovich; Mailer. No sooner had the chairman, Louis Untermeyer, called the meeting to order than Hardwick
and McCarthy began banging on the floor with their umbrellas as per
the instructions of the "goon," and then were mortified—McCarthy
especially—when Untermeyer patiently asked them to wait for the
question-and-answer period, when each would be given two minutes.
(In *Being Red*, Fast takes the credit for this courtesy. "Go ahead, tell us
the truth," he says he told McCarthy, who had insisted he would never
do such a thing.) Before he could proceed, Lowell stood to object to
his referring to Hook as a "dirty word" in his opening remarks. Untermeyer, who had a ready wit, "agreed to emend that to 'a four-letter
word,' and went on to introduce the panel members."

Like everybody at the conference, Macdonald was transfixed by
Shostakovich, "pale, slight and sensitive looking, hunched over, tense,
withdrawn, unsmiling—a tragic and heart-rending figure," who also
had no reason for being on a panel about literature. By contrast the
literary apparatchik Alexander Fadeyev was a fleshy man in a tight suit,
resembling a plainclothes detective.

There were calls from the audience for the young literary lion
Norman Mailer to speak. Although he had campaigned for Wallace
in New York and Hollywood, Mailer was not the compulsive public
performer he was to become, and in appearance he was still boyish
and skinny, diffident rather than cocky. He stood to applause, which
rapidly yielded to bewilderment.

"I have come here as a Trojan horse," Mailer confessed. "I don't
believe in peace conferences. They won't do any good. So long as there
is capitalism, there is going to be war. I am going to make myself even
more unpopular. I am afraid both the United States and the Soviet
Union are moving toward state capitalism." As for disappointing his
hosts, "all a writer can do is tell the truth as he sees it, and to keep on

writing. It is bad, perhaps, to inject this pessimism here, but it is the only way I can talk honestly."

Seated in the audience, Howe realized that Mailer was advancing, or perhaps simply parroting, a Trotskyist heresy he had learned from his friend and French translator, Jean Malaquais, whom many in his circle distrusted and considered to be the young novelist's evil genius without the genius. In his account for *PR*, Howe wrote of the episode: "Mailer's hesitant, painful, but obviously deeply felt talk was a perfect illustration of a politically inexperienced mind freeing itself from Stalinist influence . . . The audience listened quietly, with emotions one can imagine. When he was finished, there were scattered boos."

"Suddenly he became white as a shroud, then burst out with what had been the substance of our conversations, attacking the conference for what it was—a fraud." Thus, Malaquais improved on the occasion for Mailer's biographer Peter Manso in the 1980s. "Quite brave of him. I didn't have the slightest inkling he was going to do so. Lionized for starters, he was now viciously booed: he'd become an enemy. He walked off, and we all surrounded him, afraid he'd be assaulted."

Dwight Macdonald, on the other hand, was made to feel a little sorry for the Communists, so beleaguered, no longer able to impose unanimous opinion, and now deserted by what was supposed to be their most promising recruit. As for the conference's organizers, Lillian Hellman, also interviewed by Manso decades later, recalls "sitting in another room, reading or something, when somebody who worked on the committee came running in and said, 'Guess what? Come quick, Norman Mailer is denouncing all of us!' I didn't hear the speech; I read it and was shocked by it." (The indomitable Hellman's capacity for being shocked was legendary; Mailer's capacity to shock grew immeasurably with the decades.)

As promised, the saboteurs were given their two minutes. At the Wrocław Conference Fadeyev had delivered the opinion: "If hyenas could type and jackals could use a fountain pen, they would write like T. S. Eliot, John Dos Passos, Jean-Paul Sartre and André Malraux." Was such bad-mouthing of eminent Western writers likely to promote "cultural understanding"? Macdonald asked. He followed up with a question about the condition of six noted Soviet writers, including Boris Pasternak and Isaac Babel; Fadeyev not only gave his word as a Soviet citizen that all the named writers were alive and well, but he brilliantly ticked off the titles and description of the work that each particular writer was engaged upon. He described where they lived, when he had seen them, and even repeated details of their merry reaction to the "'capitalist slander' that they were being persecuted."* In fact, except for Pasternak, they all were either in prison or dead: Isaac Babel had been murdered on Stalin's orders in the Gulag in 1940. The cultural commissar struck Irving Howe as a brutal sort of bureacrat only temporarily dispossessed of prisons and labor camps to impose himself upon. "Fadeyev seemed to enjoy himself more than anyone else at the conference; he did not have to worry about maintaining good relations with Frederick L. Schuman or John Rogge [the U.S. delegates formerly associated with Wallace, specializing in foreign affairs] and just let loose berating those stupid Americans."

Mary McCarthy asked F. O. Matthiessen if he endorsed Fadeyev's comments about the literary situation in Russia. Looking as miserable as Shostakovich, Matthiessen said they were "direct and forthright"; noting that he had conscripted Emerson as a "precursor" of Lenin, McCarthy asked if his likes would be permitted to live in Russia. Matthiessen said he supposed not, but then neither would Lenin be permitted to live in America—the non sequitur of the year in Macdonald's opinion.

Shostakovich was fidgeting so badly that he could barely hold his eternal cigarette. "One wondered then: was he, as he sometimes seemed, a pathetic little man, obviously ill-at-ease and wishing to be away from these painful discussions? Or did we think him pathetic because we expected him to be?" His participation in the Waldorf Conference was the latest in the rituals of abjections that the composer had endured to be "rehabilitated," of which the least was endorsing the official view, whatever it might be. (He would sign anything, he told his family, even if it was upside-down; during his years in Stalin's disfavor he would sometimes sit up at the landing of his apartment house by the elevator so that the men coming to arrest him by night would not disturb his family.)

On the concluding night, March 27, a Thursday, the eighty-one-year-old W. E. B. Du Bois addressed a capacity crowd at Madison

---

* Fast gives the occasion as the fine arts panel cochaired by Arthur Miller and himself, but Miller says nothing about such an exchange in *Timebends*.

Square Garden. He was there to introduce the featured speaker, Harlow Shapley, but an animated Du Bois did not relinquish the podium easily. He congratulated the delegates that "in a time of hysteria, suspicion and hate," they had succeeded in bringing together one of the "largest gatherings of creative artists and thinkers the world has seen." He conceded that they were not, and probably would never be, in agreement about all matters; "but in one vital respect our agreement is complete. No more war!"

Denouncing the proposition that any of them were plotting force or violence—"it is precisely force and violence that we bitterly oppose"—he rued the successive failures of the League of Nations and the United Nations to address seriously the plagues of imperialism and racism. "I tell you, people of America, the dark world is on the move! It wants and will have Freedom, Autonomy, and Equality. It will not be diverted in these fundamental rights by dialectical splitting of political hairs . . . Whites may, if they will, arm themselves for suicide, but the vast majority will march over them to freedom . . ."

The AIF had wound up its démarche that afternoon with a counter-rally at Freedom House, a nineteenth-century mansion facing the New York Public Library across Bryant Park; the old pile was the eponymous headquarters of an organization founded in October 1941 to support American intervention in the Second World War and now, unsurprisingly, committed to the Marshall Plan and NATO. The AIF had solicited and received endorsements from André Malraux, Karl Jaspers, Jacques Maritain, Bertrand Russell, and Igor Stravinsky. When a last-minute telegram of support was received by the National Council from Thomas Mann, the AIF countered with one from T. S. Eliot. (Living up to his Nobel Peace Prize, Dr. Albert Schweitzer lent his famous name to both sides.)

In its packed hall Nicholas Nabokov assailed the fraud of artistic freedom in the Soviet Union and the exploitation of Shostakovich at the Waldorf. Shostakovich did not disagree in the memoirs published thirty years later in 1979 (how inconceivably remote that prospect would have seemed in March 1949!):

I still recall with horror my first trip to the USA. I wouldn't have gone at all if it hadn't been for intense pressure from administrative figures of all ranks and colors, from Stalin down. People sometimes say it must have been an interesting trip, look at the way I'm smiling in the photographs. That was the smile of a dead man. I answered all the idiotic questions in a daze and thought, When I get back it's over for me. Stalin liked leading Americans by the nose that way. He would show them a man—here he is, alive and well—and then kill him. Why, say lead by the nose? That's too strongly put. He only fooled those who wanted to be fooled. The Americans didn't give a damn about us, and in order to live and sleep soundly, they'll believe anything.

Despite some mild fraternizing between the saboteurs and the conferees, when Fast and Mailer invited them to a party at the Sutton Hotel after the literary panel, the crowds circumnavigating the Waldorf Astoria, and the incessant speechifying, the atmosphere was curiously solitary—or so it seemed to Arthur Miller, much later, in *Timebends*: "Even now something dark and frightening shadows the memory of that meeting nearly forty years ago, where people sat as in a Saul Steinberg drawing, each of them with a balloon overhead containing absolutely indecipherable scribbles."

The Waldorf Conference was to be a curtain raiser, if not the first act, of the "Cultural Cold War." Within a month, Fast, Du Bois, Paul Robeson, and fifty other Americans were attending a huge peace conference in Paris, organized by the Cominform, and best remembered for the dove that Picasso drew for its emblem. (In *Being Red*, Fast recalls the planetary change of going from the United States, where the Communist Party numbered a beleaguered thirty-five thousand, to France, where it was the leading party with six million members.) A year later, with Sidney Hook, James Burnham, and Arthur M. Schlesinger Jr. in the American delegation, the Congress for Cultural Freedom, which became the vehicle for the CIA's secret patronage of the arts and literature, was organized in Berlin. On either side, a great number had gone through the revolving doors of the Waldorf Astoria in March 1949, but the significance of the conference came in retrospect.

It was plain enough at the time that the conference was the end of the road for the Popular Front, which had been revived by the wartime alliance with the Soviet Union. It was the end of "Communism

Is Twentieth-Century Americanism," a credo that not even avowed Communists professed by 1949, "Americanism" having been definitively appropriated by the right; the end of Lincoln Steffens's "I have seen the future and it works"; and the end of "Russia." No one was saying, even in jest, "Come the revolution."

Eighteen months separated the bristling martial display of Harry Truman's inaugural from the outbreak of war on the Korean Peninsula. Crowded with triumphs, the interval was the "apogee" of his presidency.* In May 1949 Stalin lifted the blockade of West Berlin; the United States and Britain continued the airlift for several months, underlining their resources. (Berliners were provided a better diet than Britons, who remained for some years on rations.) In July the Marshall Plan's armed complement, the North Atlantic Treaty, establishing NATO, was confirmed by the Senate, eighty-three to thirteen, and signed on the 23rd by Truman. Domestic legislative accomplishments were sparse even with a restored Democratic majority in Congress— still, Truman enjoyed the transient satisfaction of renewed popularity.

But this second honeymoon was "the triumph of hope over experience," like Samuel Johnson's saying about second marriages. It was shaken by a series of tremendous shocks, later noted by Herbert Agar as "Hiss, Chiang, Fuchs, and the Bomb," each successively more explosive. China, about which Americans felt proprietary, was "lost," along with the American monopoly of the bomb—which Truman for one had expected to be practically eternal—its innermost secrets betrayed to the Soviets by the Los Alamos physicist Klaus Fuchs, whose connections went to Moscow by way of David Greenglass in Los Alamos and his brother-in-law Julius Rosenberg in Brooklyn. In April 1949, a month before Alger Hiss, the supposed New Deal paragon, went on trial in the federal courthouse in Lower Manhattan, indicted for perjury but accused implicitly of treason. At the end there was another war, but not yet. In *Democracy in America*, in the chapter titled "That the Aspect of Society in the United States Is at Once Excited and Monoto-

---

* According to his most celebratory biographer, Robert H. Ferrell, in *Truman: A Centenary Remembrance* (1984), 195.

nous," Tocqueville writes: "Like travellers scattered about some large wood, which is intersected by paths converging to one point, if all of them keep their eyes fixed upon that point and advance towards it, they insensibly draw nearer together—though they seek not, though they see not, though they know not each other; and they will be surprised at length to find themselves all collected on the same spot. All the nations which take, not any particular man, but man himself, as the object of their researches and their imitations are tending in the end to a similar state of society, like these travellers converging to the central spot of the forest." As in Tocqueville's allegory, there were many paths in the forest—no one knew where the Americans were about to converge.

Dean Acheson, secretary of state, being sworn in by Chief Justice Fred Vinson, January 21, 1949, with President Truman observing

PART VIII

DAYS WITHOUT END

Beyond the mountains, more mountains.

—KOREAN SAYING

In the first years of the Cold War, James Vincent Forrestal occupied a commanding position all his own. He had come up from lace-curtain-Irish origins in upstate Matteawan, a gritty town on the Hudson River, to make it to Princeton, where he edited the *Daily Princetonian*, only to leave a credit short of a degree. He became the multimillionaire president of Dillon, Read, and from official anonymity as one of FDR's confidential assistants he rose to the top of the wartime military bureaucracy, succeeding Frank Knox as secretary of the navy in 1944. "Stimson was the more venerated and by far the most experienced," Lewis L. Strauss wrote, "but was obviously in his final public post. Forrestal was on the way up politically and there was no comparable rival."* Following Knox's example and his own instinct, he made his way to the fighting fronts, where in a plain work uniform minus insignia he was photographed standing at the bridge of a cruiser or sitting in the gunner's seat in a Navy plane on a mission. "He was everywhere with the fleet," said Strauss, who was his special assistant (and former Wall Street rival). Once at Pearl Harbor he commandeered a typewriter in a vacant office; the enlisted man who came upon him and demanded to know who he thought he was almost fainted when he replied, "I'm Forrestal."

Forrestal was on the cover of *Time* in October 1945, when the great armada was at anchor in New York Harbor, lauded as the navy's "skillful pilot," who had navigated the wartime bureaucracy with all his resources, and transformed the traditionally hidebound service into "a businesslike partnership between civilians and brass hats." In the *New*

---

* *Men and Decisions* (Garden City, NY: Doubleday, 1962), 157. Stimson, on the other hand, stood atop the Manhattan Project, about which Forrestal was necessarily well informed, but without exercising authority.

York Times, Krock promoted his friend as a plausible vice presidential nominee for the Democrats in 1948: "Movie audiences were giving him more applause than almost any other public figure when his 'diffident' image" appeared in newsreels, suggesting that the stigma of being a Wall Street man had been exorcised by victory.

After the war, Forrestal remained uninterruptedly in Washington up through the crucial period when he became "the godfather of containment" and the principal architect of the national security state. Yet he often spoke of quitting government, and even told his family to be ready to return to New York at the end of 1945. That deadline passed, but he continued to talk about going into publishing, and between 1945 and 1947 at one time or another cast an acquisitive eye at the *Seattle Times*, the *Manchester Union Leader*, the *Denver Post*, the *Wall Street Journal*, the ancient *New York Sun*, and the *San Francisco Chronicle*. The *Wall Street Journal* turned out not to be for sale, and with the other papers Forrestal either lost interest, waited too long, or was outbid. After a year of keeping others and perhaps himself in suspense about his intentions, Forrestal sold his town house on Beekman Place to the celebrated songwriter Irving Berlin.

On Wall Street and while socializing on the north shore of Long Island and Hobe Sound, Florida, Forrestal had maintained an air of skeptical detachment about the glittering prizes, though he sought them avidly, and this stance continued into public life. Ever in trim physique and preppy dress, he stood out from the gray-colored men stuffed into double-breasted suits who embodied the power elite of the 1940s. Watching Truman's cabinet as they arrived in their official cars at the White House late in 1945, Jonathan Daniels marked Forrestal as the fittest physical specimen, with "a cat quality like a fighter's"; at fifty-two, he looked tougher than most of the Navy officers in his department. But his appointment as secretary of defense in September 1947 capped two years of incessant travel, bureaucratic maneuver, strenuous advocacy, and tense negotiations—all of which in the later opinion of his friend Lovett had left Forrestal "a burnt-out case."

In the long-drawn-out debate over military unification that had begun during the war, Forrestal had zealously guarded the navy's autonomy, including naval aviation, and helped to preserve the Marine Corps, which Truman privately disparaged as "the navy's police force," and longed to abolish.* In what their go-between, Clark Clifford, recalls in his memoirs as "a titanic battle of wills," Forrestal largely prevailed.†

Truman's first choice for defense secretary was Robert Patterson, but when Patterson declined, saying that after six years in Washington it was time for him to restore his finances in New York, inevitably Truman turned to Forrestal, who was sworn in by Chief Justice Fred Vinson in September 1947. Truman reasoned that if Forrestal continued as secretary of the navy, "he would make life miserable for the Secretary of Defense; if on the other hand, *he* was the Secretary, he would have to try to make the system work. It was a brilliant tactical decision that was to have a profound effect on the future of the Pentagon; but it was also to contribute to Forrestal's tragic death." Besides the National Military Establishment (NME), which preceded the Defense Department, the National Security Act of 1947 created the National Security Council and the Central Intelligence Agency approximately as they had been envisioned in the plans Forrestal had drawn up with Ferdinand Eberstadt during the war, along with mechanisms for coordinating their activities.

"Once again, the central figure was Forrestal. He should have been pleased, for he had won a decisive victory over the Army and had created a structure that fully protected the Navy and the Marines," says Clark Clifford, who was present at the creation. *"Moreover, positions he had long advocated toward the Soviet Union were gradually becoming American policy.* He was, at that moment, equal in stature to anyone else in Washington other than the President and General Marshall."‡

---

* One can imagine the obscene objections he would have made if some prophet had informed him that sixty-odd years later the Marines would be fighting in the mountains of Afghanistan.

† This of course abbreviates and radically simplifies a long, tortuous, sometimes byzantine tale of politics high and low, including bureaucratic lobbying and public relations. Forrestal's role is superbly told in *Driven Patriot*, chapters 23–27.

‡ Emphasis added. Almost casually, Clifford resolves from the point of view of a supreme insider who was "the first cold warrior" in the Truman administration—not Truman, who wavered at least until late 1948; nor William Bullitt, who was out of office and power, nor an outlier like George Earle, the two other men Forrestal believed understood the Russians in 1944, when, in his opinion, the Roosevelt court did not. Hoopes and Brinkley, 353.

But Forrestal did not seem pleased to be vindicated, and he entered upon his new duties with no great enthusiasm. To his friend Robert Sherwood he wrote mordantly, "This office will probably be the greatest cemetery for dead cats in history."

Private life for him was not a distraction—he barely had one. He and his wife, the former Josephine Ogden, lived separate lives; a beauty in the 1920s when they married, she was a heavy drinker who frequented café society and began spending long periods in Europe after the war. Forrestal never criticized her behavior but lived in terror that she would make a drunken scene—as she memorably did the time she appeared at the top of Prospect House's grand staircase, an hour after a party had begun, and loudly wondered, "What in the world do you people have to say to one another?" Even his recreations seemed excessively strenuous. His friends—not to mention his aides, who had no escape—dreaded an invitation for golf or tennis because of the grim and compulsive way he played both games, barely bothering to make conversation before or after, let alone during. One year when he asked his aide Marx Leva to play golf on Christmas, Leva countered with an invitation for dinner, which Forrestal gratefully accepted. Then he went back to work alone in his vast office in the Pentagon.

Forrestal had managed to save naval aviation during the unification battle but could not prevent the creation of a separate Air Force. Its first civilian chief, W. Stuart Symington, was a zealous convert to the "wild-blue-yonder" tenets that held strategic bombing as the future of warfare, and the Air Force therefore should be supreme. In his diary Forrestal prophetically noted that in public life one often had the most trouble with one's friends. But then, Stuart Symington was never a close friend, as he was of Clark Clifford; Forrestal had always somewhat distrusted him, and his distrust was justified. In the battle for air power Symington threw in with the younger officers, the B-29 brigade, who regarded the Defense Department as a merely provisional arrangement until the air force's supremacy could be asserted.

Truman was committed to a balanced budget in which military expenditures would account for no more than a third, preferably much less, and total spending would decline (from $13 billion in fiscal year 1948 to $10 billion in 1949). His calculations reflected, as Alonzo Hamby noted, his fiscal conservatism (essentially, his shopkeeper's mentality), a number of wistful illusions and prejudices ("the citizen-soldier," for example), along with his sense of what Congress would agree to. Also, he and Marshall believed that a war-weakened Soviet Union would be constrained by America's monopoly of the bomb, limiting the need for conventional arms.

"To the extent he assumed that Congress would place a strict limit on national security resources as possible into foreign economic aid, such a decision had much to recommend it. But he also locked himself into a rigid and dangerous budgetary formula that tolerated a growing disparity between escalating commitments and military capabilities."

As defense secretary, Forrestal was caught in a "reality gap," as Hamby calls it—obliged to defend a budget that he believed was inadequate for the nation's security, even as he was struggling to reconcile the various and costly demands of the three services, and fought a losing battle to wrest the physical custody of the bomb from the civilian Atomic Energy Commission. But the controversy that most embittered his relationship with the White House was Israel. In Forrestal's view support for an Israeli state jeopardized essential American interests in the Arab world, especially access to its oil; to his enemies his anti-Zionism reeked of anti-Semitism. At the beginning, Truman was ambivalent; what was unchanging in his shifting positions was his sense that the matter of Palestine was, politically speaking, a New York affair. "I am not a New Yorker," he was heard to say during the controversy over the Grady-Morrison plan. "I am an American."

The unification controversy exhausted Forrestal physically and mentally, but the matter of Palestine was yet more punishing and possibly broke him. He was a man subject to obsessions, mild and strong: physical fitness, dialectical materialism, the British civil service, and the socialist political scientist Harold Laski among them. It was not on its people's account that Palestine became one, but rather because of its strategic relation to "Saudi Arabian oil," which is first mentioned in Forrestal's *Diaries* in July 1945, when he met with Jimmie Byrnes at Potsdam: "I told him that, roughly speaking, Saudi Arabia, according to oil people in whom I had confidence, is one of the three great puddles left in the world, the other two being the Russian Caucasus and the Caribbean." It went without saying that a break with the Arabs over a Jewish homeland in Palestine might imperil the flow of oil, which Forrestal felt was of utmost importance. As Walter Millis noted, this consideration helps to explain his "strong interest" in all aspects of Mediterranean strategy and so in the controversy over Palestine, "which," he understated, "was later to involve him in much adverse criticism."

The British for their part were sick to death of their mandate by 1947, incensed by Zionist terrorist attacks, and eager to maintain good relations with the Arab world. The foreign secretary Ernest Bevin openly considered the project of Israel to be a plot hatched in New York (alternatively, a device for keeping an influx of Jews out of New York); his principal advisor in the Foreign Office, Harold Beeley, was an Arabist in his sympathies as well as his expertise. It was the same at Foggy Bottom, where the State Department was relocated after the war from the old State, War, and Navy Building across from the White House. Along with the "striped-pants boys," as Truman liked to deride career diplomats, the entire upper echelon of the department, including Marshall, Acheson, Loy Henderson, and Lovett was opposed to an independent Jewish state. Aramco, the American oil consortium in Saudi Arabia, was terrified that King Ibn Saud would cancel its concession in retaliation for recognition of Israel.

None of these actors imagined that the Zionist Yishuv could defend itself against a concerted Arab offensive in support of Palestinian Arab resistance, nor did American military planners imagine it would be possible to rescue it. The prospect was of millions of Arabs being launched into battle, sweeping the Jews into the sea, and creating a region-wide tumult that the Soviets would be swift to exploit. In the worst case the Arabs would be swept into the Russian orbit and (once again) America's access to their oil would be lost. Truman was enduringly resentful of how the striped-pants boys had condescended to him when he assumed the presidency, expecting him to defer to their expertise, and was unmoved by their and Forrestal's argument that America should follow Britain's example in cultivating the Arabs. The plight of the displaced Jews touched him as the bitter complaints of the Arabs did not; and political calculation led him to where his sympathies already lay.

Forrestal disliked Roosevelt, according to his friend Herbert Elliston, the editor of the *Washington Post*, and even more some of his close associates. Forrestal had risen into the monied New York world in which FDR was born, and could negotiate it with reasonable ease; he could never accustom himself to the blowsy atmosphere Truman brought to the White House afterhours, but lacking the self-confidence simply to stay away, like Acheson and Harriman, he joined stag occasions where he was visibly bored and uncomfortable.

Forrestal seemed to embody everything Truman resented about New York and his suspicion of the foreign-policy establishment in a way that Harriman, a plutocrat, or Acheson, whose hauteur was famous, somehow did not, making it easier for his enemies at the White House to pursue their vendettas. As their campaign intensified during the Palestine controversy, one or the other had the satisfaction of reporting to Drew Pearson that after Vaughan brought him yet another complaint Truman had denounced Forrestal in an Oval Office rant as a "goddam Wall Street bastard."

Forrestal's views on Palestine did not seem connected to anti-Semitism. He had grown up in a casually anti-Semitic milieu in Matteawan and exchanged it for another on Wall Street and in his clubs in Washington and New York. Forrestal might not have thought Jews were his social equals, but then he was perfectly aware that WASP grandees did not think that an Irishman like himself was their equal either. Everybody on Wall Street knew that his mentor Clarence Dillon was born Clarence Labowski, the son of a Jewish immigrant from Poland; Bernard Baruch and Lewis Strauss were his friends and counselors; and he promoted captain Ellis M. Zacharias to rear admiral over the fierce opposition of navy officialdom, whose anti-Semitic promotions policy was a cherished tradition. When he hired Marx Leva as a confidential assistant, he told him that his being Jewish would never help nor hinder him; when Leva turned out to be able and devoted, Forrestal gave him his complete confidence, indicating a fair-mindedness. His friend Elliston maintains that his views on Palestine were based on what he considered to be objective estimates of the national interest, including an assured petroleum supply, and were informed by what the intelligence services in the military services and the State Department told him. Personally, he was indifferent to the competing claims of Arabs and Jews in Palestine—and unmoved by the plight of its prospective new settlers, the displaced European Jews who more than once he suggested could be resettled in Peru or somewhere else in Latin America. The fears and apprehensions that he shared with the State Department turned out to be unfounded. There was no Arab uprising, no rout of the Jews, no descent into regional chaos threatening global war. The Israeli army's superior training, arms, and spirit carried the day. "The Arabs turned out to have no mass, there was not even the slightest chance of a jihad, and what was more important, the Jews had *élan*, and an electrical amount of it," Elliston writes. "The result should have been foreseen." Forrestal several times telephoned the Israeli ambassador, Eliahu Epstein, formerly the representative of the Jewish Agency in Washington, to confess he had been mistaken; since the expectation of the Yishuv's destruction was almost universal, his apologies seem overblown, possibly a sign of his mental deterioration.

But Forrestal's prominence and power guaranteed that he would be reviled in Zionist and pro-Zionist circles—the American counterpart to Ernie Bevin. Truman, who had reserved this issue for himself, disregarded Forrestal's warnings as reflecting the prejudices of a Wall Street banker and the baseless fears of a perennial alarmist. The defense secretary was not invited to the climactic deliberations at the White House in the second week of May 1948, in which the fate of Palestine was debated between the State Department and the White House political functionaries whose very presence General Marshall found unseemly. Even these meetings were for show, as we have seen, Truman having made up his mind to recognize a Jewish state once it had been proclaimed.

In his less than two years as defense secretary, Forrestal had raised an international host of enemies, this in addition to the vindictive clique that was poisoning Truman's mind against him in the White House. Aside from his position on Israel, his biographers Hoopes and Brinkley mentioned: "Through his strenuous personal efforts to deny the communists an electoral victory in the 1948 Italian elections, he had incurred the hostility not only of European communists and their Soviet mentors, but also of elements on the radical left in the United States, including the followers of Henry Wallace, who insisted that the cold war was essentially a Wall Street imperialist plot . . . Owing to these several grievances, Forrestal became the target of increasingly reckless attacks."

None were as reckless or damaging as those launched by Drew Pearson and Walter Winchell—respectively, a muckraker and a gossip, who were the two highest-paid media personalities in the world. Pearson's "Merry-Go-Round" column, syndicated out of New York to six hundred newspapers, earned him $2,000 a week, and his radio broadcasts to an audience of 10 million another $5,000. Winchell had an even bigger print and radio audience, eight hundred newspapers and, he claimed, 25 million listeners, and in 1948 earned almost half a million dollars, most of which, he complained, went to pay income taxes. In their columns and radio broadcasts, Pearson and Winchell tarred Forrestal as a tax evader and the financial enabler of the Nazis during their rise; a warmonger with the Soviets; a physical coward; an enemy of the Jews; and last, as we shall see, a madman who had been entrusted with every state secret, including the atomic. Their broadcasts on Sunday evenings, when both appeared on sponsored shows on ABC, were weekly nightmares for Forrestal.

His tormentors were self-made phenomena. With his sometime partner Robert S. Allen, Pearson had pioneered the political insider's column and successfully translated it to radio. In July 1948, when he was in mad pursuit of Forrestal, *Time* put Winchell, the "Querulous Quaker," on the cover, calling him the author of "a brand of ruthless, theatrical, crusading, high-voltage hypodermic journalism that has made him the most intensely feared and hated man in Washington." Franklin Roosevelt was the first of many presidents to brand him a liar. Forrestal's deadliest sin in Winchell's eyes was his perceived hostility to Israel. Winchell found Forrestal's realpolitik deeply suspect, and probably rooted in the anti-Semitism that was typical of his Wall Street milieu.

Pearson, who fancied himself a moralist, comprehensively disliked *everything* Forrestal supposedly stood for; it was as if all of his black beasts and phobias—"Wall Street, Big Oil, the military, everything German, and all opposition to a homeland for the Jews"—had been concentrated in one man, and then placed on the heights where he could lead the world toward war. James Vincent Forrestal was "the most dangerous man in America," the "Trojan Horse of the Right" within the walls of the administration, and "the Cabinet Judas," whose downfall was Pearson's mission from the day Forrestal became secretary of defense. Pearson's vendetta against him began much earlier than Winchell's, and, week after week, was pursued more consistently.

In retrospect, his friends and associates noticed signs of Forrestal's decline in spring 1948, or even as early as 1946, during the grueling battle over unification. His composure and powers of concentration were noticeably affected by the strain of responsibility, although his worsening relationship with Truman had to be the chief anxiety of a person anxious to keep his job. He developed a nervous tic of scratching at a spot on the back of his head until it bled, and the disconcerting habit of staring blankly ahead at meetings; lucid and sometimes still even brilliant in the mornings, he would forget what he had said by midafternoon. His golf and tennis games became more frantic and compulsive, even as his health weakened. It was at this very time in the fall of 1948 that Forrestal conceded the inadequacy of the compromise National Military Establishment Act of 1947, which he had overseen, and moved to strengthen his office, in the process deeply angering many of his former allies.

All this time Forrestal further harassed himself by a private study of Marxism. "It is only possible to get into a fright about the communists by reading what they say they are going to do instead of what they have done," A. J. P. Taylor wrote in 1966, quoting Forrestal as a "good example": "He played a large part in inventing the Cold War. He drove himself mad by reading the works of Marx and Engels." In fact, like many professing Marxists in the American intelligentsia, Forrestal mostly read *about* Marx and Engels—in his exalted position, mostly memoranda by the intellectual members of his staff—sufficient to inflame paranoia; George Kennan's "X" article in *Foreign Affairs*, one of the main documents of the Cold War, was originally written for "Mr. Forrestal's" edification, as Kennan writes in his *Memoirs*. Soon after Forrestal was installed as defense secretary, George Kennan approached him with a plan for a "guerrilla warfare corps" to take the fight against the Soviets underground. Forrestal endorsed the plan, as did Acheson, and a series of NSC directives codified the scheme. NSC 10/2 and NSC 20, drafted during the winter war scare, and signed by Truman the following summer, authorized in the first instance such covert operations as propaganda, economic warfare, sabotage, and anti-sabotage, "subversion against hostile states, including assistance to underground resistance movements, guerillas and refuge liberation groups"; and in the second, specifically for recruiting and training Soviet defectors and minorities within the USSR to wage guerrilla warfare with an eye to destabilizing the regime in the long run, but also to do immediate damage should war arrive sooner.

Within the State Department an Office of Special Projects had been established under Kennan's supervision, anticipating the covert activities to come; it was headed by a Mississippi-born lawyer, Frank Wisner, who before the war had been a partner at Carter, Ledyard & Milburn, the venerable Wall Street law firm where FDR had once been a boastful and not overly diligent associate. In line with the NSC resolutions Wisner recruited secret armies of dissident and disaffected soldiers from farther east: "Rumanian, Hungarian, Bulgarian, and Ukrainian refugees for possible future armed missions into their former homelands."

Nightingale (for Nactigall) was the code name for a remnant of the Organization of Ukrainian Nationalists (OUN)—an underground independence movement in existence since the 1920s, which had split into factions during the war: Nightingale in particular had collaborated with the Nazis, hunting down Jews and informing on Red Army sympathizers, and continued to maintain a stronghold in the Carpathian Mountains after the war. Wisner made shadowy arrangements to enlist its already fiercely anticommunist leaders, bring them to the United States for training and indoctrination, and parachute them back into Ukraine to carry on their war with the Soviets, at the same time that another CIA branch was hunting down as war criminals these Ukrainians who had joined up with the Nazis. Disdained for their wartime collaboration, spied upon by Soviet agents, and betrayed by England's master spy in Washington, DC, Kim Philby, few lived long after their translation back to the homeland.

Taken by surprise when Truman did not announce Forrestal's departure in January 1949, when George Marshall and Robert Lovett announced their resignations, his enemies renewed their attacks; his friends, including Lovett and John J. McCloy, regretted this lost opportunity at once to go out "with all flags flying," and to disburden himself after nearly eight years of crushing responsibility. Five months of suspense followed, prolonged by Truman's capriciousness and vacillation, in which Forrestal was able to delude himself about his chances of remaining indefinitely in office, even after it had been established that Louis Johnson, a man he despised and even Truman distrusted, would be his successor.* There ensued, for Washington insiders and at length the nation, the spectacle of one of the world's most powerful men subjected to violent abuse in the media and visibly cracking under its impact.

That winter the political class in Washington and New York was lining up for and against Forrestal's staying in place. Truman deeply resented all the advice he was receiving, especially from the likes of Winchell and Pearson, and it is probable that he delayed Forrestal's departure simply to frustrate his critics. "No S.O.B. could tell him what changes to make to his cabinet," David Lawrence reported him as saying. Rumors had reached him that Forrestal believed that he was being followed and his telephone tapped. The head of the Secret Service, U. E. Baughman, was assigned to investigate. "Baughman's 'first assumption,' which was probably shared by the President, was that if Mr. Forrestal thought he was being followed he probably *was* being followed." (Forrestal had received death threats because of his stand on Israel, as had Robert Lovett.) Forrestal's butler confidentially told Baughman, "Mr. Forrestal had become so overly suspicious that whenever the front door was opened or the bell rang, he would go and peer out secretly to see who was there." He had become so forgetful and distracted that he kept his hat on in the house and, on one occasion, wandered into the kitchen and asked the loyal retainer, "Where's my butler?" He accumulated a large stash of sleeping pills and rewrote his will.

On January 9, Winchell went on the air to denounce the National Security Act, which Forrestal had crafted, authorizing the president to "throw the country into war without even notifying Congress." He exhumed the old story that Forrestal had evaded taxes by forming a dummy Canadian corporation in 1929, and predicted he would be out within the week. Two days later, after a private talk with Truman at the White House, January 11, 1948, Forrestal was cross-examined by

---

* Forrestal told his former assistant William Smedberg, who had been appointed superintendent of the Naval Academy, "Smeddy, this is a bad day for the Navy [*sic*]. The man knows nothing. He is incompetent and a braggart." As quoted in Hoopes and Brinkley, 438–39.

reporters about the pro forma resignation which, Charlie Ross had reminded them, it was customary for cabinet members to submit when a new administration took office. Forrestal said that his letter of resignation would be sent in time for Truman's inauguration.

"Do you anticipate its acceptance?"

"No."

"Do you want to and expect to continue as secretary of defense?"

"Yes, I am a victim of the Washington scene."

On Sunday night, January 16, Drew Pearson told his 10 million listeners that the only reason the "Cabinet Judas" remained in office was because Truman, who indeed had intended to accept his resignation that week, decided otherwise because he was enraged with Winchell, and did not want to vindicate any prediction of his. Warming to his attack, Pearson reprised the charges of tax avoidance, and then, exceeding himself, regaled his listeners with a phony story about an episode at Beekman Place in 1937 that branded Forrestal a physical coward. (Supposedly, he had fled out the back door while his wife was being robbed at the entrance.) Although he confided some qualms about his pursuit of Forrestal to his diary later on, Pearson took the attitude that almost any means were justified in removing from office a mental incompetent who was being protected by his friends in the Establishment. Pearson's source for the story was probably Stuart Symington; knowing what actually happened that night, Symington would also have had to know it was untrue. The secretary of the Air Force was ever the Iago.

Forrestal's final days underscored the melancholy adage, attributed to Delmore Schwartz, that "even paranoids have real enemies." On January 21, the day after Truman's inauguration, Eisenhower, who might have been the nominee of either party for president (but who wanted to be drafted by both, and so was nominated by neither), arrived at the Pentagon as Forrestal's chief military advisor, charged with supervising war plans; as he had done in England before D-Day, Ike dealt with a tense job by chain-smoking as many as four packs of cigarettes a day and permitting himself the occasional temper tantrum. Forrestal drugged himself with fatigue and long hours, and worried his close friends Ferdinand Eberstadt and Justice William O. Douglas with his troubles. His calendar was a blur of receptions, interviews, working breakfasts, cocktails, black-tie events, white-tie events; the McCloys after dinner; the Mayflower, the Sulgrave, and the Shoreham hotels, a tour of the Pentagon for the Boy Scouts of America; award ceremonies; and meetings of the Joint Chiefs of Staff at which he was "not expected." At a white-tie dinner at the Sulgrave or the Wardman Park he would suggest a walk in the dark with his friend Justice Douglas, as the latter related in his memoirs. "He would say, 'Bill, something awful is about to happen to me.'"

On March 1, Forrestal was summoned to the White House off the record ("Use East Entrance") and told by Truman that his resignation was wanted within the month. Enough time, perhaps, had passed for Truman to be sure that no one could accuse him of buckling to critics like Drew Pearson. The interview, which lasted about an hour and a half, ending at 12:30, was a "shattering experience," Forrestal told his friend Eberstadt, whom he consulted in New York as he sat alone at Prospect House drafting his formal letter of resignation, "effective on or about March 31," which was delivered to the White House twenty-four hours after it was requested. Truman's "Dear Jim" letter of acceptance stated that he was "fully cognizant" of Forrestal's reasons for resigning and recalled that it was because of "his personal" urging that Forrestal had remained in Washington "far beyond the time when he had expressed a hope of leaving government service."*

Oppressed by a terrible sense of foreboding, Forrestal kept up the busy schedule of a great man of affairs, evidently in the desperate hope of remaining one; the most poignant indication of his changed status was the notation that appeared on his calendar next to meetings of the Joint Chiefs of Staff: "You are not expected." His last appearance as secretary of defense was scheduled for noon, when Louis Johnson was to be sworn in. That morning, according to his naval aide, Captain Robert Dennison, Harry Truman took a telephone call from Forrestal, which Dennison overheard from the Oval Office. "Yes, Jim, that's the way I want it," Truman concluded. Hanging up, he explained, "That

---

* In correspondence with Arnold A. Rogow in 1959, Truman continued to maintain that Forrestal had in fact wished to leave earlier and that he had urged him to remain, which he naturally now regretted. It seems likely in context that he was referring to 1945–46, when all of Roosevelt's other cabinet appointees (except for Henry Wallace) were leaving the cabinet, more or less willingly, and when Forrestal, as noted, was exploring a return to Wall Street or a new career as a publisher.

was Forrestal. He wanted me to tell him whether I really wanted him to be relieved by Louis Johnson today."

The retiring secretary was composed—resigned—at the brief ceremony at the Pentagon, but composure broke when he arrived at the White House minutes later to bid the ritual goodbye to the president and found that Truman had gathered the cabinet, the service chiefs, and other high-office holders to honor him with a citation for "meritorious and distinguished service," and the Distinguished Service Medal, which he pinned to his coat lapel. Visibly overcome, Forrestal stammered, "It's beyond me . . . beyond my . . ." Truman interposed: "There you are. You deserve it, Jim." Later, this might seem ominous behavior, but Forrestal had recovered himself and displayed his usual superb "sportsmanship" when he appeared at a cocktail party and black-tie dinner for the incoming secretary at the Mayflower Hotel that evening.

It was the last appointment in his last official day as a public man, but at another ceremonial on Capitol Hill, he was honored by the House Armed Services Committee, chaired by his old friend and ally Carl Vinson of Georgia. With his old fluency, Forrestal in reply praised the committee's work, "their high and their customary zest and force," in building the Navy and in preparing the way for building a unified defense force, "which I know will be ably guided by Colonel Johnson, my successor." He praised his service secretaries in discriminating terms: Kenneth Royall for "loyal service," and Stuart Symington for "zeal and high devotion to his beliefs," not quite the same thing. Vinson, Johnson, and Forrestal stood together for Forrestal's last-known photograph: Vinson holding the engraved silver bowl, a chalk-striped Forrestal extending a hand gingerly, a fat-faced Johnson holding a pipe and looking on impassively. A cascade of mail and telegrams awaited Forrestal at the Pentagon, where a temporary office had been assigned him. With his aides Leva and Ohly, he was about to enter his car when Symington approached, saying, "There is something I want to talk to you about."

But all that is positively known is what happened immediately after. "Poking his head" into Forrestal's office, Marx Leva discovered him sitting in a rigid posture at his desk, where the silver bowl had been placed, still wearing his hat and staring fixedly at the blank wall opposite. "Is there anything the matter?" Leva asked and had to repeat. "You are a loyal fellow," Forrestal replied distractedly. Frightened, Leva again asked what he could do, and this time Forrestal replied that he wanted his car so he could go home. It seemed to "daze" him when he realized that he no longer had an official limousine to command, although Leva—a resourceful man—ordered Dr. Vannevar Bush's chauffeur to drive them back to Georgetown in Bush's car.* In the meantime Leva had gone back to his office and telephoned Forrestal's closest friend, Ferdinand Eberstadt. Together, they decided that Forrestal must be persuaded to leave the capital and fly to Florida for a long rest at Hobe Sound, that great resort of the New York rich since the 1920s, where his wife and old friend Robert Lovett were staying. Eberstadt phoned him from downtown and drove straight to Prospect House, disturbed by Forrestal's initial refusal to come to the phone and his cryptic advice not to come "for your own sake."

Depressed and jittery, Forrestal warned Eberstadt that the house was wired, and, pointing through a parted window blind, that he was being spied on by the two men loitering on the corner. Rehearsing the scene, it seems impossible that his oldest friend and late-night confidant had not known of Forrestal's belief that he was being followed and spied upon. But there was more. "In the privacy of his home Forrestal confessed to Eberstadt that he was a complete failure and that he was considering suicide. He also expressed the conviction that a number of individuals—Communists, Jews, and certain persons in the White House—had formed a conspiracy to 'get' him, and had finally succeeded." Some of them were probably in the house at that moment, he whispered; and probably not for the first time, he went to search the closets and other possible hiding places.

Eberstadt managed to steal away long enough to telephone Louis Johnson, who immediately agreed to put an Air Force Constellation on the ready to fly Forrestal to Hobe Sound; Robert Lovett, to alert him

---

* Arnold Rogow notes that in 1948 Forrestal had begun to show a concern for the mental state of other powerful men with grave responsibilities, including Bush, who had been highly placed in the Manhattan Project: "Not his mind, but just he's drawn pretty fine, I think." [343] In the 1940s, Washington, DC, was a cabinet of talents and a collective bundle of nerves to an extent it would not see again until the Vietnam War era.

of the flight; and Marx Leva, to drive them to National Airfield. Remy packed a suitcase of sports clothes and Forrestal's golf bag. Only the crew accompanied Forrestal on his flight to Florida. Back in New York, Eberstadt consulted the *Times*'s medical editor, Dr. Howard Rusk, who recommended "the most eminent psychiatrist in the country," Dr. William C. Menninger, the cofounder (with his father and older brother Karl) of the famous Menninger Clinic in Topeka, Kansas, and who was president of the American Psychiatric Association.

The small party that met Forrestal at the airfield, including his wife, were mostly his old friends from the twenties: the fashionable playwright Philip Barry and his wife, Ellen; Robert and Adelle Lovett; and his partner's son Douglas Dillon. Robert Lovett made a wan joke about beating him at golf. "Bob, they're after me," Forrestal replied. The sense of being targeted and surveilled never lifted, as Robert Lovett realized one day when they were strolling together on the beach and Forrestal, pointing to the sockets for umbrellas fixed in the sand, said: "We had better not discuss anything here. Those things are wired, and everything we say is being recorded." Reported back to Drew Pearson, Forrestal's fears of a Communist invasion explain the most notorious episode of his stay in Hobe Sound, which almost certainly did not happen as Pearson reported on his radio program several weeks later. On April 1, on his first full day there, Forrestal and everyone else in the house were awakened by a fire siren in the town that went off at six a.m., and everyone dashed outside to see the cause. When it appeared the alarm did not concern them, they went back to their beds, but rumors soon reached Washington that Forrestal had run around in his pajamas, screaming, "The Russians are attacking" (or, as the phrase entered the language, "The Russians are coming"). Once again, on King Claudius's principle that "madness in great ones must not unwatch'd go," Truman sent Baughman of the Secret Service to investigate; this time Baughman's report, marked "secret," was that Forrestal had suffered a "mild nervous breakdown"—which was hardly the case, although it corresponded to what would be the administration's official line until his death.

Hospitalizing him at a general hospital would protect Forrestal's reputation and spare the general public the knowledge that one of the nation's former top officials, de facto the second-most-powerful man in the executive branch, had suffered a psychotic break. On April 2, he was given heavy sedatives and secretly flown on a military plane to Washington, where his party was met by a private car at a remote corner of the airfield; he was accompanied by his old friend King Eber, his former aide Admiral Gringrich, and Dr. Menninger. During the flight Forrestal had been "in a state of extreme agitation," about "them," who confronted him everywhere, and wondering aloud whether he was being punished for being a "bad Catholic" and marrying a divorced woman. As he was being driven to Bethesda, Forrestal tried to jump out of the car several times and had to be forcibly restrained. When he arrived at the great hospital which had once been part of his domain, he forcibly declared that he would never leave it alive.

For the remaining six weeks he had left to live James Forrestal was confined in the sixteenth-story V.I.P. suite that had been outfitted for Franklin Roosevelt should he have needed it; it was never intended for a mental patient with suicidal tendencies, and indeed his supervising physician, Captain George N. Raines, would have preferred that his patient, as Forrestal had become, be housed in one of Bethesda's adjoining one-story buildings where psychiatric cases were customarily placed. But word had come from "downtown," meaning the White House, that Forrestal should be where access was easily restricted. Raines put heavy screens on the windows, so they could not open wide.

Raines's diagnosis of Forrestal's case was "involutional melancholia," whose etiology was subtly different from Menninger's "reactive depression." The latter essentially attributed Forrestal's breakdown to accumulated stress; when Lovett wondered how such a physically fit specimen could collapse so abruptly, Raines replied that Forrestal had "used up" his physical and spiritual resources in repressing his anxieties for so long, especially during the previous year. "Involutional melancholia," with its antique sound, was typically a disease of the accomplished middle-aged man, a "tendency to bewail the past and feel the future has nothing more in store." To the layman, both sound equally plausible and similarly glib—in any case clinical, psychiatric terminology has moved on, abandoning "melancholia" along the way.

In the first five weeks Forrestal was subjected to the chemical regime customary at the time for his symptoms of paranoia, extreme anxiety, and depression: a week of "narcosis," in which he was sedated into passivity, followed by four weeks of "subshock" or "subcoma" insulin therapy to produce periods of "clouded consciousness" lasting about an hour. The former treatment succeeded in calming Forrestal, but the results of the second were "less successful than Raines had hoped for, but he decided not to use the more controversial electric treatment," at least not until the milder alternatives had been exhausted. At Forrestal's insistence the curtains were kept drawn against assassins, and at least once he ordered Rear Admiral Sidney Souers, the executive secretary of the National Security Council, to "sweep" his room for listening devices; when none were detected, Forrestal's reply was that "they" had known Souers was coming, and would replace their devices when he was gone.

In their daily, hours-long sessions of "talking" therapy, Forrestal referred to his religious anxieties but also confessed to worldlier regrets. He obsessed about his failure to alert the nation to communism's menace, beginning as early as 1943. "On one occasion, when Forrestal read several newspaper editorials praising him for his record of public service, he threw them to one side, exclaiming, 'The fools. Don't they know that I betrayed my country?'" The public was told that he had been hospitalized for extreme "exhaustion," that he required rest, and that a full recovery was expected; the White House did not discourage speculation that he would undertake a round-the-world inspection tour on the president's behalf after he was released. The hundreds of letters expressing gratitude and good wishes that were addressed to him at Bethesda, from navy wives to admirals, an ex-lover, and former cabinet colleagues, suggest that some great as well as small were deceived about his state. But in the bastions of the Establishment, at the Cosmos Club and along Embassy Row, in congressional committee rooms and executive suites in Manhattan, word circulated that Forrestal's condition was serious: the former head of Dillon, Read, secretary of the navy, and secretary of defense was not simply a desperately tired man.

It outraged Drew Pearson's Quaker soul that "the most dangerous man in America" had gone mad, and his "cabal" was still at work protecting him, successfully imposing an "iron wall of secrecy" between the truth and the public. On April 9, Pearson convened a war council ("or what passed for a council under his authoritarian regime," Jack Anderson qualifies), and wondered aloud: "How long had Forrestal been demented? What orders, policies, or security breaches might be attributable to his condition? Why was his malady not detected or acted upon until he had disintegrated into a raving lunatic?" And so on. Admittedly, this exposure would hand the Russians a tremendous propaganda coup (the levers of power in America had been wielded by a madman, and who knew for how long?), but the nation was strong enough to be told the truth. Aware of the obloquy it would bring upon to "break the taboo," Pearson determined to broadcast the facts on his radio program.

From ABC headquarters in New York, executives had been sent to take Pearson off the air if he uttered the word "insanity," and specifically forbade him to accuse the administration of having knowingly allowed an insane man to remain in office. Undeterred, Pearson departed from his script, sneaking in phrases like "temporary insanity" and "out of his mind," and recounting the fairy tale about "The Russians are coming." Uncensored, he returned to the attack in "Merry-Go-Round" the next day.

But much to his shock the taboo held. The administration kept to its line that Forrestal "was not seriously ill and that his complete recovery was probable, even certain," as Rogow summed it up, and the Establishment press repeated its earlier diagnosis of nervous and physical exhaustion. It was easy to dismiss and refuse to repeat Pearson's charges as "sensationalism," considering the source, and even easier to belittle them when they were echoed by Walter Winchell.

Raines was satisfied that Forrestal was improving despite his continued paranoia, one sign being that his anxiety became less acute each week as Sunday, the day that Pearson and Winchell broadcast, approached; although not allowed to listen to their programs, on Mondays Forrestal "made" Raines tell him what they had said. From this and from the episode with Souers, it is evident that his old habit of command never quite deserted him. Like Hemingway, the other famous American whose rumored madness was confirmed by suicide, Forrestal also knew how to use his charm and the aura of his fame on his keepers. After Forrestal's death, Captain Raines praised him for being "the most honest and idealistic man I ever met, and one of the most intelligent," which is exactly the impression Forrestal had always striven to present; he befriended Edward Prise, one of the young corpsmen assigned to watch over him, and offered him work "as chauffeur, valet, man Friday" after his discharge. "It was my one big chance," Prise mourned years later, of his lost entrée into the great world.

Optimistic about Forrestal's progress, Dr. Raines took what he later called "calculated risks" in relaxing his regime, encouraging him to roam the rest of the sixteenth floor and chat with nurses and patients, and to make use of the kitchen pantry across the corridor. Although he later conceded that according to his diagnosis Forrestal was entering a phase of his illness in which suicide became an acute threat, Raines thought it safe, indeed advisable, for Josephine Forrestal to leave Washington on May 12 for one of her usual European trips. Meanwhile, he discontinued his daily session with Forrestal on May 14, and on May 18 left for a weeklong psychiatric convention in Toronto.

As the weekend of May 21–22 approached, Forrestal showed high spirits rather than his usual anxiety about Sunday night's broadcasts. On Saturday, when the commanding officer at Bethesda, Rear Admiral Willcutts, joined him for lunch, Forrestal ate a large steak, seeming eager for the afternoon's scheduled visitors, including his teenaged son, Peter. After passing a quiet evening, Forrestal told corpsman Prise, who was going off duty at midnight, that he intended to sit up late reading and did not need a sedative or sleeping pill. Prise later confessed to some vague foreboding as he left the sixteenth floor, to be replaced by a corpsman who would be on duty with Forrestal for the first time. The former checked on Forrestal at 1:45 a.m., Sunday, and observed him copying on loose-leaf papers from a book, a red-leather, gold-embossed gift edition of Mark Van Doren's *An Anthology of World Poetry.*

Forrestal copied part of a line from Sophocles's *Ajax:* "Of the lone bird, the querulous nightingale," stopping at night without finishing. He inserted the pages he had copied into the back of the book, which he left open on his nightstand. The new corpsman was away, apparently running an errand Forrestal had assigned him. Wordlessly, he stole across the corridor to the pantry, where he tied one end of his dressing-gown sash to the radiator below the window, the other around his neck, and having removed the window screen from its hooks, jumped into the night. If Forrestal had intended to hang himself, the attempt failed when the cord around the radiator broke or slipped loose. Fingerprints found on the outside windowsill and surrounding cement suggest that for a terrible moment he might have reconsidered, then tried and failed to climb back inside, or perhaps just reflexively scrabbled at the wall as he hung suspended. But it was only a moment. He fell to his death. At 1:50 a.m. a nurse on the seventh floor heard a loud crash, the noise of Forrestal's body landing on the roof of a passageway connecting two wings of the hospital at the third floor. The silk sash was still around his neck, and his watch was still running; the Montgomery County coroner concluded that his death was instantaneous.

"In the dark night of the soul," Scott Fitzgerald had written of his own "crack-up," "it is always three o'clock in the morning." James Vincent Forrestal, the first secretary of defense, had lived almost until two. At the White House Harry Truman officially learned of Forrestal's death from a seven a.m. radio broadcast. He was "inexpressibly shocked and grieved."

About ten o'clock on the evening of Saturday, June 24, 1950, the white telephone that connected the secretary of state, Dean Acheson, with the White House switchboard rang at Harewood Farm, his place in Sandy Spring, Maryland, where he and his wife were spending a quiet weekend. The secretary, if he followed his usual routine, had spent some of the afternoon gardening (he raised dahlias, which he liked to present to his friends in bushels) and then dressed for dinner in one of the flamboyant costumes he liked to wear at home, "a pleated cotton wedding shirt from Mexico or the islands, lime green slacks, no socks, sandals or Mexican *huaraches* on the feet, an orange sash around the waist falling to the knee." The eighteenth-century farmhouse, sitting on eighteen hundred acres, was "very small, very quiet, and very secluded," Acheson recalled for one of Truman's biographers. Five months of Senator Joseph McCarthy's blackguarding him as a coddler of Communists—if not far, far worse!—had led to an alarming increase in crank mail, so that he was now attended by day and night shifts of bodyguards, "a regimen not conducive to relaxation."

Dean and Mary Acheson were reading when the phone rang. The secretary stood up in his *huaraches*, put down his book—which might have been anything from Thucydides to Tobias Smollett, Dickens, or Shakespeare, or a book of Victorian history—and picked up the phone.

On the line was Dean Rusk, the assistant secretary for Far Eastern affairs, who had dashed to the department's new headquarters in Foggy Bottom after a press aide found him at Joseph Alsop's house in Georgetown, bearing the news that United Press International had received a cable from its correspondent in Seoul reporting a major Communist offensive. Just as Rusk arrived at the State Department, another cable came in from the American ambassador to South Korea, John Muccio, an officer with a rare sympathy for, and expertise in, Korean matters, confirming that heavily armored troops from the pro-Communist north were mounting a massive attack across the 38th parallel on the forces of the Republic of Korea (ROK), allied to the United States.

Though privately skeptical to the point of cynicism about the purpose and capabilities of the United Nations, Acheson approved a suggestion from another of his deputies on the phone that the Security Council should be convened to call for a cease-fire, and ordered the necessary steps to be taken, subject to correction by the president. Then he put through a call to Truman, who was in Independence, Missouri, enjoying the first getaway to his hometown in six months; his white telephone rang in the hall off the small, crowded library at 119 North Delaware Street, where he, his wife, daughter, and formidable mother-in-law, Madge Gates Wallace—who owned the house and forever treated him as a glorified boarder—were reading and chatting after an early dinner. It was a hot summer night in Independence.

"Mr. President," Acheson said, "I have very serious news. The North Koreans are attacking across the thirty-eighth parallel."

Truman said he would return to the capital immediately. But Acheson advised against a hastily arranged night flight as an unnecessary risk, and one that might alarm the public. (The night before, a Northwest Orient airliner on a transcontinental flight out of La Guardia had disappeared in a squall over Lake Michigan around 1:30 a.m., with a presumed loss of all fifty-eight passengers and crew aboard—the worst aircraft disaster in America to that date.) The intentions of the North Koreans and the extent of their offensive remained unclear; in the last year they had launched guerrilla operations involving as many as fifteen hundred troops. Was this really an all-out attack, or just another incursion, perhaps a feint?

Acheson asked Truman to await another call from him the next day as the situation became clearer. "And I agreed," Truman recalls in his

Memoirs. "I went to bed, and that was one night that I didn't get much sleep." In her biography, Margaret Truman writes, "My father made it clear, from the moment he got the news, that he feared this was the opening round of World War III."

In the capital, George Kennan, the retiring head of the State Department's planning board and the architect of the administration's containment policy toward the Soviet Union, learned of the events in Korea only from the headlines in the Sunday newspapers after returning to Washington from an overnight stay with his wife, Annelise, at their farm in Berlin, Pennsylvania, where there was no telephone in the house or newspaper delivery.

"Nobody had thought to notify me, and perhaps there was no reason anybody should have," Kennan writes in his *Memoirs*, considering that he was leaving government in the next month to become a fellow at the Institute for Advanced Study in Princeton, "but I could not help but reflect that General Marshall would have seen that this was done." Dean Acheson was less solicitous of Kennan's counsel than his predecessor, and was known to say—at least once to Kennan himself, who was in one of his intellectual funks—that he might be better off standing on a street corner waving a "The End is Nigh" sign.

Perhaps the end *was* nigh. As Kennan recalls, there had been signs and portents and voices in the air that spring for those with the privileged access to hear them.

"At some time in late May or early June, some of us who were particularly concerned with Russian affairs in the department were puzzled to note, among the vast 'take' of information that flows daily into the ample maw of that institution, data suggesting that somewhere across the broad globe the armed forces of some Communist power were expecting soon to go into action. An intensive survey of the Soviet situation satisfied us it was not Soviet forces to which these indications related. This left us with the forces of the various satellite regimes, but which?"

Now that the question was so unexpectedly answered, Kennan ruefully recalled that on a trip to Japan in 1949, after the American troops' withdrawal from the peninsula, he had been assured by MacArthur's command that an attack from the north "was practically out of the question: the South Koreans were so well armed and trained; so clearly superior to those of the Communist north, that our greatest task, we were told, was to restrain the South Koreans from resorting to arms to settle their differences with the north," and that at any rate, any trouble in that vicinity could be dealt with by airpower launched from Okinawa. "Having no grounds to challenge this judgment, I accepted it (I have always reproached myself for doing so) and we passed on to other things. But nowhere else, understandably enough, could we see any possibility of an attack, and we came away from the exercise quite frustrated."

Korea, whose name means "Land of the Evening Calm"—a fact American soldiers came to find bitterly ironical—had barely existed for American policy makers between 1905, when Theodore Roosevelt effectively handed over the ancient kingdom to Japan in the settlement of the Russo-Japanese War, and November 1943, when Franklin D. Roosevelt proposed a "free and independent Korea" at the Cairo Conference with Churchill and Chiang Kai-shek. In his seigneurial way, FDR might well have regarded Korea's unhappy state after almost forty years of Japanese occupation as a piece of unfinished business.

In 1905, in cheerful violation of an 1882 American pledge to support Korea's independence, and without informing the State Department, let alone submitting his policy to the advice and consent of the Senate, Theodore Roosevelt had secretly authorized William Howard Taft, his secretary of war, to inform the Japanese prime minister, Count Katsura, of his readiness not to interfere with Japan's intentions on the peninsula in exchange for the empire's acceptance of the American colonization of the Philippines. Taft's occult mission was hidden in plain sight. His talks with Katsura occurred in the course of a diplomatic junket that he led across the Pacific, from San Francisco to Hawaii, Japan, Korea, and the Philippines—a huge, showy affair with a score of congressmen and seven senators. As an irresistible distraction for the press, it included Roosevelt's oldest child, Alice, a rebellious, high-spirited beauty of twenty, who smoked cigarettes in public, bet on horse races, and carried a pet snake to parties, and whose handsome features adorned cigar boxes and sold rotogravure newspapers. "I can be President of the United States, or I can attend to Alice. I can't possibly do both!" TR once exclaimed to his friend Owen Wister; but now he found a way to turn her celebrity to use. As Warren Zimmerman writes, "While Alice reaped the publicity, Taft, to protect a vulnerable American acquisition close to the Asian mainland, quietly made the deal to sell out the Koreans."

Disingenuously offering himself as a mediator between the tsar and the mikado in the war they fought in 1904 and 1905 to determine who would be master in Manchuria and Korea—a conflict that conclusively showed the debility of the Russian Empire and confirmed Japan as the rising power in Asia—Roosevelt had deftly overseen the negotiations at Portsmouth, New Hampshire, and Oyster Bay, Long Island, that led to a peace agreement in which Korea was ceded to Japan as a protectorate. After crushing losses at sea, there was no way that Russia could have dislodged Japan anyway. In the end the more serious obstacles to a treaty had been the status of Sakhalin Island, which was divided between them, and Tsar Nicholas II's absolute refusal to pay reparations. The Korean emperor (formerly king), heir to the five-hundred-year-old Joseon dynasty, was disabused of his illusion that America was Korea's benevolent elder brother. For his good work Roosevelt was awarded the Nobel Peace Prize. "Korea is absolutely Japan's," he wrote in a private letter. "To be sure, by treaty it was solemnly covenanted that Korea should remain independent. But Korea was itself helpless to enforce the treaty, and it was out of the question to suppose that any other nation . . . would undertake to do for the Koreans what they were utterly unable to do for themselves." As a historian, Roosevelt knew well what the Athenians had told the Melians: "The powerful exact what they can, and the weak grant what they must." Korea was formally annexed to Japan in 1911. By secretly abetting Japan's imperial pretensions on the Asian mainland while publicly posing as an "honest broker" in its conflict with the Russians—whom he regarded as a degenerate "race," compared to the rising Japanese—Roosevelt helped set the train of events that led directly to the Pacific War, its clash of civilizations, and its thirty million dead.

What the Oyster Bay Roosevelt had taken away in 1905, the Hyde Park Roosevelt proposed to restore in 1945. After the vague declarations at Cairo, a free and unified Korea was more emphatically endorsed at Yalta at FDR's insistence. Deferring to the president, Stalin asked if foreign troops were to be stationed on the peninsula. "Roosevelt replied in the negative, and Stalin expressed his appreciation of this." It was vaguely agreed that a brief trusteeship of the Big Four would precede independence. When the war ended in August 1945, the U.S. and the USSR agreed to what was supposed to be a provisional division of the Korean Peninsula at the 38th parallel in order to accept the surrender of Japanese troops on either side. At the Pentagon, according to MacArthur's biographer William Manchester, a colonel protested futilely that Korea—as its economy had been organized by the Japanese—was a political and economic unit and could not be divided; but a gaggle of one-star generals overruled him: "We have got to divide Korea, and it has to be done by four o'clock this afternoon." Dean Rusk, then an army staff officer, drew the line across the peninsula's waist—according to one version, with a pencil and a ruler on an old *National Geographic* map. In *Plausible Worlds*, his subtle and sparkling philosophical study of contingency and causation in history, Geoffrey Hawthorn, in considering divergent interpretations of the Korean War, poses the question of when the conflict became inevitable. His answer, to abridge an intricate argument, is when the peninsula was divided at the 38th parallel.

In the big chill between the United States and the Soviet Union after the war, the joint trusteeship languished, and by mid-1948 both the Russians and the Americans had largely withdrawn, and client states with a strongman had been installed: in the industrial north, the People's Republic of Korea, it was Kim Il-sung, a Communist militant in his thirties, who had attained the rank of major in the Red Army; in the more populous, agricultural south, Syngman Rhee, a venerable "patriot" who had been in exile in the United States for forty years, where he had diligently acquired degrees from George Washington University, Harvard, and Princeton. Both insisted that Korea must be unified; each, that it should be under his auspices. MacArthur, who had shown scant interest in Korea until then, made a proconsular appearance at Rhee's inauguration and, succumbing to his superb instinct for the dramatic gesture, assured him, "If Korea should ever be attacked by the Communists, I will defend it as I would California."

But that was so much bravura on MacArthur's part, as at least his entourage understood. The Pacific War had bypassed Korea, and most Americans could not have located it on an unmarked map. As for the few men who were stationed there, Clay Blair in his monumental history says flatly: "The Army occupiers hated South Korea." In 1948 they could hardly bear to wait for their scheduled withdrawal. The Americans found its mountainous landscapes poor and monotonous; they abominated the sultry-hot and bitter cold extremes of the summer and winter seasons, and the stench from the night soil that fertilized the rice paddies. (Henry Adams made the same complaint in Japan in the 1880s.) Almost all of them distrusted the Koreans: they were, their commander, General John Hodge, said, "the same breed of cat as the Japanese." Perversely, Hodge chose to keep the hated Japanese police force in place during the first months of occupation, poisoning many Koreans' opinion of their supposed liberators, whose "trusteeship" came across as simply another colonialist regime. After the division, a spirited left-wing opposition to Syngman Rhee sprang up in the south, but the Americans chose not to parley with it, although personally Truman thought little of Rhee.

The first month of 1950 was a hinge in the history of Truman's administration. On January 31, the same day that he announced his decision to mount a crash program to build a hydrogen bomb, he secretly authorized the drafting of the state paper that became known to history as NSC-68, the foundational document of the National Security Council for which Kennan's Long Telegram and "X" article had provided some of the rationale.

Almost three weeks earlier, January 12, 1950, Acheson had delivered a speech about American policy in Asia at the National Press Club in Washington, which the China lobbyists and the right-wingers whom he called the "primitives" soon consigned to the annals of infamy.

"It was a supercharged moment to be speaking on Asian affairs," he admitted later. Chiang Kai-shek, the Nationalist leader in China who was a hero for the China lobby, and admired by millions of less fervid Americans, had fled across the sea—undone, according to Senator Taft, by a left-wing cabal in the State Department. A triumphant Mao Zedong was in Moscow negotiating with Stalin. Acheson's view was that Chiang—implicitly condemned as inept and corrupt—had at last exhausted the patience of the Chinese people despite the vast military advantages he enjoyed at the end of the war, and there was nothing the United States could have done to prevent his fall. This was the burden of the unsparingly candid white paper that the State Department published after the Communist takeover; himself unsentimental about China, Acheson could never understand why it was so ill received by those who blamed the administration for its "loss." Americans had never had the territorial designs on China that Russia historically did, he noted in his speech at the Press Club; therefore, "we should not deflect from the Russians to ourselves the righteous anger and hatred of the Chinese people."

Acheson was clearly prepared to cast adrift the generalissimo ("a refugee on a small island off the coast") and, implicitly, to accommodate American policy to Mao's regime, while attempting to detach it from Russian tutelage. In embryo, Acheson's China policy at mid-century was that of Nixon and Kissinger a quarter-century later, including the delivery of China's seat in the Security Council to "Red" China; at the time—or to be exact, when running for vice president in 1952—Nixon accused Adlai Stevenson of holding a Ph.D. from "Dean Acheson's College of Cowardly Communist Appeasement."

In a passage that subsequently caused Acheson much grief, he defined a "defensive perimeter" running from the Aleutians to Japan to the Ryukyu Islands (Okinawa) to the Philippines. The American "line of defense" was thus located at "the very edges of the Pacific," excluding the entire Asian mainland, South Korea and Indochina, as well as the island of Formosa (Taiwan), where the generalissimo was bunkered. No person could guarantee these "other areas" from military attack; in the event of one, "the initial reliance must be upon the people under attack to resist it, and then upon the United Nations, which so far has not proved a weak reed to lean on by any people who are determined to protest their independence against outside aggression." The last clause was disingenuous; the secretary, as earlier mentioned, held the UN in contempt, and believed it was a superstition to think of it as an entity in itself, as if it could have some existence apart from its membership— and regarding membership, he felt it was absurd that a tiny, remote country should have the same vote in the General Assembly as a great power. If Acheson had thought more highly of the UN, he might not have made such adroit use of its Security Council a few months later. If he intended to discourage aggression by the reference, he expected subtler readers than he got.

It was a typical, bravura Acheson performance, including his fatal gift for the memorable phrase (although "defensive perimeter" did not seem to be one at the time). His speech was overshadowed by the stormy withdrawal of the Soviet representative to the Security Council, Yakov A. Malik, in protest of its refusal to remove the Chinese Nationalists and seat the Communists. South Korea was not mentioned in the *New York Times*'s story until the thirty-second paragraph, where it was mistakenly included inside the "defensive perimeter." (The North Koreans must have been reading the *Times*, because they included their southern neighbor among the "subjugated states" in America's thrall.) In his memoirs Acheson writes that since his "defensive perimeter" was exactly the same as the "line of defense" which the Joint Chiefs of Staff and General MacArthur had articulated, "it did not occur to me that I should be charged with innovating policy or political heresy." (MacArthur had declared the Pacific Ocean to be an "Anglo-Saxon lake," with American defenses deployed along its fringes.) But the Joint Chiefs of Staff and MacArthur had laid down their line before China fell to Mao, while Acheson's speech, coming after, seemed to view with composure the "loss" of yet another country on the Asian mainland, even if it did not, as Joseph McCarthy and Richard Nixon later charged, seem to solicit it.

Intimately involved in all the great foreign-policy undertakings of Truman's first term, Acheson made his friendship with the president into one of the defining facts of his second; when Korea came, it seemed almost to be Mr. Acheson's war as much as Mr. Truman's. Yet, of all the lieutenants Truman inherited from Franklin Roosevelt and promoted to higher office, Dean Gooderham (pronounced "GOOD-rum") Acheson might have seemed the very least likely to win not only his admiration and affection but his complete trust. In appearance and manner, they seemed to represent two entirely different species of public man. It is easy to see why Truman, who had nursed a secret desire to be great since boyhood, was mistaken for a common man, so much did he embody the popular idea of one. "He looked like Truman," John Steinbeck writes of a drab character in *The Wayward Bus*, a best-selling novel in 1947, "and like the vice-presidents of companies and like certified public accountants. His glasses were squared off at the corners. His suit was gray and correct, and there was a little gray in his face too."

Dean Acheson (as Alistair Cooke pictured him in the *Manchester Guardian*) was a magnifico, a "six-foot-two Velázquez grandee who has submitted himself, with a twinkling eye, to his present reincarnation in fine tweeds as a Connecticut Yankee." His tailored suits and candy-striped shirts with starched white collars and French cuffs, linked by gold; his elaborately cosseted mustache—especially, the mustache, which Averell Harriman begged him to shave off during the early excesses of the McCarthy era; his accent (which in anyone else Truman would have called Harvard but was actually upper-class Connecticut Valley); his gilded path from Groton to Yale to Harvard Law to clerkships at the Supreme Court and a white-shoe law practice; his undisguised assumption of intellectual superiority (James Reston said that "he was smarter than most of his colleagues in Truman's cabinet but not smart enough not to show it"); even his height, which made the two of them look like Mutt and Jeff in the comics: all this *might* have told against him, but in the mysterious alchemy of friendship, traits and distinctions that could have been fatal in anyone else were discounted or came to be regarded fondly.

Though a Connecticut Yankee, Acheson was not the patrician blueblood he looked every inch to be, but rather, on both sides, a first-generation American, whose parents were "Anglo-Canadian middle-class." His father, a soldier's son who had migrated to Canada as a boy and fought against an Indian uprising, was an Episcopal clergyman, who married the daughter of a whiskey distiller and banker in Toronto and became the bishop of Connecticut; as their son liked to recall, both were still loyal subjects of Queen Victoria when he was born in 1893.

After what he remembered as a Tom Sawyerish boyhood in Middlebury, Connecticut, Acheson did not distinguish himself academically at Groton, which he hated, and where he was instructed in rowing by a young Averell Harriman, or at Yale, where he was dismissive of the curriculum and known as something of a playboy; he was elected to Scroll and Key and acquired a lively circle of friends, including Archibald MacLeish, who charmingly remembered him as "the typical son of an Episcopal bishop—gay, graceful, gallant," and Cole Porter, with whom he shared excursions to New York for the theater and nightlife. His classmates voted him "fifth most witty and tenth 'sportiest' in the class"—dubious distinctions which tend to confirm that "Yale was just a finishing-school for boys in those days." Acheson went on with his friends to Harvard Law School, where he and Cole Porter shared a house on the Gold Coast. At the suggestion of the dean, Porter switched to music, and went on to other things; Acheson stuck with the hard mistress. It was at Harvard Law, under the tutelage of Felix Frankfurter, who became his lifelong friend, that he said he discovered "the power of thought." After his graduation, Frankfurter arranged for him to clerk for Justice Louis Brandeis; he stayed for two years at the Supreme Court and helped with the arrangements at Brandeis's brainy afternoon "at-home" gatherings. Acheson admired Brandeis for his liberal principles and lofty character, although for some reason he named Justice Oliver Wendell Holmes Jr., whom he met at this time, and General Marshall as the two great men he had known, putting Brandeis among the "near-great"; reminded of the omission, he added Harry Truman to the greats. In 1921, Acheson, who had accepted a job in Boston, was invited to join the young Washington law firm of Covington & Burling, where his logical flair, analytical finesse, and forensic skills quickly established him as an appellate lawyer, despite his losing the first fifteen cases he argued before the Supreme Court. George Roblee, another senior partner, remembered their catch as "the shiniest fish that ever came out of the sea," words that William James had originally applied to George Santayana. Covington & Burling prospered on Burling's insight that, having become accustomed to regulating business on a large scale during the war, the government was unlikely to lose the habit; and after he was made partner in 1926, Acheson's personal finances were secure. In 1922, well in advance of fashion, he and Alice had bought a substantial brick house, later much enlarged, on P Street in Georgetown, and, soon after, the farmhouse in Sandy Spring, which lacked electricity until after the war; and in both they helped Washington to live up to Henry James's description of the capital as "the city of conversation." Acheson's politics were liberal—he had considered becoming a labor lawyer—and their guests included Sinclair Lewis, the labor leader John L. Lewis, the Greenwich Village radical journalist Norman Hapgood, and "lots of La Follettes." As his biographer Robert L. Beisner pictures the rising Acheson: "He thrived, discussing law, literature, and politics with smart people in a city that never bored him. He had already figured out that the center of American power was shifting from New York to Washington, and he was an ambitious man."

"You have to remember this about Acheson. He was basically a Washington lawyer, not a diplomat. The fact that he looked like a diplomat confused people, but it didn't make him one. He had never lived abroad, knew no foreign languages, knew nothing about the outside world," George Kennan told John Lewis Gaddis. He did, however, know where to position himself to rise as high as he did. If he had been a career diplomat, he would never have been appointed secretary of state by Harry Truman, in which office, it was said, he "protected the Foreign Service from the President, and the President from the Foreign Service."

There had been no such closeness with Roosevelt, for whom he felt "admiration without affection." His friend Clark Clifford believed that Acheson's warmth for Truman was increased by his resentment over what he considered FDR's regal and patronizing ways, which, he said, made him feel as if he were a promising stable boy taking orders from his milord, and was expected to tug his forelock.

"It was ironic that Acheson felt this way about Roosevelt, since so many people felt something similar when in the presence of Dean Acheson," Clifford goes on. "In a city filled with large egos, he was the most self-confident man I ever encountered. Fortunately, his intellect and seriousness of intent justified his demeanor." Actually, they did not, in the majority view at the time, for Acheson not only did not suffer fools gladly, "he positively exuded an attitude that made other people feel belittled and scorned." Such—for it so clearly implied his moral superiority—was his famous remark "I do not intend to turn my back on Alger Hiss," regarding a man to whom he had not been close, and may well have suspected of prevaricating; referring to "the twenty-fifth chapter of the Gospel According to St. Matthew, beginning with verse 34."

As Senator Hugh Butler of Nebraska said, "I watch his smart-aleck manner and his British clothes and that ever-lasting New Dealism . . . and I want to shout, Get out, get out, you're everything that's been wrong with this country for years."*

More than he knew then or might have wished later, Acheson's words at the National Press Club were scrupulously parsed in Moscow. As Gaddis states in *The Cold War*: "Stalin read the speech carefully—as well as (courtesy of British spies) the top-secret National Security Council study upon which it was based—and authorized his foreign minister, Molotov, to discuss it with Mao Zedong. The Soviet leader then informed Kim Il-sung that 'according to information from the United States . . . the prevailing mood is not to interfere.' Kim in turn assured Stalin that the attack will be swift and the war will be won in three days."

After a month in Moscow—his first trip outside China—Mao was exasperated by Stalin's remote, manipulative, and dilatory behavior. "Am I here just to eat, shit, and sleep?" he complained to his entourage. Irritated by Acheson's charge that Russia was "detaching the northern provinces of China . . . and attaching them to the Soviet Union," Sta-

* The latter charges were false. Acheson's suits were tailored by Farnsworth-Reed in Washington, DC, and his shirts and ties were mostly Brooks Brothers and Sulka. His biographer Robert L. Beisner delightfully quotes Truman's biographer David McCullough's youthful memory of seeing "Acheson emerge from a New Haven clothing store looking 'like a strapping handsome actor all dressed up to play the part of Dean Acheson.'" Acheson was a staunch Democrat, having followed his noncitizen father into the party, and an admirer of Woodrow Wilson, but his economic instincts were conservative, and, after a few months of service as undersecretary of the treasury in 1933, during which he was acting secretary during the illness of William Woodin, he resigned after a dispute with Roosevelt regarding the latter's unorthodox gold policy. FDR carelessly announced his resignation before he had tendered it, but Acheson made no fuss, and even made an appearance at his successor's swearing-in, impressing the president with his sportsmanship. "Dean Acheson knows how to resign," Roosevelt said later, in pointed contrast with others who departed noisily and disloyally. In 1940, as war approached, he brought him back into the administration. On the wardrobe, see Beisner, 88–89; on the resignation, Schlesinger, *The Coming of the New Deal*, 241–42; Beisner, 11–12.

lin demanded, via Molotov, that Mao denounce the speech through his foreign ministry, assuring him that Outer Mongolia and Russia would do the same. Although he complied with Stalin's order, Mao signed the statement with the name of a lowly press officer and slyly included Outer Mongolia as a Chinese province. An exasperated Stalin called him in for a tongue-lashing delivered in front of Mao's right-hand man, Zhou Enlai, in which he all but accused him of turning into China's "own Tito." After completing this performance, Stalin invited the Chinese comrades to come to his dacha for dinner, but Mao sulked throughout the meal, and pettishly refused to join in the dancing when Stalin turned on his gramophone, although several men tried to pull him up. Considering the trouble the speech later caused him, it might have consoled Acheson to know that it was the occasion for an awkward time in Moscow, although in the end Mao's visit ended with the signing of a treaty signaling Chinese solidarity with Russia, on terms greatly (and secretly) advantageous to Russia, and while he was in Moscow, his regime was formally recognized by Great Britain.

In late April 1950 Truman was presented with the highly classified paper known to history and bureaucracy as NSC-68. The remotest origins of the paper went back to George Kennan (he was appalled by the final product, which he found crude and melodramatic); the moving force was Dean Acheson; the principal author, Paul H. Nitze, the Wall Street banker who was Kennan's deputy and successor as head of the State Department Policy Planning staff and, like the late James Forrestal and Ferdinand Eberstadt, an alumnus of Dillon, Read.

As a member of the Strategic Bombing Survey in Germany and Japan, Nitze was among the first Americans to see the devastation caused by the atomic bombs. But as he conceived it, his task was to measure, "with calipers," the damage, not to brood over it. "While others saw the bomb as the ultimate proof of the futility of war, Nitze saw it as a weapon that could and probably would be used again. The damage in Hiroshima, he reckoned, was simply the equivalent of an incendiary bombing raid by 210 B-29s." NSC-68 is equally cold-blooded on the subject.

In his memoirs Acheson does not dispute a Washington insider's later description of NSC-68 as "'the most ponderous expression of elementary ideas' he had ever come across." In its alarmist and hortatory tone, and Manichaean worldview, NSC-68 really resembled the DAR primers to which Kennan ruefully compares the "X" article in his *Memoirs*. There was no recourse to national psychology, however crude; no ambiguities such as literary airs and graces might have insinuated. But its blinding obviousness was part of the exercise. "The purpose of NSC-68 was to so bludgeon the mass mind of 'top government' that not only could the President make a decision but that the decision could be carried out."

Truman considered NSC-68 so explosive that he had all the copies collected and then locked them in his office safe. NSC-68 was not declassified until 1975, when historians petitioned for its release, and in 1969 Acheson, in many ways its true author, was still not able to quote it. But Acheson had promoted the tenets of what he called "total diplomacy" at the time, and the mass mind of the public was not spared some bludgeoning of its own. At all times, he confessed, it was necessary to be "clearer than truth."

No, communism was monolithic, pure and simple: implacably hostile to America and the Free World it led, and intent on world conquest. Its essence was, exactly, "the priority given by the Soviet rulers to the Kremlin design, world domination, contrasted with the American aim, an environment in which free societies could exist and flourish." (Acheson echoes Nitze, who repeatedly contrasts the Kremlin's malefic "design" or designs with benign American "aims" or "purposes.")

As an early reader, the president's counsel Charles Murphy was so undone that he did not go to work the next day but stayed home and brooded. (It was he who suggested that the document be assigned to the nascent National Security Council.) What was to be done? NSC-68 had an answer for that. The Soviets' designs might be global, and thus explained virtually any losses that America or its allies and dependents might suffer, but for practical purposes a suitably mobilized America had the limitless resources to check and revert them. Without flinching at building up the nuclear arsenal with the idea in mind that it might have to be used, NSC-68 called for a massive increase in conventional arms and the size of the military establishment. By design, as it were, NSC-68 did not venture a dollar estimate of the cost, but anyone with the back of an envelope could calculate from the 20 percent of GNP that it proposed as a sustainable level of armaments that $50 billion was manageable—three times what the parsimonious Truman and Defense Secretary Louis Johnson had budgeted for 1950; indeed, in the foreseeable future, it would pay for itself as military expenditures and budget deficits invigorated the whole economy. (Nitze had consulted with Leon Keyserling, the leading Keynesian in the administration, in writing the economic parts of his paper.) Such was the formula for the military Keynesianism which came to undergird the burgeoning economy of the postwar era. The style of NSC-68 reflected an original intention that at least part of it should be made public, and it should thus be simple and stirring enough to move the masses, calling for "Hemingway sentences," as Robert Lovett put it. This plan fell prey to the administration's increasing obsession with secrecy, so that in the end, the only reader who mattered was Harry Truman. But he, who liked his memoranda "with the bark off," turned out to be the ideal reader, so captivated was he by its unvarnished imperatives that, after a short hesitation interrupted by events, he shrugged off the frugality of four years and never looked back.

For a document of such historical consequence, NSC-68 aroused no pride of authorship. Kennan, the putative "father" of containment, repudiated what he considered a bellicose misreading of his "doctrine"; Nitze disavowed any originality. As his grandson Nicholas Thompson writes in *The Hawk and the Dove:* "Years later, a student sent Nitze a master's thesis arguing that Nitze had 'militarized containment.' On his copy, Nitze crossed out that line and carefully wrote in his own view of NSC-68's objective. 'This paper *more realistically set forth the requirements to assure success* of George Kennan's idea of containment.'"

According to Margaret Truman, her father had never believed in "containment." "Our purpose was much broader," he said. "We were working for a united, free and prosperous world." What might all this cost? In a speech delivered in 1952, Truman noted that NSC-68 "meant a great military effort in time of peace. It meant doubling or tripling the budget, increasing taxes heavily, and imposing various kinds of economic controls. It meant a great change in our normal peacetime way of doing things." By the time he spoke, most suitably, at a service reunion at the Shrine Mosque in Springfield, Missouri, the United States had been mired in Korea for two years. "Even so," Acheson concedes in his memoirs, regarding the "bludgeoning," "it is doubtful whether anything like what happened in the next few years could have been done had not the Russians been stupid enough to have instigated the attack against South Korea and opened the 'hate America' campaign.'" Or, as he elsewhere put it more simply, "Korea saved us."

"The news was growing rather grim," Margaret Truman understates, when Acheson gave his report to Truman at 12:35 p.m., Central Standard Time. A massive tank column was treading toward Seoul and its Kimpo Air Base; the North Koreans had staged seven amphibious landings on the eastern coast. Although Ambassador Muccio had brave things to say about the ROK troops, they were falling apart, and Syngman Rhee and his government were soon in panicky flight.

Truman readily assented to Acheson's proposed resolution in the Security Council condemning North Korea's "armed attack" on its southern neighbor as "an unprovoked act of aggression" (subsequently downgraded to "a breach of the peace"). Truman asked Acheson to draw up recommendations and arrange for the top people at the State and Defense Departments to confer with him that evening at Blair House, his official residence while the White House was undergoing a restoration. Before he hung up, he said, "We've got to stop the sons of bitches, no matter what." Then he ordered his airplane, the *Independence*, readied for takeoff. The flight back to Washington took three hours, ample time for reflection.

"In my generation, this was not the first occasion when the strong had attacked the weak. I recalled some earlier instances: Manchuria, Ethiopia, Austria. I remembered how each time that the democracies failed to act it had encouraged the aggressors to keep going ahead. Communism was acting in Korea just as Hitler, Mussolini, and the Japanese had acted ten, fifteen and twenty years earlier." As often, Truman reflected that the only new thing in the world was the history you had not read.

Waiting for the president at National Airport when he arrived at 7:15 p.m. were Acheson, Louis Johnson, and Budget Director James

Webb. "By God," he said to Webb when they were inside his limousine, "I am going to let them have it." Johnson, who was in a front seat, leaned back and fervently shook his hand.

Korea, Stephen E. Ambrose writes in *Rise to Globalism*, was the crisis Truman needed if a parsimonious Congress was going to enact the warfare-state legislation contemplated by NSC-68, and if the administration was to find a way to demonstrate its anticommunist credentials, which had come under attack by the Republican demagogue, the senator from Wisconsin, Joseph McCarthy. Until February 9, 1950, McCarthy was little known outside his own state, and even in Wisconsin there were many who believed that he was actually a battle-scarred war hero, "Tailgunner Joe," when his service was in air combat intelligence, and his only injury came from a drunken shipboard stumble. On that date, McCarthy electrified an audience in Wheeling, West Virginia, by brandishing a sheet of paper supposedly containing the names of fifty-seven card-carrying Communists in the State Department (and, it was clearly implied, known to be such by Dean Acheson), which had been given to him by a good American in government "whose name I shall never reveal." The number of miscreants was later blown up to 205, dropped to as few as 10, upped to 81; what did not change was the accusation that Acheson was their protector, and probably their co-conspirator.

To be sure, McCarthy was following the lead of other Republican senators, including Robert Taft and Styles Bridges, the so-called China lobby, and a regiment of right-wing editorialists in denouncing Truman and Acheson, but he brought a coarse brio to the task, denouncing Truman as "drunk on bourbon and Benedictine" (how Truman must have resented being charged with swilling a liqueur!), and "the elegant and alien Acheson" for abetting the "loss" of China to "atheistic slavery." Outdoing itself, the *Chicago Tribune* called Acheson "another striped-pants snob who ignored Asian peoples and betrayed true Americanism to serve as a lackey of Wall Street bankers, British lords, and Communistic radicals from New York." The attack of the primitives was thus already well launched when McCarthy erupted on the scene, but he deserves his due. As Acheson later wrote: "One could have said his name, like those of Judge Lynch and Captain Boycott, had enlarged the vocabulary."

Walter Lippmann blamed the failure of the administration's containment policy and the missteps and arrogance of Acheson in particular for the rise of the movement that had now found its metonym. His increasingly dim view of the secretary was confirmed when he found out that, having provided his enemies with a cudgel in the form of the "defensive perimeter," he declined to pick up one given him by the columnist Marquis Childs, who invited him to join a discussion at his house with Lippmann, Edward R. Murrow, Elmer Davis, and other leading journalists on how to blunt the influence of the China lobby by revealing its secret and unsavory finances. (In a striking foreshadowing of the Iran-Contra affair, its operatives had used monies derived from drug trades and refunneled American aid to China to finance its public-relations campaigns and to reward its friends in office.) After some consideration Acheson demurred, Lippmann suspected, because too many important Democrats were implicated.

On the left, the fact that the Korean War came so quickly to Truman's aid, as well as Chiang's and Rhee's, predictably led to the suspicion that it might have been orchestrated for that purpose. I. F. Stone, the storm bird of radical journalism, whose byline had successively appeared in *PM*, Bartley Crum's *New York Star*, and Ted. O. Thackeray's *Daily Compass*, claimed to detect such a pattern in his 1952 *Hidden History of the Korean War*. (Having run out of radical newspapers to write for, and shunned by the mainstream press, Stone founded his legendary *I. F. Stone's Weekly* the next year.) It remains doubtful that American aims in Korea were concerted quite so deftly, although at the time policy makers did quite successfully obfuscate the fact that America was intervening in a civil war, as, later, in Vietnam, as well as the likelihood that they were aware some sort of large-scale intervention was coming.

In later years Truman would say that his decision to go to war in Korea was almost instantaneous. There were, however, two war councils before it was announced. From his plane, Truman had ordered that a "Very Important Dinner" precede the conference on Sunday evening at Blair House, to which General Omar Bradley, the service secretaries, and the service chiefs were added as well as the party that met him at the airport. A meal of fried chicken, shoestring potatoes, asparagus, biscuits, and, for dessert, vanilla ice cream with chocolate sauce: everyone agreed that it was excellent, but there was little else to discuss, since Truman had forbidden any talk about why they had gathered until the meal was finished—Louis Johnson tried to read a statement and was cut off—and the servants had gone. (Why did he bother with the dinner? Was it because of some instinct that a warriors' banquet was in order on such a momentous occasion? On December 7, 1941, keeping an earlier date, FDR had dined on sandwiches and beer with Edward R. Murrow.)

After the table was cleared, Acheson was invited to begin, which he did with "a darkening report of great confusion." The air filled with the clouds of cigarette smoke—the invariable accompaniment in the forties to serious deliberation and intellection, as well as socializing, and which the nonsmoking Truman had learned to tolerate. Rather than dominating the war council, Truman let Acheson lead the discussion, although Truman had been heard to say earlier, "We can't let the UN down! We can't let the UN down!" in indicating his position. Everyone was canvassed for his opinion, and their undisputed consensus was that a line had to be drawn somewhere, and here it was. Within the year, Dean Acheson would say: "If the best minds in the world had set out to find the worst possible location to fight this damnable war, politically and militarily, the unanimous choice would have been Korea."

Once again, as after Pearl Harbor nine years before, the tense hours were filled with meetings in Washington, DC, and New York. At the conclusion of his first war council, Truman ordered the Seventh Fleet to neutralize Formosa, and General MacArthur was told to empty his supply houses to provide for the South Koreans, and to offer limited air support. The next day brought more dire news, more fateful decisions. At the end of the day, after declaring that the South Koreans would receive the unreserved assistance of American navy and army forces in the Far East, Truman declared sorrowfully to his advisors: "I do not want war. Everything I have done in the last five years has been to try to avoid making a decision such as I have had to make tonight."

(So much for his vainglorious declaration twenty years later that it had not cost him more than a moment's reflection.)

Of course, as he conceived the situation, there was no alternative. Korea, which Acheson and the Joint Chiefs of Staff had so recently considered irrelevant to America's strategic interests in Asia, was now poised "like a dagger" at Japan. Standing by the enormous globe that Ike had used during the war and presented to him as a gift, he told George Elsey "that Korea was 'the Greece of the Far East,' and that if the United States acted as it had in Greece, it might stop further aggression. 'But if we just stand by, they'll move into Iran and they'll take over the whole Middle East . . . and keep right on going and swallow up one piece of Asia after another . . . and no telling what would happen in Europe."

"Step by step, in six fateful days, searching for alternatives before each move, my father found himself fighting his third war." Margaret Truman's précis is not that of an eyewitness, but undoubtedly represented how her father saw his role in the latest crisis. If on Sunday night he hoped that it might be sufficient to arm and assist the South Koreans, his course was set by Tuesday evening when another war council was convened, and a message circulated from MacArthur saying that a collapse of the ROK seemed to be "imminent." The next day, MacArthur flew to Korea for an inspection tour, after which, predictably, he reported that only American troops could prevent a North Korean takeover. On Thursday morning, in Washington, Truman ordered three regiments be deployed to the peninsula and sent into action, thus launching the war on the Asian mainland that, only a few months before, MacArthur had warned would be "madness." (Twelve years later, he gave the same advice to John F. Kennedy, who nonetheless then sent "advisors" to Vietnam.)

There were some missteps along the way, and another, which might have been disastrous, was averted when Acheson persuaded the president, against his original inclination, *not* to accept Chiang Kai-shek's offer of thirty thousand troops. Acheson argued that the troops would be poorly trained, badly armed, and more trouble to transport from Formosa than their services would have been worth. More important, no doubt, in the secretary's calculations was that it would have given the generalissimo a leverage in Asian affairs which few sensible China hands, as opposed to the China lobby, wished to see. It was odd, in any case, that Truman would ever have wished to be indebted to a regime of bloodthirsty brigands, as he thought of the Nationalists.

Truman took great satisfaction in how the United Nations had been brought into the affair, from the first resolution condemning the aggression of North Korea to the subsequent resolution in the Security Council authorizing an armed response, and another in the General Assembly affirming it. In a historic press conference on Wednesday, June 29, Truman stated, in response to the question a reporter said "everyone is asking in this country," "We are not at war." "No comment," he replied when asked whether ground troops or the atomic bomb was being considered; he characterized the North Korean invasion as a "bandit raid" and agreed, with utmost casualness, that it would be correct to characterize the United Nations response as a "police action." At the end of the six days he sent a handwritten note to Dean Acheson regarding his actions that week, whose results showed "you are a great Secretary of State."

The Americans congratulated themselves on making the most of the Russians' "colossal blunder" in continuing to boycott the Security Council, enabling the Americans to pass their resolutions and to enlist more than a dozen members of the organization in their campaign, with Great Britain and, oddly, Turkey contributing the most troops. Years later, Dean Acheson explained for the television cameras why the Soviet Union's decision making was too ponderous to reverse a disastrous mistake in time. Actually, as we now know, Stalin knew perfectly well what he was doing, whether it was wise or not. Malik, who had expected to return to the Security Council, was ordered not to; Stalin calculated that the intervention in Korea would fail, and the UN's involvement would do grave damage to an institution that was then dominated by the United States.

In the six days after the North Korean incursion, anxious crowds could observe the crush of official cars at the White House gates heightening the atmosphere of history-in-the-making, although the making went on in cloistered rooms. Truman paid obeisance to the spirit as well as the letter of bipartisanship when he invited the congressional leaders of both parties into the deliberations. (Only Robert Taft ventured some sharp qualifications of his support.) On Friday, Congress, the public, and the apparatus of opinion joined in applauding the rush to war, although, significantly, there were no great massed expressions of enthusiasm in New York or anywhere else comparable to what had happened in 1917. If, as Robert Sherwood wrote of the Second World War, the soldiers who waged it were disillusioned before it began, it could be said of the Korean War that the public was already weary of it. After V-J Day the green flash of Utopia spread, for a moment, along the historical horizon; now it was the battlefield that loomed again; as William Manchester writes, after 4:00 a.m. on June 24 in Korea, when the North Korean howitzers led the attack, it had been "wartime once more, on all the Angeluses of the world."

The national magazines and the big daily newspapers that had been divided on intervention in Europe up to Pearl Harbor joined the lords of the Hill, whom Truman had ceremoniously consulted, the Republican establishment, and the Democratic politicos in supporting intervention on the mainland of Asia. John Foster Dulles, the pontifical Wall Street lawyer who had been Dewey's secretary of state in waiting, and had joined the administration to negotiate a peace treaty with Japan, had addressed the Korean Parliament on June 19, assuring them: "You are not alone." He rejoiced in Truman's decision to act, telling an aide traveling with him that he was "the greatest President in history." Old antagonists lent their support. "I whole-heartedly agree with and support the difficult decision you have made," Governor Dewey cabled—although he wrote his mother in Oswego, Michigan, that the administration had gotten itself into a situation that "a more skillful diplomacy and stronger action" might have prevented. Talking with his friend George Gallup, Dewey censured Acheson's Press Club speech, but gibed that Truman "wasn't smart enough" to know that Korea was part of the Asian mainland.

On the newsstand, the *New York Times*, the *Herald Tribune*, the *Wall Street Journal*, *Time*, *Life*, the *New Republic*, and the *New Yorker* (but not the *Nation*) all stood in support. Particularly striking is the brief season of favor that Truman enjoyed with Time Inc., which of all American media empires seemed to be most formidably of the hour after the war, the most proprietary about how to maintain the American empire (had not *its* proprietor, Henry Luce, proclaimed the "American Century"?), the most Asia-minded? His biographer Alan Brinkley writes of Luce being "uncharacteristically supportive of the Truman administration" at this time. A typically mind-reading editorial in *Life* claimed: "The reaction of the plain man seems to have been, 'At last! It was the only thing to do!' Both the President and the plain man are to be congratulated for . . . good judgment on a very complicated matter." But it *was* a very complicated affair; and although John Lewis Gaddis states that the shock of the North Korean invasion was equal to that of Pearl Harbor, and the effect on American policy as profound, yet the psychological effect on the public was not comparable: there was none of the rage and, as it turned out, little of the lasting resoluteness. The decision to intervene in Korea brought another of those brief, intense, ultimately delusive moments of national unity that had occurred before in Truman's turbulent regime: at his ascension after Roosevelt's death, on the V-Days, on his election in his own right.

"East, west, north, and south, American newspapers reported overwhelming support of the President in their areas. 'The White House gang is today enormously popular, incredibly popular,' even the *Chicago Tribune* found itself saying." So Eric Goldman recalls the summer of consensus, when even McCarthy was silenced for a moment, and the White House wondered that Robert Taft, who had disgraced himself by embracing McCarthy, was said to have "joined the United Nations."

"For one moment," Goldman writes, "suspended weirdly in the bitter debates of the postwar, the reckless plunge of the North Korean Communists and the bold response of Harry Truman had united America, united it as it had not been since the distant confetti evening of V-J."

Among the thousands of Americans who wrote to the White House to applaud the march to war there were undoubtedly many who expressed some version of the sentiment quoted in David McCullough's biography: "'You may be a whiskey guzzling poker playing old buzzard, as some say,' wrote a Republican from Illinois, 'but by damn, for the first time since old Teddy left there in March of 1909, the United States has a grass roots American in the White House.'"

It hardly matters that Truman's correspondent mistook the patrician Theodore Roosevelt's common touch for grass roots; what he meant was that Truman was *one of us*. So much greater the frustration, within a matter of weeks, for those who saw him in that light when it became clear that he was not only standing by Acheson, but reposing even more trust and responsibility in the northeastern elitists whom they associated with the New Deal. One of the first things that Truman did after the invasion was to recall Averell Harriman from Paris, where as the "ambassador to Europe" he had been the important American on the Continent, to be his de facto national security advisor; he did so on the advice of Acheson. General Marshall agreed to serve as secretary of state, he hoped for no longer than six months, on the condition that Robert Lovett, who had been his deputy at the State Department, would be appointed his undersecretary and successor.

By the end of July it was back to rancor as usual. The turbulent political climate of Truman's remaining years in office was owed largely to the fortunes of war, which in Korea seemed to consist of nothing but reversals of fortune. There was a near-rout of the outnumbered, out-armored, undertrained United Nations forces in the first weeks of the war; some who surrendered or were captured were bound and bayoneted or shot. In an almost Homeric episode, their field commander, Major General William Dean, was separated from his men during a retreat and was presumed dead; actually, he wandered, lost, for six weeks, sick and wounded, before he was turned over by some South Korean peasants to the Northern command, which secretly kept him prisoner until the truce. Whether advancing or retreating, the GIs came to fear and loathe the plunging gorges, the gullied paths, and the fetid, stinking rice paddies that defined the terrain. "I thought the Hürtgen Forest was bad and Normandy, but they were nothing like this," said a sergeant caught up in the early retreat from Taegu. "This was awful." MacArthur made his daring landing behind North Korean lines at Inchon, and, joining with the American troops pushing north from Pusan, sent the North Koreans reeling across the 38th parallel, reclaiming Seoul along the way. At their conference at Wake Island in October, General MacArthur assured Truman there was no likelihood that the Chinese would enter the war, although their "volunteers" had been seen far south of the Yalu River; on November 26, he was obliged to report that they had come in "with both feet." Their nightly attacks, heralded by trumpet blasts and tinkling cymbals, badly shook the American troops and their allies, and sent them into a retreat down the peninsula. The UN forces began to inch back in the new year.

Averell Harriman called Korea "the sour little war"—presumably in contrast to the Spanish-American, which John Hay called "the splendid little war." From the beginning, it seemed an inglorious affair. The big war might have been fought in a mood of unreality, as we have quoted C. Wright Mills, and been clouded with disillusionment from the start, but it was fought with an unwavering resolve, and as the end approached, the GIs could afford to comport themselves with the bravado of conquerors ("Kilroy was here") even if the *Yank* cartoonist Bill Mauldin's perennially unshaven and shabby Willie and Joe hardly looked the part, shuffling into some Italian hill town; whereas in Korea a grim fatalism was the best that could be mustered by the troops. "That's the way the ball bounces," they said. The policy which justified their sacrifices was marked Top Secret and locked away in Truman's safe.

In 1945, the apocalypse had come and gone, and with its end came a sort of Egyptian sense that the world might be settling into a pattern down whose grooves things might run for hundreds of years— who could tell for how long? George Orwell, Stephen Spender, Lewis Mumford, and the young Robert Lowell all testified to this sense, as in a few years did the Beats. The post-historical transit was evident even, or especially, in movies turned out by the dream factories in Culver City and Burbank with titles like *Tomorrow Is Forever* and *Kiss Tomorrow Goodbye* and *Till the End of Time* and, most famously, *From Here to Eternity*. In New York City, soon after the war, a young veteran, Louis Simpson, threw his wristwatch from a high window "because we are all living in Eternity now," and after a few other extravagances the future Pulitzer Prize winner for poetry was carried off to the madhouse; later, Allen Ginsberg put the episode into *Howl*: "who threw watches off the roof to cast their ballot / for / Eternity outside of Time, & alarm clocks fell on their heads / every day for the next decade." What did the imagination of disaster expect? Perhaps it would be something like the Spenglerian "Second Religiousness" expected by the Beats, perhaps something as monstrously evil as Orwell imagined in *1984*, or, as later on appeared rather likelier, something more subtly oppressive, like an endlessly prolonged Eisenhower administration, in Gore Vidal's phrase, "the dull terror of the Great Golfer."

Of course, that is not at all what happened, although in the "tranquilized *Fifties*" it seemed it might. The green light of Utopia that briefly flashed at the end of the war would appear again, and retrospect discerns vivid patterns in the late forties that were invisible then. Ahead lay an allegorical landscape: an Age of Anxiety peopled by an Invisible Man, an Irrational Man, an Organization Man, dominated by a Power Elite and promising (a mirage) the Affluent Society. In this landscape, New York remained, as always, the great City of Ambition. Robert Lowell sings, "and the Republic summons Ike, / the mausoleum in her heart." But in the meantime, the Lonely Crowd had reached the center of the forest and found what was there. The Brazen Age had lasted three years, ten months, and ten days.

Acknowledgments

A great town is a great solitude, in the ancient Roman phrase: *Magna civitas, magna solitudo.* Writing a book is a lonely business, too, but when for many years you write about the Terrible Town, as Henry James called New York, I find you come away indebted to a very friendly crowd that has assembled over time, even before the book is conceived.

It is a pleasure long deferred to offer enormous thanks to Sandra Dijkstra, my agent and loyal friend, as well as to her associate, Elise Capron, and all the rest of the grand team at the Dijkstra Literary Agency. Years ago, when Sandy asked if I had a book I wanted to write, I gave her a few typed pages ambitiously projecting one about postwar New York. She phoned a few hours later to point out that Gore Vidal had handed me the perfect title—*The Brazen Age.*

To my continuing good fortune, the publisher that Sandy found was Pantheon, whose early years were on "Genius Row," in Washington Square, during the Second World War, and whose founding editors came out of the intellectual migration of the 1930s and '40s, as did many of its authors. The acquiring editor at Pantheon, Sara Bershtel, has been a dear friend ever since.

Shelley Wanger inherited *The Brazen Age* when it was more of a work in contemplation than in progress; and over numerous drafts, visions and revisions, changes in direction and points of view, I have had the benefit of her lynx-like editorial eye, the pleasure of her wit and fun in conversation, the example of her Shakhanovite work ethic, and the final push over the wall, for all of which I am grateful indeed. Her able assistant, Terezia Cicelova, has been equal to any number of enormous changes at the last minute. My thanks to Kevin Bourke, my production editor, and to Athena Angelos, my photo researcher. The copyediting by Patrick Dillon was searching, meticulous, and above and beyond.

I have discovered reasons for gratitude in the past at the same time I was accumulating them in the present; long-ago conversations likely forgotten by my interlocutor, undergraduate arguments over a novel or a poem, ancient controversies whose origins are untraceable, turn out to inform one's present opinions. "The Rains of Empire: Camus in New York," an essay I published in *MLN* (1997), which I draw upon in this book, is dedicated to my teacher Claire D. Tremaine, who introduced me to existentialism when it was still in flower. My oldest friends, Patrick Mills and Ben W. Pesta, who shared my fascination with the postwar era—quickened it, really, in the case of Ben—did not live to read this book, although they encouraged its progress.

My profoundest debts are to my parents, Max and Antonia Reid, who inspired my interest in the New Deal era, and lived through it. My mother took great pride in telling how she came to cast her first Democratic ballot as an underage voter in Utah, when her Republican uncle escorted her to a polling place with stern instructions to vote for Herbert Hoover; in the privacy of the voting booth, she pulled the lever for FDR and became a lifelong Democrat. Early on, my father put me into the habit of haunting bookstores, and some of the first books he bought me were about Roosevelt and his campaigns. I still have a copy of *Behind the Ballots* by James A. Farley, signed in his green ink. I am so grateful to them both.

For illumination, information, moral support, and excellent company, I am grateful, in order of appearance, to: Jonathan Jerald, L. Randolph Skidmore III, Judith L. Kahn, Ernest W. Machen III, Jeremy Larner, Raquel Scherr, Richard Rodriguez, Joe Christiano, Sean Wolfe, Nikolas Koskoros, Lewis Klausner, Peter Manso, Ariel Parkinson, Peter Selz, John R. Gillis, the late Garrett Scott, Sam Witt, Philippe Aronson, Augustin Trapenard, Scott Mikal-Heine, Benjamin Blustein, Andrew Meyer, Julian Harake, Erik Thorrin, John H. Pujol, Sasha Sosnowski.

Leonard Michaels, a great and loyal friend for thirty years, was often on my mind as I wrote this book. Many of his most brilliant stories and essays, including "Murderers," and "The Zipper" (inspired by Rita Hayworth's performance in *Gilda*), inhabit the New York of the 1940s. When he married Katharine Ogden in the 1990s and moved to Italy, where they lived in Rome and Umbria, Lenny embraced e-mail with the fervor of an early convert, and, thanks to that medium, he and I had substantially completed what we called the "genius book"—an anthology he had conceived to combat the postmodernist prejudice that geniuses don't exist—when he was taken ill; he died suddenly and too soon, 2003. I owe to our discussions the understanding of how central the idea of genius was to the New York Intellectuals.

Rubén Martínez, a staff writer at *L.A. Weekly* when we met, is now the holder of the Fletcher Jones Chair in Literature and Writing at Loyola Marymount University, and the author of many distinguished books, including most recently *Desert America*. Keeping up with him has been an adventure, and his support has been steadfast. Rubén contributed an essay to a book I edited for Pantheon, *Sex, Death, and God in L.A.* (1992), which led to many friendships that have been great events in my life.

David Freedlander, who was until recently the senior political correspondent of *The Daily Beast*, has the greatest knowledge of current New York City politics of any journalist I know; he has also deepened my sense of its political past. Our friendship, which began in Berkeley a decade ago, has enriched and enlivened my days ever since. No one has done more for me lately in all matters New York than David.

Most of the research and almost all of the actual writing of this book has been done in Berkeley, California. At the Library of the University of California at Berkeley, I am grateful for many kindnesses over the years to Joyce Ford at the privileges desk of the Doe Library and to her worthy successor, Sean Grant. I owe a similar debt to Eric Gerlach at the Flora Lawson Hewlett Library at the Graduate Theological Union Library. The staff at the Environmental Design Library, too, has been unfailingly helpful.

I have found a view of the San Francisco Bay a fine prospect for contemplating the brilliant and terrifying last century in which New York was in some ways at the center, but in which Berkeley, its poets and its scientists, its revolutionists and its dissidents, also played no small part. But most important, at every stage and in every extremity, this book has gained from the wit, learning, fine editorial instincts, and almost unfailing patience of my cherished wife, Jayne L. Walker, to whom the dedication is the palest acknowledgment of my immeasurable debt.

Notes

INTRODUCTION

xiv "V-letters by the bale": Truman Capote, *Breakfast at Tiffany's* (New York: Random House, 1958), 16.

xiv "stories of a long-lost world": John Cheever, Preface, *The Stories of John Cheever* (1978; rpt. New York: Ballantine Books, 1980), ix.

xv "the rise of New York": Oswald Spengler, *The Decline of the West* (*Der Untergang des Abendlandes*), trans. and with notes by Charles Francis Atkinson, vol. 2 (1928; rpt. New York: Knopf, 1980), 99.

xvi "a wedge of geese": E. B. White, *Here Is New York* (New York: Harper & Row, 1949), 51.

xvi American empire: See Franz Schurmann, *The Logic of World Power: An Inquiry into the Origins, Currents, and Contradictions of World Politics* (New York: Pantheon, 1974), 4ff. Schurmann's is a classic analysis of Roosevelt's vision for a global American imperium and what the vision became under Truman and his successors. "By the end of the 1940s," he sums up, "a new American world order had clearly emerged. America 'lost' Russia in 1945 and China in 1949, it gained the remainder of the world, which it proceeded to energize, organize, and dominate in a most active way." 5. Although Schurmann considered himself an anti-imperialist, he did not regard the American empire in its original conception by Roosevelt as a globalized New Deal, as the endlessly malefic Leviathan with which "empire" is customarily identified on the Left. In *Imperium*, a sweeping essay titled "American Foreign Policy and Its Thinkers," originally published in *New Left Review*, September / October 2013, Perry Anderson writes: "Schurmann's imaginative grasp of the impending mutation in the American imperium remains unsurpassed."

PROLOGUE

3 With such news: This account of Roosevelt's campaign in 1944 draws on James McGregor Burns, *Roosevelt: The Soldier of Freedom* (New York and London: Harcourt Brace Jovanovich, 1970), 521–31; Doris Kearns Goodwin, *No Ordinary Time: Franklin and Eleanor Roosevelt: The Home Front in World War II* (New York: Simon and Schuster, 1994), 546–53; Conrad Black, *Franklin Roosevelt: Champion of Freedom* (New York: Public Affairs, 2003), 1014–23; and contemporary accounts as noted.

4   "He plays the part": Robert E. Sherwood, *Roosevelt and Hopkins: An Intimate History* (New York: Harper & Brothers, 1948), 821.

4   "I ought not": Jonathan Daniels, *White House Witness, 1942–1945* (Garden City, NY: Doubleday, 1975), 125.

5   "and make a hell": Richard Norton Smith, *Thomas E. Dewey and His Times* (New York: Simon and Schuster, 1982), 103ff.

6   "sweeping through every": John Gunther, *Inside U.S.A.* (New York and London: Harper & Row, 1947), 529.

6   mightily assisted by: On Willkie's defeat of Dewey, see Smith, 305–12.

7   "These Republican leaders": There are accounts of FDR's "Fala" speech in the biographies, including those named above. For a contemporary account, see Sherwood, 832–33.

10 "and while the rain": William D. Hassett, *Off the Record with FDR, 1942–1945* (New Brunswick, NJ: Rutgers University Press, 1958), 279.

12 "The three greatest men": On Roosevelt and African Americans, see John Hope Franklin, *From Slavery to Freedom: A History of American Negroes*, 2nd ed., revised and enlarged (New York: Alfred A. Knopf, 1956), 512–33. For an essential discussion of the devil's bargain FDR made with southern politicians to pass the New Deal, while providing employment and relief to African Americans through its agencies, see Ira Katznelson, *Fear Itself: The New Deal and the Origins of Our Time* (2013; rpt. Liveright, 2014), passim. In August 1944, as black voters had reason to consider, Roosevelt made the strongest show of federal authority to enforce civil rights since the end of Reconstruction, by giving the attorney general the means to break a company strike in Philadelphia by streetcar conductors called to protest a federal order to hire qualified blacks. On this largely forgotten episode, which presaged the armed role of the federal government in the civil rights revolution of the 1950s and '60s, see Doris Kearns Goodwin, *No Ordinary Time: Franklin and Eleanor Roosevelt: The Home Front in World War II* (New York: Simon and Schuster, 1994), 537–39, 541.

14 The furriers, however: On racketeering in the garment trade, see Steve Fraser and Gary Gerstle, eds., *The Rise and Fall of the New York Order, 1930–1980* (Princeton, NJ: Princeton University Press, 1989), 238–58.

15 "but they also came": Warren Moscow, *What Have You Done for Me Lately? The Ins and Outs of New York City Politics* (Englewood Cliffs, NJ: Prentice Hall, 1967), 59.

15 At Twenty-third Street: The canard that FDR, who appointed more Jews to high positions and relied more on Jewish counselors than any other president, repaid the adulation of Jews in America by callously abandoning to their fate the Jews of Europe, including those attempting to flee in America, is amply refuted by Robert N. Rosen in *Saving the Jews: Franklin D. Roosevelt and the Holocaust* (New York: Thunder's Mouth, 2006), a lawyerly brief which comes bearing the weighty imprimatur of Gerhard L. Weinberg, and by Richard Breitman and Allan J. Lichtman in their magisterial *FDR and the Jews* (Cambridge, MA: Belknap Press, 2013). Although he would surely have benefited from knowing what we know now, and, as a politician answerable to his constituents, from being unconstrained by the endemic anti-immigrant and anti-Semitic prejudices of the time, popular and institutional, as in his own state department—which he was not—nonetheless, the record shows that at the very least he was uniquely vehement among world

leaders in denouncing Nazi anti-Semitism before the war and to protecting Jews during it. I agree entirely with Lars-Erik Nelson that the calumnies directed against Roosevelt in regard to Yalta and the Holocaust reflect what Denis Brogan, in a famous essay called "The Illusion of American Omnipotence" (1951), according to which any great reverse or perceived danger for America can be accounted for only by the foolishness or knavery on the part of certain Americans; see Nelson, "Clinton and His Enemies," in the *New York Review of Books*, January 20, 2000.

18 FDR mixed drinks: Goodwin, 550–51.
19 "a Republican audience": Hassett, 280.
20 When John Gunther: Gunther, 64–75.
22 "So to my simple": Burns, 526; Goodwin, 559–51.
23 "Now, really—which": Burns, 529.
26 "With that phrase": Ted Morgan, *FDR: A Biography* (New York: Simon and Schuster, 1985), 113.
28 "I have no reason": Sherwood, 830.
28 "I still think": Hassett, 294.
30 Shahn's posters were: On the CIO PAC and "People's Program for 1944," see Joseph Gaer, *The First Round: The Story of the CIO Political Action Committee* (New York: Duell, Sloan and Pearce, 1944), passim.
31 "Mr. President in 1948?": Burns, 552.
32 "The 1944 election": Michael Barone, *Our Country: America from Roosevelt to Reagan* (New York: Free Press, 1990), 179–80.
32 "as cowboy, Rough Rider": Henry F. Pringle, *Theodore Roosevelt: A Biography* (1931; rpt. New York: Harcourt, Brace, 1956), 360.
33 "As the skies": Isaiah Berlin, "Franklin D. Roosevelt," in *Personal Impressions*, ed. Henry Hardy (New York: Viking Press, 1981), 26.
33 "This is what makes": Berlin, 28–29.
33 "The more businessmen": Alfred Kazin, "The Historian at the Center," in *Contemporaries* (Boston: Little, Brown, 1962), 418.
33 "the America of the future": Frances Perkins, *The Roosevelt I Knew* (New York: Viking Press, 1946), 13.
34 "Mourn for us now": W. H. Auden, *The Age of Anxiety*, in *Collected Longer Poems* (New York: Random House, 1969), 331.

PART I: EMPIRE AND COMMUNICATIONS

35 "The rumor of a great": *New York Panorama: A Companion to the WPA Guide to New York City* (1938; rpt. with a new introduction by Alfred Kazin, New York: Pantheon, 1984), 3.

1 City Lights

37 "My last image": Albert Camus, *American Journals*, trans. Hugh Levick (London: Abacus, 1990), 25.
38 For Wilson the: Edmund Wilson, review of *The Stranger*, *New Yorker*, April 13, 1946, 99–100.
38 America's most admired: Edmund Wilson, "A Dissenting Opinion on

Kafka," in *Classics and Commercials: A Literary Chronicle of the Forties* (New York: Farrar, Straus and Giroux, 1950), 383–92.

38 "Our generation had": William Barrett, *The Truants: Adventures Among the Intellectuals* (Garden City, NY: Anchor/Doubleday, 1982), 101.

39 That night, crossing: Camus, 31–32.

40 This "pioneer spectacle": Frederick Lewis Allen, *The Big Change: America Transforms Itself, 1900–1950* (1952; rpt. New York: Bantam Books, 1965), 13–14.

40 "The merciless lights": Quoted in Peter Conrad, *Imagining America* (New York: Oxford University Press, 1980), 80.

40 "For anyone interested": Gore Vidal, *United States: Essays, 1952–1992* (New York: Random House, 1993), 1068.

40 Edwin Denby, the dance: Edwin Denby, *Dancers, Buildings, and People in the Streets* (New York: Horizon Press, 1986), 262.

2 Cultural Capital

42 "The most important": John Gunther, *Inside U.S.A.* (New York and London: Harper & Row, 1947), 550.

43 But the golden age: John Cheever, "The Enormous Radio," in *The Stories of John Cheever* (New York: Ballantine Books, 1980), 37.

43 In 1945, when: Mary McCarthy, *Sights and Spectacles: Theatre Chronicles, 1937–1959* (New York: Meridian Books, 1957), 76.

43 In 1947, the year: Mary McCarthy, *On the Contrary* (New York: Farrar, Straus and Cudahy, 1961), 6.

45 "managed to define": Gore Vidal, *Palimpsest: A Memoir* (New York: Random House, 1995), 129.

45 "In the late forties": Vidal, 127.

46 "In January 1948": "Television," in Kenneth T. Jackson, ed., *The Encyclopedia of New York City* (New Haven and London: Yale University Press, 1995), 1159.

46 This standstill was: Erik Barnouw, *Tube of Plenty: The Evolution of American Television* (New York: Oxford University Press, 1975), 113.

46 "Hollywood," Eric Hobsbawm observes: Eric Hobsbawm, *The Age of Empire, 1875–1914* (New York: Pantheon, 1987), 240.

48 For the huge sum: Richard Schickel, *D. W. Griffith* (New York: Simon and Schuster, 1985), 416.

48 Gloria Swanson: Quoted in Matthew Bernstein, *Walter Wanger: Hollywood Independent* (Berkeley: University of California Press, 1994), 61.

48 During World War II: Arthur Laurents, *Original Story By: A Memoir of Broadway and Hollywood* (New York: Knopf, 2000), 32.

49 In the early twenties: On Hearst's moviemaking, see David Nasaw, *The Chief: The Life of William Randolph Hearst* (Boston: Houghton Mifflin, 2000), 305ff. and passim.

51 The Rockefellers waited: See Daniel Okrent, *Great Fortune: The Story of Rockefeller Center* (New York: Viking, 2003), 239–45.

55 As Raymond Rubicam: See Stephen Fox, *The Mirror Makers: A History of American Advertising and Its Creators* (New York: Morrow, 1984), 127–40.

57 Hamill describes Weegee's: Pete Hamill, *Piecework: Writings on Men and*

Women, Fools and Heroes, Lost Cities, Vanished Friends, Small Pleasures, Large Calamities, and How the Weather Was (Boston: Little, Brown, 1996), 17.

3 *The Greater City*

60 As the *New Yorker*: Philip Hamburger, *Friends Talking in the Night: Sixty Years of Writing for* The New Yorker (New York: Knopf, 1999), 268.

60 In fact, the real: Moscow, 2–3.

61 "In wealth, resources": Allan Nevins and John Krout, eds., *The Greater City: New York, 1898–1948* (New York: Columbia University Press, 1948), 7.

62 As the historian: Hugh Thomas, *Armed Truce: The Beginnings of the Cold War, 1945–46* (New York: Atheneum, 1984), see pages 323ff.

62 Surveying the wreckage: Stephen Spender, *European Witness* (New York: Reynal and Hitchcock, 1946), 239–40.

63 The real work was: Anatole Broyard, *When Kafka Was the Rage: A Greenwich Village Memoir* (New York: Carol Southern Books, 1993), 27.

64 "In Manila Bay": James Salter, *Burning the Days: Recollection* (New York: Random House, 1997), 109.

64 From one end: Spender, 240.

64 Just as the lights: John Gunther, *Inside U.S.A.* (New York and London: Harper & Row, 1947), 549.

64 The cities of the West: Edmund Wilson, "A Dissenting Opinion on Kafka," in *Classics and Commercials: A Literary Chronicle of the Forties* (New York: Farrar, Straus and Giroux, 1950), 47.

66 From her youth: Marya Mannes, *The New York I Know* (Philadelphia: Lippincott, 1961), 15.

66 "There is some sense": Felix Riesenberg, *East Side, West Side* (New York: Harcourt, Brace, 1927), 12–13.

67 Thumbing through: Gunther, 553–54.

67 In the text accompanying: Andreas Feininger, *New York in the Forties* (New York: Dover Publications, 1978).

4 *Babylon Revisited*

68 "Before the Civil War": Lewis Mumford, "The Metropolitan Milieu," in *America and Alfred Stieglitz: A Collective Portrait*, ed. Waldo Frank et al. (New York: Literary Guild, 1934), 33.

68 As late as 1800: Henry Adams, *History of the United States of America During the Administrations of Thomas Jefferson* (New York: Library of America, 1986), 20.

68 New York entrepreneurs: Raymond Vernon, *Metropolis 1985* (Cambridge, MA: Harvard University Press, 1960), 7.

69 In 1815, as the Napoleonic: Eric E. Lampard, *Industrial Revolution: Interpretations and Perspectives* (American Historical Association, 1957), 1–2.

70 Toward the end: Edith Wharton, *A Backward Glance* (London: Appleton-Century, 1934), 79.

70 Mark Twain, passing: Bayrd Still, *Mirror for Gotham: New York as Seen by Contemporaries from Dutch Days to the Present* (New York: New York Uni-

versity Press, 1956). For Twain and other observers in the 1840s, see pp. 125–39.

71 Henry Adams wrote: Henry Adams, *The Education of Henry Adams: An Autobiography* (Boston: Houghton Mifflin, 1918), 499.

71 Unlike Chicago's, most: Jean-Paul Sartre, "Individualism and Conformity in the United States," in *Literary and Philosophical Essays*, trans. Annette Michelson (New York: Criterion, 1955), 104.

72 In John Dos Passos's novel: John Dos Passos, *Manhattan Transfer* (1925; rpt. Boston: Houghton Mifflin, 2000), 49.

72 Edwin G. Burrows and Mike Wallace note: Edwin G. Burrows and Mike Wallace, *Gotham: A History of New York City to 1898* (New York: Oxford University Press, 1999), see pp. 111–31.

73 "A map of Europe": Konrad Bercovici, *Around the World in New York* (New York: Century, 1924), 20–21.

74 Not so Jews, who: Henry James, *The American Scene* (1907; rpt. with an introduction and notes by Leon Edel, Bloomington: Indiana University Press, 1968), 132.

74 James toured the slums: James, 137.

74 Of the museum: James, 192.

75 After the Armistice: Quoted in Still, 291.

75 And New York by night: Paul Morand, *New York* (New York: Henry Holt, 1930), 39.

76 "Mongrel Manhattan": Ann Douglas, *Terrible Honesty: Mongrel Manhattan in the 1920s* (New York: Farrar, Straus and Giroux, 1995), passim.

77 Touring Ellis Island: Morand, 49.

77 Paradoxically, the quotas: Alan Dawley, *Struggles for Justice: Social Responsibility and the Liberal State* (Cambridge, MA: Belknap Press of Harvard University Press, 1991), 290.

77 Once, somewhere out west: See Donald Burner, *The Politics of Provincialism: The Democratic Party in Transition, 1918–1932* (Cambridge, MA: Harvard University Press, 1986), 210–16.

78 "It was characteristic": F. Scott Fitzgerald, "Echoes of the Jazz Age," in *The Crack-Up*, ed. Edmund Wilson (New York: New Directions, 1945), 14.

79 Langston Hughes's rueful: Langston Hughes, *The Big Sea* (New York: Knopf, 1940).

79 At the time, Alain Locke: See Douglas's rich synoptic account, 303–45.

79 As Peter Conrad observes: Peter Conrad, *The Art of the City: Views and Versions of New York* (New York: Oxford, 1984), 205.

80 Abroad when the stock market: Arthur M. Schlesinger Jr., *The Crisis of the Old Order, 1919–1932* (Boston: Houghton Mifflin, 1957), 145.

80 "Then I understood": Fitzgerald, "My Lost City," in *The Crack-Up*, 32.

80 Murray Kempton had noted: Murray Kempton, *Part of Our Time: Some Ruins and Monuments of the Thirties* (1955; rpt. New York: Modern Library, 1998), 4.

80 And as for the once: Edmund Wilson, "The Literary Consequences of the Crash," in *The Shores of Light: A Literary Chronicle of the Twenties and Thirties* (New York: Farrar, Straus and Young, 1952), 498.

81 At a drunken fund-raising: Tess Slesinger, *The Unpossessed* (New York: Simon and Schuster, 1934), 330–31.

81 The cafeteria at City College: Alfred Kazin, *Starting Out in the Thirties* (Boston: Little, Brown, 1965), 5.
81 In places like the Greenwich Village: Kazin, 66.
82 "Besides, New York": Saul Bellow, *Humboldt's Gift* (1975; rpt. New York: Avon, 1976), 11.

5 *Wandering Rocks*

83 The publishing heir: Cecil Beaton, *Cecil Beaton's New York* (Philadelphia: J. B. Lippincott, 1938), 238.
84 In *New York Intellect*: Thomas Bender, *New York Intellect: A History of Intellectual Life in New York City, from 1750 to the Beginning of Our Time* (New York: Knopf, 1987), 324–28.
84 "The drink, till Prohibition": Virgil Thomson, *Virgil Thomson* (New York: Knopf, 1967), 216.
85 One night in Harlem: Thomson, 217.
86 "I only know": Thomson, 217.
86 "The large colored night-clubs": Beaton, 168.
87 Tyler is writing: Beaton, 236.
87 "Handsome and as coolly": Alfred Kazin, *Starting Out in the Thirties* (Boston: Little, Brown, 1965), 15–16.
88 A great walker: Kazin, 134–35.
88 "Otis hated them": Kazin, 50.
89 Out of such poor: Kazin, 28–31.
89 Later in the thirties: Kazin, 137.

PART II: CITY OF REFUGE

1 *Exiles and Émigrés*

93 As Virgil Thomson: Virgil Thomson, *Virgil Thomson* (New York: Knopf, 1967), 337.
94 "And the writers fled": Benjamin Appel, "The Exiled Writers," *Saturday Review of Literature*, October 1940.
94 The few so-called: *Life*, October 1940.
95 "All the events": Appel, October 1940.
95 "The attractiveness of America": Appel.
96 It was only toward: H. Stuart Hughes, *The Sea Change: The Migration of Social Thought, 1930–1965* (New York: Harper & Row, 1975), 23.
96 Comparing their exile: Peter Gay, *Weimar Culture: The Outsider as Insider* (New York: Harper Torchbooks, 1970), xii–xiv.
97 About three-quarters: Introduction, Donald Fleming and Bernard Bailyn, *The Intellectual Migration: Europe and America, 1930–1960* (Cambridge, MA: Belknap Press of Harvard University Press, 1969), 3–10.
97 Out of Hungary: Kati Marton, *The Great Escape: Nine Jews Who Fled Hitler and Changed the World* (New York: Simon and Schuster, 2006), passim.

99 "God bless the U.S.A.": W. H. Auden, "On the Circuit" (1963), in *Collected Poems*, ed. Edward Mendelson (1976; rpt. New York: Modern Library, 2007), 731.

99 And since almost all: Quoted in Helmut F. Pfanner, *Exile in New York: German and Austrian Writers After 1933* (Detroit: Wayne State University Press, 1983), 39–41.

99 Thus, the novelist: Quoted in Pfanner, 38.

99 "God, what a terrifying": Christopher Isherwood, *Christopher and His Kind* (1976; rpt. New York: Avon, 1977), 339.

100 The sheer forbidding: Quoted in Pfanner, 39.

100 These imaginary examples: Mike Davis, "The Flames of New York," in *Dead Cities and Other Tales* (New York: New Press, 2002), 1–4.

100 "What will finish": H. L. Mencken, "Totentanz" (1924), in *A Second Mencken Chrestomathy*, ed. and with an introduction by Terry Teachout (New York: Knopf, 1994), 183.

100 Hans Natonek recalled: Quoted in Pfanner, 44.

100 Anyone whose papers: Quoted in Pfanner, 47.

101 Attracted by the commotion: Andrew Field, *Nabokov: His Life in Part* (New York: Viking Press, 1977), 232.

101 The driver: "'Lady'": Field, 232.

102 To the contrary: Field, 21.

102 Moreover, he was: Field, 16–17.

103 It is doubtful: Laura Fermi, *Illustrious Immigrants: The Intellectual Migration from Europe, 1930–1941* (Chicago: University of Chicago, 1968), 28–29.

104 "Perhaps it is for": Jeffrey Mehlman, *Émigré New York: French Intellectuals in Manhattan, 1940–1944* (Baltimore: Johns Hopkins University Press, 2000), 46–47.

104 There were the usual: Pfanner, 87.

104 "Not to grin": Jean-Paul Sartre, *Iron in the Soul* (*La Mort dans l'ame*), trans. Gerald Hopkins (London: Hamilton Hamish, 1950), 15.

105 "Once when I": Pfanner, 68ff.

105 In the thirties: See Fermi on the constellation, 4–11.

106 In the first years: Pfanner, 79.

106 Usually with little fuss: Pfanner, 78–81.

106 The novelist Claudia Martell: Pfanner, 98–99.

107 But the one language: Thomas Mann, *Letters of Thomas Mann, 1889–1955*, selected and trans. Richard and Clara Winston (New York: Knopf, 1971), 470.

107 The academy, within limits: Fermi, 74–78.

108 Between 1933 and 1940: Fermi, 372–73.

109 The Nuremberg Decrees: Fermi, 113.

109 Americans seemed genuinely: Erwin Panofsky, *Meaning in the Visual Arts: Papers in and on Art History* (Garden City, NY: Anchor, 1955), 326–27.

110 "I fondly remember": Panofsky, 321.

110 Cook had had a genius: Panofsky, 332.

110 The IFA graduated: Fleming and Bailyn, 570–73.

110 Under his entrepreneurial: Fleming and Bailyn, 570–73.

110 Panofsky was offered: Panofsky, 322.

111 "Where the communications": Panofsky, 328.

2 *The City at War*

112 "the great arsenal of democracy": "The Arsenal of Democracy: Introducing Lend-Lease," in Russell D. Buhite and David W. Levy, eds., *FDR's Fireside Chats* (Norman: University of Oklahoma Press, 2010), 163–73. The introduction of the phrase "national security" into national discourse is noted by Conrad Black, *Franklin Delano Roosevelt: Champion of Freedom* (New York: Public Affairs, 2003), 607. The "Fourth New Deal," in which jobs were created by rearmament and conscription, is proposed on 606.

112 "Wartime spending had brought": Thomas Kessner, *Fiorello H. La Guardia and the Making of Modern New York* (New York: McGraw-Hill, 1989), 539.

113 La Guardia appealed to Roosevelt: Kessner, 539–40.

113 The redistribution of population: Richard Rovere, "The Decline of New York City" in *American Mercury*, December 1944.

113 "I marveled at this city": Eric Sevareid, *Not So Wild a Dream* (1946; rpt. New York: Knopf, 1965), 29.

114 "a then-irresistible novel": James Salter, *Burning the Days: Recollection* (New York: Knopf, 1997), 85.

114 "The city was saturated": John Tytell, *Reading New York* (New York: Knopf, 2003).

114 "city without a country": Quoted in Bayrd Still, *Mirror for Gotham: New York as Seen by Contemporaries from Dutch Days to the Present* (New York: New York University Press, 1956), 189.

115 "a great and awed respect": Quoted from Carlos P. Romulo, *My Brother Americans* (1945), in Still, 328.

115 Edward Robb Ellis notes: Edward Robb Ellis, *The Epic of New York City*, with drawings by Jeanye Wong (1966; rpt. New York: Kondansha International, 1997), 58–59.

116 "After the shabbiness": Cecil Beaton, *Portrait of New York* (London: Batsford, 1948). Although announced as a revised edition of the 1938 *Cecil Beaton's New York*, this is a substantially different book in tone and contents; a postwar production.

PART III: WORDS, WORDS, WORDS

1 *Books Are Bullets*

120 Paul Fussell, who quotes: See the chapter "Reading in Wartime," in Paul Fussell, *Wartime: Understanding and Behavior in the Second World War* (1989; rpt. New York: Oxford University Press, 1990), 228–50. The figure for ASE editions is from Yoni Applebaum's useful article, "Publishers Gave Away 122,951,031 Books During World War II," *The Atlantic*, September 10, 2014.

120 "Isn't this in the spirit": Malcolm Cowley, *The Literary Situation* (New York: Viking Press, 1954), 116.

120 Between July 1943: On the ASE paperbacks, see Fussell, 239–42.

122 "Wartime was notably": Fussell, 244, 247.

123 "There were five, all Viking Portables": James Jones, *Some Came Running* (New York: Scribner, 1957), 23.

123 During the war: See Alice Payne Hackett, *Sixty Years of Bestsellers, 1895–1955* (New York: R. R. Bowker, 1956), 179–80.

124 "Literature as a business": Malcolm Cowley, "American Literature in Wartime," in *The Flower and the Leaf: A Contemporary Record of American Writing Since 1941*, ed. and with an introduction by Donald W. Faulkner (New York: Viking, 1985), 3.

124 "might as well have been mailed by slow boat": Cowley, 3.

125 "The one thing for which they were not prepared": Cowley, 10.

125 "If a student of taste wants to know": James D. Hart, *The Popular Book: A History of American Literary Taste* (New York: Oxford University Press, 1950), 281.

125 *Dangling Man*, Saul Bellow's: James Atlas, *Bellow: A Biography* (2000; rpt. New York: Modern Library, 2002), 102.

127 "astounded and terrified": Edmund Wilson, *Classics and Commercials: A Literary Chronicle of the Forties* (New York: Farrar, Straus, 1950), 204–08.

127 "people who don't matter": Alan Ansen, *The Table Talk of W. H. Auden*, ed. Nicholas Jenkins (Princeton, NJ: Ontario Review Press, 1990), 8.

127 Spiritual disquiet sold: "Maugham's Half & Half," in Gore Vidal, *United States: Essays, 1952–1992* (New York: Random House, 1993), 242–44.

128 In her historical study: Hackett, 6.

128 Maugham "dominated the movies": Vidal, 237.

129 "dissolving forms": Daniel J. Boorstin, *The Image: A Guide to Pseudo-Events in America* (1961; rpt. New York: Vintage, 1992), 145ff.

129 "A book or a story is a 'property'": Joan Didion, "In Hollywood," in *The White Album* (New York: Simon and Schuster, 1979), 159.

130 a whim of iron: Lucius Beebe, "New York's Most Glamorous Restaurant," in Alexander Klein, ed., *The Empire City* (New York: Rinehart, 1955), 135.

130 "But there is one thing": John Steinbeck, "The Making of a New Yorker," rpt. in Klein, 474.

130 "I don't think John Steinbeck": Elia Kazan, *A Life* (New York: Knopf, 1988), 785.

130 "Thus the multiplying kinds of images": Boorstin, 149.

130 "The electric light": Marshall McLuhan, *Understanding Media: The Extensions of Man* (2d ed., rpt. New York: Signet, 1964), 23.

2 *New York Discovers America*

131 "New York is not America": Ford Madox Ford, *New York Is Not America* (New York: A. & C. Boni, 1927).

132 "smacked of psychological regression": James D. Hart, *The Popular Book: A History of American Literary Taste* (New York: Oxford University Press, 1950), 279.

132 "So the new literature": Alfred Kazin, *On Native Grounds: An Interpretation of Modern American Prose Literature* (1942; rpt. New York: Harcourt Brace Jovanovich, 1970), 510.

132 Earlier, Malcolm Cowley ventured: On the 1930s, see Malcolm Cowley, *The Dream of the Golden Mountains: Remembering the 1930s* (New York: Penguin, 1981), passim.

133 "by upsetting established relations between citizen and government": Hart, 159.

133 To placate the Marxists: Jerre Mangione, *The Dream and the Deal: The Federal Writers' Project, 1935–1943* (1972; rpt. New York: Avon, 1996), 105.

134 Philip Rahv, the cofounder: Mangione, 173.

134 "The Grand Canyon, Yellowstone Park, Jim Hill's mansion": Mary McCarthy, *On the Contrary* (New York: Noonday Press, 1962), 7.

134 "and chided the Daughters of the American Revolution": Eric Foner, *The Story of American Freedom* (New York: W. W. Norton, 1998), 214.

135 "the party of Bill Foster and Big Bill Haywood": Howard Fast, *Being Red: A Memoir* (New York: Laurel/Dell, 1990), 141–42.

136 "The peculiar power": V. S. Pritchett, *Complete Collected Essays* (New York: Random House, 1991).

3 *Limousines on Grub Street*

138 *"Roosevelt's Psychiatrist's Egg Ranch"*: James D. Hart, *The Popular Book: A History of American Literary Taste* (New York: Oxford University Press, 1950), 279.

138 "Limousines on Grub Street": Malcolm Cowley, "American Literature in Wartime," in *The Flower and the Leaf: A Contemporary Record of American Writing Since 1941*, ed. and with an introduction by Donald W. Faulkner (New York: Viking Press, 1985), 89–98.

139 "a brief period at the end of World War II": Malcolm Cowley, *The Literary Situation* (New York: Viking Press, 1954), 171.

139 more of a "soporific . . . than an aphrodisiac": Alice Payne Hackett, *Sixty Years of Bestsellers, 1895–1955* (New York: R. R. Bowker, 1956), 180.

139 John Updike recalls reading: John Updike, *Hugging the Shore: Essays and Criticism* (1983; rpt. New York: Vintage, 1984), 196–99.

140 In a letter to Louise Bogan: Edmund Wilson, *Letters on Literature and Politics, 1912–1972*, selected and edited by Elena Wilson (New York: Farrar, Straus and Giroux, 1977), 437.

141 "It may seem naive, and even stupid": Edmund Wilson, *The Cold War and the Income Tax: A Protest* (New York: Signet, 1963), 11.

4 *Scenes of Writing*

142 the "ideological seat": *New York Panorama, A Companion to the WPA Guide to New York City* (1938; rpt. with a new introduction by Alfred Kazin, New York: Pantheon, 1984), 176.

143 "three gardeners, a houseboy": Anthony Burgess, *Ernest Hemingway* (1978; rpt. London: Thames and Hudson, 1986), 94.

144 "and despite occasional efforts at reconciliation": "Paleface and Redskin," in Philip Rahv, *Literature and the Sixth Sense* (Boston: Houghton Mifflin, 1970), 1.

144 the most exquisitely mannered: Dwight Macdonald, *Against the American Grain: Essays on the Effects of Mass Culture* (New York: Random House, 1963), 175.

144 "One seems to become a myth": Peter Ackroyd, *T. S. Eliot: A Life* (New York: Simon and Schuster, 1984), 289.

144 "It was the moment of gallantry in heartbreak": Edmund Wilson, *The Wound and the Bow* (Boston: Houghton Mifflin, 1941).

144 "There are individuals in America": Jean-Paul Sartre, "Individualism and Conformism," in *Literary and Philosophical Essays*, trans. Annette Michelson (New York: Criterion, 1955), 105.

145 "writers in New York": Ernest Hemingway, *Green Hills of Africa* (1935; rpt. London: Penguin, 1966), 25.

145 "complicated and obsessive relationship": Ann Douglas, *Terrible Honesty: Mongrel Manhattan in the 1920s* (New York: Farrar, Straus and Giroux, 1995), 108–09.

146 "Have you ever noticed that no American writer": Quoted in Stefan Kanfer, "City Lights," *City Journal*, Autumn 2010, 3.

147 "emerged from the womb of the depression crying": William Phillips and Philip Rahv, "In Retrospect: Ten Years of *Partisan Review*," in William Phillips and Philip Rahv, eds., *The Partisan Reader: Ten Years of* Partisan Review, *1934–1944: An Anthology* (New York: Dial Press, 1946), 679.

148 "as if the editors in choosing this place were returning": William Barrett, *The Truants: Adventures Among the Intellectuals* (Garden City, NY: Anchor, 1982), 35.

149 "However intense in its personalities": Barrett, 58.

150 "tweedy professors of English": William Barrett, "The Resistance," *Partisan Review*, Autumn 1946.

150 "I know pedagogy is a depressing subject": Lionel Trilling, *The Moral Obligation to Be Intelligent: Selected Essays*, ed. and with an introduction by Leon Wieseltier (New York: Farrar, Straus and Giroux, 2000), 381.

151 "Without a Ph.D. I had no hope": Irving Howe, *A Margin of Hope: An Intellectual Biography* (New York: Harcourt Brace Jovanovich, 1982), 123.

151 "The United States was born in the country": Richard Hofstadter, *The Age of Reform: From Bryan to F.D.R.* (New York: Knopf, 1955), 23.

151 "When you visited": Alfred Kazin, *Writing Was Everything* (Cambridge, MA: Harvard University Press, 1995), 107–09, 112.

152 "Seeing him get his mail downstairs": Peter Manso, *Mailer: His Life and Times* (New York: Simon and Schuster, 1985), 99.

PART IV: THAT WINTER—AND THE NEXT

153 "There was a time when New York": Harvey Swados, "Nights in the Gardens of Brooklyn" (1960), in Swados, *Nights in the Gardens of Brooklyn: The Collected Stories of Harvey Swados* (New York: New York Review Books, 2004), 3.

1   *A Fractious Peace*

155 "in a way, the celebration": Eric F. Goldman, *The Crucial Decade—And After: America, 1945–1960* (1956; enlarged edition: New York: Knopf, 1960), 4.

155 Within the month: See Goldman, 19ff. See also Joshua Freeman et al., *Who Built America? Working People and the Nation's Economy, Politics, Culture, and Society*, vol. 2, *From the Gilded Age to the Present*, American Social History Project, City University of New York, Herbert G. Gutman, founding director (New York: Pantheon, 1992), 469–77.

157 The strike wave reached New York City: See Joshua Freeman, *Working-Class New York: Life and Labor Since World II* (New York: New Press, 2000), 3–6 and passim.

157 "Until the strike was settled": *Time*, February 18, 1946.

158 "We are all equally children": *New Yorker*, February 16, 1946.

159 "In New York": Freeman, 4.

160 "New Yorkers had suffered since V-J Day": *Time*, February 18, 1946.

160 "In other ways, too": Frederic Prokosch, *The Idols of the Cave* (Garden City, NY: Doubleday, 1946), 251–52.

160 "The Englishman who crosses": Beverley Nichols in *Uncle Samson* (1950), quoted in Bayrd Still, *Mirror for Gotham: New York as Seen by Contemporaries from Dutch Days to the Present* (New York: New York University Press, 1956), 338–40.

2 New York Observed

162 Connolly compared the welcome: Cyril Connolly, "Introduction," *Horizon*, October 1947, 2.

162 "the surprising and disconcerting impression": John Lukacs, *Confessions of an Original Sinner* (New York: Ticknor & Fields, 1990), 128 and passim.

163 "entire classes of American women": Lukacs, 129.

163 "those endless 'north–south' highways": Jean-Paul Sartre, "New York, the Colonial City," in *Literary and Philosophical Essays*, trans. Annette Michelson (New York: Criterion, 1955), 120.

163 "Night on the Bowery": Albert Camus, *American Journals*, trans. Hugh Levick (London: Abacus, 1990), 42.

164 "the supreme metropolis of the present" and passim: Connolly, 3.

165 "hard and awe-inspiring": Cecil Beaton, *Cecil Beaton's New York* (Philadelphia and New York: J. P. Lippincott, 1938), 37.

165 "Why, after midnight": Connolly, 7.

166 "a high point of civilization": Connolly, 5–7.

166 "its woeful, watery macaroni": Elizabeth Hardwick, *Sleepless Nights* (New York: Vintage, 1980), 32.

166 "something in New York": Simone de Beauvoir, *America, Day by Day*, trans. Carol Cosman (Berkeley: University of California, 1999), 18.

167 "There is the wailing of the wind": Sartre, 121.

167 "the new landmarks crushing the old": Henry James, *The American Scene* (1907; rpt. with introduction and notes by Leon Edel: Bloomington: Indiana University Press, 1968), 78.

167 "the architecture of the Police State": Lewis Mumford, *New Yorker*, October 30, 1948, 49.

168 "For several years, Mrs. H. T. Miller had lived alone": Truman Capote, "Miriam," in *A Capote Reader* (New York: Random House, 1987), 3.

168 "Far away I see": Sartre, 124.

169 "the heat closed in": Truman Capote, *Local Color* (New York: Random House, 1950), 19.

169 "On some nights, New York": Saul Bellow, *The Victim* (1947; rpt. New York: Signet, 1965), 11.

3 *Soldier's Home*

170 "Probably I was in the war": Norman Mailer, *Barbary Shore* (1951; rpt. New York: Grosset & Dunlap, Universal Library, 1963), 3.

170 "to find all Gods dead": F. Scott Fitzgerald, *This Side of Paradise* (New York: Scribner, 1920), 304.

171 "psychic reconversion": Anne O'Hare McCormick, *New York Times*, December 23, 1944.

171 "Flags cracked": Jack Kerouac, *The Town and the City* (1950; rpt. San Diego: Harcourt, Brace, 1970), 443.

172 "'the disintegration of our armed forces'": Harry S. Truman, *Year of Decisions: Memoirs* (1955; rpt. New York: Signet, 1965), 560.

172 "some of the fourteen million comrades": Merle Miller, *That Winter* (New York: W. Sloane, 1948), 34, passim.

172 "After all, we had—all of us—won": Gore Vidal, *Palimpsest: A Memoir* (New York: Random House, 1995), 101.

173 "Was I to do the book of the returning veteran": Norman Mailer, *Advertisements for Myself* (New York: Putnam, 1959), 93.

173 "we were all reading": Alice Adams in conversation with the author.

174 "What did people want to believe": Paul Fussell, introduction to *Diana Trilling: Reviewing the Forties* (New York: Harcourt, Brace, Jovanovich, 1978), ix.

175 "He looked about him at the people passing by": Kerouac.

180 "The truth is": Cynthia Ozick, "Alfred Chester's Wig," in *Fame and Folly: Essays* (New York: Knopf, 1996), 52–53.

181 "People went to the New School": Anatole Broyard, *When Kafka Was the Rage: A Greenwich Village Memoir* (New York: Carol Southern Books, 1993), 14.

PART V: THE CITY IN BLACK AND WHITE

183 "As usual in New York": James Merrill, "An Urban Convalescence," in *Collected Poems*, eds. J. D. McClatchy and Stephen Venser (New York: Knopf, 2002), 127–29.

185 "A sprinkling of French and Italians": Thomas Allibone Janvier, "The Evolution of New York (Greenwich Village)," *Harper's Magazine*, vol. 87 (1893), quoted in Caroline W. Ware, *Greenwich Village, 1920–1930: A Comment on American Civilization in the Post-war Years* (Boston: Houghton Mifflin, 1935), 11.

185 "a kind of established repose": Henry James, *Washington Square*, in *The American Novels and Stories of Henry James*, ed. and with an introduction by F. O. Matthiessen (New York: Knopf, 1947), 171.

185 "as if the wine of life": Henry James, *The American Scene* (1907; rpt. with

an introduction and notes by Leon Edel, Bloomington: Indiana University Press, 1968), 88.

186 "Nearly a century of fraud": Gustavus Myers, *History of the Great American Fortunes* (1910; rpt. New York: Modern Library, 1936), 273.

187 "By 1910 the transformation of Greenwich Village": *WPA Guide to New York City: The Federal Writers' Project Guide to 1920s New York*, with a New Introduction by William H. Whyte (New York: Pantheon, 1982), 128. See "Greenwich Village," 124–43.

188 "Already the lines": Ware, 105ff.

189 "It is not too easy": William Barrett, "Greenwich Village: New Designs in Bohemia," *New York Times Magazine*, 1950; rpt. in Alexander Klein, ed. *The Empire City: A Treasury of New York* (New York: Rinehart, 1955), 97–105.

190 Kaufman decided it would be: Marion Meade, *Lonelyhearts: The Screwball World of Nathanael West and Eileen McKenney* (Boston: Houghton Mifflin Harcourt, 2010), 309. Meade gives a detailed account of the accident, 304–09.

190 Alexander Trachtenberg, the Communist Party: Alan M. Wald, *Exiles from a Future Time: The Forging of the Mid-Century Literary Left* (Chapel Hill: University of North Carolina Press, 2002), 78; Wald explains the expulsion of McKenney and Bransten from the Party, 175.

190 "*Eileen* seemed so awfully Thirties-bound": Quoted in Meryle Secrest, *Leonard Bernstein: A Life* (New York: Knopf, 1994), 196.

191 "they wanted to be": Quoted in R. G. Sperling, Preface, in Christiana Stead, *I'm Dying Laughing: The Humourist*, ed. R. G. Geering (New York: Henry Holt, 1986), ix–x.

191 "Greenwich Village, that part of New York": Stephen Spender, *World Within World: The Autobiography of Stephen Spender* (1951; rpt. New York: St. Martin's, 1994), 297–98.

1 *Berenice Abbott's Village in the City*

193 "the most phenomenal human gesture ever made": "A Woman Photographs the Face of a Changing City, *Life*, January 3, 1938, 40–44. Unless otherwise noted, quotations from Abbott and the facts about her life are taken from the short biography by Hank O'Neal in *Berenice Abbott, American Photographer* (New York: McGraw-Hill, 1982), which includes over two hundred pages of illustrations, an introduction by John Canaday, and a commentary by Abbott. *Changing New York* (1938) is reproduced as *New York in the Thirties, as Photographed by Berenice Abbott* (New York: Dover, 1973). For the complete WPA project, see Bonnie Yochelson, *Berenice Abbott: Changing New York* (New York: New Press in association with the Museum of the City of New York, 1997).

195 "The streets outside were those of Glenn Coleman's early paintings": Malcolm Cowley, *Exile's Return: A Literary Saga of the 1920s* (New York: Viking Press, 1951), 48.

195 "The Baroness was like": Quoted in Robert Reiss, " 'My Baroness': Elsa von Freytag-Loringhoven," in Rudolf E. Kuenzil, *New York Dada* (New York: Willis Locker & Owens, 1986), 81. Reiss attributes the remark to Abbott in conversation with her biographer Hank O'Neal, 101n.

198 "dozens of visits": Julien Levy, *Memoir of an Art Gallery* (New York: Putnam, 1977), 90ff.
199 "Unfortunately, it was": Levy, 93–95.
202 "Cubist historiography": Frank Kermode, *Continuities* (New York: Random House, 1968), 72.
202 "Remarkably, however, almost all of these pictures are empty": Walter Benjamin, "Little History of Photography," *Selected Writings*, vol. 2, 1927–1934, trans. Rodney Livingston (Cambridge, MA, and London: Belknap Press of Harvard University Press, 1999), 519.
202 "Abbott's images are obituaries": Peter Conrad, *The Art of the City: Views and Versions of New York* (New York: Oxford University Press, 1984), 169.
203 "Manhattan Island is a stony spine of land": *Time*.
206 "typical Village street": *Greenwich Village, Today and Yesterday*, photographs by Berenice Abbott, text by Henry Wysham Lanier (New York: Harper & Brothers, 1949). Photo captions are by Elizabeth McCausland.
207 "The whole region must have been": Abbott and Lanier. If not otherwise noted, and apart from the photo captions by McCausland, subsequent references in this section come from Lanier's text.
209 "Within a year of Daguerre's discovery": Marshall McLuhan, *Understanding Media: The Extensions of Man*, 2nd ed. (New York: Signet, 1964), 171.

2 *Gottscho's Oz*

212 Samuel H. Gottscho, a great urban romancer: Donald Albrecht, Introduction, *The Mythic City: Photographs of New York by Samuel H. Gottscho, 1925–1940* (New York: Museum of the City of New York, Princeton Architectural Press, 2005). Albrecht is my source for the facts of Gottscho's life and career.

3 *Weegee's Dark Carnival*

215 "There are lots of things I could have taken in the last five years": Bonnie Yochelson, *Berenice Abbott: Changing New York* (New York: New Press in association with the Museum of the City of New York, 1997), 23.
216 "To You, the People of New York": Weegee, *Naked City* (1945; rpt. New York: Da Capo, 1973), 5.
216 "I only take off my clothes when I have company": Weegee, *Weegee by Weegee: An Autobiography* (New York: Ziff-Davis, 1961), 64.
220 "a rather portly, cigar-smoking, irregularly shaven man": William McCleery, Foreword, Weegee, *Naked City*, 7.
223 "posed her against a background of salamis": Weegee, *Weegee's People* (New York: Essential Books: Duell, Sloan and Pearce, 1946), unpaged.
224 "in the streets of New York, Hellinger only dissipated": David Thomson, *The New Biographical Dictionary of Film* (New York: Knopf, 2010), 388,
225 "undoing as a photojournalist": Jane Livingston, *The New York School: Photographs, 1936–1963* (New York: Stewart, Tabori and Chang, 1992), 319.
225 "But all that ended": Downes, *Weegee by Weegee*, 6.
225 "the most sensitive spot": Weegee, *The Village by Weegee* (New York: Da Capo, 1989), unpaged.

PART VI: GREENWICH VILLAGE: GHOSTS, GOTHS,
AND GLIMPSES OF THE MOON

1 *Bohemia Was Yesterday*

229 "this dreamy, chaotic way of life": Albert Parry, *Garrets and Pretenders: Bohemian Life in America from Poe to Kerouac* (1933; expanded republication New York: Dover Press, 1960; rpt. with introduction by Paul Buhle, 2012), xvi.

229 "book about all Bohemias": Parry, xvi–xvii.

230 unfolds like a tragicomic cavalcade: Parry, 8ff.

230 To Poe's solitary reign: Parry, 88ff.

230 "a fearful pile of Titanic bricks": Herman Melville, *Pierre, or, The Ambiguities* (1852). In the Library of America Melville, vol. 3, 309.

230 "*Pierre*-of-Melville goof and wonder": Jack Kerouac, *The Subterraneans* (New York: Grove Press, 1958), 15.

231 "claustrophic" Lower Manhattan: Ellis Amburn, *Subterranean Kerouac: The Hidden Life of Jack Kerouac* (New York: St. Martin's, 1999), 193–95.

231 Living fast and dying young: On Ada Clare, see Parry, 14–37.

231 "We do not know of": Parry, 63.

232 "something between a black art": Edith Wharton, *A Backward Glance* (1935; rpt. New York: Simon and Schuster, 1998), 79.

232 "In the Seventies": Charles de Kay, obituary, *New York Times*, 1934.

232 Richard Watson Gilder: Thomas Bender, *New York Intellect: A History of Intellectual Life in New York City, from 1750 to the Beginnings of Our Own Time* (New York: Knopf, 1987), 213–14.

232 Gilder commissioned Stanford White: Parry, 87.

232 "distinctly fin de siècle quality": Bender, 214.

232 "an unwelcome tragedy": Parry, 87.

233 more gay Parisians to emulate: Parry, 99–109 and passim.

234 "The fiddles are tuning": Quoted in Alfred Kazin, *On Native Grounds: An Interpretation of Modern American Prose Literature* (1942; rpt. New York: Harcourt Brace Jovanovich, 1970), 166.

234 "'Hey, fellas'": Harry Kemp, *More Miles* (New York: Boni & Liveright, 1926), 28.

234 "on or about December 1910": Virginia Woolf, "Mr. Bennett and Mrs. Brown," in *The Captain's Death Bed* (London: Hogarth, 1950) and many other editions.

234 "Looking back upon it now": Mabel Dodge Luhan, *Movers and Shakers* (1936; rpt. Albuquerque: University of New Mexico Press, 1985), 39.

235 When he attempted: Floyd Dell, *Intellectual Vagabondage: An Apology for the Intelligentsia* (New York: Boni & Liveright, 1926), passim.

235 "a kind of proto–street theater": Christine Stansell, *American Moderns: Bohemian New York and the Creation of a New Century* (New York: Henry Holt, 2000), 112–14.

235 "the drift to respectability": Max Eastman, *Enjoyment of Living* (New York: Harper & Brothers, 1948), 523.

235 "Who does not know": Kazin, 166.

236 The "rebel girl": Ross Wetzsteon, *Republic of Dreams: Greenwich Village, the American Bohemia, 1910–1960* (New York: Simon and Schuster, 2002), 173–74.

236 "That's the rebel girl": *IWW Songs to Fan the Flames of Discontent: A Reprint of the Nineteenth Edition (1923) of the Famous Little Red Song Book* (Chicago: Charles H. Kerr, 2003), 36.

236 Max Eastman, the newly installed editor: Eastman, 447.

237 a New Woman: Wetzsteon, 168–71.

237 Vorse owned: Arthur and Barbara Gelb, *O'Neill* (New York: Harper & Brothers, 1962), 307.

237 "where youth lived and reds gathered": Lincoln Steffens, *The Autobiography of Lincoln Steffens* (New York: Literary Guild, 1931), 653.

238 "O life is a joy": John Reed, "Forty-Two Washington Square" (1913), rpt. in June Skinner Sawyers, *The Greenwich Village Reader: Fiction, Poetry, and Reminiscences, 1872–2002* (New York: Cooper Square Press, 2002), 49.

238 The Liberal Club: Parry, 269–73. See also Allen Churchill, *The Improper Bohemians: A Re-creation of Greenwich Village in Its Heyday* (New York: E. P. Dutton, 1959), 81ff.

238 Its guiding spirit: Churchill, 33–34.

239 Awkward but a compelling storyteller: Churchill, 63–64.

239 "Incredibly naïve": Floyd Dell, *Love in Greenwich Village* (New York: Knopf, 1924), 17.

239 No less than for her causes: Churchill, 65.

240 "At such times": Dell, *Love in Greenwich Village.*

240 Polly, as Paula Holladay was known: Churchill, 34–35. See also Parry, 270–71. See also Wetzsteon, 15–47.

241 "ugly, ugly, ugly": Luhan, 9.

241 Her spirits rose: Churchill, 43–43.

241 "Why, something wonderful": Luhan, 81.

241 "All sorts of guests": Steffens, 654–55.

242 Max Eastman puzzled: Eastman, 523.

242 "The first, and possibly the last": Carl Van Vechten, quoted in Churchill, 45.

242 "the most dangerous woman in New York": Luhan.

243 "Episode 2: The Mills Dead": Quoted in Churchill, 81.

243 "As city police charged": Churchill, 81.

243 "that it was no time for lovemaking": Luhan, *Movers and Shakers.*

244 Max Eastman recalls: Eastman, 524–25.

244 "an electric bulb with red tissue paper": Luhan.

244 "She was raving mad": Eastman, 525.

244 "Looking back on that": Jay Stevens, *Storming Heaven: LSD and the American Dream* (New York: Harper & Row, 1987), 9.

244 "not yet, not yet": Leonard Michaels, "In the Fifties," in *The Collected Stories* (Farrar, Straus and Giroux, 2007), 125.

2 *Conciliating Nobody: The* Masses *and the Villagers*

245 "every agitator who really intended to overthrow": Max Eastman, *Enjoyment of Living* (New York: Harper & Brothers, 1948), 409.

245 "Our magazine provided": Eastman, 409.

246 "a sleepy Adonis": Allen Churchill, *The Improper Bohemians: A Re-creation of Greenwich Village in Its Heyday* (New York: Dutton, 1959), 108–09.

246 The accomplished Annis Eastman: Max Eastman, *Love and Revolution: My Journey Through an Epoch* (New York: Random House, 1964), 13.

246 "the melancholy honor": Eastman, *Love and Revolution*, 12.

246 "I can't even hope for it": Eastman, *Love and Revolution*, 15.

247 "New York was not": Eastman, *Enjoyment of Living*, 265–66.

247 "the most beautiful white woman": Claude McKay, *A Long Way from Home* (1937; rpt. New York: Arno Press, 1967).

247 Eastman tells: Eastman, *Enjoyment of Living*, 266.

248 His languorous air: Eastman, *Enjoyment of Living*, 12.

248 One spring day in 1913: Eastman, *Love and Revolution*, 12. Eastman devotes a chapter to "My Self and the Old *Masses*," and parts of two others, in *Love and Revolution*, and a substantial part of *Enjoyment of Living* is devoted to this adventure, which ended him in the dock. See also the valuable accounts in Daniel Aaron, *Writers on the Left* (1961; rpt. New York: Avon, 1965), 48–67; William L. O'Neill, *The Last Romantic: A Life of Max Eastman* (New York: Oxford University Press, 1978), 30–53; Ross Wetzsteon, *Republic of Dreams: Greenwich Village, the American Bohemia, 1910–1960* (New York: Simon & Schuster, 2002), 48–91; Christine Stansell, *American Moderns: Bohemian New York and the Creation of a New Century* (New York: Henry Holt, 2000), 167–175; Albert Parry, *Garrets and Pretenders: Bohemian Life in America from Poe to Kerouac* (1933; expanded republication New York: Dover Press, 1960; rpt. with introduction by Paul Buhle, 2012), 281–304.

249 "They were inviting me": Eastman, *Love and Revolution*, 17.

249 "Bourgeois pigs! Voting!": Churchill, 107–08.

249 Ben Hecht, another Chicago bohemian: Ben Hecht, *A Child of the Century* (1954; rpt. New York: Ballantine Books, 1970), 207.

250 "Dear Max": Eastman, *Enjoyment of Living*, 442–44.

250 "Life is extraordinarily simple": Floyd Dell, *Love in Greenwich Village* (New York: Knopf, 1924).

250 "The *Masses* was a luxurious magazine": Eastman, *Enjoyment of Living*, 455, 458–61.

250 "natural genius": Eastman, *Enjoyment of Living*, 399.

250 "They draw fat women": Churchill, 281.

251 William L. O'Neill says: O'Neill, 36.

251 "The socialist idea": Eastman, *Enjoyment of Living*, 390.

251 Electorally, socialists seemed destined: See the overview in Irving Howe, *Socialism in America* (New York: 1985), 3–9.

251 its pictorial style: Eastman, *Enjoyment of Living*, 402, 445.

253 In the June 1913 issue: Eastman, *Enjoyment of Living*, 413–14.

253 Eastman suspected: Eastman, *Enjoyment of Living*, 465.

253 Eastman aimed: Eastman, *Enjoyment of Living*, 466.

253 In 1916 a group: Eastman, *Enjoyment of Living*, 548–59.

255 "pernicious neutrality": Ronald Steel, *Walter Lippmann and the American Century*, (1980, rpt. New York: Vintage, 1981), 107.

255 Unconcerned with Marxist orthodoxy: Eastman, *Love and Revolution*, 39.

256 In a landmark opinion: See Gerald Gunther, *Learned Hand: The Man and the Judge* (New York: Knopf, 1994), 151–61.

256 "I loved that gun": Eastman, *Enjoyment of Living*, 53–56.

257 "He had a powerful": Eastman, *Love and Revolution*, 28.

258 "If any man": John Dos Passos, *1919*, vol. 2 of *U.S.A.* (New York: Modern Library, 1937), 105–06.

258 "The gangsters admired": Malcolm Cowley, *Exile's Return: A Literary Saga of the 1920s* (1934; rpt. New York: Viking Press, 1965), 69.

259 "Bill, pipe all these": "MacDougal Street," originally published in *Masses*, May 1916, collected in *Mike Gold: A Literary Anthology*, ed. and with an introduction by Michael Bloom (New York: International Publishers, 1972), 23.

259 As the trio huddled: Arthur and Barbara Gelb, *O'Neill* (New York: Harper & Brothers, 1962), 359–60. On Mike Gold, see also Aaron, 102–08; Alan M. Wald, *Exiles from a Future Time: The Forging of the Mid-Twentieth-Century Literary Left* (Chapel Hill: University of North Carolina Press, 2002), 39–70.

260 "It was as though": Eastman, *Love and Revolution*, 64.

261 "Of necessity it would be": Eastman, *Love and Revolution*, 70; Wilson is quoted, 62–63.

261 "It was a little like": Eastman, *Love and Revolution*, 84.

261 "You call that a poem?": See Churchill, 138–41. It might also have weighed on the court that Bell was personally unacquainted with her supposed coconspirators, as noted by William L. O'Neill in *The Last Romantic*, 75.

262 "we were all" Eastman, *Love and Revolution*, 85.

262 Their chief counsel: Eastman, *Love and Revolution*, 83.

262 "My flag was still the red flag": Eastman, *Enjoyment of Living*, 86; see 86–91 for his account of the first *Masses* trial. See also Parry, 292–94; Aaron, 59–63; Churchill, 140–144; Wetzsteon, 76–83.

264 "War is a confused time": Floyd Dell, *Homecoming: An Autobiography* (New York: Farrar & Rinehart, 1933).

264 "a crazy foolishness": Eastman, *Enjoyment of Living*, 103–04.

265 "President Wilson is waging": Eastman, *Love and Revolution*, 151.

265 "I went out there": Eastman, *Love and Revolution*, 113, 117.

265 With Hillquit and Malone: On the second *Masses* trial, Eastman, *Love and Revolution*, 118–24. See also Parry, 293–95; Churchill, 145–46; Wetzsteon, 81–83.

266 "On our side": Eastman, *Love and Revolution*, 119.

266 "It is either": Eastman, *Love and Revolution*, 129.

266 This time, the trial: Eastman, *Love and Revolution*, 122, 136–37.

3 *Brightness Falls*

268 In *Exile's Return*: Malcolm Cowley, *Exile's Return: A Literary Saga of the 1920s* (New York: Viking Press, 1951), 67.

268 "as old as the trade of letters": Cowley, 55.

269 As in any town: Cowley, 69–71.

269 "'They' had been rebels": Cowley, 71.

270 "all wars fought": F. Scott Fitzgerald, *This Side of Paradise* (New York: Scribner, 1920), 304.

270 "Greenwich Village was not only": Cowley, 59.

270 "But the war": Cowley, 66–67.

271   "Female equality was a good idea": Cowley, 73.

271   "The truth is": Cowley, 73.

271   " 'Is yours a drinking crowd?' ": Allen Churchill, *The Improper Bohemians: A Re-creation of Greenwich Village in Its Heyday* (New York: Dutton, 1959, 108–09.

271   Admission was a dollar: Churchill, 110.

271   For the Liberal Club: Floyd Dell, *Love in Greenwich Village* (New York: Knopf, 1924), 299.

272   "The dance at the Commodore": Cowley, 67–68.

272   "that Mabel was on the hunt": Max Eastman, *Enjoyment of Living* (New York: Harper & Brothers, 1948), 537.

273   When Floyd Dell visited: Dell, *Homecoming*, 334.

273   Ingenious hucksters: On the notorious Guido Bruno, see Albert Parry, *Garrets and Pretenders: Bohemian Life in America from Poe to Kerouac* (1933; expanded republication New York: Dover Press, 1960; rpt. with introduction by Paul Buhle, 2012), 207–09; Churchill, 149–55; John Strausbaugh, *The Village: 400 Years of Beats and Bohemians, Radicals and Rogues—A History of Greenwich Village* (New York: Ecco/HarperCollins, 2013), 124–29.

273   "First Aid for Struggling Artists": Churchill, 151–55.

273   "Quite ordinary people": Quoted in Strausbaugh, 125.

273   No mere exhibitor-exhibitionist: Churchill, 150–55. See also Ross Wetzsteon, *Republic of Dreams: Greenwich Village, the American Bohemia, 1910–1960* (New York: Simon & Schuster, 2002), 304–08; Strausbaugh, 124–28.

274   "See you sagging": Djuna Barnes, *The Book of Repulsive Women: 8 Rhythms and 5 Drawings* (1915; rpt. Sun and Moon Press, 1994), unpaged.

274   "Ghastly days": Wetzsteon, 439.

274   "the king of bohemia": Parry, 308–09. For Hartmann's life and times, see also Introduction, Sadakichi Hartmann, *Buddha, Confucius, Christ: Three Prophetic Plays*, ed. Harry Lawton and George Knox (New York: Herder and Herder, 1971).

274   "I'm Sadakichi Hartmann": Gene Fowler, *Good-Night, Sweet Prince: The Life and Times of John Barrymore* (New York: Viking Press, 1944).

275   "and as for the vagaries": Ezra Pound, Canto LXXX, *The Pisan Cantos*, in Ezra Pound, *The Cantos of Ezra Pound* (New York: New Directions, 1970), 495.

275   Bohemia's "king" was born: Hartmann, xv.

275   Whitman fried eggs: Parry, 308–09.

276   "King Ludwig would have loved Hollywood": Introduction, Hartmann, xx.

276   In his early twenties: Kenneth Rexroth, *An Autobiographical Novel*, revised and expanded, ed. Linda Hamalian (1960; rpt. New York: New Directions, 1991), 68.

276   Along with Lafcadio Hearn: Kenneth Rexroth, *American Poetry in the Twentieth Century* (New York: Herder and Herder, 1971), 28–31.

277   "The other gentleman": Strausbaugh, 126.

277   "a living freak": Fowler.

277   "moved to the Village": Parry, 309.

277   "good plays by": Parry, 310.

278   Although Guido Bruno had: Parry, 310. See also Strausbaugh, 127–28.

279   In the early days: Churchill, 221–22.

279 "that blotch, that blazon": Quoted from an opinion by Hand in Gerald Gunther, *Learned Hand: The Man and the Judge* (New York: Knopf, 1994), 306.

279 Gallant flourished: Churchill, 274.

279 Mercenary instincts never: See Dan Balaban, "The 'Gypsy' Lady Who Fed Bohemia," in June Skinner Sawyers, *The Greenwich Village Reader: Fiction, Poetry, and Reminiscences, 1872–2002* (New York: Cooper Square Press, 2002), 390–97; Strausbaugh, 128–30.

280 "Do I really": Dell, 301–02.

281 "I loathed what": Dell, 302.

281 A former chorus girl: For the baroness's life and times, see Irene Gammel, *Baroness Elsa: Gender, Dada, and Everyday Modernity: A Cultural Biography* (2002; rpt. Cambridge, MA: MIT Press, 2003). For other descriptions, see Parry, 311; Strausbaugh, 144–47; Wetzsteon, 317–24.

282 When George Biddle: George Biddle, *The Story of an American Artist* (Boston: Little, Brown, 1939), 137.

282 According to Margaret Anderson: Margaret C. Anderson, *My Thirty Years' War* (1931; rpt. Westport, CT: Greenwood Press, 1971).

283 "Crime is not crime": Anderson.

283 Her sexual voracity: William Carlos Williams, *The Autobiography of William Carlos Williams* (New York: New Directions, 1967), 168–69.

283 "She was all joy": Gammel, 172.

283 A handsome teenage art student: Gammel, 216–17.

283 "Shaving one's head": Anderson.

283 The baroness lengthened: Gammel, 212.

284 "All New York is dada": The letter to Tristan Tzara, postmarked 8 June 1921, is reproduced in Gammel, 289.

284 "one of the few": Robert Hughes, *American Visions: The Epic History of Art in America* (New York: Knopf, 1997), 361–62.

284 "If there was anyone": Hughes, 362.

284 "her spirit withering": Biddle, 141.

284 "I have no chance": Gammel, 306.

284 Deeply relieved to see: Gammel, 311. See also Williams, 169.

284 "dotty old lady": Wetzsteon, 323. See also Peter Gay, *Weimar Culture: The Outsider as Insider* (New York: Harper Torchbooks, 1970); on how the outsiders became insiders, passim.

285 Her work found: Gammel, 362–64.

285 "I dared as fine": Gammel, 384.

285 In fall 1927: Gammel, 382–84.

285 In his autobiography: Williams.

285 Berenice Abbott, who had been: Gammel, 384.

285 Djuna Barnes, who had: Gammel, 384–88.

286 "One world war produced the Baroness": Rexroth, *American Poetry*, 77.

286 "I was having lunch": Floyd Dell, *Homecoming: An Autobiography* (New York: Farrar & Rinehart, 1933), 368.

286 "I would have had him": Dell, *Homecoming*, 368.

287 In *Love in Greenwich Village*: Dell, *Love in Greenwich Village*, 303ff.

287 "I went out from the noise": Dell, *Love in Greenwich Village*, 321.

287 "In the past decade": Fitzgerald, "Echoes of the Jazz Age," in *The Crack-Up*, ed. Edmund Wilson (New York: New Directions, 1945), 321.

288 "No girl was ever ruined": Wetzsteon, 384.

288 "from the unknown Scythian wastes": Ben Hecht, *A Child of the Century* (1954; rpt. New York: Ballantine Books, 1970), 435.

288 "Men of letters": Hecht, 446.

288 In *Homecoming*: Dell, *Homecoming*, 360.

289 "Way down South": Bobby Edwards, "The Village Epic" (1922), quoted in Sawyers, vii.

289 The most famous: Parry, 316–19. See also Wetzsteon, 324–33.

290 "Wall Street was flooded": Parry, 319.

290 It was "Pound's Era": Parry, 329–45.

290 "Now even New York": Cowley, 80.

290 By 1927, the American colony: Alistair Horne, *The Seven Ages of Paris* (New York: Knopf, 2002), 331.

291 Spreading out from the corner: Rexroth, *Autobiographical Novel*, 341–42.

291 "You're an expatriate": Ernest Hemingway, *The Sun Also Rises* (1926; rpt. New York: Scribner, 1954).

291 *"that American poet"*: Ernest Hemingway, "The Snows of Kilimanjaro," in *The Complete Short Stories of Ernest Hemingway* (New York: Scribner, 1987), 49.

292 Reporters had crowded: Cowley, 74–75, 79.

293 "God damn the continent of Europe": F. Scott Fitzgerald, *The Letters of F. Scott Fitzgerald*, ed. Andrew Turnball (New York: Scribner, 1963), 326.

293 In his diary: Harold Macmillan, *The Blast of War* (New York: Harper & Row, 1968), 239ff.

293 "You could have sworn": Harold E. Stearns, *The Street I Know* (1935, rpt. New York: M. Evans, 2014).

293 "In those days": Morley Callaghan, *That Summer in Paris* (New York: Coward-McCann, 1963) 114–15.

294 "Yes, even more than Hemingway": Parry, 332.

295 In 1929 Eric Blair: Horne, 332.

296 "Sooner rob than starve": George Orwell, *Down and Out in Paris and London* (New York and London: Harper & Row, 1933).

296 "had learned from a distance": Cowley, 170.

296 "the City of Anger": Cowley, 201.

296 "In fact, once the returning exiles": Cowley, 205.

297 The New Era: See the chapter "The Revolt of the Intellectuals" in Arthur M. Schlesinger, Jr., *The Crisis of the Old Order, 1919–1932* (Boston: Houghton Mifflin, 1957) 145–52.

297 Greenwich Village is again: Wilson, 357–62.

297 "For several years": Blanche Wiesen Cook, "The Radical Women of Greenwich Village: From Crystal Eastman to Eleanor Roosevelt," in Rick Beard and Leslie Cohen Berlowitz, eds., *Greenwich Village: Culture and Counterculture* (New Brunswick, NJ: Rutgers University Press, published for the Museum of the City of New York, 1993), 243–57.

298 "About midnight the moon": Rexroth, *Autobiographical Novel*, 210–11.

298 "What came after": Parry, 346.

299 At last, a procession: Parry, 356.

300 "he got drunk night after night": Malcolm Cowley, *A Second Flowering: Works and Days of the Lost Generation* (New York: Viking Press, 1974), 209.

300 It was Cowley: Cowley, *Second Flowering*, 213.
300 His life in Mexico City: On Crane's last days and apparent suicide, see John Unterecker, *Voyager: A Life of Hart Crane* (New York: Farrar, Straus and Giroux, 1969), 648ff.
300 "The periodicity of his excesses": Waldo Frank's Introduction to the 1958 *Collected Edition* of Hart Crane's poetry is included as an appendix to *The Complete Poems and Selected Letters and Prose of Hart Crane*, ed. and with an introduction and notes by Brom Weber (1966; rpt. New York: Anchor Books, 1966), 269–73; the quotation appears on 273.
301 "He wanted to escape": Frank, Introduction, 273.
301 Crane's suicide is often compared: On Harry Crosby's career and death, see Cowley, *Exile's Return*, 246–84; Geoffrey Wolff, *Black Sun: The Brief Transit and Violent Eclipse of Harry Crosby* (1976; rpt. New York: New York Review Books, 2003).
301 "In these two suicides": Parry, 357–58.
301 Albert Parry was drawn back: Parry, 364.
302 "You get a job": Parry, 365.
302 Painters were better adapted: Parry, 368.
303 "A lanky, hot-eyed Trotskyite": Parry, 370.

4 Another Part of the Forest

304 "I remember one morning hearing Riis roaring": Lincoln Steffens, *The Autobiography of Lincoln Steffens* (New York: Literary Guild, 1931), 223.
305 "It was all worked out": Jack Kerouac, *The Town and the City* (1950; rpt. San Diego: Harcourt, Brace, 1970), 410.
306 "'Everybody was very classy'": Charles Kaiser, *The Gay Metropolis, 1940–1996* (Boston: Houghton Mifflin, 1997), 12.
306 "I did enjoy my daily meetings": Gore Vidal, *Palimpsest: A Memoir* (New York: Random House, 1995), 115.
307 "From behind me, someone quotes": Vidal, 104–05.
307 "a fairy party": Gore Vidal, *The City and the Pillar* (New York: Dutton, 1948), 233 and passim.
308 the notorious photograph: Gerald Clarke, *Capote: A Biography* (New York: Simon and Schuster, 1988), 154, 158–59.
308 "I have read that I was too stupid": Gore Vidal, Preface, *The City and the Pillar and Seven Early Stories* (New York: Random House, 1995), xiii.
308 If gay liberation began as a literary movement: Christopher Bram, *Eminent Outlaws: The Gay Writers Who Changed America* (New York: Twelve, 2012).
308 "By the time I came to write": Gore Vidal, *The City and the Pillar Revised, Including an Essay, "Sex and the Law," and an Afterword* (New York: New American Library, 1965), 155.
309 "A man who could not be had": Vidal, *City and the Pillar* (1948), 236.
309 "there is of course no such thing": Vidal, passim.
309 "He did not like men who acted like women": Vidal, *City and the Pillar* (1948), 247.
309 "a half-world where normal and homosexual people met": Vidal, *City and the Pillar* (1948), 245.

310 "I give a Party": Anaïs Nin. *Diary of Anais Nin*, vol. 4, 1944–1947, ed. and with a preface by Gunther Stuhlman (New York: Harcourt Brace Jovanovich, 1971), 132–33.

310 "Everybody came": Gray Foy.

311 " 'Who does that little pig think he is?' ": John Malcolm Brinnin, *Sextet: T. S. Eliot & Truman Capote & Others* (New York: Delta/Seymour Lawrence, 1981).

311 "I saw a small, slender young man": Nin, 110.

311 "How," he addressed: Gerald Clarke, *Capote: A Biography* (New York: Simon and Schuster, 1988), 139.

312 Capote and Vidal's wary: Clarke, 141.

312 " 'What in the name of God' ": Vidal, *Palimpsest*, 114.

313 "What a strange, and strangely enchanted place": Clarke, 196.

313 "Did you see that Mary McCarthy": Alan Ansen, *The Table Talk of W. H. Auden*, ed. Nicholas Jenkins (Princeton, NJ: Ontario Review Press, 1990), 65.

313 "Dostoyevskian New York": John Clellon Holmes, *Nothing More to Declare* (New York: E. P. Dutton, 1967), 200.

313 "The reasons Americans pretend": Ansen, 80.

314 "For more than a half century": Gore Vidal, Introduction, Karl Bissinger, *The Luminous Years: Portraits at Mid-Century* (New York: Harry N. Abrams, 2003), 9.

315 "My overriding concern": Brinnin, 258.

315 Eliot impressed John Berryman: Eileen Simpson, *Poets in Their Youth: A Memoir* (New York: Farrar, Straus & Giroux, 1990), 171–73.

316 "I used to be gorgeous": Ross Wetzsteon, *Republic of Dreams: Greenwich Village, the American Bohemia, 1910–1960* (New York: Simon & Schuster, 2002), 447.

316 "You're a fast walker": Harold Norse, *Memoirs of a Bastard Angel* (New York: William Morrow, 1989), 175.

317 "During the forties and fifties": Gore Vidal, "Some Memories of the Glorious Bird and an Earlier Self," in *United States: Essays, 1952–1992* (New York: Random House, 1993), 1136.

317 " '*Partisan Review* is a 'eterosexual magazine' ": Mary McCarthy, *Intellectual Memoirs: New York, 1936–1938* (New York: Harcourt Brace Jovanovich, 1992), 80.

317 "For me the final and parting irony": William Barrett, "New Innocents Abroad" (1949), rpt. in Chandler Brossard, ed., *The Scene Before You* (New York: Rinehart, 1955), 299.

318 "The American mother who fears": Barrett, 304–05.

318 "the bright-eyed poet-novelist-editor": Vidal, *Palimpsest*, 114.

5 *Culture and Anarchy: "The Sublime Is Now"*

319 E. B. White noted: E. B. White, *Here Is New York* (New York: Harper, 1949). White's valentine first appeared in *Holiday* in the same year.

319 "like *Who Walk in Darkness* and *Go*": Malcolm Cowley, *The Literary Situation* (New York: Viking Press, 1954), 61.

320 After leaving the *Liberator:* Eastman's further adventures are recounted in *Love and Revolution: My Journey Through an Epoch* (New York: Random House, 1964). His version of the beginnings of his disillusionment with Trotsky and the contretemps with Hemingway are told in *Great Companions: Critical Memories of Some Famous Friends* (New York: Farrar, Straus and Giroux, 1959), of which parts are reprinted in *Love and Revolution.*

320 "five blocks from the publisher's office": White, 10.

321 "you have sunk beneath all tolerance": Quoted in Daniel Aaron, *Writers on the Left* (1961; rpt. New York: Avon, 1965), 333.

321 Eastman got it right: Victor Serge, *Memoirs of a Revolutionist* (1951), trans. by Peter Sedgwick et al. (New York: New York Review Books, 2012), 308.

321 "The main difference": Norman Podhoretz, *Making It* (1967; rpt. New York: Harper & Row, 1980), 99–100.

321 a portentous exercise: Milton Klonsky, "Greenwich Village: Decline and Fall," rpt. in Chandler Brossard, ed., *The Scene Before You: A New Approach to American Culture* (New York: Rinehart, 1955), 16–28.

322 "The mood which infects them": Klonsky in Brossard, 26.

323 "As he was the illegitimate son": Broyard, "A Portrait of the Hipster," in Brossard, 113–19.

323 An ingenious theory: For a useful, if not entirely persuasive, summary, see John Leland, *Hip: The History* (2004; rpt. New York: Harper Perennial, 2005), 22–28.

324 Broyard described his apotheosis: Broyard, "A Portrait of the Hipster," in Brossard, 119.

324 "'Whodya like in prose'": Seymour Krim, "My Favorite Intellectual," in Mark Coh, ed., *Missing a Beat: The Rants and Regrets of Seymour Krim* (Syracuse: Syracuse University Press, 2010), 33.

324 famous anatomy of hip: Norman Mailer, "The White Negro: Superficial Reflections on the Hipster," in *Advertisements for Myself* (New York: Putnam, 1959), 347.

325 "If it hadn't been": Broyard, *When Kafka Was the Rage*, 30, 133, 135.

325 young enough to be a runaway: Herbert Gold, *Bohemia: Where Art, Angst, Love, and Strong Coffee Meet* (New York: Simon and Schuster, 1993), 215–16.

325 "unleashed zazous": "Hip, Cool, Beat—and Frantic," rpt. from the *Nation,* November 16, 1957, in Herbert Gold, *The Age of Happy Problems* (New York: Dial Press, 1962).

326 "just too tough": Barry Silesky, *Ferlinghetti: The Artist in His Time* (New York: Warner Books, 1990), 43.

326 "uneasy intersection": Michael Harrington, *Fragments of the Century: A Social Autobiography* (New York: Saturday Review Press, 1973), 39–40.

327 "Every bright kid": Ronald Sukenick, *Down and In: Life in the Underground.*

328 "two hours by car": James Merrill, *A Different Person: A Memoir* (New York: Knopf, 1993), 3.

328 "an hour or two": Merrill, 4.

329 Night after night: Merrill, 3.

329 "beat before there were beats": Tennessee Williams, *Memoirs* (1975; rpt. New York: Bantam, 1976), 105.

330 Early in 1951: The composition of the so-called "scroll" version of *On the Road* is variously told by Kerouac's friends and biographers. For the Cannastra connection, see Gerald Nicosia, *Memory Babe: A Critical Biography of Jack*

Kerouac (New York: Grove Press, 1983), 343ff. Nicosia tells of Cannastra's last days and strange death, 330–33.

330 "ill-dressed, underfed, overdrunken": William Gaddis, *The Recognitions* (1955; rpt. New York: Avon, 1974), 327.

331 "clerks, messengers, office boys": Quoted in Dore Ashton, *The New York School: A Cultural Reckoning* (1972; rpt. New York: Penguin, 1985), 147.

331 "It's hard to describe": John Gruen, *The Party's Over Now: Reminiscences of the Fifties: New York's Artists, Writers, Musicians, and Their Friends* (New York: Viking Press, 1972).

332 "the place where the money is": Florence Rubenfeld, *Clement Greenberg: A Life* (New York: Scribner, 1997), 98.

332 "Someday it will have to be told": Clement Greenberg, *Art and Culture: Critical Essays* (Boston: Beacon Press, 1961), 230.

333 "motionless Alexandrianism": Greenberg, 4.

333 "international Bohemia": Rpt. in Greenberg, vol. 2, 166ff. In this essay Greenberg made his famous judgment that "the most powerful painter in contemporary America and the only one who promises to be a major one" was named Jackson Pollock. He goes on: "Pollock's strength lies in the emphatic surfaces of his pictures, which it is his concern to maintain and intensify in all that thick, fuliginous flatness which began—but only began—to be the strong point of late cubism." The latter constituted a concise prophecy of the direction that Pollock would soon be taking in his "all-over" paintings, but also of his own criticism.

333 "The alienation of Bohemia": Greenberg, vol. 2, 194.

334 "helplessness before the void": Robert Hughes, *The Shock of the New* (New York: Knopf, 1983), 259–60.

334 "The sublime is now": The essay originally published in *Tiger's Eye* (1948), rpt. in Charles Harrison and Paul Wood, eds., *Art in Theory, 1900–1990: An Anthology of Changing Ideas* (Oxford: Blackwell, 1992), 572–74.

334 "It is disastrous": For the debate, see B. H. Friedman, *Jackson Pollock: Energy Made Visible* (1972; rpt. New York: Da Capo, 1995), 109–10.

335 "Life as it is lived": Loudon Wainwright, *Life: The Great American Magazine: An Inside History of Life* (1986; rpt. New York: Ballantine Books, 1988), 198–99.

336 With this debacle in mind: Naifeh and Smith, 590–91.

336 Their interviewer was: Seiberling became art editor of *Life* in 1952, continuing there until the magazine ceased weekly publication in 1972, when she went to work as an art editor at Clay Felker's *New York* magazine, and later to the *New York Times* as deputy editor of the *Sunday Magazine* under Abe Rosenthal. She married and divorced the art critic and historian Leo Steinberg.

337 "cool-hunter, *avant la lettre*": Joan Schenkar, *The Talented Miss Highsmith: The Secret Life and Serious Art of Patricia Highsmith* (New York: St. Martin's, 2009), 235.

337 "'Look at him'": Naifeh and Smith, 595.

338 bought a hundred copies: Naifeh and Smith, 597.

338 The bare wooden floors: Calvin Tomkins, *Off the Wall: Robert Rauschenberg and the Art World of Our Time* (1980; rpt. New York: Penguin, 1983), 58. Tomkins is the source for most of the biographical material that follows, and the delightful quotation from Steinberg.

340 contemporary art market: Peter Watson, *From Manet to Manhattan: The Rise of the Modern Art Market* (New York: Random House, 1992), 285.

340 Now that *Life:* See Naifeh and Smith, 597–601, regarding the opening at Parsons and events surrounding it.

342 In April 1950: Naifeh and Smith, 602–03.

PART VII: 1948

1 *Verdict*

345 "Great displays of war might": Jack Kerouac, *On the Road* (New York: Viking Press, 1957), 135.

346 "Harry Truman has never been elected": Zachary Karabell, *The Last Campaign: How Harry Truman Won the 1948 Election* (New York: Knopf, 2000), 113.

346 "Not only all the commentators": Jonathan Daniels, *The Man of Independence* (Philadelphia: J. B. Lippincott, 1950), 25.

346 Along with a unanimity: Alistair Cooke, "Harry S Truman: A Study in Failure," *Manchester Guardian*, November 1, 1948.

347 "I don't care how the thing is explained": David McCullough, *Truman* (New York: Simon and Schuster, 1992), 712.

348 And yet, the senator from Ohio: David Halberstam, *The Fifties* (New York: Villard Books, 1993), 9.

348 "Up from the country came a long loud guffaw": Eric F. Goldman, *The Crucial Decade—and After: America, 1945–1955* (1956; enlarged ed., New York: Knopf, 1960), 88.

348 "FDR had stolen the faith of people": John Gunther, *Inside U.S.A.* (New York: Harper & Brothers, 1947), 523.

349 "with much justice and without detracting": Walter Lippmann, "Today and Tomorrow," *New York Herald Tribune*, November 8, 1948.

349 "In spite of the great contrast": Rexford Guy Tugwell, *A Chronicle of Jeopardy, 1945–1955* (1955; rpt. Chicago: University of Chicago Press, 1974), 159–60.

350 "Labor did it": Alonzo Hamby, *Man of the People: A Life of Harry S. Truman* (New York: Oxford University Press, 1995), 494.

350 "The farm vote switched": Richard Norton Smith, *Thomas E. Dewey and His Times* (New York: Simon and Schuster, 1982), 544.

351 "and to lose in New York, New Jersey": McCullough, 713.

352 But in Brooklyn: As told to the author by David Meltzer.

352 "I kept reading about that Dewey fellow": Goldman, 89.

352 "The plain fact of the matter": *Life*, November 10, 1948.

353 In 1944 Paul Lazarsfeld: Paul Lazarsfeld, *The People's Choice: How the Voter Makes Up His Mind in a Presidential Campaign* (New York: Columbia University Press, 1948).

353 "the streams of voters": Samuel Lubell, *The Future of American Politics* (1952; rev. 2d ed., New York: Anchor, 1956), 6.

354 "One doesn't have to question Truman's sincerity": Lubell, 218–27.

354 "furiously dead center of stalemate": Lubell, 24.

355 ideal "border-state politician": Lubell, 13.

355 In this regard, Sam Lubell tells: Lubell, 8.

356 "It was because": Lubell, 12.

356 "Why is it that": Lubell, 210ff.

357 "The people who had elected Roosevelt would vote for him": Lubell, 5.

358 "Where was Gideon's army?": Lubell, 218–27. Apart from Lubell, the following draws on Karabell, 115–26; and for the flavor of the campaign and its distinctive rallies, Curtis D. MacDougal, *Gideon's Army* (New York: Marzani & Munsell, 1965), vol. 3 passim.

359 "We want Wallace!" MacDougal, vol. 1, 154–55.

360 "We have assembled a Gideon's army": John C. Culver and John Hyde, *American Dreamer: The Life and Times of Henry Wallace* (New York: Norton, 2000), 456.

361 "urban frontier": Lubell, 219.

362 Lubell calculates: Lubell, 336–227.

363 "The 1948 elections confirmed": Henry Steele Commager and Samuel Eliot Morison, *The Growth of the American Republic* (New York: Oxford University Press, 1950), 793–94.

363 "To save the peace": MacDougal, 882–83.

365 Clark, a buffoon: See Merle Miller, *Plain Speaking: An Oral Biography of Harry S. Truman* (New York: Putnam, 1974), 225–26. "It's just that he's such a dumb son of a bitch. I think he's about the dumbest man I've ever run across." Truman elevated him to the Supreme Court. See also Jonathan Bell's provocative and persuasive *The Liberal State on Trial: The Cold War and American Politics in the Truman Years* (New York: Columbia, 2006) on anti-Semitism.

366 "having commanded his own twelve years": Murray Kempton, "The Trouble with Henry (and Harry)," in *Rebellions, Perversities, and Main Events* (New York: Times Books, 1994).

366 "It would have been a national catastrophe": John Lukacs, *1945: Year Zero: The Shaping of the Modern Age* (Garden City, NY: Doubleday, 1978), 134.

370 "Almost every major Abstract Expressionist already active": David Anfam, *Abstract Expressionism*, World of Art series (New York: Thames and Hudson, 1990), 53.

370 "The receipt of a check from the United States government": Dore Ashton, *Life and Times of The New York School* (New York: Viking Press, 1972), 46.

371 "white gods": Tom Wolfe, *From Bauhaus to Our House* (1981; rpt. New York: Pocket Books, 1982), 41–59.

371 In the introduction: David Riesman, *The Lonely Crowd: A Study of the Changing American Character*, in collaboration with Reuel Denney and Nathan Glazer (1950; abridged ed., New Haven: Yale University Press, 1970).

372 "But then it is a waste of time to wonder": Kempton, 436.

372 "the underground river returned to earth": Norman Mailer, *Some Honorable Men: Political Conventions 1960–1972* (New York: Little, Brown, 1976), 176.

2 *Last Hurrah at the Waldorf*

373 "My idea was to organize a great meeting": Howard Fast, *Being Red* (Boston: Houghton Mifflin, 1990), 199.

374 "three thousand middle-class Wallaceites": Irving Howe, "The Cultural Conference" (1949), in Edith Kurzweil, ed., *A Partisan Century: Political Writings from* Partisan Review (New York: Columbia University Press, 1996), 92–97.

374 "the largest and most important": Fast, 200.

374 "And on the morning of the conference": Arthur Miller, *Timebends: A Life* (New York: Grove Press, 1987).

374 "Dupes and Fellow Travelers": *Life.*

375 an inveterate signer of petitions: Meryle Secrest, *Leonard Bernstein: A Life* (New York: Knopf, 1994), 171.

375 "the sharp postwar turn": Miller, 234.

375 international cultural congresses: See Daniel Aaron, *Writers on the Left* (1961; rpt. New York: Avon, 1965), 321; Roger Shattuck, "Having Congress," in *The Innocent Eye: On Modern Literature and the Arts* (1984; rpt. New York: Washington Square Press, 1986), 3–37.

375 The League issued calls: Aaron, 372–74.

376 "in addition to the breathless middle-brows": Howe, 92.

376 "no adequate compensation": Howe, 92.

377 "As waiters staggered into the suite": Frances Stonor Saunders, *The Cultural Cold War: The CIA and the World of Arts and Letters* (New York: New Press, 1999), 45–46. Another useful synoptic account, "The View from the Waldorf," appears in Neil Jumonville, *Critical Crossings: The New York Intellectuals in Postwar America* (Berkeley: University of California Press, 1991), 1–47.

378 An academic wunderkind: See his autobiography, *Out of Step: An Unquiet Life in the Twentieth Century* (New York: Harper & Row, 1987).

378 "some goon from the Intelligence Freedom Committee": Quoted in Michael Wreskin, *A Rebel in Defense of Tradition: The Life and Politics of Dwight Macdonald* (New York: Basic Books, 1994).

379 "Go ahead, tell us the truth": Fast, 202.

379 "agreed to emend that to a 'four-letter word'": Wreskin, 217.

379 "pale, slight and sensitive looking": Wreskin, 217.

379 "I have come here as a Trojan horse": Quoted in Mary V. Dearborn, *Mailer: A Biography* (Boston: Houghton Mifflin, 1999), 71.

380 Seated in the audience: Peter Manso, *Norman Mailer: His Life and Times* (New York: Simon and Schuster, 1985), 135.

380 "Mailer's hesitant, painful, but obviously deeply felt talk": Howe, 97–98.

380 "Suddenly he became": Manso, 134.

380 "I didn't hear the speech": Manso, 136.

381 "Fadeyev seemed to enjoy himself": Howe, 97.

381 "One wondered then: was he": Howe, 97.

382 "in a time of hysteria, suspicion and hate" and passim: W. E. B. DuBois, quoted in David Levering Lewis, *W. E. B. DuBois: The Fight for Equality and the American Century, 1919–1963* (New York: Henry Holt, 2000), 543.

382 "I still recall with horror my first trip to the USA": Dmitri Shostakovich, *Testimony: The Memoirs of Dmitri Shostakovich* (New York: Harper & Row, 1979). On the terrible trip, see 141–42.

383 "something dark and frightening": Miller, 235–36.

383 In *Being Red:* Fast, 213.

383 A year later: see Stoner, 85–104.

PART VIII: DAYS WITHOUT END

410 "a pleated cotton wedding shirt from Mexico": Robert L. Beisner, *Dean Acheson: A Life in the Cold War* (New York: Oxford University Press, 2006), 89.

410 "very small, very quiet, and very secluded": Quoted in Merle Miller, *Plain Speaking: An Oral Biography of Harry S. Truman* (New York: Berkley, 1974), 269.

410 "a regimen not conducive to relaxation": Dean Acheson, *Present at the Creation: My Years in the State Department* (New York: Norton, 1969), 402.

411 John Muccio, an officer with a rare sympathy: Acheson, 402.

411 "Mr. President," Acheson said: Harry S. Truman, *Memoirs*, vol. 2, *Years of Trial and Hope* (1956; rpt. New York: Signet, 1965), 378.

411 "And I agreed": Quoted in Miller, 270.

412 "My father made it clear": Margaret Truman, *Harry S. Truman* (New York: Morrow, 197), 455.

412 "Nobody had thought to notify me": George Kennan, *Memoirs, 1925–1950* (1967; rpt. New York: Bantam, 1969), 512; further quotations below from Kennan, 511–13.

413 "Having no grounds to challenge this judgment": Kennan, 512.

413 "free and independent Korea": On the Cairo Conference, see Robert E. Sherwood, *Roosevelt and Hopkins: An Intimate History* (New York: Harper & Brothers, 1948), 771.

413 secretly authorized: James Bradley, *The Imperial Cruise* (New York: Little, Brown, 2009), 348.

414 "I can be President": Variously quoted; see, for example, Stacy A. Cordery, *Alice: Alice Roosevelt Longworth, from White House Princess to Washington Power Broker* (New York: Viking, 2007).

414 "While Alice reaped the publicity": Warren Zimmerman, *First Great Triumph: How Five Americans Made Their Country a World Power* (New York: Farrar, Straus and Giroux, 2002), 470.

414 "Korea is absolutely Japan's": Quoted in John Morton Blum, *The Republican Roosevelt* (Cambridge, MA: Harvard University Press, 1977), 131.

415 "Roosevelt replied in the negative": Sherwood, 868.

415 "We have got to divide Korea": Quoted in William Manchester, *American Caesar: Douglas MacArthur, 1880–1964* (Boston: Little, Brown, 1978), 638.

415 His answer, to abridge an intricate argument: Geoffrey Hawthorn, *Plausible Worlds: Possibility and Understanding in History and the Social Sciences* (Cambridge, MA, and New York: Cambridge University Press, 1991).

415 "If Korea should ever be attacked": Clay Blair, *The Forgotten War: America in Korea, 1950–1953* (New York: Times Books, 1987), 44.

416 "The Army occupiers hated South Korea": Blair, 42.

416 "the same breed of cat as the Japanese": Quoted in Blair, 38.

416 "It was a supercharged moment": Acheson, 355.

417 "Dean Acheson's College of Cowardly Communist Appeasement": Quoted in Herbert S. Parmet, *Richard Nixon and His America* (Boston: Little, Brown, 1990), 228–29.

417 "the initial reliance must be upon the people": Acheson, 357.

418 "it did not occur to me that I should be charged": Acheson, 357.

419   "He looked like Truman": John Steinbeck, *The Wayward Bus* (1947; rpt. New York: Penguin, 2006), 30.

419   "six-foot-two Velázquez grandee": Quoted in Beisner, 88.

419   "he was smarter than most of his colleagues": Quoted in Beisner, 92.

421   "He thrived, discussing law, literature, and politics": Beisner, 10.

421   "You have to remember this about Acheson": Quoted in John Lewis Gaddis, *George F. Kennan: An American Life* (New York: Penguin, 2011), 339.

421   "protected the Foreign Service from the President": Beisner, 113.

421   "admiration without affection": Acheson, 7.

421   "he positively exuded an attitude": Clark Clifford, *Counsel to the President: A Memoir* (New York: Random House, 1991), 143

421   "I do not intend": Acheson, 360.

422   "I watch his smart-aleck manner": Beisner, 305.

422   "Stalin read the speech carefully": John Lewis Gaddis, *The Cold War* (New York: Penguin, 2005), 42.

422   "Am I here just to eat, shit, and sleep?": Jung Chang and Jon Halliday, *Mao: The Unknown Story* (New York: Anchor, 2006), 347–48.

423   "While others saw the bomb as the ultimate proof": Walter Isaacson and Evan Thomas, *The Wise Men: Six Friends and the World They Made: Acheson, Bohlem, Harriman, Kennan, Lovett, McCloy* (New York: Simon & Schuster, 1986), 485.

424   "'the most ponderous expression of elementary ideas'": Acheson, 374.

424   "clearer than truth": Acheson, 374–75.

424   "the priority given by the Soviet rulers": Acheson, 375.

425   "Hemingway sentences": Quoted in Isaacson and Thomas, 497.

425   "Years later, a student": Nicholas Thompson, *The Hawk and the Dove: Paul Nitze, George Kennan, and the History of the Cold War* (New York: Henry Holt, 2009), 114.

425   "Our purpose was much broader": Quoted in Margaret Truman, 430.

425   "meant a great military effort in time of peace": Harry S. Truman, *Public Papers*, vol. 3 (Washington, DC: United States Government Printing Office, 1965), 158.

426   "Even so," Acheson concedes: Acheson, 374.

426   "Korea saved us:" Isaacson and Thomas, 504.

426   "The news was growing rather grim": Margaret Truman, 456.

426   "We've got to stop the sons of bitches": Quoted in Alonzo L. Hamby, *Man of the People: A Life of Harry S. Truman* (New York: Oxford University Press, 1995), 534.

426   "In my generation, this was not the first occasion": Harry S. Truman, *Memoirs*, vol. 2, 379–90.

427   "By God," he said to Webb: David McCullough, *Truman* (New York: Simon and Schuster, 1992), 776.

427   the crisis Truman needed: Stephen E. Ambrose, *Rise to Globalism: American Foreign Policy Since 1938* (London: Allen Lane, Penguin, 1971), 192.

427   the *Chicago Tribune* called Acheson: Beisner, 305.

427   "One could have said his name": Acheson, 362.

428   Acheson demurred: Ronald Steel, *Walter Lippmann and the American Century* (1980, rpt. New York: Vintage, 1981), 469

428   two war councils: See Harry S. Truman, *Memoirs*, vol. 2, for Truman's ver-

sion of these events, 378–85; see also McCullough, 775–79; Hamby, 535–39; Beisner, 340–45.

429 "We can't let the UN down!": Beisner, 340.

429 "If the best minds in the world had set out": Quoted in David Halberstam, *The Coldest Winter* (New York: Hyperion, 2007), 2.

429 "I do not want war": Quoted in McCullough, 780.

430 "Korea was 'the Greece of the Far East' ": Quoted in Beisner, 342.

430 "Step by step, in six fateful days": Margaret Truman, 469.

431 Truman took great satisfaction: Margaret Truman, 469–71.

432 "wartime once more": Manchester, 645.

432 "You are not alone": Leonard Mosley, *Dulles: A Biography of Eleanor, Allen, and John Foster Dulles* (1978; rpt. New York: Dell, 1979), 282–83.

432 "I whole-heartedly agree with and support": Quoted in Richard Norton Smith, *Thomas E. Dewey and His Times* (New York: Simon and Schuster, 1982), 561.

433 "uncharacteristically supportive of the Truman administration": Alan Brinkley, *The Publisher: Henry Luce and His American Century* (New York: Knopf, 2010), 364–65.

433 the shock of the North Korean invasion: Gaddis, *Cold War*, 43.

433 "East, west, north, and south, American newspapers reported": Eric F. Goldman, *The Crucial Decade: America, 1945–1955* (New York: Vintage, 1961), 171–73.

433 " 'You may be a whiskey guzzling poker playing old buzzard' ": Quoted in McCullough, 781.

434 "I thought the Hürtgen Forest was bad": Quoted in Goldman, 175–76.

435 "the sour little war": Quoted in Halberstam, 2, and numerous other places.

435 In New York City: See Allen Ginsberg, *Howl: Original Draft Facsimile, Transcript & Variant Versions, Fully Annotated by the Author, with Contemporaneous Correspondence, Account of First Public Reading, Legal Skirmishes, Precursor Texts, and Bibliography*, ed. Barry Miles (New York: Harper Perennial, 1995), for his recollection of the episode and Louis Simpson's response to his query in 1985, 135.

Selected Bibliography

"The greatest part of a writer's life is spent in reading, in order to write; a man will turn over half a library to make one book": Samuel Johnson. Having mustered my sources in interminable endnotes, I confine myself here almost entirely to the books, many of them still on my desk or on shelves nearby, on which I have most relied in writing *The Brazen Age*, and which I recommend for consultation or as further reading.

Except alphabetically, the books at the top of the list are *The Encyclopedia of New York City*, edited by Kenneth T. Jackson, my daily companion for many years, and *New York 1930* and *New York 1960*, the relevant volumes in the series of architectural and urban studies by Robert A. M. Stern and colleagues. Of the innumerable memoirs and biographies that shed light on the period, I have included only an essential few, for their superior powers of evocation. That most democratic literary form, the anthology, enjoyed a golden age in the 1940s; a select few, reflecting the sense and sensibilities of different decades, are recommended here, as a door into the time machine.

Abel, Lionel. *The Intellectual Follies: A Memoir of the Literary Venture in New York and Paris*. New York: W. W. Norton, 1984.

Barrett, William. *The Truants: Adventures Among the Intellectuals*. Garden City, NY: Anchor, 1982.

Bender, Thomas. *New York Intellect: A History of Intellectual Life in New York City, from 1750 to the Beginnings of Our Own Time*. New York: Knopf, 1987.

Berman, Marshall. *All That Is Solid Melts into Air: The Experience of Modernity*. New York: Penguin, 1988.

Bloom, Alexander. *Prodigal Sons: The New York Intellectuals and Their World*. New York: Oxford University Press, 1986.

Brinnin, John Malcolm. *Sextet: T. S. Eliot & Truman Capote & Others*. New York: Delta/Seymour Lawrence, 1981.

Burrows, Edwin G., and Mike Wallace. *Gotham: A History of New York City to 1898*. New York: Oxford University Press, 1998.

Cohen-Solal, Annie, Paul Goldberger, and Robert Gottlieb. *New York Mid-Century 1945-1965*. New York: Vendome Press, 2014.

Conrad, Peter. *The Art of the City: Views and Versions of New York.* New York:
   Oxford University Press, 1984.
Corbett, William. *New York Literary Lights.* Saint Paul, MN: Graywolf Press,
   1998.
Cowley, Malcolm. *Exile's Return: A Literary Odyssey of the 1920s.* New York: Viking
   Press, 1951.
———. *The Flower and the Leaf: A Contemporary Record of American Writing Since
   1941,* ed. Donald W. Faulkner. New York: Viking Press, 1985.
———. *The Literary Situation.* New York: Viking Press, 1954.
Cumings, Bruce. *The Korean War: A History.* New York: Modern Library, 2010.
Davis, Mike. *Prisoners of the American Dream: Politics and Economy in the History of
   the U.S. Working Class.* London: Verso, 1986.
Denning, Michael. *The Cultural Front: The Laboring of American Culture in the
   Twentieth Century.* London: Verso, 1997.
Dickstein, Morris. *Dancing in the Dark: A Cultural History of the Great Depression.*
   New York: W. W. Norton, 2009.
Dijkstra, Bram. *American Expressionism: Art and Social Change, 1920–1950.* New
   York: Harry N. Abrams: in association with the Columbus Museum of Art,
   2003.
Douglas, Ann. *Terrible Honesty: Mongrel Manhattan in the 1920s.* New York: Far-
   rar, Straus and Giroux, 2004.
Edmiston, Susan, and Linda D. Cirino. *Literary New York: A History and Guide.*
   Peregrine Smith, 1991.
Eisenger, Chester E. *The 1940s: Profile of a Nation in Crisis.* New York: Anchor,
   1969.
Freeman, Joshua B. *Working-Class New York.* New York: New Press, 2000.
Guilbaut, Serge. *How New York Stole the Idea of Modern Art: Abstract Expressionism,
   Freedom, and the Cold War,* trans. Arthur Goldhammer. Chicago: University of
   Chicago Press, 1983.
Halberstam, David. *The Fifties.* New York: Villard Books, 1993.
———. *The Powers That Be.* New York: Knopf, 1979.
Hall, Peter. *Cities in Civilization.* New York: Pantheon, 1998.
Halliday, Jon, and Bruce Cumings. *Korea: The Unknown War.* New York: Pan-
   theon, 1988.
Hardwick, Elizabeth. *Bartleby in Manhattan and Other Essays.* New York: Random
   House, 1983.
Jackson, Kenneth T., and David S. Dunbar, eds. *Empire City: New York Through
   the Centuries.* New York: Columbia University Press, 2002.
Jackson, Kenneth T., ed. *The Encyclopedia of New York City.* New Haven: Yale Uni-
   versity Press, and New York: New-York Historical Society, 2010.
Jukes, Peter. *A Shout in the Street: An Excursion into the Modern City.* New York:
   Farrar, Straus and Giroux, 1990.
Kaiser, Charles. *The Gay Metropolis, 1910–1996.* Boston: Houghton Mifflin, 1997.
Kazin, Alfred. *New York Jew.* New York: Knopf, 1978.
———. *Starting Out in the Thirties.* New York: Atlantic Monthly Press, 1965.
Kennan, George F. *Memoirs, 1925–1950.* Boston: Little, Brown, 1967.
Kennedy, David M. *Freedom from Fear: The American People in Depression and War,
   1929–1945.* New York: Oxford, 1999.
Kluger, Richard (with the assistance of Phyllis Kluger). *The Paper: The Life and
   Death of the New York Herald Tribune.* New York: Knopf, 1986.

Koolhaas, Rem. *Delirious New York: A Retroactive Manifesto for Manhattan*. New York: Monacelli Press, 1994.

Kunstler, Howard. *The Geography of Nowhere: The Rise and Decline of America's Man-Made Landscape*. New York: Touchstone / Simon and Schuster, 1994.

Kurzweil, Edith. *A Partisan Century: Political Writings from* Partisan Review. New York: Columbia University Press, 1996.

Laskin, David. *Partisans: Marriage, Politics and Betrayal Among the New York Intellectuals*. New York: Simon & Schuster, 2000.

Liebling, A. J. *The Press*, 2d rev. ed. with an introduction by Jean Stafford. New York: Ballantine Books, 1975.

Lipsitz, George. *Rainbow at Midnight: Labor and Culture in the 1940s*. Urbana: University of Chicago Press, 1994.

Lopate, Phillip. *Waterfront: A Walk Around Manhattan*. New York: Anchor, 2005.

Lopate, Phillip, ed. *Writing New York: A Literary Anthology*. New York: Library of America, 1998.

Lukacs, John. *1945: Year Zero*. Garden City, NY: Doubleday, 1978.

———. *The Passing of the Modern Age*. New York: Harper & Row, 1970.

Mehlman, Jeffrey. *Émigré New York: French Intellectuals in Wartime Manhattan, 1940–1944*. Baltimore: Johns Hopkins University Press, 2004.

Morris, Jan. *Manhattan '45*. New York: Oxford University Press, 1987.

Patterson, James T. *Grand Expectations: The United States, 1945–1974*. New York: Oxford University Press, 1996.

Perl, Jed. *New Art City: Manhattan at Mid-Century*. New York: Knopf, 2004.

Pfanner, Helmut F. *Exile in New York: German and Austrian Writers After 1933*. Detroit: Wayne State University Press, 1983.

Phillips, William, and Philip Rahv, eds., with an introduction by Lionel Trilling. *The New Partisan Reader, 1945–1953*. New York: Harcourt, Brace, 1953.

———. *The Partisan Reader: Ten Years of Partisan Review, 1934–1944: An Anthology*. New York: Dial Press, 1946.

Sanders, James. *Celluloid Skyline: New York and the Movies*. New York: Knopf, 2001.

Saunders, Frances Stonor. *The Cultural Cold War: The CIA and the World of Arts and Letters*. New York: New Press, 1999.

Sawyers, June Skinner, ed. *The Greenwich Village Reader: Fiction, Poetry, and Reminiscences*. New York: Cooper Square Press, 2001.

Scott, William B., and Peter M. Rutkoff. *New York Modern: The Arts and the City*. Baltimore: Johns Hopkins University Press, 1999.

Stansell, Christine. *American Moderns: Bohemian New York and the Creation of a New Century*. New York: Owl, Henry Holt, 2000.

Starr, Paul. *The Creation of the Media: Political Origins of Modern Communications*. New York: Basic Books, 2004.

Stern, Robert A. M., Gregory Gilmartin, and Thomas Mellins. *New York 1930: Architecture and Urbanism Between the Two World Wars*. New York: Rizzoli, 1987.

Stern, Robert A. M., Thomas Mellins, and David Fishman. *New York 1960: Architecture Between the Second World War and the Bicentennial*. New York: Monacelli Press, 1997.

Stevens, Mark, and Annalyn Swan. *De Kooning: An American Master*. New York: Knopf, 2004.

Still, Bayrd. *Mirror for Gotham: New York As Seen by Contemporaries from Dutch Days to the Present*. New York: New York University Press, 1956.

Strausbaugh, John. *The Village: 400 Years of Beats and Bohemians, Radicals and Rogues: A History of Greenwich Village*. New York: Ecco/HarperCollins, 2013.

Talese, Gay. *Fame and Obscurity: Portraits*. New York: World, 1970.

———. *The Kingdom and the Power*. New York: World, 1969.

Thomson, Virgil. *Virgil Thomson*. New York: Knopf, 1967.

Wald, Alan M. *Exiles from a Future Time: The Forging of the Mid-Twentieth-Century Literary Left*. Chapel Hill: University of North Carolina Press, 2002.

———. *The Rise and Decline of the Anti-Stalinist Left from the 1930s to the 1980s*. Chapel Hill: University of North Carolina Press, 1987.

Weil, François. *A History of New York*, trans. Jody Gladdings. New York: Columbia University Press, 2004.

Wetzsteon, Ross. *Republic of Dreams: Greenwich Village, the American Bohemia, 1910–1960*. New York: Simon & Schuster, 2002.

White, E. B. *Here Is New York*. New York: Harper & Row, 1949.

Yagoda, Ben. *About Town:* The New Yorker *and the World It Made*. New York: Scribner, 2000.

Index

Office of Price Administration (OPA), 113, 156, 168
Office of War Information (OWI), 4, 54, 124, 373
Ogilvy, David, 54–5
Oh, Lady! Lady! (Kern, Bolton and Wodehouse), 273, 278
O'Hara, John, 80–1, 83, *184*, 271
Ohio, 6, 16, 27, 203
Ohio State University, 194, 195
Oklahoma! (Rodgers and Hammerstein), 43, 45, 136
On Active Service in Peace and War (Stimson and Bundy), 138
O'Neal, Hank, 196
O'Neill, Eugene, 43, 195, 200, 235, 238, 240, 243, 258–9, 278, 280, 286
O'Neill, William L., 251
"On Flying" (Vidal), 40
On Native Grounds (Kazin), 88
On Photography (Sontag), 183
On the Road (Kerouac), xiv, 330, 345, 466
On the Town (Bernstein, Comden and Green), 43, 114
On the Waterfront (film), 208
Oppenheim, James, 257–8
Oppenheimer, J. Robert, 96, 376
Orage, A. R., 84
Oral History of the World (Gould), 299
Organization of Ukranian Nationalists (OUN), 399
Orgen, "Little Augie," 14
Orizaba, 300–1
Orphans of the Storm (film), 48
Ortega y Gasset, José, 208
Orwell, George, 295–6, 435
Ossorio, Alfonso, 340
Oswego, Mich., 432
Othello (Shakespeare), vii, 338
Other Voices, Other Rooms (Capote), 308
Otis, Elisha Graves, 71
Our Country (Barone), 32, 358*n*
Ozick, Cynthia, 180–1

Pacific Ocean, 64, 170, 418
Paine, Tom, 18, 186
Palestine, 393–5
Paley, William S., 212

Palimpsest (Vidal), 172, 306–7, 318
Palmer raids, 266–7
Panofsky, Erwin, 96, 109–11
Paradiso (Dante), 91
Paramount Pictures, 47, 48, 288
Paramount Theater, 43, 49, 177, 222
Parents terribles, Les (Cocteau), 315
Paris, 38, 51, 59, 61, 62, 86, 132, 143–5, 168, 196–200, 202, 243, 274, 284–5, 293–4
  American colony in, 290–2
  Latin Quarter in, 231, 233, 280
Parker, Dorothy, 121, 123
Parry, Albert, 229–30, 232, 233, 259–60, 277, 289, 294–5, 298–9, 301–3, 324
Parsons, Betty, 338–40
Partisan Review, 38, 43, 44, 84–7, 99, 127, 134, 147–51, 165, 176, 247*n*–8*n*, 257, 295, 305, 312, 317, 321, 323, 331–3, 374, 377
Paterson Strike Pageant, 243
patriotism, 75, 262
Patterson newspapers, 22, 216
Paul, Maury, 306
Pavia, Philip, 331
Paz, Octavio, 323
Peace Corps, 180
Pearl Harbor, 389
  Japanese attack on, 94, 112, 432
Pearson, Drew, 395, 397–8, 400–2, 405, 407–8
Pendergast, Tom, 346, 355
Penguin Books, 120
Pennsylvania, 27, 275
Pennsylvania Station, 114, 218
Percy, William Alexander, 132
Pericles, 33
Perkins, Frances, 33
peyote, 244
Pfanner, Helmut, 104
Phi Beta Kappa, 19, 246
Philadelphia, Pa., 22, 50, 53, 64, 68, 282
Philby, Kim, 399
Philippines, 3, 19, 64, 94*n*, 237*n*, 413, 417
photography, 47, 57, 67, 191, 193–4, 196–207, 209, 212–26

Dwight Macdonald, et al. *(Courtesy of Vassar College Library)*

Henry Wallace and schoolchildren *(Courtesy of Rutgers University Libraries)*

Alexander Fadeyev, Norman Mailer, Dmitri Shostakovich, Arthur Miller, and Olaf Stapledon *(Associated Press)*

James V. Forrestal, Kenneth C. Royall, John L. Sullivan, and Stuart Symington *(Courtesy of Prints & Photographs Division, Library of Congress)*

Edward R. Murrow and Eric Sevareid *(Courtesy of Prints & Photographs Division, Library of Congress)*

Jack Kerouac and Neal Cassady *(Photofest)*

A NOTE ABOUT THE AUTHOR

David Reid is the editor of *Sex, Death and God in L.A.* and *West of the West: Imagining California* (with Leonard Michaels and Raquel Scherr). His essays, articles, reviews, and interviews have appeared in *Vanity Fair*, *The Paris Review*, *The New York Times*, *The Washington Post*, the *Los Angeles Times Book Review*, and in various anthologies, including the Pushcart Prize collections. He lives in Berkeley, California.

A NOTE ON THE TYPE

This book was set in Janson, a typeface long thought to have been made by the Dutchman Anton Janson. However, it has been conclusively demonstrated that these types are actually the work of Nicholas Kis (1650–1702), a Hungarian. The type is an excellent example of the influential and sturdy Dutch types that prevailed in England up to the time William Caslon (1692–1766) developed his own incomparable designs from them.

Composed by North Market Street Graphics, Lancaster, Pennsylvania
Printed and bound by Berryville Graphics, Berryville, Virginia
Designed by Maggie Hinders